Cyberpower and National Security

Cyberpower and National Security

Edited by Franklin D. Kramer,
Stuart H. Starr, and Larry K. Wentz

CENTER FOR TECHNOLOGY AND NATIONAL SECURITY POLICY

NDU
Press

NATIONAL DEFENSE UNIVERSITY PRESS

POTOMAC BOOKS, INC.

WASHINGTON, D.C.

Library of Congress Cataloging-in-Publication Data
Cyberpower and national security / edited by Franklin D. Kramer, Stuart H. Starr, and Larry K. Wentz. — 1st ed.
    p. cm.
  Includes bibliographical references and index.
  ISBN 978-1-59797-423-3 (pbk. : alk. paper)
  ISBN 978-1-59797-933-7 (electronic edition)
  1. National security—United States. 2. Information technology—Government policy—United States. 3. Cyberspace—Government policy—United States. 4. Cyberterrorism—United States—Prevention. I. Kramer, Franklin D., 1945– II. Starr, Stuart H. III. Wentz, Larry K.
  UA23.C929 2009
  355.3'43—dc22

                                                                    2009003301

Printed in the United States of America on acid-free paper that meets the American National Standards Institute Z39-48 Standard.

Potomac Books, Inc.
22841 Quicksilver Drive
Dulles, Virginia 20166

First Edition

10 9 8 7 6 5 4

Contents

Part III. Cyberpower: Military Use and Deterrence

Part IV. Cyberpower: Information

Part V. Cyberpower: Strategic Problems

Part VI. Institutional Factors

Illustrations

Figures

Tables

Preface

THE cyber domain is undergoing extraordinary changes, many of which present exceptional opportunities to the users of cyberspace. This evolution is apparent in the increasing numbers of participants in cyberspace and the quality of their participation, both technically and socially. As an example, it is projected that by the year 2010, approximately 2 billion people will be connected to the Internet. In addition, if the participants in the MySpace Web site were to comprise a nation, it would be the 11th largest country in the world. However, trends in cyberspace also raise major challenges. These arise from the use of cyberspace by malevolent actors (such as terrorists and criminals) and the many security vulnerabilities that plague cyberspace (for example, challenges in attribution, denial of service attacks, and exfiltration or corruption of sensitive data).

In order to exploit these opportunities and to overcome these challenges, we must begin to assemble a balanced body of knowledge on the cyber domain. This book by the Center for Technology and National Security Policy at the National Defense University provides the foundation for that body of knowledge. It is unique in that it has assembled an extraordinary set of world-class experts to provide a holistic view of the complex issues that characterize the cyber domain.

One of the major contributions of this book is that it frames key cyber issues in the appropriate context and formulates sound recommendations for policymakers to pursue. Of equal importance, it identifies key cyber questions that senior decisionmakers will have to address in the near future. These include building the human capacity to address cyber issues, balancing civil liberties with national security considerations, and developing the international partnerships needed to address cyber challenges.

We heartily recommend this book to those of you who will be fortunate enough to realize the opportunities of the cyber domain and overcome its challenges.

Introduction

THIS book is intended to help create a coherent framework for understanding and utilizing cyberpower in support of national security. Cyberspace and cyber-power are now critical elements of international security. Yet, as was noted during the course of the Department of Defense's (DOD's) 2006 Quadrennial Defense Review (QDR),[1] DOD lacks a coherent framework to assess cyber-power policy issues. To redress that shortfall, the Under Secretary of Defense for Policy directed the Center for Technology and National Security Policy (CTNSP) at the National Defense University to undertake a study of the subject area. As the study's terms of reference stated, "There is a compelling need for a comprehensive, robust, and articulate cyber power theory that describes, explains, and predicts how our nation should best use cyber power in support of United States (U.S.) national and security interests."

The book is a result of that study. It is divided into six broad areas. The first part provides a foundation and overview of the subject by identifying key policy issues, establishing a common vocabulary, and proposing an initial version of a theory of cyberpower. The second part identifies and explores possible changes in cyberspace over the next 15 years by assessing cyber infrastructure and security challenges. The third part examines the potential impact of changes in cyberspace on military use and deterrence. The fourth part analyzes informational levers of power. The fifth part addresses the extent to which changes in cyberspace serve to empower key entities such as transnational criminals, terrorists, and nation-states. The final part looks at key institutional factors, which include issues concerning governance, legal dimensions, critical infrastructure protection, and organization.

The chapters for this book were the product of several workshops at which experts from government, think tanks, industry, and academia presented their views on the major subject areas. Based on the feedback from those discussions, each presenter developed a chapter for this book. This introduction provides a bottom-up perspective of these chapters, summarizes the major themes of each, and identifies potential next steps.

Foundation and Overview

Part I is designed to provide a holistic perspective of the cyber domain by identifying and discussing major policy issues, providing key definitions, and formulating a preliminary theory of cyberpower.

In chapter 1, "Cyberpower and National Security: Policy Recommendations for a Strategic Framework," Franklin D. Kramer identifies and explores many of the key policy issues that senior decisionmakers will have to confront over the next decade. He aggregates these issues into the categories of structural issues (security, human capital and research and development, governance, and organization) and geopolitical issues (net-centric operations, computer network attack, deterrence, influence, stability operations, and doctrine, organization, training, materiel, leadership and education, personnel, and facilities [DOTMLPF]).

In chapter 2, "From Cyberspace to Cyberpower: Defining the Problem," Daniel T. Kuehl establishes a common vocabulary for the cyber realm. These include the following key definitions:

Cyberspace is a global domain within the information environment whose distinctive and unique character is framed by the use of electronics and the electromagnetic spectrum to create, store, modify, exchange, and exploit information via interdependent and interconnected networks using information-communication technologies.[2]

Cyberpower is the ability to use cyberspace to create advantages and influence events in all the other operational environments and across the instruments of power.

Cyber strategy is the development and employment of strategic capabilities to operate in cyberspace, integrated and coordinated with the other operational domains, to achieve or support the achievement of objectives across the elements of national power in support of national security strategy.

In addition, Kuehl discusses two related terms: *information operations* and *influence operations.*

In chapter 3, "Toward a Preliminary Theory of Cyberpower," Stuart H. Starr develops an initial version of the theory of cyberpower, which was requested in the 2006 QDR. This preliminary theory addresses five key areas: it *builds* on the key definitions provided in chapter 2; it gives structure to the discussion by *categorizing* the key elements of the theory; it *explains* the elements in these categories by summarizing relevant events and introducing key frameworks; it seeks to *anticipate* key trends and activities so that policy can be germane and useful; and it *connects* the various elements of the subject so that key issues can be treated comprehensively.

Cyberspace

The six chapters in part II characterize the structure of cyberspace, identify evolutionary trends (particularly in the area of security), describe the relationship of cyberspace and critical infrastructures, and explore potential revolutionary changes to cyberspace.

In chapter 4, "A Graphical Introduction to the Structural Elements of Cyberspace," Elihu Zimet and Edward Skoudis display and explain ways in which the different layers of cyberspace interact with each other and how elements interact within each individual layer. In addition, they identify and discuss major trends in cyberspace (for example, convergence and the increased move to Internet protocol [IP] version 6; merging of hardware and software and the rise of embedded "computers" with hard-wired programming; and broadband and wireless proliferation).

In chapter 5, "Cyberspace and Infrastructure," William D. O'Neil identifies and discusses the vulnerabilities that characterize our critical infrastructures. To counter those vulnerabilities, he recommends that the United States create a more reliable and robust grid for electrical transmission and distribution and implement directive regulations for infrastructure firms at the process level.

In chapter 6, "Evolutionary Trends in Cyberspace," Edward Skoudis focuses on the private-public relationship of how cyberspace is maintained and run. He identifies and discusses key trends in computers and networks (broadband proliferation, wireless proliferation, the transition from IP version 4 to IP version 6) and major social trends (worldwide technological development with localized emphases, and the rise of online communities, collaboration, and information-sharing).

In chapter 7, "Information Security Issues in Cyberspace," Edward Skoudis explores the various technology-related Internet security issues from the viewpoints of both attackers and defenders. He focuses on those forms of attacks that are associated with current Internet technologies and are most likely to continue to present a substantial challenge in the near future. He cautions that the security concerns associated with the use of the Internet today have originated from the application of technologies in ways unanticipated by their original designers.

In chapter 8, "The Future of the Internet and Cyberpower," Marjory S. Blumenthal and David D. Clark raise eight policy issues that they deem relevant to the future of cyberspace. These policy issues include security, object provenance, identity, location-aware computing, location sensing, open sensor networks, open vehicle networks, and networks in times of crisis. In particular, they note that future networks may focus on an architecture for information-handling services built out of distributed servers and staged delivery. Attention to architecture at these higher levels may provide an alternative to today's focus on common packet formats and allow the lower layers of a future network to more directly exploit features of diverse technology.

In chapter 9, "Information Technology and the Biotech Revolution," Edward Skoudis explores the blurring of lines between the computer and the human. Trends suggest that innovative interfaces are possible that will enable humans to effectively and efficiently harness machine computing power (for example, enhanced prostheses, or mental control of computers).

Cyberpower: Military Use and Deterrence

In part III, the potential impact of changes in cyberspace on the military and for deterrence is explored in four chapters.[3]

In chapter 10, "An Environmental Approach to Understanding Cyberpower," Gregory J. Rattray provides a historical perspective by assessing the common features of environmental power theories (for example, Alfred Thayer Mahan on naval power; Giulio Douhet on airpower; Halford J. Mackinder on land power; Colin Gray and Geoffrey Sloan on spacepower). Based on these earlier efforts, he identifies four common features of environmental power theories that are germane to cyberpower: technological advances, speed and scope of operations, control of key features/bottlenecks, and national mobilization.

In chapter 11, "Military Cyberpower," Martin C. Libicki addresses the question of whether networking operators permit a measurable improvement in operational effectiveness. Currently, the picture is ambiguous. In selected cases (such as air-to-air engagements), experiments demonstrate that networking can give rise to appreciable improvements in loss exchange ratios.[4] However, in more complex ground-based operations (for example, the Stryker Brigade Combat Team), networking appears to be of value, but more experimentation will be needed to assess quantitatively how much it helps.[5]

Chapter 12, "Military Service Overview," by Elihu Zimet and Charles L. Barry, provides an overview of Service initiatives in cyberspace and cyberpower.

In chapter 13, "Deterrence of Cyber Attacks," Richard L. Kugler asserts that although the U.S. Government is aware of the risks, it does not currently have a well-developed, publicly articulated strategy for deterring cyber attacks. As attacks may be launched as part of an adversary's strategic agenda, deterrence is a matter of not only defensive and offensive capabilities, but also the capacity to influence the adversary's motives, cost-benefit calculations, and risk-taking propensities. Recognizing the various actors and agendas that are likely to pose a cyber threat, the author proposes that a policy of "tailored deterrence" as cited in the 2006 QDR is needed to prevent attack. He concludes by noting that the message of a declaratory policy must be tailored for the types of adversaries likely to be faced. U.S. objectives, as well as an actor's specific motives and capabilities, will determine the response to an attack (which may use levers of power outside of the cyber realm).

Cyberpower: Information

Complementing the perspectives on the military lever of power are four chapters in part IV that address the informational lever of power and discuss the role of military and influence levers of power in a whole-of-government approach to stability, security, transition, and reconstruction (SSTR) operations.

Chapter 14, "Cyber Influence and International Security," by Franklin D. Kramer and Larry K. Wentz, explores the strategic and operational levels of influence. The authors identify three key elements of influence operations: expertise in the application of principles of influence; domain experience in arenas where the principles are to be applied; and experience in the use of cyberspace. They conclude that if the United States is to enhance its influence in cyberspace, it will require a multifaceted strategy that differentiates the circumstances of the message, key places of delivery, and sophistication with which messages are created and delivered, with particular focus on channels and messengers.

In chapter 15, "Tactical Influence Operations," Stuart H. Starr introduces a framework that links operational influence objectives to DOTMLPF initiatives. Two perspectives illustrate this framework. Looking backward, the activities of Colonel Ralph Baker, USA, former Brigade Combat Team leader in Baghdad, are mapped onto the framework to characterize DOTMLPF changes needed to enhance tactical influence operations.[6] Looking to the future, the chapter explores the potential role of Web 2.0 technology to enhance emerging influence operations.

In chapter 16, "I-Power: The Information Revolution and Stability Operations," Franklin D. Kramer, Larry K. Wentz, and Stuart H. Starr explore how information and information communications technology (I/ICT) can significantly increase the likelihood of success in SSTR operations. The chapter identifies a five-part strategy for the effective application of I/ICT: ensure that the U.S. Government gives high priority to a joint civil-military activity; require the military to make I/ICT part of the planning and execution of the SSTR operation; preplan and establish I/ICT partnerships with regular participants in SSTR operations; focus the intervention on the host nation; and harness key ICT capabilities to support the strategy.

In chapter 17, "Facilitating Stability Operations with Cyberpower," Gerard J. Christman complements the preceding chapter by identifying and discussing many of the institutional and policy activities that have recently been undertaken (for example, the promulgation of DOD Directive 3000.05, identifying SSTR operations as a core mission for DOD). However, there is still a need for developing follow-on instructions to the Services. Furthermore, additional effort is needed to foster trust and improve collaboration and information-sharing between the Government and other participants in SSTR operations (such as nongovernmental and international organizations).

Cyberpower: Strategic Problems

In part V, three chapters deal with ways in which changes in cyberspace can empower criminals, terrorists, and nation-states. In chapter 18, "Cyber Crime," Clay Wilson identifies and discusses the characteristics of and trends in cyber crime. The chapter concludes with a summary of policy issues to be considered to reduce cyber crime: seeking new ways and incentives for private industry and government to cooperate for reporting cyber crime and increasing cyber security; creating new agreements to encourage more international cooperation among law enforcement agencies to improve accuracy for attribution of cyber crimes and for pursuing malicious actors across national borders; and developing more accurate methods for measuring the effects of cyber crime.

In chapter 19, "Cyber Terrorism: Menace or Myth?" Irving Lachow analyzes the terrorist use of cyberspace. He notes that terrorists have gravitated toward the use of cyberspace because of the low cost of entry, the opportunity to achieve sanctuary, and its value in supporting a wide variety of key functions (recruiting, raising funds, propagandizing, educating and training, and planning of operations). However, Lachow maintains that terrorists are more likely to employ kinetic means, in the near term, to support terrorist operations.

In chapter 20, "Nation-state Cyber Strategies: Examples from China and Russia," Timothy L. Thomas discusses alternative nation-state perspectives on the use of cyberspace. In the case of China, the author examines the evolution of its cyber philosophy and how peacetime activities may be part of a cyber preemptive strategy (such as ongoing espionage activities). Based on an assessment of open source documents, he hypothesizes that China may intend to use electrons as they once used forces: packets of electrons might be used to fulfill the stratagem, "kill with a borrowed sword." As a result, Chinese strategy relies on preparation and mobilization to ensure that a cyber operation could be conducted suddenly, to gain the initiative by "striking the enemy's information center of gravity and weakening the combat efficiency of his information systems and cyberized weapons." Similarly, the author examines the terminology and strategic thought used in Russia to create a picture of Russia's potential cyber strategy. Russian theorists speak of "reflexive control" and seek to locate the weak link in the system and exploit it. Thomas affirms that Russia is replete with technical cybertalent, making it a potentially challenging cyberpower opponent.

Institutional Factors

In part VI, four chapters address the host of institutional issues that confront the cyber decisionmaker. First, in the area of governance, the contentious issues of governance of the Internet and the U.S. Government's role in that process are examined. Second, in the area of legal issues, selected elements of international law have been analyzed. These include the issue of attack assessment in cyberspace and the selection of suitable responses. Third, an assessment has been made of the performance and effectiveness of the actions of the Department of Homeland Security in the defense of critical infrastructures in the Nation. Finally, it is important to consider cyber issues from a whole-of-government perspective. This requires a viewpoint that considers the Presidential perspective.

In chapter 21, "Internet Governance," Harold Kwalwasser says that the mechanism for governance of the Internet is exceedingly complex (that is, there is considerable overlap among the functions and activities of the participating organizations). To assess the performance of the existing governance process, he introduces eight criteria: open, democratic, transparent, dynamic, adaptable, accountable, efficient, and effective. When evaluated against these criteria, the Internet governance process is assessed to have performed remarkably well to date. However, because of pressures from other nation-states, the U.S. Government needs to develop a viable strategy for achieving "Internet influence."

Chapter 22, "International Law and Information Operations," by Thomas C. Wingfield, describes appropriate frameworks and employs them to analyze the legal issues associated with two classes of problems: *jus ad bellum* (the lawful resort to force) and *jus in bello* (the use of force in wartime). In the area of *jus ad bellum,* the key question faced by cyber operators is, "When does an information operation (or group of operations) rise to the level of a 'use of force' under international law?" To address that question, the author introduces and applies the Schmitt framework (a multi-attribute utility approach to the factors of severity, immediacy, directness, invasiveness, measurability, presumptive legitimacy, and responsibility). In addressing the subject of *jus in bello,* Wingfield focuses on the key issue: "Once at war in cyberspace, what rules apply?" To address this question, he introduces and discusses four areas: discrimination, necessity, proportionality, and ruses of war and perfidy.

Chapter 23, "Cyberpower and Critical Infrastructure Protection: A Critical Assessment of Federal Efforts," was written by John A. McCarthy with the assistance of Chris Burrow, Maeve Dion, and Olivia Pacheco. The chapter makes the major observation that the cyber infrastructure has become vital to the national defense infrastructure, the U.S. Government, and the global economy. However, the authors caution that there is the potential for a catastrophic cyber incident. They conclude that the best way forward is for the Government to serve as an organizational model, develop and test emergency procedures, and bring its expertise to the private sector to be leveraged. In order to play those roles, the Government will need to provide clear policy direction, develop operational guidance that includes roles and responsibilities, and shift its research and development priorities and its distribution of resources to the task of managing catastrophic issues.

Chapter 24, "Cyberpower from the Presidential Perspective," by Leon Fuerth, addresses the cyber organizational issue from a "whole of government" perspective. The author notes that the organization problem is a complex, poorly structured issue that is in the class of "wicked problems." In his assessment, he considers the possibility of a Cyber Policy Council at the White House level that might be analogous to the Council of Economic Advisors.

Potential Next Steps

Although this cyber effort has been very broad in its scope, it should be regarded as an initial foundation for further work. Several areas will require additional research and deliberation. First, many of the trends associated with cyberspace are highly nonlinear (for example, global growth of the Internet and cellular technology; participation in social network systems). There is a need to perform in-depth technology assessments to anticipate when those trends begin to stabilize. Second, in the area of cyberpower, the book takes only the first steps in addressing the military and informational levers of power. Further research is needed, including about how changes in cyberspace are affecting the political, diplomatic, and economic levers of power. Third, in the area of cyber strategy, steps should be taken to assess how changes in cyberspace are affecting the empowerment of individuals, corporations, nongovernmental organizations, and international organizations. Fourth, in the area of institutional factors, it is important to explore the balance between civil liberties and national security. Overall, there is a need to develop and assemble analytic methods, tools, and data to help perform the assessments needed by senior decisionmakers to formulate sound cyber policies. Specifically, the community must develop and apply risk assessment methods to support the identification of key vulnerabilities and to identify preparatory steps to mitigate those vulnerabilities.

Part I
Foundation and Overview

CHAPTER 1

Cyberpower and National Security: Policy Recommendations for a Strategic Framework

Franklin D. Kramer

CYBERPOWER is now a fundamental fact of global life. In political, economic, and military affairs, information and information technology provide and support crucial elements of operational activities. U.S. national security efforts have begun to incorporate cyber into strategic calculations. Those efforts, however, are only a beginning. The critical conclusion of this book is that the United States must create an effective national and international strategic framework for the development and use of cyber as part of an overall national security strategy.

Such a strategic framework will have both structural and geopolitical elements. Structural activities will focus on those parts of cyber that enhance capabilities for users in general. Those categories include heightened security, expanded development of research and human capital, improved governance, and more effective organization. Geopolitical activities will focus on more traditional national security and defense efforts. Included in this group are sophisticated development of network-centric operations; appropriate integrated planning of computer network attack capabilities; establishment of deterrence doctrine that incorporates cyber; expansion of effective cyber influence capabilities; carefully planned incorporation of cyber into military planning (particularly stability operations); establishment of appropriate doctrine, education, and training regarding cyber by the Services and nonmilitary elements so that cyber can be used effectively in a joint and/or multinational context; and generation of all those efforts at an international level, since cyber is inherently international and cannot be most effectively accomplished without international partners.

Achieving these goals will require greatly expanded efforts by the United States in terms of people, resources, and partnerships. The potential of cyber is so great, and the costs of failing to accomplish these goals so significant, that a truly national effort must be undertaken.

Preliminaries: Understanding Cyber

Creating a strategic framework for cyber requires both understanding what cyber is now and having a sense of where it is going in the future.

Definitions

Cyber can be defined in many ways. One recent study found 28 definitions of *cyberspace*. Accordingly, one of the most important lessons in this realm is to recognize that definitions should be used as an aid to policy and analysis, and not as a limitation on them. In the context of this book, *cyber* is used to encompass technical, informational, and human elements. Daniel Kuehl defines *cyberspace* as an operational domain framed by the use of electronics and the electromagnetic spectrum to create, store, modify, exchange, and exploit information via interconnected and Internetted information systems and their associated infrastructures.[1] That definition is broad and technically focused but is a useful platform from which to begin discussion. As one looks at different elements of cyberpower, the Kuehl definition provides a common base for analysis, but other aspects will tend to be added or emphasized, and the technical definition will be less critical to the development of policy and strategy. By way of examples:

- cyber influence activities will include the Internet as well as radio, television, communications such as cell phones, and applications for all
- cyber military activities will include network-centric operations, computer network attack and exploitation, geopolitical influence operations, and security
- cyber security will include not only technical issues such as viruses and denial-of-service attacks, but also human matters—such as insider deception as well as normal human mistakes—and the problems of governance, both national and international.

The policymaker who faces the cyber world needs to do so with the understanding that the arena is very broad and, as discussed below, still developing. For some policy issues, that breadth will need to be continuously maintained; for analysis of others, the focus will be narrowed. Furthermore, there needs to be recognition that there is often overlap between what might initially be considered different areas of cyber. For example, while some military communications structures are physically differentiated from civilian communication structures and run by separate software and people, others rely partially or entirely on civilian networks, riding on civilian infrastructure or using civilian protocols such as Internet transmission control protocol/Internet protocol (IP). To make good judgments about cyber issues, policymakers need to understand the scope, purpose, and effects of the cyber realm in connection with the strategic issues being reviewed.

The Cyber Future: Strategy in a Dynamic Context

Cyber has a number of characteristics that suggest its future may differ importantly from its present. Policymakers must, therefore, establish cyber strategy in a dynamic context—not knowing what the future will be, but nonetheless creating structures, processes, and people sufficiently flexible to adapt to change. Cyber is malleable because, although it exists in the physical world of electrons, transmission capabilities, and computers, it is a manmade creation subject to the power of human invention.

The degree of change that the fundamentally manmade aspect of cyber can create is considerable. By way of comparison, cyber is certainly not the first important human construct subject to major alteration—money would be a significant example. In recent years, money has led a highly dynamic existence. Among many instances, new currencies such as the euro have been created, new instruments such as financial derivatives have been widely used, and new flows of funds worldwide have become an important part of the global dynamic.

Like money, cyber is highly dynamic. In classic business analysis, an S curve often shows the rate of growth, with the high slope at the bottom indicating rapid change. Cyber currently is in such a period of rapid technological, organizational, and other change.

One of the reasons for such change is that, at least in parts of the cyber arena, the barriers to entry are low. At the moment, the message content of cyber rides on transmission capabilities that are not constraining, at least not in the civilian world—in short, lots of people can use cyber for lots of things at a reasonable price (the issue of transmission capability, usually put in terms of band capacity, is more significant in the military arena). Similarly, the development of applications, including negative applications for launching various types of cyber attacks, is a relatively low-cost endeavor, allowing numerous entities to develop important new capacities. Each of these factors is enhanced by the speed of transmission and the widespread penetration of cyber throughout the world. The broad context for the policymaker is that in making judgments, "facts" about cyber, which are true today, may be altered significantly in the future—and such a prospect of changed facts may well alter what would be the most appropriate judgments. Indeed, one of the fundamental issues for policymakers will be when to take steps that will affect changes in facts.

With the understanding of the breadth of cyber and its dynamic nature, we can turn to 10 key policy issues that will affect the establishment of a strategic framework for cyberpower in a national security strategy.

Structural Issues

Security

The cyber world is not secure. Each level of cyber—physical infrastructure, operational software, information, and people—is susceptible to security breakdown, whether through attack, infiltration, or accident.

There have been numerous evaluations of the U.S. infrastructure, including the electric grid and the transmission elements of cyber itself. Vulnerabilities of those infrastructures to both kinetic and cyber attack are well documented. By way of example, *The National Strategy to Secure Cyberspace* states:

> By exploiting vulnerabilities in our cyber systems, an organized attack may endanger the security of our Nation's critical infrastructures. The vulnerabilities that most threaten cyberspace occur in the information assets of critical infrastructure enterprises themselves and their external supporting structures, such as the mechanisms of the Internet. Lesser-secured sites on the interconnected network of networks also present potentially significant exposures to cyber attacks. Vulnerabilities result from weaknesses in technology and because of improper implementation and oversight of technological products.[2]

The breadth and capacity of cyber attacks is likewise well documented. Periodically, significant virus or denial-of-service attacks are featured in the media. Whether publicized or not, the annual number of attacks is extremely large, and they often occur against significant targets. For example, the Government Accountability Office has stated, "Significant information security weaknesses continue to place federal agencies at risk. . . . In 2006, agencies reported a record number of information security incidents to US-CERT [Computer Emergency Readiness Team]—the DHS [Department of Homeland Security] unit responsible for collecting such information."[3]

Cyber is hardly the first system subject to attack and breakdown. The monetary system is susceptible to counterfeiting, fraud, and robbery, yet it obviously is widely relied upon. The fundamental questions for the cyber policymaker are what level of protection is appropriate and whether and how it may be achieved.

In evaluating the level of protection that seems appropriate, an important immediate question is whether the level might be differentiated by use and user. The United States already makes such a differentiation in protecting its military and intelligence capabilities, with some built on entirely separate networks.

A second fundamental issue is how to reach the appropriate balance between exploiting the positive aspects of cyber versus accepting the risk that costs may arise as a consequence. To put it another way, increased functionality has often been associated with increased vulnerability—for example, increasing the number of sites one visits on the Internet, which broadens the access and usefulness of the Internet, concomitantly increases the likelihood that a virus will be downloaded onto one's computer. In making such an evaluation, the consequences of the risks need to be assessed—not only the probabilities but also the lasting costs. Taking down the electric grid for a day would be costly and arguably unacceptable, but taking it down for a year would be unquestionably catastrophic.

The U.S. Government is well aware of these issues and is taking steps. The Department of Homeland Security has the governmental lead, and, as recent newspaper reports have indicated, the Department of Defense (DOD) through the National Security Agency is enhancing its efforts to protect critical governmental networks. Nonetheless, as the Government Accountability Office has annually reported, the protection of government cyber is wholly inadequate, and the private sector is at least equally and often more vulnerable. The continuing nature of this well-recognized problem derives from a combination of the difficulties of effective response, prioritization, and determining who should decide upon the appropriate security measures.

To deal with these concerns, we recommend that the Federal Government take a more directive approach to ensuring cyber security, for both governmental and private cyber. Specifically, we prescribe a two-step approach to addressing vulnerabilities. First, a differentiation should be made among *indispensable, key,* and *other* cyber capacities. *Indispensable* cyber would include critical military and intelligence capacities and other capacities that the Nation could not afford to lose for even a short time. *Key* cyber would include critical functionalities that could not be lost for any length of time but for which short-term workarounds might be available, and functionalities whose exploitation (as opposed to loss) by adverse parties would have consequences for the Nation. Included in this category might be the electric grid and certain critical financial networks (although a determination would have to be made whether they need to be in the *indispensable* category), as well as capacities such as the defense industry that are necessary for key work for military and intelligence functions. The great bulk of cyber would fall into the *other* category, but that categorization would still involve a higher degree of security requirements.

Second, for each of the three categories, appropriate security measures would be required or encouraged. For indispensable cyber, the government would provide security, including monitoring for attacks, providing protection, and generating responses as appropriate, including the possibility of reconstitution or the establishment of redundancy. For key cyber, the government could require certain levels of security protection and could itself provide monitoring, response, and support. For other cyber, the government could require and/or encourage security through regulation, incentives, information, and coordination (such as working more closely with software vendors). In this necessarily large category, differentiations could be made among the sizes of businesses and the nature of users.

The cyber security situation that the United States currently faces is reminiscent of the early days of the environmental protection movement. Affirmative action by the Federal Government was required (as by the Clean Air and the Clean Water Acts), and a level playing field had to be maintained to be fair to industry. In our view, a comparable effort is now required for cyber. The executive branch and Congress should generate a full program to deal with the problem of cyber security.

A differentiated security program ought to be proposed by the executive branch and presented to Congress for full review. Hearings should take place with executive branch, industry, and individual participation. From such an effort a framework can be created for appropriate regulatory establishment of security arrangements, including appropriate allocation and/or sharing of costs. This effort should be given high priority by the Executive and the Congress.

Human Capital and Research and Development

Cyber is a manmade construction and one that particularly relies on human ingenuity and technological capacity. For the United States to maintain leadership in the cyber world, both individual capacities and research and development (R&D) must be maintained at the highest levels. Doing so in a changing cyber world will require a substantially enhanced governmental effort.

On the human capacity side, two fundamental and related changes have occurred. The first is that countries other than the United States and its traditional partners are graduating numerous students in the science, technology, engineering, and mathematics (STEM) fields. In China and India, the annual number of STEM graduates is considerably greater than in the United States and Western Europe, though there are important differences in quality. The second change is that these STEM personnel in other countries have the capacity to do work that is currently being done in the United States, putting a significant number of (and perhaps potentially nearly all) U.S. STEM personnel in competition with offshore workers.[4]

There are substantial disputes about whether there are enough U.S. graduates in the STEM fields and about the impact of the offshoring of STEM capacities that has already occurred or may occur in the future. There is, however, no dispute that the United States needs to maintain a vibrant STEM capability to maintain its technological capacities and its global leadership position.

To accomplish those goals, two obvious but crucial actions need to be undertaken: teachers at all levels in the STEM arena need to be recruited and rewarded on a continuous basis; and a steady pipeline of students who will work STEM problems for their productive careers needs to be maintained. Numerous ways have been proposed to accomplish those goals, but the fundamental recommendation we have is that it is time to stop talking and start acting. A joint executive branch–congressional effort that provides a high degree of certainty of accomplishment in the human capital STEM arena will do much to help ensure continued U.S. leadership in cyber.

Maintaining human capital is not sufficient if there are not adequate resources for that capital to use. The United States has traditionally relied on specialized government laboratories to complement private industry efforts in accomplishing key national security goals. That arrangement has been operative in both the nuclear and energy areas, but in the cyber arena, no such structures have been developed, and governmental efforts are limited. For example, the Department of Homeland Security cyber R&D budget for fiscal year 2007 was less than $50 million. Similarly, as Vice Chairman of the Joint Chiefs of Staff General James Cartwright has stated, "We as a nation don't have a national lab structure associated with [cyber] so we aren't growing the intellectual capital we need to . . . at the rate we need to be doing."[5] In short, fundamental R&D activity through the combined efforts of the public and private sectors is insufficient to ensure the United States continues to develop its cyber leadership capabilities.

The needs are significant. For example, security is a major vulnerability for the United States. A structured R&D approach to security would seek to develop specific new capabilities, analyze the costs and benefits of developing and implementing alternative systemic approaches to security, and support and integrate both governmental and private efforts. Examples could include large programs to eliminate flaws from existing widely used software or to create secure, underlying operating systems. Beyond security, there could be a national program on semiconductor research, the development of integrated cyber and biological capabilities for medical treatment and other uses, and the creation of new architectures and software capacities for more effective usage of cyber.

A three-part program of establishing national cyber laboratories, substantially increasing R&D funding for governmental agencies, and enhancing private sector activities through direct contracts and incentives would significantly increase the medium and long-term capacities of the United States. At a time when other countries are advertently adding to their cyber capacities and placing them in direct competition with those of the United States, it is critically important to respond to such challenges.

International Governance

The existing international cyber governance structure is a creature of history more than of logic. It nonetheless has worked well for the United States (and the world), as cyber in all its manifestations has continued to develop. There are, however, two important factors that call for the United States to undertake a thorough review of international cyber governance.

The first is that the portion of the international cyber governance that guides the Internet is both sufficiently ad hoc and perceptually U.S.-dominated that there have been significant calls by other countries to revise the structures. Harold Kwalwasser has set forth the system in detail,[6] but the essence is that some important elements are run by private organizations such as the Internet Corporation for Assigned Names and Numbers (ICANN). While those organizations have been quite effective, their longevity is not guaranteed. For example, in 2010, the government's contract with ICANN (which is part of the overall arrangement) comes up for renewal, and a call for change is likely at that time.

The second factor is that no effective international arrangement deals with the security and law enforcement aspects of cyber. However, given cyber's international character, national security and enforcement efforts will necessarily be less effective than what could be accomplished by an integrated international effort. The United States, for example, has developed statutory rules against various types of cyber crimes. The European Union has organized, and nearly 30 nations have joined, a Convention on Cybercrime. However, much of the world is not covered by focused efforts, which creates a haven from which criminals can operate.

Given the probability of an international call for significant change in Internet governance and the desirability from the U.S. point of view for changes to enhance security and law enforcement, our recommendation is that the executive branch undertake a prompt and substantial review to generate an international proposal around which a consensus can be built.

Failure to create such a proposal does not mean that the United States will not face a call for change. In recent years, a number of international efforts ranging from the International Criminal Court to the land mine convention have gone forward without U.S. participation. It is likely that the current arrangements will not continue and that alternatives could end up being negotiated despite U.S. reservations. Especially because important American interests are not met by existing approaches, undertaking a review as a prelude to organizing a serious international negotiation will be important to keeping cyberspace as effective as possible.

Organization: Cyber Policy Council

The dynamic nature of cyber means that numerous issues have arisen that will need governmental consideration. The government will not always need to take action: its choices will include standing aside and letting the private sector take the lead (as has been done, for example, in the development of cyber applications), taking enabling action (through tax incentives or the creation of enabling environments, such as the development of the international governance structure for the electromagnetic spectrum), or implementing a purposive strategy in which it is substantially engaged (as it does in the military arena and could do on other aspects of cyber, such as some security).

However, there needs to be a policy organization to purposefully consider the choices the government confronts. The need is particularly acute because of the multiplicity of issues, including some already noted such as private-public interface, security, human capital, research and development, and governance, but also others such as the implications of the increased volume of traffic, the potential move from IPv4 to IPv6, net neutrality, and the nature of the U.S. global role. The problem of the multiplicity of issues is exacerbated by the numerous authorities that exist in multiple arenas working on cyber. While the government is moving to coordinate intergovernmental security arrangements, even in the security arena coordination with the private sector needs much more active consideration—and, as noted, there are a host of other issues not involved in security.

Our recommendation is to create a new organization—a Cyber Policy Council along the lines of the Council of Economic Advisors. The council would focus on policy issues that need a White House perspective, bringing together all elements of government but incorporating the Presidential perspective. Such a council could integrate or at least coordinate and review key issues. We would not recommend, at least not initially, that the council have implementing authority; for now, that power should remain with the relevant departments and agencies. But we would give the council the authority to review budgets on cyber and to make recommendations as part of the budgetary process. The council might ultimately take a more strategic directive role (as has been contemplated for the National Counter-Terrorism Center in its area), but we would have the council work for a while before the President determined whether to make it more than a policy office.

Geopolitical Issues

Cyber is both an element of, and a support for, power—for nations, for individuals, and for other entities including businesses, nonprofit organizations, and criminals and terrorists. While "cyberpower and national security" issues could therefore be defined to include the whole scope of societal activities, in this part to create more effective analysis and recommendations, we have focused on traditional geopolitical activities—the grist of international politics, including the use of diplomacy, influence, and force by both nation-states and nonstate actors.

Two preliminary issues deserve review in this connection. First is the question of whether "cyber" is a domain, comparable to other domains—land, sea, air, and space—regularly analyzed in geopolitical contexts. Authoritative DOD publications have described cyber in similar terms as the global commons.[7] Gregory Rattray has fully compared the cyber context to other domains,[8] and the comparability clearly seems to be there. From the perspective of the policymaker, however, it is critical to recognize that nothing—repeat, nothing—follows from that conclusion alone. Being in the status of a domain is not like being in the status of, for example, marriage from which various rights and obligations flow for historic, religious, and legal reasons—for example, the right to community property in some jurisdictions. Indeed, as the community property example shows, even for true forms of status such as marriage, the rights and obligations flowing from that status need to be prescribed. Some states are community property states, some are not—yet there are marriages in each. The consequence of cyber being a domain is simply that its important implications need to be determined.

Second is the question of whether dominance—meaning overwhelming superiority—can be achieved in cyberspace. The high probability is that it cannot. By comparison to sea, air, and space, where military dominance can reasonably be sought, cyber shares three characteristics of land warfare—though in even greater dimensions: number of players, ease of entry, and opportunity for concealment.

The world's most powerful navy has only some 300 ships, there is only one geosynchronous orbit with the number of satellites limited, and a military airplane can easily cost more than $100 million, a satellite system more than $1 billion, and a warship more than $3 billion. By contrast, there are billions of cyber users around the world and untold pathways between cyber site A and cyber site B. An Internet connection costs perhaps $40 a month, a good computer can be purchased for $600 (or rented for $10 an hour), and complex software can be created by a single person or downloaded off the Internet.

The point of the complexity and low cost of much of cyber is that success in cyber will be more like success in land warfare than in sea, air, and space warfare. On land, dominance is not a readily achievable criterion. During the Cold War, the United States and its allies had an effective land capability but did not have dominance vis-à-vis the Soviet Union. While the first phase of the 2003 Iraq War suggested land dominance, the more recent—and much longer and more costly—counterinsurgency/stability operations phase has demonstrated absence of dominance. A more realistic set of goals in land warfare is effectiveness and achieving objectives. That likewise is a sensible set of goals for cyber. The United States will engage in a cyber landscape where there are opponents, major and otherwise, who have consequential capabilities. We should seek to prevail—and apply the resources to do so—but we should expect a competitive environment, one in which the opponent maintains important capabilities. Indeed, if any further proof is required, it should be clear that if we were capable of dominance, we would have gotten rid of hackers instead of being subject to thousands of attacks and probes on a daily basis.

Network-centric Operations

Network-centric operations are a fundamental approach used by the U.S. military. We have been highly successful in their use, and substantial efforts are ongoing to expand such capacities. We strongly support those efforts but raise the following question: By focusing so heavily on network-centric capabilities, are we creating vulnerabilities that may be exploited by opponents to our substantial detriment?

Since the Gulf War of 1991, U.S. conventional warfare capabilities, which are grounded in network-centricity, have been deemed extremely powerful by virtually all who review them. For this reason, opponents are expected to attempt to use asymmetric means when engaged in conflict against the United States. Computer network attack against U.S. networks—both military and those civilian networks supporting the military—would be one type of asymmetry.

To offset such a potential problem, we recommend three specific DOD efforts, all of which would fall under the purview of achieving mission assurance—the ability to accomplish the objective despite significant opposition.

First, a review should be initiated to determine the operational vulnerability of network capacities. The review should include full red team efforts designed to determine what negative effects could be created under operational conditions and would presumably require a number of exercises. Since some important networks will be run by the private sector, it will be necessary to create a process by which such networks can be evaluated. The focus should not be just on red-teaming. On the blue side, efforts should be made to determine what workarounds and capacities exist even after networks become degraded. Networks hardly would be the first wartime systems or materiel to sustain degradation, and, in other arenas, we certainly plan to move forward despite the problems created.

Second, having assessed vulnerabilities, a determination should be made as to the most important research, development, and/or acquisition efforts necessary to overcome key vulnerabilities. To the extent that important vulnerabilities are found to exist in the private sector, a public-private approach will need to be generated.

Third, as part of both the R&D and acquisition processes as well as in future exercises, the implications of risk in cyber from potential network vulnerability need to be systematically assessed.

Computer Network Attack

The potential for cyber warfare has long been discussed, and the attacks on Estonia's cyber capabilities in 2007 made the prospects even clearer. DOD has been equally clear. As Lieutenant General Keith Alexander stated, "The focus of cyber warfare is on using cyberspace (by operating within or through it) to attack personnel, facilities, or equipment with the intent of degrading, neutralizing, or destroying enemy combat capability, while protecting our own."[9]

While General Alexander's goal for DOD is clear enough, a fundamental obstacle stands in its way: cyber warfare—generally called *computer network attack* (CNA) by DOD—is not integrated with other overall planning because of the highly compartmented classification that cyber activities receive. Senior military leaders have been entirely clear about the problem, with one stating: "I do not want to see the cyberspace train drive off down some dark alley and set up shop and nobody knows what the hell they've been doing. They need to be integrated."[10] Of course, as the Vice Chairman of the Joint Chiefs of Staff has said, that is difficult because of the compartmentalization/classification problem: "We make sure the recce teams don't tell the defenders what they found, or the attackers, and the attackers go out and attack and don't tell anybody they did. It's a complete secret to everybody in the loop and it's dysfunctional."[11] The negative results are clear enough, according to General Cartwright: "The geeks turn it into a special language behind a bunch of closed doors so that a warfighter has no idea how to use it."[12]

The remedy (and our recommendation) for this problem is to reduce classification and to enhance integration of CNA with other planning. This has not been done previously out of concern that knowledge of DOD capabilities would allow potential adversaries to take offsetting measures in advance. However, with other capabilities such as electronic warfare, which have great similarity to computer network attack, we have been able to offset those problems. While specific electronic warfare techniques have higher classification, general capabilities have lower classification and are fully accessible to planners. Moreover, capabilities that can be discussed at the conceptual and engineering levels are entirely unclassified, as even a quick review of the numerous DOD publications on electronic warfare will demonstrate. While potential adversaries will know that we have such capacities in general, that will hardly come as a surprise inasmuch as significant capacities for computer network attack can simply be downloaded off the Internet, attacks (in the thousands) occur each day, and hacking is discussed regularly (in both constructive and nonconstructive ways) in both open literature and private groups. To put it bluntly, we are kidding ourselves when we undertake to classify CNA in the fashion that we do—and, more importantly than kidding, we are harming our own capacity to use CNA to the extent it deserves.

Deterrence

Cyber attacks—hacking of various kinds—are a fact of modern life. Nation-states, such as China, have been publicly accused of hacking for espionage purposes, and nonstate actors, such as criminals and terrorists, likewise have substantial capabilities. The steady state of modern life is that thousands of intrusions occur each day, some with important consequences. More ominously, there are concerns that attacks could be undertaken for geopolitical purposes by states or nonstate actors that would have far greater negative impact than has thus far occurred. The capacity to deter such attacks would be enormously valuable.

Cyber deterrence has been considered challenging because of the difficulty of attributing the source of cyber attacks. While attribution unquestionably is a consequential issue, we believe that deterrence in the context of cyber is a viable strategy and one on which the United States ought to embark much more advertently. The components of such a strategy would consist of the following elements, some of which would require development as discussed below.

First, any approach to deterrence of cyber attacks needs to be considered in an overall concept of deterrence, not as a separate cyber arena. Such an effort would use a combination of potential retaliation, defense, and dissuasion. It would be based on all elements of national power so that, for example, any retaliation would not necessarily be by cyber but could be by diplomatic, economic, or kinetic—or cyber—means, depending on the circumstances. Retaliation, when and if it occurred, would be at a time, place, and manner of our choosing.

In generating policy, some important differentiations could be consequential. State actors generally act for classic geopolitical aims and often are susceptible to classic geopolitical strategies. Retaliation of various sorts might be more available against state actors, and dissuasion likewise might be more effective. By contrast, nonstate actors could be less susceptible to classic geopolitical strategies (though indirect strategies, such as affecting the country in which they are based, may have impact). Cyber defense, law enforcement, and, for terrorists, classic counterterrorist techniques may be most effective.

One important question is whether there is a threshold at which more significant responses become appropriate. It bears restating that there are a great many intrusions already ongoing, and responses to them have not been dramatic. In analyzing this issue, it may be useful to separate what might be termed *high-end* attacks from *low-end* attacks. If one hypothesized a serious attack that rendered, for example, military or key financial systems inoperative, the probability would be that an extremely robust response would be appropriate. A state actor that undertook a high-end attack should certainly understand that the United States could carry out a countervalue response that would not be limited to a response on cyber assets. The potential of a response against the high-value elements of a state should add considerably to deterrence. Likewise, it should be clear that an attack in the context of an ongoing conflict, whether against a state or a nonstate actor, likely will receive a very significant response. Dealing with cyber actions by an actor with whom we are militarily engaged, such as al Qaeda or the insurgents in Iraq, seems different than dealing with a new problem where force has not already been used.

On the other hand, even if, for example, it was clear that an identity theft ring was being operated out of a particular country, law enforcement and diplomatic responses probably would be used. The degree of damage generally would not be deemed sufficient to require a significant response. Such restraint, however, might not always be appropriate in circumstances that usually are the province of law enforcement. Historically, some instances of criminal behavior have led to consequential U.S. efforts, such as the 1989 invasion of Panama and the capture, trial, and incarceration of its president for drug trafficking. Moreover, an effective response against criminal use of cyberspace could add credibility to the prospect of a response against other actors.

One important difference between high-end and low-end attacks might be that attributing the high-end attack to its source would be easier. Because states normally act for geopolitical reasons, a high-end cyber attack by a state probably would occur in a context in which it might be possible to determine the source. Nonetheless, attribution is a significant challenge, and a major part of a deterrence policy will be to create greater capabilities to assist in attribution. Those efforts should include developing more effective technical means, such as monitoring and intrusion devices as well as traceback and forensic capacities, and it might involve other technical efforts such as new architectures, protocols, and types of servers and routers. In addition to technical responses, intelligence capabilities and law enforcement capabilities might be expanded. An important element of deterrence will be expanding protection beyond governmental entities. We have recommended a differentiated response to security, and a vital component will be to make the appropriate private networks "hard targets."

Finally, inasmuch as cyber is inherently international, working with the international community will be indispensable to generating effective deterrence of both high-end and low-end attacks. At the high end, a common approach will be important to establish the international framework that will help end the conflict on the most desirable terms to the United States. Likewise, allies and partners may have important technical and other capabilities to help enhance retaliation, defense, or dissuasion. At the lower end, greater cooperation will advance law enforcement and diplomatic capacities.

To accomplish both high-end and low-end goals, the United States will want to lead a variety of efforts, including assuring that the North Atlantic Treaty Organization (NATO) treaty is understood at a minimum as including high-end attacks as a matter of treaty consequence; developing binding law enforcement mechanisms, possibly modeled on the European Union Convention on Cyber-crime; and generating a new international regime that provides internal guidance, as well as requirements for cooperation, for all countries—potentially modeled on United Nations Security Council resolutions undertaken in the light of the 9/11 attacks. As a critical element in undertaking such action, significant policy and legal review will be imperative to determine relevant constitutional and statutory considerations (including the possibility of revising statutes) and generate an effective international diplomatic strategy. Ultimately, it may be worthwhile to expand the current limited U.S. declaratory policy regarding cyber, but such a decision should await the results of any review.

In sum, the United States needs a much more robust cyber deterrence policy than it has. Such a policy will include both generating capabilities and undertaking political action.

Influence[13]

Cyber influence is an ongoing source of power in the international security arena. Although the United States has an enormous cyber information capacity (estimated to produce annually about 40 percent of the world's new, stored information and a similar share of telecommunications), its cyber influence is not proportional to that capacity. For example, a British Broadcasting Corporation poll of some 26,000 people in 24 countries (including the United States) published in 2007 stated that the "global perception of the U.S. continues to decline," with the populace of only 3 of the 24 countries surveyed saying the United States had a mainly positive impact on world affairs.[14] The mismatch between U.S. information capabilities and the actuality of U.S. influence is obvious.

Impediments to American cyber influence include the vastness and com-plexity of the international information environment, the multiplicity of cul-tures and differing audiences to which communications must be addressed, the extensiveness and significance of contending or alternative messages, and the complexity and importance of using appropriate influential messengers and message mechanisms.

Enhancing the influence of the United States in cyberspace will require a multifaceted strategy that differentiates the circumstances of the messages, key places of delivery, and sophistication with which messages are created and delivered, with particular focus on channels and messengers. To improve in these areas, the United States must focus on actions that include discerning the nature of the audiences, societies, and cultures to which messages will be delivered; increasing the number of experts in geographic and cultural arenas, particularly in languages; augmenting resources for overall strategic communications and cyber influence efforts; encouraging long-term communications and cyber influence efforts along with short-term responses; and understanding that successful strategic communications and cyber influence operations cannot be achieved by the United States acting on its own—allies and partners are needed both to shape our messages and to support theirs.

To accomplish those ends, U.S. policymakers can undertake a variety of specific actions.

First, and perhaps most important, greater focus must be placed on the nature of audiences and of the societies and cultures into which cyber-transmitted messages will be delivered. The intended recipients need to be clear. For example, in the context of a counterterror effort, there likely will be a difference among messages to populations at large—those who do not support terrorists, those who are terrorist sympathizers, those who are active supporters of terrorists, and those who are terrorists. Moreover, those varying audiences might well be reached by different types of communications—for example, television for broader audiences and Web sites for potential terrorist recruits. In this context of differentiated messaging, a further consideration needs to be an understanding of the types of persons who have influence with the message recipients and the types of contexts in which that influence will be most effective.

Second, it will be necessary to increase the number of experts in geographic, cultural, and linguistic arenas. Such expertise can help build a societal/cultural map of influencers, key communications nodes, and cultural patterns to guide strategic communications and influence operations.

Added to these cultural experts should be experts in psychology and marketing who can help generate messages and ensure that communications are effective. Finally, experts are needed in the use of television, radio, the Internet, and cell phones. In short, an interdisciplinary approach is required.

Third, leaders must realize that while there may be a consistent base message, that message will be presented in multiple theaters. These areas will differ significantly, and to be effective, messaging should likewise differ. For example, the society, culture, and influential persons in Indonesia are significantly different from those in Pakistan, and both are significantly different from those in Egypt.

It is also worth noting that the Internet has created coherent, nongeographic communities. Numerous studies and reports document the Internet's effectiveness in transmitting messages that sympathize with, give support to, and recruit for terrorist efforts. The Internet must be a focused arena for strategic communications and influence operations.

Fourth, greater resources must be given to overall strategic communications and influence efforts. For example, expanding the capacities of the Broadcasting Board of Governors, Embassies, and other outlets of the State Department would be enormously valuable. As noted, the Internet is a key mechanism. The State Department runs Web sites, but a broader and more multifaceted Internet strategy—both globally and regionally—would be highly desirable. The Government Accountability Office has found that while Embassy posts are supposed to have a strategic communications plan, they are generally ineffective and lack focus and resources.[15] Enhancing U.S. Government capabilities is a critical requirement.

Fifth, long-term communication efforts must be encouraged along with short-term responses. It is possible to change attitudes over time. As an example, consider the American attitude toward smoking, which has transformed significantly over the last 30 years. In the battle of ideas, the U.S. Government is seeking a long-term change—and so there is a need to adopt long-term policies. Transmitting messages over DOD Web sites and the Web sites Southeast European Times and Magharebia, which provide news, analysis, and information, is a productive, long-term approach that will not affect attitudes immediately but can have significant consequences over time.

Sixth, we must fully appreciate that facts speak louder than words. Some policies generate considerable opposition, and strategic communications and influence operations are not panaceas that can overcome all real-world actions. In the earliest planning stages, the communications consequences of actions must be discussed. In conflicts such as those in Iraq and Afghanistan, the impact of violent activities will significantly change the worldviews of not only those immediately impacted but also those who are indirectly affected and those to whom those effects are communicated. Every battle commander in these irregular wars soon finds out that the communications battle is critical—because the center of gravity for success is the population. But all too often, our commanders have to learn this on the ground. Especially in this globalized world of instant communications, tactical actions can have strategic consequences. Cyberspace is a creative and cultural commons defined by information, perception, cognition, and belief, and it is becoming the preeminent domain of political victory or defeat. Increased support for training and resources for cyber-enabled communications will be critical elements of effective counterinsurgency and stability operations. Communication—to one's supporters, to the population at large, and to the opposition—is of crucial importance. The government needs resources and training for our people on these issues, and these must be undertaken not only by DOD, but also in a joint DOD-State context.

Seventh, the U.S. Government should not expect success at strategic communications and influence operations acting on its own. Rather, it should use an alliance and partnership approach, both to expand capacities and to increase effectiveness. In the business world, it would be the rare American company that would seek to enter another country without the guidance and support of local business, whether as partners, joint ventures, or advisors—and often as all three. In military and diplomatic arenas, our allies and partners are recognized as enormous sources of strength. In the strategic communications and influence operations arena, we need to develop those alliances and partnerships, both to shape our own messages and support theirs.

Stability Operations[16]

Cyber, through information and information technology, can increase considerably the likelihood of success in stability operations—if engaged as part of an overall strategy that coordinates the actions of outside interveners and focuses on generating effective results for the host nation. Properly used, cyber can help create a knowledgeable intervention, organize complex activities, and increase the effectiveness of stability operations by integrating them with the host nation. The critical decision for policymakers is to utilize on a systematic and resourced basis the capabilities that cyber provides.

The benefits from adopting such an approach are substantial. First, proper use of cyber can help create a "knowledgeable" intervention. Even before the intervention, and certainly as it progresses, the interveners will need information of many kinds about both planned and ongoing respondent activities and about the host nation. An information strategy supported by information technology provides an opportunity to share information among the stability operations respondents themselves. This cooperation will facilitate the generation of a common approach and can help in the effective use of scarce resources.

A second key benefit of a cyber-supported strategy will be the help it provides in organizing complex activities. Normally, a stability operation will be undertaken on a countrywide basis. For even the smallest countries, this means a significant geographic area, with all the difficulties of maintaining connectivity. The intervention also will undoubtedly be of some duration, and cyber will be valuable to maintain an updated approach as conditions on the ground change.

The third key benefit from cyber will come from the ability to use distributed information to integrate the stability operations respondents with the host nation. The objective of a stability operation is not a "good intervention" but rather an "effective host nation" as a result of the intervention. To accomplish this difficult task, given that the host nation is likely fragmented, disrupted, and ineffective, the interveners need to stay connected to the host nation so that the results are adopted and adoptable by the populace on whose behalf the effort is being undertaken.

An effective cyber strategy would involve the host nation (likely in numerous manifestations) in the ongoing activities of the intervention.

The fourth benefit is to integrate the host nation and make it more effective. Effectiveness can be enhanced by using cyber capacities to identify key requirements and target scarce resources. Host nation capacity can also be created by the use of cyber. Government operations can be reestablished with the proper use of information technology. Both the information systems and the training to use them will be required, but information capacity often can be generated far more quickly than other infrastructures—and can enable other effective actions.

Five key elements are required to generate an effective cyber strategy for the United States to use in stability operations. The first requirement is for the U.S. Government to make the fundamental decision that such a strategy is a mandatory element of all stability operations. That is no small statement because the reality is that the United States has never—in any of its many stability operations—made such a decision. But the rationale for such a conclusion is clear: information and information technology are crucial elements to the success of stability operations.

Although the problems of stability operations go far beyond military, the second element of an effective cyber strategy recognizes that, doctrinally, the military requires a cyber strategy as part of the planning and execution of any stability operation. Accordingly, in both joint and Service documents—plans and the rules and guidance for their development and execution—a cyber strategy is a required element.

The third element of a cyber strategy for the U.S. Government for stability operations is to establish partnerships with key stability operations participants in advance. It is important to emphasize the word *key*. It is not possible, and would not be effective, to try to establish partnerships with all of the many players who would take part in a stability operation. But there are some very key parties who would regularly be involved and participate in planning.

The fourth element of an effective cyber strategy is to focus on the host nation. Establishing host nation effectiveness cannot be overemphasized—it is the main goal. Informing host nation decisionmaking, enhancing governmental capacities, and supporting societal and economic development are all crucial elements of an effective cyber strategy. However, when cyber technology is considered, efforts with respect to the interveners too often are emphasized as compared to creating effectiveness of the host nation. This is backward. An effective cyber strategy is one that makes the host nation effective. Nothing else will do. Thus, a critical element of the strategy is a cyber business plan for the host nation and an intervener support strategy that aims to enable the host nation business plan.

In sum, policymakers can substantially enhance U.S. capabilities in stability operations by adopting a cyber strategy as part of the overall effort.

Doctrine, Organization, Training, Materiel, Logistics, People, and Finance

The concept of doctrine, organization, training, materiel, logistics, people, and finance is a DOD construct intended to ensure that an activity is looked at in its full dimensions. Cyber needs such a review by DOD because as a new activity, it has generated a host of initiatives that need to be better coordinated. In general, we applaud the various actions taken, such as the designation of U.S. Strategic Command (USSTRATCOM) to have authority over cyber or the Air Force's decision to have a new cyber command. But there are numerous open questions that need consideration, and a significant internal review should lay them out for decision. Among the key questions are:

- What should be the relationship between cyber efforts and information operations, and does the latter need redefinition?
- How should USSTRATCOM relate to the regional commands in practice?
- What component commands should be established to support USSTRATCOM, and should they all perform the same functions?
- How should the Joint Information Operations Command relate to the public diplomacy activities of the State Department?
- What should the role of cyber be in exercises, both Service and joint, and does there need to be greater interagency exercising?
- What education and training should personnel involved in cyber receive, and what career paths should be developed?
- What cyber research and development should DOD engage in, and how should that be conducted?

As part of the review, we have two recommendations. First, we believe cyber needs to be regularly integrated into exercises, both through red teams and otherwise, since the cyber world is the real world we face. Second, just as we have nuclear and energy laboratories, we believe there need to be government "cyber laboratories." The precise mechanics can be determined, but the critical point is that there needs to be focused and substantial government research on cyber. We recognize that the private sector conducts significant and highly valuable cyber research. The private sector, however, is understandably motivated by profit, and there are issues that government needs to address because the appropriate level of effort will not be generated through market activity alone. The government can, of course, rely in part on the private sector for such R&D, as it does in other national security areas. However, creation of government cyber laboratories will establish the ability to delve deeply into key questions under government control in a way that cannot always be accomplished through the contracting process.

Finally, in connection with the DOD review, we think that a government "cyber corps" should be considered. Such a group could be joint and multi-disciplinary—and probably should be looked at as a potential interagency approach. Operationally, a cyber corps could integrate influence, attack, defense, and exploitation in the operational arena—and could help support those efforts in particular, more specialized agencies.

The Need for International Action

The nature of cyber itself and the discussions thus far should make it readily apparent that cyber cannot sensibly be considered solely on a national basis. Cyber in many of its manifestations is a creature of globalization, and it needs to be analyzed and reviewed with an international framework and international consequences in mind. The fundamental issues are the same internationally as they are from the U.S. perspective—including security, governance, uses in geopolitical context, and others—and their solutions will require, or at least be enhanced by, international actions.

Three international issues call out for immediate action. First, the 2007 cyber attacks on Estonia should make clear that NATO needs to undertake a comprehensive review of its cyber policies. The review would include the obvious question of when an "armed attack" in terms of the treaty has occurred, and whether the treaty or its interpretation needs to be revised to include the ability to act jointly. But the review should also raise the issue of whether NATO has the appropriate security arrangements for its forces to allow for secure interconnectivity and for its nations to protect them from outside harm. Moreover, the review needs to determine whether NATO has the proper capacity for deterrence (retaliation, defense, and dissuasion). Finally, it needs to analyze NATO capacity to use cyber in stability operations and for influence. In short, a major NATO effort concentrating on cyber is called for.

Second, international influence and international public diplomacy need to be strengthened. A battle of ideas is likely to continue in the 21st century. The United States will need significant international support to prevail.

Third, the international governance structure for cyber needs to be strengthened. In the law enforcement arena, greater cooperative measures need to be created. In the overall governance area, there undoubtedly will be a major review.

Cyber offers important prospects for individuals, organizations, and governments. But it will require forceful steps to ensure that its potential is best fulfilled. Accomplishing the major recommendations of this study will go far toward enabling that end.

CHAPTER 2

From Cyberspace to Cyberpower: Defining the Problem

Daniel T. Kuehl

THIS CHAPTER has several ambitious objectives that are critical for this book: to lay out the central concepts for what we mean by *cyberspace* and *cyberpower*, to suggest definitions that capture the logic behind these concepts; and to establish a set of foundations upon which future work can build. *Cyberspace* has been in our lexicon for two decades, since William Gibson used it to describe "a consensual hallucination" in his science fiction novel, *Neuromancer*, but there certainly is no consensus on its meaning in the world of the 21st century.[1] While organs of government attempt to define its meaning in the real, operational world— Gibson's approach obviously will not suffice—the approaches we develop toward this domain will shape how it interacts with other domains and affects relationships among the other elements and instruments of power, especially how humans and the organizations we create use that power.

The march of technology and progress guarantees that even while we debate this definition—regardless of exactly how we define it now and refine it in the future—our use of cyberspace has already reached the point where an increasingly wide range of social, political, economic, and military activities are dependent on it and thus are vulnerable to both interruption of its use and usurpation of its capabilities. This chapter offers definitions of both *cyberspace* and *cyberpower*, suggests some of the ways they relate to and impact other domains, and explores how they are shaping new operational concepts such as information operations, new technological combinations such as the global information grid, and other instruments of power. It suggests an approach for a national cyber strategy and provides links to this book's following chapters, which explore key topics and issues in greater detail.

Cyberspace: A New Domain

From the start of recorded history until about a century ago, mankind had only two physical domains in which to operate, the land and the sea, each of which had dramatically different physical characteristics. The sea was usable by humans only with the aid of technology—the galley, sailing ship, steamship, nuclear submarine—because we could swim for only so long. Other than by simply walking, the land was usable only through the exploitation of technology—the wheel, the plow, the war chariot (up to and including the modern main battle tank). The great change was a century ago, when we added a third physical domain—the aerospace—to the mix,[2] and while its military aspects outweighed its commercial applications for many years, the economic, social, and political aspects of air travel and transportation for the 21st-century are enormous. In 1957, we added a fourth to our mix, and while outer space is not yet as militarily or commercially pervasive as the air, it has deep and essential links to operations and activities in all other environments. Each of these four physical domains is marked by radically different physical characteristics, and they are usable only through the use of technology to exploit those characteristics.

To these domains we have now added a fifth: cyberspace. Joint Publication 1–02, *Department of Defense Dictionary of Military and Associated Terms*, had a definition of cyberspace dating to the early 2000s, but there was almost universal agreement that it was insufficient: "the notional environment in which digitized information is communicated over computer networks."[3] Cyberspace is hardly "notional," and confining it to the realm of being "digitized and computerized" is far too limiting, failing to reflect the massive technological and social changes with which cyberspace is interwoven.

Defining Cyberspace

Since the mid-1990s, a number of authors (see table 2–1) have offered useful insights that have helped shaped thought on this issue, and the definition proposed in this chapter draws heavily from them. Several consistent threads run through these insights, including the role of electronics, telecommunications infrastructures, and information systems.[4] A crucial and useful perspective was offered by the 2003 *National Strategy to Secure Cyberspace*, which defined cyberspace as the "nervous system—the control system of the country . . . composed of hundreds of thousands of interconnected computers, servers, routers, switches, and fiber optic cables that allow our critical infrastructures to work."[5] The Joint Staff in early 2006 initiated an important and much-needed effort to develop the *National Military Strategy for Cyberspace Operations*, and when it was approved in December 2006 by Chairman of the Joint Chiefs of Staff General Peter Pace, it included a definition that closely mirrored the one suggested by this book: "Cyberspace is a domain characterized by the use of electronics and the electromagnetic spectrum to store, modify and exchange information via networked information systems and physical infrastructures."[6]

Two additional official definitions were issued in early 2008. One came out of the White House, with President George W. Bush's signature of National Security Presidential Directive (NSPD) 54/Homeland Security Presidential Directive 23, "Cybersecurity Policy," on January 8, 2008. While NSPD 54 itself is classified, its definition of cyberspace is not: "Cyberspace means the interdependent network of information technology infrastructures, and includes the Internet, telecommunications networks, computer systems, and embedded processors and controllers in critical industries." Whatever the strengths and weaknesses of this definition, it is important to consider that it was issued within the context of a specific issue, the safety and security of military and government information networks.

TABLE 2-1. Definitions of Cyberspace

- Greece: *kybernetes* (the steersman) or *cybernetics*, the study of control processes, which was the basis for Tom Rona's concept (1976) of "information warfare."

- William Gibson, *Neuromancer* (1984): "a consensual hallucination."

- Edward Waltz, *Information Warfare: Principles and Operations* (1998): The "cyberspace dimension" refers to the middle layer—the information infrastructure—of the three realms of the information warfare battle-space. These three realms are the physical (facilities, nodes), the information infrastructure, and the perceptual.

- Google: "The electronic medium of computer networks, in which online communication takes place. . . . a metaphor for the non-physical terrain created by computer systems. . . . the impression of space and community formed by computers, computer networks, and their users. . . . the place where a telephone conversation appears to occur. . . . the place between the phones."

- Winn Schwartau, *Information Warfare: Chaos on the Electronic Superhighway* (1994): "That intangible place between computers where information momentarily exists on its route from one end of the global network to the other. . . . the ethereal reality, an infinity of electrons speeding down copper or glass fibers at the speed of light. . . . Cyberspace is borderless . . . [but also] think of cyberspace as being divided into groups of local or regional cyberspace—hundreds and millions of smaller cyberspaces all over the world."

Continued

Table 2–1 continued

- Winn Schwartau, *Information Warfare: Chaos on the Electronic Superhighway* (2d ed., 1996): "[National] cyberspace are distinct entities, with clearly defined electronic borders. . . . Small-C cyberspaces consist of personal, corporate or organizational spaces. . . . Big-C cyberspace is the National Information Infrastructure. . . . add [both] and then tie it all up with threads of connectivity and you have all of cyberspace."

- *Oxford English Dictionary* (1997): "The notional environment within which electronic communication occurs."

- Walter Gary Sharp, *CyberSpace and the Use of Force* (1999): "The environment created by the confluence of cooperative networks of computers, information systems, and telecommunication infrastructures commonly referred to as the Internet and the World Wide Web."

- Dorothy Denning, *Information Warfare and Security* (1999): "The information space consisting of the sum total of all computer networks."

- Gregory Rattray, *Strategic Warfare in Cyberspace* (2001): "A physical domain resulting from the creation of information systems and networks that enable electronic interactions to take place. . . . Cyberspace is a man-made environment for the creation, transmittal, and use of information in a variety of formats. . . . Cyberspace consists of electronically powered hardware, networks, operating systems and transmission standards."

- *Merriam-Webster Third New International Dictionary* (2002): "The on-line world of computer networks."

- *National Military Strategy for Cyberspace Operations* (2006): "A domain characterized by the use of electronics and the electromagnetic spectrum to store, modify and exchange information via networked systems and physical infrastructures."

- National Security Presidential Directive 54 (2008): "The interdependent network of information technology infrastructures, and includes the Internet, telecommunications networks, computer systems, and embedded processors and controllers in critical industries."

- Deputy Secretary of Defense Gordon England (2008): "A global domain within the information environment consisting of the interdependent network of information technology infrastructures, including the Internet, telecommunications networks, computer systems, and embedded processors and controllers."

Just over 4 months later, in May 2008, the Department of Defense (DOD) expanded this definition in a memorandum from Deputy Secretary of Defense Gordon England that defined cyberspace as "a global domain within the information environment consisting of the interdependent network of information technology infrastructures, including the Internet, telecommunications networks, computer systems, and embedded processors and controllers."[7] The memo also advises that DOD will use this definition "until further notice," a wise acknowledgment that the rapidly evolving nature of the field will likely generate further refinement. This memo thus nullified the definition contained in the 2006 *National Military Strategy for Cyberspace Operations*, which will incorporate the new definition whenever it is formally revised. While both definitions are useful and advance our conceptual understanding of cyberspace, they lack a critical piece of information: what makes cyberspace unique? If cyberspace is a domain alongside land, sea, air, and outer space, what are its unique and defining physical characteristics?

All of these various approaches combine to suggest that cyberspace is more than computers and digital information. This chapter offers a definition that builds upon those threads cited above and yet is different in some crucial regards: cyberspace is *a global domain within the information environment whose distinctive and unique character is framed by the use of electronics and the electromagnetic spectrum to create, store, modify, exchange, and exploit information via interdependent and interconnected networks using information-communication technologies.*[8]

This definition blends the best elements of both Secretary England's approach and that contained in the *National Military Strategy for Cyberspace Operations*. These interdependent and interconnected information networks and systems reside simultaneously in both physical and virtual space and within and outside of geographic boundaries. Their users range from entire nation-states and their component organizational elements and communities down to lone individuals and amorphous transnational groups who may not profess allegiance to any traditional organization or national entity.[9] They rely on three distinct yet interrelated dimensions that in the aggregate comprise the global information environment as outlined in Joint Publication 3–13, *Information Operations*, and to which (hopefully) Secretary England's memo was referring: the physical platforms, systems and infrastructures that provide global *connectivity* to link information systems, networks, and human users; the massive amounts of informational *content* that can be digitally and electronically sent anywhere, anytime, to almost anyone, a condition that has been enormously affected and augmented by the convergence of numerous informational technologies; and the human *cognition* that results from greatly increased access to content and can dramatically impact human behavior and decisionmaking.[10]

While the fundamental technological aspects of cyberspace that require the use of manmade technology to enter and exploit seem to support an argument that cyberspace is a manmade environment, this situation is actually no different from any of the other four domains. We also need manmade technologies to enter and exploit the other domains, the only difference being that we can more easily see and sense those domains.[11] It is, however, important to note that while the physical characteristics of cyberspace can be delineated and come from forces and phenomena that exist and occur in the natural world, in a real sense cyberspace is also a designed environment, created with the specific intent of facilitating the use and exploitation of information, human interaction, and intercommunication.[12]

At the risk of being reductionist, it might be useful to break down the definition offered in this chapter and examine some of its key elements. First, cyberspace is an *operational* space where humans and their organizations use the necessary technologies to act and create effects, whether solely in cyberspace or in and across the other operational domains and elements of power.[13] In this sense it is like any of the other four physical domains—land, sea, air, and outer space—in which we operate, and one of the explicit objectives of this definition is to place cyberspace firmly within the bounds of the operational domains and elements of power within which the national security community operates. The business community uses cyberspace to facilitate global trade, exchange funds, manage far-flung enterprises, and do innumerable other vital things. In a real sense, cyberspace is where we create and use the digital information that fuels the global economy. Every day, the global business community exchanges trillions of dollars via cyberspace, transactions in which not a single dime or euro of hard currency is moved. The political strategist cannot ignore cyberspace, because its effective use may well mean the difference between victory and defeat in the electoral process.[14]

In the effort to influence—whether focused on an individual, an organization, or an entire society—cyberspace is a key operational medium through which "strategic influence" is conducted, and daily we see increased references to "Jihad.com" and other ways in which the terrorists and so-called jihadists and irhabists are using cyberspace as a critical medium for their operations.[15] Warfare of the 21st century involving opponents possessing even a modicum of modern technology is hardly possible without access to cyberspace, and entire new operational concepts such as network-centric warfare or fighting in an "informationized battlespace" would be impossible without cyber-based systems and capabilities.[16] The ability to reprogram the targeting data within a weapon on its way to the target, then rely on real-time updates from a global positioning system satellite to precisely strike that target, is possible only through the use of cyberspace. In many ways, the entire debate on whether DOD is "transforming" itself revolves around efforts to better employ and exploit cyber-based capabilities.[17]

The second part of the definition is what truly makes cyberspace unique and distinguishes it from the other environments, for it is the use of *electronic* technologies to create and "enter" cyberspace and use the energies and properties of the *electromagnetic spectrum* that sets cyberspace apart. Even without detailed definitions and analyses, we can clearly see that the physical characteristics of these different domains are what differentiate them from each other.[18] The argument that cyberspace is a manmade environment is only half-true. The electronic technologies that we create and employ to use cyberspace are its counterparts to the vehicles, ships, airplanes, and satellites that we have created to exploit the other domains, but the unique characteristics of each domain are naturally occurring phenomena of the physical world.[19] Any definition of cyberspace that omits this fundamental condition—the blending of electronics and electromagnetic energy—is thus flawed by not recognizing the central features that make cyberspace distinct.

This brings us to the third aspect of our definition, because we exploit those characteristics and properties not to sail the seas or orbit the earth, but rather to "*create, store, modify, exchange, and exploit*" information via those electronic means. This may seem self-evident, but that may be because we see so many different trees around us that we do not realize the extent of the forest. The way that cyberspace has changed (some would argue is expanding astronomically) how we can create, store, modify, exchange, and exploit information has transformed how we operate in the other domains and use the instruments of national power. We literally can capture any kind of information—the human voice on a cell phone, the contours of a fingerprint, the contents of the *Encyclopedia Britannica*, or the colors of ice and dust as "seen" by a spacecraft on the planet Mars—store that information as a string of bits and bytes, modify it to suit our purposes, and then transmit it instantly to every corner of the globe.[20]

It is the fourth aspect of our definition, the *networking of interdependent and interconnected networks using information-communication technologies* that are the backbone of those systems, that has brought cyberspace to the forefront of debates over its impact on and importance to national security and international affairs.[21] We began to network and interconnect modern, technologically based information systems with the invention of the telegraph, which has been called the "Victorian Internet," before we began using the air, the subsurface of the sea, or outer space.[22] The telegraph functions by the use of small amounts of electricity (the early ones were powered by battery) to transmit information in the form of dots and dashes over a wire, a process remarkably similar to today's use of fiber optic cables to perform the same basic function—albeit in a form and volume that Samuel Morse could not have imagined. The extension of these dots and dashes into the ether came with the invention of the wireless, which had followed by not many years the telephone, and preceded by even fewer years the transmission of voice over wireless—radio.

All of these functions were uses of cyberspace, even though the invention of the electronic computer was decades away. Once the microchip was developed, all the elements were present for what we have come to call the information revolution, and even though this revolution took place in an evolutionary manner—as do almost all revolutions—we now see that in myriad ways, our daily life is essentially inseparable from cyberspace. The definition of cyberspace proffered in this chapter thus begins with those physical characteristics that make cyberspace unique before emphasizing the key interaction of communications to exchange information. It is the inseparable linkage of the technology, the human users, and the impact of the interconnectivity in the modern world that differentiates these kinds of information networks from earlier ones—such as the Pony Express of the 1860s—and that hints at cyberspace's future impact.

What does this definition of cyberspace offer us that the other definitions do not? Two key issues manifest themselves. First is its foundation in the physical world: it is based not on any list of activities that take place within that domain but rather on the unique physical characteristics that set it apart from the other domains. What makes cyberspace neither aerospace nor outer space is the use of the electromagnetic spectrum as the means of "movement" within the domain, and this clear distinction from other physical environments may be crucial to its further development within the national security structure.

This leads to the second key issue: clarity. As contrasted with some of the definitions surveyed earlier, the definition presented here clearly focuses on the technologies that exploit cyberspace's unique characteristics and their resultant effects. If the information being "created, stored, modified, exchanged, or exploited" depends on the use of electronics and electromagnetic energy, then it is being done in cyberspace; if the information is carried by a rider on a pony or a messenger riding a motorcycle, it is not. A computer connected to an area network or a broadcast platform transmitting television signals to a set of receivers is exploiting cyberspace, regardless of whether that computer or transmitter is being carried in a ship, an airplane, the international space station, or by a Special Forces Soldier riding a horse.[23]

Cyberspace and Information Operations

One issue that has engaged DOD in a surprisingly contentious debate is the relationship between cyberspace and information operations (IO). Joint Publication 3–13 defines *IO* as:

the integrated employment of the core capabilities of Electronic Warfare, Computer Network Operations, Psychological Operations [PSYOP], Military Deception, and Operational Security in concert with specified supporting and related capabilities, to influence, disrupt, corrupt or usurp adversarial human and automated decision making while protecting our own.[24]

This definition does not particularly help sharpen this debate, because it constitutes a list of activities, whereas cyberspace is a domain within which those activities are often conducted. To add another element of potential confusion to the debate, Joint Publication 3–13 provides an insightful and useful description of the information environment, as discussed earlier in this chapter: three separate but related and synergistic dimensions, which in this chapter are termed *connectivity, content*, and *cognition*. The first of these, the physical/interconnected dimension, is the primary means by which cyberspace touches and shapes the information environment, because the technological aspects of an interconnected world are dominated by cyberspace.

However, there are other forms and means of connectivity that do not come from cyber capabilities and are outside the definition of cyberspace: the posting of broadsides of the Declaration of Independence that were distributed by horse, hand, or post throughout the 13 colonies in 1776 was an example of connectivity, as is an American battalion commander sitting down to meet with a group of tribal elders in a province in Iraq. The printed material on the broadside, or the subject of the conversation with the tribal elders, would be an example of the content. A PSYOP leaflet may be printed on a hand-operated printing press in Afghanistan, and when the battalion PSYOP officer meets with that leaflet's intended audience to gauge its impact, content has been exchanged without any help from cyberspace. But content is also created in cyberspace: a growing amount of the information that is carried and delivered via the interconnectivity just discussed is created, modified, and stored via electronic/cyber means. Thus, it is erroneous to equate cyberspace with IO. Instead, the most accurate view of cyberspace is to see it as one critical aspect of the overall information environment within which IO is conducted, but not the entire environment, a view that coincides with Secretary England's definition of cyberspace as "a global domain within the information environment."[25]

While information operations include all three dimensions of the information environment, cyberspace comprises only a part—albeit perhaps a large part—of the connectivity and content dimensions.[26] Cyberspace is thus shaping and changing the three dimensions of the information environment: how we create information content itself (a Web page, for example), how we share that content through new forms of connectivity (the Internet links that make that

Web page accessible to over a billion people), and how human interaction and communication are affected.

Another way of looking at this is to portray cyberspace as having multiple layers. At the foundation is the set of physical characteristics that create the basic frameworks of how we enter and use cyberspace. The next layer consists of the platforms and technological systems that we create and employ to create, store, modify, exchange, and exploit information in all its myriad forms. This is where we design and build cyberspace, because each of these cyber platforms is created with a purpose, and we combine them to create even newer and more complex/capable systems and networks. The next layer is the information itself. Finally, and most importantly, is the human element—the people who use the connectivity and the content to affect cognition and do the different things that people do with information. Each layer is important, and each is affected and shaped by the others.[27]

If cyberspace is but one element of the information environment—albeit perhaps the most important one in many cases—are there other issues that arise from this relationship? There are likely many, but two that immediately come to mind are the organizational and doctrinal aspects as related to warfare and the military component of power. Even as the U.S. military comes to grips with a definition of cyberspace, the Services and the joint force are responding with organizational and doctrinal adaptations. Both the Navy and Air Force took action in 2006 to improve their abilities to operate in cyberspace. In October 2006, Admiral Mike Mullen, then Chief of Naval Operations, tasked his Strategic Studies Group at the Naval War College to develop a concept for "Fighting in Cyberspace in 2030" and to examine the operational, procedural, and technological improvements needed for the Navy to master the cyberspace warfighting realm. Admiral Mullen called cyberspace a "new dimension in warfare," and he wanted to determine the relationships between cyberspace and the traditional realms such as the maritime environment. What will warfare be like in cyberspace, he asked, and how will a "1,000 ship Navy go to cyberspace?"[28]

The group's report, which examined the "Convergence of Sea Power and Cyber Power," surveyed nearly 30 definitions of cyberspace and attempted to plot them on an x-y scale that measured each definition against two metrics: its degree of human versus technical centricity, and its present-day versus future focus. It assessed the definition in the 2006 *National Military Strategy for Cyberspace Operations* as quite present-day and tech-centric, then offered its own definition of cyberspace as:

> an unconstrained interaction space . . . for human activity, relationships, and cognition . . . where data, information, and value are created and exchanged . . . enabled by the convergence of multiple disciplines,

technologies, and global networks . . . that permits near instantaneous communication, simultaneously among any number of nodes, independent of boundaries.[29]

While there is much wisdom and perceptive insight in this approach, it has two problems. One is that it is unwieldy and suffers from the understandable attempt to include detailed examples and explanations. The other is that it is not grounded in what makes cyberspace unique—namely, electronic technologies and the electromagnetic spectrum.

The Air Force's move into cyberspace attracted much greater attention because of the more visible and public manner in which it was accomplished. On the anniversary of the bombing of Pearl Harbor in 2005, Air Force Chief of Staff General Michael Moseley and Secretary of the Air Force Michael Wynne signed a new Air Force mission statement declaring that the mission of the Air Force was to "fly and fight in the Air, Space, *and Cyberspace* [emphasis added]." Early in 2006, General Moseley established a task force to explore concepts for how the Air Force should respond to the emergence of this new warfighting environment. In September 2006, General Moseley and Secretary Wynne signed a joint memo directing the creation of an "Operational Command for Cyberspace" that would "enable the employment of global cyber power across the full spectrum of conflict."

Two months later, on November 1, General Moseley designated the 8th Air Force as the Air Force Cyber Command and gave it the added mission of extending the Service's reach and capability into the "domain of electronics and the electromagnetic spectrum." The eventual goal was to develop a plan to "organize, train, and equip" the Air Force as a fully capable cyber force, and for the 8th Air Force to become the cyber equivalent of the Air Force's major commands for air and space sometime in the future (2007 was the target for an "initial operational capability"). The Air Force established a goal of "full operational capability" by late 2009, and was building cyberspace into its programs and budget plans a decade into the future.[30] The Cyber Command's "Strategic Vision" described the cyber domain and strategic environment and established the goal of "dominating cyberspace" so that the Air Force would be able to "establish, control, and use" the domain. Talking about developing capabilities is one thing, but putting resources—money, people, and organizations—into cyberspace is another, and it appeared that the Air Force was not only "talking the talk" about cyberspace, but "walking the walk" as well.[31]

However, suspicion arose among the other Services that the Air Force's movement was a grab for cyber turf, and in the wake of Secretary of Defense Robert Gates' relief of both Secretary Wynne and General Moseley in early summer 2008, the new Air Force Chief of Staff, General Norton Schwartz, called a halt to all actions on Air Force Cyber Command: "Transfers of manpower and resources, including activation and re-assignment of units, shall be halted." While it is unclear how much influence Secretary Gates and Chairman of the Joint Chiefs of Staff Admiral Mullen had on this action, it will certainly have a negative impact of the development of cyber capabilities in the Air Force and perhaps across DOD.[32]

The Army and the Marine Corps are also developing concepts and capabilities for cyber operations, albeit to less of a degree than the Navy and Air Force. The Army sees cyberspace not so much as its own unique warfighting domain but rather as a critical enabler for two vital functions: intelligence and command and control of forces and operations, or "networked enabled battle command." Army Field Manual 3.0, *Operations*, reorganized a series of five tasks related to information and cyber, none of which are cyber-specific, which is congruent with the Army's institutional reluctance to consider cyberspace as an operational domain.[33] But in June 2008, the Army established a Network Warfare Battalion (Provisional), which may herald a more aggressive approach to cyberspace. The Marines' cyber concept is somewhat similar and looks at cyberspace from the perspective of command, control, communications, and computers.

In 2002, a change to the Unified Command Plan assigned responsibility for information operations to U.S. Strategic Command (USSTRATCOM), which undertook a wide-ranging reorganization that included the creation of several joint task forces (including one for global network operations) and joint functional component commands (including one for network warfare). The former includes important elements of the Defense Information Systems Agency and emphasizes protecting and defending military cyber capabilities, while the latter includes capabilities for that aspect of IO known as computer network attack. These changes were made to improve USSTRATCOM's ability to operate in cyberspace and carry out critical missions in support of military and national security strategy, but they also hint at an inherent tension between offense and defense, with the offensive and defensive components divided into two entirely different organizations.[34] This particular and somewhat unusual organizational structure reflected the desire of then USSTRATCOM Commander General James Cartwright to push the authority and responsibility for conducting IO away from the central headquarters and out to the organizations that actually had capabilities and resources. Whether this organizational structure endures in its present form or is modified is perhaps less important than the continued development of real capabilities to plan and conduct IO.

Alliance Perspective
Since cyberspace is global in nature, it is fitting to include the perspective of our single most important alliance, the North Atlantic Treaty Organization (NATO).

In 2008, NATO issued its final draft of "Policy on Cyber Defence." Its intent was to enhance NATO's protection against cyber attacks on communication and information systems of "critical importance to the Alliance," meaning those that support military and political decisionmaking. Data processing systems and supporting services needed for functioning and consultations of Allied nations, intelligence-sharing, decisionmaking, and planning and conduct of NATO missions are the most critical functions to be protected.[35] This interest in cyberspace was intensified by the events in Estonia in mid-2007, which contributed to the creation of several organizations to support this protection. These included NATO's Computer Incident Response Capability, the Cyber Defence Management Authority, and the NATO Cooperative Cyber Defence Centre of Excellent, to be located in Tallinn, Estonia.[36]

These efforts will almost certainly receive added impetus as a result of the "cyberwar" waged as part of the Russian-Georgian confrontation in August 2008. While Russian conventional military operations were conducted in Georgia during the crisis, there reportedly was a "coordinated Russia versus Georgia cyber attack in progress" as well. But there was probably far more smoke than actual fire in this situation. While someone acted to deface and otherwise interfere with a wide range of Georgian governmental Web pages and sites, there was no attribution of these actions to the Russian government, nor were there any cyber attacks against actual Georgian infrastructure or systems critical to the life and well being of the populace or the capability of its military forces. Rather crude defacements of Georgian government Web pages—replacing the image of Georgian President Mikheil Saakashvili with one of Adolf Hitler, for example—or denial of service attacks against other Georgian governmental Web sites appeared to be the extent of the "cyberwar."[37] This limited action should not, however, be interpreted as a lack of Russian capability. Far more likely was the lack of appropriate targets in Georgia, along with the reluctance to expose what might have been very specialized and hard to acquire capabilities. Instead of focusing on cyber attacks against infrastructure, the confrontation featured widespread use of cyberspace by both sides for influence and propaganda purposes, activities that are just as real and strategically vital as potential actions against cyber-connected supervisory control and data acquisition systems.

Cyberspace is slowing finding its way into the doctrinal lexicons of all the Services, and one of the issues that will be contentious is the meaning of *superiority*. Unfortunately, Joint Publication 3–13 defines *information superiority* as "the operational advantage derived from the ability to collect, process, and disseminate an uninterrupted flow of information while exploiting or denying an adversary's ability to do the same." This definition uses a measurement of effort, not impact, and has a communications or intelligence flavor to it. The Air Force developed a significantly different approach, describing *superiority* as "that degree of information advantage of one force over another that permits the conduct of operations at a given time and place without prohibitive opposition."[38] While this definition has a decidedly martial tone, this approach is better because it is based upon an effect—"degree of advantage"—rather than a sterile and perhaps misleading measurement of effort.

An even better approach was offered in the 2004 edition of Joint Publication 1–02, *Department of Defense Dictionary of Military and Associated Terms*, which defined *information superiority* as "that degree of dominance in the info domain which permits the conduct of operations without effective opposition." If one substitutes the word *aerospace* or *maritime* for *information*, General Hap Arnold or Admiral Chester Nimitz would have understood and agreed. Taking the next step and substituting *cyberspace* for *info realm* produces a workable definition of *cyber superiority*: "the degree to which one can gain advantage from the use of cyberspace while if necessary preventing one's adversaries from gaining advantage from it. Cyber superiority includes offensive/proactive and defensive/protective operations."

The question that immediately comes to mind, however, is whether such a concept is at all appropriate to or workable in cyberspace. If cyberspace inherently includes all of the practically endless networks and information systems that are globally interconnected, how can one speak of having "superiority" in it or "dominating" it? If cyberspace has become part of the global commons that the entire world has access to—such as the aerospace or the sea—how can one speak of controlling it? A materially based view is clearly inappropriate, because the issue is not controlling electrons or electromagnetic forces, but rather influencing the use of cyberspace, in the same way that air or naval superiority is not about controlling molecules of air or water but rather controlling how the physical domain is used. It is a measure of effect or impact on human affairs and processes. Attaining operational superiority requires action at both ends of the spectrum: offensive or proactive efforts to use cyberspace and perhaps actively negate someone else's use of it, while simultaneously defending our uses of it and taking protective measures to prevent as much as possible anyone else from interfering with our use.

Cyberpower

This brings us to a second major objective of this chapter: to define and explore cyberpower. Earlier, this chapter drew a strong analogy among the domains of air-land-sea and outer space and cyberspace, and those same analogies hold true for a concept of cyberpower as drawn from seapower or airpower. Surprisingly, however, although much has been written about airpower and seapower, simple and clean definitions of them are lacking. The "father of American seapower,"

Admiral Alfred Thayer Mahan, wrote extensively about the factors that led to naval supremacy and how a government could spur national attitudes toward power on the seas, but he never clearly and simply defined what he meant by the term.[39] A definition of *seapower* published by two professors at the U.S. Naval Academy shortly after World War I—"a nation's ability to enforce its will upon the sea"—was clearly influenced by Mahan's thinking and emphasized effects rather than means, although it ignores seapower's relationship to other aspects of power, such as national economic strength.[40] Obviously, the professors were not referring to controlling the sea itself but rather to controlling human and national activities on the sea and how that physical medium was used to affect events and operations.

Giulio Douhet, the man most closely associated with the concept of airpower, also did not clearly define it, although he created elaborate scenarios to demonstrate its impact on future warfare. Nor did Billy Mitchell, one of the pioneers of American airpower, define it in detail, although his pithy statement that "airpower is the ability to do something in the air" captures several critical aspects of any form of power. Yet it, too, suffers from the same narrow perspective as Mahan's definition and ignores, for example, the huge economic impact of American dominance of the civilian airliner market for many years.[41] But all of these pioneers would have understood—and likely agreed with—an approach that concentrated on the ability to use and exploit the physical environments, "the ability to use the sea to advantage," or "the ability to use the air for our purposes." This leads to the definition of *cyberpower* as "the ability to use cyberspace to create advantages and influence events in all the operational environments and across the instruments of power."[42] This definition is broader than the Mahanian or Douhetian approaches to seapower or airpower because it includes explicit reference to other forms of power and is meant to emphasize cyberpower's synergistic impact on and integration with other forms and instruments of power.

This instrument of power is shaped by multiple factors. While cyberspace as an environment simply "is," cyberpower is always a measure of the ability to use that environment. Technology is one obvious factor, because the ability to "enter" cyberspace is what makes it possible to use it. That technology is constantly changing, and some users—countries, societies, nonstate actors, and the like—may be able to leap over old technologies to deploy and use new ones to dramatic advantage. Organizational factors also play an important role, because the organizations we create reflect human purposes and objectives, and their perspectives on the creation and use of cyberpower will be shaped by their organizational mission, be it military, economic, or political. All of these different factors shape how we employ cyberpower to impact and influence the elements of power.

The element that is most closely tied to cyberpower is information. Cyberspace and cyberpower are clearly dimensions of the informational instrument of power under the PIME (political, informational, military, economic) model, one of several current approaches to elements of power, and we can see myriad ways that cyberpower links to, supports, and enables the creation and exercise of the other instruments. Cyberpower is playing an increasingly vital role in economic strength. The National Security Strategies published by the Reagan administration in the 1980s were laced with insights and references to the role that information and the new information technologies would play in strengthening the American economy. In the global economy of the 21st century—the economy of a globalized and interconnected "flat world"—cyberspace is perhaps the single most important factor linking all the players together, boosting productivity, opening new markets, and enabling management structures that are simultaneously flatter yet with a far more extensive reach.[43]

Cyberpower's impact on political and diplomatic affairs is hardly less extensive. The world's most ubiquitous influence medium remains satellite television, which is carried by systems and networks that connect via cyberspace. The influence campaigns waged by the U.S. Government or by the shadowy terrorist nets of al Qaeda are both using cyperpower as a crucial capability in the struggle for minds and ideas.[44] Militarily, cyberpower has been perhaps the most influential instrument of the past two decades. From the Russian concept of the "military technical revolution" in the 1980s to the development of net-centric concepts and defense transformation in the U.S. military, cyberspace and cyberpower have been at the heart of new concepts and doctrines. Across the levels of conflict, from insurgency to main-force conventional warfare, cyberpower has become an indispensable element of modern technologically based military capability.

Cyberpower is exerting itself as a key lever in the development and execution of national policy, whether it be counterterrorism, economic growth, diplomatic affairs, or one of myriad other governmental operations. In state and even local affairs, cyberpower is shaping how governments connect with their citizens to provide services in ways that could not have been imagined a decade ago. It does the same for the development of new technologies, in their creation, exploitation, and measurement of success. One is hard pressed to think of a technology today that is not affected or improved by a cyber component; just look at the number of computers and information systems embedded within the typical new automobile for an example of how cyber capabilities are improving technologies that at first glance seem to have no connection to cyberspace at all. As cyberpower has exerted increasingly widespread impact across society during the past two decades, we are forced to adapt to those impacts in new ways, as seen in the current debate over how to draw the limits on government surveillance of the citizenry and access to their personal information, from financial records to communications.

Cyberpower creates synergies across the other elements and instruments of power and connects them in ways that improve all of them. Cyberspace is literally transforming how we create data itself, the raw material that fuels our economy and society. Because of new forms of content—images, sounds, information in a thousand and one forms—and the connectivity that we use to transmit and exchange that content, we are transforming how we exert influence and employ "smartpower" in the pursuit of strategic goals, whether as part of the war of ideas against violent extremism or to enable a traditional town hall meeting. These latter uses hint at what is perhaps the most significant and transformative impact cyberspace and cyberpower are having, that of linking people and organizations in new ways in an increasingly wired world in which traditional borders and boundaries are being altered and new relationships among people being forged. Where once only governments spoke to other governments, now we see governments and individuals interacting with each other, often across national borders. Listing all of the many ways (some of which are not yet known) that cyberspace and cyberpower will drive and facilitate change is impossible, but they are already driving it. The whole of the cyber revolution is greater than the sum of its parts, and not only will its impact be nearly ubiquitous, but also it will increase.

A National Strategy for Cyberspace

The existence of cyberspace as a new global domain presents fresh opportunities for its employment and vulnerabilities to be defended against, as discussed previously, and the strategist will be challenged to integrate its capabilities with other elements and instruments of power. In short, it demands the crafting of strategy—a *cyber strategy* that looks to enable and exploit the capabilities that cyberspace offers while protecting and defending against the vulnerabilities it simultaneously presents. To do this, we must first define our terms: what is a cyber strategy? The Joint Staff defines *strategy* as "the art and science of developing and employing instruments of national power in a synchronized and integrated fashion to achieve theater, national, and/or multinational objectives." This is a good starting point, but the approach toward defining any strategy in terms of an operational realm, such as an *air strategy*, must be grounded in that realm. Thus, the approach this chapter uses is that "cyber strategy is the development and employment of strategic capabilities to operate in cyberspace, integrated and coordinated with the other operational domains, to achieve or support the achievement of objectives across the elements of national power in support of national security strategy."

To develop a national strategy for cyberspace, therefore, is to simultaneously create cyber resources and procedures that can contribute to the achievement of specific national security objectives. Those means/resources might be technological (Internet Protocol Version 6), or organizational (the Joint Functional Component Command–Network Warfare or a Computer Emergency Response Team), or even human (trained and certified chief information officers.) At a foundational level, those objectives might focus on the creation of the resources and procedures themselves in the same sense that an airpower strategy must first consider what airpower means are available or needed, then examine how those resources could be used. This is a fundamental first step in the sense that one could not have an air or space strategy without first having the airplane or satellites that enabled the use of those realms; the concepts and doctrines for the use of those planes and satellites follow. This must be a strategy of partnership, given the definition of cyberspace presented in this chapter, because the private sector is inseparable from government and the military in cyberspace. Indeed, in many crucial ways—at least in the United States—the government and Armed Forces are heavily and increasingly dependent on the private sector for the development, maintenance, and security of cyberspace capabilities.[45]

This perspective is no different from the way that we view seapower or airpower. Mahan enumerated several factors necessary for the development of national seapower, among them geography, industry, populace, national character, and governance. While Douhet did not do the same for airpower, others have, such as Stefan Possony, who listed no fewer than 15 elements, including industry, research and development, aircraft, and manpower.[46] These attributes are closely tied to the private sector and national industry, and this is as, if not more, true of cyberspace as these other forms of power. There are important parallels to—and differences from—cyberspace. While no modern nation possessing and employing seapower or airpower has lacked any of these attributes, this might not always hold true for cyberspace. Small nations may be able to create significant cyber capabilities—look at the example of Estonia, which has infused cyberspace throughout much of its daily life, to significant economic and societal benefit—and the human side of the equation does not requires thousands of trained troops, perhaps only dozens or hundreds.[47]

A large part of the cyber strategy issue concerns the ends for which these cyber capabilities might be used. These ends are part of the larger military, political, economic, diplomatic, and national security objectives being sought. Cyberpower is not created simply to exist, but rather to support the attainment of larger objectives. Nations do not expend national resources to create seapower or airpower or spacepower except in the expectation that those efforts will help to achieve strategic goals across the elements of national power—political, diplomatic, informational, military, and economic—as a means of satisfying the vital national needs and interests of national security strategy. The national security strategies of the Reagan administration in the 1980s made explicit reference to the links between information and economic power, including specific recommendations concerning computers and advanced information technologies. Toward the end of the Clinton administration in the 1990s, the role of information in diplomatic, military, and economic affairs was explicitly recognized and explored. While the George W. Bush administration did not make these connections in its two national security strategy documents, lower level strategies such as the *National Strategy to Secure Cyberspace* or the *National Military Strategy for Cyberspace Operations* did. The key contribution for a national strategy for cyberspace will be to clearly demonstrate how it makes possible the support of all the other strategies, especially the national security strategy, and the achievement of their critical and interrelated objectives. This is the challenge for the future.

CHAPTER 3

Toward a Preliminary Theory of Cyberpower

Stuart H. Starr

THIS CHAPTER represents an initial effort to develop a theory of cyberpower. First, the terms of reference that were provided to the National Defense University (NDU) team are characterized. Next, the components of a theory of cyberpower are characterized. Consistent with that characterization, key terms are identified, and straw man definitions of those terms are put forth. Specific objectives that are addressed in this theory are identified. In accord with those objectives, a holistic framework to categorize and discuss key categories is presented. The intellectual capital required to address these issues is discussed within this holistic framework.

Subsequently, theoretical dimensions of the key categories—cyberspace, cyberpower, cyber strategy, and institutional factors—are discussed. In addition, the challenges associated with connecting across these categories and anticipating future cyber activities and issues of interest are contemplated. The chapter concludes by summarizing major findings and identifying the next steps that should be taken to refine this preliminary theory of cyberpower.

Terms of Reference

In the 2006 Quadrennial Defense Review (QDR),[1] requests were made to develop theories of spacepower and cyberpower. The Institute for National Strategic Studies (INSS) and Center for Technology and National Security Policy (CTNSP) at NDU were tasked with developing, respectively, theories of spacepower[2] and cyberpower.

As stated in the terms of reference for the cyberpower task,[3] "there is a compelling need for a comprehensive, robust and articulate cyberpower theory that describes, explains and predicts how our nation should best use cyberpower in support of U.S. national and security interests." Consistent with that broad goal, the terms of reference identified four specific areas for which the theory should account:

- the Nation's increased use of and reliance upon national security, civil, and commercial cyber capabilities
- other nations' and nongovernmental actors' use of cyberspace
- direct challenges to U.S. use of cyberspace
- the changed and projected geostrategic environment.

Elements of a Theory

A theory of warfare should address five key issues.[4] First, it should introduce and define the key terms that provide the foundation of the theory. Second, it should give structure to the discussion by categorizing the key elements of the theory. Third, it should explain the elements in these categories by summarizing relevant events and introducing key frameworks or models. Fourth, it should connect the various elements of the subject so that key issues can be treated comprehensively. Finally, it should seek to anticipate key trends and activities so that policy can be germane and useful.

This framework for a theory raises one immediate issue. The terms of reference identified the need to predict, rather than anticipate, key activities. However, as described below, the cyber problem is in the midst of explosive, exponential change, creating an environment of exceptional uncertainty in which making reliable predictions is infeasible. Thus, the NDU team adopted the less challenging task of anticipating key trends and activities.

Finally, the following caveat must be stressed: since this is a preliminary effort to develop a theory of cyberpower, the emerging theory will not be complete. Furthermore, as discussed below, early efforts to develop a theory for any discipline inevitably were somewhat wrong.

To provide some context for theoretical developments, it is useful to note the challenges posed to the theories associated with physics over time. Contemporary physics theory has evolved over hundreds of years, dating back to the seminal contributions of Galileo Galilei and Isaac Newton. In this discipline, there is a common base of knowledge, although there are significant variants for specific subareas (for example, quantum mechanics, classical dynamics, and relativity). In addition, there are strong links to other hard science disciplines, such as mathematics, chemistry, and biology. Although the definitions of key terms and concepts are generally established, it should be noted that there were many false starts; a hundred years ago, for example, physicists had (incorrectly) postulated the existence of an ether through which electromagnetic waves propagated as they traversed a vacuum. Even in contemporary times, questions persist about the fundamental definitions of matter (for example, quarks with a variety of properties).

Within the subareas of physics, there is broad agreement about key categories (for example, solid, liquid, and plasma physics) for which mathematical models have generally been developed drawing on experiments and observations. Many of these mathematical models have proven to be extremely accurate and precise in explaining and predicting outcomes. However, efforts are still under way to connect many of the key subareas of physics. For example, there is considerable work ongoing in the area of string theory to develop a unified understanding of basic phenomena, although some critics have argued that this effort is likely to be a dead end.[5]

To highlight the challenges facing the "cyber theorist," it is useful to contrast the discipline of physics with that of cyberspace. The cyberspace of today has its roots in the 1970s, when the Internet was conceived by engineers sponsored by the Advanced Research Projects Agency (ARPA). Detailed analysis of cyberspace issues often requires even broader cross disciplinary knowledge and skills than does analysis of physics. Experts with requisite skills include, inter alia, computer scientists, military theorists, economists, and lawyers. Each of these disciplines has its own vocabulary and body of knowledge. Thus, it is quite challenging for these stakeholders to communicate effectively. This difficulty is manifested in debates about the most basic of terms (for example, *cyberspace*) where key definitions are still contentious. Consistent with the heterogeneous nature of the problem, it is not surprising that prior efforts to characterize this space have not been successful. At present, there is no agreed taxonomy to support a comprehensive theory.

As noted above, key attributes of a theory include its ability to explain and predict (or at least anticipate). Among the many reasons why prior cyber theory efforts have foundered are the facts that key facets of the field are changing exponentially, there is little or no agreement on key frameworks, and the social science element of the discipline (for example, understanding of cognition and human interactions in virtual societies) makes it difficult to develop models that reliably explain or anticipate outcomes. Finally, the disparate elements of the field cannot be connected because a holistic perspective of the discipline has not yet been created.

Objectives

This chapter addresses the five elements of a military theory: define, categorize, explain, connect, and anticipate. In the areas of *explain* and *anticipate*, the focus is on identifying and characterizing rules of thumb and principles for cyber elements. More extensive explanations of and anticipation for cyber elements will be found elsewhere in this book.

The scope of the chapter is restricted to two major areas. First, the national security domain is the focus of attention. Changes in cyberspace are having a major effect on social, cultural, and economic issues, but they are addressed only tangentially. Second, attention is limited to the key cyberpower issues confronting the national security policymaker. Thus, no attempt is made to generate a comprehensive theory of cyberpower that touches on broader issues.

Approach

To achieve these objectives, the NDU team employed the following approach. First, we drew insights from observations of cyber events, experiments, and trends.[6] Second, we built on prior national security methods, frameworks, theories, tools, data, and studies germane to the problem. Finally, we formulated and hypothesized new methods, frameworks, theories, and tools to deal with unexplained trends and issues.

We implemented this approach through a series of workshops that drew upon world-renowned leaders in the areas of interest. This included representatives from government, industry, academia, and think tanks. At each workshop, the author of a chapter presented preliminary thoughts and conjectures to the participants. Based on feedback from the participants and reactions from the NDU team, the authors generated the material that is contained in this book.

The NDU team has adopted the holistic cyber framework depicted in figure 3–1. This framework is patterned after the triangular framework that the military operations research community has used to deconstruct the dimensions of traditional warfare. In that framework, the base consists of systems models, upon which rest more complex, higher orders of interactions (for example, engagements, tactical operations, and campaigns). Historically, the outputs from the lower levels provide the feedback to the higher levels of the triangle.

By analogy, the bottom of the pyramid consists of the components, systems, and systems of systems that comprise the cyber infrastructure. The output from this cyber infrastructure enhances the traditional levers of power: political/diplomatic, informational, military, and economic (P/DIME). These levers of power, in turn, provide the basis for empowerment of the entities at the top of the pyramid. These entities include, among others, individuals, terrorists, transnational criminals, corporations, nation-states, and international organizations. While nation-states have access to all of these levers of power, the other entities generally have access to only a subset of them. In addition, initiatives such as deterrence and treaties may provide the basis for limiting the empowerment of key entities. The pyramid suggests that each of these levels is affected by

FIGURE 3-1. Broad Conceptual Framework

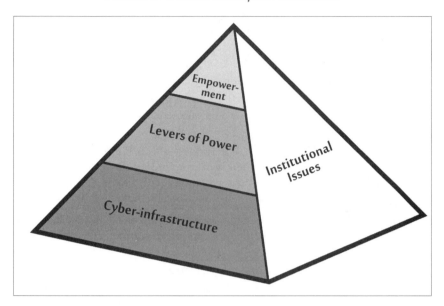

institutional issues that include factors such as governance, legal considerations, regulation, information-sharing, and consideration of civil iberties.

This framework is merely one of many that could be constructed to conceptualize the cyber domain. However, it has proven useful to the NDU team in deconstructing the problem and developing subordinate frameworks to address key cyber issues.

Key Definitions

As noted above, there is a continuing discussion about the appropriate definitions for key cyber terms. For example, in its study of the "Convergence of Sea Power and Cyber Power,"[7] the Strategic Studies Group (SSG) identified 28 candidate definitions of the term *cyberspace*. To categorize and compare those terms, the group introduced a two-dimensional space that featured the axes *focus* (present-day versus future) and *centricity* (technology versus human). They observed that the definition posed by William Gibson, in his 1984 book *Neuromancer*,[8] fell in the upper right quadrant of this space (futurist with some consideration of the human dimension): "A consensual hallucination . . . a graphic representation of data abstracted from banks of every computer in the human system."

For the purposes of this theory, the NDU team adopted a variant of the formal definition of cyberspace that the Joint Staff employed in the *National Military Strategy for Cyberspace Operations*: "An operational domain whose distinctive and unique character is framed by the use of electronics and the electromagnetic spectrum to create, store, modify, exchange, and exploit information via interconnected and internetted information systems and their associated infrastructures."[9] This definition does not explicitly deal with the information and cognitive dimensions of the problem. To do so, the NDU team has introduced two complementary terms: cyberpower and cyber strategy.

Cyberpower is defined as the ability to use cyberspace to create advantages and influence events in the other operational environments and across the instruments of power. In this context, the instruments of power include the elements of the P/DIME paradigm. For the purposes of this preliminary theory, primary emphasis is placed on the military and informational levers of power.

Similarly, *cyber strategy* is defined as the development and employment of capabilities to operate in cyberspace, integrated and coordinated with the other operational domains, to achieve or support the achievement of objectives across the elements of national power. Thus, one of the key issues associated with cyber strategy deals with the challenge of devising tailored deterrence to affect the behavior of the key entities empowered by developments in cyberspace.

The definition that the NDU team has adopted for cyberspace begins with the phrase *an operational domain*. This raises an issue that is hotly debated by the military Services: Is cyberspace a domain?

The term *domain* is not defined formally in key national security and military products. However, it is cited in selected policy documents. For example, the 2004 National Military Strategy states that "the Armed Forces must have the ability to operate across the air, land, sea, space, and cyberspace domains of the battlespace.[10] Furthermore, the 2006 QDR notes that "the [Department of Defense] will treat cyberspace as a domain of warfare." Joint Publication 3–0, *Joint Operations*, identifies several key features of a domain: it can be described physically; there are distinctions in means, effects, and outcomes; and military and combat operations can be conducted in and through the domain.[11]

One can make the argument that cyberspace is a domain through the following logic. It is widely accepted that (outer) space is a domain. In comparison to space, cyberspace has the following bounding attributes that suggest that it is a military domain: it is subject to ongoing levels of combat (see below); it is characterized by greater ease of access; and it is more difficult to identify and track military operations within it.

The acceptance of cyberspace as a domain has significant practical implications for the requirement to allocate resources to support organization, training, and equipping of "cyberforces," the need to develop a culture that is consistent with cyber activities, and the development of a professional cadre and establishment of a structured career progression.

Thus, for the purposes of this preliminary theory, cyberspace will be assumed to be "an operational domain" (as stated in the NDU team definition). Consistent with that definition, the elements of the holistic framework can be recast as depicted in figure 3–2.

Required Intellectual Capital

Dealing with the rich array of cyber policy issues that confront senior decision-makers will require a diverse set of intellectual capital. Figure 3–3 suggests the differing types of knowledge needed to address issues within and across the categories of interest.

For example, in the realm of cyberspace, there is a need for physicists, electrical engineers, computer scientists, systems engineers, and system-of-systems engineers. These professionals will play key roles in developing the hardware components (such as microprocessors and hard drives), software protocols and standards (for example, implementing Internet Protocol version 6 [IPv6]), applications and services, and the systems that exploit this hardware and software (command, control, and communications systems).

In the realm of cyberpower, subject matter experts who are qualified to deal with P/DIME issues are needed. This implies extensive reliance on micro- and macroeconomists and social scientists with training in such diverse fields as

FIGURE 3-2. Cyberspace, Cyberpower, Cyber Strategy, and Institutional Factors

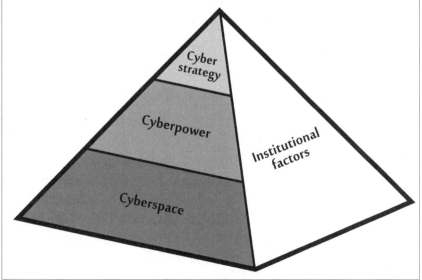

FIGURE 3-3. Required Intellectual Capital

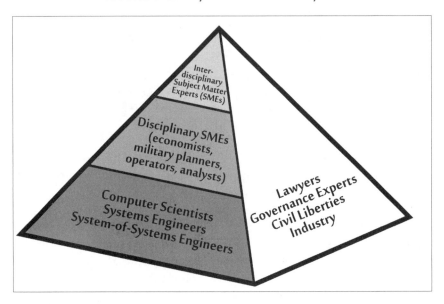

sociology, cultural anthropology, psychology, and demographics. Furthermore, in the area of military knowledge, participation by military planners, operators, and analysts is necessary.

In the realm of cyber strategy, interdisciplinary experts are required who are able to deal with the full range of political, military, economic, social, informational, and infrastructure (PMESII) issues associated with entities empowered by changes in cyberspace. In particular, analysts are needed who have had experience in addressing deterrence among these entities.

Finally, in the realm of institutional factors, the key skills needed are legal, governance, civil liberties, and industrial experience.

Cyber policy decisionmakers are expected to be among the main users of this intellectual capital. They will also need operations analysts to help orchestrate and harness this heterogeneous intellectual capital and futurists to help conceptualize possibilities that require unfettered imaginations.

Theoretical Perspectives

Three of the major objectives of a theory of cyber are to help explain, connect, and anticipate key aspects of the problem for the decisionmaker. Doing so will require the formulation of conceptual models for the various categories introduced above. In formulating these conceptual models, it is useful to recall the famous saying by the statistician George Box: "All models are wrong; some are useful."[12] The challenge for the theorist is to suggest and apply appropriate models that are useful for the decisionmaker and to delineate the range of their utility.

This section systematically introduces a variety of models that are germane to the many policy questions associated with cyber issues. Structurally, a bottom-up approach is pursued and cyberspace, cyberpower, cyber strategy, and institutional factors are addressed.[13] For each area, we introduce a variety of models and frameworks that help the decisionmaker explain key observables and conceptualize the issues of interest. This is followed by an articulation of rules of thumb and principles that highlight major issues of interest.

Theoretical Aspects of Cyberspace[14]

This section briefly explains key cyberspace trends in five main areas: growth in users, features of major components (such as microprocessors and hard drives), architectural features (for example, Internet protocols), and military systems of systems.

Growth in users. The most remarkable aspect of the Internet has been the exponential growth in users worldwide. Figure 3–4 illustrates that growth over a 33-year period. User population increased from approximately 1 million users

FIGURE 3-4. Number of Internet Users

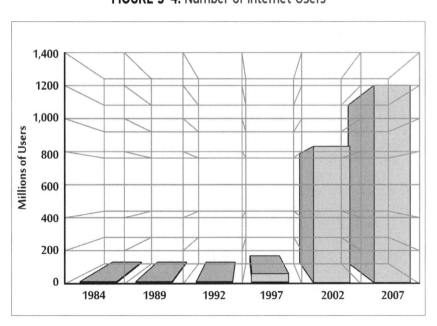

in 1992 to 1.2 billion users in 2007. It is projected that the Internet will have 2 billion users by 2010. This number is projected to grow substantially if the One Laptop Per Child project, which aims to get millions of low-cost laptops to children in underdeveloped countries, is brought to fruition.

The SSG report depicted this growth from another perspective. The researchers set 50 million users as a benchmark for penetration of a mass medium. That level was achieved by radio in 38 years, television in 13 years, and the Internet in 6 years (beginning with the introduction of the World Wide Web).

Another key element of cyberspace is cellular telephony. As a point of reference, the first cell phone call was made in 1973. It is estimated that today, 35 years later, approximately 3.3 billion cell phones are in use worldwide.

Components. From a theoretical perspective, the physics of the hardware that supports cyberspace has a significant impact on its performance. This is particularly manifested in the design of microprocessors and hard drives.

Microprocessors. Clock cycles of modern microprocessors exceed 2 gigahertz (GHz). Therefore, under ideal circumstances, electrons can move a maximum of 0.15 meters in a single processor clock cycle, nearing the size of the chip itself. With clock cycles going even higher,[15] electronic signals cannot propagate across a chip within one clock cycle, meaning elements of the chip cannot communicate with other elements on its other side. Thus, this limitation maximizes the effective size of a single integrated microprocessor running at high clock speeds. Addressing this limitation is one of the reasons that various processor manufacturers have moved chip architectures toward multicore processors, where multiple, semi-independent processors are etched on a single chip. Current chips have two or four cores, with substantial increases expected for the future.

Hard drives. Figure 3–5 depicts computer hard drive storage capability (in gigabits per square centimeter) over the last 25 years. It is notable that the improvement in memory was negligible for the first 20 until IBM engineers applied the phenomenon of giant magnetoresistance.[16] Currently, improvements in memory are manifesting exponential improvement, making it feasible to create portable devices, such as iPods, with extremely high storage capability.

These two examples suggest that a careful technology assessment is needed to determine if and when bottlenecks in technology that limit current performance will be overcome.

Architectural features. Figure 3–6 schematically depicts the architecture of the existing Internet. The key innovations of this architecture revolve around the protocols and standards instantiated in the transmission control protocol/ Internet protocol (TCP/IP) stack and the use of a router to transmit packets from the sender to the user.

Originally, this architecture was devised by a group for whom security was

FIGURE 3-5. Hard Drive Capacity

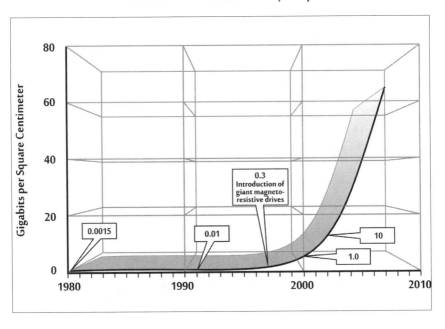

a secondary issue. Thus, the primary emphasis was to implement an architecture that facilitated the interoperability among heterogeneous networks. In addition, a decision was made to implement IP addresses that consisted of 32 bits (or approximately 4 billion addresses).

These two decisions have led to several major limitations in the current architecture. In light of the security shortfalls in the existing architecture, there is interest in alternative architectures designed around different priorities (for example, highest priority being security, second priority being connectivity among highly mobile users). Consistent with those revised priorities, new architectural efforts are under way at the National Science Foundation and Defense Advanced Research Projects Agency (DARPA).

Second, the constraint on IP addresses (as well as concern about enhanced security and mobility) has led to the adoption of IPv6. Since it allocates 128 bits to IP addresses, it will give rise to an extraordinarily large number of IP addresses.[17]

Both of these innovations pose a problem to the cyberspace community: how can one transition from the current architecture to an alternative architecture efficiently and effectively without creating new security vulnerabilities? This is an ongoing challenge that the computer science community must confront over the next decade.

FIGURE 3-6. Protocol Layering and Routing Packets across a Network

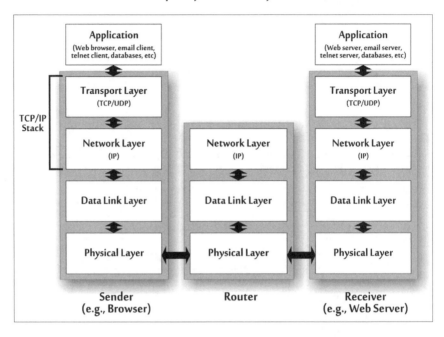

Military systems-of-systems. The military community has embraced the underlying computer science principles associated with the Internet, although it has enhanced security for classified systems by developing airgapped networks (such as the Secret Internet Protocol Router Network and the Joint Worldwide Intelligence Communications System). Figure 3–7 provides an illustration of that implementation for the notional global information grid (GIG).

There are several distinctive aspects of the evolving GIG. First, for the transport layer, the plan is to employ a heterogeneous mix of satellite (for example, transformational satellites), airborne (selected joint tactical radio systems), and surface (fiber optic) telecommunications media. As a side note, the military is finding it difficult to develop many of these elements within acceptable levels of performance, schedule, and cost.

Second, there is interest in employing a service-oriented architecture to provide loose coupling among key systems. Third, the military has developed communities of interest to address the challenges associated with the data that will flow through the systems (for instance, specify metadata; deal with issues of pedigree). The military wishes to transition from the principle of "need to know" to "need to share." Finally, it hopes to assimilate the Services' visions of future systems into the GIG (for example, the Army LandWarNet, Navy ForceNet, and

Air Force Command and Control [C²] Constellation). Achieving this vision will require the concerted efforts of the military's system-of-systems engineers.[18]

Cyberspace rules of thumb and principles. To help explain the various trends in cyberspace, one can provide several rules of thumb and straw man principles. Several broad guidelines employed in the community are incorrectly characterized as laws. For example, Moore's "law" indicates that the number of transistors on a chip approximately doubles every 18 months.[19] This growth has contributed to the production of smaller, less expensive devices that have enhanced computational power. Although this trend is generally representative of past behavior, there is concern that it may be extremely difficult to sustain in the indefinite future without a fundamental, expensive change in the underlying technology (such as transition to nanotechnology). Second, as noted in figure 3–5, recent breakthroughs in physics have put the growth in hard drive capacity on an exponential versus a conservative linear curve. Ultimately, this curve will reach a level of saturation (an "S-curve") that is representative of a mature technology. Lastly, the current limitation in IP addresses will be dramatically overcome once the transition to IPv6 is implemented.

Several straw man cyberspace principles can be articulated. First, the offense has the advantage, in part because of the target-rich environment that

FIGURE 3–7. A Framework to Characterize the Global Information Grid

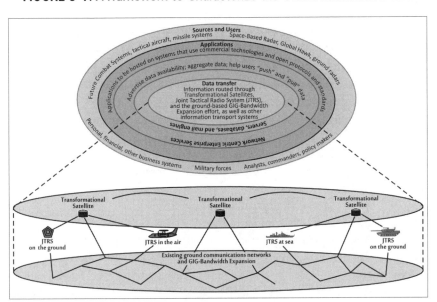

Source: Government Accountability Office, *The GIG and Challenges Facing its Implementation* (Washington, DC: Government Accountability Office, July 2004).

an adversary faces. This situation makes it difficult for defense to prioritize and defend selected targets. In addition, the existing architecture makes it challenging to attribute an attack if an adversary seeks anonymity. If cyberspace is to be more resistant to attack, it will require a new architecture that has "designed-in" security. However, it will be a challenge to transition effectively and efficiently from the current legacy system to a more secure objective system.

Theoretical Aspects of Cyberpower

This section briefly explains key trends in the military and information dimensions of cyberpower.[20] It focuses on changes in the principles of war, environmental theories of power and risk, net-centric operations (NCO), and the mission-oriented approach to influence operations.

Principles of war. Historically, military intellectuals have developed a set of principles of war to support the planning and execution of operations. These principles have evolved over hundreds of years through the writings of key military analysts.[21] Although the precise set of elements in these principles of war is variable, most lists would include unity of command, objective, offensive, mass, maneuver, economy of force, security, surprise, and simplicity. In general, a contemporary general officer would regard these factors as essential dimensions of a plan and subsequent operations. Thus, he would test his straw man plan by thinking deeply about each of these principles.

It is argued that a revised set of modernized principles of war is appropriate for 21st-century operations. One of the participants in this debate has updated the list to include perceived worthiness, informed insight, durability, engagement dominance, unity of effort, adaptability, and culminating power.[22] As illustrated in table 3–1, most of these revised principles represent combinations of and linkages to the classical set of principles of war.

This preliminary theory of cyberspace has not focused extensively on the issue of the appropriate principles of warfare in an information age. However, it does acknowledge that the impact of changes in cyberspace may warrant a basic reassessment of the appropriate principles of contemporary warfare. Thus, it identifies this area as one worthy of continued research.

Environmental theories of warfare. In the discussions that led to this study, the observation was made that the naval theories of Alfred Thayer Mahan played a major role in shaping U.S. perspectives and strategies on naval power. It was suggested that cyberpower needed a comparable perspective to shape its strategy in cyberspace. Consistent with that interest, this study reevaluated the various environmental theories of power. These included analyses of land power,[23] naval power,[24] airpower,[25] and spacepower.[26] Based on these analyses, four common features of environmental power theories were identified: technological

TABLE 3-1. Evolving Principles of War

MODERNIZED PRINCIPLES	RELATIONSHIP TO TRADITIONAL PRINCIPLES
Perceived worthiness	Morale: what makes it worthwhile to risk one's life in combat?
Informed insight	Sensemaking, cognition, surprise
Strategic anchoring	Concentration on and prominence of the offensive
Durability	Incorporate security into plan; depends on logistics
Engagement dominance	Incorporates and simplifies maneuver; impose/oppose surprise
Unity of effect	Draws on unity of command; reinterprets economy of force, mass, maneuver
Adaptability	Presupposes flexibility but does not mandate simplicity
Culminating power	Power needed to attain satisfactory closure at a given level of conflict

Source: Charles Dunlap, "Neo-Strategicon: Modernized Principles of War for the 21ˢᵗ Century," *Military Review* (March-April 2006).

advances, speed and scope of operations, control of key features, and national mobilization.

Consistent with each of these features, the following implications were drawn for a theory of cyberpower. With respect to technological advances, it was observed that dependency on cyberspace has given rise to new strategic vulnerabilities. This vulnerability has been dramatized by the specter of a "cyber Pearl Harbor" and the realization that the existing cyberspace is vulnerable to a variety of adversary attacks (for example, denial-of-service attacks, exfiltration of sensitive but unclassified information, or potential corruption of sensitive data). In addition, due to the diffusion of low-cost cyberspace technology, the power of nonstate actors (such as individuals, terrorists, transnational criminals, and corporations) has been greatly enhanced (see below).

Improvements in cyberspace have also enhanced the speed and scope of operations. These upgrades are manifested in the speed at which global operations can be conducted (for example, the ability to successfully engage time-sensitive targets anywhere in the world). In addition, they have led to improvements in the ability to automate command and control, dramatically decreasing the classic observe-orient-decide-act loop process.

In the environmental theories of power, emphasis was placed on controlling key features. For example, in naval theories, this entailed the domination of chokepoints (such as the Straits of Malacca), while in spacepower theory, there was interest in controlling geosynchronous orbit locations. In the case of cyberspace, the key features are manmade. Thus, for example, there is interest in defending "cyber hotels" where information and communications technology systems are concentrated. In addition, while the chokepoints in the physical world tend to be immutable, they may change relatively rapidly in cyberspace (for example, the location of extensive server farms).

Finally, national mobilization is a vital measure of cyberpower. To ensure that it is available when needed, the United States must assure access to a cadre of cyberspace professionals. This argues for reexamining career progression for cyberspace professionals in the military Services. In addition, it is important to establish links to the private sector where the bulk of cyberspace professionals reside. This suggests that a reservoir of Reservists should be established to provide access to this intellectual capital in the event of national need.

It is argued in this book that the U.S. Government has tended to focus on the opportunities offered by changes in cyberspace rather than the risks assumed. To summarize that dichotomy, table 3–2 identifies the opportunities and risks associated with military activities at the strategic, operational, and tactical levels.

The risks at the strategic level include loss of technical advantage (due to the diffusion of cyberspace technology), potential rapid change in the operating environment (such as the possibility that nations such as China could leapfrog the United States by transitioning rapidly to IPv6), and the vulnerabilities associated with military dependence on key systems (for example, the GIG). At the operational level, the diffusion of cyberspace technology could result in the U.S. loss of advantage in operational pace. Finally, at the tactical level, advances in cyberspace could generate a new front for adversaries to build resources. These observations suggest that the U.S. Government might be assuming significant, unknown risks by failing to take a balanced perspective of key cyberspace trends. It also implies the need to undertake more extensive risk assessments to understand the potential downside of key dependencies.

To begin to deal with these risks, steps should be taken at the strategic, operational, and programmatic levels. At the strategic level, actions should be taken to ensure the resilience of supporting critical infrastructures, such as electric power generation and transmission. At the operational level, it is vital to plan for operations against an adversary that is highly capable of cyberwarfare. This should include the creation of an opposing force that would be employed extensively in experiments and exercises. Finally, at the programmatic level, emphasis should be placed on addressing cyberspace implications in the development process.

TABLE 3-2. Military Opportunities and Risks in Cyberspace

LEVEL	OPPORTUNITIES	RISKS
Strategic	• Net-centric warfare–enabled • New centers of gravity opportunities (for example, deterrence, virtual conflict)	• Loss of technical advantage • Rapidly changing operating environment • Military dependence on key systems (for example, the global information grid)
Operational	• Phasing of operations • Enhanced force structure mix (for example, cheaper, more precise)	• Loss of advantage in operational pace
Tactical	• Discover and track adversaries using cyberspace	• New front for adversaries to build resources

This should include placing higher priority on the challenges of information assurance. Overall, an improved analytic capability is required to address each of these issues.

Net-centric operations. As one aspect of the analytic capability, work is needed to enhance and apply the existing conceptual framework for NCO. As illustrated in figure 3–8, the NCO process involves consideration of the interactions among the physical, information, cognitive, and social domains.[27] There is a need to develop better analytic tools for all aspects of this process, particularly in the cognitive and social domains. One potential source of intellectual capital is the forthcoming initiative by the Director of Defense Research and Engineering in the Office of the Secretary of Defense (OSD) to improve human, social, and cultural behavior models and simulations. This issue is discussed later in this chapter.

Mission-oriented approach to influence operations. In the area of influence operations, a straw man framework has been developed to help the community plan for and implement influence operations (see figure 3–9). This framework represents an extension of the mission-oriented approach developed and applied to a variety of C^2 issues in the 1980s.[28]

This approach begins with the articulation of the nature of the problem of interest. It then poses a sequence of questions. First, what is the operational objective of the mission? A reasonable objective may be to establish a trust relationship with the indigenous population (versus "winning hearts and minds"). Second, how should this operational objective be accomplished? Again, a decision was made to work with surrogate audiences, including the local media, religious leaders, educational leaders, political leaders, and tribal leaders, in order to reach the undecided population. Organizations and processes were established to reach out to those audiences effectively. At this point, one can characterize the existing doctrine, organization, training, materiel, leadership and education, personnel, and facilities (DOTMLPF) activities and compare them to the operational needs. This will give rise to DOTMLPF shortfalls and the articulation of options to mitigate them. It may also prompt the operator to reevaluate the operational goals and the operational activities to support them.

This process should be refined and applied to a broader variety of strategic, operational, and tactical influence operations. In particular, it can be used to explore the utility of employing new options in cyberspace (media such as the Internet and social networks) to improve future influence operations.

Cyberpower rules of thumb and principles. One of the so-called laws of cyberpower was formulated by Bob Metcalfe.[29] He postulated that the value of a telecommunications network is proportional to the square of the number of users of the system (n^2). However, there is no empirical data to support this law. A recent article suggested that the value is closer to $n\log(n)$.[30]

From an analytical perspective, the former Office of Force Transformation has supported a number of studies to relate the impact of net-centricity on enhancements in cyberpower (primarily in the military domain). These ongoing studies have demonstrated that net-centricity can have a substantial impact on mission effectiveness for selected mission areas. For example, the use of jam-resistant Link 16 radios by airborne interceptors in M-on-N combat can enhance air-to-air loss exchange ratios by approximately 2.5.[31] However, the complexity of modern conflict is such that it is difficult to assess the effect of net-centricity on complex missions (for example, air-land operations or stability and reconstruction operations). This suggests that additional experiments will be needed to assess the quantitative value of net-centricity for complex missions, in which better control is exercised over potentially confounding variables.

Theoretical Aspects of Cyber Strategy[32]

The NDU team has identified an extensive list of entities that are being empowered by changes in cyberspace that includes individuals, "hacktivists,"[33] nongovernmental organizations (such as the Red Cross), terrorists, transnational criminals, corporations, nation-states, and international governmental organizations (such as the United Nations).

For the purposes of this study, attention has been focused on a subset of these entities that includes terrorists, transnational criminals, and certain nation-states (China and Russia). From a U.S. Government national security perspective,

FIGURE 3-8. Conceptual Framework for Net-centric Operations

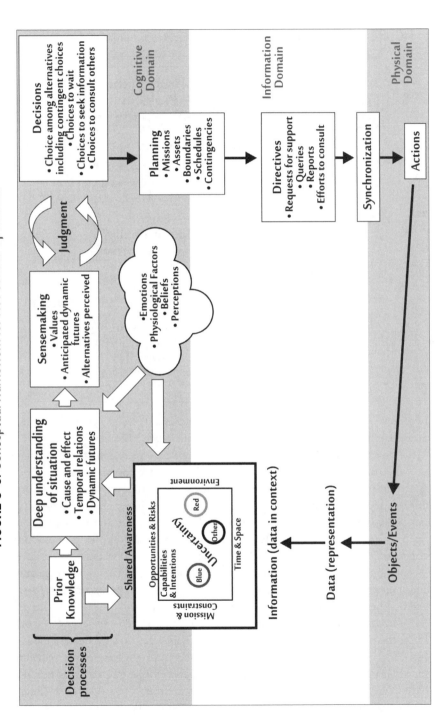

FIGURE 3-9. Straw Man Framework for Analyzing Influence Operations

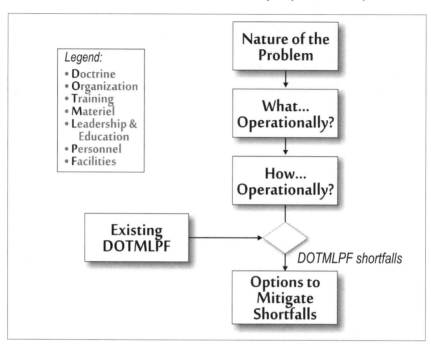

two issues stand out. First, is it feasible to achieve tailored cyber deterrence? Second, what steps should be taken to deal with cyber espionage?

Terrorist use of cyberspace. Terrorists are empowered substantially by changes in cyberspace. With the loss of physical sanctuary in key areas (such as Afghanistan), they have been turning to the sanctuary of cyberspace to perform important interrelated functions that include recruiting malleable candidates, raising resources to support operations, planning operations (employing such open-source tools as Google Earth), commanding and controlling operations, conducting influence operations (for example, disseminating their perspectives of operations in Iraq to sympathetic and uncommitted audiences), and educating and training supporters on a variety of subjects (such as interpreting the Koran and building and deploying improvised explosive devices).

Terrorists have found cyberspace an attractive milieu for several reasons. First, the cost of entry is low. One can acquire the latest cyber technology for hundreds to thousands of dollars and exploit key open-source software. In addition, terrorists can take full advantage of the extraordinary sums that have been invested by the commercial sector in cyber infrastructure (including communications and navigation systems). Second, cyberspace provides rapid, worldwide reach. Thus, terrorists are able to transcend the limited geographic reach of their prior physical sanctuary and perform the key functions cited above. Third, it has been posited that the next generation of terrorists is being radicalized by online interactions.[34] Finally, there is concern that terrorists are developing linkages with transnational criminals who are able to provide terrorists with cyber knowledge while profiting from the relationship.

Recent reports suggest strategies for the U.S. Government to counter the terrorists' use of cyberspace. For example, a special report on Internet-facilitated radicalization formulated five recommendations to address the cyber threat posed by terrorists:

- craft a compelling counternarrative for worldwide delivery in multimedia, at and by the grassroots level
- foster intra- and cross-cultural dialogue and understanding to strengthen the ties that bind communities at the local, national, and international levels
- recognize and address the need for additional behavioral science research into the process of radicalization both online and offline
- deny or disrupt extremist access to, and extremist efforts through, the Internet via legal and technical means and covert action, where appropriate
- remedy and resource capability gaps in government.[35]

The many actions associated with these recommendations are summarized in table 3–3. From the perspective of this chapter, some of the more interesting actions involve developing a strategic communication plan based on a compelling narrative, implementing an innovative program on behavior science research, and addressing U.S. Government shortfalls in knowledge of culture and language.

Nation-state use of cyberspace. From a nation-state perspective, different combinations of levers of power are employed to generate desired effects. From a theoretical perspective, these nations formulate their strategy through a mix of P/DIME activities. The effects of these activities are manifested in the areas of PMESII. Tools are being created to explore how alternative P/DIME activities can give rise to differing PMESII effects.

The United States. Using the P/DIME–PMESII paradigm, one can begin to characterize how cyber changes have empowered the United States. In the political dimension, changes in cyberspace have encouraged democratic participation by the population. The Internet has provided a forum for individuals to articulate their views through blogs and contributions to wikis. In addition, political candidates are finding the Internet to be a useful vehicle for raising resources from grassroots supporters. Furthermore, Internet sites such as YouTube have enhanced the accountability of candidates.

TABLE 3-3. Options to Counter Terrorist Use of Cyberspace

RECOMMENDATIONS	PROPOSED ACTIONS
Craft compelling multimedia counternarrative for worldwide delivery	• Challenge extremist doctrine • Offer compelling narrative • Use graphics • Deliver message through authentic sources • Amplify, augment grass-roots nonextremist voices
Foster intra- and cross-cultural dialogue at all levels	• Address perceptions, realities of American Muslim alienation, marginalization • Enhance civic engagement • Increase people-to-people exchanges • Deal appropriately with the media
Address need for behavioral science research	• Deepen understanding of radicalization process • Apply social networking theory
Deny or disrupt extremist use of Internet	• Employ legal means • Undermine trust that binds adversary networks • Exploit convergence of human intelligence and cyberspace
Address capability gaps in U.S. Government	• Address cultural and linguistic deficiencies • Reclaim high ground • Develop strategic communications plan • Expand community policing programs

In the military dimension, the concept of NCO has enhanced effectiveness in selected operational domains (for example, air-to-air combat). Efforts are still required to quantify the military benefits that are achievable for more complex military operations (such as air-land maneuver).

Economically, the commercial sector has seen dramatic improvements in industrial productivity (for example, Boeing's use of computer-aided design tools to support the development of the 777 and 787 aircraft). These cyber-based advancements are giving rise to considerable improvements in responsiveness by reducing time to market and cost reductions (for example, by outsourcing "backroom operations" to other nations).

The development of cyberspace has increased social interactions in several ways. Tens of millions of users participate in social networking sites such as MySpace and FaceBook. In addition, millions of users worldwide participate in virtual reality environments such as Second Life. In fact, terrorist organizations are rumored to be using virtual reality environments to explore prototypical operations.

In the information dimension, the Internet has increased dissemination of information worldwide. The argument can be made that the U.S. dominant position in entertainment and advertising provides a strong forum for promoting soft power.[36]

Finally, many critical infrastructures have been using the Internet to facilitate more efficient and effective operations. However, this constitutes a double-edged sword because of the potential vulnerability of supervisory control and data acquisition systems.

Overall, it must be stressed that empowerment is more than the sum of the individual PMESII factors.

Near-peer use of cyberspace. Nations such as China and Russia use a different vocabulary in discussing cyberspace and cyberpower. For example, Chinese writings on the subject focus on stratagems, objective and subjective reality, and dialectic (that is, "reasoning that juxtaposes opposed or contradictory ideas and seeks to resolve conflict").

Two key aspects of the Chinese view of the revolution in military affairs are particularly germane: "War with the objective of expanding territory has basically withdrawn from the stage of history, and even war with the objective of fighting for natural resources is now giving way to war with the objective of controlling the flow of financial capital." Furthermore, "If we go our own path to develop military theory, weapons, and equipment, we will develop something never seen before in places that no one has ever thought of before; others will be unable to anticipate or resist our 'self-accommodating systems.'"

As an illustration of "self-accommodating systems" against a superior foe, three ways are cited for making a cat eat a hot pepper: "Stuff it down his throat, put it in cheese and make him swallow it, or grind it up and spread it on his back. The latter method makes the cat lick itself and receive the satisfaction of cleaning up. The cat is oblivious to the end goal. This is strategy."

Cyber deterrence. A vision for tailored deterrence was articulated in the 2006 QDR. Consistent with that vision, a recent strategy paper identified three aspects of tailoring:

- tailoring to specific actors and specific situations. This recognizes that tailored deterrence is "context specific and culturally sensitive."
- tailoring capabilities. One dimension of this factor deals with the associated resource implications.
- tailoring communications. This relates to the kinds of messages that the United States would send in words or actions to deter specific actors in peacetime and crisis situations.[37]

TABLE 3-4. The Calculus of Tailored Deterrence

- What are the nation's or group's values and priorities? How are they affected by its history and strategic culture?
- What are their objectives in the particular situation?
- What factors are likely to influence their decisionmaking?
- Who makes decisions, how does the leadership think, what is their worldview and experience with and view of the United States?
- How do they calculate risks and gains?
- What do they believe their stakes to be in particular situations?
- How risktaking is the leadership?
- How much latitude does the leadership have (to provoke, conciliate, and so forth)?
- What are their alternative courses of action?
- What do they believe the costs and benefits of constraints to be?
- What do they perceive America's answers to these questions to be?

Source: M. Elaine Bunn, *Can Deterrence Be Tailored?* Strategic Forum 225 (Washington, DC: National Defense University Press, January 2007).

To deal with the various dimensions of tailored deterrence, a variety of questions must be addressed that include the social, cultural, and historical aspects of the adversary, including his calculation of risks and gains. As noted in table 3–4, a critical element of this calculus deals with the adversary's perception of the U.S. position on these key questions.

There is a debate within the analytic community as to whether tailored deterrence is a viable concept for the full spectrum of U.S. adversaries.[38] That issue represents an important element of the research agenda for the community. However, the NDU study team believes that the full set of P/DIME options should be considered in developing a course of action to respond to a cyber attack.[39]

Cyber strategy rules of thumb and principles. Three key insights emerged during the course of this study. First, low-end users (such as individuals, hacktivists, terrorists, and transnational criminals) have enhanced their power considerably through recent cyberspace trends. A tailored deterrence strategy will be needed to keep these entities in check.

Second, potential near-peer adversaries are aggressively exploring options to exploit attributes of cyberspace. In the near term, this exploitation is being manifested through acts of espionage that have resulted in the exfiltration of massive amounts of sensitive governmental and industrial data. In the longer term, the United States must be prepared to deal with unique "cyber stratagems" that reflect the particular cultural and military history of important nations such as China and Russia.

To deal with the emerging cyber threat, the United States must conduct experiments and exercises that feature a creative and aggressive cyber opposing force. It would be naïve and dangerous to assume that future adversaries will not seek to negate the benefits that the United States hopes to achieve through net-centric warfare.

Theoretical Aspects of Institutional Factors

This section focuses on two critical institutional factors: governance of cyberspace and the legal dimensions of the problem. The section concludes by identifying key institutional issues and principles.[40]

Governance. Table 3–5 characterizes key governance functions in cyberspace and the organizations that participate in them. The mechanisms for governance of the Internet are exceedingly complex. Organizational activities often overlap or fit end-to-end, requiring the expenditure of considerable resources in multiple forums to achieve objectives. Consequently, a core set of participants (generally in the private sector) is involved in several of these organizations.

In an effort to evaluate the performance of Internet governance, the following criteria are introduced: open, democratic, transparent, dynamic, adaptable, accountable, efficient, and effective. When measured against these criteria, recent Internet governance has performed remarkably well.

However, in the future, the U.S. Government will be challenged to alter its position on Internet governance. Preliminary views on this subject are being articulated at the ongoing Internet Governance Forums (IGFs). In fact, a recent white paper on the subject observed:

> Internet Governance is an isolating and abstract term that suggests a nexus with an official government entity. The term also implies a role for the U.S. Congress in Internet decision-making. It is a misnomer because there is no true governance of the Internet; only a series of agreements between a distributed and loosely connected group of organizations and influencers. A more fitting term may be "Internet Influence," or for long-term strategy purposes, "Internet Evolution."[41]

Cyber law. One of the most challenging legal issues confronting the cyber community is whether cyber attack is an act of war. Legalistically, the answer is often presented as one of three possible outcomes: it is not a use of force under United Nations (UN) Article 2(4); it is arguably a use of force or not; it is a use of force under UN Article 2(4).

TABLE 3-5. Governance of Cyberspace

Function / Group	Domain names	International domain names	Core Internet functions	Telecommunications standards	World Wide Web standards	Product standards	Development	Cyber security**
Internet Corporation for Assigned Names and Numbers	X	X						X
Internet Society*			X					X
International Telecommunication Union		X		X		X	X	X
Organization for Economic Co-operation and Development							X	X
Council of Europe								X
European Union							X	X
International Organization for Standardization						X		X
International Electrotechnical Commission						X		X

Institute of Electrical and Electronics Engineers		X	
World Wide Web Consortium			X	
United Nations				X

* Internet Society and related organizations (Internet Engineering Task Force, Internet Engineering Steering Group, Internet Architecture Board)
** As well as national governments

Several frameworks are being considered by the legal community to address this issue. Michael Schmitt has formulated a framework that defines and addresses seven key factors: severity, immediacy, directness, invasiveness, measurability, presumptive legitimacy, and responsibility. Once one has assessed each of those factors, one should employ multi-attribute utility theory to weight each of them and come to a determination. As an example, the application of this framework in chapter 22 of this volume, "International Law and Information Operations," implies that the recent attack against Estonia was not a use of force under Article 2(4). An associated challenge is to formulate responses to that attack consistent with the legal tenet of proportional response.

Overall, the area of cyber law is in its infancy. Although there have been preliminary rulings on sharing of music, there are major issues on the questions of sovereignty, intellectual capital, and civil liberties. These issues will be areas for research for the foreseeable future.

Institutional principles. Based on the insights developed during the course of this study, four major straw man principles have emerged in the arena of institutional factors.

First, given the complexity of the governance mechanisms, one should seek influence over cyberspace versus governance. Second, the legal community has barely addressed the key issues that must be resolved in the cyber arena. For example, considerable research is needed to assess the following questions:

- What is an act of (cyber)war?
- What is the appropriate response to an act of (cyber)war?
- What is the appropriate way to treat intellectual property in the digital age?
- How can nations resolve differences in sovereign laws associated with cyber factors?

Third, there is a need for a framework and enhanced dialogue between champions of civil liberties and proponents of enhanced cyber security to establish an adequate balance. Finally, guidance and procedures are required to address the issue of sharing cyber information between the U.S. Government and industry. This approach should be based on the concept of risk management.

Connections

At the beginning of this chapter, it was noted that one reason for a theory was the need to connect diverse elements of a body of knowledge. In general, the community is focusing on the issue of connecting the knowledge within a stratum of the pyramid. Even though this is challenging, it generally involves communicating among individuals with a common background and lexicon.

It is far more difficult to have individuals connect across the different strata of the pyramid. This effort requires individuals from different disciplines to work effectively together. Doing so requires a holistic perspective on the measures of merit for cyber issues.

Figure 3–10 suggests a potential deconstruction of the measures of merit associated with the cyber problem. It identifies four linked sets of measures: performance, functional performance, effectiveness, and measures of entity empowerment (MOEEs). Since this field of endeavor is still in its infancy, the material is meant to be illustrative and not exhaustive.

Measures of performance are needed to characterize the vital computer science and electrical engineering dimensions of the problem. A key measure is the amount of bandwidth available to representative users of cyberspace. As the bandwidth increases to the megahertz/second range, the user is able to access advanced features such as imagery and video products. A second measure is connectivity. For circumstances in which the cyber-infrastructure is fixed, a useful measure is the percent of people in a country who have access to the Internet. However, in many military operations, the cyber-infrastructure and the users are mobile. Under those circumstances, a more useful measure is the performance of mobile ad hoc network users (for example, their ability to stay connected). Third, one can introduce measures of the "noise" that characterizes the cyber-infrastructure. For example, the extent to which the quality of the Internet is degraded can be characterized by the unwanted email that it carries, which can subsume a considerable subset of the network's capacity. In early 2007, approximately 90 percent of the traffic on the Internet was estimated to have been spam.[42] In addition, the integrity of the information is further compromised by phishing exploits in which criminal elements seek to employ the Internet to perpetrate economic scams. Finally, measures of performance can be introduced to characterize resistance to adversary actions, including denial-of-service attacks, propagation of viruses or worms, and illicit intrusion into systems.

It is useful to introduce measures of functional performance that characterize how successfully selected entities are able to perform key functions, taking advantage of cyberspace. In the case of the U.S. military, the concept of net-centricity is to employ advances in cyberspace to perform essential functions, which include the ability to enhance the performance of increasing levels of information fusion (for example, at level one, the ability to generate a timely, complete, accurate picture of blue forces). Similarly, a basic tenet of net-centricity is to propagate commander's intent so that the participants in the operation can synchronize and self-synchronize their actions.

Measures of effectiveness are needed to characterize how successful entities can be in their key missions, taking advantage of cyberspace. In the context of

FIGURE 3–10. Measures of Merit

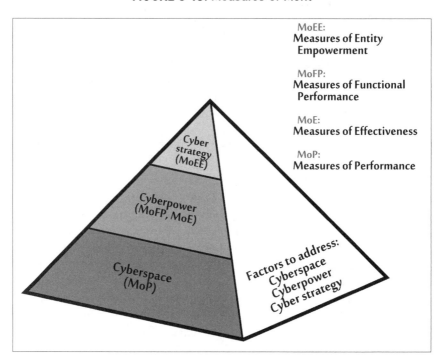

major combat operations, measures of effectiveness are required to characterize the ability to exploit cyberspace in multiple dimensions. At one extreme, enhancements in cyberspace have the potential to reduce the time to conduct a campaign and the casualties associated with the campaign. At the other extreme, enhancements in cyberspace may substantially enhance blue force loss exchange ratios and the amount of ground gained and controlled.

From the perspective of cyber strategy, there is interest in characterizing the extent to which enhancements in cyberspace can empower key entities. In the case of nation-states, potential measures of entity empowerment might include selected PMESII variables. As an example, it might address the ability to leverage cyberspace to influence a population, shape a nation at strategic crossroads, and deter, persuade, and coerce an adversary.

Table 3–6 suggests some candidate measures of merit that may be employed in future analyses of cyber issues.

Anticipation

From the perspective of the decisionmaker, the primary challenge is to anticipate what will occur next in the cyber domain and to formulate coherent policy to cope with those developments. To begin to address that challenge, this section deals with four aspects of anticipation. First, it identifies key trends expected to characterize cyberspace. Second, it identifies the research activities that should be conducted to address those trends. Third, it briefly identifies the major policy issues that decisionmakers will need to address. Finally, it discusses the assessment needs that must be addressed to support the formulation and analysis of policy options.

Cyber Trends

To anticipate key changes in cyberspace, various chapters of this book have identified several key trends. However, it is difficult to provide quantitative estimates as to how rapidly these trends will be manifested. Thus, the following should be regarded as a partial, qualitative list of some of the most significant potential changes.

TABLE 3-6. Selected Measures of Merit

MEASURES	REPRESENTATIVE MEASURES
Cyberstrategy— entity empowerment	• Political reforms (for example, participation in democratic elections) • Military efforts to enhance security (for example, reduction in number, severity of insurgent, terrorist attacks) • Economic reforms (for example, reconstruction projects completed) • Social reforms (for example, reconciliation of warring parties) • Information (for example, gaining trust of host nation population) • Infrastructure (for example, improvement in delivery of electric power, clean water)

Effectiveness (against targeted groups)	• Informational
	  o Media: number of positive/negative stories
	  o Clerics: tone of mosque sermons
	• Military: loss exchange rates

Functional performance	• Informational
	  o Time to create, validate, disseminate influence messages
	  o Number of meetings held with surrogate groups

Performance	• System performance (for example, latency, bandwidth, reliability) • Resistance to adversary attack (for example, ability to withstand a denial-of-service attack)

First, there is an increased move to adoption of IP-based systems. As a consequence, one can anticipate a convergence of telephone, radio, television, and Internet. As one example, there is a dramatic use of voice over Internet protocol (with attendant security issues) in the area of telephony. Second is the emergence of sensor networks that feature an extremely large number of heterogeneous sensors. One manifestation is the netting of enormous numbers of video cameras in urban areas, raising issues in the civil liberties community. Third is an inexorable trend toward proliferation of broadband and wireless. An example of this trend was the plan to have citywide deployment of worldwide interoperability for microwave access. However, this trend suggests the difficulty in predicting when a trend becomes a reality. Nextel had made this objective the key to its strategy; however, the company has recently observed that the technology has not matured sufficiently to implement it in the near term.[43] Fourth is the enhancement of search capabilities, both for local systems and the entire Internet. A driver for this trend has been industrial competition to develop improved search engines (in part, to enhance advertising revenue). Fifth are extraordinary efforts to enhance human/machine connectivity. One example is the development of direct nerve and brain connections to computers or prostheses, arising from efforts to treat soldiers injured by improvised explosive devices in Iraq.[44] Finally, there are dramatic increases in user participation in information content. This trend is manifested through the proliferation of blogs, contributions to wikis, participation in social networks, and involvement in virtual reality environments.

Opportunities for Cyber Research

As an application of the emerging theory of cyber, table 3–7 identifies the major areas where cyber research should be pursued.

Cyberspace research. In the area of cyberspace, improved technology projections are needed to identify major breakthroughs (comparable to the discovery of giant magnetoresistance) that may substantially affect measures of performance for cyberspace. Second, malevolent actors inevitably will gain access to the U.S. Government and defense industrial base cyberspace. This suggests that research is needed to protect the essential data in cyberspace from exfiltration or corruption. Finally, additional research is needed to formulate an objective architecture for cyberspace that is inherently more secure than the existing architecture. Consistent with that effort, there is a need to address the challenging issue of transitioning from the existing to the objective architecture.

Cyberpower research. Due to resource constraints, this preliminary assessment of cyber theory has not adequately addressed the political, diplomatic, and economic levers of power, and assessments should be completed for them. Second, existing assessments of the military lever of power have focused almost exclusively on the potential benefits that can accrue by creatively employing cyberspace. It is equally important to perform risk assessments to understand the potential downside of relying extensively on cyberspace. This includes conducting experiments and developing the methodology, tools, data, and intellectual capital required to perform military risk assessments. Similarly, it is important to conduct research into the potential benefits and risks associated with leveraging cyberspace developments for non-U.S. military capability (for example, North Atlantic Treaty Organization [NATO] allies that are pursuing network-enabled capabilities). Finally, in the area of information, additional research is needed to quantify the information duels likely to occur with potential adversaries.

Cyber strategy research. To deal with the challenges posed by the full array of entities empowered by enhancements in cyberspace, it is vital that information-enabled societies conduct research on tailored deterrence. This concept suggests that important alliances (such as NATO) must develop a holistic philosophy that understands the goals, culture, and risk calculus of each of the potential adversaries, develops and plans for capabilities to deter these adversaries, and devises a strategy to communicate these concepts to the potential adversaries.

Institutional factors research. Theoretical research is needed to address critical gaps in institutional knowledge in the areas of governance, legal issues, sharing of information, Internet regulation, and civil liberties.

TABLE 3–7. Areas Where Additional Theoretical Research Is Required

AREA	RESEARCH AREAS
Cyberspace	• Perform technology projections to identify key breakthroughs • Develop techniques to protect essential data from exfiltration, corruption • Formulate an objective network architecture that is more secure and identify options to transition to it
Cyberpower	• Extend analyses to other levers of power (diplomatic, economic) • Perform risk assessments to address cyber-dependence • Quantify the blue-red information duel
Cyber strategy	• Conduct research on "tailored deterrence" • Explore options to address cyber espionage
Institutional factors	• Perform research on cyber influence; legal frameworks; balance between security and civil liberties
Cyber assessment	• Develop analytical methods, tools, data, and intellectual capital to assess cyber issues

First, in the area of governance, the U.S. Government must reassess the role of the Internet Corporation for Assigned Names and Numbers in the governance of the Internet. In the future, the United States clearly must be more adroit in the area of cyber influence versus governance. This will require a thorough reexamination of all the institutional bodies that affect cyber governance and the development of a Government strategy to interact with them.

Second, cyber legal issues are in their infancy. The current situation is non-homogeneous, with inconsistent laws in various sovereign nations (for example, German hate crime laws) and limited signatories to the Council of Europe Convention on Cybercrime.[45] In particular, there is a need to clarify the issue of espionage in cyberspace—what it is and what rights of response are left to the victims. In addition, a consistent model must be adopted that can be applied to determine whether a cyber attack is an act of war.

Third, controversy continues about the sharing of information between the U.S. Government and the private sector. Research is needed to determine what information should be shared and under what circumstances.

Fourth, regulatory agencies, such as the Federal Communications Commission, have the authority to regulate Internet service providers to redress selected cyber security issues. However, to date, regulatory agencies have been reluctant to address these issues.

Fifth, the recent debate about the Foreign Intelligence Surveillance Act court has mobilized the civil liberties community to raise the specter of "Big Brother." As a consequence of the actions of civil liberties organizations, major Government programs have been terminated or modified (for example, DARPA's Total Information Awareness and the Department of Homeland Security's Multistate Anti-terrorism Information Exchange). Research is needed to clarify the appropriate balance among actions to deal with adversaries while still protecting civil liberties.

Cyber assessment research. As discussed below, our ability to perform cyber assessments is extremely uneven. As a consequence, research efforts are required to develop analytical methods, tools, data, and intellectual capital to address issues in the areas of cyberpower, cyber strategy, and infrastructure issues.

Cyber policy issues. During the course of the NDU cyber project, several major policy issues were singled out that required further attention. For the purposes of this preliminary cyber theory, these issues have served to focus the boundaries of this study, although we have also addressed a number of lower priority policy issues. Consequently, emphasis has been placed on assembling the intellectual capital required to illuminate those issues.

In table 3–8, these issues have been aggregated into the categories of cyberspace, cyberpower, cyber strategy, and institutional factors. However, most of

TABLE 3-8. Selected Policy Recommendations

Category	Area/Recommendations
Cyberspace	• Security: U.S. Government should adopt "differentiated security" approach • Resources: establish national cyber laboratories; substantially increase research and development funding for governmental agencies; enhance private sector activities
Cyberpower	• Net-centric operations: address risks (for example, exercise against highly capable cyber warriors) • Computer network attack: review definitions, classification level, integration into operations • Influence operations: adopt a holistic, multidisciplinary, interagency approach • Stability, security, transition, reconstruction: adopt I-power approach
Cyber strategy	• Organization: create a new interagency cyber policy council • Deterrence: U.S. Government should adopt a more robust deterrence policy (for example, generate capabilities, undertake political action) • Espionage: conduct policy/legal review
Institutional	• Governance: develop strategy for Internet influence • Legal: clarify definitions, reconcile international and sovereign law • Critical infrastructure protection: implement effective public-private partnership

these issues are extremely broad and contentious; consequently, additional analyses will be required to address them adequately.

Cyber assessment. One of the major challenges confronting the analysis community is to develop the methods, tools, and data needed to support cyber policy decisionmakers. Figure 3–11 suggests the relative maturity of key tools in the areas of cyberspace, cyberpower, cyber strategy, and institutional factors.

In the areas of cyberspace, the community is employing several tools to address computer science and communications issues. Perhaps the best known is the OPNET simulation widely employed to address network architectural issues.[46] From an analytic perspective, techniques such as percolation theory enable one to evaluate the robustness of a network.[47] Looking to the future, the National Research Laboratory has developed a GIG Testbed to explore the myriad issues associated with linking new systems and networks.

FIGURE 3-11. Subjective Assessment of Modeling, Simulation, and Analysis for Cyber Policy Analyses

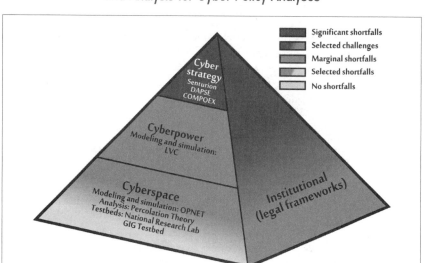

In the area of cyberpower, the community has had some success in employing live, virtual, and constructive simulations. For example, in assessments of air-to-air combat, insights have been derived from the live air intercept missile evaluation–air combat evaluation experiments, virtual experiments in the former McDonnell Air Combat Simulator, and constructive experiments using tools such as the TAC BRAWLER air combat simulator. However, the community still requires better tools to assess the impact of advances in cyberspace on broader military and informational effectiveness (for example, land combat in complex terrain).

In the area of cyber strategy, a number of promising initiatives are under way. In response to recent tasking by U.S. Strategic Command, a new methodology and associated tools are emerging (the Deterrence Analysis and Planning Support Environment).[48] However, these results have not yet been applied to major cyber strategy issues. In addition, promising tools are emerging from academia (for example, Senturion predictive analysis software and George Mason University's Pythia modeling software) and DARPA (Conflict Modeling, Planning, and Outcomes Experimentation). However, these are still in early stages of development and application.

Finally, only primitive tools are available to address issues of governance, legal issues, and civil liberties. Although some tools are being developed to explore the cascading effects among critical infrastructures (National Infrastructure Simulation and Analysis Center system dynamics models),[49] they have not yet undergone rigorous validation.

Conclusion

Consistent with the macro framework that has been adopted to characterize the cyber problem, this section summarizes the key insights in the areas of cyberspace, cyberpower, cyber strategy, and institutional factors. The section concludes by identifying the next steps that should be taken to refine the theory of cyberpower.

Key Insights

Cyberspace. Cyberspace is a manmade environment experiencing exponential growth in important measures of performance. There is an extraordinary diffusion of knowledge among all the stakeholders of cyberspace, including malevolent users. As a consequence of this diffusion of knowledge, cyberspace is being degraded by noise (such as spam) and a broad variety of cyber attacks. The most troubling of these attacks includes denial of service, exfiltration of data, and the potential for corruption of data. In each instance, recent experience has demonstrated that these attacks are relatively easy to implement technically and financially and are extremely difficult to attribute.

These vulnerabilities arise from the basic architecture that has evolved from the original ARPANET. A new cyberspace architecture may be required to halt the perceived erosion of security. However, there will be substantial difficulties in transitioning from the current architecture to one that is more robust against adversary action.

Cyberpower. As cyberspace evolves, it has the potential to enhance each of the levers of national power. This chapter has focused on two of these levers: military and information.

In the area of military power, studies are under way to characterize the extent to which enhancements in cyberspace can enhance key measures of effectiveness. These studies tend to be unambiguous in the area of air-to-air combat where experiments suggest that enhanced digital communications can enhance loss-exchange ratios by a factor of approximately 2.5. Although studies of other military operations have also been undertaken, the results are generally confounded by other factors such as mobility and protection.

To complement these experiments, an assessment of theories of environmental warfare was undertaken that critically reassessed the theories of land, sea, air, and space theory. Based on that assessment, it was concluded that a theory of cyberpower should focus on four factors: technological advances, speed and scope of operations, control of key features, and national mobilization.

From the perspective of information, the chapter has addressed influence operations from a strategic and tactical perspective. Based on prior experiences and an adaptation of earlier analytical frameworks, an approach was developed for linking operational objectives and processes to DOTMLPF requirements. These assessments suggest that developments in cyberspace can substantially affect future efforts to enhance influence operations (for example, to implement precision-guided messages).

Cyber strategy. The evolving theory of cyber has identified a range of entities that will be empowered by enhancements in cyberspace. These include terrorist groups, which are employing cyberspace to recruit, raise money, propagandize, educate and train, plan operations, and command and control operations; hacktivists, who are employing cyberspace to conduct "cyber riots" and implement exploits in cyberspace; transnational criminals, who pursue a variety of techniques (such as phishing and denial-of-service attacks) to raise substantial funds (reputed to be more than the money derived from drug trafficking); and nation-states, the most advanced of which are employing cyberspace to enhance all dimensions of PMESII activities.

However, changes in cyberspace have given rise to unintended consequences. Many of the entities at the low end of the spectrum (terrorists, hacktivists, transnational criminals) are making life more dangerous for information-enabled societies. In particular, these entities tend to be much more adaptable than nation-states, causing the latter to respond, belatedly, to the initiatives of the former. In addition, research about selected near-peers (China, Russia) suggests that they have new perspectives on cyber strategy that will present information-enabled societies with new challenges in cyberspace.

Institutional factors. From an institutional perspective, issues are emerging that will affect all aspects of cyber theory. This chapter has high-lighted the challenges that exist in cyber governance, legal issues, exchange of cyber informa-tion between governments and industry, and the balance between national security and civil liberties.

From a theoretical perspective, one of the major challenges emerges from the difficulty in characterizing and responding to an attack in cyberspace. As demonstrated by recent events, it is extremely difficult to attribute an attack to an adversary that chooses to act anonymously. In light of that ambiguity, it is difficult to formulate a coherent response to such an attack. For example, it is still unclear how an alliance, such as NATO, might respond to a cyber attack against one or more of its members. It is anticipated that these issues will be addressed in subsequent analyses.

Next Steps

As stated earlier, this effort constitutes a preliminary theory of cyberpower. To refine this product, it is recommended that the following steps be pursued.

Define. Although there is still confusion about the definitions for the key terms in a theory of cyberpower, the community should find it relatively straightforward to go from the current base to agreement on terms. However, additional work is still required to establish the linkage between cyber terms and the terms associated with information operations.

Categorize. The cyber pyramid has proven to be a useful taxonomy in "binning" major concepts. However, there is still a need to develop specific cyber frameworks and models to explore policy issues that confront senior decision-makers.

Explain. This theory of cyberpower was anticipated to be incomplete. Additional efforts are needed to address issues beyond the scope of this book. In the area of cyberpower, there is a need to assess how potential changes in cyberspace will affect political, diplomatic, and economic functionality and effectiveness. In the area of cyber strategy, the extent to which key entities are empowered by advances in cyberspace and cyberpower must be assessed. These entities include individuals, nongovernmental organizations, transnational corporations, selected nation-states, alliances, and international organizations. Finally, in the area of institutional factors, there is a pressing need to assess the effect of changes in cyberspace on the balance between civil liberties and national security. In assessing these issues, it would be useful to employ a risk management approach.

Connect. Currently, we have relatively little understanding about the appropriate measures of merit to employ in cyber assessments or the relationships among them. For example, we do not have a clear understanding about how changes in cyberspace affect U.S. levers of power or empowerment. At a minimum, it is important to develop preliminary relationships so that a decisionmaker can understand the implications of how potential changes in cyberspace or institutional factors will affect cyberpower and cyber strategy.

Anticipate. Cyberspace is in the midst of explosive, nonlinear change. It is vital that more detailed technology assessments be undertaken to anticipate and understand potential breakthroughs in cyberspace. Furthermore, efforts should be made in the development and application of models, simulations, and analyses to assess the impact of these changes on cyberpower and cyber strategy. These developments in methodologies, tools, and data should provide decisionmakers with the analytic support needed to explore the long-range effect of alternative cyber options.

Appendix: Timeline of Key Cyber Events

This appendix summarizes several of the key events associated with the evolution of cyberspace, cyberpower, cyber strategy, and institutional factors. These observations have affected the formulation of the preliminary theory of cyberpower.

Evolution of Cyberspace

Figure 3–12 provides a timeline of recent events that have shaped cyberspace. It is notable that this timeline is scarcely 40 years old. Among the events of interest are the creation of the Internet (and the associated development of the TCP/IP) and the evolution of the domain name service (DNS). A major enabler was the proliferation of inexpensive personal computers with operating systems that made it relatively simple for any user to employ the technology. Other seminal events include the creation of the World Wide Web and the Mosaic browser that made the information easily accessible to individual users.

Google, founded in 1998, has become the world leader in popular search engines. By virtue of its advertising revenue, it has developed a viable business model.

Another important development involves the launch of the Wikipedia in 2001. Its open-source software is widely used by government entities (for example, Intellipedia and the Joint Data Systems of the Office of the Secretary of Defense).

In 2001, Apple began to sell the iPod, a device able to provide high capacity in an extremely small package due to the discovery of giant magnetoresistance.

Finally, in 2007, Microsoft released Vista, a new operating system. The oft-delayed product was revised to deal with the many security problems that afflict cyberspace.

Evolution of Cyberpower

The timeline in figure 3–13 identifies events that have shaped the military's perspectives on the use of cyberspace. The timeline begins in 1983, when MILNET split off from ARPANET (subsequently becoming the Defense Data Network). Subsequently, the intellectual underpinnings of military cyberpower were refined by the publication of *Joint Vision 2010*.[50] That was complemented by the Advanced Battlespace Information System, which was cosponsored by Vice Admiral Arthur Cebrowski, Director, J6, Joint Staff, and Anita Jones, Director of Defense Research and Engineering, to orchestrate evolving network concepts of

FIGURE 3-12. Evolution of Cyberspace

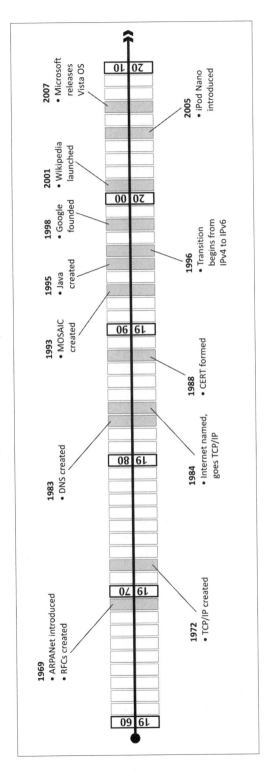

FIGURE 3-13. Evolution of Cyberpower: Military Perspective

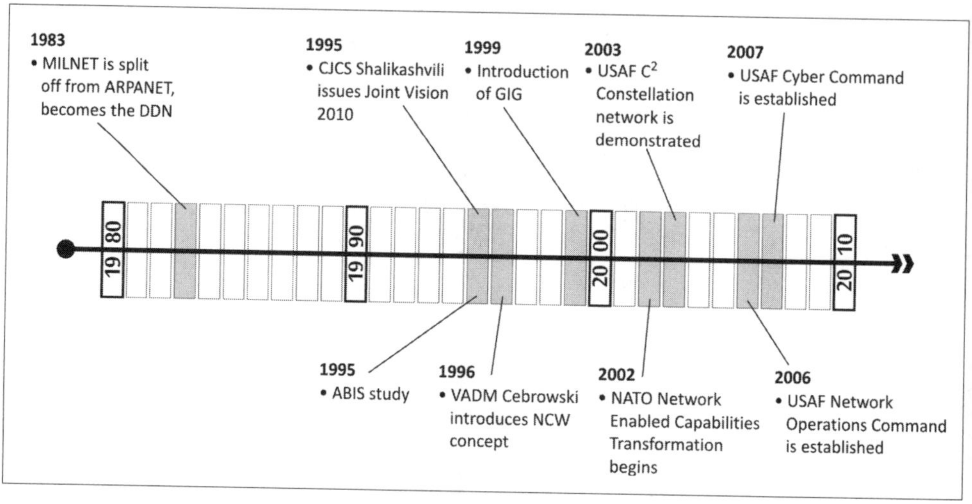

1983
- MILNET is split off from ARPANET, becomes the DDN

1995
- CJCS Shalikashvili issues Joint Vision 2010

1999
- Introduction of GIG

2003
- USAF C² Constellation network is demonstrated

2007
- USAF Cyber Command is established

1980 — 1990 — 2000 — 2010

1995
- ABIS study

1996
- VADM Cebrowski introduces NCW concept

2002
- NATO Network Enabled Capabilities Transformation begins

2006
- USAF Network Operations Command is established

operations and science and technology investments.[51] Subsequently, Vice Admiral Cebrowski and John Garstka wrote a seminal paper introducing the concept of net-centric warfare.[52] Building on that base, OSD launched the concept of the Global Information Grid, and the individual Services formulated their visions of subordinate networks (LandWarNet, ForceNet, and C² Constellation). In addition, selected NATO and Partnership for Peace nations developed tailored strategies to implement variants of net-enabled capabilities. More recently, the Air Force has modified its mission space to include operations in cyberspace and reorganized to create an Air Cyber Command.[53]

Although the current NDU effort has not specifically addressed the economic and diplomatic levers of power, these issues are being actively discussed elsewhere. For example, Thomas Friedman has identified 10 critical steps on the road to increased economic globalization.[54] As shown in figure 3–14, these steps have their roots deep within the use of information technology (for example, the age of the personal computer, the advent of the Internet, and the revolution in Internet search engine capabilities). The extent and impact of globalization are being actively debated in the academic community.

Similarly, the diplomatic community is beginning to assess the impact of cyberspace on its operations. The global availability of information has affected the roles of Embassies. Whereas the Embassy was once the primary source of indigenous information, the capital city frequently has access to information not easily available to the Embassy. Furthermore, the Department of State has begun to explore "blog" diplomacy to provide "digital outreach."[55]

Evolution of Cyber Strategy

The cyber strategy timeline in figure 3–15 emphasizes selected attacks and responses in cyberspace. At the onset of the timeline, the key elements of malware included worms (1979) and viruses (1983). An early example of an attack on sensitive but unclassified U.S. Government systems occurred in 1998 with Solar Sunrise. Although this was ultimately attributed to two California teenagers (linked to a subject matter expert in Israel), it dramatized the vulnerability of selected Government databases to intrusion. Subsequently, events such as Moonlight Maze (beginning in 1999 and attributed to sources in Russia) and Titan Rain (beginning in 2003 and attributed to sources in China) suggested the vulnerability of U.S. Government and defense industrial base data sources to cyber espionage. In the case of Titan Rain, Chinese sources were estimated to have exfiltrated on the order of 10 terabits of data.

More recently, attacks have featured distributed denial of service, drawing on herds of penetrated zombies or bots. As examples, in February 2007 there was a generally unsuccessful attack on the core DNS servers[56] and a reasonably successful "cyber riot" against government agencies, the financial sector, and media outlets in Estonia.[57] In many of these events, it has proven exceedingly difficult to attribute the source of the attack.

FIGURE 3-14. Evolution of Cyberpower: Economic Perspective

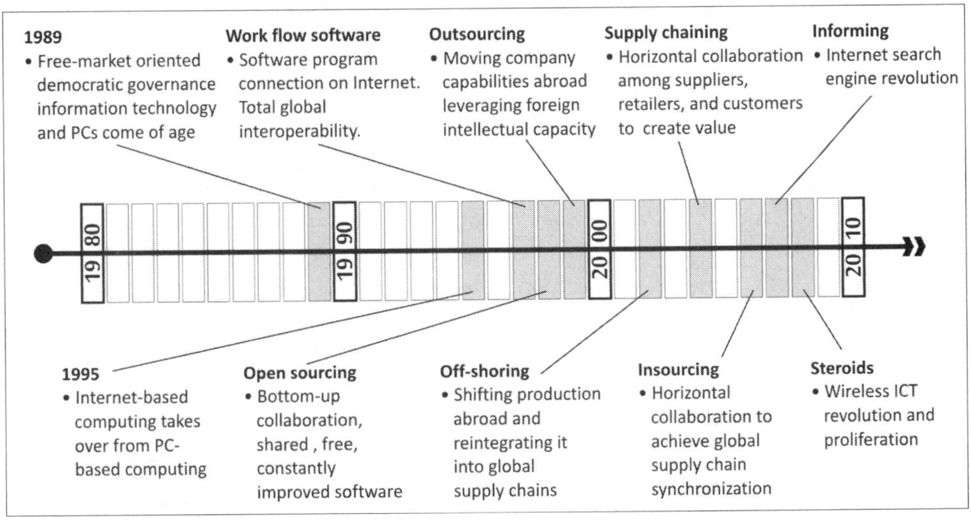

1989
- Free-market oriented democratic governance information technology and PCs come of age

Work flow software
- Software program connection on Internet. Total global interoperability.

Outsourcing
- Moving company capabilities abroad leveraging foreign intellectual capacity

Supply chaining
- Horizontal collaboration among suppliers, retailers, and customers to create value

Informing
- Internet search engine revolution

1995
- Internet-based computing takes over from PC-based computing

Open sourcing
- Bottom-up collaboration, shared, free, constantly improved software

Off-shoring
- Shifting production abroad and reintegrating it into global supply chains

Insourcing
- Horizontal collaboration to achieve global supply chain synchronization

Steroids
- Wireless ICT revolution and proliferation

Source: Thomas L. Friedman, *The World Is Flat: A Brief History of the Twenty-first Century* (New York: Farrar, Straus and Giroux, 2005).

FIGURE 3-15. Evolution of Cyber Strategy: Selected Attacks and Responses

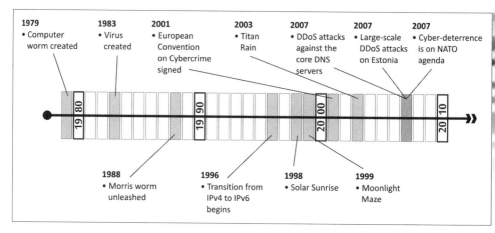

The attack against Estonia has prompted NATO to reevaluate its position on cyber defense. For example, Estonia is in the process of establishing a Computer Defense Center of Excellence, and NATO is addressing cyber deterrence in senior meetings. With respect to the latter, there is ongoing discussion about the implications of a cyber attack against a NATO Ally (Is an attack against one an attack against all? Does it have ramifications for Articles 4 and 5?).

Evolution of Institutional Factors

Figure 3–16 provides a timeline of key institutional events. Several of the early events (demonstration of the ARPANET, introduction of TCP/IP into the Internet, creation of the DNS) were discussed above.

In the 1980s and 1990s, organizations were created to provide governance for the Internet: the Internet Engineering Task Force and the Internet Research Task Force. In 1992, they morphed into the Internet Society, and the World Wide Web Consortium was formed. Subsequently, the Internet Corporation for Assigned Names and Numbers was created in 1998.

In 1998, the President's Commission on Critical Infrastructure Protection was formed under the leadership of Tom Marsh. That effort focused public attention on the issues associated with critical infrastructure protection.

Institutionally, the events of September 11, 2001, gave rise to significant organizational and legal activities. These included the creation of the Department of Homeland Security and the passage of the USA PATRIOT Act. One unintended consequence was the formation and cancellation of the Total

Information Awareness program at DARPA, due in part to concerns voiced by civil liberties advocates.

In recent years, the future governance of the Internet has been affected by two meetings of the World Summit on the Information Society in Geneva and Tunis. These have been followed by two Internet Governance Forum meetings in Athens and Rio de Janeiro.

FIGURE 3-16. Timeline of Key Institutional Events

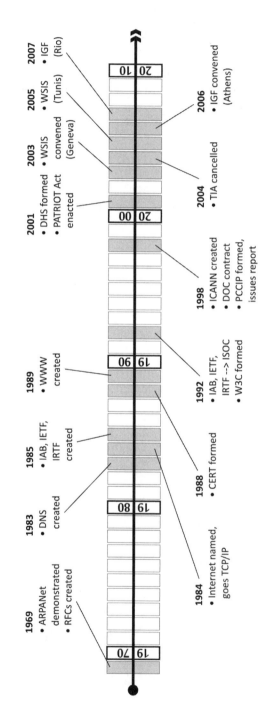

Part II
Cyberspace

CHAPTER 4

A Graphical Introduction to the Structural Elements of Cyberspace

Elihu Zimet and Edward Skoudis

THE MAJORITY of Internet users do not have (or need) much understanding of what is going on "under the hood" of cyberspace, beyond use of their keyboard, display, and favorite applications. To further the understanding of other chapters of this book by readers without a technical background, this chapter explains various elements of cyberspace, particularly the Internet, with a graphical presentation.

The purpose here is to shed light on elements of cyberspace by example, so there is little attempt to be comprehensive. The focus is on Internet technology, particularly networks using the Internet protocol (IP). However, because legacy telephone networks, cellular networks, and cable networks, as well as private enterprise, government, and military networks, increasingly use Internet technology, we discuss them briefly as well.

The structure of cyberspace will change as new technology is developed and employed in a variety of new applications and social structures. Thus, the representation here reflects a snapshot of the present only.

Figure 4–1 presents the domains of cyberspace addressed in this chapter.

The *systems domain* comprises the technical foundation, infrastructure, and architecture of cyberspace. It includes hardware and software, as well as the infrastructure items supporting them, such as the electrical power grid.

The *content and application domain* contains both the information base that resides in cyberspace and the mechanisms for accessing and processing this information.

FIGURE 4-1. Domains of Cyberspace

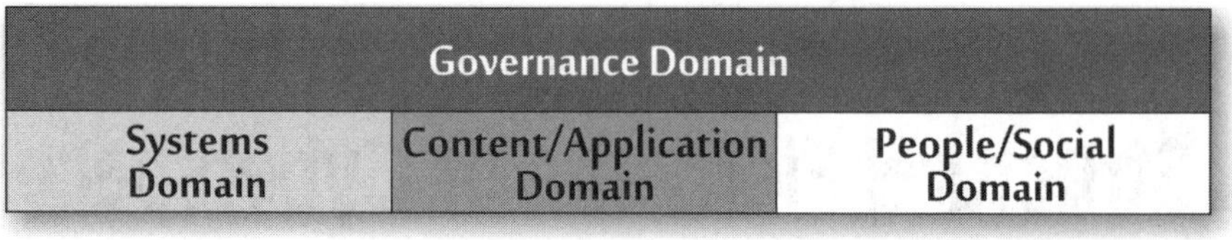

Governance Domain		
Systems Domain	Content/Application Domain	People/Social Domain

Communications among people and interactions between people and information occur in the *people and social domain*. Businesses, consumers, advocacy groups, political campaigns, and social movements are in this domain.

The *governance domain* overlays all of the aspects of cyberspace, including the technological specifications for the systems domain, the conventions for data formatting and exchange in the content and application domain, and the legal frameworks of various countries associated with the people and social domain. This chapter focuses on the first three domains defined above (the governance domain is described in chapter 21 of this book, "Internet Governance").

The Systems Domain

The systems domain of cyberspace is the infrastructure that carries, stores, and manipulates information. Hundreds of millions of computer and network systems interact in cyberspace, carrying information generated by over a billion people. A major portion of the modern economy is associated with manufacturing the components and systems of cyberspace, including computer chips, desktop computers, routers, servers, and operating systems. Another major component of the economy is associated with operating this infrastructure, including Internet service providers (ISPs), telecommunications firms, electrical power companies, and other organizations.

The global open communications backbone—including telecommunications, cable, cellular, Internet, and other public networks—is the principal infrastructure for both civil and military communications today. In addition, many militaries, governments, and commercial enterprises also employ closed private networks. Many of these private networks have interconnection points with public communications networks, either integrated as part of their design or created on an accidental, ad hoc basis.

Network Building Blocks

Most networks are made up of smaller subnetworks. For example, among the subnetworks of the telephone network are smaller telephone networks operated either by telephone companies or independent enterprises, all of which are interconnected at various points. The original telephone network employed switchboards on which telephone operators established a stable circuit between two or more parties. The circuit remained dedicated to those particular users as long as the call was maintained. In such *circuit-switched* networks, the network allocates resources—originally a physical connection using switched wires, later a timeslot in a protocol—for every communicating session, established in real time, to move information across the network. With circuit switching, then, the network is "aware" of individual communicating sessions, tracking them constantly and allocating resources for each of them.

Instead of the circuit switching of the traditional telephony network, the Internet relies on the alternative technology of *packet switching*. Instead of the network dedicating resources between the end systems for each communications stream, the data that make up that communication are broken up into separate packets or chunks of data and each is delivered independently by the network to the desired destination. "Header" information is attached to each packet to help the network move the packets to the right place. The network itself is generally ignorant of the relationships between the packets but instead focuses on getting individual packets to their destination as quickly as possible.

The fundamental packet-switching network building block of the Internet is a local area network (LAN), an extremely focused form of subnet in a relatively localized geographical area. Most enterprise networks for corporations, government agencies, and military organizations are groups of LANs. Increasingly, LAN technology is being deployed in homes so that disparate devices such as personal computers, voice over IP (VoIP) telephones, and servers can communicate with each other. Components on a single LAN are typically connected using a switch or wireless access point, perhaps using wired Ethernet or WiFi wireless technology; these simple devices send packets directly between interconnected systems over short distances ranging from one to a few hundred meters. Figure 4–2 shows a common LAN setup.

LANs are connected by routers, devices that can direct packets to their destination subnets based on the addresses in the packets themselves. Routers can also connect LANs to point-to-point links to create even larger networks. Point-to-point link technologies include T1, Digital Signal 3 (DS3, also known as T3), cable modem, fiber optic service (FIOS), and digital subscriber line (DSL), a relatively higher speed network connection over telephone network wires. The result is a network of networks, or internetwork, of a multitude of interconnected LANs, routers, and point-to-point links.[1]

Figure 4–3 depicts an internetwork of various LANs, routers, and point-to-point links, such as might be found inside a small or medium-sized enterprise.

The Internet is a publicly accessible internetwork with global reach tied together by means of common use of IP. Physically, the Internet is made up of

FIGURE 4-2. A Local Area Network

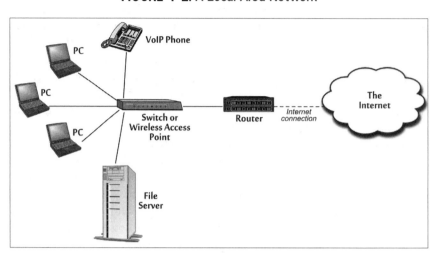

a group of "backbone" routers operated by top-tier ISPs (see figure 4–4). A few hundred high-end routers distributed around the world constitute this backbone, making up the major branches of the network architecture, moving packets across ISP networks and also between ISPs. The top-tier ISPs offer smaller ISPs access to the Internet backbone. Both the top-tier and smaller ISPs also give enterprise networks, individuals, and content providers access to the backbone infrastructure. In the United States and some other countries, numerous top-tier ISPs compete for this business. In other countries, a single dominant provider, often the legacy telephone company, acts as the only ISP.

From the introduction of the Internet in the early 1970s until today, the legacy communications network has provided connectivity for networked computers in addition to telephones. Other types of enterprises, including cable companies, wireless operators, and dedicated data communications carriers, have also begun to offer carriage of Internet data as part of their business. Bandwidth has been increased significantly through the use of better signal processing, more rapid transmitters, and fiber optic communications.

The communications networks require a significant support infrastructure, including the electrical power grid, required for operating all components of the networks. Supervisory control and data acquisition (SCADA) devices, which consist of simple computers directly connected to industrial equipment, are used to monitor and manage many types of utility networks and industrial operations, including electrical power grids, gas pipelines, and manufacturing lines. Increasingly, the SCADA devices themselves are managed remotely across a private network or even the public Internet. This approach introduces a significant dependency loop: the communications infrastructure relies on the

FIGURE 4-3. Internetworking Local Area Networks via
Routers and Point-to-point Links

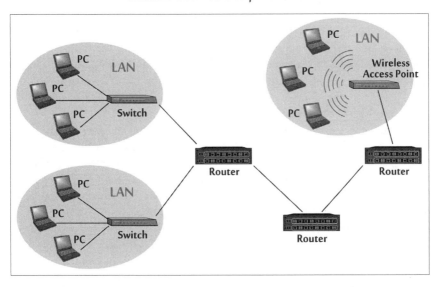

FIGURE 4-4. Internet Links to Backbone Routers
Operated by Internet Service Providers

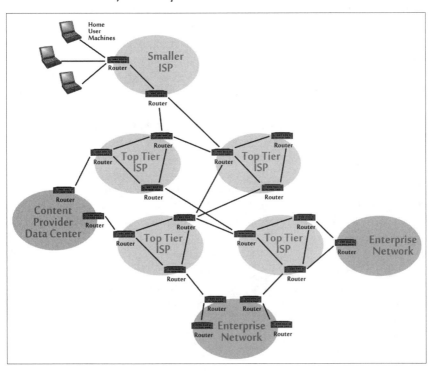

electrical power grid, which is controlled with SCADA systems that rely on the communications infrastructure. There is thus is a risk of cascading failures. Another vital aspect of the support infrastructure is the manufacturing base, which creates the physical equipment that makes up the various systems of cyberspace. These, too, may rely on SCADA systems and their communications networks, again raising the risks of interdependency.

Another View: Protocols and Packets

So far, this chapter has analyzed how internetworks and the Internet itself are built up of smaller building blocks such as LANs and point-to-point links. To further analyze the elements of the systems domain of cyberspace, a different view of networking can be helpful: the protocol and packet view. This view helps explain how different machines connected to the same Internet communicate with each other by sending packets according to standard protocols.

Protocol layering is a critical concept underlying this view of network communications. In 1980, the International Organization for Standardization released the Open Systems Interconnection (OSI) Reference Model, a generic description of how computer-to-computer communications could operate using protocol layering. In this model, a series of small software modules on each system perform a set of tasks that allow two computers to communicate with each other. For example, one module might focus on making sure that data are formatted appropriately, another takes care of retransmitting lost packets, and yet another transmits the packets from LAN to LAN across the network. Each of these modules, referred to as a *layer*, has a defined small job in communication (see figure 4–5).

The software of a given layer on the sending machine communicates with the same layer on the receiving machine. A layer is a collection of related functions that provides services to the layer above it and receives service from the layer below it. For example, one lower layer might send packets on behalf of the higher layer that is focused on retransmitting lost packets. This higher layer, in turn, serves an even higher layer that generates the data in the first place. In the example of figure 4–5, a layer of software inside a Web browser generates data to send to a Web server. This Web browser application passes the data to the transmission control protocol (TCP) layer software on the sending machine, which provides several services, including retransmitting lost packets. The TCP layer passes the software down to the IP layer, which provides the service of carrying the packet end to end through all the routers on the network. Although one layer relies on another to get things done, the layers are designed so the software of one layer can be replaced with other software, while all other layers remain the same. This modularity has proven especially useful in deploying new types of networks—for example, as IP version 4 (IPv4) networks are transitioned to IP version 6 (IPv6), the successor protocol for the Internet.

FIGURE 4-5. Protocol Layering

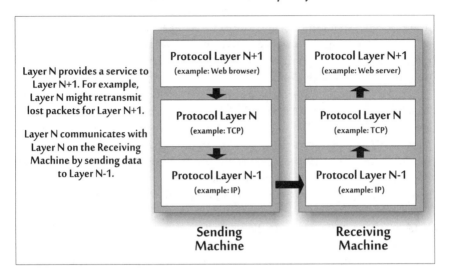

The communications modules taken together are called a *protocol stack* because they consist of several of these layers, one on top of the other. The OSI conceptual model defined by the International Organization for Standardization in 1980 includes seven such layers, each with a defined role in moving data across a network. At the "top," layer seven, the *application layer*, acts as a window to the communications channel for the applications themselves by interpreting data and turning it into meaningful information for applications. The application might be, for example, a Web browser or server, an email reader or server, a peer-to-peer file copy program, or an enterprise financial system.

Layer six, the *presentation layer*, deals with how data elements will be represented for transmission, such as the order of bits and bytes in numbers, the specific method for encoding textual information, and so on.

Layer five, the *session layer*, coordinates sessions between two communicating machines, helping to initiate and maintain them as well as to manage them if several different communications streams are going between them at the same time.

Layer four, the *transport layer*, supports the reliability of the communications stream between two systems by offering functions such as retransmitting lost packets, putting packets in the proper order, and providing error checking.

Layer three, the *network layer*, is responsible for moving data across the network from one system, possibly across a series of routers, to the destination machine. This layer is absolutely critical to making the network function end to end.

Layer two, the *data link layer*, moves data across one "hop" of the network, getting it from one system, perhaps to its destination on the same LAN, or to the nearest router, so it can be sent between LANs or to a point-to-point link.

At the "bottom" of the stack, layer one, the *physical layer*, actually transmits the bits across the physical link, which could be copper, fiber, wireless radio transmitters and receivers or another physical medium.

Today's Internet is loosely based on the OSI model, but it does not break out each layer exactly as the OSI model specifies. Most commonly, IP is paired with a transport protocol called the transmission control protocol (TCP)—hence the term TCP/IP to refer to the duo of protocols in most common use on the Internet today. TCP/IP is roughly equivalent to layer four (transport) and layer three (network) of the OSI Reference Model, plus a little interaction with layer two (data link). Everything above TCP/IP is left to the application with the application, presentation, and session layers (seven, six, and five) of the OSI Reference Model all folded into the application program itself. TCP/IP is mainly responsible for transmitting data for that application. It is important to note that the application layer is not TCP/IP itself: the application comprises the particular program trying to communicate across the network using TCP/IP. The application might be, for example, a Web browser and a Web server, or two mail servers, or a video player communicating with a streaming video server, or a file transfer protocol (FTP) client and server. Based on the OSI model, the application layer is often referred to as *layer seven*, even in TCP/IP networks.

The transport layer could be the transmission control protocol or its cousin, the user datagram protocol (UDP), a simpler but less reliable protocol. The transport layer ensures that packets are delivered to the proper place on the destination machine. For those applications requiring such functionality, TCP also delivers packets in the proper sequence or retransmits packets.

The network layer is based on the IP. Its purpose is to deliver packets end to end across the network, from a source computer to a given destination machine. Using terminology from the OSI Reference Model, the IP layer is sometimes referred to as *layer three*.

The data link layer transmits each packet across each hop of the network. For example, this layer moves data from a home computer to a router that connects the LAN to the Internet. Then, the router uses its data link layer software to move the data to another router. In the OSI Reference Model vernacular, the data link layer is often referred to as *layer two*.

The physical layer, called *layer one*, is the physical media, such as the wire, fiber optic cable, or radio frequencies, across which the information is actually transmitted.

To illustrate how these layers on IP networks typically communicate, figure 4–6 shows an example in which two computers, the sender machine and the receiver machine, communicate. Suppose a user on the sender machine wants to surf the Internet with a Web browser application such as Internet Explorer or Firefox to access a Web site. The browser on the sender needs to communicate with the Web server on the receiver, so it generates a packet and passes it to the TCP/IP stack software running on the sender machine. The data, which consists of a Web request, travel down the communications layers on the sender to the physical layer and get transmitted across the network (which usually consists of a series of routers). The packet is sent through one or more routers this way, until it reaches the receiver machine. It then travels up the receiver's communications stack.

To start this process, the sender's transport layer (that is, TCP software running on the sender machine) takes the packet from the browser application and formats it so it can be sent reliably to the transport layer on the receiver. This TCP software also engages in a packet exchange (called the TCP Three-Way Handshake) to make sure all of the sender's packets for this connection arrive in sequence. (Other types of transport layer protocols, such as UDP, do not care about sequence, so they have no such packet exchange for ordering packets.)

FIGURE 4-6. Protocol Layering to Transmit Packets on an Internet Protocol Network

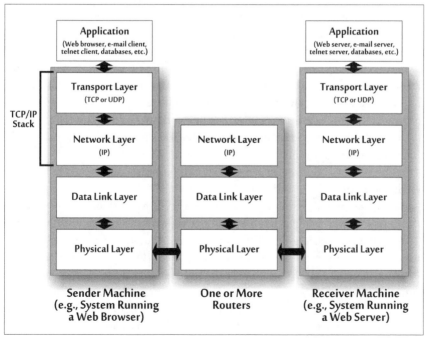

Just as the two applications, here the Web browser and the Web server, communicate with each other, so do the two transport layers. On the sender, the transport layer passes the packet down to the network layer, which delivers it across the network on behalf of the transport layer. The network layer adds the source and destination address in the packets, so they can be transmitted across the network to the receiver's network layer. Finally, the data are passed to the sender's data link and physical layers, where it is transmitted to the closest router on the way to the destination. Routers move the packet across the network, from subnet to subnet. The routers include the network, data link, and physical layer functions required to move the packet across the network. (Because these routers are focused on moving packets, not receiving them, they do not require the transport or application layers to deliver the packet to the receiver.) On the receiver side of the communication, the message is received and passed up the protocol stack, going from the physical layer to the data link layer to the network layer to the transport layer to the ultimate destination, the application.

This passing of data between the layers is illustrated in figure 4–7. Each layer attaches some information in front of (and in some cases, behind) the data it gets from the layer above it. The information added in front of the data is called a *header*, and it includes critical information for the layer to get its job done. As figure 4–7 shows, the application generates a packet. This packet might be part of a Web request, for example, or a piece of an email message. The transport layer adds a header to this data, which is likely to include information about where on the destination machine the packet should go. When TCP is used, the resulting header and data element is called a TCP *segment*. The TCP segment gets passed to the network layer, which adds another header with information about the source and destination address in the IP header. This header is analogous to an envelope with a postal address for the data. The resulting packet is called an IP *datagram*. This package is sent to the data link and physical layers, where a header (and a trailer) are added to create a *frame* that makes it possible for the data to be transmitted across the link.

The packets sent between machines pass through different layers of this stack and have various headers in front of them. The one layer that all systems and routers communicating with each other on the network must conform to is the network layer; for the Internet, the network layer is the Internet Protocol. Today's Internet relies on IPv4 from one end to the other. Certain subnets and routers also support the successor protocol, IPv6. Every packet sent across the Internet today using IPv4 has the structure shown in figure 4–8. It includes a source IP address (a 32-bit number indicating the network address of the system that sent the packet) and a destination IP address, which routers use to determine where to send the packet.[2] Other fields of the IPv4 header are associated with

FIGURE 4-7. Protocol Layering Applying Various Headers and a Trailer

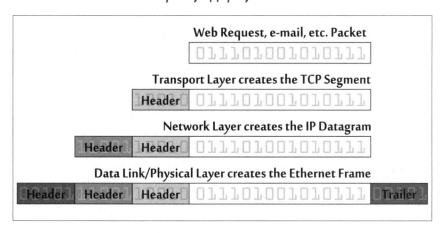

FIGURE 4-8. An Internet Protocol Version 4 Packet

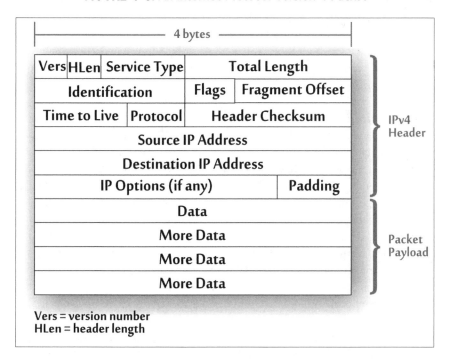

controlling the number of hops a packet can take as it traverses the network (the time-to-live field), fragmentation (which breaks larger packets into smaller ones), and other network functions.

Although the packet in figure 4–8 looks two-dimensional, that formulation is done purely for diagram purposes. Each field is transmitted on the wire (or wireless radio) one byte after another, linearly. The version number (such as IPv4) goes out first, followed by the header length (the size of the overall header in front of the data), field by field as shown, through total length, the identification field, which is associated with fragmentation, and so on. Bit after bit, the packet leaves the sender source. When it reaches a router, the router absorbs the packet on one network interface, inspects its various fields, and moves it to the appropriate network interface for transmission to its destination, or one router hop closer to its destination. In this way, a packet is sent and routed across the Internet.

The Content and Applications Domain

The systems domain of cyberspace provides the technical underpinnings of the network, but it is merely an infrastructure on which to store, transmit, and manipulate content or information using various software applications. The content and applications domain rides on top of the systems domain and provides the usable applications and the information they handle. This section describes some of the common methods for content storage in cyberspace, provides an overview of various application architectures, and outlines some of the most common application types used today.

Content Storage

Although content is stored on computer systems in cyberspace in many ways, two methods of information storage dominate: hierarchical file systems and relational databases. Nearly all cyberspace applications rely on at least one of these concepts; most applications use both. In a hierarchical file system, as shown in figure 4–9, one or more computers stores information in individual files, which themselves are made up of small sections of the hard drive or chunks of memory, depending on the computer system. Files on a typical computer system include the software of the operating system itself (such as Windows, Linux, or Apple's Mac OSX), executable programs that make up the applications of the computer (such as Adobe Acrobat, a Web browser, or a word processing program), configuration files that hold settings for the programs on the machine, and the data stored on the system by the application and its users, such as document files. Files are located inside of directories (also called folders on some operating systems). The directories themselves may contain subdirectories. This results in a hierarchical structure.

Today, many computer users take this structure for granted, and may assume that this organization of content is the way that computers necessarily work. But early computers did not have such a structure. Development of the hierarchical file structure revolutionized human interactions with machines. A hierarchical file system is useful because it provides an unambiguous way to refer to files, indication that there is a relationship between files—for example, files in the same directory are likely to have some common purpose—and a method for navigation between files. This paradigm is so useful for information storage that it is found in all of the major general-purpose operating systems available today—including Windows, Linux, UNIX, Mac OSX, and others—across various kinds of computing equipment, including laptop computers, desktops, and servers as well as many cell phones, music players, and video storage devices. Even systems without hard drives are increasingly likely to use a file system implemented in memory.[3]

Another common method for storing content involves a relational database. As illustrated in figure 4–10, a relational database stores information in a series of

FIGURE 4-9. A Hierarchical File System

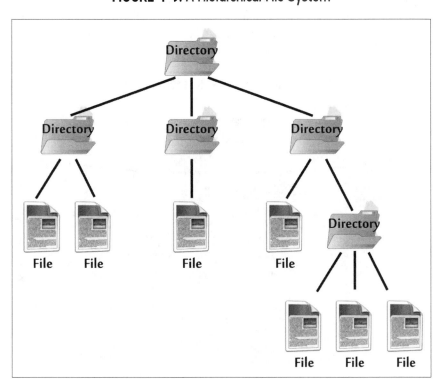

tables. The tables specify a number of fields under which specific types of data, called values, are stored. In the value section of each field, all of the elements in a given row of the table relate to each other as a single record in the database. Two or more tables may have the exact same field in them to forge a relationship between them. Such a relationship is illustrated by field C in the figure.

For example, suppose the database in the figure is associated with electronic commerce. Table 1 might hold transaction information, perhaps indicating items various people have bought from an online store. Table 2 might hold customer credit card information. Within table 1, fields A, B, and C could be, respectively, the date, the item purchased, and the account number of the purchaser. Table 2 could also hold field C, the account number, and, in addition, field D, the credit card number for that customer. Data are presented in these tables discretely, for flexible search and update. A program or user could write a query and pull out or update information directly from table 1, analyzing transactions or adding new ones as purchases are made. Because of the relationship between the tables, which is embodied in field C (the account number), database query software can research, for example, the number of times a given credit card number (table 2 data) was used on a given date (table 1 data). This "join" operation offers significant flexibility in handling and manipulating content. Of course, figure 4–10 is a highly simplified diagram to illustrate the fundamental constructs of a relational database. Most real-world databases have dozens or hundreds of tables, each with 2 to 20 or more fields and thousands to millions of rows.[4]

FIGURE 4-10. A Simple Relational Database

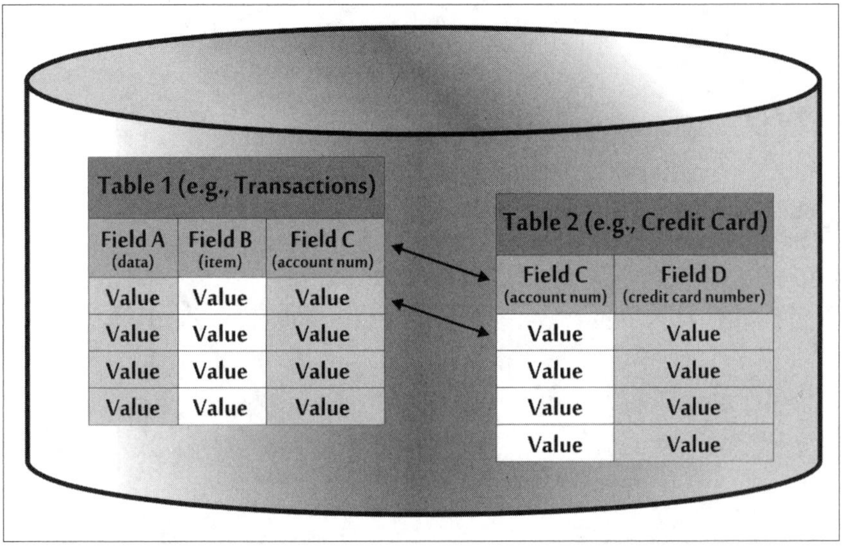

Relational databases are the most popular form of database storage today in market share. However, other kinds of database storage options are available, including hierarchical databases, object-oriented databases, and flat files, each offering different performance and functions from relational databases.

Although relational databases and hierarchical file systems are fundamentally different paradigms for organizing content, the two have some connections. Relational databases are, for example, almost always implemented as software running on top of a hierarchical file system. That is, the database programs themselves consist of a group of hierarchically organized files. The database tables and their contents exist inside of files as well. Just as large-scale packet-switched networks are often built up of point-to-point links from circuit-switched networks, relational databases are an overlay on top of a file system, offering a more flexible way of organizing information for query and update. In addition, most applications in cyberspace today are a mixture of files interacting with a back-end database using a variety of application architectures that manage the interaction of the files and the database. Such systems are referred to as back-end infrastructure to differentiate them from the front-end systems such as browsers that users run to initiate transactions.

Application Architectures

From the 1950s through the 1970s, computer applications typically resided on mainframe computers. Users logged into the system from "dumb" terminals. These terminals displayed information stored and processed on the mainframe but did no processing themselves. They were connected to the mainframe using fairly limited network protocols. All aspects of the application were stored on the mainframe itself.

Starting in the 1980s, personal computers (PCs) with limited processing power began replacing dumb terminals. In the 1990s, many mainframes were replaced with lower cost and smaller server machines. Both enterprise and public networks connecting PCs and servers began to make significant use of IPv4. A variety of new, distributed application architectures arose. Figure 4–11 depicts some of the common consumer and business application architectures in use today on enterprise networks and on the Internet.

The common applications architecture depicted on the left of figure 4–11 is a traditional client-server application. The client consists of a custom program dedicated to that application running on a desktop or laptop computer. The client handles the user interface, some data processing, and communications with a server, accessed across the network. The server may include database software, although some client-server applications instead place the database on a separate machine, as shown in the second architecture of the figure. This separate database can then support multiple application servers.

One of the concerns of the architectures on the left half of figure 4–11 is the distribution and update of specialized client-side software. Each application has a custom program that controls access to the server. Thus, synchronization of updates to several different client applications is rather complex. In the mid-1990s, various applications began to move to the third architecture of the figure, which involves using a Web browser as a generic client that formats, displays, and processes information for the user, relying on a single program—the browser—for multiple applications, thus simplifying client-side updates. This generic browser accesses a server across the network, which in turn accesses a back-end database server. This so-called three-tier architecture is the dominant enterprise and Internet application architecture today. Some applications introduce an additional element, an application server, shown in the fourth example of the

FIGURE 4-11. Common Modern Application Architectures

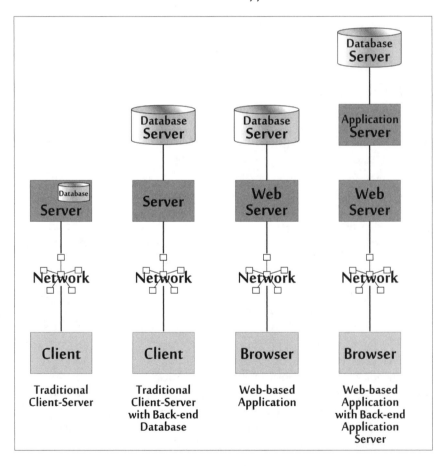

figure. The application server handles some of the critical information processing capabilities that were previously handled by the Web server.

While the three-tier architectures shown on the right side of figure 4–11 will continue to be dominant for several years, a newer architecture paradigm started to emerge in the mid-2000s: the so-called service oriented architecture (SOA) model. Figure 4–12 illustrates this approach. In this model, client-browser software still accesses Web servers; often, this interaction relies on the Extensible Markup Language (XML), a flexible format for defining data structures to be exchanged on the network. Web servers may, similarly, interact with other Web servers using XML to pull together information for the client, processing information in a distributed, coordinated fashion on the network. This is sometimes called computing "in the cloud." Using this SOA model, different functions, such as geographical mapping, product search, or price calculation and comparison, can be distributed across different servers. Applications can be stitched together by information flows between different Web-enabled services. An example might offer a user a way to create a consumer grocery shopping list that minimizes cost and travel time. A user enters a desired grocery shopping list and starting location into a browser. The browser sends XML requests to a grocery pricing Web service that responds with prices at various local grocery stores. This Web service might pass on a request to a separate street maps Web service, asking for directions between the consumer and different stores. The service might then forward a request to a traffic service that provides information about clogged highways. All of the information is reassembled at the user's browser, indicating the most efficient options for buying the desired groceries.

Common Application Types

The architectures shown in figures 4–11 and 4–12 are used to create many application types on internal networks and the Internet. New applications are constantly being devised and becoming popular. Some of the most common applications on today's Internet include email, instant messaging, search engines, and others described below.

Email is one of the oldest and most widely used applications of the Internet. Many companies are heavily dependent on their email infrastructure for communication between employees and also as the technical underpinnings of vital business processes. Email servers exchange email messages, which are accessed by users running either specialized email reading software or a general-purpose Web browser. In addition to user-to-user email, hundreds of thousands of mailing lists are used by communities with shared interests to exchange information to all subscribers. Email is also used to spread malicious code and online scams.

FIGURE 4-12. A Service-oriented Architecture

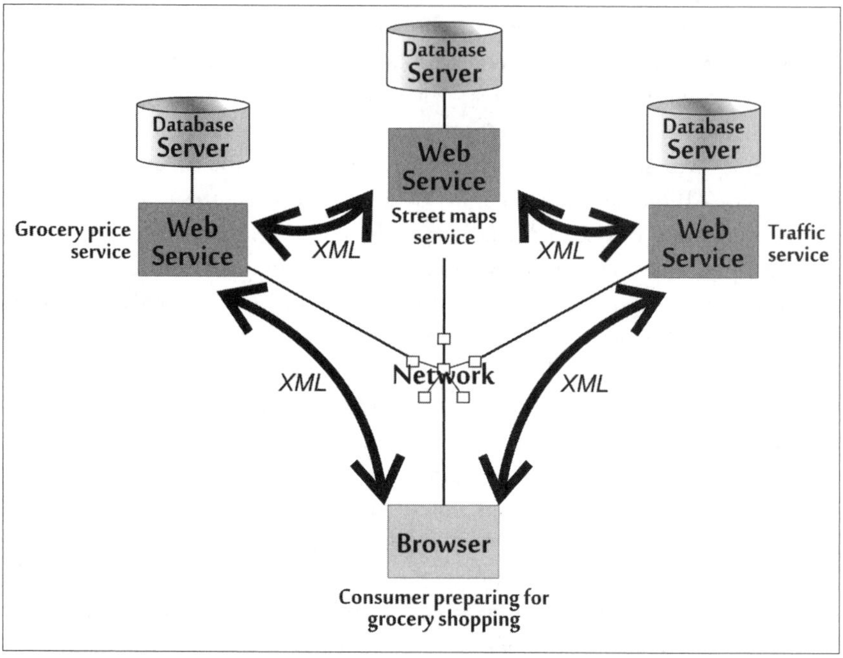

Consumer preparing for
grocery shopping

Email is store-and-forward technology: messages wait for users to access them. By contrast, instant messaging focuses on real-time exchange of messages between users. Many such chats occur one-on-one, as two users send information to each other. Chat rooms allow many users to exchange information simultaneously. America OnLine, Yahoo! Messenger, and Microsoft Messenger, as well as independent, open standards for messaging such as Jabber and Internet Relay Chat, are widely used on the Internet. An alternative technology used for cell phones, called Short Messaging Service, has much the same functionality but different underlying communication protocols.

Search engines are another important set of applications on the Internet. Search engines employ their own specialized browsing machines, known as crawlers, to fetch billions of pages from the Internet by following links from one page to the next, discovering new pages as they are posted and linked to other pages. The search engine company's software then assembles a searchable index of the pages fetched by the crawlers, offering users a Web-based front-end service by which users can search the massive index, which is stored in a distributed database maintained by the search engine company.

E-commerce applications have burgeoned since the late 1990s, as retailers have set up Web sites to sell products and services to users. Consumer e-commerce companies such as Amazon.com and Apple's iTunes Store are among the most familiar. Numerous business-to-business e-commerce applications are also in use.

Business management systems have moved online to automate business purchasing, payroll, supply-chain management, and other vital aspects of enterprise operations. Many organizations have deployed enterprise resource planning and enterprise resource management systems such as those offered by SAP, PeopleSoft, Oracle, and Microsoft.

Wikis are Internet-based applications that use specialized Web server software to inventory, categorize, and store information about a given topic or group of topics and allow it to be created and updated quickly. The most widespread and widely used wiki is Wikipedia, a comprehensive encyclopedia of information that can be updated by anyone who wishes to contribute to the information.

Blogs (a shorted form of "web logs") are another important kind of Internet application, made up of online diaries that are frequently updated. Most blogs are devoted to a single topic, such as politics, news, sports, a business or industry, or hobbies. Hundreds of thousands of blogs are available today, and some acquire readership numbering in the hundreds of thousands of users per week.

Social networking sites, another fast-growing form of Internet application, allow users to store information online in a personal profile and then link that profile to those of friends or business associates. By following these links, people with related interests can reach out to each other, keeping personal relationships up to date via socially oriented services such as MySpace or Friendster, or making business connections using professional services such as LinkedIn and Orkut.

In other applications, users are increasingly turning to the Internet for audio and video news, information, and entertainment. Such services are packaged as podcasts, audio or video shows that are automatically downloaded to user machines periodically when new content is published by the podcast author. Radio shows, television programs, and content from other mass media are published in tens of thousands of free and commercial-subscription podcasts on a daily basis. Downloadable and streaming video services with short-form videos are also becoming quite popular; offerings include those of YouTube and Google Video. Increasingly, entire television programs and movies are available on the Internet through related services, such as Amazon's Unbox and the television studios themselves.

Peer-to-peer file-sharing services allow large number of users to share files on the Internet, copying music, movie, and other files automatically between user systems. User machines that join the peer-to-peer network are used to store files that are redistributed to other users without any direct user interaction. Some of the most popular peer-to-peer networks are BitTorrent, Gnutella, and eDonkey. Many of these networks are used to exchange song and movie files in violation of copyright, but they are also increasingly used by legitimate publishers to distribute movies and television shows on a pay-per-view basis.

Internet telephony applications such as Gizmo and Skype offer free or very low-cost telephone calls from a user's computer across the Internet. Gizmo and Skype carry calls from end-user machine to end-user machine without traversing any intermediary servers. Vonage, on the other hand, carries calls via VoIP servers, which provide value-added services, such as voice mail. Because they often undercut the cost of long distance and international calls, both kinds of Internet telephony services are starting to supplant more expensive traditional telephone calls.

Another important kind of Internet application bridges cyberspace and the real world: mapping applications. These tools, often offered for free on the Internet, provide comprehensive street maps and driving directions on the Internet; MapQuest and Google Maps are dominant.

With virtual reality sites, users are presented with a well-developed "virtual world" that they can explore using an avatar, a digital icon representing their online persona. People meet in virtual reality sites for a variety of reasons, including social interactions, business relationships, and online gaming. Second Life is one of the most popular virtual reality sites, in which users interact in social and business settings. Many online games are also a form of virtual reality simulation, including the popular World of Warcraft game. Within some virtual reality simulations, different "cities" are founded with different focuses, such as a given hobby or business pursuit.

While these are among the most popular applications on the Internet today, the content and applications domain of the Internet is constantly changing and growing. New applications rise to prominence frequently, as they empower people to interact with their information and with each other on a more flexible basis.

The People and Social Domain

Cyberspace is a human-made artifact, created to gain access to information and share it between people and machines. With the increasing presence of cyberspace in modern life, the underlying systems domain and content and applications domain have given rise to a new people and social domain as individuals build communities in cyberspace. Numerous types of online communities exist in cyberspace, visited by users from around the world who share personal, business, political, or other interests. These communities are sometimes built using a single application: a community may be entirely based on an email list of hobbyists. More commonly, however, online communities consist of people who use multiple applications for different aspects of their community; the hub might consist of a particular blog, augmented with mailing lists, sections in video-sharing sites, chat rooms, or cities within a virtual reality simulation, as shown in figure 4–13.

Such cyberspace communities have been founded for numerous purposes. New communities form on a regular basis and older communities dry up. Flourishing communities today include those built around social interactions, such as dating sites, teenage hangouts, and corporate "virtual water coolers." Nearly every hobby imaginable—model rocketry, chess, recipes, and more—has a Web site, and many have full-blown online communities.

Online news communities include the Web sites of major news services such as CNN and the *New York Times*, local newspapers, local television news, professional bloggers who work as independent journalists supported by online ads, and amateur bloggers who fact-check other news sources and provide commentary. Over 50 million Americans read news online, according to a 2006 survey by the Pew Internet and American Life Project, and the number is trending upward rapidly.

Numerous online communities are devoted to discussions of a given type of technology, helping users understand and relate to the technology more effectively, such as the Web sites Slashdot, devoted to open-source software and related technologies, Ars Technica, focused on detailed aspects of PC hardware and software, and Gizmodo, focused on technical gadgets and consumer electronics.[5]

Many health care–oriented online communities help doctors and patients share information to better understand and cope with various medical conditions. Online support communities offer help for people suffering from particular diseases.

Adherents of many religions, major and minor, have created online communities for proselytizing, fundraising, and placing their messages and beliefs in front of a wider audience.

Political communities on the Internet are used for debate, analysis, and fundraising activities. Several popular blogs from nearly every aspect of the political spectrum, and their associated mailing lists and online video distribution sites, are increasingly helping to shape political messages and candidacies.

Both business-to-consumer and business-to-business communities have flourished in cyberspace, helping to make business processes more efficient. Sites such as eBay and Amazon.com offer storefronts through which numerous other organizations and individuals sell to consumers. Some industries have established their own online communities to improve efficiencies in bidding and service delivery. For example, American and some international automotive companies created the Automotive Network Exchange.

Not all communities in cyberspace have beneficial impacts. Terrorists rely on cyberspace to recruit, plan, and spread propaganda. International criminals

FIGURE 4-13. Online Communities Built of One or More Applications

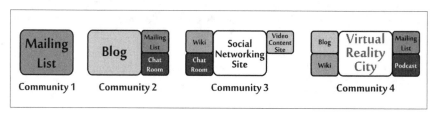

likewise use cyberspace to commit crime and track their business ventures, as described in more detail in chapter 18, "Cyber Crime."

The walls between these types of communities are permeable: a single individual may participate in numerous communities. The communities themselves may also interconnect: communities created for social interactions may flow into hobbyist communities or start to engage in political debate.

Conclusion

As cyberspace continues to expand, the diversity of elements in all of the domains discussed in this chapter is likely to increase. The underlying networks will become more complex, pulling in other kinds of technologies and other protocols. The application mix will be updated as people apply technology to new uses. Online communities will continue to evolve and merge as technology grows more immersive and people grow more accustomed to living various aspects of their lives in cyberspace.

This evolution of cyberspace also appears to be increasing in speed. Much of cyberspace got started in the 1970s as computers were interconnected and primitive email systems were established. In the 1990s, Web sites for information distribution became popular. In the early 2000s, search engines and e-commerce flourished. Many of the most popular applications and online communities are even newer, such as blogs, wikis, and virtual reality applications. With this pace of evolution continuing to accelerate, cyberspace is likely to have an increasing impact on the economy and society in coming years. For this reason, policy decisionmakers need to understand the underpinnings of the technology and its rapidly changing status to help inform their actions.

CHAPTER 5

Cyberspace and Infrastructure

William D. O'Neil

THIS CHAPTER addresses two related subjects: protecting cyber, electrical, pipeline, and other infrastructures against cyber attack, and protecting cyber infrastructure against all forms of attack. After a brief history of infrastructure attack and a review of the nature of networks, it outlines threats and responses, including systems engineering and dependability. Existing U.S. policy for infrastructure protection is described, along with government and industry responsibilities. The chapter next examines policy issues for protecting infrastructure against cyber attack and protecting cyber infrastructure, and then closes with specific policy recommendations.

The History of Infrastructure Attack

Infrastructure attack is a story as old as war. Time out of mind, attackers have sought to cut off their target's water supply and transportation, often with decisive results. The rise of modern infrastructure systems starting in the 19th century brought heightened concerns about vulnerability. As one widely read futurist and social critic put it in 1929:

> [S]omething on the order of one hundred key men, opening its veins of water, power, gas, sewage disposal, milk supply, [and] communication, could bring the life of a great city to an end—almost as neatly as though its every crevice had been soaked with poison gas. Even in rural areas with the growing use of electric power, the telephone, gasoline, and imported

foodstuffs, the factor of dependence on an unknown technology is very great. . . . The machine has presented us with a central nervous system, protected with no spinal vertebrae, lying almost naked for the cutting. If, for one reason or another, the severance is made, we face a terrifying, perhaps mortal crisis. . . . Day by day the complexity, and hence the potential danger, accelerates; materials and structures ceaselessly and silently deteriorate. One may look for some very ugly happenings in the next ten years.[1]

Especially in the United States, early airpower enthusiasts drawing on these currents of thought became convinced that infrastructure attack held the key to victory in modern war. Infrastructures—especially the electric grid—were seen as relatively easy to take down and so critical that their slightest disruption would severely affect warmaking potential and economic activity in general.

When World War II came, however, Air Corps planners decided that electric power was not as critical as previously thought and turned their attention to other target complexes. Later analysis suggested that this was probably an error and that attacking powerplants could have been quite effective. German electric production was curtailed when attacks on the rail infrastructure cut back coal shipments severely, but concerted attack on transportation was not decided upon until late in the war. Electric production in Japan, which was largely hydroelectric, was affected less by bombing.[2]

Of the 1.5 million tons of air ordnance delivered by U.S. forces against German and German-held targets in 1943–1945, 41 percent fell on transportation targets, largely rail, and 6 percent on oil, chemical, and synthetic rubber targets.[3] In the war against Japan, naval submarine and surface forces as well as air forces devoted much of the weight of their attack to enemy transportation, particularly at sea.[4] It was later concluded that attacks on transportation infrastructure had severely affected the enemy war effort and that even greater effort against transportation would have been worthwhile.[5]

Wars since 1945 have continued to feature attacks on transportation and often on oil as well. The 1991 Gulf War included major campaigns against both, as well as systematic attacks on Iraq's communications infrastructure. Since World War II, U.S. bombing campaigns generally have made electric power infrastructure a major target. The best documented case is the Gulf War: 88 percent of Iraq's electric grid capacity was knocked out, most in the first few days.[6] Guerrilla and terrorist forces have also frequently targeted infrastructure. Since the invasion of Iraq in 2003, there have been repeated attacks on Iraq's infrastructures, especially those for electric power and oil.[7]

So far as has been publicly revealed, however, there have not yet been military campaigns against the infrastructure of cyberspace, nor any military cyber attacks on other infrastructures. But there have been a great many attacks by hackers, whose identities and motives often are shadowy; some observers believe that some of these attacks have been state-sponsored.

Below, lessons of this history for defending infrastructures are examined, but first the nature of infrastructures themselves is explored.

Networks

Infrastructures often depend on networks: we speak of the road network, the rail network, the telephone network, the electricity network, and more recently the Internet. The theory of networks is important to a great many fields of science and technology.[8] A network consists of the points of supply or origin, the routes of transportation or movement, and the points of destination or consumption. Nodes may function both for origin and for destination. The whole set of nodes of origin and destination, together with the linking routes, comprises a network.[9] A wide variety of manmade and natural physical, biological, and social systems can be analyzed in network terms. Each infrastructure is physically distinct, but, as the terminology suggests, they share something important at the level of abstract structure.

While infrastructure networks are not truly random, they are complex and irregular; as a result, many of the applicable tools of network theory are statistical in nature.[10] Large, irregular networks—like most infrastructures—can be seen in two broad classes. In one type, most of the nodes have roughly the same number of links. Only a few nodes have many links. Networks with this sort of egalitarian structure are often called *exponential networks* (because highly connected nodes are exponentially unlikely) or, more descriptively, *uniform-random networks* (see figure 5–1).[11]

In the other major class, most nodes are connected to nodes that also already have a great many connections (although there is still a random or random-like element). These are called *power-law networks* (for technical mathematical reasons that reflect the relative abundance of highly connected nodes) or, more commonly, *scale-free networks*, a reference to their lack of a dominant typical or average scale in the sense of number of connections per node. A more descriptive term might be *hub-and-spoke random network* (see figure 5–2).

If an accident or attack were to disable a node picked at random from the exponential network in figure 5–1, it usually would disconnect only a handful of other nodes that happen to have no connections other than to the one disabled. In the scale-free network, a random disablement would likely do even less damage, since so few nodes have any other node that connects only through them. However, the worst case in a scale-free or power-law (hub-and-spoke) network (figure 5–2) is worse than in a random-like exponential network because taking down only a few highly connected hubs does a lot of damage.

FIGURE 5-1. Exponential or Uniform-random Network

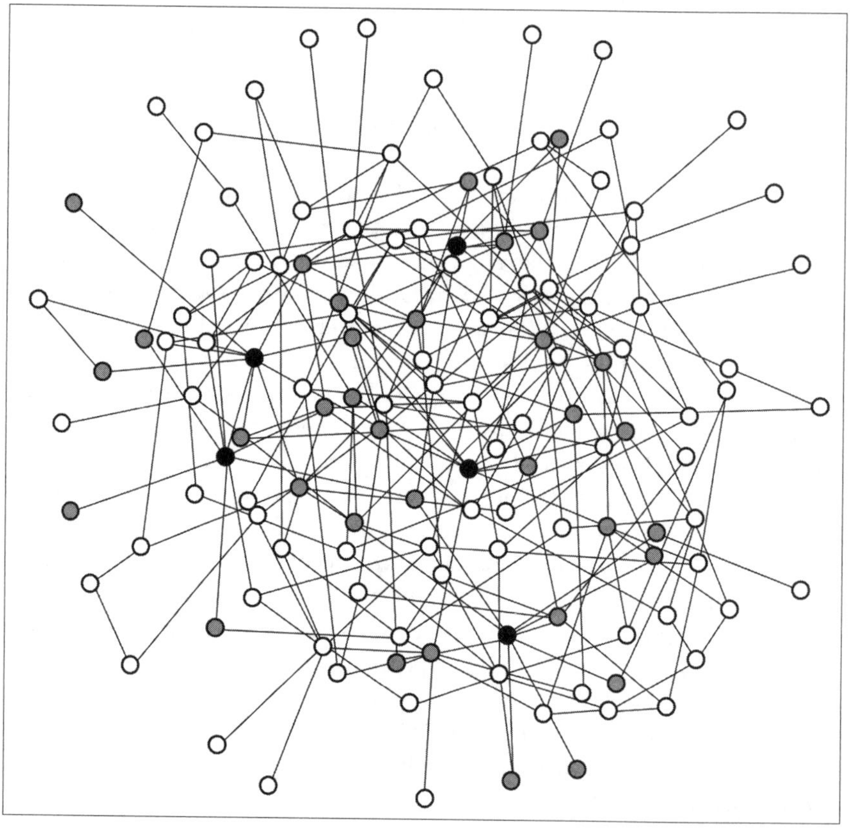

Cyber Networks

So far we have addressed the topology of the networks: the logic of how nodes and links connect. We also need to look at the physical nature and spatial location of these elements. Infrastructures are not only networks, but also networks upon networks (as outlined with respect to cyberspace in chapters 6 and 8 in this volume, "Evolutionary Trends in Cyberspace" and "The Future of the Internet and Cyberpower"). As table 5–1 shows, cyber content rests on a structure of physical elements that have physical properties and locations. Even though its topology is not identical with that of the network layers it is built upon, cyberspace itself, like other infrastructure networks, has a geography as well as a topology, and both affect its vulnerability and survivability.

The topologies of the Internet and World Wide Web are the subject of particularly intense study, for reasons including their complexity, availability for study, and practical importance.[12] No simple model can fully capture the complexity of these structures, but in broad terms, both are power-law or scale-free networks.

Scale-free networks arise typically through growth, as new nodes link preferentially to old nodes that are already highly linked, forming highly connected hubs. It is easy to see how this happens in the Web: it costs no more to link a Web page to a richly connected hub Web site such as Google or Wikipedia than to an isolated site run by a specialized organization, such as <ndu.edu>, or by an individual, such as <analysis.williamdoneil.com>.

Internet nodes consist of computers (or devices that incorporate computers). The simplest case is a single isolated computer in a home or small business. The cheapest possible connection would involve running a cable or wireless link to the computer next door. In most cases, however, this would not accomplish much, since usually only a small portion of our information

FIGURE 5-2. Scale-free or Power-law Network

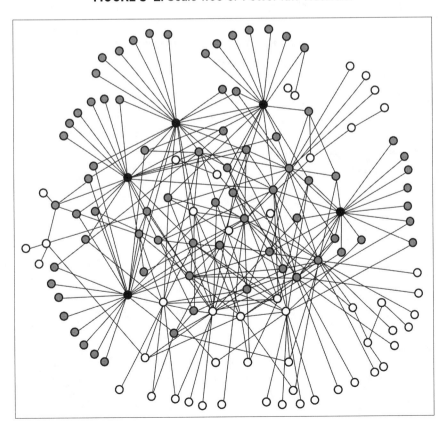

needs can be supplied by our immediate neighbors. Of course I might be able to piggyback on the information channels available to my neighbor, but this would cut into the bandwidth available to him and so would be unattractive from his standpoint. Even though it costs more, therefore, we generally buy our service from an Internet service provider (ISP), which offers a connection to its hub or server bank (a group of high-speed computers, usually housed in a single warehouse-like building) via some miles of telephone wire, coaxial cable, fiber optic cable, wireless cellular radio link, or satellite radio link. Higher bandwidth connections that provide greater information capacity cost more, but most users find the expense worthwhile.

An ISP whose server bank services thousands of high-speed connections over an area of many acres or square miles faces similar choices. Connections to nearby ISPs would be relatively inexpensive in terms of the cost of the cable but would not meet ISP needs for a rich flow of data to meet its customers' demands. Thus, the ISP finds it worthwhile to pay for a very high bandwidth connection to a major hub with a massive server bank that handles a great deal of Internet traffic in order to tap its riches. Processes such as these, repeated

TABLE 5-1. Simplified Schematic Overview of Levels Involved in Cyberspace

LEVEL	DESCRIPTION	EXAMPLES
Cyber	Intellectual content	Data, commands, knowledge, ideas, mental models
Logical net	Services employing physical signals to carry logical messages	Telephones, broadcast radio and TV services, cable TV service, public Internet, private Internet protocol (IP)–based networks carried on common-carrier infrastructure, private-infrastructure IP-based networks, supervisory control and data acquisition networks
Hard net	Infrastructures formed from base elements that carry electrical or electromagnetic signals	Common-carrier telecommunications networks, tactical radio systems, dedicated wireline systems, community cable systems, cell phone systems
Base	Physical elements that underlie telecommunications services	Cable headworks, optical fiber, coaxial cable, radio transmitters and receivers, radio transmission paths, communications satellites, Internet routers, modems

at all levels, drive the Internet toward a hub-and-spoke scale-free architecture resembling that shown in figure 5–2.

Scale-free networks are, for reasons described above, robust in the face of random or untargeted failures, which fall most heavily on the large numbers of nodes with only a few connections. The experience of the Internet reflects this: nodes often fail or are shut down for a variety of reasons, but this has scarcely any discernible effect on overall network performance. Even more massive failures, such as those caused by widespread power outages or the 9/11 attacks, have been quite localized in their effects. (Of course, such incidents can generate a surge in traffic that may itself slow response, but this is not a vulnerability of the Internet per se.)[13]

There have been many random outages but few that preferentially target the Internet's major hubs. Nevertheless, what is true in theory would hold equally true in practice: successful attacks on many of the biggest hubs would have severe and pervasive effects, leaving many Internet nodes isolated or able to communicate with only a small number of other nodes. Thus, protection of major Internet hubs is a cornerstone of rational policy for cyberspace infrastructure defense.

Link outages might be much less worrisome than outages of key nodes in a scale-free network like the Internet: severing links could not do as much damage to network connectivity as disabling an equal number of critical nodes. A closer look at the physical layers underlying the Internet, however, shows that this may be too sanguine a view in practice. Links that are logically and topologically separate may in fact be carried over the same physical communications infrastructure through multiplexing. Indeed, entirely separate networks, having no logical interfaces at all, may be multiplexed via one fiber optic strand. Even if they use physically separate communications lines, it is possible that those lines may share the same conduit or otherwise be vulnerable to the same damage agents. Thus, a single attack might take out thousands or tens of thousands of links at one time, potentially cutting off multiple nodes from the network. The places where this can occur must be protected to assure cyberspace infrastructure integrity. This is a particular concern for nodes located in physically isolated sites, as are many that are critical to national security. Where economy or convenience is the dominant consideration, such sites are often served by only one or two pathways for all communications links.

The Electrical Network

Loss of electricity does not ordinarily take down a major Internet hub—at least not at once, since most hubs have emergency backup power sources that can carry them for hours or days. In a larger sense, however, the Internet, like practically our entire society, is critically dependent on electric supply.

If we examine specific electric grids, we find that while there are core areas representing major centers of population and industry, there are no hubs connected directly to large numbers of nodes, and most nodes have more than one link. The topology of electric grids is more like the uniform-random (exponential) network depicted in figure 5–1. Although the electric grid, like the Internet, grows and changes as nodes and links are added, modified, and sometimes deleted, its economic and technological forces are quite different from the Internet and result in a different kind of pattern. These forces are changing in important ways today, and the resulting grid will no doubt eventually look quite different, as discussed below. We must look first at historical forces to understand today's grid.

Even though it comes in different forms—alternating or direct current at any of a number of voltage levels—electricity is all of a kind.[14] With suitable conversion of form, any electrical energy will serve any electrical load.[15] It is a bulk commodity both in the sense that it is lacking in the specificity that distinguishes information and that it shows strong economies of scale. Because electricity is most economically generated at large scale, the resulting grid is dominated by a relatively small number of large central station plants, usually located at or near their energy sources. (This may well change as the costs of carbon emissions and other environmental damage are figured into the cost of generation; some generating technologies with low environmental impact, such as wind turbines and solar-electric systems, may favor smaller scale operation.) Electricity is also most economically transported in bulk, at high levels of energy and voltage.[16]

Neither bulk generation nor bulk transmission in itself dictates a uniform-random electric network. A key reason for this type of network is that in the United States, most electrical transmission is in the form of alternating current (AC) at high voltages, and most electrical use is AC at lower voltages. A relatively simple passive device, the transformer, allows high-voltage AC (HVAC) to be tapped at lower voltage with scarcely any loss of energy. Thus, major corridors are served by a few high-capacity HVAC lines along which distribution stations are located that feed local bulk users and local retail distribution networks. The corridors themselves are determined by economic geography: they go to where the customers are. (Of course, customers may also find it economical to locate in corridors served by major transmission facilities.)

Except for those who use electric power on truly massive scales, it is more economical for customers to draw power from a nearby distribution station than to run lines directly to a distant central station. Because the distribution station draws its power from a major HVAC line, it can supply large quantities, and since all power is the same, it makes no difference where it comes from as long as there is enough. This is why, when we look at a portion of the electric grid, we see a network that more closely resembles the uniform-random pattern of figure 5–1 than the scale-free hub-and-spoke layout of figure 5–2. Thus, the electric grid is a fundamentally different kind of network from the Internet.

The earliest commercial electric utilities used direct current (DC). AC won out as the U.S. standard, in large part because it is less difficult and costly to tap HVAC transmission lines with transformers to produce lower voltage for distribution and final use than to step down from HVDC.[17] DC continued in use for specialized local applications (such as shipboard electrical systems) for some decades, but these applications too gradually died out. For moving very large flows of energy over long distances, however, HVDC lines can be more economical than HVAC. This fact has led to the use of HVDC intertie lines to connect distant "islands" of intense electric use across wide stretches with little use, where distribution stations are not needed.[18] Today, the North American electric grid (encompassing the continental United States, Canada, and a small portion of northwestern Mexico) is divided into four large regions that connect almost entirely via HVDC links. This greatly reduces the risks of a continent-wide grid failure.

When there are two or more possible routes from generator to load, electricity by its nature will flow over all of them, with the greater amount following the paths with lower resistance. If one path is cut off, the flow automatically redirects itself over the remaining links. When the flow in a transmission network is near the limits of its capacity to handle power flow, the failure of one link would throw more load on remaining links than they can carry. This would lead to a cascade of failures, as links either break down due to overheating or are shut down (by automatic switches or by human intervention) to save them from damage.

On an AC network, the current must alternate at the same frequency everywhere in what is called synchronous operation. Any failure of this frequency synchronization would produce unbalanced forces that could literally tear equipment apart. Synchronization failures also can cascade, as generation or transmission equipment drops offline to avoid catastrophic failures.

The loading on the grid varies from moment to moment, and the organizations responsible for its operation have only limited tools for managing it. Users can add loads by throwing a switch; generators and transmission equipment can go offline for a variety of reasons. Grid operators may have the ability to shed some loads (temporarily cutting off customers who have bought "interruptible power" at reduced rates), but load-shedding capacity is limited. In an emergency, a block of customers in a particular area may be blacked out to shed loads, but many systems are not set up to allow it to be done quickly, and utilities are reluctant to do this except as a last resort. An overstressed link or node may have to be shut down, which increases the load on other components. If local overloading drags the frequency of a generator down, then it and the area it serves must immediately be disconnected from the grid. On a wide scale, this can cut the grid up into isolated islands, many or all of which might fail under local load imbalances.

Could such a failure cascade engulf the entire North American electrical grid, leaving the whole continent in the dark? Two factors make this unlikely. First, like the ripple caused by a rock thrown into a pool, the disturbance following a major fault in the grid weakens as it disperses. Second, the HVDC intertie lines that link the four major synchronous regions in North America also isolate each region from frequency disturbances in the other regions. Regardless of what may happen in any one region, the others should be able to adjust and continue normal operation without major disruption.[19]

Prior to the mid-1960s, widespread grid failures were unknown because with a few exceptions (mostly involving large hydropower systems), most electric power was generated, distributed, and delivered within a compact area served by a local power utility that enjoyed a regulated monopoly. This "cellular" rather than networked structure meant that there was little opportunity for failures to spread beyond a single utility. Moreover, regulators held utilities responsible for reliability of service and could apply effective sanctions when reliability fell short.

Although this regime led to steadily decreasing electrical prices for decades as the utilities incorporated new technology, in the 1970s and 1980s economists and political leaders argued that the monopolistic structure, even with regulation, was economically inefficient and led to added cost. At the same time, new technologies appeared to offer the potential to generate and transmit electricity economically on scales that were beyond the capacity of even large individual utility companies. Thus, starting in the mid-1970s, the Federal Government moved to deregulate electricity—in fact, to change the regulatory basis so as to encourage competition in generation and transmission. States have followed suit, although not in a uniform way, leading to fragmentation of ownership and control over generation and distribution equipment and operation.[20]

Deregulation in general has not been followed by further significant decreases in the costs of electricity, although proponents argue that it resulted in avoidance of large increases and had other benefits. It has, however, opened the way to other problems not fully anticipated and still being worked out.

Because every part of the grid influences every other part, it has been difficult to construct a deregulation regime that would allow the truly independent operation necessary for fully effective competition. In 2000 and 2001, for example, Enron Corporation and other power producers and speculators exploited the physical properties of California's electricity grid in combination with its deregulated operating rules to manipulate prices to their great advantage, at the same time causing or exacerbating electricity shortages in the state. Analyses of this event show how difficult it is to ensure the smooth running of the physically tightly coupled but economically fragmented electric market system.[21] The same limitations that permit participants to impose costs on others without inherent limits (other than those interposed by the remaining regulators) equally allow serious technical problems to develop and spread without any individual participating firm or organization having a clear interest in taking corrective action.[22]

Legislators and public officials nevertheless retain a strong commitment to deregulation, but even if restoration of the earlier regime of regulated local vertical-power monopolies were politically and economically feasible, it is not clear how it could work physically today. Many regions have come to depend on power generated far away and transmitted over long distances. Heavy long-distance power flows have become a fact of life, and any attempt to redivide the grid into relatively small, self-sufficient cells operated by separate local firms would involve major investment costs and serious environmental concerns. But without some such structure, there is no simple way to assign responsibility for maintaining adequate and reliable power service.

The physics of electricity simply does not allow a fully laissez-faire, every-man-for-himself operating regime. Just as on the highway, there must be some consistent set of operating rules that everyone is constrained to obey if the system is to operate stably and safely. Despite warnings, this realization has been somewhat slow in emerging, perhaps in part because authorities were thinking in terms of analogies with networks that were not as tightly coupled as the electricity grid and thus less in need of highly disciplined operation. Below, we discuss what has been done to address the policy issues raised by these facts and what more may need to be done.

Lessons from a Blackout

Major outages demonstrate how tightly coupled the grid is and what this implies for its operation and protection. The most recent major outage in North America occurred on August 14, 2003, and eventually covered large areas of the northeastern United States and Canada, affecting electric service to approximately 50 million people for an extended period.[23] The extent of the blackout is illustrated in figure 5–3.

Investigation revealed a number of hardware and software failures, together with faulty operational procedures on the part of both the local utility operator and the organization responsible for ensuring the reliability of the grid in the region. Most of these did not directly contribute to the blackout, but many of them clearly could have led to major failures under slightly different circumstances. Many aspects of the operation were in violation of accepted industry standards (which were then voluntary). Even if all equipment and software had been functioning properly and fully in compliance with existing standards, however, the tools available to the operators for system awareness were critically limited.

The process that led to blackout started after 3 p.m. near Cleveland, Ohio. August 14 was hot and air conditioning loads were heavy, although not near peaks that the system had handled before. The immediate cause of the blackout was a series of instances in which high-voltage transmission lines contacted trees that had been allowed to grow too tall into the lines' rights of way. Autonomous safety systems sensed the resulting ground faults and automatically disconnected or "tripped" the lines to prevent more serious damage and fires. Over a period of 8 seconds starting at 4:10:37 p.m., automatic safety relays all over the Northeast shut down lines and generators that had violated preset acceptable operating limits; these shutdowns severed grid links and blacked out areas throughout the region.[24]

Operator response was poor, in part because critical warning and analysis systems had failed due to design defects and operator error. One by one, the faults accumulated until the point at which human intervention could no longer be effective. Even given the various hardware and software failures, the huge blackout would never have occurred as it did if the operators had been well

FIGURE 5-3. August 2003 Blackout

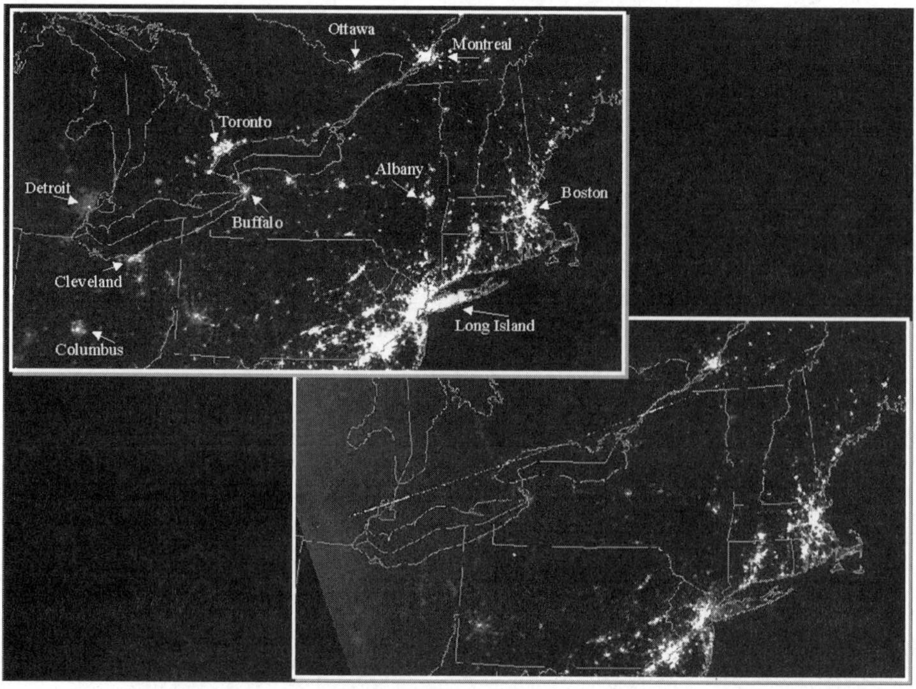

trained and effective in applying the existing procedures, despite their limitations. At worst, a very limited area with a few tens of thousands of customers might have been affected for a few hours. Instead, part of the problem arose from excessive and inappropriate operator reliance on limited and fallible warning and diagnosis systems.

Coming just a month before the second anniversary of September 11, the blackout caused many to wonder whether it was caused or worsened by terrorist attacks. Indeed, claims of responsibility purportedly from al Qaeda appeared within a few days of the outage. The "Blaster" Internet worm had first been seen just a few days earlier on August 11; this led to speculation that it might have been involved in the blackout. Investigation showed that neither al Qaeda nor Blaster was responsible, but it did reveal significant potential vulnerabilities.[25]

The process that set the stage for the August 2003 Northeast blackout included software failures that denied operators the information tools they were accustomed to. These failures were accidental or were intrinsic to the system design, but comparable failures could have resulted from cyberspace attacks. In general, the operators of the grid rely on a variety of cyberspace services to gather operating information, communicate with other control personnel, and issue instructions. Of particular concern are supervisory control and data acquisition (SCADA) systems and energy management systems (EMS). These gather data on the operational parameters of equipment throughout a particular segment of the electric grid, report it to a central location and present it to operators, and change setpoints for equipment controllers in response to operator decisions about system configuration and operation. We address the policy and standards efforts being undertaken to meet these problems later in this chapter.

The (Secure) Grid of the Future?

Engineers and policymakers have devoted considerable attention and development effort to defining the future of the electric power grid. The visions generally involve a "smart grid" able to adapt to failures in real time with limited if any degradation.[26] In a sense, this would resemble a return to the cellular structure of the pre-deregulation grid, but with smaller cells that are regulated by adaptive software rather than governmental agencies, and with provision to take advantage of distant power sources. One key is distributed local power sources and perhaps power storage systems. Fuel cells in particular appear to promise small-scale but highly efficient generating units that could serve these purposes.[27]

Growing concern about global climate change may affect these visions in various ways. One possibility is a renewed emphasis on very large nuclear central-station generating plants. This offers zero emissions of greenhouse gases—even better than fuel cells—but would involve greater concentration of power generation.[28] Solar power is another zero-emissions option and could integrate more naturally into a cellular structure, although efficient and economical means to store the energy from solar systems for release in the hours of darkness must be found if they are to become a major electrical source.[29] Effective use of wind power at large scale depends on solutions to the challenges posed by the irregularity and unpredictability of its flow.[30] Various other advanced technologies for energy production are more speculative at this time.[31] None of the alternative sources so far conceived can obviate or substantially modify the need for a more reliable and robust grid for electrical transmission and distribution. In most cases, they would add complexity, due to their limited ability to provide steady and continuous power or to vary their output rapidly in response to load fluctuations.

Practically all proposed schemes for improved electricity delivery depend on networked "smart control," which is to say that they depend more on cyberspace. Most proposals have devoted little attention to security against cyber attack. Clearly, this must change before much more work is done along these lines in order to ensure that efforts to improve the reliability and efficiency of power distribution do not increase vulnerability to attack.

Pipeline Networks

The electrical infrastructure is unique both in its degree of coupling and in its central role, but other infrastructures—particularly two other major energy-sector infrastructures, oil and natural gas—present parallel concerns, even if overall risk levels are lower.[32] Both oil and natural gas are also networked infrastructures, with about 170,000 miles of oil pipelines and 1.4 million miles of natural gas pipelines.[33] More than 75 percent of U.S. crude oil supplies flow by pipeline, as do about 60 percent of refined petroleum products, and almost all natural gas.[34]

Notwithstanding the obvious dangers of pipes filled with flammable and potentially explosive fluids, the overall safety record of U.S. pipeline systems is good. Despite their vulnerability to sabotage, there have been few attacks or attempts on U.S. pipelines. So far, all publicly known threats have been of attack by physical rather than cyber means.

Both oil and gas pipelines make use of SCADA and operational management systems, although not at the same level as the electrical infrastructure. The issues of cybersecurity in these infrastructures are generally similar to those affecting electricity.

Infrastructure Threats

The operators of infrastructure systems of all types routinely face a spectrum of threats, from natural causes such as lightning, earthquakes, or hurricanes; from intrinsic faults such as stuck valves or circuit breakers, failing electronics, or unstable software; and from criminal action by vandals, thieves, extortionists, or hackers. Motivated by a community sense of responsibility, regulatory and legal requirements, and economic self-interest, operators take action to avert these threats, minimize their potential damage, and recover rapidly from damage when it does occur. Many national security threats resemble more intense and deliberate versions of these normal infrastructure threats. This emphasizes the need to integrate all aspects of infrastructure protection.

Our special focus here is on cyberthreats. There have been a number of attacks on the cybersystems serving infrastructure, but they have not been coordinated large-scale attacks. Damage has been limited so far. However, the Central Intelligence Agency (CIA) has warned of the threat of cyber attack, especially against electrical utilities, noting that "cyber attackers have hacked into the computer systems of utility companies outside the United States and made demands, in at least one case causing a power outage that affected multiple cities." The agency reportedly did not know "who executed these attacks or why, but all involved intrusions through the Internet." According to a CIA analyst, "We suspect, but cannot confirm, that some of the attackers had the benefit of inside knowledge."[35] There have been other attacks, some domestic, but generally they have received no publicity in an effort to avoid giving the attackers useful feedback.[36]

In some cases, cyber-extortionists clearly were behind the attacks, but in most, the identity and motivation of the attackers are unclear. Following the September 11, 2001, terrorist attacks, it was widely predicted that al Qaeda would follow up with massive cyber attacks on infrastructure targets, but these have not materialized, and the likelihood of large-scale cyber-infrastructure attacks by terrorists is disputed.[37]

Even if terrorists never find the means or motivation to do so, there is little doubt that a conventional state enemy determined to mount a military attack on the United States could launch massive coordinated cyber attacks on infrastructure as a part of an overall strategy of infrastructure attack. Thus, we need to ask how much damage could be done by cyber means and what may be done to limit it.

A crucial question is the extent to which systems can be accessed via the Internet. Wide-open access is rare, but many systems may have some Internet portals through which an attacker might reach critical functions. Active efforts are widespread to close these or at least provide highly secure protection, and to the extent these efforts succeed, it will be impossible to attack systems from the Internet. This does not rule out attacks via individuals with inside access, however.

The consequences of failures are always foremost in the minds of the engineers who design infrastructure systems and components. Well aware that complex systems in general and software in particular are prone to failure, they design to limit the consequences. Where possible, critical control functions with the potential for severe equipment damage are lodged within simple, entirely autonomous, self-contained systems such as governors and overload trips. Thus, an EMS might be able to overload a transmission line with current but could not prevent the circuit breakers from tripping and opening the circuit to forestall damage.

This strategy is not universally applicable, however. In an aircraft with a fly-by-wire control system, for instance, a runaway of the system conceivably could fly the airplane into the ground or exceed its limiting flight loads. When such vulnerabilities are unavoidable, engineers may go to extraordinary lengths to assure the reliability and integrity of the critical control system, as they do in the case of aircraft controls. Yet there may be cases where care is inadequate, leaving vulnerabilities that cyber attackers might exploit with devastating results. Systems engineering disciplines do exist to minimize the chances of this, but they require high costs and intrusive oversight and thus are unlikely to be uniformly applied. Moreover, many systems were designed before the risks of cyber attack were recognized.

There are many proponents of commercial-off-the-shelf (COTS) or open-source systems for practically all uses; such approaches can save sub-stantial amounts of time and money, and thus suppliers and customers may be tempted to incorporate such subsystems and software modules into a system. However, they can greatly increase vulnerability to common modes of attack, perhaps catastrophically so in critical applications such as EMS or SCADA systems. Thus, their use should be guided by policies that assure management of risks and by adequate weighing of risks and costs.[38]

There is also danger in policies of commonality—that is, the widespread use of the same systems or the same family of systems in an organization or industry. No doubt this can reduce costs, but it means that exploitation of a single vulnerability could affect a wide range of operations. Here, too, care should be taken to weigh savings against risk.

Concerns about security of infrastructure systems emerged in the 1990s and have been heightened by recurrent hacker attacks. Even though these attacks have not so far gone beyond the nuisance stage (at least domestically), when the grid is operating under stress, a successful denial-of-service attack on a SCADA system or an EMS could, at least in theory, lead to a situation comparable to what occurred by accident and inattention in August 2003, when the blackout spread because operators lacked important information or could not exercise effective control. If appropriate operator action is hindered or prevented by cyberspace attack, this could set the stage for a massive failure cascade.

Worse still could be capture of a SCADA system or an EMS by attackers who could then use it to control generating and transmission equipment. An attacker who had sufficient information and understanding of the affected portion of the grid and enough access could increase stress on the system by configuring it inappropriately. An attacker who could simultaneously block or spoof system reporting and operator control functions could render the manual safeguards ineffective or even counterproductive, whether the capture was effected by physical intrusion or by remote means via cyberspace.

There are some limits, however, on how much an attacker could accomplish simply by capturing control of an EMS or a SCADA system. SCADA and energy management systems are designed to lack the capability to override self-contained automatic safety relays associated with generators, transmission lines, and transformers. Design engineers, aware of the possibilities of SCADA and EMS failures for a variety of reasons, avoid giving them more control authority than is strictly necessary for their intended functions. Unless an attacker knew of and could exploit a serious design flaw, capture of a SCADA system or an EMS generally would not, by itself, allow the attacker to inflict major long-term damage on the electrical system, nor could the attacker initiate a major failure cascade in the absence of heavy external system loading.[39] If combined with effective physical attacks on critical equipment, however, capture of the control systems could allow an attacker to inflict much greater damage. Even without coordinated physical attacks, a cyber attacker with sufficient access and knowledge could trigger a widespread blackout comparable, within the affected area, to the Northeast blackout of August 2003. As that experience showed, it could take several days to restore full service, and there could be large economic losses, as well as risk to life and property.

SCADA systems and EMS are cyberspace systems, according to the definition used in this book, but their susceptibility to attack by cyberspace means varies. Industry standards call for them to be isolated from contact with the public Internet and other sources of possible outside cyber entry.[40] (The standards also call for them to be protected from physical intrusion and from surreptitious insider takeover.) Many instances have been found, however, in which the systems have failed to meet these standards fully. In some cases, deficiencies have been revealed through hacker attacks, but most have been discovered in the course of testing.

One potential threat that is often overlooked is that of Trojan horses introduced in the process of developing or maintaining the software. A concealed fault deliberately planted in a device or software program is a familiar fictional device,[41] but little has been done to forestall such threats, perhaps in part because no actual cases have been publicized. Although more complex to mount than a virus or denial-of-service attack, a surreptitious fifth column attack of this sort could be more damaging and more difficult to diagnose and correct. The danger is greatest in the case of open-source systems, where there is little control over who may have modified the code. But COTS and even purpose-built systems are at risk, because they might have incorporated key modules supplied by obscure low-tier subcontractors with little oversight.

While an attacker who finds and exploits a key cyber vulnerability may be able to do severe and lasting damage to a particular system, many systems will be competently and conscientiously designed and operated and will not offer such opportunities. If an attacker targets a system for which he cannot identify a catastrophic cyber vulnerability, he would have to employ physical attack to do major damage to it.

In general, moreover, it is necessary not only to do physical damage, but also to do enough of it to saturate the capacity for near-term restoration. Electrical utility companies, for instance, generally are well prepared to restore considerable numbers of downed transmission lines quickly, since natural causes such as ice storms or hurricanes can do damage of this sort. If the attacker's goals involve putting the system out of operation for more than a few days, it would do better to attack other elements. There is only very limited capacity to replace large transformers quickly, for instance, and even less to replace major generator facilities. The dangers are greater if the attacker is able to interfere with repair and restoration activities, or to mount repeated attacks with little cost, as in Iraq.[42] In any event, the importance of physical security for key facilities is clear. In recognition of the threat posed by attacks on transformers and generators, efforts are being made by utilities and coordinating groups to improve capabilities for restoring them quickly, an effort that should be wider.

Systems Engineering and Dependability

Engineers in many fields have long sought to make systems perform their intended functions dependably despite a wide spectrum of threats. They have developed a body of practice, usually referred to as systems engineering, that encompasses specification, analysis, design, and testing practices to ensure that a system will meet definite standards of dependable operation. Although it is not always fully effective, thorough application of systems engineering practice greatly improves dependability.

However, application of systems engineering has been notably weak in most areas of software development. The techniques for effective systems engineering for software are well understood and documented,[43] but the structure of the industry has not supported their application in most commercial software (making it cheaper but less dependable). However, most customers find it easier to assess and evaluate price than dependability in the abstract.

Securing infrastructures against cyber attack is impossible without dependable software. Thus, any program for infrastructure protection must mandate good software systems engineering in order to be effective.

Policy and Organization

Concerns regarding protection of infrastructure are long standing, but it was in the second Clinton administration that the first steps toward a comprehensive policy were taken. A Presidential commission, convened in 1996 and reporting in 1997, emphasized government-industry cooperative efforts.[44] On May 22, 1998, President Bill Clinton signed Presidential Decision Directive (PDD)/National Security Council 63 (PDD 63), "Critical Infrastructure Protection." Although now superseded, PDD 63 was the root of most current U.S. infrastructure protection policy. The principal policy directives regarding infrastructure protection as of mid-2008 are described in this section.

The primary focus of the Executive Order on Critical Infrastructure Protection, signed by President George W. Bush on October 16, 2001, is "continuous efforts to secure information systems for critical infrastructure, including emergency preparedness communications, and the physical assets that support such systems." It assigns to the Secretary of Defense and the Director of Central Intelligence (DCI) the responsibility:

> to oversee, develop, and ensure implementation of policies, principles, standards, and guidelines for the security of information systems that support the operations under their respective control. In consultation with the Assistant to the President for National Security Affairs and the affected departments and agencies, the Secretary of Defense and the DCI shall develop policies, principles, standards, and guidelines for the security of national security information systems that support the operations of other executive branch departments and agencies with national security information.

However, the policy and oversight structure set up by this executive order has been considerably modified since its promulgation, as outlined below.

The Homeland Security Act of 2002, signed into law by President Bush on November 25, 2002, established the Department of Homeland Security (DHS) and assigned it lead responsibility for preventing terrorist attacks in the United States, reducing national vulnerability to terrorist attacks, and minimizing the damage and assisting in recovery from attacks that do occur. It gives DHS broad responsibilities for protection of critical infrastructure in the United States against both terrorism and natural disaster. DHS, however, was not given responsibilities for protecting critical infrastructure from intrinsic or natural faults such as those involved in the Northeast blackout of August 14, 2003, or from nonterrorist attacks.

The National Strategy for the Physical Protection of Critical Infrastructures and Key Assets (NSPPCIKA) was approved by President Bush in February 2003. The focus is on protection against terrorist attack, rather than protection generally. It lays out a cooperative effort to be shared among various levels of government and the private sector without, for the most part, specifying definite responsibilities.

The National Strategy to Secure Cyberspace was approved by President Bush in February 2003. It does not focus on terrorist threats to the extent that the NSPPCIKA does, mentioning criminal threats and threats of military attacks as well. Its overall structure and approach, however, are similar to that of the NSPPCIKA. Its stated purpose is "to engage and empower Americans to secure the portions of cyberspace that they own, operate, control, or with which they interact." It identifies the private sector as "best equipped and structured to respond to an evolving cyber threat" but acknowledges that in "specific instances . . . federal government response is most appropriate and justified," such as "where high transaction costs or legal barriers lead to significant coordination problems" and "[where] governments operate in the absence of private sector forces," and to resolve "incentive problems that lead to under provisioning of critical shared resources" as well as "raising awareness." The role of DHS is emphasized and explained in detail.

Homeland Security Presidential Directive 7, "Critical Infrastructure Iden-tification, Prioritization, and Protection," signed by President Bush on December 17, 2003, establishes U.S. Government policy "to identify and prioritize United States critical infrastructure and key resources and to protect them from terrorist attacks." The Department of Defense (DOD) is assigned specific responsibility for protecting infrastructure relating to the defense industrial base. DHS is given responsibility for protection of most other national-level infrastructures, including many critical to DOD operations, from terrorist attacks.

National Infrastructure Protection Plan (NIPP) 2006 was agreed upon by multiple agency heads, including then–Secretary of Defense Donald Rumsfeld, in June 2006. The goals of the NIPP are "enhancing protection of the Nation's CI/KR [critical infrastructure/key resources] to prevent, deter, neutralize, or mitigate the effects of deliberate efforts by terrorists to destroy, incapacitate, or exploit them; and to strengthen national preparedness, timely response, and rapid recovery in the event of an attack, natural disaster, or other emergency." In military terms, the NIPP is analogous to a strategic plan, whereas the other directives more closely resemble broad statements of policy. Sector-specific plans under the NIPP are in the process of development and approval.

The NIPP integrates terrorist and natural-disaster threats into the infrastructure and gives brief attention to criminal threats. Like the other directives, it does not address threats of warlike attack or intrinsic failure. This is an opportunity for improvement in U.S. policy: it would be more effective and efficient to deal with such threats in an integrated and comprehensive way.

Aside from the now-superseded Clinton administration PDD 63, the focus of all these directives is strongly on terrorist threats. Criminal and military threats receive some limited treatment but practically no attention to damage that might result from intrinsic, accidental, or natural causes.

The government has policies with respect to these other threats, but, for the most part, they are scattered among many laws, regulations, and directives relating to the responsibilities and functions of specific departments, agencies, and organizations. For that reason, we turn next to an organizational perspective.

Organizational Responsibilities

The duties of DHS are the subject of the policy documents just described. U.S. infrastructures are operated by thousands of commercial and other organizations, almost all of which take measures to ensure reliability and security of operations. The rest of this section concentrates on other organizations.

The DOD Role

Regardless of other considerations, each Federal department and agency must see to protecting its own infrastructures against all threats, cooperating and coordinating with other agencies where appropriate. In addition, DOD must defend the Nation's infrastructures against military attack and participate with allies in doing the same. It may be called upon to aid in protecting and restoring the Nation's infrastructure or those of allied or friendly nations against natural disasters. A comprehensive DOD policy regarding infrastructure defense and protection must deal with all these needs.

As a practical matter, however, DOD concerns cannot stop there. Infrastructure by its nature is pervasive and highly networked and may be largely invisible. Few clear boundaries can be drawn. Although DOD makes great efforts to be self-sufficient, it is dependent on many infrastructures not under its control. Even though defending them against some kinds of threats is not within its defined responsibilities, DOD cannot afford to neglect them.

Moreover, the distinctions among threat sources—military, terrorist, criminal, natural, or intrinsic—often are not operationally meaningful: it can be difficult or impossible to discern the actual source of a threat in time to affect operations. For instance, it may not be feasible or prudent to await definitive information about whether a specific problem is the result of military attack before taking defensive action.

Thus, the DOD policymaker confronts a dilemma regarding infrastructure protection. It is impossible for DOD to simultaneously stick solely to its own business and fulfill its responsibilities. There will inevitably be ambiguities and overlaps of responsibility and spheres of action, and consequent potential for costly conflict with other agencies and entities. There can be no bureaucratic "good fences" to make "good neighbors" with other agencies and organizations in infrastructure protection. Unless close and cooperative give-and-take relationships can be developed in advance, counterproductive friction is likely to hamper needed efforts.

None of these issues or considerations is new to DOD, which has long confronted them in various forms. But the changing nature of the threats, as well as new organizational responses in other areas of the government, has led to significant changes. These are reflected in three key policy and doctrine documents. The Department of Defense Strategy for Homeland Security and Civil Support, approved by Deputy Secretary of Defense Gordon England in June 2005, is a broad statement of policy and approach. DOD Directive 3020.40 of August 19, 2005, on Defense Critical Infrastructure Program (DCIP), also approved by Deputy Secretary England, specifically defines DOD policy with respect to protection of defense-related critical infrastructure and assigns responsibilities. Third, Joint Publication 3–27 of July 12, 2007, *Homeland Defense*, is especially lengthy, reflecting the complexity of the issues involved, and provides commanders at all levels with authoritative guidance covering a wide range of situations and contingencies.

Only experience will tell whether DOD policy and doctrine will prove adequate, and be adequately implemented, but what has been produced is encouraging.

Other Federal Agencies

Five major Federal agencies share responsibilities relating to energy infrastructure: DHS, the Department of Energy (DOE), Department of Transportation (DOT), Federal Energy Regulatory Commission (FERC), and Nuclear Regulatory Commission (NRC). DOE and FERC are both involved in protection of all energy infrastructures (electrical, oil, and natural gas) against natural and intrinsic threats and share terrorism-protection responsibilities with DHS. NRC plays a comparable role with respect to nuclear energy infrastructure. DOT has responsibility for pipeline safety, exercised by its Office of Pipeline Safety, and coordinates with DHS regarding pipeline security.[45] DOE has several national laboratories (outgrowths of the development of nuclear weapons); its Idaho and

Sandia National Laboratories are active in energy infrastructure security research and development.

The Federal Communications Commission (FCC) has responsibility for all Federal communications regulation. In the past, it commissioned a recurring series of Network Reliability and Interoperability Councils (NRICs), composed of representatives of a broad spectrum of communications industry entities as well as concerned government organizations, and chartered to provide recommendations to the FCC and to the communications industry to help "assure optimal reliability and interoperability of wireless, wireline, satellite, cable, and public data networks."[46] The commission's Public Safety and Homeland Security Bureau works with DHS on security and protection issues.

National Communications System
The National Communications System (NCS) is an outgrowth of a Cold War initiative from the 1960s intended to assure critical executive branch communications under any circumstances, including nuclear attack. An interagency group long run by DOD, it is today lodged in DHS.

Rather than build dedicated government-owned communications infrastructure, the NCS stressed close cooperation with the telecommunications industry to assure the necessary reliability. The closely related National Security Telecommunications Advisory Committee (NSTAC) provides industry-based advice to the executive branch on communications security issues.

North American Electric Reliability Organization and North American Electric Reliability Corporation
The first widespread power outage in North America was the Northeast blackout of November 1965, which affected large areas of Ontario, New York, New Jersey, and New England. In response, regional reliability councils were formed, to be coordinated by the National Electric Reliability Council (NERC). The regional councils and NERC operated under Federal authority but were funded and staffed from the utility industry; their standards were consensual, and industry compliance was voluntary and self-policed. Experience showed that this was not adequate and that the same causes cropped up again and again in power failures. Industry leaders urged that NERC—which by then had become the North American Electric Reliability Council, including coverage of Canada and a small portion of Mexico whose grid is linked to that of California—needed to be given teeth so it could formulate and enforce mandatory standards.[47] Finally, after the August 2003 Northeast blackout, necessary legislation was passed.

Under the Energy Policy Act of 2005, FERC was given responsibility and authority for the reliability of the bulk electric power delivery system throughout the United States. It was authorized to designate an independent Electric Reliability

Organization (ERO), which it was hoped would also be recognized by Canada and Mexico, to set and enforce standards throughout the North American electric grid. NERC had become the North American Electric Reliability Corporation, subsidiary to the council; it reorganized itself to comply with the requirement that it be independent and submitted its proposal. Certified by FERC as the U.S. ERO in July 2006, it is empowered to establish and enforce reliability standards, subject to FERC approval, with penalties for infraction. Among these are standards for security, including cybersecurity. Inevitably, the standards reflect a balance among security and other considerations, notably cost. They have been reviewed by concerned government and industry organizations and are widely but not universally believed to be adequate. The standards were approved by FERC in January 2008 and went into effect in March 2008.[48] The standards are oriented toward both processes and objectives and are broad enough to cover a range of situations. The ERO issues implementing instructions and assesses compliance, recommending action to the FERC to correct problems that cannot be resolved administratively.

State Agencies
Although states have embraced deregulation in various ways and degrees, state governments retain their inherent powers to regulate infrastructures operating in their territories. Most states have one or more independent agencies devoted to these functions. In addition, state and local law enforcement agencies play major roles in protecting infrastructure systems.

Information Sharing and Analysis Centers
In 1998, PDD 63 called for the establishment of an Information Sharing and Analysis Center (ISAC) as part of the Federal apparatus for critical infrastructure protection. This evolved into a series of 11 organizations: Communications ISAC, Electricity Sector ISAC, Emergency Management and Response ISAC, Financial Services ISAC, Highway ISAC, Information Technology ISAC, Multi-State ISAC, Public Transit ISAC, Surface Transportation ISAC, Supply Chain ISAC, and Water ISAC. Loosely coordinated by an overall council, the ISACs serve as conduits for government-industry and industry-industry communication about operational threats and protective measures.

The Communications ISAC is the National Coordinating Center for Tele-communications, an arm of the National Communications System. The Electricity Sector ISAC is the NERC.

DHS Councils and Partnerships
DHS has established or assumed sponsorship of a number of organizations intended to advise the government on infrastructure protection matters and co-

ordinate government and private-sector efforts. These include the Federal Inter-agency Security Committee, the State, Local, Tribal, and Territorial Government Coordinating Council, the Critical Infrastructure Partnership Advisory Council (CIPAC), and the National Infrastructure Advisory Council.[49]

Partnership for Critical Infrastructure Security

Representatives from the CIPAC Sector Coordinating Councils comprise the Partnership for Critical Infrastructure Security, a cross-sector coordinating organization established in December 1999 under the auspices of the Department of Commerce and now subsumed under the CIPAC.

Policy Issues

Since PDD 63 was issued in 1998, a great deal has been accomplished to make the Nation's critical infrastructure systems more secure and robust and to improve their protection against cyber as well as physical attack, with emphasis on defense against terrorists. In the same period, law enforcement agencies have greatly stepped up their activities in the area of cyber crime. Yet potential threats also have burgeoned. It is a race in which to stand still is to fall seriously and swiftly behind.

Throughout this period, cyber attacks have mounted rapidly. Many have been directed at the infrastructure of cyberspace itself, and a smaller but still substantial number against other infrastructures via their SCADA and management systems. In the majority of cases, it has been impossible to determine the identity or the motivations of the attackers. Vandalism, criminal gain, terrorism, intelligence-gathering, or even covert military attack are all possibilities, and usually there has been no way to tell.

These cyber attacks have been costly, but their effects, in terms of deaths, economic losses, and sheer misery and inconvenience, have been much less than those stemming from other sources of infrastructure damage. Many more Americans have been far more seriously affected by loss of electrical, com-munications, transportation, natural gas, and oil service resulting from stressful weather, geological disaster, accident, and intrinsic faults in design or construction. As a logical result, our society invests more attention and capital in averting and containing these more common and costly problems.

In practice, however, it often is not clear whether damage was initiated by human or natural attack. After the August 2003 Northeast blackout, it took months to determine that the cyber infrastructure failures that had an important bearing on the extent of the damage had not been caused by hostile attack. In fact, very similar damage might have been produced by a combination of physical attacks on transmission lines and cyber attacks on EMS and SCADA systems.

At the physical and engineering level, there is thus a large area of overlap in the measures needed to guard infrastructures against damage from whatever cause. To ignore this underlying unity in framing policy is to fight against nature, and it cannot fail to generate needless conflicts, gaps, and duplications of effort. Yet our survey above of the welter of policies and governing organizations reveals little evidence of unity in dealing with infrastructure protection.

A Basis for Unified Policy

A fundamental axiom of U.S. policy in every field is that, to the greatest extent possible, responsibilities should be assigned to specific individuals or small, unified groups, and that responsibility and authority should always be closely aligned. That is the basis for our free enterprise system, for restricting the powers of government as narrowly as possible, and for assigning governmental powers to the lowest and most local level possible.

We are also wary, as a society, of the hazards of mixed motives and conflicting interests. We know all too well how difficult it is to serve two masters or pursue divergent interests.

These principles have informed America's decisions about infrastructures. Thus, for example, unlike many countries, we have never made the telecommunications, rail, or petroleum infrastructures into government departments. The Internet, created at Federal Government initiative, was divested as soon as it seemed feasible. Governmental control and operation of other infrastructures is quite limited and largely confined to local authorities.[50]

Yet we have seen how the private enterprise structure in electrical power distribution has contributed to conflicting interests and mismatches of responsibility and authority, leading to massive artificial shortages and huge blackouts. The companies involved found that they could increase profit potential by withholding electricity (as in the California energy crisis of 2000–2001) or by neglecting safeguards (as in the August 2003 blackout). They understood that these actions were undesirable from the standpoint of American society as a whole, but it is our society, after all, that mandates such powerful incentives to individual and company profit. This was predictable and even predicted, but no effective preventive measures were established. If we wish different outcomes, we must either restructure the marketplace to assure that profit motives align with society's needs, or else impose effective regulation to prevent companies from finding profit in damaging or dangerous actions.

Market Solutions

Aligning profit motives with needs for infrastructure protection against attack would be most desirable, providing maximum delegation of power and responsibility while minimizing conflict of motive and interest. The most direct approach to this is to make companies bear the costs that result from successful attacks on their facilities and services. This in principle would motivate them to do what is needed to avoid or mitigate damaging attacks, including banding together as necessary to take collective action. This would be the pure free-market solution and the one that is arguably best aligned with American principles and values.

Scarcely anyone in our society questions the efficacy of the free market in providing well-defined products and services to meet customer demands at the lowest price. But in a case such as this, experience and theory combine to raise a series of issues to be considered. First, because the incentives would take the form of threat of need to repay money already collected from customers, they would depend on the credibility of some external enforcement mechanism, inevitably governmental in character. The government would have to be prepared not only to act in a rigidly punitive fashion but also to convince the companies that it would act. It has always been difficult for democratic government to do this.

The companies most affected would be limited-liability corporations, and their inherent limitations of liability would imply a cutoff in threat response. That is, any threat severe enough to endanger the viability of the company should evoke the same level of protection, regardless of whether its effect on society was catastrophic or only serious. Thus, a second issue is that society might be relatively underprotected against the gravest threats.

A third issue arises because any corporation is run by agents—its executives—whose own incentives may be more or less misaligned with those of the corporation's owners, its shareholders. Alignment of executive and owner interests is essential to any free-market solution to the infrastructure protection problem. But this alignment is difficult to achieve when income and cost are separated in time and the magnitude of cost is uncertain. This is a case where cost may be imposed a long way in the future and where its amount (and even incidence) is wildly uncertain. In such circumstances, it is extremely tempting for executives to focus on present-day income and neglect the highly uncertain future costs of infrastructure attack.

Finally, many of the most effective potential responses to threats of attack involve intelligence collection in foreign countries, or the exercise of police powers or military force. Broad delegation of such powers to individuals or corporations would raise issues regarding the nature of our nation and government that far transcend the bounds of this discussion.

Regulatory Solutions

Unless some way can be found to avoid problems that are inherent in a market-based approach, security for our infrastructures will have to depend on direct government control or regulation. Direct government control would raise the issues of delegation of responsibility and control and of alignment of motivations discussed earlier.

In principle, the most desirable way to regulate infrastructure security might well be by private orderings, in which industry participants, recognizing self-interest or social responsibility, evolve structures upon which society could rely. This could minimize the costs of regulation.[51] Internet governance is a prominent example of such private ordering. But there seem to have been no serious efforts yet to develop proposals for private orderings for infrastructure security. For the moment, it is an open question and a challenge to policy analysts.

In the absence of serious suggestions regarding private orderings, we turn to public orderings. In broad principle, all regulation operates by manipulation of the incentives of income and costs. There is a great difference in practice, however, between regulation that threatens to cost executives their freedom and that which merely promises to modify the firm's profit and loss calculus. Here we distinguish between incentive regulation and directive regulation.

A well-known example of incentive regulation is pollution credits (also discussed under the rubrics of emissions trading or cap and trade). The regulator creates a certain number of credits, each conferring the right to emit a defined quantity of pollutants—for instance, 10 million tons of carbon dioxide per year. The credits are allocated to firms by administrative fiat or by auction, and thereafter firms are free either to keep a credit and emit that quantity of pollutant or to sell the credit to another firm. The price of a credit acts as an incentive to the firm to invest in pollution reduction so it can sell the credit. The net effect, ideally, is to concentrate investment in pollution reduction in areas where the greatest improvements can be achieved at the least cost to society as a whole.

There are pitfalls for regulators in such schemes, and they do not always work well. As outlined earlier, the incentive regulation regime employed to regulate electricity and natural gas distribution in California in the early 2000s offered opportunities for gaming, which were exploited by Enron and other suppliers to gain billions of dollars in extra profits without public benefit. There is wide (although by no means universal) agreement, however, that where they can be appropriately designed and well implemented, incentives provide the most efficient means of regulation.

There are, however, many areas of regulation where incentive regimes have not yet been found feasible or attractive. For instance, issuance of credits permitting a firm to cause a certain number of deaths or maimings probably would not be publicly accepted as a substitute for affirmative direct regulation of safety measures, regardless of any theoretical merits of such a scheme.

Basing regulation to decrease vulnerability to infrastructure attack on such incentives seems open to similar objections. Beyond this, however, attacks themselves are infrequent and variable enough in nature and intensity to raise severe problems in measuring vulnerability. It is a very different situation from that of carbon dioxide emissions or even workplace accidents, where it is possible to gather relatively immediate and direct data on the impact of any control measures.[52]

Thus, it appears that in many areas, effective protection of infrastructures against attack can best—and perhaps only—be assured through directive regulation of infrastructure firms. To the greatest possible extent, this regulation should take the form of performance-oriented requirements that leave to the individual firm the choice of means by which the necessary performance is to be achieved. In safety-related regulation, however, there generally are areas in which the regulators must, as a practical matter, mandate the use or avoidance of specified procedures and equipment. The problems of this sort of regulation are significant: regulators are given power to impose costs without having to answer to the firm's owners, whose only recourse is through administrative, legal, or political appeals. The regulators present the same agency problems as management and may be even less accountable to owners. The only mitigation is that, unlike managers, regulators are not able to profit personally by actions that might damage the firm.

In any event, good practice in process- and equipment-oriented regulation always dictates that firms should be given the opportunity to propose alternatives based on an evidentiary case that what they propose will produce results at least as satisfactory as those mandated in the regulation. Regulators also must be attentive to industry arguments that change in technology or circumstance results in a need for regulatory revision.

One important variant of public ordering is public ordering with private enforcement, in which the rules are publicly determined but are enforced in part or in whole by private appeal to the courts or administrative tribunals. In principle, this offers opportunities to reduce both costs and opportunities for costly bureaucratic meddling. A variant of this is now being employed in regulating electrical system reliability, and it merits attention.

The quest to improve the security of the electrical power infrastructure against natural and intrinsic threats, as well as against many forms of attack, has led recently to the establishment of a formal Electric Reliability Organization. The ERO takes the form of a private nonprofit corporation with close ties to the electric power industry, but endowed with regulatory powers under the supervision and control of a Federal agency, FERC. Earlier experience with NERC (which now runs the ERO) had demonstrated that admonition and appeals to industry-wide and national interest were not adequate, but it is expected that the ERO will not have to regulate with a heavy hand and will not be a source of significant needless cost for the industry and its customers.

This system of regulation is only now starting to operate, and we cannot be certain how well it will fulfill expectations. Even if it operates exactly as hoped, it will not eliminate blackouts, for that is not possible with an electric grid anything like the one we have. It should be able to reduce their frequency and greatly limit their severity. If it is successful in establishing and enforcing appropriate standards, based in present knowledge, then a blackout like that of August 2003 should never happen again.

It is not possible to be as confident about ERO potential to protect the grid from deliberate attack because our experience with attack is not as comprehensive as that with natural and intrinsic casualties. But analysis and experience indicate that consistent enforcement of ERO standards should make the risk of damage from an attack significantly lower.

The ERO model offers promise as a mechanism for regulation to improve the survivability and operability of many kinds of infrastructures in the face of attacks as well as natural and intrinsic threats.

Cyberspace Infrastructure

Many U.S. infrastructures are shared to some degree with Canada and Mexico, and actions to protect them need to be coordinated closely with those taken by the governments of these nations.

The cyberspace infrastructure has far greater international connections and dependencies than other infrastructures. This raises unique problems of governance and regulation. In electrical power, the United States can and does operate with standards that differ considerably from those used in distant countries, even in such basic matters as AC distribution frequency (60 hertz here but 50 hertz in many other places). In cyberspace, however, international coordination issues are much more complex. Many details of cyberspace infrastructure protection policy must therefore be coordinated with foreign and international bodies.

How Much Is Enough?

The most fundamental of questions in defense planning is always, "How much is enough?" What level of protection is needed? There is no absolute answer, but the question must be addressed explicitly and systematically.

How are we to weigh warnings of threats to cyberspace infrastructure, and to other infrastructures, against other threats? How much of our attention and resources should be devoted to countering them? Our limited experience with such threats makes the problem much more difficult.

Examples drawn from other risk fields help to illustrate the issues. For example, in 2001, about 5,000 extra people died in U.S. traffic accidents because more than a quarter of car and truck occupants failed to wear seatbelts.[53]

In the same year, drownings killed 3,300.[54] Both tolls exceeded that of terrorist attacks and continue year after year, but public concern about terrorist attacks is far higher than concern about seatbelt use or water hazards, and far more resources are devoted to combating terrorism.

Another comparison is illuminating. The average annual toll from asteroid impacts is estimated to be lower than that from machinery accidents, but the two averages are arrived at in different ways. Machinery accidents occur frequently and relatively regularly, each involving a small number of deaths. By contrast, fatal asteroid impacts are rare, coming at intervals of 1,000 years (for relatively small incidents) to 100 million years or more (for catastrophic ones), but they could involve huge numbers of fatalities and even extinction of our species. Until recently, the asteroid threat was generally discounted, but over the past two decades, public concern has increased as evidence of historical impacts has been discovered and analyzed.[55]

Surveys and experimental studies analyzing how we evaluate and respond to perceived risks confirm, as these examples suggest, that people are not rigorously logical about such matters. The perceived dreadfulness of a threat has a lot to do with response to it, as does the form in which information regarding its probability of occurrence is received.[56] We are prone to be less concerned, relative to objective quantitative risk level, about common and familiar risks such as heart disease or motor vehicle accident than about shadowy and little-understood menaces such as cyber attack.

A further complicating factor is the concern decisionmakers often feel regarding public reactions to attacks or failures, such as fear of mass panic.[57] Less immediately, decisionmakers fear weakening of public support for necessary measures or sacrifices. For instance, almost every wartime President since Abraham Lincoln has worried that the people would be unwilling to accept casualties as the price of victory.

Social scientists find, however, that support for a conflict depends not so much on particular levels of casualties as on belief in the cause for which it is fought and the probability of success.[58] Similarly, it is found that mass panic is very rare, even in circumstances that might seem to provide ample justification.[59] For most people, emotional factors play the dominant role in determining overall response to issues such as demand for defense, but this by no means implies that the public is irrational about such subjects.[60] Our emotional apparatus evolved as it has because it aided survival in threatening environments, and it continues to serve us in this role.[61] Decisionmakers often resort to measures intended to manipulate the public's emotional responses to gain support, but while manipulation can seem effective in the short term, it often evokes a backlash over the longer term.

Ultimately, the question of how much is enough infrastructure protection can be answered only by the public through the political process. Policymakers hoping for a sound answer will do well to provide the public with clear, credible information.

Policy Recommendations

The foregoing examination of infrastructure protection issues has revealed a lack of broad and systematic policy. The following 10 recommendations to remedy this are presented for consideration at the highest levels of government.

Unify Policy Direction

It is unrealistic to expect that all of the aspects of policy relating to infrastructure protection can or should be united under a single governmental department or agency, but it is essential that a positive mechanism be put in place to assure effective interagency coordination. Because essentially the same actions are required to protect each infrastructure against natural disasters, accidental and intrinsic failures, and threats from terrorist, military, and criminal attack, the interagency mechanism must encompass them all. The precise organization of this mechanism requires further study by Congress and the Executive.

Specialize Policy Direction

While there should be unity in overall direction, policy direction for the various infrastructures should be tailored to their specific nature and needs. Thus, for each infrastructure there should be a subordinate interagency process involving the agencies that have specialized knowledge and responsibility.

Strengthen and Unify Regulation

While directive regulation of infrastructure firms at the process level has important pitfalls, there is no evident substitute for it with regard to protection of infrastructures. Absence of effective regulation leaves firms exposed to commercial pressures that work against protection and tend to prompt a "race to the bottom." For each infrastructure there should be a single, well-informed regulator with the knowledge and incentives to strike the right balance between risk and economic benefit. The ERO represents a promising approach, which should be studied as a potential model for other infrastructures.

Define State and Local Roles

State primacy in policy and regulation for infrastructures has been undercut by the trend toward larger interstate networks, but state and local government agencies nevertheless retain a very important role. The Federal interagency mechanism for infrastructure protection policy and related regulatory apparatus must be linked closely with the relevant state agencies. How this is to be accomplished must be worked out directly with the states.

Define International Interfaces

Cyberspace infrastructure networks depend on international connections, but in this they differ in degree rather than in kind from other infrastructures. In practically all cases, it is necessary to coordinate international action to secure infrastructures most effectively. Again, the ERO appears to offer a promising model, with the United States playing a positive leadership role by offering a structure with mutual benefit and by demonstrating readiness to modify its positions to meet the legitimate interests of others.

Mandate Effective Systems Engineering for Infrastructure-related Software

Undependable software is one of the greatest vulnerabilities of infrastructure systems. The cost-driven trend to wide use of undependable COTS and open-source software is exacerbating the risks. Software dependability will not achieve the necessary standards unless effective systems engineering is mandated for infrastructure systems.

Don't Take No for an Answer

There will be some in the infrastructure industries who resist any directive regulation, regardless of justification. Their objections must not be accepted. It is instructive to look at the 40-year struggle to avert massive electrical blackouts without directive regulation; that struggle culminated in the August 2003 Northeast blackout, whose magnitude was multiplied by widespread failure to comply with existing voluntary standards. Any decisionmakers who are tempted to give in to industry pressures against regulation should consider carefully what they would say if that decision cleared the way for a successful attack.

Establish and Implement Clear Priorities

While there is no clear limit to potential threats against infrastructures, there are limits to the resources that can be used for protection. An attempt to protect everything against all possible threats will result in failure to protect the most crucial targets adequately against the most important threats. Setting and keeping priorities for the allocation of financial and management resources are essential in order to provide effective protection.

Inform the Public Clearly and Accurately

Many of the decisions regarding protection of infrastructures will be technical and should be made by those with appropriate expertise. It is a serious error, however, to imagine that the key decisions in this area can be held within any closed group. The integrity of infrastructures affects everyone in our society, and the public will demand that its views be heeded at critical junctures. A systematic ongoing effort to make full and objective information available is the best guarantee of informed and considered public input. It also is the best way to ensure that the public will feel confidence in those who direct infrastructure protection efforts and will pay appropriate attention to their recommendations.

Conduct a Continuing Program of Research

Many important questions remain unsettled and more will arise as threats, technology, and economic conditions change. The policy and regulation institutions must have the authority, resources, and responsibility to sponsor and guide broadly conceived programs of research to serve their information needs. Knowledge can be expensive, but its absence can be much more so.

CHAPTER 6

Evolutionary Trends in Cyberspace

Edward Skoudis

CYBERPOWER is built on the rapidly shifting terrain of cyberspace, which includes not only the Internet, but also the legacy telephony infrastructure, cellular phone technologies, and wireless data services. The technologies underlying all of these aspects of cyberspace—such as bandwidth, interconnectedness, processor speed, functionality, and security vulnerabilities—have evolved over decades. The purpose of this chapter is to identify these evolutionary trends and to extrapolate their implications, creating a view of possible and likely aspects of the future of cyberspace.

This chapter focuses on the accumulation of incremental evolutionary change over long periods. Even individually small quantitative changes, when compounded over time, can bring about great qualitative changes on their own. In addition to evolutionary trends, revolutions are also possible, but revolutionary discontinuities are difficult to predict, and so they are not discussed here (but see chapter 8 in this volume, "The Future of the Internet and Cyberpower").

Trends that have long-term staying power and transformative implications will be examined, while fads and "flash-in-the-pan" issues will be ignored, even though it is not always easy to see the difference while in the midst of major transformations.[1] While fads can help set initial conditions for future evolution, they are hard to predict as they begin. However, the follow-on evolution can be observed and extrapolated into the future. This chapter attempts to identify real changes affecting cyberspace and to filter out passing fads.

With that goal in mind, three types of trends will be examined: computer and network, software, and social. Computer and network trends include:

- increases in computer and network power
- proliferation of broadband connectivity
- proliferation of wireless connectivity
- transition from Internet Protocol version 4 (IPv4) to IPv6.

Software trends include:

- increases in software complexity
- enhanced capabilities for search both across local systems and Internet-wide
- widespread virtualization of operating systems
- convergence of technologies
- increased noise in most aspects of cyberspace
- increased vulnerability due to advancement of computer and network attack and exploit methodologies.

Social trends in the use and development of cyberspace include:

- worldwide technological development, with different local emphases
- rise in online communities, collaboration, and information-sharing.

While cyberspace evolution is proceeding on a multitude of fronts, these trends were identified by a team of authors associated with this book as the sources of a great deal of the momentum for the evolution of cyberspace. The trends in this list represent the evolution of the underlying elements of cyberspace itself as the basis for a variety of other technological, social, economic, and related changes.

Taken in their totality, these trends point to a future in which cyberspace becomes far more pervasive, touching most aspects of daily life in some way for a majority of the world. Two longstanding trends—significantly lower cost of processor performance and increases in flexible network connectivity—will facilitate the incorporation of cyberspace into more and more products. If these trends continue, some form of intelligence and network communication will eventually be embedded in most electrically powered devices: if you plug it into a wall socket today, it is likely to have some cyberspace functionality in the future. Indeed, with advances in wireless and battery technologies, even many objects that do not get plugged into the wall will also have cyberspace components. These trends mean that cyberspace is increasingly becoming an overlay technical infrastructure to our physical world, as it increasingly becomes involved in monitoring, analyzing, and altering the physical landscape.

Computer and Network Trends

Among the computer and network trends likely to have lasting effect are increases in power, proliferation of broadband and wireless connectivity, and upgrades in the fundamental protocols of the Internet.

Increases in Computer and Network Power

Moore's law describes a major component of the evolution of the information technology industry. Originally observed in 1965 by Gordon Moore, co-founder of Intel Corporation, Moore's law posits that industry's ability to produce integrated circuits continually improves, so that the number of microcomponents that can be etched on a chip will double at regular intervals.[2] There is some variation in the specific interval cited for the doubling timeframe observed by the law. Gordon Moore originally predicted doubling each year but later revised the timeframe to 2 years. Historically, the timeframe has varied between 1 and 2 years. Most current estimates focus on the 2-year timeframe.

The doubling in the density of circuitry translates to increased processor performance and lower costs. Although the slowdown and even ultimate demise of Moore's law are predicted from time to time, the pace it describes has continued for over 40 years. It should be noted that, although Moore's observation is commonly referred to as "Moore's law," it is an observation and an industry goal, not a "law" in the physical sense.[3]

As individual machines grow more powerful, they are also increasingly interconnected in networks. The benefits of the increase in interconnectivity are addressed in Metcalfe's law, named after Robert Metcalfe, one of the inventors of Ethernet technology. Metcalfe posited that the value of a telecommunications network is proportional to the square of the number of its users. According to this hypothesis, as more users are brought onto a shared communications network, the value of the network to the overall community grows not just at a linear rate, but as the square of the number of users. A related hypothesis, Reed's law, estimates the value even higher, saying that the utility of a network can scale exponentially with the number of participants in the network.

Unlike Moore's law, which has demonstrably reflected reality for the past 40 or more years, Metcalfe's and Reed's laws cannot be quantified: they are more a metaphorical statement of the value and power of networks than a quantifiable observation or prediction. Furthermore, Metcalfe's and Reed's laws have been challenged; some observers have said that they overstate the increase in value of a network when new users join.[4] Still, it is generally agreed that the value of a network grows faster than at a linear rate of the number of users.

Well established technological and economic trends led to the observations known as Moore's law and Metcalfe's law; these trends suggest that the future of cyberspace will see faster computing devices interconnected in more powerful and valuable networks. With the compounding impact of these trends over time, cyberspace will continue to grow in importance and influence as more economic, military, and even social activity migrates to that realm.

Broadband Proliferation

Another major evolutionary trend in cyberspace is the widespread deployment of broadband Internet services. Cyberspace experienced at a speed of just 56 kilobytes per second (kbps)—allowing rudimentary Web surfing and data exchange—is very different from cyberspace at 400 kbps or more. Widespread access to faster connectivity by desktops, laptops, personal digital assistants, and cell phones enables new business models and new social interactions. Just as business and social models were transformed by the move from trains and ocean liners to jet airline flights in the past century, today the richer audio, video, and networked applications supported by higher speed Internet connections make cyberspace significantly more valuable to its users. Many face-to-face transactions and physical exchanges can be supplanted by much less expensive software-based interactions. New services not previously associated with the Internet, including telephony and television, are moving to this plentiful, cheap bandwidth. Widespread fiber optics, cable modems, digital subscriber loops/lines (DSL), and broadband wireless services are the technological underpinnings allowing broadband access by consumers or businesses throughout the world.[5] These technologies have higher speeds (typically greater than 400 kbps) and are also always on, not requiring time-consuming dial-up "handshakes." While broadband deployment is already a reality in many parts of the world, it is not yet universal. Some set of users probably will continue to use dial-up access for some time, but there are likely to be fewer and fewer.

Broadband connectivity to the endpoints of computer communication is only possible if the Internet backbone itself can carry all of the extra traffic generated by these end systems. Internet backbone providers have deployed more high-speed links, using new fiber technologies such as OC–48 and OC–192 (operating at speeds of 2.488 Gigabits per second [Gbps] and 10 Gbps, respectively).[6] Higher speed satellite and microwave towers are interconnecting high-speed networks around the world. Interconnectivity between various backbone providers has increased to carry more traffic more quickly. As this interconnectivity grows, the topology of the Internet backbone becomes more complex from a design and management perspective.

As client computers increasingly rely on broadband access, and as the Internet infrastructure is refined to carry all of those bits, the servers to which the communications are directed likewise need additional computational and network power to provide new services. Faster servers can help deal with some of these needs, but most large Internet companies are instead relying on larger numbers of less expensive servers, distributed across one or more campuses around the world. Large Internet companies, among them Google, Amazon, eBay, and Microsoft, are constructing vast "server farms." By some estimates, Google's server count is at over half a million computers in 2007 and rising quickly.

Business models are also evolving, as Internet service providers (ISPs) try to furnish value-added services and applications on top of their increasingly commoditized bandwidth business. To realize the business value in the telephony, video, and various other applications and content being distributed via their "pipes," some ISPs are partnering with, buying, or building in-house application services and content. Such services and content are directly affiliated with that ISP, in contrast to other services that are not affiliated but that are accessed through that ISP by its customers. This evolution has led some ISPs to consider charging nonaffiliated application service providers and users a premium for their use of high bandwidth. Those that do not pay extra may face lower performance, with their traffic handled at a lower priority than higher paying affiliated users and application providers. This economic friction between ISPs and application service providers is a worldwide phenomenon and has been termed the "Net neutrality" issue. Some argue that governments should require the equal or "neutral" handling of affiliate and nonaffiliate traffic alike by ISPs, to foster interoperability and prevent the fragmentation of the Internet into various ISP enclaves. Others argue that allowing economic advantages for an ISP's affiliated services will encourage investment in new and improved services by the ISPs.

Several countries are grappling with this complex and contentious issue. Net neutrality issues are being studied by Japan's Ministry of Internal Affairs and Communications to determine a reasonable balance among the competing factors. The European Union has tentatively supported neutral networks, but companies such as Deutsche Telekom and Telecom Italia are beginning to lobby for changes to the existing European approach. A Net neutrality bill being debated in the U.S. Congress would require ISPs to handle traffic independently of their business relationships. Such legislation is hotly contested, and it is not yet clear how the issue will evolve.

In the future, bandwidth to the end system and on the backbone will likely grow even faster, with more widespread deployment of 10 megabits per second (Mbps) or higher rates to the home and a corresponding backbone to support it. Video applications will almost certainly increase, as today's nascent Internet television business grows much larger and video conferencing is more widely used.

Wireless Proliferation

Cyberspace connectivity is increasingly moving to wireless communication, in the form of wireless local area networks (WLANs), wireless broadband, and similar technologies. One of the major vectors of this move is often overlooked in discussions of cyberspace: the cell phone. An estimated 2 billion people have access to cell phones. Over 150 million camera phones have been sold to date, each supporting voice, text, and image transfer. Even with low bandwidth text messaging, their small size, decentralized communications capacity, and relatively low cost have made cell phones an increasingly important technology underlying social change. Rioters in France in late 2005 and early 2006, people involved in Ukraine's Orange Revolution in the winter of 2004/2005, and terrorist organizations have all relied on cheap and ubiquitous cell phone text-messaging to exercise command and control and to disseminate information.

Where today's cell phones have simple text messaging and still cameras, future cell phones with higher bandwidth applications and full video capabilities are likely to have even greater impact as they gain the capabilities of modern personal computers (PCs) and become, in effect, pocket-sized television studios. The hand-held video cameras of the late 1980s and early 1990s led to countless major news stories, such as the 1992 Rodney King riots in Los Angeles. However, that technology was limited: few people carried cameras with them most of the time, and the technology required the cumbersome handling of physical videotapes, typically delivered by hand or by courier. By contrast, when a major portion of the world's population carries cell phone–based video cameras wirelessly linked to the Internet at all times, cell phones will likely have a much larger impact on society, as when camera-equipped cell phones disseminated graphic pictures and video, albeit of low quality, of the execution of Saddam Hussein in 2006 within minutes of the event.

Today's grainy cell phone photos and simple videos will be replaced by much better multi-megapixel video cameras integrated into cell phones as video capture technology becomes smaller, cheaper, and more widely disseminated. Already television news outlets in some countries ask members of the public to submit cell phone video of events immediately after they happen. Web sites offer to broker the sale of videos of hot news events taken by private individuals. These trends decrease the time between an event's occurrence and its coverage in the news, further shrinking the news reporting cycle and the time available for the public and policymakers to analyze events.

Numerous other wireless technologies are transforming the nature of cyberspace. WLANs, in their most popular form, are implemented according to a set of standards denominated "802.11." Such "WiFi" networks allow nearby systems (within perhaps 100 meters) to communicate with one another or gain access to the Internet. Untethering computers from wired access makes it possible to use them for a wider variety of applications, ranging from industrial use to home appliances. By minimizing the need for costly wiring installations, WLANs allow for more rapid network deployment at much lower costs. A variety of organizations have taken advantage of this: stores in shopping malls use wireless for point-of-sales terminals and inventory control, and military deployments can rapidly deploy computer networks. WLAN technology is pushing the boundaries of the definition of "local" as well: originally designed for shorter distances, 802.11 signals have been successfully carried several miles and have been detected at over 200 miles under ideal circumstances (atop mountains on a clear day). Wireless signal transmission for computer devices often outpaces the distances it was designed to span. While WLAN technologies were created for distances up to 100 meters, their propagation across a mile or more has significant implications. Most consumers would be surprised to hear that the WLANs they have deployed in their homes can be detected and even accessed many blocks or miles away. Wireless data communications opens up computer network access over longer distances, making computers more accessible to both their users and would-be attackers.

With widespread deployment of WLANs, numerous wireless networks often occupy overlapping physical spaces. Activating a wireless detection device in any major city typically reveals at least a half-dozen nearby WLANs ready for a connection. Systems may appear on a WLAN for a short time, use it to transmit some vital information, and quickly disappear; this makes it hard to determine which assets are part of a given organization's network and which are not. For enterprises, maintaining a list of computing assets in such environments is difficult. And if an enterprise does not know which machines are part of its network and which are not, managing and securing those assets becomes impossible.

Another rapidly rising wireless technology is evolution data optimized (EVDO) service, by which cellular networks make possible high-speed data transmission from PCs and cell phones. EVDO is an evolutionary descendant of code division multiple access (CDMA) technology used by some cell phones for wireless data transmission. In the United States, a handful of carriers have deployed networks that use EVDO and CDMA technology, allowing business users and consumers in most major cities wireless connectivity at 128 kbps to 2 Mbps over distances of a mile or more. With a simple PC card, cell phone and PC users can gain wireless broadband access to the Internet from most major population centers in the United States. Such services could supplant cable modems and DSL, allowing more mobility at high bandwidths over longer distances.

Another emerging wireless technology is Worldwide Interoperability for Microwave Access (WiMAX), designed to obviate expensive copper and fiber solutions for the "last mile" to consumers' homes. Although it has a maximum throughput of 70 Mbps and a maximum distance of 70 miles, WiMAX in real-world circumstances achieves approximately 10 Mbps over about 2 miles.

WiMAX deployment is beginning to be used in urban and suburban areas to link WiFi LANs and to connect users to their ISPs.

Other wireless technologies, such as Bluetooth, are interconnecting the components of an individual computer wirelessly over distances of up to 10 meters. Bluetooth capabilities are built into many modern laptops, keyboards, computer mouse devices, cell phones, headsets, and music players. While designed for distances of only 10 meters, hobbyists have discovered that Bluetooth signals can sometimes be detected over a mile away. With numerous Bluetooth-enabled devices in close proximity, it can be hard to determine which assets are part of a given computer and which belong to another, again complicating the management and security of assets that are increasingly ephemerally tied to the network via wireless.

Another rapidly rising wireless technology is Radio Frequency Identifier (RFID) tags, very small, simple computer chips that send a unique identifier number. They are being used to support inventory activities, augmenting and possibly someday supplanting the familiar universal product code barcodes found on nearly all products today. With RFID tags, which are about the size of a grain of rice, a given product's code can be read without line-of-site viewing or direct physical access, as long as the radio frequency transmission can be read. RFIDs were designed to communicate over short distances (originally 1 to 10 meters, but hobbyists have demonstrated reading such tags over 100 meters away). Codes identifying equipment can be read without physical contact over such distances, with possible privacy implications as RFID applications spread.

Several organizations have expressed interest in using RFID technology for large-scale inventory management, including Wal-Mart Corporation, the U.S. military, and the Chinese government. The U.S. State Department has begun using RFID tags in electronic passports. As RFID deployment becomes more prominent, implementation vulnerabilities are likely to be discovered and scrutinized. Researchers have begun to devise methods for attacking RFID infrastructures, devising hypothetical worms that could spread from tag to tag, infecting large numbers of systems with very simple code. Research on attacks against RFID readers, including the transmission of malicious code to such readers, is also under way. RFID spoofing, whereby an attacker makes a bogus RFID tag impersonate another legitimate tag, is an active area of research today with implications on cloning passports. Skimming is the process of surreptitiously reading an RFID tag to extract its vital information, which may later be used in a spoofing attack to clone the tag. With RFID information embedded into consumer products, sensors deployed in a city could instantly determine the products carried by citizens who walk within 100 meters of the sensors, allowing monitors to determine the make and model of various devices carried by the user—an issue with significant privacy implications. Very invasive remote search of pedestrians or houses by government and law enforcement officials (as well as thieves) becomes possible with the technology.

Transition from IPv4 to IPv6

The current Internet infrastructure is based on the widely deployed IPv4, a specification originally created in the late 1970s that spread widely in the early 1980s and throughout the 1990s as the Internet grew. This protocol far exceeded its original expectations, becoming the common language for communication across the Internet and large numbers of private networks, and allowing a huge variety of devices—from mainframe systems to cell phones—to communicate. Despite its unprecedented success as a protocol, the original IPv4 design had significant drawbacks: a limited number of network addresses that were distributed inefficiently, no built-in support for security, a lack of quality-of-service features, and limited support for mobile devices. To address these shortcomings, the Internet Engineering Task Force set out in the mid-1990s to define a next-generation Internet protocol, termed IPv6.[7]

While the IPv6 specifications were completed some time ago, full deployment has been slow. Most modern operating systems have IPv6 software, but few use it. Pockets of IPv6 networks exist in specialized laboratory and educational environments. Small IPv6 networks have been overlaid on the existing IPv4 Internet, with network nodes run by academics, researchers, and hobbyists around the world.

One of the major reasons IPv6 deployment has moved slowly involves the innovative retrofitting of its various concepts into the existing IPv4. For example, the Internet Protocol Security (IPsec) specification was designed to be mandatory in IPv6. However, the cryptographic protections supported by IPsec—such as confidentiality protection, integrity checks, and system authentication—have also been included in many IPv4 implementations at least since 1997, reducing the incentive to move to IPv6. The limited 32-bit network address space of IPv4 was to be supplanted by the vast 128-bit address space of IPv6 to allow for more systems on the global Internet, increasing the number of IP addresses from about 4 billion (4×10^9) to 3.4×10^{38}. However, most organizations have deployed various network address translation devices to shuffle and reuse private network addresses, somewhat alleviating the original constraints of IPv4's 32-bit addresses. Likewise, quality-of-service and mobility options have been implemented in IPv4. These adaptations to IPv4's limits have eased many of the "pain points" driving the demand for IPv6.

Although IPv6 deployment has started slowly, it is expected to ramp up; both the Chinese government and the U.S. military have announced intentions to move to IPv6 by 2012 to support the modernization of their large networks. Even so, some Internet experts have viewed IPv6 deployment as a perpetual "five years in the future"—always predicted, but never actually occurring. However, over the next decade, IPv6 deployment seems very likely, given the momentum of decisions by large buyers, large vendors (including Cisco and Microsoft, whose products support the protocol), and the Internet Engineering Task Force, which crafts the specifications for the protocols used on the Internet.

What are the implications of true widespread IPv6 deployment? Although IPsec is mandatory in IPv6, that does not necessarily mean that the newer protocol will immediately boost security. To speed and simplify deployment, users sometimes implement IPv6 with IPsec without the necessary trusted encryption keys, in effect blindly trusting any system on the network. Some IPv6 implementations use blank ciphers, leaving data unencrypted. Such deployments nullify any authentication and confidentiality benefits of IPsec within IPv6. Even with the careful use of trustworthy keys and ciphers, systems supporting IPv6 may still have a large number of security flaws, at least initially, in their protocol stacks. These could allow for remote denial-of-service attacks that cause a system crash or that exhaust all processing or memory resources, or they could permit system compromise and control by an attacker. Building and maintaining IP stacks is very difficult, even using the far simpler IPv4 protocol. The software development community has required a full 20 years to scrub similar problems due to faulty code out of their IPv4 implementations.[8] IPv6 software is likely to go through a similar process as vulnerabilities are discovered and fixed. While it may not take another 20 years to get IPv6 right, it will certainly require significant effort to discern flaws in the numerous implementations of this vastly more complex protocol. The Internet and its users may be exposed to attacks for some time.

IPv6 also raises other security implications. The very large address space can make it easier for systems to hide: an attacker who modulates a network address across a very large address space can hide systems more easily than within the smaller and simpler IPv4 landscape.

Increases in Software Complexity

Although underlying hardware and network speeds have increased, most new computers do not seem to their users to be significantly faster than their predecessors for very long after their introduction. This is largely due to increases in software complexity, as additional features, increased error-handling capabilities, and more complex security facilities sap the processing gains reflected in Moore's law and in higher bandwidth. This phenomenon is sometimes referred to as Wirth's law, named after Niklaus Wirth, a Swiss computer scientist and inventor of Pascal and several other programming languages. Wirth's law states that software is decelerating faster than hardware is accelerating.

Modern software includes a proliferation of features, some important and useful to large numbers of users, and others providing utility to only a small fraction of the user base. Users demand that new programs do more than their old software, and vendors cater to this expectation. Software vendors introduce these features to entice new customers to purchase their products, as well as to inspire existing customers to continue on the treadmill of constant software upgrades. Unfortunately, some software vendors do not spend the resources necessary for thorough development, integration, and testing of these features and modifications.

More complex software is more likely to have flaws, which may manifest themselves in broken features, software crashes, or security vulnerabilities. When a software flaw is discovered, especially one with major security implications, the software vendor typically releases a "patch" to alleviate the condition. Microsoft, for example, releases patches once per month, each typically including between five and a dozen major fixes, often requiring upwards of 10 megabytes of new code. With such massive changes pushed to over 100 million systems, the patching process for Windows alone is a monumental worldwide undertaking on a monthly basis, involving not just Microsoft, but also hundreds of thousands of enterprise users and consumers, not all of whom test such patches carefully before installing. Moreover, multiple patches applied over time could introduce additional flaws. The constant accumulation of patches can make systems more "brittle," requiring even more complexity to patch adequately without breaking functionality.

Unfortunately, complexity is often the enemy of security, as subtle vulnerabilities linger in highly complex, perhaps poorly understood code. To address such vulnerabilities, security tools—antivirus tools, antispyware software, and intrusion prevention systems—are common defenses for systems today. Many of these tools operate in a reactive fashion, to clean up after an infection has occurred, and most defend against specific vulnerabilities that have already been found, not against as-yet-undiscovered security flaws. Compounding the problem, these security tools themselves often have flaws, so they need patches as well. This, again, increases the overall complexity of computer systems and makes them even more brittle.

Antivirus, antispyware, and other anti–malicious code technologies use a mixture of techniques to detect such "malware," analyzing protected computers on which they are installed at a granular level to police the system for infection and attacks. The need for such defenses is turning into a significant security tax on the increases described by Moore's law and is boosting complexity.

Enhanced Search Capabilities

With increasingly complex software used for a greater number of applications, more and more vital data is accumulating in databases and file systems. On a local system, data are typically stored in multi-Gigabyte or even Terabyte (1,000

Gigabyte) file systems. On large servers or even networked groups of systems, databases often exceed 100 Terabytes. These data are only useful if users and applications can search for information; high-quality search functionality is therefore vital, and the data must be organized, stored, and presented in useful structures. The metadata that describe the data, tagging, and visualization technologies are thus increasingly critical.

Because of their involvement with these crucial functions, Internet search engines are currently at the center of activity in cyberspace evolution. As search engines acquire more data sources, including phone books, highly detailed satellite imagery, and maps, users are presented with more powerful search directives and operators.[9] Such options let users hone in on specific items they seek, using a complex array of search directives instead of merely grabbing data with a specific set of search terms located in it. In addition, simple text-based searches are expanding to searches for images, sound, or videos.

With so much information on the Internet, many users need help to find what they need. Users might not even know precisely what to search for and would benefit from a ranking system of interesting or useful sources of information. To address this need, other sites on the Internet act as aggregating front-end portals that organize data from multiple data sources and process it to provide users with extra value. Sites such as digg.com and del.icio.us contain lists of popular articles and sites that are voted on by users, giving other users a guide to information in a variety of categories.

The need for search capabilities is not limited to the Internet. Internal network searching is increasingly important for locating useful information from an organization's internal servers and desktop computers. To address this need, Google offers an appliance that explores an internal enterprise network and creates a "mini-Google" for that organization, searchable in the same manner as the Internet-wide Google itself. Many other players are also moving into the internal enterprise network search market.

Local system search tools are also being deployed, including Google's Desktop Search software, Apple's Spotlight for Macintosh, and Microsoft's enhanced search capabilities for Windows machines. These tools let users formulate queries to find important information stored on their local hard drives rapidly. Current search capabilities of local products have only a limited syntax of search directives and operators, but these technologies will improve.

Search capabilities are particularly vital to analysis of very large centralized data repositories. Services such as LexisNexis (for searches in published news sources and legal documents), credit reporting agencies, and fraud detection tools for financial services organizations require extremely rapid search of large databases maintained by a small number of companies and government agencies. These data sources are used for data mining, correlation, and detailed analysis to discern trends and important outliers. Many of the operators of such databases sell search services to their clients; major economic decisions may be based on the results of searches of these data repositories. System downtime of a credit-reporting database, for example, could have major economic impact.

Novel search strategies made Google what it is today; its Page Rank algorithm for associating pages together provides a fast and reliable method for searches. In the future, as data sources and the amount of information stored grow, searching and prioritizing information are likely to become even more important, and new search strategies and new companies will arise to help people use data.

Widespread Operating System Virtualization

Virtual machine environments (VMEs) such as VMware, Microsoft's Virtual Server, and Xen let a user or administrator run one or more guest operating systems on top of a single host operating system. With such VME tools, for example, three or four instances of the Microsoft Windows operating system can run as guest systems on top of a single Linux host operating system on a single PC or server. The concepts of virtualization were pioneered in the mainframe world but are now migrating to standard PCs and even to cell phone systems. Such virtualized environments are used for clients as well as servers in a variety of commercial, government, and military organizations, and their deployment is increasing very rapidly for several reasons. First, VMEs improve server operations by helping to cut hardware costs, simplify maintenance, and improve reliability by consolidating multiple servers onto a single hardware platform. Second, they may lower the cost of providing user access to multiple networks having different sensitivity levels. By means of VMEs, some government and military agencies and departments may use one PC, with different guest operating systems associated with each separate network a user may need.

Third, numerous "honeypot" defensive technologies rely on VMEs because they can be more easily monitored and reset after a compromise occurs. Honeypots are used to detect attacks, research attackers' motives and methods, and provide a limited environment, isolated from critical facilities, in which to engage attackers. Given VMEs' ability to reset an infected system quickly, most malicious code researchers utilize them to analyze the capabilities of the latest malware and to construct defenses. If a malware specimen under analysis infects and damages a guest virtual machine, the VME lets a researcher revert to the last good virtual machine image, quickly and easily removing all effects of the malware without having to reinstall the operating system.

Finally, systems that are directly accessible from the Internet have a high risk of compromise; in multi-tiered e-commerce environments, it can be expected that the front-end system will be compromised. Increasingly, therefore, these exposed hosts are installed on VMEs to minimize downtime, increase security, and simplify forensic procedures.

Computer attackers are, accordingly, becoming very interested in detecting the presence of VMEs, both locally on a potential VME and across the network. If malicious code (such technologies as spyware or keystroke loggers) detects a VME, it might shut off some of its functionality to keep researchers from observing it and devising defenses. Researchers might not notice its deeper and more insidious functionality or may have to work harder to determine what the code would do when not in the presence of a VME. Either way, the attacker buys time, and with it, additional profit. VME detection is useful to attackers who seek to avoid wasting time on honeypots. Attackers also have other motivations for discovering whether a given system is running in a VME. If, for example, an attacker could find out that a group of five systems were guest virtual machines all on a single host, launching a denial-of-service attack against the host machine would be a far easier way to cause more harm to the target organization.

As VMEs are deployed more widely, even perhaps to a majority of machines on the Internet, their detection may become a less significant issue, as attackers may come to assume they are always in a guest machine. However, other security implications of VMEs would come to the forefront. VME detection could become a precursor to VME escape, whereby an attacker might leak classified information from a more sensitive guest machine to a more easily compromised guest, undermining isolation and exposing sensitive data. An attacker or malicious code that detects a VME might try to move from a guest machine to the host machine or to other guests, compromising security, infecting other guest systems, or breaking into higher levels of security classification.

Technological Convergence
Digital convergence, which has been predicted at least since the late 1970s, is starting to happen rapidly.[10] Previously disparate technologies, such as telephones, radio, television, and desktop computers, increasingly use a common set of underlying technologies and communications networks. Convergence has recently been manifested with the migration of PC-based technology—hardware such as processors and hard drives as well as software such as operating systems and browsers—to non-PC products. Internet telephony, for example, is growing rapidly in companies, government agencies, and households, and new phone companies are being formed to provide related services. Many radio stations stream their audio across the Internet to augment their broadcast service and reach new audiences around the world. Music sales on the Internet have been a small share of music sales (6 percent in 2007), but the percentage is increasing rapidly.[11] Some music playback and video equipment incorporates hard drives to store digitized music files or video footage. Apple, Google, and others now sell or distribute television shows on the Internet, both for streaming (ABC's most popular shows, for example) and for download (YouTube, Google, and

others). YouTube announced that it handled over 100 million video downloads per day as of mid-2006.[12] These are typically homemade videos or captured broadcast or cable television snippets ranging from 2 to 5 minutes in length. Through services such as Google Earth and other satellite and mapping services, cyberspace is influencing perception and use of the physical world. High-quality, easily available maps allow people to understand their surroundings and even to manipulate them better.

Convergence can help to lower transmission costs for content because a single network—the Internet—can deliver disparate services. Consumers can move content among different types of systems—from a portable music player to a computer to a television, for example. However, from a security and reliability perspective, convergence brings new risks. An attack or an accidental disruption can have a more significant impact because a larger population of users and organizations is relying on a common infrastructure using common technologies. Such disruptions may affect services that users may not realize are related. For example, if an enterprise's Internet connection goes down, most users will expect to be unable to get email, but in some enterprises, critical business functionality might also become inaccessible if it depends on Web applications residing on third-party servers on the Internet. Major upgrades of converged infrastructure may be more complex because their implications for multiple services must be considered but perhaps cannot all even be anticipated. Most organizations, and the ISPs they rely on, strive not to have potential single points of failure in their physical deployments, but their use of common operating system software (typically Windows, variations of UNIX and Linux, or Cisco's Internetwork Operating System) may raise the risk of downtime and attack.

As significant services such as telephony, television, and business transactions move to broadband Internet connectivity, modern economies increasingly depend on the Internet infrastructure and on the ISPs. In many countries, competing ISPs have taken on a role filled by monopolistic telephone companies in the past as stewards of the nation's communications infrastructure. In the United States, the older system was dominated by the Regional Bell Operating Companies and their parent company, AT&T, which provided this stewardship under significant Federal, state, and even local regulatory control that constrained the rates they could charge for service and set standards for service reliability. In most countries, such regulations do not exist for the collection of ISPs and Internet backbone providers, who have nonetheless provided the United States at least with relatively high reliability.

There are even bigger implications as the networks used to manage various critical infrastructures converge with the Internet itself. The super-visory control and data acquisition (SCADA) systems associated with control of electrical power distribution, water distribution, pipelines, and manufacturing are increasingly managed using PC- and Internet-related technologies. Although most SCADA systems are not directly connected to the Internet itself, they are managed via maintenance ports that use the same technologies as the Internet, and even isolated SCADA systems sometimes communicate with laptop PCs that also connect to the Internet from time to time. These maintenance ports could offer a backdoor avenue for attack, exposing SCADA systems. Once convergence occurs, attacks, infections, and disruptions launched from other aspects of cyberspace could have amplified economic effects. Convergence of technologies also implies convergence of threats and vulnerabilities that thus amplify risk, perhaps in unexpected ways. Even if the SCADA systems themselves could withstand such an attack, the management systems controlling them might be disabled or impaired, affecting control of critical infrastructure facilities and thus preventing alerts and corrective actions in response to an emergency.

Another area of network convergence is the rise of voice over Internet protocol (VoIP) services. The most familiar aspect of VoIP involves end-user telephony; for example, cable companies and others advertise phone service carried over broadband Internet connections. VoIP, however, is not limited to carrying calls from individuals to their local phone companies: many long-distance companies are already transporting at least some of their long-distance traffic by means of IP-based networks to take advantage of the lower costs associated with transporting such calls over broadband pipes that mix Internet data and voice. Even users relying on traditional phone lines—the so-called Plain Old Telephone Service (POTS)—may thus have their calls carried in part over the Internet, unaware that VoIP was associated with the call made POTS-line to POTS-line. A major concern is that the existing non-VoIP long-distance network may not be able to handle all of the long-distance traffic if the Internet and its VoIP systems were impaired. Because design of local and long-distance telephony capacity now presumes that a certain call volume will be handled via VoIP, the telephony infrastructure might not be able to handle the entire load if all VoIP became unavailable due to an Internet attack or outage. This is of particular concern for emergency organizations that must rely on public facilities to communicate, including law enforcement, government, and military groups. The converse could also be a problem, if a cellular outage caused a surge in VoIP calls, overloading the carrying capacity of the Internet.

As convergence continues, many more services will be delivered to homes, government agencies, and military operations via combined networks. Even when multiple networks exist, gateways may shuttle information between one network and another, resulting in a network of interconnected networks. The resulting converged systems and networks will offer some highly useful synergies, but at the cost of increased risk.

Increased Noise in Most Aspects of Cyberspace

As cyberspace has grown, various aspects of it have become more full of *noise*, or apparently random data without meaning to most users or applications. Consider spam, or unsolicited email that typically has a commercial message: spam comprised about 30 percent of all email in 2003, has gone to over 80 percent today, and continues to rise. Newsgroups often host messages full of apparent nonsense that just takes up space. Another form of cyberspace noise is the clutter of advertisements on major Web sites today, including pop-up ads. Search engine results often include noise, either from mistaken matches returned by search engine software or Web sites that deliberately try to fool search engines in order to be included inappropriately in search results. Uniform resource locators, which point to Web pages, are increasingly cluttered with complex symbols and in some cases even small software snippets designed to run in browsers. Roving, automated Web crawlers search the Internet looking for Web sites with forms to fill out, which they then populate with advertisements or political messages. The Internet even sees raw packet noise. "Sniffing" software that monitors an unfiltered Internet connection with no regular use will see a significant amount of nonsense traffic, as users around the world inadvertently type incorrect IP addresses, attackers scan for weak target sites, and backscatter is generated by spoofed attacks against other sites. The Internet is indeed a noisy place, and it is growing noisier.

Noise is helpful to those wanting to hide: a noisy environment can let covert channels blend in, so attackers can communicate and coordinate. An attacker might send spam messages, newsgroup postings, or even raw packets to millions of targets on the Internet just to obscure delivery of a single encoded message meant for a single individual or group. Such a message is not likely to be noticed in the day-to-day noise distributed via these same mechanisms. What's more, the location-laundering mechanisms pioneered by the spammers would make it very difficult to find the source of such a message and, given that the message is spewed to millions of destinations, locating the true intended recipient is likewise a major hurdle. Finding an information needle in the haystack of noise data is difficult, and as noise increases, it becomes harder.

In the future, the Internet will likely become even noisier, as many new services are deployed that are filled with advertising and nonsensical inform-ation. Computer attackers and political dissidents will likely increasingly use this noise to camouflage their plans and communications with each other.

Advancement of Computer and Network Attack and Exploitation Methodologies

A major trend fueling the evolution of computer attacks and exploits involves the rising profit motive associated with malicious code.[13] Some attackers sell to the highest bidder customized malicious code to control victim machines. They may rent out armies of infected systems useful for spam delivery, phishing schemes, denial-of-service attacks, or identity theft. Spyware companies and overly aggressive advertisers buy such code to infiltrate and control victim machines. A single infected machine displaying pop-up ads, customizing search engine results, and intercepting keystrokes for financial accounts could net an attacker $1 per month or more. A keystroke logger on an infected machine could help the attacker gather credit card numbers and make $1,000 or more from that victim before the fraud is discovered. With control of 10,000 machines, an attacker could set up a solid profit flow from cyber crime. Organized crime groups may assemble collectives of such attackers to create a business, giving rise to a malicious code industry. In the late 1990s, most malicious code publicly released was the work of determined hobbyists, but today, attackers have monetized their malicious code; their profit centers throw off funds that can be channeled into research and development to create more powerful malicious software and refined business models, as well as to fund other crimes.

When criminals figure out a reliable way to make money from a given kind of crime, incidents of that kind of crime inevitably rise. Computer attackers have devised various business models that are low risk, in that the attackers' chances of being apprehended are very small when they carefully cover their tracks in cyberspace. They can make hundreds of thousands or even many millions of dollars.

A factor fueling the growth of cyber attacks is bot software. Named after an abbreviated form of the word *robot*, this software allows an attacker to control a system across the Internet. A single attacker or group may set up vast botnets—groups of infected machines—scattered around the world.[14] Bot-controlled machines give attackers economies of scale in launching attacks and allow them to set up virtual supercomputers that could rival the computer power of a nation-state. They can use that resource to conduct a massive flood, to crack crypto keys or passwords, or to mine for sensitive financial data used in identity theft.

Bots and other computer attack tools have become highly modular, using interchangeable software components that allow attackers to alter functionality quickly to launch new kinds of attacks. Common bots today include 50 to 100 different functional modules; an attacker could shut off or remove those modules not needed for a given attack, while more easily integrating new code features. Other modular attack tools include exploitation frameworks, which create packaged exploitation code that can infiltrate a target machine that is vulnerable (because it is misconfigured or unpatched). Just as interchangeable parts revolutionized military equipment in the early 19th century and consumer manufacturing in the early 20th century, interchangeable software components today offer computer attackers and exploiters significant advantages in flexibility and speed of evolution.

Speeding up evolution further, attackers increasingly rely on exploit and bot code that morphs itself, dynamically creating a functionally equivalent version with different sets of underlying code. Such polymorphic code helps attackers evade the signature-based detection tools used by the dominant antivirus and antispyware technology of today. This dynamically self-altering code is also harder to filter, given that it constantly modulates its underlying software. This "moving target" of code also makes analysis by defenders more difficult. Polymorphic code furthers attackers' goals because the longer the attackers have control of a botnet by evading filters and signature-based detection, the more money they can realize from the infected systems.

Another trend in attacks involves "phishing" email: an attacker pretending to be a trusted organization or individual sends email that aims to dupe a user into revealing sensitive information or installing malicious software. Attackers often spoof or mimic email from legitimate e-commerce and financial services companies to try to trick a user into surfing to a bogus Web site that appears to be a retailer or bank. When the unsuspecting user enters account information, the attacker harvests this data, using it for identity theft. More recent phishing attacks include so-called spear phishing attacks that target a particular organization or even individuals. Such phishing email may appear to come from a trusted individual, such as a corporate executive, government manager, or military officer, and exhorts the recipient to take some action. Simply clicking on a link in a spear-phishing email could allow the attacker to exploit the victim's browser, installing a bot on that machine that would act as the attacker's agent inside of the victim enterprise.

In phone phishing, an attacker sends email with a phone number for the victim to call or even leaves POTS voice mail with a recording asking the user to call back. The calls appear to go to a major U.S. or European bank, perhaps by using the area code of 212 associated with New York City. Attackers use VoIP technology with standard voice mail software to transfer the calls outside of the United States or Europe to a voice mail system located elsewhere; a friendly recorded voice then asks the user for confidential account information. Phone phishing is automated, telephone-based criminal social engineering on a worldwide scale.

The attack and exploitation issues described in this section reinforce one another, allowing the attackers to dominate more "ground" for longer times in cyberspace, evading authorities and making money while doing so.

Social Trends

Finally, we turn to the social trends that may result from changes in cyberspace.

Worldwide Technological Development, with Different Localized Emphases

Throughout the 1980s and much of the 1990s, the locus of cyberspace evolution was the United States and Europe. There, for example, the Internet originated with the Defense Advanced Research Projects Agency, many of its standards were developed by the Internet Engineering Task Force, and the World Wide Web standards were created at CERN in Geneva. More recently, however, the trend is toward more internationalization of cyberspace deployment and technological development. A large fraction of the planet's population is now online; over 1 billion people had at least rudimentary access to the Internet by 2007.[15] The Internet is, however, only one aspect of cyberspace: today, cell phones give more than 2 billion people the ability to tap into the world's telephony network. This lowers barriers to entry and allowed players from around the world to participate in cyberspace activities, for good or ill. While this trend is broad-based, various countries have carved out particular niches of their focus in cyberspace. For example, China has aggressively moved into manufacturing computers, network equipment, and telecommunications infrastructure and devices. India offers various services using the distribution media of the Internet, including call center support, software development, tax preparation, and other knowledge-based services. Europe, South Korea, and the United States have widespread broadband access and major software development, both by commercial companies and open-source initiatives. Europe has been particularly strong in cell phone development and Japan in hand-held gadgetry such as games, digital cameras, and video players.

A typical computer, network router, or operating system involves hardware and software assembled from several countries; the true source of given components may be difficult or impossible to track down. Thus, the involvement of more countries in the advancement of global high-tech infrastructures means that covert monitoring and control capabilities for exploitation and disruption could be added at numerous points in the supply chain outside of the United States.

These overall national areas of technological dominance are blurring with time. Some countries are making major investments in underlying bandwidth and tweaking incentives so they can become havens for high technology and new corporate development. Such activities have diminished the overall U.S. dominance of cyberspace as more and more significant contributions are made on a worldwide basis, not just by U.S.-based or European companies. Even U.S.-based companies, such as Microsoft and Google, are investing in research and development operations outside of the United States, particularly in China. Such a shift has significant intellectual property implications, as innovations devised outside of the United States by international corporations offer fewer avenues for U.S. control and increased control by other countries.

From an economic perspective, the U.S. tendency has been to rely generally on a broad free-market approach to technological development. Some other countries have relied on targeted incentives for specific technologies in an attempt to leap ahead of other players. These differing approaches have contributed to the trend of different emphases in various countries' technological development.

The trend toward internationalization of cyberspace technological change is especially visible in the realm of computer and network attacks. In the 1990s, most attacks, and indeed almost all publicly released computer attack tools (both free and commercial), came from the United States or Europe. In the early 2000s, however, computer attacks went international. Several widespread worms have been released by citizens of countries not commonly associated with high technology: in 2000, the Love Bug computer virus was released by a student in the Philippines, and in 2005, the Zotob bot was released by a developer from Morocco, funded by an individual from Turkey.[16] There have been plausible allegations of Chinese probing of cyberspace, including the highly publicized Titan Rain series of attacks against U.S. military facilities.[17] North Korea, not a typical bastion of computer technology, has boasted of its cyberwar hacking abilities and is rumored to run a hacking training program.[18]

Not just attack tools but attacks themselves have taken on a more pronounced international flavor. Ten years ago, the origin of most attacks across the public Internet was within the United States and Europe, usually a single spot. Attacks typically now come simultaneously from multiple countries, often a dozen or more. Some of these attacks are conducted by one individual in one location using bot-infected machines in other countries to mask the source of the attack, while other attacks are launched by coordinated attackers located in multiple countries. Attackers sometimes log in to U.S. systems from outside the country and use them as a base for attacks against other targets or for hosting propaganda. Some attackers motivated by geopolitical or nationalism issues launch an attack from one country against another hostile country, while others choose to launch an attack between friendly countries, hoping it will escape scrutiny. Thus, attacks sometimes come from Canada to the United States when the attackers themselves, located elsewhere, use the Canadian machines in an effort to blend in with normal traffic between the two allies.

These trends are likely to continue, as broadband access, technical training and expertise, and high-technology industries spread. For decades, students from overseas received training in high technology at U.S. academic institutions, and many took their expertise back to their home countries. More recently, world-class high-technology universities have been established in India (including the Indian Institute of Technology) and China (with its University of Science and Technology of China); thus, many students worldwide now receive high-tech training indigenously. The gap between levels of technological skill in the United States or in Europe and those in the rest of the world is shrinking and will continue to do so. Of course, the United States and Europe will keep pushing ahead to new technologies, and their existing base is an advantage, but yesterday's gaps have significantly narrowed.

Rise in Online Communities, Collaboration, and Information-sharing

Another major cyberspace trend is the rise in online communities made up of people or organizations with common interests who coordinate in cyberspace to share information and achieve other goals. As the term is most commonly used, an *online community* refers to a social setting in cyberspace, such as MySpace, LinkedIn, and Orkut, where consumers with common interests communicate and share personal profiles, business contacts, and so forth. Such sites have flourished recently; MySpace had over 300 million accounts for users around the world as of 2007.[19] Such social online communities also yield information- and data-mining opportunities to law enforcement, as users provide detailed information about their lives and their network of acquaintances. Unfortunately, there have also been high-profile cases of stalkers misusing this information to target children. While today's specific most popular online communities might be a mere fad (the Friendster site saw its popularity plummet with the rise of MySpace, only to rebound later), the concept of online communities in the form of social networking sites is likely to be an enduring trend.

Another type of community is the blog, an online diary where a writer shares information and commentary about politics, hobbies, or other interests. Most bloggers allow others to provide comments on their blog, resulting in a community of sorts. The blogosphere (as all of the blogs on the Internet are collectively known) is witnessing very rapid growth: there were over 20 million blogs in January 2006.[20] Some blogs have become quite popular and have helped shape political debates and news stories. Blogs will likely become more consequential as the distinction between the blogosphere and traditional news media blurs. Many major newspapers have started their own blogging operations, for example, or have hired bloggers to write content for the Internet and for printed media.

Making use of social networking and blogging for a very different objective, terrorist organizations have also formulated online communities, to aid in fundraising, recruitment, propaganda, and command and control of their operations.[21] Some of these sites are available to the public, especially those associated with propaganda, fundraising, and communiqués from terrorist leadership, while other sites, containing more sensitive information about the organization, are available only to those specifically invited.

Another use of online communities involves integrated supply chains, in which a given manufacturer relies on a host of suppliers, who in turn rely on their own suppliers, distributed in countries around the world, the whole controlled through cyberspace. With an integrated supply chain, messages regarding inventory, capacity, and payment can be transferred quickly, allowing the manufacturer to cope more efficiently with changes in demand and possible disruptions to supply. Dell Computer famously relies on integrated supply chains using Internet technology; many other companies are also heavy users of these technologies, including United Parcel Service and Wal-Mart.[22] Given the transnational nature of such supply chains, each individual country through which the chain passes has some form of cyberpower over that chain, with the ability to tax, slow down, or even shut off a vital component of the chain. However, with the economic importance of these chains, and their corporate owners' ability to use cyberspace to reroute capacity and demand or to set up new chains rapidly, most countries will probably use some restraint in their exercise of such power.

Online communities also encompass sites associated with consumer commerce, such as Amazon.com and eBay; these have created a lively interchange of buyers and sellers, with complex ranking, preference, and voting systems for products and providers. Some online communities involve participants in even deeper immersion in the cyber world. An example is Second Life, a site run by Linden Research, which describes their offering as a "3D online digital world imagined, created, and owned by its residents." Users of this community create their own avatars, or online representatives, to explore and alter the virtual reality space inside of the community and to create objects to use or buildings to inhabit. People meet, have relationships, and conduct business transactions inside of Second Life, which even has its own currency.[23] While Second Life is targeted at adults, a special area within the Second Life world is geared to teenagers. Another example, for children 5 to 10 years old, is an online world of game-playing and avatars called Webkinz created by the toy company Ganz; it, too, has its own digital economy. There are many other such communities.

Conclusion

Where are these evolutionary trends heading? The future of cyberspace is likely to involve the embedding of Internet and PC technology deeply into many everyday objects, including not only technical items such as computers, telephones, radios, and televisions, but also items not now associated with cyberspace, such as home appliances, consumer products, clothing, and more. These everyday objects will incorporate software intelligence, processing information delivered wirelessly by a broadband connection. Global positioning systems and RFID tags will allow these everyday objects to locate and interact with each other in the physical world. Cars, ships, airplanes, weapons systems, and their components will all become more intelligent and interactive, increasingly without direct human control. The economies of developed nations will rely on this interconnected grid of objects.

Unfortunately, however, the grid is built on technologies not consciously designed to handle information of such an extent and value. Security flaws will let attackers establish widespread collections of infected objects they can use to exploit other objects, manipulate target organizations, and possibly disrupt countries and economies. Such actions are not at all far-fetched, based on the accumulated evolutionary trends of the past decade. Revolutionary changes, such as those described elsewhere in this book, could have an even bigger impact on cyberspace.

CHAPTER 7

Information Security Issues in Cyberspace

Edward Skoudis

THIS CHAPTER examines attacks and defenses associated with Internet technologies, defined as systems that are either directly or indirectly connected to the global Internet, relying on the transmission control protocol (TCP)/Internet protocol (IP) communications suite.[1] As described in chapter 4, cyberspace relies on a vast collection of underlying technologies. Security issues associated with these technologies will be analyzed from an attack and a defense perspective to provide a better understanding of the technological options available to both attackers and defenders and of various policy issues associated with security technologies. This chapter focuses first on the most common attacks today and those that will likely pose a significant threat for the foreseeable future. It then discusses the most widely available defensive technologies, how they thwart attacks, and various public policy issues associated with each defense.

With the increasing convergence of technology, Internet-based systems are among the fastest growing components of cyberspace. Phone, television, radio, and financial transactions increasingly rely on the Internet. This chapter focuses on Internet attacks and defenses; analogous concepts, if different technologies, can be applied to other cyberspace elements not associated with the Internet. For example, an attacker might deliberately cause widespread Web site outages via a denial-of-service flood against various Internet components (comparable to jamming or overwhelming a radio communications channel to block the exchange of information). With these Web sites down and the links connecting them to the Internet clogged with flood traffic, other ancillary services that use the same network, such as Internet telephony, streaming radio, and television services, could likewise be impacted.

Internet Attacks

Various forms of cyberspace attacks occur every day on the Internet, ranging from virus infections to massive automated credit card thefts involving millions of consumers. In this chapter, attacks are categorized as small- or large-scale.[2] Small-scale attacks may cause limited damage to a relatively small number of people (from one to many thousands). For example, most viruses today infect hundreds or thousands of people and represent a nuisance that can typically be cleaned quickly with an antivirus program. Examples of spyware, programs that surreptitiously undermine a user's privacy, fall into this small-scale category as well. While spyware infections in their totality may affect 100 million machines or more, each individual falls into the small-scale range.

Large-scale attacks are those that have potential impact on millions of users, possibly disabling pieces of the Internet so users within a given country or geographic region cannot get access at all, or compromising the accounts of millions of users to steal sensitive information for committing fraud.

Small-scale Attacks

Attacks on the small scale are far more common than large-scale attacks. Throughout the 1990s, the dominant threats to systems connected to the public Internet came from hobbyists experimenting with viruses and other malicious code and small-scale criminals looking to cash in on isolated cyber crime. More insidious threats may have existed, such as organized crime or nation-states engaging in Internet-based reconnaissance, but these were not a major issue at the time. However, around 2002, the threat quickly changed: organized crime groups began to use a variety of cyber crime techniques, including shady advertising schemes, online scams, and other attacks, to make money. Today, worldwide criminal businesses are based on cyber crime. This section summarizes the most common of these attacks.

Spyware. Many contemporary small-scale attacks on the Internet are carried out using spyware, which focuses on gathering information from and about users and is installed on a user's machine without notice or consent. Very aggressive companies and cyber criminals use spyware to gather information about users, often treading in a gray area of legality. Some online advertisers, gaming companies, pornographic Web sites, and others stray into violating users' privacy with spyware as they carry out various money-making practices. Spyware is installed on an end-user's desktop or laptop computer by an attacker either exploiting software vulnerabilities on the machine or tricking the user into installing the spyware by bundling it with some other program. Once installed, such spyware might track user activity, inject advertisements into a user's browsing session, or even steal confidential information or documents.

The most benign forms of spyware track user interactions across a series of Web sites. Advertisers and other organizations have a financial interest in determining user Web surfing habits so they can customize advertisements to maximize sales of a product or service. The simplest form of spyware is a tracking cookie, a small piece of data that a Web site pushes to a user's browser for storage on the user's machine. Whenever the browser accesses that Web site again or other sites affiliated with the spyware company, the cookie is presented back to the associated site, and by this means the user's access of all affiliated sites can be tracked. Tracking cookies are only transmitted to and from Web sites affiliated with the site that originally sent the cookie to the user's browser and can only be used to track user actions between affiliated sites, not all of the user's surfing outside of the affiliate sites.

To get around these limitations, more aggressive spyware companies may install software on a user's machine that tracks all Web surfing activities to any sites. Instead of relying on a cookie, the spyware companies install software on the user's machine that watches the user's activities. The data entered into Web sites and the date and time of each interaction may be transmitted to the spyware company across the Internet. This stolen data may include credit card numbers and passcodes, which a thief can use to make illicit charges against the victim's account.

Other forms of spyware make use of duplicitous advertising and redirection to try to cash in on Internet-based advertising, a multibillion-dollar-a-year business. The advertiser typically pays the referrer (the Web site that forwarded a user to the ad Web server) a fraction of a cent or more for each ad displayed in a user's browser. If the user clicks through on the ad, the rate of pay is higher. These small payments aggregate to billions of dollars. Spyware purveyors may surreptitiously install software on users' computers that fetches ads from the Internet and presents them on the browser or via a popup ad. Some of the more aggressive spyware customizes ads to appear inside the content of other Web sites. For example, spyware may wait for a user to perform a search at a popular search engine such as Google, Yahoo!, or MSN Search. Before the results are displayed in the browser window, they are edited by the local spyware on the victim's machine. This spyware might reorder search results, or inject its own ads inline onto the browser screen. Ads that appear to come from Google might actually be generated by locally installed spyware on a machine.

Some spyware redirects browsers to affiliates of the spyware creator. When the user tries to access a major search engine, for example, the spyware may redirect the browser to a search engine that displays advertisements for which the spyware creator is paid. The user's browsing is hijacked and directed to locations chosen by the spyware creators. For example, when a user tries to access a major retailer online, their browser may automatically jump to a different retailer associated with the spyware creator.

Some spyware focuses on stealing information from users by searching a hard drive for sensitive or proprietary documentation that it sends to the attacker. One of the most insidious forms is a keystroke logger, which records everything typed into the keyboard of an infected machine, such as account numbers typed into a financial services Web site login page, and transmits the information to an attacker.

Bots and rootkits. An attacker may use *bot* software—the name is derived from the word *robot*—to get complete control of an infected machine across the Internet. Such an attacker is sometimes referred to as the *bot-herder.* A collection of bot-infected machines is known as a *botnet* and may range in size from a few thousand machines to many millions of systems.

By controlling an infected system, bots can be used as a form of spyware, tracking user Web surfing habits, stealing files, or logging keystrokes. Bot-herders can also do more damage by harnessing the computing and network resources of a botnet to achieve other goals. For example, software distributed to all systems in a botnet could operate as a distributed supercomputer to crack encryption keys or passwords many thousands of times faster than a single computer could. Attackers can send spam email via the botnet at a much faster rate than they could with only a single computer. Bots can launder the Internet source address of an attacker who configures bots as anonymous packet forwarders, which strip information from packets directed through them. Forwarding information through a dozen or more anonymizing bots makes tracking criminal activity back to an individual attacker much more difficult for investigators.

Bot-herders interact with and control their botnets in a variety of ways. They may, for example, place commands on a Web page, either one maintained by the attacker or a public one such as a social networking site. Alternatively, they may control their botnet using an Internet Relay Chat (IRC) server, which is designed for chatting but also is useful in sending messages to large numbers of systems. Such methods expose attackers to a single point of failure: if an IRC server, social networking Web site, or user profile controlling the bots disappears due to the work of diligent investigators, the botnet becomes headless. Thus, some bot-herders have turned to distributed peer-to-peer communications protocols, similar to the Internet telephony service Skype. Instead of relying on a centralized point of control, individual nodes seek and find other nearby nodes in peer-to-peer networks. Diligent investigators may shut down hundreds or thousands of bots in the network, but they will still have disrupted only a small fraction of the botnet.

Large-scale removal of bots would undermine the attacker's business model, so bots are increasingly bundled with rootkits, software that alters the operating system to lie about and hide the attacker's files, programs, and network communications, thus concealing the attacker's presence on a machine. Some bots prevent antivirus and personal firewall protections of the system from working. Bots hidden by rootkits are widely used by cyber criminals today.

Spam and phishing. Unsolicited commercial email, commonly known as spam, makes money. Millions of email messages daily advertise pharmaceuticals, software, and consumer electronics goods. Most spam is merely an annoyance and can be controlled with antispam email filters, which look for common patterns associated with spam. However, the infrastructure created by spammers to send email is increasingly being used to commit scams, fraud, and cyber crime.

Phishing attacks are one of the most common forms of online scam. They typically involve millions of emails, apparently from a legitimate company such as an online bank or merchant, announcing a problem with the recipient's accounts. The emails try to dupe users into clicking on a link that appears to point to a legitimate business Web site but actually takes the user to an imposter site controlled by the attacker and designed to resemble the e-commerce site. The site asks the user for a login name and password or other account information, which the attacker's software retains for fraud and criminal use. There are over 100,000 phishing Web sites on the Internet, and millions of phishing emails are sent every day.[3] Phishers are also increasingly using email that appears to come from taxing authorities, government benefits organizations, and other government agencies.

Increasingly common is *spear-phishing*, in which phishers choose a particular group of target recipients either more likely to succumb to a scam, such as the elderly, or who have access to sensitive information, such as some military personnel.

Spam and phishing email distribution infrastructures have become more resistant to suppression by law enforcement. From 1999 to 2003, thwarting schemes that used a dozen or so email servers to send spoofed email was quite straightforward. Once investigators detected the large number of bogus email messages originating from the spammer's mail servers, they could add each server's address to a blacklist to be blocked by legitimate mail servers around the world. Once on the blacklist, the attacker's email servers would be shut down, forcing the attackers to interrupt their business as they moved to different servers.

Starting around 2003, however, spammers and phishers began using mail servers operated by others that had been configured inappropriately to act as mail relays. Mail relays accept email and forward it to other mail servers. The attackers would send their spam through these innocent but poorly configured third-party mail servers, which in turn would forward the spam to other mail servers and to its recipients. Again, the Internet community did a reasonable job of handling this problem, typically through blacklists. When the third-party mail server being used by the attacker was added to a blacklist, mail servers around the world would start dropping messages from all users on that server, regardless of whether the mail was legitimate or not. The legitimate users of the third-party mail server would complain about the dropped messages, and the company would quickly turn off mail relaying, a function seldom needed on Internet-accessible mail servers today.

Attackers responded with further refinements, such as relying on botnets of 100,000 or more systems instead of a dozen mail servers or 100 mail relays. Disabling or even blacklisting such an enormous number of systems is impractical. Because consumer end-user computer systems almost never need to act as mail servers or relays, many Internet service providers (ISPs) block any normal mail server traffic on their networks that is associated with end-user computer systems. Unfortunately, most ISPs outside of the United States and Europe do not implement such defenses, due to the costs and lack of perceived direct benefit to the ISP itself. Furthermore, such defenses only apply to consumer systems, because most enterprise networks require mail server traffic.

Credit card fraud and identity theft. The Internet is a major vehicle for the theft and illicit use of consumer credit card accounts. Attackers steal card numbers in a variety of ways. Bot-based keystroke loggers and phishing attacks are two methods for stealing such information from end-users one at a time. Other attackers focus on sources of aggregated information, such as companies that accept credit cards. Every week, new incidents are reported involving data breaches that affect 50,000 to 1 million or more users. Attackers can sell credit card account information on the black market; card-selling exchanges on the Internet are hosted in a variety of countries, especially in Eastern Europe. Other information is also useful in fraud, such as credit histories, mortgage information, and Social Security numbers. By exploiting Web site vulnerabilities, poorly secured wireless network access, or improperly configured corporate networks, attackers frequently infiltrate systems to steal such information from companies and government agencies in order to commit fraud.

Credit card fraud usually starts with a small charge against the account to make sure that it is working. Next, the attackers continue increasing the amount they charge until the activity is detected by automated antifraud systems operated by credit card companies and issuing banks. Then the account is usually deactivated and a new card issued to the consumer. The consumer suffers the inconvenience of waiting for a new credit card, while the back-end banks typically write off the fraudulent charges.

Some attackers establish complete dossiers of information about individuals. Cyber crime organizations compile vast databases of user information from multiple breaches over time, with fields including Social Security numbers, multiple credit cards, and mortgage loan information. Given enough information, attackers can engage in identity theft. Posing as that user, criminals may acquire new credit cards or even mortgages, destroying the victim's credit in the process.

Corporate information theft. Cyber criminals may seek to steal corporations' business operations data, including trade secrets, business strategies, and other sensitive corporate information. Using the same technical means used to steal credit cards, attackers may compromise corporate networks to steal corporate secrets. Such secrets can be used for gaining competitive advantage or causing economic damage to the company. Such attacks have received little press attention, due to the reluctance of victimized companies to disclose them publicly.

Denial-of-service extortion. A particularly disruptive form of attack involves sending a large number of packets to one or more target machines to overwhelm their ability to communicate on the network, a technique known as packet flooding. With a small-scale botnet of a mere 1,000 machines, attackers could hobble the Web site of a typical medium-sized organization with a packet flood. For some organizations, such as Internet merchants, such a packet flood could have catastrophic economic consequences. If customers cannot reach the site, some companies are, in effect, closed for business. Cyber criminals have capitalized on this possibility through the use of extortion, demanding payment to prevent a flood or offering to provide "security" or "protection" services for a price and threatening dire consequences if payment is withheld. Attackers can usually sustain a flood for 3 days to a week; any longer and most ISPs can differentiate the flood traffic so that they can start shunning it. This type of extortion scheme proliferated in the mid-2000s, first targeting online gambling and commercial pornographic Web sites, then small- to mid-sized mainstream e-commerce sites and financial services institutions. A variety of companies have paid under such threats; others have refused and may have suffered the consequences.

Large-scale Attacks

In the early 2000s, the dominant threats on the Internet shifted from hobbyists and isolated criminals to organized crime groups. The major threat vector could evolve again, possibly toward larger scale attacks waged by nation-states or nonstate actors seeking to cause widespread damage. The Estonian cyber attacks in spring 2007 could be a harbinger of future attacks: for several weeks, waves of packet floods targeted major financial institutions and government agencies in Estonia, which is heavily reliant on its Internet infrastructure.[4] Filters and shunning technology blocked the attack only after extended downtime for some sites. The attack may have been retaliation for a decision by Estonian officials to move statues commemorating the Soviet victory over the Nazis in Estonia during World War II. It is unclear whether the attack was directed by individuals inside or outside the Russian government; Russian officials have denied government involvement. Either way, this directed attack represents the first explicit large-scale computer attack for political rather than economic purposes.

Four types of cyber attack could damage a large target population: denial-of-service packet floods, exploitation of infrastructure components, damage of client systems with widespread botnets, and mass credit card fraud with identity theft. Each uses existing capabilities and technological means already accessible to sufficiently funded and motivated nations and nonstate actors. For each type of attack vector, smaller scale historical examples from the past decade suggest the shape of larger scale attacks in the future.

Denial-of-service packet floods. Web servers of various companies and organizations are frequently subject to packet-flooding attacks by disgruntled customers, political opponents, or others. These are small-scale attacks by the definition offered in this chapter, but attackers might also target systems that have a larger impact, as this section explains.

Today, most flood traffic originates with a botnet of perhaps 100,000 to millions of machines, a size already commonly used by organized crime. The largest botnet publicly documented to date used 1.5 million machines. Dutch law enforcement authorities documented such a botnet in October 2005. A handful of other multimillion-system botnets controlled by organized crime groups have also been identified.

Although most of today's botnets are used by criminals in small-scale attacks to make money, some of the larger botnets have been used in large-scale flooding attacks against specific Web sites or the Internet's infrastructure. A large-scale attack might involve flooding critical Web sites and related systems of a given organization, business sector, or country. In 2000, for example, many major e-commerce sites in the United States, including stock-trading firms Ameritrade and E*Trade, were attacked with a packet flood. The 2007 attacks against Estonia were a similar large-scale operation, launched from several cooperating botnets. In a similar fashion, several major e-commerce retailers might be flooded in an effort to strangle a whole country's financial transactions.

Alternatively, to broaden the damage, attackers might seek to flood the Internet infrastructure of a target country or even the Internet as a whole. While the Internet was devised to have redundancy and the ability to bypass interruptions of traffic flow, an attack against certain portions of the Internet infrastructure could restrict traffic flow and impact millions of users.

Of particular concern from an infrastructure perspective are the domain name system (DNS) and backbone routers. DNS is a network service that converts a system's name (such as <www.ndu.edu>) into a numeric IP address. When a user types a domain name into a browser, software on the browsing machine queries a nearby DNS server, which in turn queries other servers in the DNS hierarchy to retrieve the domain-name-to-IP-address mapping, a so-called address record. The destination IP address for the given Web site is placed in every packet of data for that site, so that the network can carry the packets to the right location. Thus, DNS represents a critical component of the Internet, mapping human-entered names into network-understandable and -routable IP addresses.

At the top of the DNS hierarchy are 13 root servers that are distributed around the world; they provide information about various lower level DNS servers.[5] When lower level servers are booted up, they may contact the root DNS servers to retrieve and cache information about other components of the DNS hierarchy so that they can start responding to user queries. If one root name server is unavailable, software automatically adjusts, moving to the next root name server to retrieve the information requested.

However, if all 13 root name servers could not be accessed because of a packet flood of bogus DNS requests, the Internet itself, for most users, would decay as more and more IP addresses could not be fetched. The decay would be gradual, because lower level DNS servers temporarily hold on to records in their local cache for a period that typically varies between a few seconds and a few days, depending on how frequently the owner of the record plans on updating DNS entries. If the root DNS servers were all annihilated, more and more systems on the Internet would become unavailable to users as records expired over time, except those users who had memorized or stored name-to-address mappings for sites that they wanted to access.

Flood attacks against the 13 root DNS servers were attempted in 2002 and again in 2007.[6] In 2002, 9 of the 13 servers were taken offline in a massive flood. While the four remaining root DNS servers were able to handle the load, the attack did cause a great deal of concern about the robustness of the DNS infrastructure. To help alleviate this concern, the operators of most of the root name servers deployed a technology called *anycast*, which allows multiple distributed machines to act together as one server. Therefore, while there are still 13 named root DNS "servers," many of them are really collections of dozens of machines deliberately distributed across different continents. As a result of anycast deployment, the next attempted DNS root server flood in February 2007 was far less successful: only two of the root name servers were significantly affected, and the vast majority of Internet users did not even notice the attack.

Besides floods against DNS servers, backbone routers operated by ISPs represent another critical infrastructure component. These routers are the central points in the network through which traffic flows. Routers are essentially specialized computers that move traffic from subnetwork to subnetwork between different physical interfaces of the router itself. These backbone routers are operated by large ISPs. Many major countries rely on several ISPs, although some lack such diversity. In some countries, a single legacy telecommunications provider offers Internet access; elsewhere, corporate mergers may be decreasing the number of unique ISPs. Typically, all traffic is directed through 10 to 100 backbone routers (or perhaps as many as several hundred) that constitute the main infrastructure of an ISP. A determined attacker with a large botnet—perhaps hundreds of thousands or millions of machines—could target the infrastructure routers of a single ISP, or the ISPs of a whole country, to try to overwhelm them with bogus traffic. With all of the routers choking on bogus packets, users and servers within that country would have difficulty accessing systems within the country and could be completely blocked from accessing systems outside of the country.

Of the three packet flood targets for large-scale attacks described above, the most likely to succumb to such a flood are the e-commerce and e-government Web servers, followed by DNS servers, followed by ISP backbone routers, because of the redundancy introduced by DNS with anycast technology and the redundancy of the ISP architectures of most countries. While major e-commerce Web site operators often have 10 or more redundant Web sites, these systems are not as robust as the DNS or ISP infrastructure.

Among the different kinds of packet floods, the most frequent today are synchronize (SYN) floods, hypertext transfer protocol (HTTP) floods, and DNS amplification attacks.

The first widespread SYN floods started in the United States in 1996 and have since become a daily occurrence on the Internet around the world. SYN floods involve undermining the session initiation technique used by the TCP. Most Internet-based services rely on TCP as a transport protocol, including the HTTP for Web surfing, file transfer protocol (FTP) for file transfer, and secure shell for remote system access and administration. One of the crucial properties of TCP involves the sequencing and reliable transport of packets. TCP is designed to ensure that packets arrive and that they arrive in order.

To achieve these properties, TCP depends on sequence and acknowledgment numbers that it embeds in the headers of packets. All legitimate TCP connections begin with the TCP three-way handshake, a simple interaction designed to exchange sequence numbers for that connection. To start a connection, the initiating machine (such as a Web browsing machine) generates a TCP SYN packet that includes an initial sequence number for packets going from the initiator to the receiver of that connection (say, a Web server). If the receiving machine is configured to accept the connection request, it responds with the second portion of the three-way handshake, a SYN–ACK (acknowledgment) packet, indicating that it acknowledges the sequence number it received and that it will synchronize around a new initial sequence number for all response packets. To complete the three-way handshake, the initiator then sends an ACK packet, acknowledging the sequence number the recipient wants to use. Thus, the two systems have exchanged sequence numbers, so that all packets that follow on the connection will increment the appropriate sequence number for each byte of payload data transmitted.

A SYN flood exploits this three-way handshake by stalling it two-thirds of the way through the connection initiation. The attacker sends a SYN packet, to which the recipient responds with a SYN–ACK packet. The attacker never sends the ACK to complete the three-way handshake, leaving a dangling, half-open connection on the destination machine. If this incomplete exchange is repeated thousands or millions of times per second, the target machine can become unable to respond to other requests.

In recent years, most ISPs have deployed traffic sensors to detect the distinctive traffic pattern associated with SYN floods.[7] If it is detected, they start shunning such traffic automatically, lowering or even eliminating the damage from a SYN flood. Although such technologies are increasingly widely deployed, attackers still attempt SYN floods and are sometimes successful.

Because of ISP success in preventing SYN floods, some attackers are evolving new kinds, including HTTP floods. An HTTP flood looks like legitimate traffic but involves a massive number of legitimate-looking requests. Automated tools designed to detect flood patterns have more difficulty in differentiating these attacks from normal traffic and thwarting them.

ISPs do have some mechanisms for dealing with HTTP floods. Analysts at the ISP can study the bogus HTTP request traffic coming from bots and try to characterize patterns in that traffic, such as a repeated request for a given Web page with certain parameters. Attackers seek to make their traffic difficult to identify by removing patterns that might allow an ISP to differentiate the flood traffic from the legitimate traffic. More sophisticated attackers are better at disguising their traffic.

Another flood type is a DNS amplification attack. The attacker sends small query packets to hundreds of thousands of third-party DNS servers; each query causes each server to send a larger response packet, resulting in an amplification of the traffic load. To direct this traffic load at a victim machine, the attacker sends each query from a spoofed source address, as if it came from the targeted machine. Responses addressed to the victim overwhelm the victim's network connection. The servers are not themselves the targets, but rather are used as amplifiers to inundate another victim machine with a flood.

Since 2005, DNS amplification has generated flood rates in excess of 20 gigabits per second, equivalent to the bandwidth of some backbone routers and very large e-commerce facilities. An attacker using this technique could interrupt the service of even large e-commerce players unless their ISPs can devise signatures to characterize and thwart the spurious DNS responses.

Flood attacks of these types would likely have significant impact over short periods, affecting millions of users for 12 to 72 hours. ISPs would then most likely be able to characterize that specific flood's traffic and devise methods for filtering it. However, a more persistent and technically adept attacker might plan methods for altering the characteristics of the flood as it occurs, perhaps starting with SYN floods, then simple HTTP floods, followed by even more complex traffic forms. Keeping up with such an adversary could prove difficult, and an attack might be sustained over several weeks or more. Moreover, while the ability of U.S. ISPs to devise a signature and coordinate its deployment of filtering is quite good, coordination with overseas organizations could be difficult.

Exploiting infrastructure components. Another avenue for large-scale attack involves exploiting vulnerabilities in infrastructure systems, such as backbone routers or DNS servers. The software at the heart of major infrastructure devices may have bugs or flaws; most are mere annoyances, but attackers might deliberately trigger some flaws to harm a system. Software programs to trigger such vulnerabilities are known as *exploits*.

Some software vulnerabilities could allow an attacker to cause a target machine to crash, resulting in a denial-of-service condition, or could compromise a system, with the attacker taking over administrative control of the machine and bypassing normal security measures. An attacker could simply shut the system down or use it to conduct even more insidious attacks. Having taken control of critical infrastructure components such as routers or DNS servers, attackers could redirect traffic to other destinations anywhere on the Internet so that, for example, all traffic destined for a given country's banks would be directed to a different country. System compromise might let attackers capture traffic going across the Internet, such as sensitive financial transactions, management data associated with the infrastructure itself, or business communications, which could be recorded for later analysis and use.

Once or twice a year for the past decade, independent researchers have discovered vulnerabilities in parts of the Internet infrastructure that could be exploited.[8]

Two examples illustrate the issues underlying these types of vulnerabilities and the large-scale attacks that could have resulted from them. In early 2004, researcher Paul Watson identified a TCP reset technique that could prevent routers from exchanging routing updates with each other.[9] This approach could disable routing updates on the Internet, which would have caused the network itself to degrade over several hours, ultimately resulting in a loss of connectivity for chosen segments of the Internet, such as the entire United States, or perhaps all systems associated with U.S.-to-Europe connectivity. Before this vulnerability was exploited, however, Watson publicized its existence, and large ISPs around the world and government, commercial, and military enterprises deployed a patch to mitigate the vulnerability.

Similarly, in July 2005, researcher Michael Lynn discovered a way of exploiting routers manufactured by Cisco Systems, Inc., that could have been used to crash or take over the routers and reroute traffic.[10] Lynn announced his approach to Cisco and made a presentation on it at a hacker conference; the associated vulnerabilities were then patched. This type of vulnerability could go beyond denial of service to rapid takeover and crashing of large numbers of key routers. The fix for this type of flaw would be difficult to distribute and deploy if the Internet itself were down.

Popular DNS server implementations have also had significant vulnerabilities over the past decade.[11] To launch a large-scale attack involving the exploitation of critical infrastructure systems, attackers would have to find vulnerabilities before vendors or well-intentioned security researchers do. In the past two decades, most of such flaws publicly disclosed have been discovered and publicized by independent hobbyists, commercial researchers, and the vendors themselves. Would-be attackers do not need to do any tremendously difficult analysis to find these flaws; their discovery involves looking for a series of known kinds of flaws in commercial products. Product evaluation methodologies, applied in a comprehensive fashion, can discover a significant number of these flaws. Because ISPs rely on much of the same routing software that smaller institutions do, and because other Internet infrastructure components run on software that is free or available inexpensively, a well-stocked research lab for finding these kinds of flaws can be created for between $3,000 and $20,000, a relatively small investment to discover high-impact security flaws.

The amount of time between discovery of a security vulnerability and the public release of exploit code by malicious attackers that could take over a target machine is shrinking, from 6 to 12 months in 2000 to a few days or less in 2007. Both legitimate researchers and attackers have developed automated methods of finding security-related flaws and creating exploitation code. Exploitation has begun to appear "in the wild" before vendors or legitimate security researchers discover flaws; only when systems start succumbing to the exploit is the vulnerability detected. Such attacks using previously undisclosed vulnerabilities are occurring regularly against desktop and laptop computers today. In the future, they could be used to target routers, domain name servers, and other critical infrastructure components.

Other kinds of infrastructures are increasingly being managed and controlled using the TCP/IP protocol suite and other Internet technology, including commercial-off-the-shelf switches, routers, and operating systems. Historically, supervisory control and data acquisition (SCADA) systems, which are used to manage complex installations such as nuclear power plants and electric grids, were based on proprietary communications protocol and isolated networks. This arrangement made it difficult for would-be attackers to find vulnerabilities in the technology, which was relatively difficult to acquire. Now, however, such systems—including aviation systems of commercial aircraft, military equipment, nuclear power plant monitoring, and other technologies—are increasingly using standardized TCP/IP components.

The move toward using Internet technology to interface with and manage other types of systems is based on simple economics as the technology has grown cheaper, smaller, and lighter. Internet technology is especially attractive where minimizing weight and size are important, such as in aircraft avionics and control. Rather than design and deployment of a massive and expensive network of custom equipment for managing an electrical plant, use of off-the-shelf Internet technologies can significantly lower costs.

With TCP/IP spoken by most computing systems, from mainframe computers and desktop machines to cell phones, use of commonly available hardware and software makes systems more flexible, with the ability to interface with numerous inexpensive devices. However, use of standardized protocols and common implementations by sensitive infrastructures introduces significant risk. There are tradeoffs between cost and security. Most secure would be air-gapped or isolated networks that use entirely different protocols from others; a sensitive network, such as the aviation controls of an aircraft, the SCADA systems controlling components of a power grid, or military command and control systems, could use custom network technology (not Internet protocol version 4 [IPv4]) on a network that is completely separate from the Internet. On the other end of the spectrum is integration using a common network protocol such as IPv4 on networks that are interconnected. Some protection might be offered by a firewall that polices the traffic, filtering out unneeded services and potential attacks. Even with such filters, at this end of the spectrum, there is some connectivity.

Other possible topologies strike different balances between economic benefit and lower security risk. For example, a single physical network with two or more different network protocols could achieve, if not complete isolation, at least some separation of traffic. But such solutions still involve security risk. To see why, consider one physical network with systems that use two different network protocols; call them Protocols X and Y. In this hypothetical multiprotocol network, most rank-and-file users might rely on Protocol X, whereas some special and important equipment uses Protocol Y. Only the special equipment has endpoint software to speak Protocol Y. The routers that comprise the network may, in the simplest but least secure solution, understand both Protocols X and Y so they can route packets for both protocols across the network. However, instead of making the routers aware of both Protocol X and Y, another option for implementing a multiprotocol network is to use a process whereby the entire network, including all endpoints and routers, speaks Protocol X, but only certain specialized endpoints (not routers) on the network have software that embeds Protocol Y inside of Protocol X packets. Such a "tunneling" solution is used for implementing mixed networks of IPv4, the current dominant Internet protocol, and IPv6, its successor, whose deployment is under way.

Multiprotocol networks, whether implemented with routers that speak multiple protocols or through tunneling, do yield some isolation. Attackers who had software that only spoke Protocol X could not directly attack Protocol Y systems; however, they might create, buy, or find software that can speak Protocol Y. To lower this concern, all Protocol Y traffic could be encrypted as it traverses the network, so the attacker would also have to break the encryption keys or find a flaw in the implementation of Protocol Y.

Even with encryption of Protocol Y traffic, another security problem frequently encountered in multiprotocol networks arises with the use of network gateways. With shared physical infrastructure, some users almost always will want to move data associated with Protocol X applications to Protocol Y applications. To speed up the process of such conversion, these users may introduce gateways that speak Protocol X on one side and Protocol Y on the other so they can shuttle data between the two. Even if encryption is used for all Protocol Y traffic, the gateway may act as an endpoint for the encryption.[12] A gateway may be introduced by users who are unaware of how it undermines the security of the Protocol Y machines, and such gateways could allow an attacker with only Protocol X software to exploit the machines.

Multiprotocol networks are at risk of denial-of-service flooding attacks. Even an attacker with only Protocol X software could launch a flood attack against the routers, consuming them with so many bogus Protocol X packets that they drop Protocol Y altogether, leaving the special equipment that uses only Protocol Y unreachable. Some networks configure routers to favor Protocol Y over Protocol X, but a deluge of Protocol X packets would overwhelm such a prioritization scheme.

If there is a flaw in the Protocol X routing software in the routers (such routing flaws are fairly common), an attacker could send exploit packets to compromise the routers via the Protocol X flaw, gaining control of the router, which handles both Protocol X and Protocol Y. The attacker could then intercept Protocol Y traffic, and possibly decode it, gaining the capability of using the

Protocol Y software to compromise the special equipment (in a sense, exploiting a router to create its own gateway between Protocol X and Y to exploit the specialized equipment). Multiprotocol networks offer better security than having all network components speak the same protocol, but they are not as secure as air-gapped networks in protecting against the compromise.

Real examples of such mixed networking include the Internet's most common protocol, IPv4 (usually referred to as simply IP), and Novell's old IPX protocol. Although the acronyms IP and IPX sound similar, the two protocols are very different. IP is an open protocol with numerous vendor implementations for use on the Internet, while IPX is a proprietary protocol used by Novell for some of its older enterprise network products. In the 1990s IP and IPX were often mixed on corporate networks, with IP used for Internet access of Web sites and email, and IPX used for Novell file and print sharing. Protocols X and Y could represent a myriad of other protocols as well.

Damaging client systems with widespread botnets. Another form of large-scale attack directly targets massive numbers of end-user systems such as desktop and laptop computers, cell phones, personal digital assistants, and other computing devices. Attackers could affect millions of users with bot software installed on end-user systems to cause harm to the systems themselves, such as deleting critical files or damaging the video card, hard drive controller, processor, or other hardware. An attack might corrupt files, such as financial information associated with purchases or tax preparation software. Each of these attacks could be done on a small scale, but accomplished across a large botnet, such malicious activity could have an impact on large numbers of users. Although criminal enterprises have the capacity to engage in this type of attack, such disruptions have not occurred, because of the more lucrative use of botnets for small-scale criminal activities discussed earlier.

To construct a large-scale botnet, attackers rely on various methods for compromising new hosts, such as the use of worms, self-replicating code that spreads across a network infecting vulnerable machines. With a worm, one infected machine scans for and finds other vulnerable systems. The worm then spreads to those new victims, copying its code; victim machines then find other targets, and worms may spread exponentially. Since at least 2004, worms have been used to carry and install bot software, allowing the attacker to control the newly infected machines.

Some bots are distributed as executable email attachments, duping users into installing the bot by claiming that an important attachment needs urgent attention. Despite publicity warning against reading email attachments from unknown senders, a significant number of users succumb to this form of subterfuge. Attackers also use spear-phishing attacks for bot distribution. Bots are also bundled with apparently benign or useful applications, such as system add-ons or games.

A frequently used bot distribution mechanism involves exploiting a client-side program, such as a Web browser, a document-viewing application such as a word processor or slide viewer, a video-viewing application, or music-playing software. Every month, numerous vulnerabilities are discovered in these types of applications. If a user views content posted by an attacker on a Web site, the content itself (which could be a document, audio file, or other file format) could trigger the vulnerability in the client program, making it install the attacker's bot software. Some refer to this technique as a drive-by download of malicious code known as *malware*.

As cell phones, music-playing devices, and personal digital assistants become more powerful, attackers are compounding the problem by devising worms and bots to attack them, too. A botnet made up of millions of Internet-capable cell phones could cause significant damage.

Mass credit card fraud to disable accounts. Large-scale credit card fraud and identity theft could be another attack vector via cyberspace. Today, most of the fraud committed by theft of credit card account numbers falls into the range of small-scale attacks. Attackers might grab a million credit cards from a merchant that suffers a breach, but automatic fraud detection tools operated by the credit card companies and issuing banks detect the fraud and react rapidly. Software running on the credit card companies' computers rapidly determines that the given merchant has had a breach, given the uptick in fraudulent activity tied to cards used at that merchant recently. These cards are then disabled, along with other cards used at that merchant, foiling the attacker's chance to use the other stolen account numbers. Quite often, the credit card companies detect a breach based on the fraudulent use of cards before the merchant that suffered the breach realizes it. Thus, despite the large number of compromised accounts, the actual amount of fraud committed with stolen credit cards has been kept between 1 and 4 percent of all credit card transactions.

However, the antifraud systems could also be used to instigate a large-scale attack. When a breach is detected and card accounts are disabled, consumers may have to telephone the issuing bank to either reactivate an account or to request issuance of a new card. An attacker who wanted to cause economic damage could purposely generate bogus transactions for tens of millions of credit cards, triggering mass account shutoffs. In the 1990s, generating that number of credit card transactions was difficult if not impossible, but today, a million-system botnet could initiate transactions through thousands of e-commerce sites. Consumers would not be able to use their cards unless credit card and bank personnel temporarily suspended automated antifraud account shutdown functions. Such an attack could have a noticeable impact on the economy.

Defensive Technologies and Associated Public Policy Issues

This section surveys common and powerful cybersecurity defensive technologies, explaining the concepts underlying each and some policy options and questions they pose. The discussion examines network- and host-based defenses as well as defensive concepts that apply to both.

Public policy decisionmakers can influence network-based and host-based defenses in different ways. Network-based defenses differ in that they tend to be more scalable and applicable within enterprises and government agencies, and possibly even nationwide, through the deployment of systems at network interconnection points to protect large numbers of computers on the given network. For example, an ISP might deploy defensive technologies that can benefit all of its customers through a relatively small number of critical network junctions; perhaps 10 to 100 systems can coordinate in the defense of all hosts on the ISP's network. Network-based defenses might be required of network operators, including ISPs and large enterprises, or vendors of network equipment and software might be required to offer certain security capabilities with their products.

Host-based defenses, by contrast, involve installing software on a system-by-system basis; they can protect large numbers of machines, but with a more expansive, invasive, and usually more expensive technological deployment. For widespread host-based defenses, software would have to be deployed on perhaps millions of machines or more, including consumer, commercial, and government systems. Such defenses can be incorporated into the operating system itself or as standard features of other widely used packages, such as productivity suites or antivirus tools.

Requirements for host-based defenses could be applied either to end-users or to vendors (of operating systems, browsers, databases, office suites, and the like). Given most users' relative lack of rigor and technical sophistication in configuring complex security software, requirements placed on software vendors are likely to have greater impact in improving host-based security.

Network-based Defenses

Operators of large-scale networks, including commercial ISPs, major enterprises, government agencies, and the military, must weigh the impact of a variety of competing goals, including performance, manageability, and scalability, against the impact of security measures. A security technology that combs all network traffic looking for signs of attack with a high degree of accuracy but that slows the network to a crawl would be unacceptable. Also unacceptable would be security technologies that make the network so complex that it cannot be managed effectively or that impair its ability to grow enough to support its entire user base. For this reason, the vendors offering security technologies and the network operators using them must carefully vet their security tools before deploying them. While each of the technologies covered in this section has been applied successfully in large-scale networks, not every defensive technology is suitable for every network provider.

Firewalls. Firewalls filter network traffic, allowing certain types into a network while blocking others, based on the firewall's configuration. Most firewalls filter based on the type of network services; they may, for example, allow Web traffic while blocking network management traffic arriving from the Internet. More advanced firewalls may allow specific source or destination addresses to be blocked. The most sophisticated firewalls provide content inspection, analyzing the data inside packets to determine whether it contains application data, key words, attack patterns, or specific phrases that should be blocked. Network firewalls are often deployed at the interconnection points between two networks, such as the border between an enterprise network and the Internet. Such firewalls are usually configured to allow inbound access to specific Internet-accessible Web servers, mail servers, and other related systems. In most organizations, outbound filtering is far more open; many organizations choose to allow all traffic out of their networks. Because exfiltration of sensitive information from corporate and government networks represents a risk, some organizations also filter outbound access.

Some countries, notably China and Saudi Arabia, firewall all of their outbound traffic, using numerous firewall machines operating in parallel to suppress access to Web sites and other Internet activities associated with unwanted political ideas or religious expression. However, such firewall deployments are not perfect. Political and religious dissidents have devised methods to fool them, often using tunneling technologies to carry controversial traffic that might otherwise be blocked inside of innocuous-looking packets, sometimes applying encryption to minimize the chance of inspection by authorities.

Even with the possibility of small-scale evasion of firewalls, these country-level firewalls provide a capability for near-complete disconnection from the Internet for the countries that operate them. The network architecture of these countries is built around a large number of firewall chokepoints through which traffic must pass for analysis. If, due to a geopolitical crisis, these countries wanted to shut off both inbound and outbound Internet access, they could leverage their firewall infrastructure to block access very quickly, likely within a few minutes. In late 2007, Burma severed its Internet connectivity during political unrest, severely limiting the flow of information into, and perhaps more importantly, out of the country.[13] Countries without such firewalls and where international connectivity has blossomed with large numbers of ISPs and foreign interconnections would have a harder time doing such thorough blocking so quickly. It is unlikely, for example, that the United States would ever move to firewall all Internet connectivity or even contemplate the full-scale breaking of international connectivity, due both to the severe economic implications and the widespread connectivity offered by its multiplicity of ISPs.

However, given that some countries have the capability of rapidly implementing firewall-based isolation, the United States may want to consider methods for gaining access to the Internet infrastructure of a country that has employed firewall filtering on a countrywide level. Such methods could include satellite links, connections via international companies operating inside the country, or covert agents operating inside the firewalled country itself. Even if such connections cannot politically or diplomatically be implemented unless a definitive crisis offers an immediate justification, the United States may want to draw up plans for the rapid establishment of such connectivity for operations in various countries, should such access ever be needed.

Network-based intrusion detection systems. Network-based intrusion detection systems (NIDS) monitor Internet traffic looking for attacks.When an attack is discovered, the NIDS tool alerts network management personnel, operating like a network burglar alarm. Many commercial and government enterprises deploy NIDS monitoring sensors at their Internet gateways, just inside their firewalls, to determine if an attacker has penetrated their "front door." Some organizations deploy NIDS sensors throughout their internal networks, monitoring for attacks throughout.

Most of today's NIDS technology focuses on signature-based detection. For each known attack, the NIDS vendor creates a specific definition of telltale signs in packets that would indicate such an attack is under way. For example, a given software flaw may lead to a vulnerability in a router that attackers can exploit to take over the router. A NIDS vendor may write a signature describing the pattern of packets that have specific settings that indicate an exploit is attempting to trigger the vulnerability. Such signatures are published regularly, with many thousands available on a free and commercial basis.

Some NIDS technology also uses behavior-based protection, based on identifying deviations from "normal" usage of protocols in a given network. A NIDS sensor may detect an attack due to unusual protocol behavior, such as repeated SYN, SYN–ACK patterns, without completion of the TCP three-way handshake seen during SYN flood attacks described earlier. Another form of behavior-based NIDS tool looks at connection flow information, analyzing the source and destination points of connections going across a network, and the services associated with each flow, to determine whether it matches the normal expected patterns for the given network.

Attackers have an interest in devising methods for evading detection of both signature-based and behavior-based NIDS tools. Exploits may split up and encode data so that it still functions against the target but without displaying signatures to NIDS tools. Attackers may also seek to make their attack mimic legitimate traffic in order to evade behavior-based defenses. Such stealth capabilities are increasingly available in commercial or free open-source hacking tools.

Attackers work to evade detection, but most attacks, especially very large-scale ones such as denial-of-service floods against infrastructure targets, are detected based on the immediate impact of the attack itself. Most major commercial enterprises and government agencies have some form of NIDS capability. Some, but not all, ISPs likewise have deployed NIDS tools on their networks. However, coordination and analysis across these NIDS do not exist in many industries. A determined, countrywide attack might not be recognized until it has already caused significant damage. Some industries have formed information sharing and analysis centers (ISACs), cooperative groups of information security professionals, to share information about attack activity. The financial services ISAC was one of the first, and they have been established for information technology, energy, state government, and other sectors. ISACs provide a window into activity associated with only one industry and, as might be expected, companies may hesitate to share information that could damage their reputation or competitive advantage. For these reasons, ISACs do not provide a comprehensive detection capability for widespread attacks against the United States.

To make them more useful against countrywide attacks, NIDS tools could be deployed on ISP networks at points of interconnection with other countries. The U.S. Government or military could apply such tools to monitor all traffic coming into or going out of the country, looking for coordinated attacks. ISPs may be reluctant to have such monitoring devices on their network, and privacy advocates might be concerned about intrusive monitoring. However, a program could be devised that minimizes impact by looking only at packet header or traffic connection flow information. If applied to the major fiber optic connections into and out of the country, monitoring could cover most but not all Internet traffic. A small segment of traffic that would be more difficult to monitor is satellite communications carrying IP traffic into the United States, due to their geographically widespread distribution, the lack of publicly available information about all satellite connection points in the United States, and the ephemeral nature of such connections. However, even a monitoring capability focused only on fiber-based transmissions could provide significant warning of widespread attacks.

Due to the large amount of traffic flowing in and out of the country through ISPs, a monitoring solution of this type probably would focus only on traffic flows and not individual packets and their contents. Such a detection capability at the network borders would be analogous to the U.S. Coast Guard's monitoring of the Nation's ports or the U.S. military's early warning missile launch detection systems, applied to the cyberspace borders of the United States.

Network-based intrusion prevention systems. While firewalls focus on allowing or denying particular services and NIDS tools detect attack activity, network-based intrusion prevention system (NIPS) tools combine these two concepts. NIPS devices monitor network traffic looking for attacks. When packets associated with an attack are detected, the NIPS may drop those packets or reset the connection, stopping the attack from functioning and thereby protecting the end system. Due to the risk of blocking traffic if NIPS misidentifies legitimate traffic as an attack (known as a false-positive condition), some NIPS tools are tuned so that attacks commonly associated with false positives generate an alert rather than a blocking action. False positives could cause significant problems in an enterprise environment, breaking important applications if their traffic accidentally matched the attack patterns the NIPS is configured to detect. A NIPS tool configured merely to alert for some types of attacks takes on the same behavior as a NIDS tool. Like their NIDS cousins, NIPS products detect attacks using a signature-based approach, behavior-based identification, or a mixture of both techniques.

Some NIPS tools operate inline: traffic flows pass through the NIPS for inspection and possible blocking. Other NIPS tools sit beside the network and sample its traffic to detect attacks. Inline NIPS tools can provide a comprehensive view of attack activity in the stream because they inspect each and every packet. Inline NIPS tools can also effectively block unwanted traffic simply by dropping a packet and not allowing it through. NIPS tools that sit beside the traffic flow, on the other hand, may miss some dangerous packets in a fast stream. Furthermore, if an attack is detected, the NIPS tool that samples the traffic may not be able to reset the connection quickly enough, and an attacker might cause damage before it can be blocked. Thus, from a purely defensive measure, inline NIPS tools offer some advantages, but from a network performance and operations perspective, inline NIPS tools could become a performance bottleneck, slowing network traffic to inspect it. Because inline NIPS tools must both inspect and forward packets, the tools could become overwhelmed by a high traffic load; this could give attackers a way to launch a denial-of-service attack against the network by clogging up the inline NIPS tools with bogus packets. NIPS that sit beside a network sampling its traffic typically do not suffer from this performance bottleneck.

In variations of NIPS technology, some ISPs and large enterprises have distributed sensors throughout their networks to detect unusual traffic flows that might be attacks, especially denial-of-service floods. These tools may have the ability to throttle such traffic, holding back the onslaught of packets to a level that a target machine might be capable of handling, a technique called *traffic shaping.* Such sensors—the same technology as the packet-flood shunning concepts described earlier—are becoming more able to recognize attacks in an automated fashion and shun the traffic associated with the flood.

Either NIDS or NIPS tools could be used for a nationwide cyber monitoring system at the U.S. "borders." NIDS provides detection capabilities but cannot block or throttle an attack. Functionality for blocking the attack would have to come from other systems, perhaps the machines under siege. If NIPS tools were the early warning system, the United States could use the system to shun the attack, but this capability comes at the price of potentially lower performance and the risk of false positives.

Network encryption. The original Internet protocol specification included neither network-level encryption to prevent eavesdropping nor authentication mechanisms to identify machines or users. Security functionality was left to end-user computers and applications developers; the network pro-tocols were geared more toward moving packets end-to-end than providing security. In the absence of network-level encryption, three end-to-end encryption technologies became popular in the 1990s. While any of the three could be used to encrypt any kind of data moving across the Internet, each found favor with a different segment of Internet applications and technology. The pretty good privacy (PGP) program created by cryptographic hobbyist Phil Zimmerman was commonly applied to encrypting email and files. The Secure Shell (SSH) suite was applied primarily to protect remote login capabilities in which an administrator or user gained remote access to a system across the network. The most widely deployed encryption tool, the Secure Sockets Layer (SSL), was usually applied to securing communication between Web browsers and Web sites. These three technologies are still widely used to encrypt data flowing across the Internet, but each requires that both ends associated with the communication, the sender and receiver, have special software and encryption keys in order to use the application-layer encryption.

In the mid-1990s, the Internet Engineering Task Force[14] recognized the need for having network equipment, rather than end systems, encrypt packets and authenticate their origin. Thus, they defined Internet Protocol Security (IPsec), a protocol that was "retrofitted" into IPv4 and incorporated in IPv6 to provide network-level encryption. Any application on the end systems could thus take advantage of cryptographic protections from the network itself, without any changes to the application (unlike PGP, SSH, and SSL). In recent years, a variety of vendors have released IPsec-compatible software in operating systems, routers, firewall equipment, and a variety of other devices. IPsec is a very complex protocol with numerous options; it required rigorous compatibility testing and implementation fixes. Today, the most popular operating systems, including Windows, Linux, Mac OS X, and others, support IPsec, as does major network equipment.

IPsec offers various kinds of security capabilities via cryptography, including confidentiality, so no one can read the contents of packets without the decryption key; authentication, identifying which user or machine sent each packet; and integrity, to verify that a packet's contents were not altered. IPsec was designed to operate with traditional IP on the network so that secure and unsecured communications could coexist.

IPsec communication can be deployed in a variety of ways. The simplest example is a point-to-point connection between two end systems, such as two workstations or a workstation and a server. A system administrator can configure the two systems with a preshared encryption key, which in turn is used to exchange other keys that encrypt the data going from system to system. In network-to-network encryption, a network administrator can configure two routers or firewalls on the Internet so that all traffic going between the two systems is encrypted. Thus, two enterprises engaged in a joint venture can encrypt all traffic going between their two networks across the Internet by applying IPsec at their Internet gateways and configuring them with encryption keys. Or, in another example, encrypting data between many end-user computers and a network gateway, such as a router or firewall, allows a large number of users to access a corporate network, for example, in a secure fashion.

In each of these three deployment scenarios—system-to-system, network-to-network, and system-to-network—IPsec is used to create a virtual private network (VPN) to carry sensitive data securely across the public Internet. Such VPN capabilities are significantly less costly than dedicated dial-up or point-to-point facilities.

While IPsec, PGP, SSH, and SSL encryption can provide a great deal of security, a major impediment to universal deployment is that each requires distribution of encryption keys, which are essentially series of secret strings of numbers. Ensuring that encryption keys are distributed only to legitimate users and that they are protected from attackers is thus paramount. The simplest deployments of IPsec among a very small number of users or networks can use basic preshared keys, configured by administrators, but such deployments are unworkable beyond about a dozen intercommunicating systems because of the complexities of key distribution and secrecy in a larger organization.

To scale to larger user and network populations, various organizations have devised management systems to distribute keys in a trusted fashion. Technologies for secure key distribution rely on one or more parties, trusted by all users of the keys, to digitally sign all keys in the system. These key signing entities are referred to as certificate authorities (CAs), because they generate certificates, or data packages that include a user's or network's key, name, and other attributes. Digitally signed by the CA, a certificate acts like a digital identity card, verifying users' or systems' identities and allowing them to encrypt communications for others who trust the CA that issued each system's certificate. The complexity of determining whom to trust to sign keys has limited their widespread deployment. Isolated pockets of encrypted communication use IPsec, PGP, SSH, or, to some extent, SSL. For example, many organizations have signed and distributed their own IPsec keys for use by their employees and business partners. Many individuals have created and signed their own PGP keys for use by their business associates. System administrators create and sign SSH keys for the users of their machines. But each of these uses results in pockets of communicating systems, not an all-encompassing encryption scheme. Each system may use the same software technology and encryption algorithms, but if they do not all trust the same CA, they cannot communicate with each other securely. A variety of companies offer commercial CA services to the public and to enterprises, but there is no interoperability between the certificates of different CAs. Some government agencies have contracted with a commercial CA or have started to issue their own certificates, acting as a CA for their own interactions with the private sector.

Market forces may lead a small number of trusted CAs to offer inter-operability between their certificates; this would result in a federated certificate infrastructure that Internet users could rely on. However, each commercial CA has an interest in selling its own certificates in a market with heavy competition. Various CAs have different standards for security and for issuing certificates.[15] An all-encompassing federated certificate infrastructure established by market forces might cater to the lowest common denominator of CAs, resulting in less security than some companies and government agencies require. For these reasons, government regulation or standards for CA practices might be necessary to establish a reasonable level of security. Multiple layers of security, each with its own set of security practices for CAs, might support different values and types of transactions.

While network-based encryption can provide security for information in transit, it can cause problems for the defensive technologies described earlier. When packets are encrypted, tools such as firewalls, NIDS sensors, and NIPS solutions cannot inspect the contents of the packets in order to detect attacks. Network floods and attacks that violate protocol specifications can still be detected based on traffic volumes, unusual network behavior, and signatures associated with packet header information. But most other forms of attack could be obscured by network-based encryption, especially those associated with the exploitation and compromise of a target machine or component of the network infrastructure. In order for firewalls, NIDS, and NIPS defenses to examine these packets, they would need to be configured with encryption keys for traffic flows.

Either individual cryptographic keys from each system or user or universal keys for decrypting traffic for large groups of systems would need to be distributed to numerous network components. In most networks, however, placing keys on such network equipment results in significant privacy concerns, as well as increasing the risk that an attacker could steal the keys and completely undermine the cryptographic protection. Network-based encryption is therefore not a security panacea. Even if widespread key distribution issues could be solved with a set of trusted CAs, numerous security issues will remain. As network-based encryption becomes more common, attackers will be able to exploit systems across encrypted connections with diminishing risk of detection.

Host-based Defenses

Host-based defenses are those that protect individual systems against attack. They contrast with network-based defenses, which benefit from having a wide view of activity against a large number of machines but often cannot discern the details of action against individual hosts. This problem is compounded as attackers increasingly rely on network-based encryption technologies to obscure their attacks from network sensors. Host-based defenses, however, can see the action on a single machine and discern the details of an attack.

Host-based defenses protect both client machines and servers. Client systems include traditional workstation and laptop computers, as well as cell phones, personal digital assistants, and consumer electronics such as televisions and stereos that are controlled by built-in general-purpose computer systems. Server systems include Web, email, DNS, and file servers, and an increasing number of media servers that provide video and audio content to individuals. All of these types of hosts, both clients and servers, could utilize some form of host-based defenses, but current defensive technology has focused on workstations, laptops, and servers. As more valuable information and processing capacity propagate to other types of technologies, the types of defenses honed for traditional computer systems will likely be repurposed to these new platforms. This section analyzes some of the most common and widely used host-based defenses applicable to all of these types of machines.

Anti-malware tools. Today's malicious code takes many forms. Viruses were one of the first types of malware; these are self-replicating code snippets that infect files, copy themselves throughout a victim computer's file system, and spread wherever files are shared between machines via file servers, email, or the Web. Worms, a close cousin of viruses, also self-replicate, copying themselves across a network, usually by exploiting software vulnerabilities. Spyware, bots, and rootkits—other forms of malware described earlier—are also proliferating. Collectively, there are hundreds of thousands of specimens of malware, and attackers are continuously creating new examples.

Antivirus and antispyware tools are the most common defenses against such malware. Originally two different segments of the market, antivirus and antispyware tools have largely converged into a single product category of host-based protection suites, centered around an anti-malware scanner. Offered by a variety of commercial vendors, these tools scan a computer's hard drive and memory to detect and eradicate malware. Generally speaking, most modern anti-malware tools apply some combination of three approaches to detecting malware: signatures, heuristics, and behavior-based detection. Each approach has benefits and weaknesses.

Commercial solutions with signature-based malware detection have been available since the 1980s. With these products, vendors regularly publish a database of malware signatures (essentially cryptographic fingerprints of viruses, worms, and other specimens), which their customers install on each system. As the anti-malware tool runs, it can detect and block the copying of malicious code onto the computer, and if malware is somehow placed on the machine, the anti-malware tool can prevent it from running. In the 1980s and 1990s, vendors told their customers to update their signatures approximately every month so that they could be protected against the latest threats the vendors identified in "the wild." As the rapid growth of the Internet in the late 1990s spurred the quick spread of new malware, monthly signature updates became inadequate, and most anti-malware vendors now publish new signatures every day or two to keep up with the rapidly evolving threat.

Attackers have a financial interest in holding on to compromised end-user machines for as long as possible and, to that end, increasingly rely on polymorphic code, that is, software that modifies itself as it runs or as it spreads to each newly infected machine. Even daily signature updates may not be enough to keep up with such attacks, but it is not realistic for most organizations and computer users to update their anti-malware signature databases more than once per day, given technical limitations on the architectures for distributing signatures and verifying their effectiveness. Thus, although signature-based solutions are helpful against the most widespread and least dynamic malware, other detection approaches are needed too.

Many modern malware attacks are thwarted using heuristic detection techniques. Whereas signature-based solutions look for an exact match of malware code against a signature, heuristic solutions look for partial matches of elements of the malware, including chunks of the malware's file, the configuration settings associated with the malware, and its file name. Heuristic defenses are "fuzzy" signatures that take advantage of the fact that attackers frequently reuse functional building blocks of code from previous malware in their new creations. Anti-malware vendors analyze malware specimens to isolate the most common element of the code, such as the instructions associated with polymorphic behavior, code used to infect sensitive portions of the computer system, or software that interacts with the network. Even out-of-date heuristic tools have a chance of detecting the newest strains of malware if the attackers reused some code, as they often do. In today's anti-malware tool suites, most of the protection is provided by heuristic capabilities.

Heuristics have their own limitations: an attacker who creates new malware without reusing any code is just as invisible to heuristics as to detection using strict signatures. An attacker may have a significant motivation for creating and using custom malware to evade signatures and heuristics in extremely targeted attacks against high-value systems.

A third common anti-malware approach is based on detecting the typical behavior of malicious code as it runs on a machine. By monitoring every running program on the protected computer, the anti-malware tool can look for aggressive behaviors such as the rapid opening, writing, and closing of thousands of files on the file system, typically associated with virus infection. For example, spyware often alters a user's browser settings to make it easier to inject ads and capture keystrokes from the victim; bots sometimes reconfigure the system in predictable ways to enhance the attacker's control of the machine. By looking for these actions as programs run, an anti-malware tool can stop the misbehaving program, uninstall it, and attempt to restore the computer's settings to their pre-malware configuration.

Behavior-based solutions afford a good deal of security, but with some fairly significant costs. First, such solutions tend to lower performance; monitoring every running program taxes system processor and memory resources. Next, the anti-malware tool has to let the malware run at least briefly to observe its behavior before detecting it. Significant and possibly irreversible damage could occur during that time, such as the deletion or alteration of important data stored on the machine. Behavior-based solutions also have a much higher risk of false-positive detections than signature or heuristic solutions. In an enterprise environment, if the anti-malware tool identifies a legitimate program as being malicious, it could disable the program and might break a critical business application. Because impairing a corporate application could result in financial losses, some anti-malware vendors have tuned their behavior-based detection capabilities to be far less sensitive. Other vendors have avoided behavior-based solutions, focusing their energies on signature and heuristic defenses.

Anti-malware vendor solutions offer differing mixes of signature, heuristic, and behavior-based defenses that reflect that vendor's philosophy toward detection. The particular mix is typically not communicated to customers, who may assume that anti-malware protection is essentially interchangeable and that they are safe as long as some form of anti-malware tool is running. The vendors may claim that the subtle tradeoffs represented in their detection regimens are too complex for their customers to understand, which is certainly true for general consumers. Large enterprises, however, especially those associated with critical business, government, and military operations, are well able to apply technical understanding and analysis to these tradeoffs during the product selection process, and availability of such information would help to improve the match between business needs and the security tools chosen.

Host-based intrusion prevention systems. Like their network-based counterparts, host-based intrusion prevention system (IPS) tools detect various forms of attack and block them. But instead of analyzing network traffic for attacks, these tools focus on policing the running programs on each end host. The goal of network-based and host-based IPS tools is the same—blocking exploitation of target machines—but the technology and its implications are quite different. Some host-based IPS tools look for alterations in the memory of running programs that indicate that an attacker has injected exploit code into the machine. Others analyze the calls made into the underlying operating system kernel by programs as they run, checking to see if these calls are typical for the given program on that machine. Unlike most anti-malware tools that are focused on detecting malicious programs the attacker has placed on a machine, host-based IPS tools tend to look for existing legitimate programs that are misbehaving because they have come under the control of an attacker. Host-based IPS tools are an active area of research in academia and commercial security companies, given their relatively new status, the lucrative market for such solutions, and their great potential for blocking exploitation and takeover of end systems.

Host-based intrusion detection system tools that merely detect but do not block attacks have largely been subsumed into the host-based IPS market. Today's host-based IPS can be configured to detect or to block attacks.

Because host-based IPS tools by their nature analyze the activities of legitimate programs in order to look for deviations from normal program activity and enforce certain rules, they too face a risk of false-positive detections that could break important applications. In the past few years, some host-based IPS tools have gotten a reputation for overly aggressive enforcement, leading some companies to remove or disable the protection to restore an application. Some host-based IPS tools require lengthy and complex configuration sessions by experienced administrators to "train" the tool about what is normal activity for a given application. Even after this training is completed, a new patch for the application may alter its behavior, requiring further tuning. While such tuning activities are costly, they can significantly improve the security of a system, making it immune to many of the common exploitation techniques in widespread use today.

Personal firewalls. Personal firewall software protects end-user computers and servers from network-based attacks by allowing only certain traffic into or out of the system from a specified list of programs configured by an administrator or user. For example, the personal firewall may allow the browser to make Web connections outbound to Web servers on the Internet, but it may block inbound connections seeking access to files on the protected machine unless file sharing is enabled. Personal firewalls block access to the network by malware installed by the attacker or injected into programs that would not normally require network access.

While personal firewalls do improve the security of a system, attackers have crafted numerous techniques for subverting them. Many modern techniques exploit programs such as Web browsers that are allowed access to the Internet, and then use the allowed program as a means to communicate with the victim machine. Because the personal firewall allows users to surf the Internet with a browser, the malware mimics a user's actions in the browser while polling an attacker for its commands and sending information taken from the victim machine. However, even though they can be bypassed, personal firewalls do provide some protection.

Microsoft bundled firewall technology in Windows XP Service Pack 2, released in 2004, and all subsequent versions of Windows. This personal firewall was designed in large part as a response to the significant number of worms that had infected Windows machines earlier in the decade. Although it was a very crude personal firewall in its configuration and capability, the protection thus made widely available helped to reverse an alarming rise in worm attacks from 2000 to 2004. The built-in Windows personal firewall is an example of how bundling security capabilities with an underlying operating system can help ensure that large numbers of consumers and enterprises have these protections. Other companies offer free or commercial personal firewalls that are far better than the fairly minimal capability offered to Windows users, which tech-savvy consumers and enterprises can deploy, but the Internet as a whole is better protected when these capabilities are built in.[16]

However, bundling security technologies into the underlying operating system has economic and political complexities. In the 1990s, for example, Microsoft bundled a Web browser into Windows but this resulted in significant antitrust litigation with the U.S. Department of Justice, several states, and some European countries. While the Windows personal firewall was largely successful, Microsoft has shied away from building anti-malware scanning capabilities into the operating system by default, perhaps fearing legal challenges from competitors in the security industry. Microsoft has released several anti-malware tools, some for free, but only as separate downloads that are not built into Windows. Microsoft has also altered recent versions of Windows, including Vista, to provide some capabilities of host-based IPS tools, such as preventing certain areas of memory usually associated with data from being used to run code, a technique often employed by malware. But these are only the lowest hanging fruit of host-based IPS capabilities, picked up by Microsoft as Windows evolves.[17]

Host-based encryption—file-level versus drive-level. Encryption technology can protect data on a host either by encrypting individual files and directories or by encrypting the entire hard drive, including the operating system and software applications. File-level encryption is often faster than encrypting the entire drive. Drive-level encryption tends to offer better security, however: an attacker is less able to subvert the operating system and the encryption tool because the code for these programs is itself encrypted on the drive. Many organizations are deploying host-based encryption in light of the high number of cases involving loss of account information for millions of consumers due to theft of a laptop or compromise of a back-end database to steal the accounts.

Over 30 states and several countries have passed laws requiring disclosure of any breaches of personally identifiable consumer information. As of this writing, the United States does not have a Federal law regarding breach disclosure, but even without such a law, many breaches in the United States are disclosed nationwide. If a given e-commerce site has customers in a state that has a breach disclosure law, the organization is legally considered to be doing business in that state and must disclose the breach to its customers in the state. Most, therefore, disclose the breach to all of their customers, which makes such laws de facto a nationwide standard.

Many host-based encryption tools can be bypassed in various ways, which could have significant implications for breach disclosure laws. One method for bypassing cryptographic protections involves finding hidden temporary files created by the cryptographic tool during the encryption operation. For example, the built-in Microsoft Windows Encrypting File System technology leaves such files with the unencrypted data on the system until a user or administrator removes them manually or they are overwritten by another program, a fact that would come as a surprise to many users. Another method for bypassing host-based encryption tools involves exploiting an account or software running as a legitimate user on the system. Because the user or the software run by the user has the privileges and encryption keys to access the protected data, an attacker who compromises the account or exploits the software will gain exactly the same access to the data. In effect, because the encryption solution has to decrypt the data for legitimate users, an attacker can exploit software vulnerabilities to use those functions to retrieve the data.

A third way to bypass the encryption tools involves the attacker retrieving the decryption keys, usually stored on the system itself, often protected with a user's password. An attacker might be able to determine a user's password, either by guessing it or by launching a password-cracking tool, a process that might take a few minutes or many years, depending on how difficult the password is to guess for an automated tool that can try hundreds of thousands of guesses per second. An attacker who has determined the password can gain access to the data encryption keys and decrypt the data. For this reason, some encryption solutions do not rely exclusively on a user password, but augment protections with smart cards (credit card–sized computing devices that can store crypto keys), tokens, or biometric authentication. However, the majority of host-based encryption solutions deployed today rely exclusively on password protection.

If an attacker steals a laptop or gains access to a back-end database, the organization that suffered the breach is only required to disclose the breach if the attacker actually gained access to the consumer data. With host-based encryption solutions, a company may conclude that breach notification is unnecessary, given that the data was encrypted so the attacker should not be able to gain access to it. However, the attacker might be able to bypass the encryption and read the consumer data. Thus, while host-based encryption does improve security, it could decrease the breach disclosure rate, making consumers unaware of violations of their privacy or potential compromise of their financial accounts.

Issues Applying to Network- and Host-based Defenses
This section describes some issues that apply to both network-based and host-based defensive approaches, including issues of patch management and the human factor. Their broad application offers significant opportunities for thwarting major attacks in cyberspace.

Patch management. Software vendors regularly release critical patches for their products that fix security vulnerabilities, either by tweaking the existing software or by issuing a whole new version of the product. The vast majority of security patches for consumer, enterprise, and infrastructure software products are downloaded through the Internet. Some systems, especially consumer machines, are configured to receive and install patches automatically. On other systems, such as those used by enterprises, a system administrator installs patches. This manual process slows down the application, but it allows administrators to vet patches carefully to make sure they will not break any enterprise applications.

Patch distribution through the Internet offers vendors the ability to disperse patches quickly but raises the chicken-and-egg problem of relying on the Internet to distribute patches for components of the Internet itself. If a major attack were to render the Internet unusable for a time, patch distribution could come to a halt. A few ISPs and other large enterprises have made plans for manual distribution of patches on physical media, such as CDs or DVDs with the software, carried by airplanes in the event of a catastrophic network failure. However, not all have done so.

Some vendors include a rating of the criticality of each patch to help organizations focus on the most severe vulnerabilities. Other vendors, including some associated with critical enterprise infrastructure applications, do not provide any criticality estimate but presume that their clients will install every patch they release. Unfortunately, because a bad patch can cause systems to crash or introduce additional security vulnerabilities, some enterprises choose to delay patching for issues of intermediate criticality, sometimes for many months. During that timeframe, the organization's systems are exposed to attack, and the organization may not even realize the threat if the vendor fails to specify a criticality rating with a patch.

Another concern with the state of software patching in cyberspace is the lack of vendor liability in most countries for security flaws in their original programs and for issues associated with patches. Most software contracts and license agreements explicitly disclaim vendor liability for flaws in their products, even blatant security vulnerabilities and the damage associated with exploited systems. The market does drive vendors to release patches, because of their customers' implicit threat not to repurchase or renew product license agreements. However, many software vendors have their customers locked in, as the customers' business processes are tightly intermingled with the vendors' software. This undermines market pressures to produce secure products. This situation creates incentives for vendors to push products out the door quickly, with plans for fixing security flaws later by means of patches. In the meantime, systems have exploitable vulnerabilities, and hundreds of new flaws are discovered and publicized each month.

The human factor. Technological solutions may improve security, but only if solid security practices are followed by the human users and administrators of the systems. A user who reveals a password over the phone or is tricked into installing malicious software on a machine can undermine the most hardened enterprise or carefully configured operating systems. Enterprise administrators who fail to install a critical patch because they do not understand the security issues it fixes likewise leave their systems exposed to attack. Thus, user awareness education is just as vital a tool in protecting cyberspace as the latest firewall or encryption technology.

Many corporations and government agencies have, at best, rudimentary cybersecurity user awareness programs. Once a year, users may be exhorted to choose robust passwords, to avoid running untrusted programs downloaded from the Internet, and to avoid revealing sensitive information in email. While such advice is sound, enterprises handling sensitive data or operating critical infrastructures need to strive for a culture of information security, not just a yearly reminder that users quickly forget. Regular reminders of security practices are vital, as well as periodic audits to ensure that those practices are being followed. Given their access to and control over vital computing assets, system administrators and other information technology professionals are among the most important enterprise staff members to educate in comprehensive security practices. Enterprises themselves should require cybersecurity education of their system administrator staff, potentially with government requirements or oversight.

The sorry state of information security awareness for the public at large is an even bigger problem than the relative lack of security awareness in enterprises. Operating system and security software vendors may incorporate more and more defensive technologies into their products, but they are fighting a losing battle unless the public can be trained to use them. The large numbers of users who fall for phishing scams, lack anti-malware tools, run unpatched systems, and choose easily guessed passwords for their accounts indicate that the public is either not aware of sound security practices or does not understand the threats. The state of information security in cyberspace could be significantly improved by public service announcements and education campaigns. Like the anticrime, environmental awareness, and antismoking television ad campaigns of recent years, a comprehensive and repeated program of public awareness could help instill fundamental security principles to make cyberspace safer and more secure. Some agencies (including the Department of Homeland Security in the United States) and countries have experimented with small-scale user awareness initiatives for the public, but more and broader initiatives are necessary. Such awareness programs should point out that securing one's own computer not only lowers the risk for that individual, but also helps improve the security of cyberspace and the country as a whole.

Conclusion

The security concerns associated with today's Internet are based on the rapid evolution of technology, applied in ways unanticipated by its original designers. The Internet has grown considerably beyond the scope of the original experimental ARPANET. The Internet's architects did not design the network or its protocols to handle the level of sensitive data and economic activity that they routinely carry today. The network has scaled to hundreds of millions of users around the globe, a vast and diverse population. The computers that the Internet connects typically use general-purpose processors and operating systems that can run any program presented to the machine, making them flexible and extendable. However, this flexibility results in the possibility of infection by numerous varieties of malicious code, such as viruses, spyware, worms, and bots. As significant vulnerabilities are routinely discovered in workstations, servers, and network equipment, and large numbers of malicious code specimens are introduced every day, the state of Internet security is cause for concern.

Today, small-scale attacks are commonplace. Attackers have the technical capabilities, but usually not the financial motivation, for large-scale attacks. Over the past two decades, the threat landscape has increased from experimental hackers and hobbyists to include organized cybercriminals. We may face a further evolution of the threat as terrorist groups and nation-states seek to utilize cyber attacks as a form of warfare.

However, as various threats grow and vulnerabilities proliferate, security technologies have been developed for the Internet and the computers it interconnects. These technologies can provide a good degree of security if they are judiciously deployed and carefully maintained by system administrators and users who are informed about good security practices.

CHAPTER 8

The Future of the Internet and Cyberpower

Marjory S. Blumenthal and David D. Clark

THE PURPOSE of this chapter is to provide a forward-looking perspective on cyberspace that will support effective cyberpower analysis. The development and implementation of any cyberpower policy will take time. If the policy is to be relevant and not out-of-date before it is implemented, it must be based on a future view of cyberspace, not what cyberspace is today. Looking forward even 10 years, the shape of cyberspace will likely be much changed from today. There are many possible outcomes for the future of cyberspace, driven not only by the evolution of component technologies (see chapter 6 in this volume, "Evolutionary Trends in Cyberspace"), but also by the decisions and interactions of many actors whose interests may not be aligned: the research community, innovators in technology, investors in communications facilities and the services that use them, government entities at all levels, and the multitude of individual and organizational users. Indeed, the technical fact of information convergence—that all information can be digitized and carried as strings of bits—has driven industry sectors that used to be separate, such as cable and telephone providers, into vigorous competition and contention. It is the actions of these powerful players that will define the future, not the fact that bits are bits. Out of their decisions and actions will emerge new conditions for connectivity and performance, kinds of content, and contributions to cognition, as well as degrees of choice (for connectivity and content) and credibility (for content and hence cognition). Whichever of the many possible outcomes is realized will affect the level, distribution, and balance of cyberpower. We argue that a number of trends combine to point to a cyberspace that, 10 years from now, will more fundamentally blend technical, economic, and social elements in complex ways. However, we are only beginning to be able to analyze such trends, let alone predict them.

This chapter looks at eight factors that will influence the future of cyberspace:

- the present and future character of the Internet, since it is a central component of cyberspace today: it is an example of the *platform* character of cyberspace
- the future shape of computing devices, which will shape networking (and thus cyberspace in general) and define the basis for the user experience in cyberspace
- the changing nature of information and the tools and mechanisms to deal with it
- the emergence of network design principles at a layer higher than simple data transfer
- the nature of the future user experience in cyberspace, drawing on today's research
- the challenges associated with security and responses thereto
- the role of private sector investment in defining the future
- the health and character of research on the science and technology of cyberspace.

For each factor, our discussion tries to bring out issues and implications for cyberpower, such as the tools for control and the balance of power among different actors and stakeholders. We also note places where we can expect differences in the nature of cyberspace in different nations.

Platforms: The Centrality of the Internet Today

There are many aspects to cyberspace, from the computing and communications infrastructure, through the information that is processed and transported, up to the users that operate in cyberspace. We consider a number of these aspects in this chapter, but we focus on the Internet because of the central role it plays in so many of these dimensions.

The importance of the Internet arises from its design and the purpose for which it was conceived. The Internet was designed not to support a specific application, but with the goal of generality. In contrast to the telephone network, for example, which was initially designed specifically to carry telephone calls, the Internet was designed to support a wide range of applications, even those not yet thought of. And indeed, new applications such as the World Wide Web were later conceived and deployed to extend the general service provided by the Internet.

The Internet provides a general platform for applications and services on top of a variety of network technologies, ranging from high-speed optical links and local area networks to wireless connections. This generality means that the application designer need not be concerned with the technical details of specific network technology. The use of different technologies can, however, affect the way different parts of the Internet perform, so one can design an application and later adjust parameters such as throughput or resilience by changing the technology over which the application is operating.

The Internet illustrates a critical characteristic of cyberspace: that it is built out of components that provide services, and these services are designed so that they can be composed and combined to form ever more complex services. Low-level services include program execution environments, mechanisms for data transport, and standards for data formats. From these are built applications, such as a word processor, a database, or the World Wide Web. By combining these, more complex services emerge. For example, by combining a database with the Web, we can get dynamic content generation and active Web objects. Cyberspace features the continuous and rapid evolution of new capabilities and services, based on the creation and combination of new logical constructs, all running on top of the physical foundations. Cyberspace is a sequence of platforms on which new capabilities are constructed, each of which in turn becomes a platform for the next innovation; it is thus very plastic. Cyberspace has emergent qualities: it is the consequence not of a coherent or centralized design, but of the independent contributions of many actors with various motivations and capabilities.

Technically, the essence of the Internet, defined by the Internet protocol (IP), is a set of standards that describe how data to be sent is broken up into *packets* (small units of data together with instructions for delivery). IP defines the format of those packets, how the destination of the packet is specified, and so on. The specification at this middle level, above the transmission technology and below the application, has sometimes been illustrated by drawing the Internet as an hourglass (see figure 8–1); diverse transmission technologies support the packet transport service of the Internet, and diverse applications sit on top of this service. Defining a level of standardization (the narrow waist in the illustration) supports a wide range of diversity and innovation in other parts of the system (the wide top and bottom in the illustration).

Today's wireless technology illustrates how different kinds of networks that came into being at different times may coexist within the Internet, with different implications. Cellular systems are centrally administered and have global reach; WiFi networks are deployed at the edge of, but are seen as part of, a global network; Bluetooth wireless systems are very small scale, operating without wide-area connectivity but capable of serving as edge systems if connected to a global network. All of these technologies, sitting "below" the narrow waist in figure 8–1, are being used today to carry packets as part of the Internet.

What Does *Internet* Mean?

The term *Internet* can mean a number of things, which we must tease apart. In most cases, the term is synonymous with the public Internet—the globally interconnected service so many of us use. The term can also refer to the standards—the specification of the technology of the Internet—and to the technology base itself, the set of products consistent with those standards. This distinction is important because many of the Internet products purchased

FIGURE 8-1. Internet Protocol

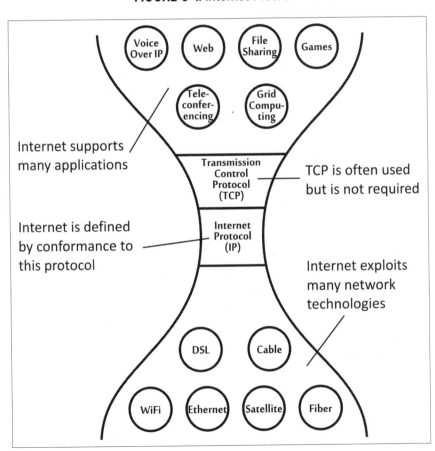

Source: Computer Science and Telecommunications Board, *Realizing the Information Future* (Washington, DC: National Academies Press, 1994), 53.

today do not end up in the public Internet, but in private deployments, restricted to a corporation, government, or other actor. It is often carelessly said that "in the future, all communications will be over the Internet." It is easy to see how this assertion might be made, as telephony and television begin to migrate to the Internet, and it is used to build control systems (such as supervisory control and data acquisition [SCADA] systems for the power grid and other critical infrastructure, as described in chapter 5 in this volume, "Cyberspace and Infrastructure"), and so on. However, this masks an important distinction: these applications are being redesigned to take advantage of Internet technology, but this does not mean that they will all be carried over the public Internet. Many private or closed networks, including networks for telephone and television as well as for large users in government and the private sector, are being built out of Internet technology, because it is general-purpose, inexpensive, and available.

An example of both other services being carried on an "Internet" base and IP networks separated from the public Internet is provided by Britain's telephone provider, BT Group, and its ongoing effort to transfer all its communications traffic to an IP backbone. This offers simplification and savings in the costs of future upgrades. In contrast to "Voice over IP" (VOIP) services that run on top of the public Internet, BT Group's telecommunications system will operate in essence as a separate, private Internet. This isolation is intended to enhance security and reliability.[1]

All uses and forms of the Internet are not equivalent: there is tremendous diversity in the variety of technology, the degree of interconnection, the range of use, and the controls on that use. Recognition of this point, with careful choices about technology, the degree of interconnection, and so on, may affect cyberpower.

In general, the architecture of the Internet helps to define what it is used for, how it works, and how it is composed. The interaction of use, operation, and structure points the way to potential paths for change as well as to levers or targets for cyberpower. Possible revolutionary change in cyberspace will influence both the future of the "public Internet" and the future penetration of Internet technology, potentially in different ways.

An Alternative to the Present Internet

One of the goals of this chapter is to illustrate the myriad possibilities for the future of cyberspace. *Virtualization* is an example of an alternative approach that might lead to a very different global network in 10 to 15 years. Virtualization has the objective of providing a greatly enhanced ability to exploit different network technologies. The Internet's service, characterized by the narrow waist of the hourglass in figure 8–1, can be implemented over a range of network technologies, since it only requires the technology to carry strings of bytes as packets. If these technologies have other capabilities, the applications sitting on top of the IP layer cannot exploit them. The simplicity of the IP layer is both powerful (in terms of generality) and limiting (in terms of exploiting technology features). For example, radio is intrinsically a broadcast medium, but the broadcast feature cannot be exploited in the Internet. Fiber is capable of carrying a very high bandwidth analog signal with very low distortion, but this quality cannot be exploited using the Internet design.

Virtualization, a very familiar concept in computer science and electrical engineering, attempts to make the advanced features of any network technology directly available to the application. It is a set of techniques that divide a physical set of technology resources among multiple uses in a way that gives each use (or user) the illusion of having a separate and distinct copy of these resources, essentially identical except that the copies run slower than the actual technology base that is being virtualized. We know how to take a computer and use software that creates a number of *virtual machines*.[2] We can divide up and virtualize circuits, memory, and so on. Now research seeks to virtualize all the resources found in a global network and then give *virtual global networks* to different classes of users or uses.[3] There is no commitment to a common packet format (indeed, to packets at all) or to any of the other current conventions of the Internet. Different applications can use the resources in ways best suited to their needs: one set of users might run something like the Internet in one virtual global network, while another set of users might use a virtualized fiber optic path to carry analog signals, and a third set of users might use a virtual global network for global dissemination of bulk data, with a totally different approach to packetization and routing. User behavior, and consequences, such as traffic patterns, might become less predictable.

Compared to the illustration of the Internet, this approach moves the point of agreement—the narrow point of the hourglass—down, to the technology base. It demands of each technology not that it be able to carry packets, but that it be able to "virtualize itself."

So there is an interesting turbulence in the future of networking. As many industries (such as the cable television industry) are moving away from their current approach (transmission of analog signals) to a digital approach based on the existing Internet technology, in order to exploit the benefits of a low-cost integrated platform, the platform might evolve in an attempt to support what these industries already do.

One particular application area that might benefit from the ability to exploit the specific features of underlying technology is the use of wireless technology on the battlefield. This extremely demanding and hostile environment may require that we abandon the generality of the existing Internet design for a new kind of generality that allows applications to more directly exploit and benefit from the features of advanced wireless systems. But how best to do this, and what this means for a global network of the future, is still a question for the research community. Research along these lines has been a priority for the Defense Advanced Research Projects Agency (DARPA).[4]

Thus, a future global network might be based not on a common packet format, but on a set of conventions at a "lower layer," that is, the ability of the resource to be shared using virtualization. This approach, if successful, could lead to a network in which applications are able to exploit the native capabilities of current and future network technologies. If the virtualization approach provides more flexibility to the application in how it exploits underlying technology, it also raises fundamental architectural questions about the division of function between the virtualization layer and the layers above it—questions about security, management, the economics of the industry, and so on. And it invites the question of whether the associated generality is actually more valuable than the generality of the Internet of today. This concept, if it proves itself and moves out of the research community, could offer a very different future global network.

The Changing Face of Computing: Getting Fast and Getting Small

The shape of tomorrow's networks will be defined by the shape of tomorrow's computers. In 10 years, the range of networked computers will be much more diverse than what we see today; one trend leads toward massive server farms and other high-end computing platforms, and another toward dense universal deployment of very small and inexpensive computers embedded in everything. This changing nature of computing will influence many aspects of cyberspace. It will greatly expand the range of applications and functions that can practically be supported, and it will change the nature of the Internet; since the Internet was designed to connect computers, as computers evolve, so does the Internet. The early Internet of the 1970s featured long-distance access to large, centralized mainframes by so-called dumb terminals; the last two decades, by contrast, have been dominated by personal computers (PCs), small systems that bring computing intelligence to the user. PCs popularized computers and the things that could be done with them, thanks to continued reductions in size and weight and the progressive linking of computing with communication, first through private networks and then the commercialization of the "public" Internet, while numerous innovations in software made more and more activities first possible and then easier. In an important sense, the Internet and the PC have co-evolved, and the apparent stability and maturity of the Internet is due to the maturity of the PC.

Now we are at a point where advances in computing are overturning the PC as the dominant paradigm. Thus, the next decade may be marked by rapid changes in the nature of computing and networking. PC-based computing as a dominant paradigm may well be displaced by embedded computing, sensors, and other applications of small, inexpensive processing. Proliferation rather than convergence of devices should be expected.

Continuing reductions in size and cost for equivalent performance will lead to the embedding of computing in other devices. This trend, in concept a decades-old phenomenon, is facilitated by the emergence of smaller and smaller complete platforms, which today can be the size of a stick of chewing gum or smaller.[5] Much of the value of such devices may come from their ability to communicate—they are likely to use networks, if intermittently—to share information or to give or receive directions.

The second trend in computing is at the high end, where Moore's law (see chapter 6 in this volume, "Evolutionary Trends in Cyberspace") brings ever more powerful processing. What is important is not so much the continued rapid improvements in the speed of single processors as the emergence of parallel processing at all scales. Even consumer PCs today have multiple processors ("cores") in them. Much high-end processing is based on various sorts of parallel processing. This trend will continue. What this implies for applications depends on the nature of the application itself. Some classic, computation-intensive applications, traditional drivers of supercomputing, are difficult to implement on a parallel processor system.[6] On the other hand, many important applications are naturally parallel, such as various sorts of search, pattern recognition, media formatting, and transformation. This sort of parallel processing can be seen today across processing platforms that are networked at all scales, from integrated multiprocessors, to grids (collections of computers hooked together by high-speed Internet functionality), to massively parallel processing performed on consumer PCs connected by residential broadband.[7] Such distributed, consumer-based problem solving can be seen as a positive and intentional version of the "botnets" used by criminal hackers (described in chapter 7 in this volume, "Information Security Issues in Cyberspace").[8] To the individual, this trend toward collaborative, massive, highly parallel computing can be seen as the next stage, after citizen empowerment by the PC, in the democratization of computing. All of these paradigms of parallel processing have implications for the performance and scale of the networks that connect them. The current trend is to push the function and performance of the Internet in directions that support this class of application.

The future Internet will thus be pulled in two directions by these trends in computing: toward higher speeds, by the need for high-performance parallel processing, and toward lower cost and ubiquitous access, by embedded processing. In 10 years, a single network architecture might evolve that can serve this greatly diverse set of demands, or we might instead see a split in the technology and architecture, with high-end processing and embedded processing being served by different Internets.

How computers are used is changing with their physical form. There has already been movement, especially in developed countries, from the one-PC-per-person model of the early 1980s to multiple computing devices per person, including not only conventional PCs but also other devices that incorporate computing capabilities. We can assume that in another decade or so, the typical person, in the developed world at least, will be immersed in a pervasive matrix of computing and computers, including both the processors that the person carries and the processors embedded in the environment. All of these devices will interact, which will have many new implications for the architecture of cyberspace.

A third trend in computing is the rise of massive commodity server complexes.[9] The low cost of PCs has benefited not only the consumer, but also the application designer who can build a service that runs on a huge array of such devices. More than just a special case of parallel processing, the scale of current server complexes warrants special recognition.[10] The high-end server farms run by Google, Yahoo!, and Microsoft are so large that they are recognized in the industry as effective supercomputers.

Thus, we see a number of trends that signal a major change in the way applications are designed.[11] Google Search, for example, is highly parallel, running on servers that are physically centralized and under central control.[12] Projects such as SETI@home are also controlled centrally, are highly parallel, and run on commodity PC platforms, but they differ in that ordinary consumers contribute the processors as a volunteer gesture. Consumers also contribute their processing capacity to activities with little or no central control, such as peer-to-peer music sharing. Multiple approaches coexist and support different kinds of applications; there is no single preferred or more likely outcome (especially absent any steering or constraints from law or regulation). The broad trend, illustrated by evolving grid systems, is for increasing distribution—of data, software, and/or computational resources—and for benefit to individual entities from exploitation of distributed resources.

Another broad trend is a movement from people communicating with devices, or through devices to other people, toward devices communicating with each other. This trend raises questions about who or what is a "user" of the Internet (or cyberspace), an issue complicated by customary use of *user* to apply to both individuals and organizations, and to both producers and consumers of content and applications.

Embedded Sensor Networks

Many of the issues discussed above are illustrated by the development of networks of embedded sensors. Considerable work is under way in the research community to develop sensor networks embedded in a variety of physical environments. These networks will monitor such phenomena as ecological processes, microclimates, seismic activity, and pollution (for example, contaminant and fluid flow). Complementing remote sensing via satellite systems, these networks enable in situ exploration of an environment. Such sensor nets can feature from tens to thousands of devices of different sizes that connect to each other using wireless communication. They are constrained in terms of power, capacity to store information, and capacity to communicate, but technology development is improving all of these factors. These networks may be more or less dense and may be long- or short-lived; improvements in technology and reductions in cost will even enable disposable or redeployable networks for some applications. Researchers' use of the term *smart dust* captures the potential.[13]

Current sensor networks use the public Internet to a limited degree, as systems that connect to it at its edge. For example, clusters of sensors in a given location, which process information collected locally at a local server before passing it on, may feed into networks serving a larger area; they, too, may undertake processing and aggregation of information before passing it to a higher level network.[14] The Internet of today, per se, may not be engaged directly by clusters of sensors, let alone individual sensors, but it does play a role in their interconnection.

There are many other kinds of sensors currently deployed that may have communications links but tend to be focused either on a local task or on the central monitoring of information from remote points. Examples include traffic control, home and industrial automation, industrial and infrastructure control (SCADA systems), and deployment of communicating identifiers (radio frequency identification [RFID] systems) for such applications as supply-chain management. It can be assumed that in the future, these sorts of applications will be fully networked and integrated into the larger cyberspace context. Cars and other motor vehicles, which have long had embedded sensors and computers that operate as parts of a closed system, present possibilities that range from peer-to-peer communication between vehicles (somewhat analogous to the peer-to-peer communication between airplanes that is contemplated for air traffic control) to communication between cars and other systems that could contribute to traffic monitoring and control.[15] Taken together, networks of embedded sensors all involve proliferating information technology that, to varying degrees, collects data, processes it, communicates, and automates those processes.

Contemporary sensor network research has focused on a class of networks that are self-configuring (deployed sensors establish a network among themselves), self-monitoring, and, if a problem is detected, self-healing. These features contribute to making these systems of sensors relatively autonomous and easy to deploy. Automation intended to enhance management of the system also presents the prospect of added vulnerability, because it implies dependence on programming and therefore the potential to be compromised. On the other hand, automated sensor systems also increase people's ability to interact with sensors in order to monitor data quality and control their data collection or movement in real time; thus, systems may be more responsive both to circumstances and to the controller's interests. Again, however, a benefit for functionality may also generate vulnerability if the ability to interact with sensors cannot be controlled perfectly.

Research points to the potential for sensor networks to become more versatile. For example, some systems are gaining actuation capability, the ability to control other systems. Historically, many control systems (for example, for machine tools or building access) have been automated, but only locally; people had to intervene periodically. By contrast, removal of the need for people in or near the control process presents both opportunities and vulnerabilities. In addition to controlling other systems, some sensors may be able to actuate themselves: to move to where they can be more effective, or to explore different points in their general vicinity.

The introduction of sensor networks into social situations also presents possibilities. Leveraging lessons from natural environment applications, more research is focusing on urban situations that combine features of the built environment and human behavior. They might, for example, make use of worn or carried devices, perhaps cell phones, and a human propensity for exhibitionism or voyeurism, such as Webcams, installed either by people recording themselves, or by government entities or other organizations. The ability to download software to cell phones for new functions allows cell phones to aggregate and communicate sensed data as well as to support interpersonal communication. Cell phones also illustrate how unpredictable the mix of automation and human agency can be. For example, a cell phone can be seen as a networked sensor that can operate independently (as opposed to being part of a sensor network by design), which raises questions about the potential to engage groups of cell phones as impromptu or ad hoc sensor networks.[16] The use of cell phones to trigger flashmobs (and even invoke vigilante justice), and the emerging use for relaying official emergency alerts, suggests their use as actuators, if indirect, for human behavior.

Implications of Sensor Networks

Sensors can be cheap, especially those without sophisticated instrumentation; technology development is likely to continue to decrease costs as well as size. Sensors are available to virtually anyone.[17] The proliferation of cell phones and of new uses for them indicates how ordinary citizens seek to monitor their environment and communicate the results with each other, illustrated by the sharing of photos via cell phones (and the further sharing of cell phone–captured images on the Web). Over time, more kinds of sensing modalities are likely to become available in consumer devices. Easy acquisition of sensors and their connection via open standards suggest possibilities for broadening commercial, public, and citizen use of sensor networks. We can anticipate that in the coming decade, any interested individual could deploy a set of sensors. More use of sensors may imply added societal vulnerability, for example, to electromagnetic interference (perhaps intentional); electromagnetic pulse, which could destroy large clusters of sensors; or tampering (as more and more sensors are scattered in the physical environment without supervision). More use of today's wireless technology itself implies added vulnerability, which sensor networks compound.[18]

Some sensor networks (for example, those the government uses in connection with weather) are deployed and managed top-down, while others are bottom-up, with sensors connecting according to choices made by users. A bottom-up system can operate in the same arena as a top-down system; for example, the Weather Underground system, using aggregated information from a wide range of local sensors,[19] complements government weather data. The ability to connect from the bottom up, peer to peer, can provide resilient connectivity: such networks may use a kind of cell structure, in which independent cells continue to operate even if one cell is knocked out. That independence can also increase the challenge to those who seek to monitor or control such networks. The emergence of botnets and the varied motives of their controllers suggests the analogous possibility of commercially useful sensor networks and their deployment and exploitation for productive rather than malignant purposes.

If sensor networks proliferate, how might they be interconnected? A future Internet might provide the technical means, but there are also organizational and even political issues. For example, current sensor networks are deployed by different owners, with different attitudes about the merits of interconnection. In the research community, a collaborative ethos and the incentive of funding drive efforts to interconnect different environmental sensor networks to promote greater understanding of the natural environment;[20] this also fosters greater understanding of sensor network interconnection per se. These projects suggest prospects for dual use, inasmuch as data collected for one purpose might be used for others; indeed, a hallmark of cyberspace is abundant data used (eventually) for abundant purposes. Although current efforts to interconnect sensor networks seem to emphasize hierarchy, which implies some degree of coordination and control, broader trends make it easy to envision more peer-to-peer activity.

Information Ecology

Cyberspace is defined not just by technology and standards for communication: the purpose of information technology is the manipulation, storage, and communication of data. The nature of information is changing as fast as the technology that processes it, and the trends surrounding information will be a key determinant of a future cyberspace. We consider several major trends. First, there is an increase in the volume of sensor-based information, complementing the business data and the human-created content that dominate today's information. Second, the highly distributed and decentralized creation of content, from blogs and wikis to mashups,[21] challenges the traditional models of professional creation and editorship and, by encouraging a proliferation of information and sources, may impede any single party's ability to get its message out. Another implication is that the proliferation of information sources will allow users to ask to see only what they prefer to see, which may reinforce the polarized positions and opinions of special interest groups.[22]

In addition, the landscape of search is changing: search tools such as Google provide the power to search the whole Web, tools emerge for search of nontext content such as recorded speech, and metadata systems are more broadly implemented. These tools are available to everyone, not just to specialized high-end users, and their power and capabilities will increase. Another trend is that information as it is presented to each user is increasingly personalized: each person may see a version of the content expressly generated for that individual.

These trends raise important concerns about control, quality and reliability, sharing, and options for manipulation and distortion.

New Sources of Information

The two traditional sources of online information have been human creativity—the collections of writings, utterances, and images produced by people for other people to consume directly[23]—and business data, such as the capture of online transactions, inventories, and so on. The proliferation of sensor networks predicted above would accelerate increases in the volume and variety of information that is available. Sensor data may call for different treatment than business data. With business transactions, it is important to capture and record each event reliably. With sensors, however, individual readings may not be so important, and together they are too voluminous to store individually; what is important are the trends, aggregates, and summaries of the raw data. Some researchers are exploring options for sensor output processing and aggregation, and others are exploring the designs of new sorts of databases.

A larger trend, accelerated by the emergence of embedded sensors, is geolocation: people (cell phones), things (RFID), and information (data tags) are increasingly being associated with their locations, both at a given point in time and over time, as they move around. Where sensor networks target people or social behavior, and even sometimes when they do not (as with routine utility monitoring), there can be privacy impacts, inasmuch as these systems collect personal information and permit inferences about behavior. Growth in sensor-delivered information also puts a spotlight on its quality: sampling can affect the trustworthiness of sensor readings or interpretation, and sensors can have faults and might be tampered with.

That there is more information also implies that there is more potential for information to be manipulated and more incentive to do that manipulation. In one sense, manipulation is a goal in itself: collaborative generation of content implies, or makes explicit, an invitation by the originators of information to others to manipulate it and improve on it. This is the concept behind Wikipedia (and of wikis in general).[24] A related concept can be seen in blogging, where the blogger elicits comments and responses. At present, the phenomenon may be too new to predict where the revolution will end up, and among some "digerati," there is a vigorous debate about the relative wisdom of the collectivity versus the expert.[25] New streams of information also imply new possibilities for combining information from different sources.[26] New businesses may offer to sell that capability.

As more individuals take advantage of ease of access to generate and share content, more questions arise about the impact of the resulting volume of information, the ability to find useful elements, and the role of editorship. A related question for a national cyber strategy might be what it takes to get a nation's message out to a desired audience. At a national level, this may be like asking what the Radio Free Europe–equivalent of cyberspace could be. Given the uneven history of national broadcasting to foreign populations, putting a national brand on information dissemination may or may not be practical or desirable. A future analog of a Radio Free Europe might instead be more concerned with providing access to a wide range of information rather than packaging and disseminating selected information. This view is consistent with recent U.S. Department of State activities relating to information and communication policy.[27] (See chapter 14 in this volume, "Cyber Influence and International Security," for more on these issues.)

Search

Finding useful information is a perennial challenge. Two trends may combine to transform the way searches are carried out in cyberspace. The first is the growing power and sophistication of software for automated recognition and understanding. Today, text-based processing and analysis support tools ranging from Google to LexisNexis. Emerging from the research lab are programs for image recognition, speech recognition (now used commercially in a variety of contexts), and language processing. Tools such as these may make it possible to search an audio file, such as a recording of a conversation, a commercial broadcast, or a podcast, the same way that text is searched today. The other trend is the emergence of the Semantic Web, a set of standards and methods that allows the creator of a Web site, or a third party, to tag that site with information about its content (called metadata) in a form that is easily processed by a computer program.[28] How the information is labeled or described creates the potential for finding and combining information, but also for hiding from or redirecting searchers.[29]

We can expect individual elements of information to be embedded in a rich context of linkage, metadata, translation, transcription, search aids, and commentary. The ability to control this context—what the user can find or is prevented from finding—may be as important in an analysis of cyberpower as is access to the elemental information itself. If information systems are your "eyes," part of a cyberstruggle will be to blind you, lie to you, or cause hallucinations.

The immense processing power of Google, made available to all users of the Internet for free, may be one of the most profound examples of the leveling of the playing field that is associated with the Internet. Nations desiring to control information access have found ways to moderate Google's impact, but this is only a change in degree.

Systems such as Google raise other questions. First, like other existing search systems, it can only search the Web pages it can find. There is also a so-called dark or deep Web that is not reached by the current crawlers, and perhaps because the information has no links that point to it so the crawlers cannot know it is there, is protected from open access or crawler access, or it is created only on demand. If an increasing amount of information resides in this deep Web, the scope of information and the validity of search results will be affected. Second, the economic value of search and the complementary products generated by Google have inspired an attempt in France and Germany to mount an alternative.[30] Meanwhile, in China, a national effort to degrade Google service quality has made indigenous alternatives more competitive.[31] The ability to shape the user's view of search results is clearly seen as cyberpower on a national scale.

Dynamic Information and the Personalization of Content

Another important trend is the dynamic generation of information in response to queries. More Web pages are generated on the fly out of component parts when a user asks to retrieve them, so that each user gets a personalized version of specially selected content. This personalization can be done for many reasons; for example, an online newspaper might be tailored to the interests and priorities of each reader; different advertising might be presented to each user based on the profile maintained on that user by the advertiser; or different pricing might be offered at an e-commerce site.

There are a number of implications of dynamic, personalized information. For librarians and archivists, this trend implies that there is no definitive version of a piece of information—no reference version that can be universally referenced or cited. Any producer of information may, literally, say something different to each person.

Future Architectural Concepts at a Higher Level

Current research may lead to higher level services that might define an Internet of tomorrow. These services would involve not just simple point-to-point data carriage, but more complex functions closer to what the user is trying to do and further away from moving bytes. These future services will better match the needs of sophisticated applications. We describe three examples of such research: support for an information architecture; support for the creation and management of services that depend on functions placed on servers distributed across the network; and support for communication among nodes and regions of the network that are connected only intermittently.

A Future Architecture for Information

Some current research aims at an architecture for information as opposed to an architecture for byte carriage. Some examples of what such an architecture might capture are outlined here.

On the Internet today, the authenticity and provenance of an information object are validated by where it comes from. For example, in today's Internet, the only way a user can be sure that a Web page that appears to be from the Cable News Network (CNN) is legitimate is to try to retrieve it from CNN. Once it is retrieved, there is no trustworthy information associated with the page itself that captures and conveys the provenance of the information. If one user downloads a page and then sends it on to a second person, there is no way for that second person to be sure it is not a forgery. If the validity of the information were associated with the information itself, perhaps using some sort of encryption scheme to sign the information, then we could use a much richer set of mechanisms for information dissemination. These might include peer-to-peer systems, third-party caching, archiving, and forwarding, or casual user-to-user transmission via email. This richness would provide a network that was more diverse and efficient.

An architecture for information could include a means to name information. Current Internet names (domain names) and addresses do not name information objects; rather, they name physical endpoints—that is, computers attached to the edge of the network. The Web provides one scheme for naming objects, the uniform resource locator. There has been much research on other schemes for naming objects, ranging from Internet Engineering Task Force research on universal resource names[32] and centrally managed schemes such as the Handle scheme proposed by the Corporation for National Research Initiatives,[33] to highly decentralized schemes that allow users to pick local names and share them.[34] All of these schemes imply some solution to the location problem: given a name for an object, can I find the object itself? Some solutions to the location problem would involve a centrally managed catalog of objects; others would use a more decentralized approach, with location services run by different operators in different regions of the network; some schemes would be completely decentralized, based on a user broadcasting a request for an object until a copy is found. These different schemes have very different implications for control, resilience, performance, and utility. Our concern here is the implications for control, a core aspect of cyberpower.

The problem of *search* is distinct from the problem of *location*. The location problem is to find a copy of an object once I know exactly what I am looking for. The analog in the real world is to ask what library or bookstore has the closest copy of a specific book. The *search* problem is to look for objects that may match certain selection criteria, analogous to seeking a book on the history of baseball that costs less than $20. Google's approach for finding a good match to given search criteria, for example, is quite complex and sophisticated, but Google facilitates the search process by keeping a centralized copy of every candidate page from the Web that it can discover. This massive database is very complex and costly to maintain, but it simplifies the subsequent search process. An important search question is whether it is possible to perform useful and effective searches without centralizing all the candidate material.[35] Another problem that has a critical influence on searches is the emergence of dynamic information, described above, that is generated on demand for each user. It is not clear that current search systems reliably or consistently index information that only exists when a particular user asks to retrieve it. There is ongoing research in the design of advanced search engines that could search or otherwise deal with dynamic content.

The importance of this research to the future of cyberspace is that, depending on how such efforts succeed, we may be able in the future to place either much more or much less confidence in the validity, authenticity, completeness, and persistence of information in cyberspace. Fraud and forgery could destroy all important uses of online information or, at the other possible extreme, cyberspace could become the only important and relevant source of information.

An Architecture for Services and Service Construction

The architecture of the current Internet really recognizes only two sorts of devices: the devices that make up the Internet itself—the routers that forward packets—and everything else, including all devices attached to the edges of the network, between and among which the Internet packets are transported. The dominant examples of edge devices now are the PCs that belong to the users and the servers that provide content to users. In the Internet architecture, there is no consideration of what these servers do, what patterns of communication connect them, or how applications actually exploit servers to build up their services.

Most applications today display a somewhat complex structure of servers and services to implement their functions. Content may be prepositioned on servers near the ultimate recipient to improve performance and resilience.[36] Communication among end nodes is often relayed through intermediate servers to realize such functions as mutual assurance of identity, selective hiding of certain information, logging of transactions, or insertion of advertising. Some servers, such as email servers, hold information for recipients until they choose to connect to the network to retrieve it. This allows nodes to communicate even if they are not simultaneously connected and active.

Once we recognize this rich structure, it is natural to ask whether the design of the Internet should take account of it in some way. For example, today's Internet does not provide a direct way to ask the question, "Which of these servers has the shortest path to a specified set of recipients?" The routing system knows the answer to this question, but there is no easy way for an application to retrieve the information. In another example, the Internet has no way to take account of or respond to the different traffic patterns from different clients and different sorts of servers. A particular server may, for example, typically receive content from only a certain set of sources but send information on to any number of clients. If the network could incorporate this knowledge, it might be able to detect nonstandard patterns of communication as a security attack.

The emergence (and recognition) of systems that incorporate servers and services may signal a move of processing and control from the edge of the network—the computers of the end users—toward the center, locations operated by providers. Providers might include those who supply the basic packet carriage of the Internet, as well as specialty providers of specific application services and providers of commodity platform computing on which many services can be hosted.[37] These types of players may become important parts of the Internet experience of tomorrow. At the moment, there is no evidence that the movement of function toward the center implies the emergence of new monopolists, but this is a factor to analyze and monitor, along with potential government exploitation of such centralization. Players at many layers of the

Internet—including providers of residential broadband service, providers of core software products such as Microsoft, or higher layer providers that deal in information, such as Google—may have significant market power now or in the future. Areas that will warrant attention may include advertising, marketing, and the collection and management of information about consumers.

A basic aspect of such an analysis is to identify all the components that make up a system, and ask who controls these components and what options exist to influence that control. The emergence of servers as a distinct element raises the question of who controls the servers, who has the power to select which servers are used to realize a given service, and so on. This adds richness to the dimensions of power and control in cyberspace.

At the same time, we can see the possibility of a future with increasing regional differences and a possible balkanization of the network at these higher layers. Even at the basic packet-carriage layer of the Internet, which is defined by a very simple universal standard, there have been attempts to control the flow of information across regions of the Internet. These higher layer services are more complex, with richer structure and more visible signals that may reveal the intentions of the users, and they provide many more options for points of control. The experience may differ depending on the user's location; many actors may try to shape and limit the user's experience.[38] Differentiation and fragmentation of users' experiences have many implications for cyberpower.

One of the specific issues that arises in these more complex, server-based applications is that the physical location of the servers is relevant, and indeed sometimes critical, to the effective operation of the application. If the purpose of the server is to preposition content close to the user to increase performance and reliability, then the server, because it is physically close to the user, may be more likely to be under the same legal or governmental jurisdiction as the user. It may be that services that are designed for performance and for resilience in the face of network failures will have a quite different design than services that position the content at a distance from the user in order to avoid the imposition of local controls and balkanization.[39] Research could help to enable such geographic independence. A continuing tension between technical mechanisms and legal or other nontechnical mechanisms is likely, given competing interests in disseminating or restricting specific kinds of information in specific locales.

An Architecture for Relayed Delivery of Content

A central assumption of the current Internet architecture is that communication between pairs of nodes is interactive in real time, and since any pair of nodes may want to establish such interactive communication, the network provides this capability universally. The dominant protocol for data transfer on the Internet, the transmission control protocol (TCP), is based on the immediate confirmation to the sender of the delivery of each packet. But if applications can define restricted patterns of communication involving intermediate servers, delivery from the original source to the ultimate destination is not necessarily immediate but may instead be delayed, staged, or relayed. This pattern of communication seems to be common to many sensor applications and information dissemination applications, so it is posited that this pattern should also be recognized as a part of the core Internet architecture. A current line of research involves the investigation of delay/disruption tolerant networking (DTN), which generalizes this concept of "store and forward" networking (in contrast to "end-to-end interactive" networking).[40] DTN raises many important questions about security (how much we must trust the intermediate nodes), resilience (how the service might recover from failed intermediates), routing (who controls which intermediates are used), and assurance of delivery (whether the design provides confirmation of delivery that can be relayed from recipient to sender). At the same time, they allow the network designer great freedom in dealing with challenging contexts such as poor and intermittent connectivity or hosts with intermittent duty cycles, and they allow the application designer to hand off part of the design problem to the network.

A Long-term Outcome: Revolutionary Integration of New Architecture Ideas

Above we described an alternative network design based on virtualization, in which the basic network service is not packet carriage, but access to the network technology at a lower level and more technology-specific way. This lower layer idea gains importance when it is combined with a higher level architecture for services and delay-tolerant delivery. If information is being delivered in stages, not directly from source to destination, then the details of how the data is transmitted can be different in each stage. The requirement for a uniform and universal commitment to a single packet modality, for example, is much reduced if different parts of the network talk to each other only via a higher level server. The result, in 10 or 15 years, might blend all of these ideas in a global network that is based, at a lower level, on virtualized network technology and, at a higher level, on application-aware servers that connect parts of the network in ways that are matched to the features of the technology in that region of the network.

Compared to the Internet of today, future architecture may focus on the specification of features that are "higher level"—closer to what the application designer and the user are trying to accomplish. Future networks may focus on architecture for information-handling services built out of distributed servers and staged delivery. Attention to architecture at these higher levels may provide an alternative to today's focus on common packet formats and allow the lower layers of a future network to more directly exploit features of diverse technology.

Some basic features of the present Internet, such as global end-node packet-level connectivity, will not be as important in a future where most machines only communicate via application-level servers.

The Changing User Experience in Cyberspace

Our view of cyberspace is that it is best understood as a series of layers: technology, platform, information, and human. In this section, we complete our look at these layers by an assessment of the user experience in cyberspace. We identify several important trends:

- the increasing importance of physical location as a factor influencing what happens in cyberspace
- the increasing interconnection of real and cyberspace, with the ability of the user to move fluidly back and forth between the two viewpoints
- the importance of massively multiplayer online role-playing games (MMORPGs) and other shared virtual experiences as early signals of the rich range of options for people to interact in cyberspace
- the ability to earn money and make a living by working in cyberspace.

Users are engaging cyberspace not only more overall, but also in different ways. For example, instant messaging (and its equivalents, such as chat features embedded in different kinds of applications) introduces a new kind of immediacy to online interactions; it implies an ability of the system to monitor and register presence (whether a user is online at any given moment) and reachability. Augmented reality, combining real space and cyberspace in different ways, is becoming more common. For example, navigation systems (portable or in vehicles) can now link one's location to information about nearby businesses and other sites. Other products similarly blend the virtual and the real, based on a user's location.[41] More generally, easier access combines with different kinds of activities to make the Internet more than a place to find things to look at, read, or buy; for many, it is becoming a true alternative venue for daily life.

MMORPGs, which draw on virtual reality technology, demonstrate how cyberspace can become more engaging and immersive, hence more broadly integrated into people's lives. Evidence is the use of real currency to acquire items found and used only in games, and the use of virtual product placement as a kind of advertising. In some contexts, MMORPGs can range from being a team sport to a cause for social concern about Internet addiction; the latter is often reported in South Korea, where comparatively early widespread access to broadband facilitated extensive involvement with games. The capacity to involve people to the point of addiction or self-neglect is a kind of cyberpower, albeit presumably not one intended by the application providers.

MMORPGs embody the development of synthetic worlds, which are also being considered for a range of real-world activity such as training.[42] Some synthetic worlds and many other areas of cyberspace—from eBay to gambling sites and even some blogs and other sites that host advertisements—allow more and more people to "go to work" and make "real" money in cyberspace, sometimes obviating the need for conventional jobs. MMORPGs are also an instance of social networking, itself an evolving genre. The Internet is making possible much larger social networks, and their scale (which can range to the tens of millions of users) is already motivating researchers to understand the kinds of social links being formed, the different roles people play in diffusing information through networks (as discoverers, amplifiers, reshapers), and the potential outcomes of the interactions of large numbers of self-interested parties competing for resources in online environments. In contrast to the physical world, the software basis of the online world helps to constrain and capture the interactions, making explicit some of what might have been implicit and generating detailed records of behavior.[43]

The example of MMORPGs illustrates an important distinction between cyberspace (and the resulting features of cyberpower) and other realms of power. While realms such as sea and air are physical and are strongly constrained by physical reality, cyberspace is much more a synthetic realm, constrained less by physics than by imagination.

The potential for people to spend more time (and money) in cyberspace raises questions about distinctions between who can and who cannot do so—the so-called digital divide. In some locales, individuals have their own computing systems and personal access to cyberspace. In others, such as many locations in Asia, cyberspace is accessed communally in cybercafés and other public access places. In yet others, such as some locations in Africa, cyberspace can be accessed only in a public place from which most people are remote, and it is therefore experienced infrequently. Various "appropriate technology" projects aim to overcome limitations of local power and communications infrastructures, holding out the possibility of greater universality of cyberspace access and use over time.[44]

Frequency and continuity of access may vary by choice as well as by ease of access. For example, if the stereotype that, other things being equal, younger people enjoy being online more than older people is accurate, at least in the short term, that may indicate differences in social impact and potential susceptibility to cyberpower among nations with different age structures (most developing nations have younger age structures). More generally, it is reasonable to expect that groups of people will vary in their willingness and ability to enter cyberspace, and that may affect considerations of alternative modalities for conveying, or for interfering with, information and influence.[45]

Although the overall trend with much of the technology that makes the Internet work is toward greater ease of use and even invisibility, disparities in people's ability to use technology imply differences in their ability to wield and to counter cyberpower. At one level, information can be hidden in cyberspace in so many ways that no special expertise may be required. At another, cat-and-mouse games between dissidents and censoring governments suggest that expertise may be important in some contexts. For example, sophisticated users may be able to establish a path (called a *tunnel*) to a different part of the Internet and send their packets across it so they appear to enter the Internet from this other location. This allows a user to experience what it would be like to use the Internet from a different region where there might be fewer controls on activity.

Implications of the Security Challenge and Responses

Success at improving the security properties of the Internet will determine the range of purposes for which it can be employed. If security problems continue to grow, the Internet's utility may be limited, or it may fracture into smaller, closed user groups focused on specific activities and interactions with specific parties. If we can materially improve the security of the Internet, however, it may become the primary platform for the delivery of critical information and services.

The need to improve the security of the Internet may change its nature in important ways. For example, the basic mechanisms of the Internet must take explicit account of the level of trust among the communicating parties and either permit them unrestricted efficient communication, if they trust each other, or provide protections and constraints where they lack mutual trust. We must allow trust to form part of the basis of collective action for defense against attack. To permit users to make trust decisions, they must know the identities of the parties with whom they are communicating; this means there must be explicit attention to the integration of identity mechanisms into the network. Security mechanisms must focus on the security of the information, not just the security of the conversation. We must, therefore, design a balanced set of mechanisms in the network and in the end node to deal with the reality that large operating systems will never be free of exploitable flaws.

Such security issues can be addressed in various ways that would have profoundly different effects on the balance between, at one end of the spectrum, freedom of action and unfettered exploitation of cyberspace by the users, and at the other, better ability to control hostile or unwelcome actions by other actors. One of the most fundamental questions in an analysis of cyberpower is to determine which point along this spectrum will be in the best interest of a nation.

The security of the Internet will be very different in 10 years, not because we get better at what we understand best today—mechanisms such as encryption, key management, and user sign-on—but because we become better able to understand and address the key paradox of securing the Internet: it is the act of communication that is risky, but communication is the whole goal of the Internet.

If we only communicated with those we fully trust, as did the Internet's developers and first users, the risk would be minimal. But today, much communication is with those we do not trust: we agree to accept mail from strangers, and must deal with spam and viruses; we connect to unfamiliar Web sites, and must deal with spyware and other malicious code. The Internet provides cost-effective, high-performance paths, which are great among trusting parties but also are great at delivering attacks and other unwelcome traffic. The security community has traditionally focused on the endpoints of this spectrum: either complete trust or none. The middle condition—communication despite lack of full trust—represents the everyday norm on the Internet, as in real life, but has been the least studied.[46] If security is better in 10 years, it will be because the security community has developed a framework to understand how to deal with this middle case. Failure could lead to the realization of perils discussed for years—curtailment of participation by individuals and organizations, and balkanization as the Internet breaks into zones, each having its separate rules and mechanisms for safe interaction. Potential directions to avoid this outcome are outlined below; each would have its own implications for points of control and for cyberpower.

Trust-modulated Transparency

In the Internet as in real life, when we lack trust, we turn to constraints and trusted third parties to make the interaction safe. We use firewalls as a crude means to limit the modes of communication with "outsiders," we employ a trusted service to screen our mail for spam and viruses, and so on. But these approaches are not part of the Internet—they are afterthoughts, added piecemeal without an overall conception of what the result should be. In a future Internet, we should expect an architected solution. A *trust-modulated transparency* solution may involve a basic transport service that can morph between totally transparent and very constrained, depending on the degree of trust the endpoints have for each other. Unlike current approaches, this capability would involve support at the network level, as well as new mechanisms at the application level. It would require a relayering and reorganization of basic network functions.[47]

How fundamental the impact of trust-modulated transparency may be is illustrated by a reconsideration of connection initiation. The TCP was designed to establish a connection between two endpoints as efficiently as possible, where efficiency is largely measured in the number of round-trip delays that are required before data can be sent. But no endpoint identity validation is associated with this protocol: the TCP connection must be fully established before any identity credentials can be exchanged. Trust-modulated transparency argues for redesigning these sorts of protocols to achieve a preliminary phase for establishing identity and level of trust before the connection is completed. This redesign could allow for the "outsourcing" of that first phase to a remote machine whose sole job would be protection of the end node from untrusted or unwelcome connections.[48]

Identity Mechanisms

A future Internet would benefit from a rich set of identity mechanisms, because identity is a necessary basis for trust: if you do not know to whom you are talking, there is no way to determine a level of trust. At one end of the spectrum, a trusted third party provides the confirmation of identity and perhaps credentials of trustworthy status. This role might be played by government or reliable private sector players, as credit card companies do today for e-commerce. At the other end of the spectrum are identity schemes that are private to the parties in question: each party has a model of the identity of the others, but there are no third parties involved in confirming the nature of the identity.[49] These schemes are very different in their implications for the balancing of privacy and accountability and in the balance of power and control among the various actors.

Collective Action

A traditional mode of thinking about computer security considers each computer responsible for its own defense. But many actions, such as virus detection, spam filtering, or trust assessment, are best carried out in a collaborative or collective way; this implies creating and building on trust among the collaborating parties. Another motivation to make collective action trustworthy is the expectation of increasing collaboration for other purposes, such as use of grids for data storage or computation, or use of synthetic worlds. Collaboration will be part of the context for more and more activities and functionality.

Dealing with the Insecure End Node

Many of the immediate security problems that plague users today—viruses, spyware, zombies, botnets—are the result not of an insecure network, but of an insecure end node in an open network. A material improvement in overall security requires a holistic view of how end node and network security can be integrated. We can never assume that a system of the complexity of today's PC could be designed and implemented so it is free of flaws; we must assume that the end node will always offer some opportunities for a clever attacker. Those opportunities must be foreclosed through a combination of network controls and end node controls, which might include detecting unexpected and unfamiliar patterns of communication. Another approach to making end nodes more secure is to augment them with trusted components that provide some basic assured functions even if the larger system is compromised; this "innovation" actually harks back to the concept of a trusted computing base, developed by the Department of Defense in the 1970s.[50] A third approach is to virtualize the end node; this is similar to the approach of virtualizing the network discussed above. If the end node is operated as a number of virtual machines, each used for different purposes—the distinction might be as simple as between high security concerns and low security concerns—then a combination of functions in the end node and in trusted regions of the network might be able to materially improve the expected level of security of the end node.[51]

Securing the Information

Internet technology today focuses on protecting the integrity of information during its transfer. For example, the secure sockets layer encryption protocol provides disclosure control and integrity protection for data in transit, and also provides some assurance to the user that the server offering up the data is legitimate. But once the information has been received and stored on the receiving machine, there is no way to confirm where it came from or that it is legitimate. This pattern, adequate when the mode is predominantly direct transfer from source to destination, is unsustainable when the predominant modes are staged delivery, peer-to-peer redistribution, and retrieval of copies from archival storage (such as with Google). Trust in any of these modes to deliver legitimate information implies the ability to test the integrity of information, independently of how it was received.

Implications of Security Responses

At a superficial level, a more secure network is more stable and predictable, and when this works to the benefit of all parties, it enhances cyberpower. However, there are at least two considerations that provide a more nuanced view of the situation. First, not all parts of a design need to be standardized. Some parts must be standardized for the system to fulfill the basic need for interoperation and assurance, but beyond that point, the designers and standards writers often have latitude as to what they choose to standardize—what is always done the same way everywhere—and what they leave unspecified, so that it can be implemented differently in different places. A design that leaves more unspecified might open more opportunities for different countries to intervene in order to, for example, shape how their country's networks are designed and deployed.[52] Designs might vary in how much a country could exploit such variations.

Second, different designs will create different opportunities for various actors to exercise control and power over the system. The creation of new mechanisms often creates new opportunities for control, as well as new opportunities to fight over control.[53] Different designs can shift the balance of power among the citizen, the state, the Internet service provider (ISP), third-party actors, and others.

A crucial policy consideration is whether a nation's cyberpower is best served by giving power to its citizens—which may lead to more widespread use, cyber literacy, and innovation—or by shifting power to the state, which may foster some kinds of robustness, along with greater powers of policing and enforcement. The history of the Internet has generally featured shifts away from the state, but more recently there have been attempts to shift it back, combining basic technology elements with conditions imposed on providers or users.

Incentives and Investment

Some aspects of cyberspace, particularly networks, are capital-intensive. Since the U.S. view is that construction of network facilities is a private sector activity, the future shape of much of U.S. cyberspace will be a direct consequence of investment decisions by the private sector. In this section, we discuss factors that relate to the landscape of investment, starting with the pressures that might move the Internet and other key components of cyberspace from an open platform for innovation, toward a more closed and vertically integrated service platform. Then we note the young and highly dynamic nature of some key industry sectors, such as ISPs, which have existed for only about a decade. We examine the importance of advertising as a (perhaps underappreciated) driver of investment and capital and the interplay of regulation and private sector investment. Variations in these factors among different countries contribute to variations in their cyberpower.

One of the mantras of computing comes from technologist Alan Kay: "The best way to predict the future is to invent it." That sentiment has driven advances in computing devices and in applications for computing and networking. But invention is only one key to the future of networks: because they require the construction of physical facilities such as fiber optic transmission lines and radio towers, physical networks are capital-intensive. For the Internet, we might paraphrase Kay: "The best way to predict the future is to invest in it." The critical questions that will shape what we might see in 10 years include which players will build the future communications infrastructure; why they will invest and what they will build; and what will influence those decisions. A first pass at answers points to the obvious: in developed nations, the critical players are in the private sector; firms will invest to obtain a financial return; and they will prefer the investment that yields the greatest return without excessive risk. How they calculate the balance of potential return and risk, and what returns and risks are realized, will define the infrastructure of the future.

We review here several questions that can help to frame the alternative futures. Will the Internet be open? Who is in the Internet industry? What is the role of advertising? Will the Internet be free of regulation? What are the implications of economic factors?

Will the Network Be Open?

One of the defining characteristics of the Internet is that it is *open* in several key ways. It is an open platform: any innovator can offer a product or service that runs on top of it (see figure 8–1). It is based on open standards that are free of intellectual property limitations or licensing requirements. It therefore sustains, other things being equal, an open market: new entrants can offer Internet services alongside established players. This openness, fostered by the software that defines the Internet, contrasts with the traditional, vertically integrated model of communication networks in which the investor in infrastructure recovered its investment by selling services over that infrastructure. For example, the telephone company recovered its costs in the physical assets by selling telephone service; the cable television industry recovered its costs by selling entertainment programs. An ISP charges for access to the Internet but does not currently make additional money when a user accesses the Web, watches a video, or makes a telephone call over the Internet.

There is power in the Internet's open nature: it has stimulated all sorts of third-party innovation by the likes of Yahoo!, Amazon, eBay, Google, Facebook, and YouTube, which increase both the total value of the Internet to its users and the number of users that may be interested in exploring the Internet. Inevitably, however, the demand for the Internet will mature and growth will slow, reflecting the typical S-shaped adoption curve for new technologies.[54] The open paradigm might continue to prevail, but another outcome—signaled today by the debate over "network neutrality"—is that ISPs might move in a direction of greater control of the services offered over their networks, in an attempt to make more money by treating different kinds of users and uses differently. This prospect has aroused concern about chilling effects: on innovation in the uses of the Internet, on speech and culture, and on the economy, which has fed off the Internet in many ways.[55]

If ISPs raise costs for intensive and extensive users, such as major content providers, creation of new applications by smaller players unable to afford to pay for good access might be inhibited; this is likely to reduce innovation by such actors and decrease the attraction of the Internet for those who would use their potential products, diminishing growth in Internet use. If ISPs move toward favoring their own content and applications over those of third parties, resultant reductions in competition in the supply of content and applications—a kind of return to the pre-Internet status quo—might reduce innovation in those areas and on the part of those who would use them; this, too, could stifle growth in Internet use.[56] If ISPs eschew involvement with content and applications but, facing a commodity business with low margins, do not see a case for investment in upgrades to their facilities, there might be stagnation in the capabilities or scale of the Internet, again diminishing growth in its use. Avoiding these perilous paths implies that ISPs must be able to make enough money to continue investing.

We do not address these issues in detail, but as the kinds of networks associated with the Internet change, questions about openness can be raised more broadly. Sensor networks, for example, will present opportunities to promote or constrain openness, as will networks for such specific environments as motor vehicles.

Who Is in the Internet Industry?

Understanding Internet industry economic scenarios is confounded by the dynamic nature of the ISP industry. We associate delivery of the Internet with ISPs, but that industry is not much over a decade old (it came together with the commercialization of the National Science Foundation [NSF] backbone in 1995). Within the last decade, there has been both consolidation and realignment, not only among ISPs proper, but between ISPs and more conventional telecommunications providers such as telephone and cable companies. These moves have been aided by transitions in the technology bases of those companies, such as the diffusion of IP within the telephony infrastructure and of optical fiber in telephone distribution facilities. Among other elements of convergence, there has even been consolidation between ISPs and content providers.[57] Meanwhile, a new category of player has emerged: the overlay network of servers that support a class of applications. Interposing a service between users and ISPs, they do not conform to expectations for the operation of Internet applications and the kinds of businesses that were originally differentiated by the Internet architecture layer in which they operate.

Akamai, a third-party provider of content distribution, provides an example of an overlay network.[58] It manages a set of caches that distribute Web content globally and expedite its delivery to dispersed users: users receive content from caches that are closer to them than the servers operated directly by the source may be. Akamai recognized early on that major content producers are a special kind of user that the company could serve by centralizing and packaging the task of coordinating with multiple ISPs on cache location and service quality, allowing the content producers to offer better and more uniform content delivery to their ultimate users. In identifying this service to offer to potential customers, Akamai created a new way to make money; such a model may be influencing current ISP interest in new terms for doing business with content providers, because it amplified the business potential of Internet content. It also illustrates the need for caution about defining the industry.

What Is the Role of Advertising?

The importance of advertising in the future of the Internet may not yet be adequately recognized. Today, advertising funds most of the "free" Web sites on the Internet. It is the engine that funds Google, among others. The shift of advertising revenues away from print and other traditional channels to the Internet is causing major disruption to those channels. Advertising is also embedded in new ways, such as the mounting of attractive sites directly by advertisers.[59]

The increasing importance of advertising, in terms of both revenues and clout, will become obvious as the television experience moves to the Internet. The production of almost all television content (with the exception of content for premium channels such as Home Box Office) is funded by ad revenues. If advertisers lose confidence that television advertising is effective, it could destabilize the whole supply chain for entertainment content. Today, the TiVo digital video recorder (DVR) is a threat, but the Internet could be an even more serious threat, as content becomes something the consumer can watch at will and even modify.[60] Content producers are likely to respond with technical changes to try to produce a more stable "advertising contract;" current disputes over the protection of digital rights will pale in comparison to the fights over whether the consumer can be forced to watch an ad.

This issue is potentially of broader concern, because it may influence such basic questions as who owns the servers that provide content, and how that content is managed. TiVo provides a specific example drawing on today's experience. It is a popular device that many consumers choose to install. They pay for it, and then they own and control it (to some extent). But in 10 years, who will control DVRs? It might be the advertisers, who would give the consumer the DVR for free, and then give that user access to any content desired under a wholesale agreement (somewhat like that offered by today's cable providers), assuming they can insert the ads targeted to that viewer. Technically, one way to enforce this contract would be to provide a remote control with the DVR that has been modified so that even if you switch channels, you still have to watch the ad.[61]

The question of who owns and controls the device in your home that acts as the source of the content you can see is a question that may be critical to an analysis of cyberpower. This is a variation of the classical set of questions raised in media policy discussions: media and telecommunications analysts worry about concentration of media ownership and control of information to the consumer.

Will the advertisers end up in charge of what we can see to a greater extent than today? If so, how can they contribute to defining cyberpower?

Will the Internet Be Free of Regulation?

As framed, the question of whether the Internet will be free of regulation has an obvious answer: it is not free of regulation today, never has been, and never will be. But regulatory constraints directly on the Internet have been minimal compared to those on traditional telephone companies, broadcasters, and cable television providers; and they have tended to focus on applications and consumer protection rather than the structure or competitive conduct of the industry.[62] As more traditional players have gotten more involved in the Internet, they have brought some of their regulatory burdens with them.[63]

In 2006, Congress considered telecommunications reform legislation; the proposals point to the potential for new rules. In particular, proposals for some form of "network neutrality" protection could constrain ISP pricing schemes and investment behavior. In the wake of 1996 legislation aimed at reforming telecommunications regulation,[64] the regulatory battle in the United States focused on "unbundling," requiring telephone facilities owners to lease local-loop capacity for resale to service competitors in order to increase the number of competing service providers. This approach was challenged legally and abandoned in the United States, although it remains popular in other developed countries, especially in Europe. Where there is regulation, there typically is some expectation of formal observation or monitoring by the government (and by competitors and civil society organizations); this in itself is one reason why regulation of the Internet has been resisted.

There are other categories of regulation that bear more directly on government interests and may shape the Internet and its uses in different ways. One is the provision for law enforcement access to communications. Government can gain access (under subpoena in the United States) to usage data from ISPs; in addition, there has been movement to build in to core Internet systems—routers—the conceptual equivalent of wiretapping. This was mandated in the United States by the Federal Communications Assistance to Law Enforcement Act (CALEA), which was designed originally for telephone networks and is being extended to the Internet and to wireless communications systems.[65] An unintended consequence of adding this kind of capability is that, once available, it could be exploited by others—criminals, for example—and not just by the law enforcement agencies that were its intended beneficiaries.[66]

Another government-focused category of regulation relates to critical infrastructure and involves both government-industry cooperation and investment. Arrangements for national security and emergency preparedness (NS/EP) in telecommunications arose historically in the context of the telephone industry, and the application of these arrangements to the Internet has been the subject of exploration in the United States for about a decade. A related and parallel exploration has focused on critical infrastructure protection, which involves monitoring for potential problems, sharing of related information, and implementing protection mechanisms.[67]

The ISPs are unpredictable and potentially inconsistent players in critical infrastructure protection. At issue is their willingness and ability to invest in such approaches to protection as physical facility diversity (redundant investments).[68] Also problematic is how to coordinate and allocate planning and investment within the industry and between industry and government. In the 1960s, when NS/EP mechanisms were introduced in the United States, the telecommunications industry centered squarely on one company, American Telephone and Telegraph (AT&T). By contrast, the Internet involves a wider variety of players, most of which have little history of cooperation with the government; it also involves more instability in the market, which complicates understanding of the elements of the infrastructure and identifying who is responsible for them. The controversy beginning in mid-2006 over secret U.S. Government interception of communications and the associated backlash do not bode well for future government-industry cooperation. Were there to be mandated investment in physical robustness (as CALEA compliance was mandated), any increase in costs would affect all players in a geographic region; if not offset by other factors, such an increase could have an impact on the level or growth of use in that region, and therefore on how Internet conditions in that region might compare to those elsewhere.

A final category of regulation may emerge from the international debate about Internet governance that was prominent at the 2005 World Summit on the Information Society and the convening of the Internet Governance Forum beginning in fall 2006. So far, these activities have provided forums for discussion and debate, but there has been no movement to decision or action, in part because of the difficulty of achieving consensus among large numbers of nations and different components of national governments.[69]

Implications of Economic Factors

The Internet marketplace supports much variation, even though the providers implement common standards. Issues include the degree of openness to innovation, the degree of penetration of access (both dial-up and broadband), the extent of planning and investment in resilience and diversity of infrastructure, and perhaps the degree of state and private sector observation of ongoing activities as part of regulation. Many of these issues play out differently in different countries, leading to variation in the issues that feed cyberpower.

Several factors can shift the balance. More investment in technology and operation for resilience might increase cost and reduce penetration. A shift toward more control and monitoring might lead to a network that is easier to police but might chill innovation and emerging uses. The United States must try to determine which would be a better contributor to cyberpower. It must also decide whether to do more to encourage certain sorts of investment overseas (for example, in the developing world) or to drive faster penetration of services such as the Internet, and if doing either, it must figure out what sort of network to encourage and what its features should be in order to protect U.S. interests.

Research and Reinvention

We have looked at technical issues that might be influenced by attention from the research community. This section looks more generally at the institution of research: sources of funding, the health of the research establishment, and differences in policy and practice between the United States and other countries. At the moment, research in the United States seems disorganized compared to some other countries, which could mean a loss of U.S. economic advantage, a loss of control over the shape of cyberspace, or even loss of a seat at the table to influence the factors that shape cyberpower.

Research remains essential for the vitality of the Internet, and renewed commitment by the U.S. Government may be important to future developments. The expectation that research on the Internet will continue adds to the unpredictability of the Internet's future: research generates new options for users, for ISPs, and for a wide range of third parties in both the public and private sectors. Maturation of some aspects of the Internet makes it more challenging both to frame research and to assimilate research results. The increasing presence of industry in Internet research highlights the important role that has been played by government-funded academic basic research: such research is free to address issues not likely to be pursued by applied research in industry. An obvious example is options for maintaining openness.[70]

It is well known that the Internet and other underpinnings of cyberspace arose from research programs. However, the conditions for funding, framing, and conducting relevant research have changed considerably. The U.S. situation is characterized by significant limitations. Historic industrial research giants such as AT&T and International Business Machines have become less research-active at best, without being replaced by healthier firms (Cisco might be a candidate). The historic lead funding entity in government for large-scale computing systems—DARPA—has changed its focus. The academic research community has experienced a series of losses in personnel due to funding fluctuations and the lure of industry and focus away from basic research toward research that complements, even if it does not lead, a fast-moving marketplace.[71] Other countries, meanwhile, have increased levels of activity, support, and coordination, responding to the challenge posed by the commercial success of the United States and also to concerns about its cultural hegemony, fostered by the global reach of the Internet.[72] However, there is no evidence that activities overseas are contributing to revolutionary change in ways different from what can be seen in the United States (whose researchers, of course, also participate in international exchanges).

The U.S. National Science Foundation is mounting a pair of initiatives that hold the potential to influence Internet technology in an organized way. One, called Future Internet Design (FIND), has begun to fund research that is explicitly motivated by a vision of a future network with features radically different than ones that would result simply from incremental modification or improvement. FIND was framed with an eye toward addressing some of the problems outlined in this chapter, from deficiencies in security and trustworthiness to the economic viability concerns of ISPs. Many of the revolutionary architectural ideas described in this chapter are being explored within the NSF FIND initiative.[73]

The Global Environment for Network Innovation (GENI)[74] is an infrastructure project to complement the research funded in FIND. GENI is intended to apply ideas gleaned from FIND and elsewhere in real-world tests. It will support multiple simultaneous, independent experiments with new architectural, service, and application concepts at a large scale and with live user communities. The GENI concept recognizes that practical testing is needed not only to achieve the ambitious goals of significant changes in architecture but also to demonstrate to maturing markets what new ideas can really mean in practice. An issue being discussed that must be worked out, given that the Internet has been international from its early days, is how to achieve international participation in GENI and FIND.

Goal-directed Research: Priorities for the Future

Different funding agencies have different philosophies of research—fundamental or mission oriented, long term or short term, and so on. Currently, the only U.S. funding agency that has declared its intention to give priority to research on the future of cyberspace in general and on the Internet in particular is the NSF, an agency that traditionally has focused on long-term, fundamental research. Exploration in a number of other countries is shaped with the specific objective of giving the host nation's industry a strategic advantage in the cyberspace marketplace or creating a set of standards that will shape the future of cyberspace in a particular way. We have mentioned a number of issues ripe for research, some in detail and some in passing. There are many examples:

- *Security.* Will we have an "architecture for security" in a future Internet, or will we instead continue with a mix of point solutions to problems?

- *Object provenance.* Will we have some sort of trustworthy metadata attached to an object that provides assurance as to its origin and provenance?

- *Identity.* Will we have an architected framework to deal with the issues of identity that are going to arise in cyberspace?

- *Location-aware computing.* Will we have a coherent and unified framework to associate location information with people, devices, and objects, to facilitate location-aware search and notification?

- *Location-sensing.* The global positioning system now allows any suitably equipped device to know where it is, but only if it can receive the radio signals from the satellites. Should we work toward a next-generation location-sensing framework that allows devices to determine their location inside buildings and other places where the satellite signal does not reach?

- *Open sensor network.* Will we have an available, open, ubiquitous network suited to the needs of inexpensive sensors and embedded computers, or will sensors require the installation of a custom network?

- *Open vehicle network.* Will future automobiles offer an open network, along the lines of the Internet, or will they be closed networks, with manufacturer-provided services only?

- *Networks in times of crisis.* Will we make the necessary provisions to assure that the Internet will be available and useful even in times of disaster?

These questions and others represent forks in the road to the future. Industry may or may not decide to concentrate on some of these issues. Public sector funding agencies will also make decisions as to which of these objectives are important enough for funding and attention, and which path we should take when we reach the fork. Different countries may set different priorities and work toward different outcomes around these issues. Whatever choices are made, these issues will have a profound effect on the relative balance of cyberpower in 10 years.

CHAPTER 9

Information Technology and the Biotech Revolution

Edward Skoudis

THE SECOND half of the 20th century is sometimes referred to as the information age, the space age, or the nuclear age. The first half of the 21st century may well be dominated by rapid advances in biological technologies. By leveraging the information technology base to control and manipulate biological systems, humans are poised for a biological revolution; the first fruits of such technologies are already available. Bioinformatics has yielded improved crop performance and a better understanding of some diseases for optimizing medical treatments, while brain-computer interfaces and neuralprosthetics are helping disabled people interact with their surroundings more effectively.

The integration of information technology and biology is a long-time staple of science fiction dystopian visions that portray computers linked to biological systems that somehow supplant people or otherwise wreak havoc on society. While such technological integration could be a cause for concern, its benefits could also be quite profound in improving human lives and increasing economic efficiencies and progress. The purpose of this chapter is to survey advancements in the integration of information technology with biological systems to help the reader understand the evolutionary trends in this convergence of technologies.

Biology and cyberspace both deal with the interactions of a multitude of interconnected simpler elements, giving rise to many analogies between the two fields. Information technology has exhibited increasingly biological attributes as computers become more powerful, networks grow in size, and our overall cyberspace infrastructure becomes more complex. Some cyberspace terminology and analytical methods are lifted directly from biology. The term *virus*, first applied to self-replicating malicious software by researcher Fred Cohen in 1984, is now in the common vernacular.[1] Researchers refer to *outbreaks* and *inoculation;* experts caution against the dangers of a software *monoculture* without *diversity,* because of its lack of resilience to *digital pathogens.*[2] *Evolutionary algorithms* are used to find optimal answers to math problems by having software apply iterative, *evolutionary* steps to reach an answer.

However, the convergence of biology and information technology goes considerably beyond mere analogies of how complex systems behave. Increasingly, researchers are leveraging information technology to analyze, manipulate, and control biological systems. Research on many fronts includes two areas of particular interest that are the focus of this chapter: bioinformatics and computer-neuron interfaces.

Bioinformatics

Bioinformatics is a term sometimes used interchangeably with the phrase *computational biology* to refer to the application of modern statistical and computer science techniques to solving biological problems. Current bioinformatic analysis, modeling, and solutions may be focused on a molecular level to predict, for example, the interactions of deoxyribonucleic acid (DNA), proteins, and other vital biological chemicals. A DNA strand is made up of individual molecules, called nucleotides, which encode information. Different nucleotide sequences cause a cell to manufacture different proteins. Groups of these nucleotide sequences form genes. All of the genes for a given species make up that species' *genome.* One part of bioinformatics involves recording and analyzing nucleotide sequences and examining the implications—for the cell, the organism, and the whole species—of specific patterns in the DNA and the proteins it specifies. The bioinformatics field was born in the 1960s, when biologists began using mainframe computers to analyze data from protein biochemistry. With advances in computer technology and the rise of massively distributed computer systems, bioinformatic research has expanded significantly to model biological chemical interactions.

Bioinformatics Research Areas and Subfields

Within the broad definition of bioinformatics, research has branched out into many subfields; applications include gene finding and assembly, modeling of evolutionary processes, and analyzing mutations such as those related to cancer. The large amounts of data to parse and analyze when working with DNA, proteins, and related chemicals require massive computing capabilities. The genome of a species such as corn includes over a billion nucleotides, each storing a small amount of information about synthesizing and controlling the proteins that make up the corn. The gigabytes of data associated with this genome can be stored using an off-the-shelf computer. However, the data associated with cross-references within the genome could occupy terabytes of space. Beyond the mere storage of this genome and its cross-references, actual analysis of the data and simulation of its operation require very high-speed computing resources, usually networked computers calculating and searching in parallel.

To analyze a given species, the order of the nucleotides of its DNA must be recorded into data structures in a computer system, a process known as *sequencing*. Rather than sequencing DNA nucleotides one by one, a slow technique used in the past, many modern researchers use *shotgun sequencing*, a quicker technique that requires significant computational power from the bioinformatics arena. With this technique, the DNA of the organism under analysis is broken down at random into various chunks, which can be extracted in an efficient chemical process and entered into a distributed computer system. The computers then analyze the different piece-parts and reassemble them, sorting through millions of strands, removing overlapping segments, and finding and filling holes, to rebuild the original DNA structure. With significant computing power, the shotgun sequencing technique can improve speed over previous techniques by several orders of magnitude.

Sequencing is only the beginning, merely the capture of the raw data so it can be analyzed. Another area of bioinformatics research involves finding genes and predicting their expression in the final organism. For example, some cancer researchers are attempting to identify the gene or gene combination responsible for the expression of cancerous behavior in cells. Many of the techniques used in determining gene expression are noise-prone, as anomalous gene sequences that appear to match the desired results blur identification of correct answers. Researchers turn to the methods of bioinformatics, applying computer statistical analysis and filtering to cut through the clutter and find specific sequences associated with given behaviors or actions.

Bioinformatics studies also include the modeling of evolutionary traits and analysis of mutations by comparing genetic sequences between different and related species. For example, a *phylogenetic tree* is a depiction in a tree pattern showing similarities and deviations of natural gene mutation between different species to illustrate the relationships of different organisms.[3] This technique uses genetic similarities between species to create a sort of evolutionary map or family tree of relationships, which allows researchers to identify, at least tentatively, a genetic history of a set of species that are believed to have a common ancestor. Finding and analyzing the common patterns in these genes to create the tree require significant computational power and have spun off their own subfield within bioinformatics called *computational phylogenetics*.

Some of the statistical techniques of bioinformatics are used in a subfield called *comparative genomics*. Research in this area attempts to establish correspondence between genes of different species to help identify gene function in one species by comparing it to similar genes that have already been identified in another species. The Human Genome Project, for example, found correlations between human and mouse genes, which allowed researchers to identify gene properties in humans because the genes had the same purpose in both humans and mice. The processes involved with these techniques are heavily analytical and work with large data sets, using statistical techniques similar to those found in financial applications, including Markov chains, Monte Carlo simulations, and Bayesian analysis.

Detailed genetic analysis can allow a doctor to better understand a patient's health, analyze diseases in the patient, and predict how various drugs would affect that patient's biochemistry. With such information, the doctor can customize treatments and drugs to best match the patient's genetic profile, an approach sometimes referred to as personalized medicine. In such offerings, doctors identify biomarkers for a given disease and monitor progression of the disease on a molecular level. Treatments can then be based on individual data from one patient, rather than on generalized measurements from clinical trials over a large number of patients, the way most medical treatments are designed today. In addition, once a treatment has been administered, doctors can track a patient's response to the treatment, again on a molecular level. Personalized medicine techniques show significant promise for better diagnoses, more efficient drug development tailored to specific patients, and more effective targeted therapies.

There are ethical and public policy implications associated with the rise of personalized medicine. To apply such techniques, some portion of the patient's genetic information must be gathered and scrutinized, perhaps before any disease is identified. This genetic database would most likely include raw gene sequences as well as protein information for the individual. Should an insurance or medical company have access to its customers' genetic sequences? Is it appropriate to calculate customers' insurance rates based on the possibilities of disease indicated by their genes? Some people might be effectively uninsurable, based on such information. In the next two decades, as researchers hone analytic capabilities and better understand the genetic composition or predisposition to medical maladies, such questions will become significant.

The bioinformatics areas described so far have focused on capturing and analyzing biological information using computers. Based on these results, however, researchers have gone further: they have altered the genes of a given species and moved genetic information from one species to another, giving rise to new properties in the resulting species. Such purposeful genetic manipulation is commonplace with commercial crops in many countries.[4] The United States alone accounts for approximately two-thirds of all genetically modified crops planted globally. Modified corn, cotton, and soybeans made up 40, 60, and over 80 percent, respectively, of each crop's acreage planted in the United States in

2007.[5] These crops may be modified to make them more resistant to drought, disease, and insects or to improve their nutritional content. While such genetically modified food is controversial—some European countries have placed severe restrictions on the import of such crops—it has increased the productiveness of cropland in countries where it is practiced.

Genetic modification is also possible with livestock, pets, and even humans. Gene therapy is an experimental technology used to alter an organism's genes, planting new information in them to treat a disease. Gene therapy was used successfully in 2002 on an infant with a defective gene that caused a complete shutdown of the child's immune system.[6] Doctors extracted unhealthy cells, added corrective genes to them, and then implanted the altered cells in the boy's body, where they were able to restart the immune system. Gene therapy has since been used in many similar cases and is now considered at least as effective as a bone marrow transplant in stimulating some patients' immune systems. Researchers are analyzing numerous other gene therapy techniques that could eradicate some forms of genetic disease and possibly even curtail some nongenetic diseases by increasing an organism's immune function.

Significant ethical dilemmas are raised with one generation's ability to alter the genetic makeup of all generations that follow. Who should decide which changes to make and which to forbid: government agencies, commercial interests, or parents? If we can make people who are smarter, healthier, and longer lived, should we? Can and should humans be altered to make them more docile or perhaps more aggressive? Will improved genetic traits be available only to those who can pay for them, or will they be shared across a society? Should genetic modification techniques be applied to military uses, either from a biological warfare perspective or to improve the characteristics of warfighters? Because DNA operates like a computer programmed via its nucleotide sequences, it is quite possible that given changes will work fine for many generations but will eventually cause problems, just as a computer program may run appropriately hundreds of times before crashing. Who, then, should be responsible for unanticipated negative consequences of genetic alterations?

Over the next several decades, societies around the world will have to contend with ethical dilemmas such as these that genetic manipulation poses. Such deliberations will not happen independently within each country: even if one country decides to boycott genetic manipulation while others endorse or encourage it, the boycotting country may fall behind its competitors technologically and economically. Moreover, since people, animals, and crops move across nation-state borders, a country that attempts to eschew genetic changes may not be able to keep such changes made elsewhere from crossing its borders and planting altered genes among its population. Altered genetic information already flows across borders, as pollen from genetically modified crops blows in the wind and pollinates unmodified crops hundreds of miles away, resulting in genetically modified descendants. Such issues and their importance will certainly increase.

Research Tools and Organizations Associated with Bioinformatics

At the root of bioinformatics lies the computer technology in which the biological information is stored and analyzed. The bioinformatics research community has developed and released many free, open-source, and commercial software utilities and online services for use by researchers around the world. Some of these tools are available from the National Center for Biotechnology Information (NCBI), operated by the U.S. National Library of Medicine and the National Institutes of Health. One of the most powerful and widely used databases, offered free by NCBI, is the Basic Local Alignment Search Tool, a service that can search for regions of similarity between biological sequences in various species, including humans, mice, rats, numerous plant species, and several microbes. With a Web front-end open to anyone with Internet access, this database allows for searches of nucleotides and proteins.[7] NCBI also offers the Entrez Protein Clusters database to help researchers find protein sequence and function similarities between species, and the Database of Genotype and Phenotype to help "elucidate the link between genes and disease." Such tools rely on data mining techniques to pull meaningful information from large masses of data.

For commercial purposes, searching through vast amounts of data to find relevant results has been a major focus of Internet search engines. The skills and technologies honed to locate Web pages on the Internet are now being repurposed to the bioinformatics field. Google, in particular, has taken a keen interest in bioinformatics research and the use of Google technology to improve search capabilities. Teaming with Craig Venter from the Human Genome Project, Google has set out to apply its search algorithms to genetic data and to create an entire database of genetic information available for all to access. Google founders Larry Page and Sergey Brin have recognized the relationship between search engine technology and data mining of genetic information, spearheading genetic storage and search projects that could portend genetic information stored in a Google database and searchable with Google technology.[8]

A commercial company focused on analyzing genetic information, called 23andMe, was started in 2006. It seeks to offer people insight into their own ancestry, genealogy, and inherited traits based on the information in their genes, stored on the 23 paired chromosomes in each human cell.[9] 23andMe aims to help "put your genome into the larger context of human commonality and diversity," based on genetic information. Customers provide a sample of saliva, which is sequenced and analyzed for a fee. Then they are given detailed reports on their genetic predisposition to various traits, along with commentary about how common each trait is. Reports also include explanations for tendencies in customers, such as preferences for certain foods or character traits that are associated with specific genetic sequences. Aiming to provide more value to customers, 23andMe offers recommendations for changes in lifestyle that could lower the chance of contracting a genetically predispositioned ailment, such as heart disease. Numerous other small startups are being created to offer similar services derived from the growing bioinformatics industry.

Connecting Neurons to Computers: Neuralprosthetics and Brain-computer Interfaces

A second major area of convergence of biology and information technology involves the interface between biological neural systems and computers. Such interconnections fall into two general categories: neuralprosthetics and brain-computer interfaces (BCIs). Each could eventually allow humans to control machines using thought or improve mental faculties with computer augmentation. Neuralprosthetic technologies focus on tying computer equipment into nerves outside of the brain, such as those in the ear, eye, spinal cord, arm, or leg. BCIs involve direct interface between computers and the motor, auditory, or visual cortexes of the brain itself.

Today, BCIs are highly experimental, but some neuralprosthetic technologies are already in general use as medical devices. Cochlear implants, for example, apply computer technology to help translate sound into neural signals to allow deaf people to hear. They represent one of the greatest areas of success and commercialization of neuralprosthetics; over 100,000 patients were estimated to use these devices worldwide in 2006.[10] Artificial intelligence researcher Ray Kurzweil suggests that additional processing and computing technology could augment these implants in the future, enabling them to translate languages in real time or whisper the definitions of unfamiliar terms to the implant user.[11]

A promising near-term application of BCI is the "brain pacemaker," which injects electrical signals to alleviate symptoms of Parkinson's disease or clinical depression in patients who do not respond to traditional medications. Experimental studies since 1998 have shown improvement in patients attributable to experiments with the technique.[12] Early experiments implanted such devices directly into patients' brains, representing a medical application of BCI. Other researchers have postulated that such effects might be achievable by connecting instead to spinal cords or cranial nerves, putting the devices into the category of neuralprosthetics.

Most of the experiments to date with BCI and neuralprosthetic devices have focused on one-way communication between the computer and neurons, either writing data into neurons, such as with a cochlear implant or brain pacemaker, or reading data from neurons, such as with experimental brain control of robotic arms or computer cursors. While one-way interfaces are far simpler to construct, they offer no direct feedback, and the control they offer is much more limited than with two-way devices, which would be far more complex but will likely develop as an important area of BCI and neuralprosthetics research.

Researchers have experimented with a variety of techniques for deploying both BCIs and neuralprosthetics. The most direct route involves implanting probes directly into the gray matter of the brain, with electrodes protruding from the skull. Researcher Miguel Nicolelis at Duke University began employing this technique in 2000 in experiments that have allowed monkeys to control computer cursors and/or robotic limbs.[13] Another approach involves brain implants, placed inside the skull and touching the surface of the brain but outside of the brain's gray matter, that measure electrical signals. Sometimes called electrocorticography (ECoG), this technique was used in 2006 to enable a teenage boy to play a video game by merely thinking about controlling the movements of a joystick.[14] To obviate the need for the "tether" associated with gray matter interfaces or with ECoG inside the skull, researchers are working on plans to implant a wireless transceiver in the brain that would transmit signals through the skull. This would allow patients to be more mobile, but it imposes severe size constraints on the local sensor equipment.

For each of these approaches, several experimental technologies have been devised for connecting individual neurons to computer equipment. One method is to graft the sensor directly into the neuron itself, where it would sense the signals transmitted by that neuron. In a less intrusive approach, the sensor would touch the surface of the neuron to detect its electrical state. Some researchers are analyzing use of lasers to bounce light patterns off of individual neurons to measure the changes in their reflectance that occurs as the neurons fire. This technique, called light reactive imaging, might have a less destructive effect on the neurons than other methods.

Other approaches to BCI and neural prosthetics would avoid the cost and invasiveness of inserting sensors into the body, because surgery would not be required. Some researchers are working on probes that would make contact with skin in an approach called electroencephalography (EEG); they would require no surgery but might involve shaving certain areas of the scalp. Because the skull dampens electrical signals from inside the brain, significant amplification and noise reduction would be required to get meaningful information. This technique cannot pinpoint specific neural activities but instead gathers information from a large number of neurons. While this method presents challenges, it is noninvasive and relatively low cost. An approach that is essentially "EEG at a distance" would involve sensors that can monitor brain activity remotely. This technique would require no physical contact with the patient, but it would constrain mobility of the patient so signals could be measured across a room, and it would be limited by noise from the outside environment.

Another promising approach that is neither a BCI nor a neuralprosthetic device pulls information from muscle movements, not from neurons. It employs electromyographs (EMGs), sensors connected to or embedded in muscle tissue. By measuring small changes in muscle tension, such technologies have allowed severely paralyzed patients to interact with computer equipment so they can control a voice synthesizer, computer keyboard, or other technology by moving muscles that are not paralyzed, such as their eyelids or eyes.

Organizations Associated with BCI and Neuralprosthetics

Numerous organizations are involved in BCI and neuralprosthetics work, including Duke University, Brown University, Stanford University, and the University of Sussex in England. A prominent BCI company is Cyberkinetics Neurotechnology Systems, which is experimenting with devices that let humans control computer cursor movements using sensor arrays implanted in the motor cortex of the brain. The device, about the size of an aspirin, provides approximately 100 electrodes to interface with the brain. In experiments in 2005, a quadriplegic patient implanted with the technology controlled an artificial hand, moved a computer cursor, turned lights on, and changed television channels by simply thinking about these actions. The long-term goal is to develop devices such as "thought-controlled" wheelchairs and prosthetic limbs.

Neural Signals, another major BCI and neuralprosthetics company, focuses on restoring speech by means of both invasive and noninvasive technologies. Researchers are experimenting with probes into the speech center of the brain, called the Broca's motor area. Based on the activity they detect, a computer generates 1 of the 39 phonemes that constitute the fundamental sounds of spoken English. With training, patients may be able to make the machine speak for them simply by thinking. A noninvasive approach for discerning a patient's thoughts and converting them into speech or action involves EEG signals from probes taped onto a patient's scalp. Already, such devices can differentiate the thoughts "yes" and "no" within 10 seconds.[15] The company has also commercialized EMG sensors that, when placed on the skin of speech- and motion-impaired patients, can discern small motor movements of the eye and other muscles to control computers.

With its focus on helping disabled people, BCI and neuralprosthetics research has generated far less controversy than genetic manipulation. While genetic manipulation could affect all subsequent generations of life, and altered genes might spread unchecked, BCI and neuralprosthetics are more controllable technologies; skilled personnel apply them deliberately. Yet if these technologies continue to advance and are widely deployed, they too could result in significant changes to human civilization. Some researchers posit a future with thought-controlled robotic limbs and augmentation of human senses with computer devices. Humans with such gear embedded into their bodies could have superhuman senses or superhuman strength and endurance. Futurists and science fiction writers have also envisioned computing devices that would augment the brain to offer, for example, vast increases in human memory. A photographic memory might become the norm among people who can afford the technology, profoundly increasing economic disparities in society, giving rise to an elite class with improved capabilities baked into their genes or built into their skulls. Humans with such implants might be able to look up facts on the Internet merely by thinking about them or conduct conference calls with other people without any outside equipment, all inside their heads. Military fighters with superhuman strength or intelligence delivered by BCI and neuralprosthetics technologies could dominate in combat, although opposing forces could find a way to neutralize or counter the technology with, for example, computer network attack and exploitation techniques, just as other "ultimate weapons" have historically been countered by lower tech asymmetric strategies.

Conclusion

The applications of the integration of biology and information technology are just the start of even more profound capabilities. Taken to their extreme, biology and information technology used together could transform what it means to be human. In a "trans-human" future, people might develop a new species or groups of species to succeed humanity. However, these transitions are likely to be gradual and taken for granted by most people, as their lives improve with the accumulation of technological changes. Drastic setbacks are certainly possible: crops might fail due to poorly planned genetic manipulation, or machine-augmented warfighters might cause significant damage. Nonetheless, the advantages offered by biological technology are likely to make such advances inevitable. Noted physicist and technology thinker Freeman Dyson, referring to technologies associated with genetic manipulation as "green technologies," says:

> Before genetically modified termites and trees can be allowed to help solve our economic and environmental problems, great arguments will rage over the possible damage they may do. . . . I am not saying that the political acceptance of green technology will be quick or easy. I say only that green technology has enormous promise for preserving the balance of nature on this planet as well as for relieving human misery.[16]

In the early 21st century, information technology and cyberspace provide an ideal base for a technological revolution in biology. This next revolution could have major impact on the way we live our lives and what our lives really are.

Part III
Cyberpower: Military Use and Deterrence

CHAPTER 10

An Environmental Approach to Understanding Cyberpower

Gregory J. Rattray

CYBERSPACE has increasingly become an environment in which the United States and actors around the globe act, cooperate, and compete. Achieving their objectives will require influencing other actors by orchestrating power in this realm. We do not yet have enough historical experience to fully understand the fast-evolving nature of cyber conflict and cyberpower. However, it helps if we understand the factors that underpin it. This chapter, therefore, illuminates key aspects of cyberpower by comparing and contrasting the cyber environment in light of theories of power in other environments: land, sea, air, and space. Control of key aspects of the operating environment enhances an actor's power. Inability to obtain access or sustain control can limit the range of political, diplomatic, economic, military, and informational aspects of power. For example, control over land areas such as Asia Minor, a major bridge between Asia, Europe, and Africa through which armies and trade routes have passed for millennia, has influenced the destiny of civilizations. At sea, the ability to dominate straits such as Gibraltar or Malacca have enabled empires to ensure the rapid transit of military force and secure shipping lanes essential to their economies. For the last century, freedom to operate air forces over battlefields and provide supplies via an air bridge has been fundamental to both military operations and diplomatic successes, such as the Berlin Airlift. In space, key positions such as spots for geosynchronous orbits have become the object of competition among nations and commercial corporations because they enhance the ability to conduct communications and intelligence operations.

By analogy, we seek to understand the new environment of cyberspace. Thus, this chapter first reviews the particular characteristics of the cyberspace environment that affect its strategic features. It then summarizes previous environmental theories of land power, seapower, airpower, and spacepower. A third section reviews the sources of power in each of these environments: technological advances, changes in speed and scope of operations, control of key features, and mobilization of national resources. Two distinct features of cyberspace—offense dominance and the rapidity of change—are examined. The chapter concludes with recommendations for the United States to address challenges of generating cyberpower.

Cyberspace as an Environment

The term *cyberspace* came into broad use during the early 1990s, when cyber-space was viewed as fundamentally different than the normal physical world. However, cyberspace is actually a physical environment: it is created by the connection of physical systems and networks, managed by rules set in software and communications protocols.[1] Discussion of cyberspace in the national security realm largely evolved from the interest in information warfare, particularly computer and network warfare.[2]

The United States increasingly stresses the concept of cyberspace as an operating environment. The Nation's leaders have begun to recognize the significance of this environment for U.S. security. Since the attacks of 9/11, security objectives have changed, as recognized in this statement from the 2002 *National Security Strategy of the United States of America:* "We are menaced less by fleets and armies than by catastrophic technologies in the hands of the embittered few."[3] The *National Defense Strategy of the United States of America* asserted the need to secure strategic access and retain global freedom of action, particularly through the control of the global commons, in order to deal with traditional, irregular, catastrophic, or disruptive threats. The National Defense Strategy of 2005 identified cyberspace, along with space and international waters and airspace, as a global commons and cyber operations as a disruptive challenge. It explicitly states that "cyberspace is a new theater of operations."[4]

U.S. national policy has recognized the need to protect U.S. cyberspace. The Clinton administration issued Presidential Decision Directive 68, "Critical Infrastructure Protection," putting protection of key U.S. assets against cyber attack on par with defense against physical strikes. The Bush administration extended this effort; its 2002 *National Strategy to Secure Cyberspace* outlined key efforts necessary to:

> reduce our vulnerabilities to these threats before they can be exploited to
> damage the cyber systems supporting our Nation's critical infrastructures

and to ensure that such disruptions of cyberspace are infrequent, of minimal duration, manageable, and cause the least damage possible.[5]

The Defense Department, Department of Justice, Federal Bureau of Investigation, Intelligence Community, and other Federal agencies have established organizations and programs to deal with cyberspace issues and roles related to their respective national security missions. The Department of Homeland Security, in particular, is expressly charged with protecting the United States against terrorist attacks in cyberspace. The department set up a National Cyber Security Division in September 2003, and in the fall of 2006, an Assistant Secretary for Cybersecurity and Telecommunications was appointed, with responsibility for orchestrating the full range of the department's activities in this realm.

Cyberpower, as we use the term in this book, is the ability to use cyberspace to strategic advantage and to influence events in the other operational environments and across the instruments of power.[6] As with control of land masses, crucial sea lanes, airspace, or satellite orbits, cyberpower has risen as a key factor in the capacity of states and other actors in the international system to project influence:

> Successful military operations depend on the ability to protect information
> infrastructure and data. Increased dependence on information networks
> creates new vulnerabilities that adversaries may seek to exploit.[7]

Ensuring that we have adequate influence and control in the cyberspace commons and can keep it from becoming a launching ground from which our adversaries can strike with impunity has increasingly become a goal of U.S. national strategy. Military operations, economic activity, and transit of ideas across other domains—land, sea, air, and space—rely more and more on the effective functioning of cyberspace. Cyberpower has become a fundamental enabler for the full range of instruments of national power: political, diplomatic, economic, military, and informational.

Strategic Features of the Cyberspace Environment

Cyberspace comprises both physical and logical systems and infrastructures that are governed by laws of physics as well as the logic of computer code. The principal physical laws governing cyberspace are those related to electromagnetism and light. The speed at which waves propagate and electrons move creates both advantages and challenges: global communications across cyberspace can happen nearly instantaneously, and vast amounts of data can rapidly transit great distances, often unimpeded by physical barriers and political boundaries.

This speed and freedom of movement creates challenges and advantages for individuals, organizations, and states, but at the same time it creates weaknesses that could be exploited by adversaries.

In cyberspace, like air and space, almost all activities involve the use of technology. Cyberspace is unique in that the interactions are governed by hardware and software that is manmade, so the "geography" of cyberspace is much more mutable than other environments. Mountains and oceans are hard to move, but portions of cyberspace can be turned on and off with the flick of a switch; they can be created or "moved" by insertion of new coded instructions in a router or switch. Cyberspace is not, however, infinitely malleable: limits on the pace and scope of change are governed by physical laws, logical properties of code, and the capacities of organizations and people.

The systems and infrastructures that make up cyberspace have varying degrees of interconnectivity. A home computer with a printer but no other connection utilizes cyberspace but is a very small, isolated enclave. A radio transmitter can reach a broader number of devices in its broadcast area with a one-way message. The Internet has become the prime example of a massive global network. In cyberspace, ever-increasing numbers of hardware devices have significant degrees of interconnectivity moderated by software and protocol rules. The recent explosion of digital standards for wireless transmission is leading to a fusion of wired and wireless systems, as has the convergence of transmission control protocol/Internet protocol (IP) as the most useful standards for facilitating transit of information between systems.

Although economic imperatives and the desire to widen circles of communication have led to the rapid growth of a global information infrastructure, governments, corporations, and individuals can and do control how much interconnection they establish. Boundaries are established in cyberspace by choices in how to employ hardware, software, and standards. For example, the governments that set up the International Telecommunications Union required use of certain protocols to carry telephone traffic over international circuits under their purview. Thus, states had some sovereignty over their respective telephony systems, giving them the capacity to govern the economics of international calling and to monitor the communications of their citizens.[8] The current emergence of voice over Internet protocol as an alternative for long-distance voice conversations undermines that ability and keeps governments from using standards to establish enclaves within their political-geographic borders. Still, just as governments may jam undesirable radio and television broadcasts from outside their geographic borders, now the People's Republic of China, regimes in the Middle East, and other states endeavor to employ software filters and other techniques to limit where their citizens can traverse within the global Internet.[9]

Actors in the Cyberspace Environment

The challenge of managing the technological foundations of cyberspace means that human capital is a fundamental influence on the use of this environment. Skilled people operate the systems, engineer the infrastructures, and drive the innovations necessary for achieving advantages in cyberspace. While this is also true on land and sea and in air and space, the speed of technological change in the early 21st century ensures that, to sustain advantages in using cyberspace for military, economic, or informational purposes, nations must focus on nurturing this core resource with its constant requirement for learning and training.

The number of actors who play a significant role in cyberspace is also a distinguishing feature. States do not, and cannot, control cyberspace to the same degree as they can with land, sea, and air, or even as they could control cyberspace in the past: for example, during both World Wars, the U.S. Government took control of the operation of the Nation's predominant telephone provider, American Telephone & Telegraph (AT&T).[10] That was possible because at that time, AT&T alone provided almost all of the network hardware and determined the communications rule sets that allowed the telephone system to work (although it did so under close regulation by the government). Now, however, in the United States and elsewhere, there are myriad providers of devices, connectivity, and services in loosely woven networks with open standards. Governments would have extreme difficulty in controlling the full spectrum of telecommunications and other activities in cyberspace.

Establishing sovereignty, or deciding on rules to govern the global cyberspace commons, creates major challenges and growing national security concerns for state actors.[11] With telephone networks, governments had ways to control connectivity beyond their borders. However, over time, non-state actors—corporations, nongovernmental organizations, public interest groups—have also become influential; it is not just states that set standards or determine the rules of the road. In many respects, governance in cyberspace resembles the American "Wild West" of the 1870s and 1880s, with limited governmental authority and engagement. Users, whether organizations or individuals, must typically provide for their own security. Theories and approaches for exercising state control, and for leveraging control for national power, have not yet been developed.

Environmental Theories of Power

To understand the growing significance of cyberspace, it helps to examine how strategic theorists have addressed questions of national power in other environments. Theories related to land, sea, air, and outer space power share common elements that an environmental theory of cyberpower ought to address. We also identify unique features that distinguish these theories from one another.

Land Power

Theories of military strategy and national power have existed since the rise of civilizations, but two major, competing theories about how control over specific environments affects national power came to prominence in the late 19th century. The *heartland theory*, articulated by Halford John Mackinder, focused on the increasingly intense national competition in Europe at the turn of the 20th century. Major powers were competing globally, establishing colonies and seeking the upper hand militarily. Mackinder contrasted nations with control over the Eurasian heartland, such Germany and Russia, with nations that operated on the periphery, such as England and the United States. He noted how rapid industrialization and technologies such as the railroad and telegraph were helping transform the speed and scale of military operations. Mackinder predicted that the ability to mobilize the resources of the heartland to utilize the new transportation and communications technologies would enable the heartland nations to establish protected lines of communication and engage in military operations quickly at places of their choosing. Thus, he wrote: "Who rules East Europe commands the Heartland; who rules the Heartland commands the World-Island; who rules the World-Island controls the world."[12]

In contrast was the *rimland theory* published by Nicholas Spykman in 1944.[13] Examining the course of World War I, with attention to the security arrangements that could ensure stability after World War II, Spykman's theory contrasted sharply with that of Mackinder. Spykman saw the key sources of power in the population and material goods on the rim of the Eurasian continent, in the Western European peninsula, and in East Asia. Developments in military operations, such as amphibious warfare and carrier- and land-based airpower, would allow rimland nations to apply power at key pressure points around the Eurasian land mass and elsewhere on the globe. Spykman explicitly restated Mackinder's propositions: "Who controls the rimland rules Eurasia; Who rules Eurasia controls the destinies of the world."[14]

British, Russian, and U.S. power would, said Spykman, play the key roles in controlling the European littoral and thereby the essential power relations of the world. External lines of communication, in his view, now provided the dominant means for nations to employ military power, secure their economic interests, and provide for global stability.

Just as Mackinder and Spykman did for land power, those who would develop a theory of cyberpower must determine the key resources and focal points for transit in cyberspace.

Seapower

Focused more on the characteristics of the environment, theories of seapower arose even prior to the land power theories of Mackinder and Spykman. In 1890,

Alfred Thayer Mahan published *The Influence of Sea Power upon History, 1660–1783.*[15] This work, widely discussed in the United States and Europe, articulated principles about the relationship between a nation's seapower and its overall power. When Mahan wrote, rapid developments in technology—steam power, screw propulsion, armor for ships, and guns with longer range and increased accuracy—were changing the nature of seapower. The growth of steam power required navies to establish far-flung coaling stations and repair facilities to sustain a global naval presence.

In Mahan's view, naval power was fundamental to a nation's grand strategy, for economic power derived from maritime trade. Defining the conditions necessary for a nation to develop seapower, he stressed that mobilization of naval power in both military and merchant fleets was a national priority in order to secure global presence, maximize trade, and enable the projection of power ashore. Mahan wrote that:

> the growth of sea power in the broad sense . . . includes not only the military strength afloat, that rules the sea or any part of it by force of arms, but also the peaceful commerce and shipping from which alone a military fleet naturally and healthfully springs and upon which it securely rests.[16]

To command sea lanes of communication, Mahan advocated a large main battle fleet equipped to fight decisive battles, to maintain naval supremacy, and to guarantee secure trade with colonies. He also stressed the natural advantages of certain nations that controlled chokepoints, such as straits between key bodies of water and the approaches to major river systems.[17]

British naval theorist Julian Corbett was influenced by Mahan as well as by the German strategist Carl von Clausewitz. Writing before World War I, Corbett attributed Great Britain's success to its integration of maritime, military, economic, and diplomatic resources.[18] Naval strategy—the operational and tactical movement of the fleet—was, he argued, a subset of maritime strategy. He looked more broadly than Mahan at the utility of maritime power, examining its role in limited wars: he argued that "he who commands the sea is at great liberty and can take as much or as little of the war as he will" by putting land forces into conflicts at chosen places and times.[19] Corbett argued that a major "fleet in being" might be sufficient to deter an adversary from attempting to disrupt or deny a nation's vital commerce.

Seapower theory dealt explicitly with how control of an environment enabled global maneuver and with the impact of technological change. We can draw lessons from it for understanding the development of cyberspace. For example, much of cyberspace relies on fiber optic cables that transit the seabed; these cables and associated facilities may constitute new chokepoints.[20] Alternative routes will exist in cyberspace, such as satellites for intercontinental connectivity, but these alternatives, too, might be potential chokepoints. As such, each offers a potential locus of national control.

Airpower

The legacy of World War I influenced the airpower theorists of the early and mid-20th century, in particular Giulio Douhet of Italy, William (Billy) Mitchell of the United States, and Hugh Trenchard of Great Britain. All three were participants in the rapid development of airpower in the Great War, and they drew similar conclusions about its future role in warfare. As the technology of the airplane rapidly improved, it would enhance the capacity of airpower to strike directly at an enemy, "smashing the material and moral resources of a people," said Douhet, "until the final collapse of all social organization."[21] Trenchard asserted that "the ratio of morale to material effect was 20:1."[22] The bomber, he claimed, would dominate the air and be effectively unstoppable by defenses. "Viewed in its true light, aerial warfare admits no defense, only offense," argued Douhet, failing to anticipate defensive technology such as radar and advanced interceptors.

Future wars, argued these three theorists, would be short, and they would be dominated by those with sufficient airpower. Large land or sea forces or extensive mobilization would be unneeded. Surprise and preemptive airstrikes would constitute the strategic imperative for all advanced nations. According to Mitchell,

> The advent of air power, which can go straight to the vital centers and neutralize or destroy them, has put a completely new complexion on the old system of making war. It is now realized that the hostile main army in the field is a false objective.[23]

The airpower theorists were not particularly concerned with broader issues of grand strategy and national power, although Mitchell stressed the need to make airpower a national priority to ensure the ability to keep up with rapid technological change.[24] Mitchell argued that airpower could provide a cheap source of security and avoid the large expenditures, conscription, and taxes required to maintain standing armies. All three were dismissive of diplomatic interest in arms control to manage future conflicts. Douhet asserted: "All the restrictions, all the international agreements made during peacetime are fated to be swept away like dried leaves on the winds of war."[25]

New questions arose in the early 20th century with the rise of airpower, such as the significance of offense-defense interaction, the impact of a new kind of power on defense budgets and economic burdens, and the possibilities and limitations for international cooperation in securing control over a new domain. Such questions must now be explored with regard to cyberspace.

Spacepower

As technology advanced, nations and corporations extended military and commercial activity beyond the atmosphere into space. Control of space and how it could affect national power and global issues has become a focus for strategists. The advent of intercontinental ballistic missiles and the development of intelligence and communications satellites in the 1950s and 1960s led to strategic concern over space. National security strategists wrestled with the implications of an agreed ban on antiballistic missiles. Over time, the United States and others have increasingly focused on space as an arena for national competition. President Reagan established the Strategic Defense Initiative, envisioning the use of space-based assets to protect the United States from Russian intercontinental ballistic missiles.[26] The 2000 Space Commission report to Congress asserted the importance of the "security and economic well being of the United States and its allies and friends" to "the nation's ability to operate successfully in space."[27]

The 2005 National Defense Strategy identifies space as a global commons, a shared resource and arena, like international waters, airspace, and cyberspace.[28] Space is increasingly an area of international military competition, as China's demonstration of its antisatellite capabilities in January 2007 made clear.[29]

In a 1999 review of geopolitics and strategy, Colin Gray and Geoffrey Sloan explicitly addressed the challenges of strategy in Earth, moon, and solar spaces.[30] They stressed the strategic significance of locations in space. For example, geosynchronous orbits are prized locations for satellites whose function (such as telecommunications) requires them to match the Earth's rotation in order to remain over a specific point on the Earth. Locations where the gravitational pull of the Earth and moon is equal (known as LaGrangian points) also offer operating advantages particularly useful for space transport and maintaining the growing manned presence in space.

Mark Harter recently asserted that space is the new "high ground":

Space systems will significantly improve friendly forces' ability to strike at the enemy's heart or COGs [centers of gravity], paralyzing an adversary to allow land, sea and air forces to achieve rapid dominance of the battlespace.[31]

Space forces, he argued, will also conduct separate, parallel strategic campaigns with a global reach, such as warning and defending against ballistic missile launches. At the level of grand strategy, in his view, space systems can provide a means to exercise other "instruments of national power (diplomatic, informational, military, and economic) to force an enemy to capitulate."[32] Increasing reliance on space for achieving national military and economic goals requires dedicated U.S. efforts to ensure access and ability to defend and control the space environment. He argues, similarly to Mahan and Mitchell, that national spacepower should be part of an overall national effort involving coordinated military, governmental, civil, scientific, commercial, allied, and international efforts.

Harter explicitly identifies linkages with cyberspace, stressing the reliance on space to carry information globally, and network warfare operations that make use of space systems.[33] Space satellites and their orbital locations are chokepoints in the cyber world.

Comparing Environments: Sources of Power

This overview of environmental theories of power provides a basis for identifying their common features. We focus on four common threads:

- technological advances
- speed and scope of operations
- control of key features
- national mobilization.

While all the existing theories deal substantially with major technological changes, many failed to see how continuing technological evolution could undermine major tenets they proposed. They also dealt with how the nature of the environment enables the use of military power. Additionally, we must keep in mind that rapid political change will affect how cyberpower evolves.

Technological Advances

A major imperative for most of the theories was to predict the political-military impact of technological advances. For Mackinder, the advent of rail transportation and telegraph communication meant that the nation or nations controlling the heartland would be in position to assert global rule. As Eurasia began to be covered by an extensive network of railroads, a powerful continental nation might be able to extend its political control over the Eastern European gateway to the Eurasian landmass. As Mahan saw it, the advent of steam meant that global trade and presence through maritime power would be the primary path to success for nations that could develop such capacities.

The airpower theorists thought that the rise of unstoppable strategic bombers would mean that direct strikes at the enemy centers of gravity would decide future conflicts. The ability of man to move into space led theorists such as Gray, Sloan, and Harter to argue that sustained space presence will be an essential enabler of both military operations and control over the global information infrastructure.

The advent of the Internet, the opportunities for information exchange and social dialogue created by the World Wide Web, and the growing ubiquity of wireless and digital connectivity all have implications for the nature of political, economic, and military interactions. Use of the electromagnetic spectrum outside of visible light to achieve influence and conduct conflicts began, however, with the 19th century, not the 21st. The advent of the telegraph had major impacts on economic affairs, political reporting, and the conduct of diplomatic military operations. In both World Wars, radio broadcasts provided a major vehicle for propaganda, and governments endeavored to block these messages through jamming. Later in the 20th century, Marshall McLuhan examined the impact of the relatively new medium of television, examining how people and governments were influenced by images broadcast from the faraway war in Southeast Asia.[34] The digital age of the Internet has provided new arenas for political struggles. Hackers with political motives have taken over Web sites and placed confrontational messages and other propaganda. In the spring of 2007, dissidents with ethnic Russian sympathies organized a disruptive series of cyber attacks that affected the Estonian government, banking, and other sectors.[35]

Organizations engaged in economic competition increasingly rely on cyberspace as a source of advantage. The revolution in cost controls and just-in-time production systems by companies like Dell Computers in the 1990s was made possible by the ability to collect and process large amounts of data rapidly. New forms of e-commerce retail operations by Amazon and new markets such as those created by eBay have emerged. These activities are increasingly global; U.S. and European firms produce and deliver complex software and hardware utilizing the output of far-flung research centers and manufacturing plants in places ranging from Redmond, Washington, to Dublin, to Beijing. Satellites and undersea fiber optic cables allow companies to take advantage of human capital available at lower costs in other countries.

The evolution of cyberspace is also enabling new forms of warfare. The extension of conflict to cyberspace began as early as the Crimean War when the telegraph was used to transmit intelligence reports and to command widely dispersed forces. In World War I, radio became another major mode of long-distance communications with far-flung military forces. Competition to control the use of the electromagnetic spectrum increasingly became a major feature of air, naval, and intelligence operations during World War II. The U.S. Department of Defense is now pushing toward net-centric operations based on digital communications and ease of access to information at all levels, down to the individual soldier on the battlefield. Special forces units mounted on horseback operating against Taliban positions in Afghanistan called down global positioning system–guided precision airstrikes from B–52s they could not see. New U.S. fighter aircraft such as the F–22 carry sensor systems that allow them to share data in real time about activity in the electromagnetic spectrum both with higher headquarters and with other units conducting tactical operations. Global advantages accrue to those capable of creating information-enhanced forms of traditional military operations, but most require very deep pockets. However, smaller nonstate actors have also adapted to advances in cyberspace. With Iranian assistance, for example, Hizballah negated Israeli communications jamming and succeeded in their own efforts during the 2006 conflict in southern Lebanon.[36]

Reliance on cyberspace and issues of control over sensitive information and network availability present crucial risk management decisions to governments, corporations, and other actors (as described in chapter 7 of this volume, "Information Security Issues in Cyberspace"). A growing source of advantage to actors in cyberspace competition will be the capacity to evaluate tradeoffs related to operational value, connectivity, costs, vulnerabilities, and threats and to strike an effective balance.

The rise of digital connectivity will have transformative impacts. Just as the telegraph and railroads brought about major shifts in advantages in the age-old struggle to dominate land masses, key features of how digital communications operates will transform the landscape of opportunities in cyberspace. A crucial new feature of the Internet and the World Wide Web is the ease with which individuals and small groups can access them and send messages out to global audiences without revealing their location. The Internet was not designed to help track the origin of activity, and challenges have continued to mount as actors have devised new methods of indirection and anonymization to hide their identity and location. Dissident Falun Gong groups provide communications for their members in and outside of the People's Republic of China and have even hijacked official Chinese satellite television broadcasts.[37] Sites run by Islamic extremists on the Internet incite individual acts of violence and terrorism against Western regimes and provide detailed information regarding bombmaking techniques and other ways to target the adversaries' society (as described in chapter 19 in this volume, "Cyber Terrorism: Menace or Myth?").

The new digital media are interactive, unlike earlier radio and television broadcast media. Web sites, Internet chat rooms, and text messaging are part of a wide, rapidly merging set of global services that have resulted in an explosion of new social network opportunities. The disruptive possibilities for misuse of this connectivity extend into political competition. Terrorist groups with a variety of objectives have turned to cyberspace as an environment for conducting recruitment and fundraising.[38]

The ease of achieving anonymity on the Internet also facilitates rapid orchestration of operations across wide geographic areas with less chance of tipping off adversaries that disruptive attacks are imminent. The 2004 Madrid train bombers, for example, reportedly used "a program downloaded from the Internet by which text messages could activate mobile phones simultaneously" to set off multiple explosions.[39]

Presence in cyberspace and ease of connectivity also create new vulnerabilities to attack. Accessibility and anonymity have produced an environment in which smaller organizations and political actors, especially those who seek to avoid vulnerabilities to retribution in other environments, can achieve a disproportional increase in capabilities to conduct their operations and disrupt those of adversaries.

The increasing use of the Internet and other aspects of the cyber environment by advanced states to orchestrate the operations of their energy, transportation, and other infrastructures creates new strategic vulnerabilities (described in chapter 23 in this volume, "Cyberspace and Critical Information Protection: A Critical Assessment of Federal Efforts"). Disruptive effects on economic, military, and social activities from sustained power outages or loss of confidence in transportation systems could be more severe, involving physical damage and even casualties. Attacks against digital control systems are technologically feasible.[40] Such vulnerabilities provide asymmetrical advantages to nonstate actors that are less reliant on such control systems and infrastructures.

Cyberspace has emerged as a major new environment for political and military competition. New threats may arise from actors that may not be able to compete well in other realms. Intellectual property can be lost; adversaries can disrupt operations. Just as the expansion of global maritime trade required the development of colonies, naval fleets, and supporting infrastructures, cyberspace will call for political and military measures to protect economic and informational interests. New military capabilities and business enterprises require a conscious balancing of opportunity and risk; this demands a discipline of analysis that has not yet developed. The United States must learn how to protect its cyberspace presence in a cost-effective fashion. This may involve the development of large offensive forces that "roam the net" protecting commerce; the orchestration of international accords and norms might be able to limit disruptive activity by states against other states and punish nonstate actors; perhaps a new "cyber Manhattan project" can establish more secure technological foundations for cyberspace.

Technological advances in other environments changed the terms of competition as, for example, when the rise of steam propulsion gave advantages to those who could establish colonies and coaling stations to conduct global trade. Economic and military competitors of the United States have explicitly adopted such strategies in cyberspace, too. In the late 1990s, the Japanese set out national plans to establish the world's most advanced networks and promote the construction of ultra-high-speed Internet access for its businesses and citizens.[41] The People's Republic of China has engaged in a multifront approach: controlling public Internet access, developing proprietary operating systems for national use, and endeavoring to influence global standards evolution. Nonstate actors, too, have taken advantage of the new medium: "al Qaeda has become the first guerrilla movement in history to migrate from physical space to cyberspace."[42] Appropriately, then, the 2005 U.S. National Defense Strategy explicitly acknowledges that "disruptive challenges may come from adversaries who develop and use breakthrough technologies to negate current U.S. advantages in key operational domains."[43] Cyberspace may represent the operational domain of highest risk for the United States in the early 21st century.

Speed and Scope of Operations

The changing speed, pace, and scope of military operations were also essential concerns of each of the environmental strategists. While Mackinder and Spykman came to differing conclusions, both examined advantages based on concentrating force quickly, Mackinder advocating the dominance of interior lines of operations, Spykman exterior lines. Mahan and Corbett saw maritime power and naval operations as requiring nations to be able to generate power across the globe in order to control sea lanes of trade. For the air theorists, the speed of air operations meant that wars would be over quickly, giving dominant advantages to the party that struck first. As Douhet put it:

> Wars will begin in the air, and . . . large-scale aerial actions will be carried out even before the declaration of war, because everyone will be trying to get the advantage of surprise . . . for each side will realize the necessity . . . of ridding the air of aerial means to prevent any possible retaliation.[44]

Continuous operations with no territorial limits would be an inherent feature of the space environment, creating a new high ground that would enable those with enough spacepower to dominate operations in other environments.

The rapidity of connections offered by modern communications and information systems similarly creates both challenges and opportunities. Cyberspace can make information on new political developments across the globe available almost instantly. Commercial companies are tightening global supply chains by means of radio-frequency identification systems linked to point-of-sale electronic inventories, increasing efficiencies and lowering costs. Militarily, new forms of rapidly adaptive operations are made possible by use of these systems. Actionable intelligence can be rapidly pushed to cockpits of aircraft or other weapons systems allowing engagement of high-value targets across very wide areas, as in the U.S. strike that killed al Qaeda terrorist leader Abu Musab al-Zarqawi in Iraq.[45] More broadly, advanced militaries that can conduct network-centric operations can tightly orchestrate combined arms campaigns, pursuing full-scale combat operations at any time of the day and in any weather, so they can dominate less sophisticated militaries, as the United States did in Operations *Enduring Freedom* and *Iraqi Freedom*.

However, global connectivity to achieve rapid strategic impact has become a tool for nonstate actors as well, as described in chapter 18, "Cyber Crime," and chapter 19, "Cyber Terrorism: Menace or Myth?" Organized criminal activity, Internet posting of terrorist videos of beheadings, and malicious disruption on a global scale can all spread rapidly.[46] Cyberspace provides opportunity for alliances between organized crime, hackers, and terrorists, multiplying the risk to governments, corporations, and other potential targets.

The development of airpower in the first half of the 20th century meant that attacks could be launched against strategic centers of gravity in hours. The advent of ballistic missiles with nuclear warheads after World War II brought timelines down to minutes, and the scale of effects rose dramatically. The cyberspace of the 21st century means key events and disruptive threats can necessitate responses in seconds. National leaders are faced with tighter timelines for decisions even as it becomes increasingly imperative to orchestrate action across wider distances more quickly.

The requirement for rapid response in cyberspace can mean higher levels of automated decisions for states and other entities. The Department of Defense net-centric warfare concepts, fusing improved sensor and communications systems, enable engagement of targets that emerge rapidly but offer very limited time periods in which to take action. Balancing the need for speed with the risks of automated responses in military and other operations will prove a growing challenge. Rules of engagement will often call for high-confidence identification of potential targets, but a commander may not fully trust automated systems to make the call regarding weapons employment. The U.S. Navy shootdown of an Iranian airliner in 1988 by the Aegis air defense system provides a cautionary tale, yet caution may also lead to missed opportunities.[47] Cyberspace presents chances to hide or mislead regarding the source of malicious activity. Automated systems can be subverted and turned against their operators or used against third parties.

Cyberspace has multiplied opportunities for small or nonstate groups to achieve large effects in getting their message to a global audience, thus increasing their geographic base for acquiring resources, whether through voluntary contributions or illicit activity; it offers occasions for disrupting even the largest state opponents through new means of attack. The challenge to such groups will be to take advantage of the potential for rapid, global operations without creating a recognizable signature in cyberspace that would render them vulnerable to retaliation and thus to deterrence. Nonstate actors will seek to make cyberspace a medium where guerrilla campaigns, orchestrated dispersal, and surreptitious disruption make large land, sea, and air forces fighting decisive battles irrelevant.

Control of Key Features

The environmental theories described above also endeavored to delineate the conditions that would allow control of key features, especially logistics and lines of communication. The early 20th century brought the ability to amass forces at chosen points around the Eurasian land mass, crucial to Mackinder's assertion of the centrality of the heartland. Straits or sea lanes could be controlled by a large fleet even without direct naval engagements. Mahan detailed the role of a network of coaling stations and repair facilities located in colonies in achieving global maritime prominence. The supremacy of the bomber, according to Douhet, Mitchell, and Trenchard, meant that counterforce strikes to eliminate an adversary's striking power were essential for control of the air. Gray and Sloan sought to extend the strategic vision of geopolitics into space by identifying the key locations that would enable operations. Harter stressed the requirement "for multiple space ports from which to achieve orbit [in order] to eliminate ground choke points" as a foundation for spacepower.[48]

Cyberspace contains numerous activities, ranging from international financial transactions, coordination of global logistics, terrorist planning, or disruptive attacks on cyberdependent networks and operations. All of these activities require that actors establish the capacity to transit cyberspace. Crucial assets in cyberspace include the physical infrastructures that enable communications, such as undersea fiber optic cables and communications satellites, and major interconnection points for large global networks. The small numbers of such facilities mean they may be thought of as chokepoints, similar to mountain passes or straits between oceans. The limited number of physical paths for communications cables out of a major city can make bridges and tunnels chokepoints; for example, fiber optic networks were severely disrupted by the attacks of 9/11. Control or disruption of such cyber chokepoints could have a major impact on global communications connectivity and speed. In March 2007, authorities in the United Kingdom arrested individuals accused of planning terrorist attacks against key Internet infrastructure locations on the two U.S. coasts (known as Metropolitan Area Ethernet [MAE] East and MAE West).[49]

Logical systems and code shape the interactions of digital systems, telephone traffic, and other networks and systems in cyberspace. Thus, cyberspace is a manmade environment, unlike land, sea, air, or space. States, corporations, and other actors utilizing cyberspace can and do make choices about ownership, control, and operation of these key cyberspace features. Information infrastructures such as key network control facilities may be held in the private sector or instead may be owned and operated by the state. Standard-setting for communications systems can be in the hands of governments, such as with traditional telephone systems, or largely outside government control, as with much of Internet governance (see chapter 21 in this volume, "Internet Governance"). The diverse types of stakeholders that influence choices in forums such as the Internet Corporation for Assigned Names and Numbers include governments, businesses, technical groups, and civil-society organizations. Some key features of the cyberspace environment can change rapidly, as when the ownership of a major international satellite or fiber optic network operator changes, while others occur more slowly as, for example, IP-based telephony supplants circuit-switched voice telephone networks.

Large actors such as national governments, militaries, and multinational corporations have choices about which systems to emphasize—such as open, Internet-based communications or closed, proprietary systems—and about the pace of adoption of new standards. The United States must seek to understand constantly shifting opportunities and vulnerabilities and manage its cyber assets in light of its social, economic, and military concerns. In order to better protect cyberspace, the United States should pursue redundancy and diversity in undersea cable, satellites, ground stations, and fiber optic routing in order to minimize vulnerable chokepoints. We can worry less about precise mapping of all potential vulnerabilities (which have been a focus of many U.S. Federal Government efforts), given the constantly morphing cyberspace environment. Public and private sector actors who operate and use cyberspace for key national economic and security purposes should jointly conduct regular scenario analyses and exercises to focus investment and develop strategies to establish a robust cyber infrastructure.

In managing the evolution of the logical cyber environment, the United States should more aggressively engage those who establish protocols and standards, as competitors such as the People's Republic of China have increasingly chosen to do. U.S. choices about open versus closed systems, and more defensible versus more accessible cyberspace systems at the national level, will require balancing of intelligence, military, law enforcement, commercial, and social objectives. More secure, robust protocols and systems may allow for more options in developing networks that can be both open and trusted. Investment in a separate, more securable government network for sensitive but unclassified information may be the only way to accommodate the desire to limit government control to foster economic growth and social dialogue by encouraging growth of public networks that emphasize accessibility and innovation.

The United States and its partners should also seek more vigorous mechanisms for cooperation in the governance of the global common. While notions of "arms control agreements" to seek international control over information "weapons" have surfaced, the more appropriate approach for the United States would be securing freedom of passage, similar to regimes governing the seas and space. So far, U.S. efforts in the international community to foster a "culture of cyber security" and to leave leadership over the evolution of the Internet to the private sector have been largely successful and productive in terms of pursuing its objectives.[50]

National Mobilization

The national mobilization of essential resources, including deliberate government efforts to coordinate military and commercial activities, was a central concern for many of the environmental strategists. Mahan, for example, advocated support for colonies as global bases from which to project maritime power. The sea-, air-, and spacepower theories focused on the potential synergy between a nation's commercial and military activities and the development of professionals dedicated to securing the nation's interests.

Human capital is an even more crucial resource in the cyber environment. The cyber environment still rewards pioneers. Risks in cyberspace are less physical than they were for previous explorers. The premium is on brainpower, creativity, and ability to manage complexity. Historical U.S. strengths—advanced education, systems integration, and intellectual property development and management—should offer advantages in cyberspace competition. However, the lack of requirement for major resource investments, and the ease of leveraging global access to networks, will provide more advantages to nonstate actors in cyberspace than in other environments. Knowledge of the vital characteristics of critical infrastructures, economic flows, military dependencies, operating systems, and disruptive code can be rapidly stored, duplicated, transferred, and acted upon. Such knowledge and network access permit action in cyberspace.

Building and sustaining the expertise to leverage these assets will be a lengthy and expensive process for large actors such as governments and corporations that pursue long-term objectives through the cyberspace environment. In Western nations, expertise resides mainly in the commercial sector; the government and its military and national security establishments must effectively leverage this pool. This contrasts with the other environments related to national security. Nonstate actors can leverage fairly small cadres of skilled personnel to use cyberspace for specific purposes, whether to mobilize large numbers of people for a demonstration against globalization or to launch disruptive attacks on infrastructure.

The centrality of human expertise requires the United States, like other major actors, to compete globally to create, attract, and retain the human capital needed to construct, utilize, and engage in cyberspace. These personnel must be capable of analyzing the ever-changing opportunities and risks present in the environment, operating and protecting the large enterprises and infrastructures that sustain cyberspace, and performing other tasks ranging from forming new modes of sharing information to developing the capacity for preventing or deterring disruptive attack. For the U.S. military, the challenge is to nurture a strong cadre of cyber experts, similar to the naval, air, and space expertise that has enabled its success in other environments. This requires the vision and will to divert resources from traditional military missions to invest in the core capabilities necessary for the cyber environment.

National policy can influence the international, organizational, and individual access to and use of cyberspace. Many strategic choices exist. The People's Republic of China has begun to focus on tighter control of individual rights in cyberspace, seeking to establish a somewhat separate national cyberspace with controlled access to foster government political control and improve its ability to defend national cyber assets. The United States has taken a much more laissez faire approach: its national regulation and positions in international forums stress the economic benefits of loose control in empowering innovation and access by all to services provided via the Internet and other cyberspace media.

The impact of different national approaches on the ability to manage strategic conflict in cyberspace is not clear. A loosely controlled and diverse but robust network infrastructure may fare better than a centrally managed infrastructure with mandated barriers and defense, even if the latter retains a limited capacity for rapid adaptation in the face of new threats.

A major power such as the United States requires policy and organizational structures that can encompass the full range of interrelated economic, security, and social issues related to cyberspace. The growth of a global system of ownership and control of the technology and operation of cyberspace presents both economic opportunity and security risks. Increasingly, U.S. national security organizations and critical infrastructure providers rely on information technology and communications hardware and software that are produced by people and organizations whose loyalties and purposes are not always easy to assess, yet the Nation is part of a global economic system that has greatly fostered U.S. prosperity. National focus is required to address the challenges of coordinating multiple U.S. Government agencies and including the private sector in an orchestrated system for conducting national defense against a major threat in cyberspace.

Based on the appeals of Alfred Mahan and others, Theodore Roosevelt made the establishment of a modern blue water Navy a national priority as the United

States began to become a global power at the beginning of the 20th century. Billy Mitchell's call for national effort to develop airpower was answered by Franklin Roosevelt on the eve of World War II and played a vital role in the U.S. victories in that conflict. John Kennedy launched a program to ensure the U.S. lead in space and to put a man on the moon in response to perceived Soviet challenges in this environment. Similarly, as the strategic significance of cyberspace grows, dedicated national programs may well be required to ensure that we have the capacity to achieve our national objectives.

Analysts concerned about the lack of a strategic U.S. cyber defense have called for a national focus to pull disparate efforts together.[51] The employment of national resources on the level of a "cyber Manhattan project" may be needed. Such efforts would also require the use of diplomatic capital to secure global support across nations, corporations, and civil society groups. National policy development is needed to integrate efforts by the White House, Congress, business, and civic leaders to set balanced objectives for utilizing and defending cyberspace.

Distinctive Features of Cyberspace

Cyberspace, as we have seen, has both similarities to and differences from other environments (see table 10–1). Two differences merit focused attention: offense dominance and the rapid changeability of the cyberspace environment.

Offense dominance is sometimes characteristic of other realms, but it has very different implications in cyberspace. Both the weaknesses in the technological foundations and the economic incentives for openness between networks and systems have made many key networks vulnerable to exploitation, manipulation, and disruption by digital attack. Nonstate actors derive advantages from the ability to focus on niche objectives, utilize anonymous access, rapidly leverage expertise, and make decisions more rapidly. Thus, offense is easy, and defense is difficult.

Concerns over which actor might strike first in a conflict play out differently in cyberspace than with air and ballistic missile forces. The ease of stealthy deployment of attacking forces and difficulty in attributing the source and intent of attackers mean that damage limitation through preemptive first strikes or retaliatory strikes is largely irrelevant: an actor would have little confidence in trying to attack preemptively to remove the cyber attack forces of an even moderately sophisticated adversary. Similarly, trying to use cyber counterattack to disable attacks in progress is complicated by issues of identifying and discretely targeting a complex web of electronic points of origin of the attacker, the culpability of the networks and systems from which attacks appear to originate,

TABLE 10-1. Elements with the Cyber Environment Compared with Other Environments

	LAND	SEA	AIR	SPACE	CYBER
TECHNOLOGICAL ADVANCES	Rail and communications require focus on heartland	Steel and steam enable global power projection	Crush centers of gravity directly	Creates a new high ground	New strategic vulnerabilities; enables nonstate actors
SPEED AND SCOPE OF OPERATIONS	Drives choice of preferred lines of communication	Allows global strikes against rim of heartland	Conflicts will end quickly	Continuous global operations	Extremely fast global operations; automation of command and control
CONTROL OF KEY FEATURES	Speed of mobilization crucial for heartland advantage	Requires global basing; geographic chokepoints	First strikes against adversary airfields crucial	Ensure access with lift; control key orbit points	Environment under human control; changes quickly
NATIONAL MOBILIZATION	Location of key resources crucial	Must protect trade as key element of national power	Ensure cadre of professionals; link to private sector	Ensure cadre of professionals; link to private sector	Ensure cadre of professionals; link to private sector

and the fundamental fact that disrupting these points in cyberspace may only have a limited effect. Deterrence by retaliation is also complicated by the difficulty of attributing an attack to any identifiable target for retaliation (but see chapter 13 in this volume, "Deterrence of Cyber Attacks").

National security organizations cannot simply defend the environment by increasing the size of their military cyber forces. If the attacker has a high probability of rapid success, simply pursuing current information security approaches with more vigor is unpromising. Most attention in the national security community has focused on risks from cyber espionage or a single, time-limited strategic cyber blow from a major adversary. Counterstrategies to deal with state or terrorist nonstate actors conducting an economic guerrilla campaign in cyberspace remain almost completely undeveloped. A robust, defensible infrastructure will depend on shaping the technologies employed, the obligations of operators of key networks and infrastructures, and the ability to coordinate government–private sector investment and responses to attacks.

A second unique characteristic of cyberspace is its rapid changeability. The ability of nations to compete effectively in other environments involved technological competition; indeed, the efforts of Mackinder and Mahan were largely inspired by changes in the technologies being used to compete on land and sea. However, the fundamental physical forces and terrain of those environments do not change; scientists and technologists understood them better over time. By contrast, the manmade environment of cyberspace can change its key characteristics and dominant operating modes rapidly; for example, as the World Wide Web expands, bandwidth and memory capacities increase, and new devices become increasingly ubiquitous. Software updates and additions to networks change the ability to defend and attack many networks on a daily basis. The continually accelerating deployment of new technologies, standards, access, and legal regimes changes the landscape of technological choices, operational procedures, and risks for users, attackers, and defenders.

The mobilization of resources will require leadership, strategies, and decision-making processes that put a premium on learning and flexibility. Management and acquisition processes will need to support rapid implementation of changes to systems and networks, as well as agility in the adoption of rapidly changing rules governing access to outside networks and mission partners that balance usability and security. The conduct of military and other operations will place a premium on trusting individuals to understand the changes they see in the cyber tactical environment and adjust the execution of their operations quickly.

Moving Forward

Defense and economic institutions that are now dependent on the cyber environment cannot allow a continuing slide toward a "Wild West" of criminal and disruptive opportunities. Yet we also must strive to preserve the benefits of innovation and connectivity that have made the cyberspace environment so valuable. The United States must look for ways to embed flexibility and mechanisms for rapid change in policy, institutions, technology choices, and human capital plans. This new environment may require substantially different approaches due to its more mutable, human-driven characteristics.

Insights from biological and other complex adaptive systems might serve as useful guides to what changes might be necessary. The lesson of biology is that survival is not necessarily the reward for the biggest, strongest, or meanest but rather for the most adaptable. The ability to learn, to cooperate when fruitful, and to compete when necessary, will provide the fundamental strengths of those actors seeking cyberpower.

CHAPTER 11

Military Cyberpower

Martin C. Libicki

DOES CYBERPOWER, particularly military cyberpower, matter? This may seem to be an odd question: after all, do we ask whether airpower matters? But perhaps the question is not so odd. Airpower, when first introduced into warfare, was purely instrumental in its effects. In order to matter at that time, airpower had to (and still must) influence ground power. If airpower had zero effect on the ground—if it gave no capability to deliver supplies, drop bombs, or see something of value—then it would make scant difference that one's planes could fly anywhere at will and one's opponents' planes could not. The same is true for cyberpower. If control, influence, or competence in the medium has little to do with the delivery of military power in the more conventional realms,[1] then no one would need it, except perhaps for bragging rights.

To answer the question of whether military cyberpower matters, we first define *cyberspace* and hence, power in cyberspace, or *cyberpower*. Then we examine two experiments, one involving a Stryker Brigade Combat Team (SBCT) exercise, the other involving air-to-air and air-to-ground training sorties. We conclude that the available evidence so far does not allow us to reject the null hypothesis: that network-centric capabilities have no effect on mission effectiveness.

Distinguishing Characteristics of Military Cyberpower

On the face of it, cyberspace would appear to be the pinnacle of domains. Cyberspace is all about information; while information has always been useful in warfare, it is now essential. However, cyberspace and information are not identical because the flow of information does not define a space. No one talks about "courier-space," "mail-space," "semaphore-space," or "telegraph-space," and certainly not in a wartime context. A definition of cyberspace presumes that changes in the quantity and speed, and more specifically the density and the interactivity, of information exchange imply a change in the quality of military information and decisionmaking.

Perhaps the best defining marker is that cyberspace is about networking, the two-way transfer of information, in contrast to broadcasting, in which information is transferred only one way. Networking appears to be the essence of cyberspace for two reasons: first, because *cyber* refers to control, and control requires feedback; second, because *space* assumes a medium in which there is omnidirectional movement, in contrast to the one-directional flow that would characterize water pipes. In other words, if there were no interactivity, there would be no cyberspace.

This distinction is crucial and is often ignored. Many advocates of military transformation through networking ascribe almost magical powers to its interactivity aspect, asserting that it will permit more agile command and control, enable warfighters to cycle through their observe-orient-decide-act loops faster than the enemy can, or allow self-synchronization, eliminating the need for hierarchical command and control and facilitating the superior tactic of swarming, thereby shifting power to the edge.[2] All of this takes interaction: the peer-to-peer exchange of information, perceptions, and plans. None of these effects would be possible, however, if the only noticeable result of networking the forces were to allow them to receive more information faster.

These oft-vaunted benefits of networking will not emerge if just a pair of broadcasting flows is mistakenly called networking. One good example of two-way broadcasting is Blue Force Tracker, a system by which every "blue" unit automatically transmits its global positioning system–determined coordinates to a data fusion center. The center amalgamates these location points, superimposes them on a map, and retransmits the completed picture back to all units. History suggests that such a capacity would be extremely valuable.[3] Similarly, networked sensors could feed a data fusion center, either directly or through intermediate nodes, which could collectively illuminate the battlefield and send a picture to inform the warfighters. Nevertheless, it would be misleading to call this the emergence of a new cyberspace, largely because absent peer-to-peer information exchange, there is no interaction space as such and no basis for more sophisticated (which may often mean less) command and control. Such a capability by itself would not push power to the edge, at least not directly.[4] In other words, the hourglass topology shown in figure 11–1 does not reflect cyberpower very well. The omninode or all-point connectivity topology shown in figure 11–2 is required.

We can now revisit the central question: does the creation of cyberpower by networking the operators permit a measurable improvement in operational effectiveness? To answer this question, we must rely on the results of experiments rather than actual combat results. Despite nearly two decades of discussion about the so-called revolution in military affairs (now called *transformation*), the digitization of the armed forces has been slow. Soldiers in the 2003 invasion of Iraq who operated below the company command level had very little digital connectivity; they were often first apprised of enemy forces the old-fashioned way, by running into them.[5]

As of May 2005, three networking experiments had been completed, and only two of them had produced anything quantitative that spoke to military effectiveness.[6] The SBCT experiment was documented in a RAND report.[7] The second experiment examined the effect of equipping Air Force pilots with networking capabilities (specifically, the Joint Tactical Information Distribution System [JTIDS], also called Link-16).[8]

FIGURE 11-1. Hourglass Topology

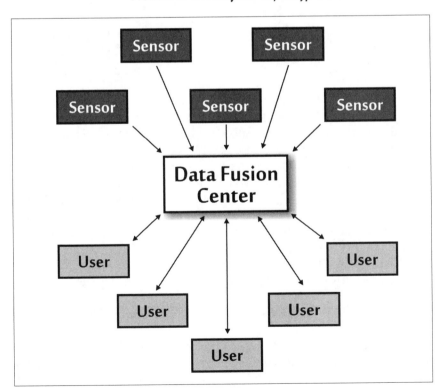

FIGURE 11-2. All-point Connectivity Topology

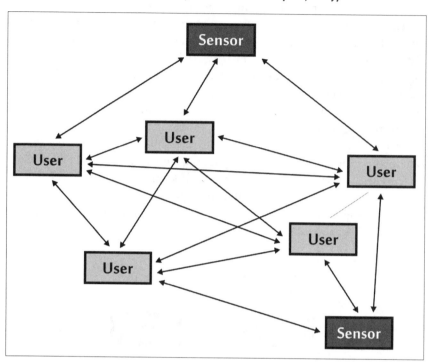

Both experiments appear to show substantial performance improvements from networking. However, the important question is: What aspects of network-centric operations best explain the improvement? Is it the network as network, that is, cyberspace, or more simply that a network meant the ability to pass more information faster? If the latter—if it was access to information per se that made the difference—comparable improvement could be provided with something similar to broadcasting. If, however, cyberpower resulted in improved information-sharing and shared situational awareness—and hence better collaboration and thus some potential for self-synchronization—this would mean that cyberpower does, indeed, matter for military power. What we found, however, was that neither experiment convincingly demonstrated without ambiguity that networking made a difference in combat effectiveness.

Results from the Stryker Brigade Combat Team Experiment

The SBCT experiment was conducted during the Joint Certification Exercise at the Joint Readiness Training Center at Fort Polk, Louisiana, in early 2004. It contrasted the performance of two similar—but by no means otherwise identical—brigades. The SBCT had dense networking between and among all vehicles, while the light infantry brigade (LIB) did not. Each attempted to take an urban target that was defended by an opposition force with armaments similar to that of current U.S. brigades.

The differences in performance were quite dramatic. The LIB—a standard force in today's Army—was able to locate and identify fewer than 10 percent of the forces it fought prior to engaging them. The SBCT was able to locate and identify 80 percent. Decisions that took the LIB 2 days to make and transmit took the SBCT only 3 hours. The LIB took as many casualties as it imposed, but the SBCT enjoyed a combat exchange ratio of better than 10:1. In the end, the LIB did not take the town; the SBCT, by contrast, succeeded.

However, it is not clear that networking accounted for all or even most of these differences. Napoleon remarked that victory favors the larger battalions, and on that count, table 11–1 is revealing. Even without information technology, the SBCT's greater size would have given it a distinct combat advantage; it was particularly well equipped with snipers.

The advantages of the SBCT do not end there. The Stryker vehicle itself had a level of firepower that the LIB lacked. Members of the LIB had to walk to the battle, 25 kilometers away, on a route with considerable potential for ambushes; the SBCT warriors had vehicles and could drive there. The SBCT thus arrived far more rested and ready for combat. Perhaps the most significant difference in terms of finding the enemy was that the SBCT had four times the number of reconnaissance units that the LIB had, and because they got there sooner, they had 60 hours available to do reconnaissance, while the LIB had just 42 hours. As a result, the SBCT had a 6:1 advantage in intelligence collection team–hours, so perhaps the 8:1 advantage in what they could find is not so surprising. Both sides had comparable use of advanced sensors: the SBCT alone had access to unmanned aircraft systems, but they were only used for confirmation of information gathered by other means.

The SBCT also enjoyed a vast advantage in connectivity. The LIB had FM radio and poor quality field voice equipment, while SBCT gear included the enhanced position location reporting system, near-term digital ratio, and satellite radios that could access military satellites and combat net radio operating over commercial channels. The SBCT enjoyed connectivity of 14 kilobits per second to every vehicle and 1.5 megabits per second to the brigade headquarters. The only equivalence between the SBCT and the LIB was in digital data connectivity to the dismounted soldier: zero in both cases.

Differences in numbers, firepower, and reconnaissance assets, as well as communications capability, meant that the SBCT had the option of pursuing different approaches to its objective. SBCT warfighters could use their superior

TABLE 11-1. Stryker Brigade Combat Team: Conventional Advantages

	LIGHT INFANTRY BRIGADE (LIB)	STRYKER BRIGADE COMBAT TEAM (SBCT)	RATIO LIB: SBCT
END STRENGTH	2,705	3,498	1:1.3
RIFLEMEN	1,062	1,353	1:1.3
MORTARMEN	132	168	1:1.3
SNIPERS	18	51	1:2.8

reconnaissance and communications assets to avoid the two-thirds of the opposition force that was fielded outside of the town and attack the town directly. It was the SBCT and not the LIB that was able to find the best avenue of approach to surprise town defenders.[9] The SBCT was able to attack the town 13 hours earlier than the LIB could, destroy the enemy force as a fighting unit, and clear every building. By contrast, the adversary was able to mass its combat power against the LIB and thereby defeat the brigade in detail, resulting in overall mission failure for the LIB.

A closer look at some of the intermediate variables shows that the SBCT had superior knowledge compared to the LIB. Both teams were asked, after the exercise, whether the information each had was complete and accurate (most of the priority intelligence requests were "where" questions). Whereas the SBCT answered *yes* in 80–90 percent of the cases, the LIB could answer *yes* in only 10–20 percent. It took an average of 12 hours to get information to the LIB from spotters, but just 2 minutes to get similar information to the SBCT. The LIB had to allow 48 hours between the creation of a war plan and its execution to get the word out to its forces. The SBCT was able to do this in 3 hours and thus could attack the town early, achieving surprise.

Specific testimony taken from surveys of the participants underscored that advantage. One infantry battalion commander in the SBCT commented, "I could see on the Common Operational Picture that the lead battalion accomplished its mission early. I moved up our attack time to achieve momentum," and presumably he gained it. Many references to distributed planning, which was likely aided by networking, were made in interviews, but the testimony does not reveal whether the primary advantage of distributed planning was that planners had superior access to each other or they simply had faster access to more reliable data. For example, one participant said that "instead of focusing discussion on the base level of knowledge and comprehension of the situation, these interactions in the SBCT were observed to reach the higher levels of analysis and application." Similarly, a Joint Readiness Training Command observer noted, "The Stryker brigade [best] exemplified [this capability] with collaborative planning between the main [command post] and the tactical [command post]. . . . VTC [video teleconferencing] capability should be extended to lower echelons . . . to enhance situational awareness [and] understanding."

To assess this experiment, we start by attempting to rule out all the hypotheses that any or all of the non-network advantages were sufficient to cause the difference in outcomes.

The SBCT had clearly superior conventional forces: more (and better rested) soldiers and greater firepower. Historically, such a modest advantage is not unknown to result in an unambiguous win. Such a win, in the absence of overwhelming force differences, however, generally requires that soldiers on the losing side recognize what fate holds in store for them and bolt from the battlefield, suffering disproportionate casualties in the process. However, in neither case did either of the combatants lose cohesion (and why would they in an experiment?), so the advantage of superior forces has to be ruled out. When forces fared badly, they fared badly in detail. Thus, one has to eliminate superior conventional force as sufficient in itself to explain such vast disparities in outcomes between the SBCT and the LIB.

Another advantage was that the SBCT had time and resources to do six times as much reconnaissance as the LIB. The fact that it was able to find more of the enemy more quickly can reasonably be correlated with this advantage. However, it may be a bit of a stretch to argue that firepower and reconnaissance alone could explain all of the difference in outcomes. Perhaps it was the SBCT's ability to fuse data more efficiently into an accurate picture of the battlefield that was more telling. For example, the SBCT was able to acquire information from spotters far faster than the LIB could. Is a combination of firepower, reconnaissance, and data fusion—which is to say, firepower and knowledge to the warfighter—enough to explain the difference in outcomes? To know the answer, one would have to compare two identical SBCT teams, one that had only the hourglass networking topology of figure 11–1, and one that was capable of taking advantage of the all-point connectivity of figure 11–2.[10] That was not done in this experiment.

Consider, finally, the SBCT's advantages of faster command and of distributed planning. The problem from the analytical point of view is that, because we cannot rule out the possibility that the other advantages already discussed—firepower plus knowledge—could account for the difference in outcomes, we cannot rule out the possibility that network-centricity per se had no additional impact on the outcomes.

Results from the Air-Air and Air-Ground Case Studies

The experiment of equipping Air Force pilots with networking capabilities, specifically JTIDS, says even less about whether cyberpower enhances military power. This has less to do with the construction of the experiment, as in the SBCT case, and more to do with the nature of air operations. First, aircraft, being expensive platforms, have always been equipped with the kind of advanced communications that mobile ground forces could only dream of. Second, there are far fewer opportunities for the kind of network-mediated collaboration in the air than there are on the ground, for reasons that are easy to imagine: flying aircraft is a demanding activity that requires continuous attention to the machine. Furthermore, while multiple aircraft do work together, it has usually been in relatively small numbers, and the pilots are often within sight of one another. The advent of long-distance networking has removed the requirement of visibility, but the numbers of coordinating units are still relatively small.

The analysis compared the mission effectiveness of "voice only" F–15 flights to that of F–15s with both voice and JTIDS capability. Adversary aircraft were assumed to have the same attributes in both cases. This study, unlike the SBCT case above, had the advantage of a large data set: 12,000 training sorties. The data was gathered through a combination of quantitative metrics and calculations as well as pilot interviews, using conservative assumptions, to examine mission effectiveness expressed in terms of kill ratios.

The improvement in kill ratios with JTIDS was, if not the 10:1 ratio of the SBCT experiment, still an impressive result of roughly 2.6 to 1 (see table 11–2).

Again, we ask what aspect of JTIDS led to such improvement. Pilots cited eight factors in particular. Two factors arise from superior knowledge: earlier, more complete individual and shared situational awareness and understanding of the adversary air picture (information completeness included knowledge of one's own aircraft formations and of enemy aircraft); and information superiority in the sense of becoming more quickly aware of and more deeply understanding of enemy air formations.

Another cited factor results from being able to acquire such knowledge faster: more decision time available for flight leads (and wingmen) and thus a greater ability to focus on the fight itself and maneuvers antecedent to it. A fourth factor results from being able to acquire such knowledge earlier (that is, prior to engagement): improved battle management and targeting before engaging. A fifth factor resembles the classic network-centric formulation: better ability to self-synchronize, or "swarm."

The remaining three factors mentioned by the pilots are the practical (and inferred) consequences of the first five: better intercept geometries, improved lethality of missile shots, and more shots per engagement.

TABLE 11-2. Improved Kill Rates with Joint Tactical Information Distribution System

	VOICE ONLY	JOINT TACTICAL INFORMATION DISTRIBUTION SYSTEM (JTIDS)	VOICE ONLY: JTIDS KILL RATIO
DAYTIME	3.10	8.11	1:2.62
NIGHTTIME	3.62	9.40	1:2.60

Both of these experiments indicate that one of the great values of networking is that it makes meetings more efficient: far less time is spent arraying and debating facts. This leaves far more time to generate and evaluate plans that depend on the observed facts. Whether better meetings lead to better warfighting, however, is another question.

One cannot, from this evidence, determine whether the one attribute that depends on the definitive characteristics of cyberpower—the ability to self-synchronize and swarm—has, by itself, a positive, null, or negative effect on the exchange ratio. It is reasonable to believe that the ability to "see" the target more quickly and earlier in the engagement cycle has an appreciable effect on mission effectiveness. It is certainly plausible, however, that the extra knowledge that is brought to the pilot through higher bandwidth and data fusion may itself account entirely for the effect.

A similar analysis applies to current and emerging capabilities for air-to-ground engagements. With JTIDS, the pilot has access to a map with potential targets indicated on it with Xs. The presented information is not good enough for precision bombing (using joint direct attack munitions), but it suffices for weapons that have the capacity to acquire the target precisely on their own if told generally where to look. It may also be good enough to cue other sensors that might identify impact points more precisely. At any rate, if accurate, it is a good synoptic picture of the battlefield. In contrast, however, JTIDS can provide much clearer communications between the forward air controller and the pilot. Compared to voice commands, digital commands can provide more information that is more clearly indicated and more persistent in the aircraft's memory.

Here, too, networking leads to better information. Pilots get more detailed data from forward air controllers faster and more reliably. They also get a much more complete and up-to-the-minute picture of adversary aircraft. Whether this fits the definition of cyberspace, such that we can say cyberspace improves performance, is much harder to determine from these results.

Conclusion

Overall, the same conclusion (or rather, absence of a conclusion) arises from both the ground and air experiments. The evidence presented does not allow us to reject the null hypothesis: that network-centric capabilities have no effect on mission effectiveness once the ability of networks to efficiently transmit data, especially consolidated data, is taken into account.

Thus, the debate must continue over whether cyberpower—as manifested in network-centricity—has any positive effect on warfighting effectiveness. This is not entirely unprecedented for new means of warfare. Take airpower, for example. Few better examples of airpower can be given than the American and British use of it against Germany in World War II. Yet even now, considerable controversy remains over whether the expenditure of resources and blood— 50,000 dead in the 8th Air Force alone—could have led the war to a speedier end had it been devoted instead to ground forces.[11]

So it is with cyberpower. In years to come, the U.S. defense establishment may conduct further experiments that test the claims of net-centricity more carefully by allowing both sides to have identical access to knowledge, but allowing only one side to enjoy the technologies that promote collaboration or faster command in general. Until then, the null hypothesis—that cyberpower does not matter—remains to be disproved.

CHAPTER 12

Military Service Overview

Elihu Zimet and Charles L. Barry

MILITARY CYBERPOWER is the application of the domain of cyberspace to operational concepts to accomplish military objectives and missions including humanitarian assistance and disaster relief (HA/DR); achieve stability, security, transition, and reconstruction (SSTR); and influence operations, as well as warfighting. Military operations such as administration, personnel management, medical care, and logistics are also enhanced with cyber tools. The growth in information technology and cyberspace has provided the military with new capabilities but has also provided new challenges, including balancing the need for new operational concepts to meet increasingly important military missions that now include appropriate and balanced use of soft and hard power with the need to jointly structure the military to accomplish these missions, including the connectivity to coalition partners. Unintended risks and vulnerabilities, especially the increased dependence of the military on civilian cyberspace capabilities, products, and services, need careful assessment to be effectively managed.

This chapter begins with a broad introduction to military cyberpower and a discussion of military operational constructs including information operations (IO), influence operations (mostly soft power), network-centric operations (NCO), intelligence operations, and the normal business and administrative use of cyberspace, followed by a discussion on military networks. Next is an overview of steps taken throughout the Department of Defense (DOD) to achieve joint network integration across the Services. Following this is an overview of current Service positions and approaches to cyberpower. The chapter concludes with observations on the DOD Global Information Grid (GIG), which is the principal common network backbone for the Services in the implementation of NCO.

Two points are made upfront. First, the growth and globalization of cyberspace technology and the corresponding need for adaptive information-based operational concepts to meet new military missions that include the use of both hard and soft power, from warfighting to HA/DR and SSTR, form the basis of the need for a military cyberpower strategy. The need to jointly structure the military to perform these operations and accomplish these missions, including the connectivity to coalition partners, provides an enduring challenge. Operational concepts such as the effectiveness of NCO in irregular warfare scenarios are still being tested.

Second, a single comprehensive network architecture designed to promote maximum connectivity and user pull based on an open commercial backbone will need separation from the secure connectivity required for sensor-to-weapon operations. The development of the GIG, the Combined Enterprise Regional Information Exchange System (CENTRIXS) program for information exchange among combined allied forces, and new technology initiatives is poised to address the issue of comprehensive networks, but not all technology objectives of these programs may be met, and vulnerabilities may exist. In the meantime, the military requires secure closed (separated) networks as well as fully connected open networks. The military also needs to wrestle with existing legacy systems to integrate them into the GIG, to leave them as standalone systems, or to terminate them.

The possession of accurate and timely knowledge and the unfettered ability to distribute this as information have always been a sine qua non of warfighting. As cyberspace has developed—particularly in the area of networked computer-based information systems such as the Internet,[1] global cellular-based networks with text messaging, personal digital assistants such as the Blackberry, and global satellite and cable networks (including radio and TV)—its impact on military operations has transformed operational concepts such as NCO and IO with the addition of new tools and procedures. In parallel with, indeed almost outpacing, the development of cyberpower in the military has been the global impact of cyberspace on all the levers of power (diplomatic/political, information, military, and economic) as well as the empowerment of individuals and groups and states. The Internet has also provided a "virtual safe haven" for nonconventional threats for the military including nonstate actors, terrorists, and criminal groups.

In the post–World War II industrial era, U.S. military superiority was structured on industrial strength; superior technology in platforms, weapons, and command, control, communications, computers, intelligence, surveillance, and reconnaissance (C⁴ISR); and a robust military infrastructure. As we have moved from the industrial to the information age, however, the diffusion of information technology has tended to change some of the parameters of warfighting, and not always to our advantage. Precision weapons and NCO have given the United States a decided advantage on the battlefield, but in irregular warfare, we have had setbacks. While the United States was the developer of the cyberspace infrastructure, it is now open and available to all who possess the means to access it. The concepts of NCO and IO are also readily available, although there is a high cost of entry in developing significant capabilities. Cyberspace is a tool amenable to asymmetric warfare because it can be used anonymously, so deterrence and retribution are difficult; its immediate effects are nonlethal, so the risk of escalation is reduced. Cyberspace can also cause lethal effects (for example, by disrupting control systems, causing things to blow up) in IO as well as NCO. For example, a computer network attack on an unprotected supervisory control and data acquisition control system of a power plant could lead to catastrophic damage to power generators and transformers.

Cyberspace has become a pillar of our national (and international) infrastructure. The military owns its tanks, ships, and aircraft but it has only limited impact on the commercially provided connectivity (such as fiber optics and satellites) that the information superhighway depends upon. Figure 12–1 characterizes the communications backbone for connectivity.

The military use of the communications backbone of cyberspace falls into three regions on this chart. The military is a general user of the global communications backbone. Due to the risks and vulnerabilities inherent in operating in an open architecture, the military has its own specific secure networks for warfighting, as shown in the shaded area outside the large circle, but it also uses networks that rely on commercial connectivity where the military controls the nodes, access, and traffic on the networks (the area of overlap of the military and the open network, for example, the Secret Internet Protocol Router Network and Secure Telephone Units). The area of overlap between the U.S. military and allied militaries represents information exchange between combined forces and the joint combat commands region to region for global operations. A single, common, global, multinational data network is being developed as the CENTRIXS program. Security technology to allow information exchange among separate, simultaneous communities of interest across common network transport remains a significant challenge.

While the military establishment and the defense industrial base have been subjected to continuous probing, disruptions, and hacking attacks, the concepts and impact of cyberwar are only now being developed in terms of military organization, operational concepts, joint doctrine, rules of engagement, and training and education.

A considerable volume of literature continues to be produced on both the structure and implications of military cyberpower. This chapter attempts

FIGURE 12–1. Cyberspace Connectivity

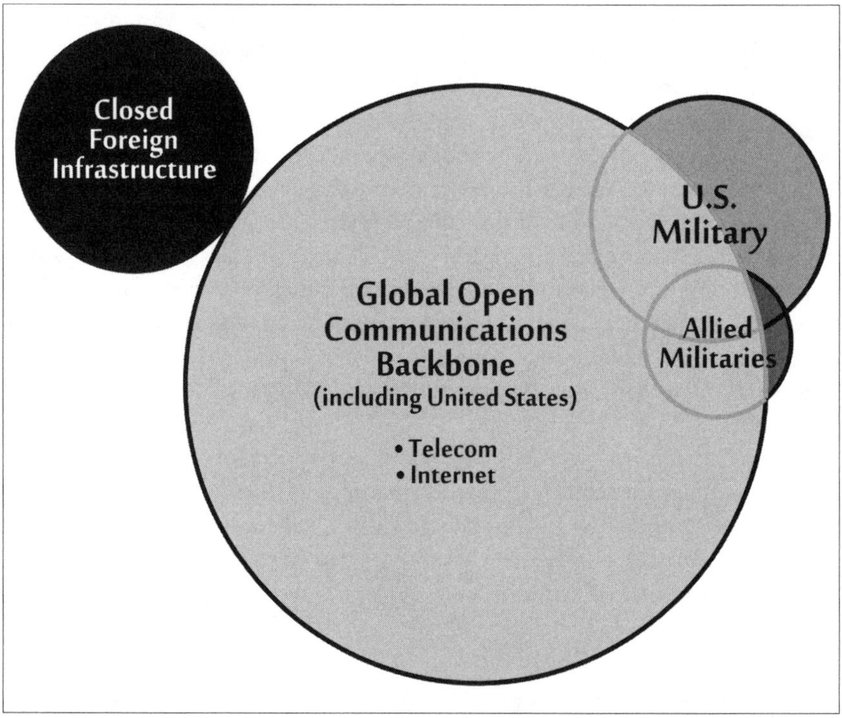

to link the capabilities enabled by cyberspace to both military missions and operational concepts. The military domain of cyberspace is characterized in two broad regimes that often require different attributes. The first regime is an open network in which collaboration, information-sharing, and situational awareness are principal measures of performance and connectivity is an essential driver. While operating within the timelines of an enemy is still essential, more latency in information transmittal is usually tolerated than in a sensor-to-shooter engagement, and shared knowledge gains in importance relative to speed of operations. The second regime employs closed, secure networks in which speed of operation, assured delivery, and integrity of information are paramount.

The concept of an open or closed network as used in this chapter is at best an abstraction in that these terms are really reference states and do not exactly correspond to actual employed networks. In fact, open networks are usually capable of supporting some secure transmissions, and some closed networks use the communications backbone. An open network is defined here as one that is open to any user who wants to dial in or log on. Security is usually provided by password protection, encryption, and computer and network protection tools. The principal measures of performance are connectivity, availability, and bandwidth. The Internet and telecom are examples (although not all of the Internet is open, and the communications backbone is also used for secure transmissions). A closed network has access by only designated nodes and is air-gapped from open networks. Principal measures of performance for closed networks are security, availability, and assuredness. An example of a closed network is the Joint Worldwide Intelligence Communications System.

Structure of Military Cyberpower

Military cyberpower is defined here as the application of operational concepts, strategies, and functions that employ the tools of cyberspace to accomplish military objectives and missions. Often, cyberpower is employed in support of operations in other domains such as maritime operations. However, at times joint cyberpower will be employed to prevail against an opponent in a contest wholly within cyberspace itself.

In order to develop this definition further, military cyberpower is represented as a pyramid in figure 12–2, where it is seen conceptually as resting on the foundation of cyberspace.

The base of the triangle is the domain of cyberspace including types of networks (open and closed) and their required attributes. Concepts such as the use of hard and soft power are broadly related to the appropriate use of networks in cyberspace for specific military missions. The second level of the triangle that is enabled by cyberspace is military cyberpower operational concepts, strategies, and functions that include NCO and IO but also the administrative function of operations including, for example, logistics, planning, training, procurement, and personnel. The apex of the triangle is "cyber-power: military missions" involving the use of cyberpower in prosecuting phase zero to phase five operations in the joint campaign plans.

Military Missions and Joint Campaign Plans

The metrics for military effectiveness are the achievement of objectives and the execution of missions. The particular framework to examine the role of cyberpower in executing military missions chosen for this discussion is taken from the six phases (phase zero to phase five) of the joint campaign planning process.[2] This planning process now covers a campaign from prehostilities to reconstruction and is at the strategic rather than tactical level of objectives.

Two caveats in the use of the joint campaign phases need to be mentioned. The first is that the phases are not entirely dissimilar from each other. For example,

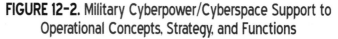

FIGURE 12-2. Military Cyberpower/Cyberspace Support to Operational Concepts, Strategy, and Functions

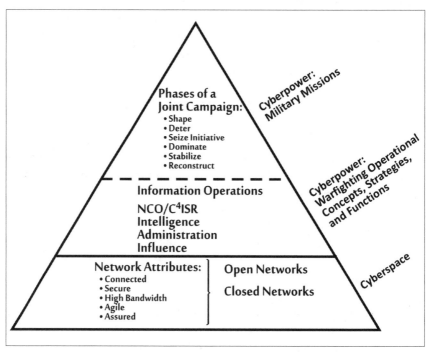

phase two, "seizing the initiative," and phase three, "decisive operations," have much in common in terms of tactics and techniques. The second caveat is that the phases overlap in time as in a "three-block war"[3] in which full-scale military action, peacekeeping, and humanitarian assistance take place simultaneously within three city blocks. Despite these caveats, the phases are useful in showing the appropriate and balanced use of soft and hard power with the appropriate uses of cyberpower at each phase:

- phase zero, shaping countries at strategic crossroads
- phase one, deterring aggression
- phase two, seizing the initiative and assuming freedom of action
- phase three, performing decisive operations and achieving full spectrum superiority
- phase four, transitioning to stability operations and establishing security (including civil security and the rule of law) and restoring essential services
- phase five, engaging in reconstruction and enabling civil authority.

Military Cyberpower Operational Constructs

The Capstone Concept for Joint Operations (CCJO) broadly describes how future joint forces are expected to operate across the range of military operations in 2012–2025 in support of strategic objectives.[4] In order to enable accomplishment of its particular objectives, the CCJO defines three fundamental actions taken by the joint force:

- establishing, expanding, and securing reach (this includes virtual reach through the use of cyberspace, as well as physical and human reach)
- acquiring, refining, and sharing knowledge
- identifying, creating, and exploiting effects.

For the objectives of this chapter and the exploration of military cyberpower, the above operations and actions are translated into the enabling (and synchronizing) hard power and soft power cyberspace concepts that support them. These are:

- information operations
- NCO, a transformational warfare concept whose scope, doctrine, and technologies are still under development and whose broad utility is still subject to debate. The debate on the effectiveness of NCO is discussed in chapter 11 in this volume, "Military Cyberpower."
- normal and routine business and administrative functions using cyberspace-based tools
- intelligence operations using cyberspace-based tools
- influence operations using cyberspace-based tools.

Information Operations

Information operations comprise electronic warfare (EW), psychological operations (PSYOPS), computer network operations (CNO), military deception, and operations security.[5] In turn, CNO includes computer network attack, computer network defense, and computer network exploitation. Capabilities that support IO include information assurance, physical security, physical attack, counterintelligence, and combat camera. There are also three military functions: public affairs, civil military operations, and defense support to public diplomacy specified as related capabilities for IO. The relationship of IO to cyberpower is not straightforward due to the eclectic nature of IO as well as the support and related capabilities. Some elements of IO such as EW might be considered in the realm of conventional weapons. PSYOPS, however, is integrated in cyberpower influence operations, while the other elements of IO are supportive of both hard and soft power.

Network-centric Operations

Network-centric operations represent a powerful set of warfighting concepts and associated military capabilities that allow warfighters to take full advantage of all available information and bring all available assets to bear in a rapid and flexible manner. The concepts of network-centric warfare (NCW) were originally applied to hard power concepts, in particular strike warfare and air defense, but, taken broadly, can also be applied to other mission areas and the appropriate and balanced use of soft power and hard power. As a comparison, an Australian view of NCO is provided by Fewell and Hazen, who define *network-centric warfare* as:

> the conduct of military operations using networked information systems to generate a flexible and agile military force that acts under a common commander's intent, independent of the geographic or organizational disposition of the individual elements, and in which the focus of the Warfighter is broadened away from the individual, unit or platform concerns to give primacy to the mission and responsibilities of the team, task group or coalition.[6]

While this definition is consistent with U.S. definitions, there is concern that in the implementation of NCO by our allies (many of whom have tailored versions of NCO), the ability to fight jointly may be compromised by nonintegrated technologies and different command and control structures. In order to head off such eventualities, DOD engages in a number of cooperative forums on interoperability with our most dependable allies, such as the North Atlantic Treaty Organization (NATO) and the cluster of so-called five eyes fora—the American, British, Canadian, and Australian Armies Standardization Program, the Multinational Interoperability Council, the Combined-Communications Electronics Board, and others. A main theme for most of these interoperability groups is multinational command and control, or determining the technologies and procedures for common information-sharing.

The tenets of NCO as articulated by DOD are that:

- a robustly networked force improves information-sharing
- information-sharing enhances the quality of information and shared situational awareness
- shared situational awareness enables collaboration and self-synchronization and enhances sustainability and speed of command
- these, in turn, dramatically increase mission effectiveness.[7]

While fairly broad in nature, these tenets imply military operations in which the principal measures of performance relate to an enhanced speed of operations and function within an opponent's observe-orient-decide-act loop. These tenets are compatible with the elements of IO in that both embrace cyberspace and deal with military operations, yet their taxonomies are quite different, with IO structured by operations and NCO defined by capability. Alternatively, IO is characterized by functionality while NCO is identified with speed of operations, connectivity, shared decisionmaking, and effectiveness. It is fair to question whether, if NCO is the enabling concept of military cyberpower, the military is best organized to utilize this growing facet of modern warfighting and has the tools to be agile, execute, and adapt.

Business and Administrative Functions

Normal and routine business and administrative functions are cyberspace-dependent components of military operations that deal with administrative rather than warfighting and SSTR dimensions. This bureaucratic element of operating the military includes the planning, programming, budgeting, and execution cycle; logistics; training and education; medical care in the field and ashore; procurement; and personnel actions and records. The principal metrics for business and crisis response networks apply here with a strong emphasis on security and information assurance.

Intelligence Operations

Intelligence operations are a major military responsibility that relies heavily on cyberspace for information retrieval and information processing and dissemination—right place, right person, right time, and right quality.

Influence Operations

Influence operations have grown in importance as the military mission set has expanded to include nation-shaping, stabilization, and reconstruction and the threat set has expanded to include counterinsurgency. The United States must now deal with the multilateral nature of the modern world rather than the two-superpower world of the past.

Service Visions and Implementation

DOD Goal of Integrating Services

Military networks, beginning with the earliest connectivity technologies—telegraph, telephone, radio, and now the Internet and private intranets—have followed Service and agency organizational structures and funding channels, connecting users along organizational lines: Service staffs with agency staffs, field units with higher headquarters, and the Pentagon with all of its subelements.

As the potential of cyberspace blossomed, DOD was getting serious about genuine joint integration across all the Services, and jointness was soon coupled with the concept of net-centric operations. Service-oriented networks had to blend into a DOD-wide capability. Successive Office of the Secretary of Defense (OSD) and Joint Staff strategic documents have called for more and better joint interoperability and networks, culminating in the drive for network-centric operations and warfighting as the emergent core of U.S. military strategy. The rapid growth and convergence of information and telecommunications technologies offer significant opportunities for creating network-enabled joint operational capabilities.

Achievement of DOD-wide network integration and operational netcentricity is a work in progress, with DOD on the cusp—perhaps just the leading edge—of that transition. Most of the communications and data exchange—strategic, operational, and tactical—in Iraq, Afghanistan, and elsewhere remains hierarchical, push broadcast, system constrained, and user limiting. Investment in modern computing and telecommunications systems alone will not create the desired transformation, which will require a far more capable global backbone, unrestrained information-sharing among commands, and truly interoperable networks wherein every authorized user can access directly and instantly any information or other user on the network. With unrelenting dedication of resources and commitment and some luck, DOD may see that goal become a reality in a decade or so.

DOD's bureaucratic processes, procedures, and organizational culture have not evolved as quickly as technology to take full advantage of the potential for network integration and interoperability. Significant Service centered cultural and programmatic biases remain, and they reinforce one another as obstacles to collaborative investments in cross-department networking capabilities. However, it is a mistake to attribute parochialism to the military departments alone; the OSD staff, Joint Staff, agencies, and combatant commands (COCOMs) all seek to protect their own organizational priorities. Breaking down such barriers is the greatest challenge to networking all of DOD.

The scope of the network integration enterprise is huge. DOD data systems are comprised of approximately 3.5 million computers running thousands of applications over some 10,000 local area networks on 1,500 bases in 65 countries worldwide, connected by 120,000 telecom circuits supporting 35 major network systems over 3 router-based architectures transmitting unclassified, secret, and top secret level information—and that is just the fixed site profile. The most important and technologically challenging networks are those of the warfighters—deployed sea, air, land, special operations, and space forces performing missions around the world—and their supporting intelligence networks.

DOD divides its networking enterprise into three mission areas: business, operational, and intelligence. Intelligence networks are not wholly managed by

DOD but are shared with other intelligence agencies. DOD business network integration arguably is equally as important as operational integration, yet it enjoys comparatively little attention. Most analysis concentrates on operations, the core of NCO.

DOD has made considerable progress toward joint networking, overcoming much parochial resistance and bureaucratic inertia and many technological obstacles along the way. Sustained emphasis on joint education, a wealth of commercial experience, and the Internet's ubiquitous presence in everyday life have been major factors in propelling a cultural shift toward broader sharing and collaboration and the breaking down of old paradigms. Most members of the military, including its leaders, demand to be connected 24/7/365 to whatever systems and users they believe essential to their mission—irrespective of parent Service, agency, or allied nation.

Across DOD, numerous commands, staffs, agencies, and contractors are committed to the goal of integrating command, control, communications, and computers (C^4) capabilities. Many billions of dollars have been spent, and ultimately hundreds of billions will have been invested. A lot of network integration is already in place, although it is still mainly *within* the Services and Defense agencies and along hierarchical lines. Incompatibilities abound. There is less progress across joint forces, especially at the tactical level. The networking and global connectivity that does exist is local. Few mobile users at the tactical level enjoy reliable, sustained Internet-based enterprise services such as real-time intelligence. However, primary joint networks do exist and have become the strategic and operational backbone of deployed forces. The interoperability goal is recognized and accepted, but as budgets tighten, all Services can be expected to cling first to internal priorities rather than joint integration when it comes to information technology (IT) and telecommunications investments. That resistance will be dampened by the forcing mechanism of essential connectivity, which drives commanders to insist on joint architectural standards so they can be continuously and reliably "plugged in" with whomever and wherever required.

Key obstacles to network integration include an unwieldy standards process, limited investment in enabling or replacing Service legacy systems, residual Service parochialism, independent-minded COCOMs, a noncollaborative culture across the officer corps, and the fact that DOD is still very much on the front end of a long timeline. Bringing the requisite technologies, processes, and systems into being will take a lot more time and investment.

In sum, DOD will get there, though budget pressures seem destined to slow progress in network integration as elsewhere. The main—and usually unrecognized—obstacle is time. It simply will take at least another 10 years of hard work, intense investment, and strong top-down emphasis before full net-centricity and network integration are achieved.

Network Integration Management at DOD

Two principal staffs driving network integration for DOD are the Assistant Secretary of Defense for Networks and Information Integration (ASD[NII]), who is also the DOD Chief Information Officer (CIO), and the Joint Staff J6 (JS J6), Director for Command, Control, Communications, and Computers, who is also the Joint Community CIO.

Under ASD (NII)/DOD CIO is the Defense Information Systems Agency (DISA), which is the operating agency responsible for DOD network operations and management worldwide. DISA is collocated with the Joint Task Force for Global Network Operations (JTF–GNO).

On the operational side, U.S. Joint Forces Command (USJFCOM) is responsible for joint force integration, including network interoperability. In this capacity, USJFCOM consolidates and harmonizes network requirements of the COCOMs and works with the JS J6 to ensure that investments in network systems include interoperability criteria as part of any approved system design.

The Services are responsible for training and equipping their forces to be joint network capable. That means investing in systems that meet interoperable protocols and common standards promulgated by OSD (NII) for their forces. There are substantial costs to meeting these requirements, and the Services routinely must make tradeoffs among priorities as they allocate investments. While the Services give every indication of full commitment to achieving network integration as soon as possible, timelines are not hard and fast, and funding is a major factor in determining progress.

The COCOMs are the managers of operational networks characterized by the architecture, standards, and systems established by DOD and provided by the Services, DISA, and JTF–GNO. Most COCOM communications and information networks are traditional hierarchical systems tethered to fixed locations, relay sites, or satellites. These are managed by the COCOM J6, who coordinates for Service requirements through the Joint Staff J6 as well as through the COCOM's subordinate component commands.

Under the 2002 Unified Command Plan, U.S. Strategic Command (USSTRATCOM) is assigned responsibility for information operations and global C⁴ISR, including the responsibility to operate and defend the global information grid. USSTRATCOM's operational arm for maintaining the GIG is JTF–GNO. The roles of DISA and JTF–GNO are similar and overlapping, which is reflected in the dual-hatting of their commander. In essence, JTF–GNO is a component command of USSTRATCOM, uniquely provided by a defense agency rather than a military department.

Many external actors are as influential in network integration as in other high-priority and costly DOD programs. Congress is keenly interested in the successful achievement of joint operational capabilities, as is evident in the continued emphasis on the goals of the Goldwater-Nichols Department of Defense Reorganization Act some 20 years after its adoption. Congressional focus on the high cost of IT systems in DOD and across the government is apparent from the 1996 Clinger-Cohen Act and a host of related legislation that seeks to ensure we can define the return on IT investments. Other external actors are industry, the policy analysis community, and international bodies such as NATO, where similar integration architectures and standards have been defined and are the subjects of considerable investment. A new arrival whose architectures and standards are not yet well defined is the interagency cluster of departments that increasingly need to network with DOD at all operational levels.

Key Guiding Documents

The number of directives and internal guidance documents issued over the past several years is one way to measure how seriously DOD takes the makeover from platform-centered operations to net-centered operations. A broad and consistent stream of authoritative guidance establishes both legitimacy and logic. It also indicates that top-level DOD management is driving toward this goal as hard as they can.

Joint Vision 2020 and Chairman of the Joint Chiefs of Staff Instruction (CJCSI) 6212.01B, "Interoperability and Supportability of National Security Systems and IT Systems" (2000); the 2003 Transformation Planning Guidance and 2006 Quadrennial Defense Review (gearing up for renewal in 2009); the Joint Technical Architecture Version 6.0, Joint Battle Management Command and Control Roadmap, and CJCSI 3170.01C, "Joint Capabilities Integration and Development System," in 2003; and the Strategic Planning Guidance and DOD Architecture Framework in 2004 are all essential references for understanding the depth of DOD-wide commitment, management engagement, and investment in network integration. These same documents also signal the complexity and magnitude of the undertaking.

Earlier foundational underpinnings beyond DOD show that the Federal Government at large has acknowledged the advent of the information age and accepted the need for government as well as industry to bring its practices into the new era. This indicates that DOD overall and not merely its military operational side must achieve network integration. Above all, there has to be a clear link between IT investment and outcomes—the return on that investment for the taxpayer. The pivotal legislation and executive regulator policies in this regard are the Clinger-Cohen Act of 1996; the Office of Management and Budget Circular A–130, "Management of Federal Information Resources," and the Information Assurance Initiative (2000 National Defense Act) of 2000; and the E-Government Act of 2002.

Role of U.S. Joint Forces Command

USJFCOM is tasked with identifying the C^4 requirements of the joint community. The command negotiates with the other joint commands to define a single, coherent set of required capabilities that can be passed to the service providers. Although flexibility and agile designs are desired, the reality is that bringing a requirement into operational use by a large force is time- and resource-intensive. Therefore, it is essential that required capabilities not be too transient or subject to frequent redefinition.

COCOMs sometimes press for standards to be loosened to encompass new and possibly immature technologies that have worked for them. In some cases, the systems may already have been procured for a pending operational requirement. USJFCOM does not yet exercise sufficient oversight to ensure that such "add-on" network systems do not actually move DOD *away* from its goal of networked forces. For example, a unique new system procured for a limited operational need by U.S. Pacific Command (USPACOM) may not be compatible with systems in use by U.S. Central Command (USCENTCOM) or U.S. European Command. However, some of the forces assigned to USPACOM for that operation may soon be ordered to USCENTCOM's area of responsibility. USJFCOM's role in achieving network interoperability is to adjudicate such inconsistencies to ensure a set of common technical standards acceptable across the joint operational user community.

USJFCOM has a primary role as well in achieving integration with interagency and multinational users. Typically, fewer close allies and agencies are involved in major combat operations than in stability operations; however, the network integration requirements for combat are more critical. The U.S. norm is for coalition combat operations, in which some allies provide niche capabilities, more partners from outside a COCOM's area of responsibility participate, and a higher level of interoperability is needed. USJFCOM has to meld multinational and interagency requirements as it does for joint operations, focusing on key allies and agencies across the range of military operations. USJFCOM then oversees these requirements as they are fed into the acquisition process, just as it does for joint matters.

The Joint Interoperability Test Command (JITC) is a test and evaluation organization established under DISA to advance global net-centric testing in support of joint operational capabilities. Its mission is to provide agile and cost-effective test, evaluation, and certification services to support rapid acquisition and fielding of global net-centric warfighting capabilities. Most of its projects are related to networks—standards, transport, services, applications, and platform integration. JITC works with industry and allies as well as DOD to certify interoperability and advance solutions as rapidly as possible.

Service Visions and Implementation

Current Service actions make clear that the tools of cyberspace have already had a significant impact on Service operational concepts and doctrine, systems development and technology, and organizational structure. There are also indications that the Services recognize that beyond being just a tool to enhance the effectiveness of conventional warfighting, cyber has changed the environment in which conflicts are played out. Cyberspace has changed the threat environment as well, creating new vulnerabilities and introducing a new level of global transparency to the execution of internal and external affairs. There is significant agreement among the Services as to the inherent capabilities of cyberpower in the networking, information/knowledge, and people/social domains. As an example, all the Services recognize the importance of cyber-dedicated educational and training facilities. But there are also major points of disagreement among the Services as to definitions and taxonomy of cyberspace, including its scope and frameworks. In addition, different organizational structures are being implemented within each Service to address this rapidly evolving source of both military opportunity and threat vulnerability. To further complicate the issue, different voices within the individual Services present diverse visions of the role of cyberpower and of their Service's role (usually that of leadership) within that vision.

Discerning substantive from semantic differences between the Service views of cyberspace and cyberpower is difficult. For example, discussion occurs about whether cyberspace is a domain in its own right and what the boundaries are between virtual and physical reality. What has become apparent is that engagements can be "fought" solely in cyberspace without resorting to the conventional domains. An example is a cyber attack on an opponent's military or civilian information networks that disrupts military connectivity and warfighting capability or degrades the country's basic infrastructures. In the emerging war of ideas and ideology, events in cyberspace are eventually manifested in the physical world. For example, the virtual haven of cyberspace has allowed terrorist organizations to recruit, plan, and execute physical acts of terrorism.

From a Service operational point of view, General James Cartwright, USMC, has critically pointed to the division of military cyberspace operations among three fiefdoms.[8] Under this approach, Joint Functional Component Command-Net Warfare is responsible for attack and reconnaissance, the Joint Task Force for Global Network Operations manages network defense and operations, and the Joint Information Operations Warfare Center oversees electronic warfare and influence operations. Strategic communications are overseen by USSTRATCOM. In addition to divisions in joint military cyberspace operations, there are potential

Service and DOD C⁴ISR interoperability issues as OSD proceeds with the development of the GIG and the Services proceed with implementations of NCW architectures.

Table 12–1 highlights Service concepts, architectural approaches, a small subset of service systems, and new organizational initiatives.

Air Force

The Air Force has put cyberpower on an even footing with spacepower and air combat and has defined cyberspace as a "fifth dimension."[9] The Air Force considers cyberspace superiority an imperative and establishes the proposition that it is the prerequisite to effective U.S. military operations in all other warfighting domains. In a discussion on what it calls the "five myths" of cyberspace and cyberpower, the Air Force asserts the following:

- The intelligence collector and the information service provider should be separate organizational functions and not dual-hatted.
- The domain of cyberspace goes well beyond the Internet. The Air Force considers cyberspace a physical domain, through interlinking by the electromagnetic spectrum and electronic systems, rather than a virtual domain.
- The battle to achieve cyber superiority in any conflict must be fought in a distributed network rather than from one location where there may be a central coordinating element.
- The control of cyber weapons effects are controllable and the targeting and collateral damage issues are no different than with effects created by explosive or kinetically destructive means.
- Defense of the cyberspace domain requires a holistic network approach rather than just increased security at each individual node.

The Air Force Transformation Flight Plan describes the C² Constellation initiative as the centerpiece of the Service's NCW implementation efforts:

The Air Force is transitioning from collecting data through a myriad of independent systems (such as Rivet Joint, AWACS [airborne warning and control systems], JSTARS [joint surveillance target and attack radar systems], and space-based assets) to a C2 Constellation capable of providing the Joint Force Commander with real-time, enhanced battlespace awareness. It will provide Ground Moving Target Indicator capabilities along with focused Air Moving Target Indicator capabilities for Cruise Missile Defense. Additionally, every platform will be a sensor on the integrated network. Regardless of mission function (C², Intelligence, Surveillance, and Reconnaissance [ISR], shooters, tankers, etc.), any data collected by a sensor will be passed to all network recipients. This requires

TABLE 12-1. Summary of Service Cyber Programs

SERVICE	CONCEPTS	ARCHITECTURES	SYSTEMS	ORGANIZATION
Air Force	Cyberspace as a warfighting domain	C² Constellation	Assurance, data integration, global information grid (GIG)	Cyberspace Command
Army	Information and cognition as a domain	LandWarNet	Future Combat System, Warfighter Information Network– Tactical, GIG	1ˢᵗ Information Operations Command, Network Enterprise Technology Command
Navy	Information operations, network-centric operations	FORCEnet	Navy Marine Corps Intranet (NMCI), GIG	Naval Network Warfare Command
Marine Corps	Net-centric operations and warfare	Marine Air-Ground Task Force– Information Operations	NMCI, GIG	Marine Corps Systems Command

networking of all air, space, ground, and sea-based ISR systems, command and control nodes, and strike platforms to achieve shared battlespace awareness and a synergy to maximize the ability to achieve the Joint Forces Command's (JFC's) desired effects.[10]

The Air Force has also introduced a significant organizational change by standing up the Cyberspace Command as the 8th Air Force at Barksdale Air Force Base. The command's mission is to prepare for fighting wars in cyberspace by defending national computer networks, running critical operations, and attacking adversary computer networks.

Army

Jeff Smith of the Army's Network Enterprise Technology Command envisions a future in which soft power and the human/social impact of cyberpower are matched with a hard power that also is transformed by cyber. Smith considers that cognition is the actual goal of military strength, which is at a level above information (which in turn is at a level above cyberspace). Cognition refers to aspects of the human element, including leadership/behavior, understanding/ decisionmaking, and problem-solving/adapting. Cyberspace is considered a subset of networks which in turn is related to information and finally cognition. In this paper, Smith collapses air/space, land, and sea into one physical environment and cognition into a second environment. His thesis is that Army doctrine, organization, training, materiel, leadership and education, personnel, and facilities are almost exclusively focused on the physical rather than the cognitive, which is the more important.

The Army implementation of NCO, LandWarNet, comprises the Service's information infrastructure and is its contribution to the GIG. LandWarNet consists of all globally interconnected Army information capabilities, associated processes, and personnel for collecting, processing, storing, disseminating, and managing information on demand—supporting warfighters, policymakers, and support personnel. It includes all Army communications and computing systems, software (including applications), data security, and other associated services. The Future Combat System (FCS), a principal development program for NCO, is a modular construct of a reconfigurable family of systems capable of providing mobile, networked C^4 functionalities; autonomous robotic systems; precision direct and indirect fires; airborne and ground organic sensor platforms; and adverse weather reconnaissance, surveillance, targeting, and acquisition.[11] The Warfighter Information Network-Tactical (WIN–T) is the Army's tactical digital communications system for providing advanced commercial-based networking capabilities under the umbrella of the GIG. The WIN–T network C^4ISR support capabilities goals are for a network that is secure, survivable, seamless, and capable of supporting multimedia tactical information systems.[12] FCS is managed by the Army, with Boeing as a lead systems integrator. The Government Accountability Office, which reviews the program annually, has questioned the technical maturity of WIN–T and the Joint Tactical Radio System in terms of Army acquisition goals.[13]

Navy

The Navy perspective on cyberpower shows a structure incorporating the elements of IO and NCW. The Navy Marine Corps Intranet (NMCI) addresses the communications network and the business and administrative functions of cyberpower in the Navy and Marine Corps.[14] The Naval Network Warfare Command includes a Navy IO core competency, which supports the combat commander's ability to shape and influence potential adversary decisionmakers' thinking prior to conflict, resulting in deterrence of hostilities; enable decisive nonkinetic (effects-based operations) to complement kinetic warfare and defeat the adversary if conflict should ensue; and engage in continuing postconflict shaping/influence operations to maintain stability. To accomplish these goals, the Navy must develop an effective structure for IO force development, integration, planning, command and control, and execution in the joint environment.

FORCEnet is the Department of the Navy's implementation strategy for performing network-centric operations. The Chief of Naval Operation's accepted definition of FORCEnet is "the operational construct and architectural framework for naval warfare in the information age that integrates warriors, sensors, networks, command and control, platforms and weapons into a networked, distributed combat force that is scalable across all levels of conflict from seabed to space and sea to land."[15] The Naval Research Advisory Committee defines FORCEnet as "a portfolio of programs to enable the gathering, processing, transportation, and presentation of actionable information in support of all aspects of joint and combined naval operations."[16] Unlike the Army's WIN–T, FORCEnet is not a specific program but rather an architecture or a group of programs that serves as the organizing principle as the Naval enablement of the GIG. The NMCI is a key component of FORCEnet and has the goal of providing the Navy and Marine Corps with a full range of network-based information services on a single intranet. NMCI has the goal of providing secure, universal access to integrated voice, video, and data communications. Eventually, the massive NMCI network will link more than 400,000 workstations and laptops for 500,000 Navy and Marine Corps users across the continental United States, Hawaii, Cuba, Guam, Japan, and Puerto Rico. Under NMCI, the program office and the prime contractor control the layout, distribution, and analysis of the system. The prime contractor, Electronic Data Systems, owns all the IT assets and leases them to the government.

In the Navy Strategic Studies Group's (SSG's) study on "Convergence of Sea Power and Cyber Power," an even broader definition of cyberpower is given:

> an unconstrained interaction space—for human activity, relationships and cognition—where data, information, and value are created and exchanged— enabled by the convergence of multiple disciplines, technologies, and global networks—that permits near instantaneous communication, simultaneously among any number of nodes, independent of boundaries.

The SSG looks to a future with a more complex world driven by many emerging challenges. Cyberpower is seen to converge with the conventional seapower concepts and to transform conventional Navy roles in sea control, power projection, naval presence (both physical and virtual), strategic lift, and strategic deterrence.

Marine Corps

The Marine Corps has focused its cyberpower vision on net-centric operations and warfare (NCOW) and is developing a Marine Air-Ground Task Force Information Operations (MAGTF-IO) strategy for operational implementation.

The future MAGTF–IO aims to enable decentralized decisionmaking that promotes taking advantage of fleeting battlefield opportunities. MAGTF–IO is a cyber strategy, a process, and ultimately a system of systems by which the Marine Corps will develop current and future capabilities and programs in order to achieve NCOW and implement the FORCEnet functional concept of providing robust information-sharing and collaboration capabilities. MAGTF–IO is the functional and conceptual equivalent of the other Service net-centric concepts of LandWarNet (Army) and C² Constellation (Air Force). It will also be integrated with NATO through the NATO NET Enabled Capability and be able to facilitate "coalitions of the willing" as needed. It entails a seamless, scalable, modular capability that is relevant across the full spectrum of military operations, from major combat operations to irregular warfare operations to humanitarian assistance operations.

DOD Implementation

Management and development of information-based technology and systems are spread through the Services. The Office of Force Transformation[17] provided an overall vision for NCO, but the Services develop their own systems in conjunction with the development of the Global Information Grid. A consideration of the GIG is essential in a discussion of military cyberpower because the GIG was mandated by DOD Directive 8100.1, "Global Information Grid Overarching Policy," in September 2002 as the physical implementation of the principles of NCW.

While all the Services recognize the GIG as the umbrella network under which they will operate, there is no commonality among them as to network architecture or their approaches to NCW. This circumstance requires that issues of interoperability be properly addressed. Each Service has special requirements, such as submarine communication for the Navy and mobile networked command and control for the Army. There are also areas where commonality should be sought, such as in aviation connectivity. How well the Services (as well as agencies such as members of the Intelligence Community) will develop their C⁴ISR NCW programs to interface seamlessly with the GIG remains to be seen.

The Defense Information Systems Agency heads the GIG project under the leadership of the CIO of the ASD (NII)/DOD. The formal definition of the *global information grid* is "the globally interconnected, end-to-end set of information capabilities, associated processes, and personnel for collecting, processing, storing, disseminating and managing information on demand to war fighters, policy makers, and support personnel."[18] The architecture for the GIG relies on Internet protocol (IP) and will depend largely on the commercial transmission infrastructure and on commercial information and network management technology.[19]

The vision and proposed architecture of the GIG are very challenging both from the standpoint of technology development and from the reliance on commercial systems to achieve information assurance. The National Security Agency (NSA) has been tasked by the ASD(NII)/DOD CIO to develop an end-to-end information assurance perspective for the GIG.[20] NSA recognizes that information assurance needs to be an embedded feature designed into every system in the GIG and that this requires a shift from today's model, which consists predominantly of link encryption and boundary protection between multiple discrete networks. In order to accomplish the GIG objectives, DOD will need to impact the commercial technologies and standards that will comprise the GIG architecture.

As noted earlier, the Services are all pursuing alternative networking architectures under the umbrella of the GIG. The GIG promises to provide a network based on commercial protocols, software and hardware for both tactical and strategic communications, data links to operate in an environment of forces on the move, and the ability to continue to operate effectively during network attacks and failures. Shortfalls exist in the GIG development to meet certain Service-specific needs. For example, with a mobile infrastructure, the Army will require protocols for a mobile ad hoc networking capability. However, commercial industry is moving toward an all-IP core network (IP version 6). The Navy may also experience shortfalls from the eventual GIG development. For example, the communications requirements for ships at sea depend on continuous high-capacity, low-latency connectivity to be provided by the transformational satellite program that is persistently being delayed for cost and technology reasons. Even when it is completed and the Navy develops suitable shipboard terminals, the Service's communications capacity will remain limited by capacity and satellite communications interruptions caused principally by antenna blockage. Also, the GIG programs do not address the challenging problem of communicating with submarines at speed and depth.[21] Another quandary for the introduction of communications systems under the GIG umbrella is funding new systems to replace legacy systems that do not fit into the new architecture. For example, Army officials must determine how to transition the Joint Network Node, a commercial, IP-based mobile communications system deployed to soldiers in Iraq, to the WIN–T.[22]

Challenges and risks also are associated with the use of commercial products such as Microsoft Windows and Office, which are typically released with bugs.

DOD does not have access to the proprietary codes to receive the patches that remedy the bugs. Additionally, commercial-off-the-shelf computers, routers, and servers often have "trap doors" for maintenance that can provide system access to hackers. Internet gateways for the Nonsecure Internet Protocol Router Network and other government unclassified networks have offered venues for attackers to exploit and disrupt. Even secure systems with multiple users are susceptible to the insider threat. The access to and the sharing of information with Internet portals have benefits, risks, and limitations that must be managed, especially for SSTR and information-sharing with other nations, international organizations, and nongovernmental organizations (NGOs).

An additional concern relating to the use of commercial products is the outsourcing of IT providers of both products and services in network operations and management in crisis situations. This practice could lead to issues such as embedded trojan horses in foreign-built equipment and software. National constraints limiting international vendors during a crisis could result in supply problems. Finally, there is a trend toward the global IT infrastructure (including IT products, services, and networks such as global Internet, cellular, telecoms, cable, and satellites) being taken over by foreign ownership that may not be friendly to U.S. policy and needs, especially the need to ensure continuity of operations during a crisis.

The full implementation of a joint, interconnected force via the GIG is still in the future. Other issues relating to multinational military actions with coalition operations as well as civil-military operations in support of HA/DR and SSTR operations will also need to be addressed. Issues to be overcome include the lack of an NCO organizing principle and architecture between the Services; related interoperability issues among Services, civil agencies, coalition partners, international organizations, and NGO communities; the impact of a changing threat environment with irregular warfare; new technology developments; the need for high bandwidth, agile connectivity, and security; and the costs associated with implementation.

Conclusion

Knowledge and information exchange have always been essential to warfighting. As cyberspace technology has evolved over the past few decades, the military has adapted the technology to its traditional warfighting paradigms of land, air-, space-, and seapower. Rather than developing its own information and communications technology knowledge base and systems, the military has relied extensively on commercial systems and increased dependence on commercial services globally, including the use of the Internet to support some elements of command and control.[23] In addition to the Internet, the military is a user of commercial products such as wireless networking, cellular phones, personal digital assistants, telecommunications, and satellite and cable-based networks, radio, and television. While it has developed the concepts of network-centric warfare to integrate land, air-, space-, and seapower, it has maintained the conventional warfighting principles of strike warfare, air superiority, and air and missile defense structured to increase the speed and timeliness of operations, to operate more effectively in extended areas of coverage, and to enhance precision. This utilization of cyberpower enhances our hard power capabilities and defines the attributes of the network to support these operations. The evolutionary growth of these capabilities has maintained the existing organizational, management, and acquisition structure of the Services in dealing with technological advances in cyberspace. Similarly, military information operations have maintained their organizational principles even in the face of the extraordinary impact that radical groups have exhibited by their adaptation of the Internet to recruit, plan, finance, and influence. Rather than speed of operations, the defining metrics here are large-scale connectivity, user pull, and collaboration. This is being accomplished by making more effective use of emerging information and communications technology and changing operations to support the increased importance of HA/DR and SSTR in phases zero, four, and five, as well as warfighting in phases one, two, and three.

In this chapter, military cyberpower has been described in terms of three dimensions: military requirements or missions as described by the joint warfighting phases; military information-based capabilities or operational concepts, including NCO, IO, military administration, intelligence collection, and influence operations; and the dimension of cyberspace, including open and closed architectures employing dedicated networks, the Internet, military tactical radios, commercial radio/TV, and telecommunications. Ideally, an integrated cyberspace architecture can be envisioned that supports all military requirements and military information-based capabilities. It would need to be reliable, available, and survivable under attack and would also need to be scalable and provide high bandwidth. While optimal, such an integrated architecture may provide multiple unforeseen vulnerabilities and introduce unacceptable cost and capability risks. A single open architecture designed to promote maximum connectivity and user pull based on IP may need separation from the secure connectivity required for sensor-to-weapon NCO operations. The GIG and new technology initiatives are poised to address these issues but may not meet all technology objectives of these programs. In the meantime, the military requires secure closed networks that restrict users and have highly controlled access arrangements and stringent security protection, as well as fully connected open networks. The military also needs to wrestle with existing legacy systems, many of which will not be interoperable with the GIG.

There is no question that the Services are already adapting to and leveraging the new environment in communications and information provided by the exponential growth in cyberspace connectivity and information storage and processing. However, risks and vulnerabilities have been introduced—especially the increased dependence of the military on civilian cyberspace capabilities, products, and services—that need careful assessment to be effectively managed. The Services are also experiencing growing pains as they deal with a different world order and the impact of new technology coupled with their evolving and changing missions in this environment including HA/DR, SSTR, and influence operations.

There is significant agreement among the Services as to the inherent capabilities of cyberpower in the networking, information/knowledge, and people/social domains. There are also currently points of disagreement among the Services as to definitions and taxonomy of cyberspace, including scope, frameworks, and leadership.

Within each Service, different organizational structures are being implemented to address this rapidly evolving source of both military operational opportunities and to defend against and respond to threat vulnerability.

While all the Services recognize the GIG as the umbrella network under which they will operate, there is no commonality among them as to network architecture or their approaches to NCO. This approach will only succeed if issues of interoperability are properly addressed.

The GIG has been mandated as the physical implementation of the principles of NCO. The vision and proposed architecture of the GIG are challenging both from the standpoint of technology development and from the reliance on commercial systems to achieve information assurance.

CHAPTER 13

Deterrence of Cyber Attacks

Richard L. Kugler

CAN THE UNITED STATES hope to deter major cyber attacks on itself, its military forces, and its allies? Creating a cyber deterrence strategy is important because such attacks are becoming increasingly likely, because they could cause serious damage to America's information networks and beyond, and because fully defending against them is problematic. If adversaries could be deterred from launching them, the United States would face fewer risks from them.

Although the U.S. Government is well aware of the dangers posed by cyber attacks, currently it does not have a well-developed or publicly articulated strategy for deterring them. Most likely, not all cyber attacks can be deterred, but if the biggest and most dangerous attacks could be prevented, this alone would be an important accomplishment. Exactly how can cyber attacks be deterred? What would be the key components and calculations of a cyber deterrence strategy? What capabilities and action agendas would it require? These important questions are addressed here.

This chapter offers a perspective that rejects the view, held by some observers, that the "attribution problem"—the difficulty of identifying actual or potential attackers—wholly paralyzes any attempt to think fruitfully about a cyber deterrence strategy. To be sure, there will be cases in which some cyber attackers successfully conceal their identities and thereby frustrate attempts to apply deterrent and retaliatory mechanisms against them. But they do not constitute the entire universe, or even the most important subset, of potential cyber attackers. In the coming years, there is likely to be a growing number of important cases—ones, for example, involving big powers such as China and other nation-states—in which adversaries use the threat of cyber attacks (or actual attacks) as a means to a larger political end or to exert coercive leverage on the United States. In these circumstances, the adversaries will be willing to make their identities known, or alternatively, their identities can be reliably inferred from the surrounding strategic circumstances. Deterrence mechanisms can be applied to such "attributable" attackers. This chapter focuses on how to develop and apply a deterrence strategy to this category of cyber attackers.

The following pages advance several core arguments. First, the prospect of major cyber attacks should not be seen in isolation, but in the context of larger global security affairs. Although some cyber attacks might be mounted purely for the purpose of damaging the United States, other attacks could be launched by adversaries whose political and strategic agenda extends beyond the cyber domain; in addition to allowing their identities to be determined, this larger context can set the stage for determining how multifaceted U.S. efforts to deter them can be forged. Second, endeavoring to deter cyber attacks is a matter both of assembling the physical capabilities for defending against them and of employing offensive capabilities—cyber, diplomatic, economic, and military tools—for inflicting unacceptable damage in retaliation. Equally important, cyber deterrence also involves a psychological and cognitive component: like other forms of deterrence, it requires the capacity to influence the motives, cost-benefit calculations, and risk-taking propensities of adversaries, in order to convince them that launching a cyber attack would not serve their interests and objectives and that the costs and risks would outweigh any sensible calculation of benefits. Assembling a proper combination of motivational instruments and physical capabilities to serve this purpose lies at the heart of forging a modern-day strategy for cyber deterrence. A one-size-fits-all approach to deterrence will not work because of the multiplicity and diversity of potential adversaries and cyber attacks, and because U.S. goals and actions may shift from one situation to the next. As a result, the United States will need a strategy of "tailored" cyber deterrence that treats each category of potential adversary, type of attack, and type of U.S. response on its own merits.

This chapter begins by portraying how official U.S. Government documents treat cyber threats and the role of deterrence in dealing with them. Then it briefly discusses the ways in which the United States is vulnerable to cyber attacks and how contemporary global security affairs are giving rise to cyber threats. Against the background of lessons from how deterrence theory evolved during the Cold War and how it operates today, the chapter then develops a general model for deterring cyber threats, based on deterrence that is tailored to influence the motivations and psychology of different cyber adversaries. An analytical section reviews the key strategic requirements of cyber deterrence strategy, including declaratory policy, situational awareness, command and control, defensive cyber security, a wide spectrum of offensive capabilities for retaliation, interagency cooperation, cooperation with allies and partners, and cyber deterrence metrics. Issues that will require further research and analysis are identified. The chapter concludes by presenting a spectrum of options for pursuing cyber deterrence.

Overall, this material articulates an underlying theme: that the United States can realistically hope to create a cyber deterrence strategy that works, perhaps not perfectly, but well enough to make a big difference and that offers considerably greater security from cyber threats than exists today. Creating such a rewarding and affordable strategy, however, will require concerted thought and coordinated actions of the sort that have characterized deterrence since it first appeared as a strategic concept over 50 years ago.

Cyber Deterrence Strategy in Official U.S. Documents

Deterrence of cyber attacks is discussed in some key U.S. strategy documents. *The National Strategy to Secure Cyberspace*, issued by the White House in February 2003 in response to the prospect of growing cyber threats, articulates three broad goals: to prevent cyber attacks, to reduce U.S. vulnerability to them, and to minimize damage and recovery time.[1] However, it contains little on how to prevent cyber attacks. In terms of deterrence, it only says briefly that a U.S. response might not be limited to criminal prosecution of cyberspace criminals and that the United States reserves the right to respond in an appropriate manner. A companion document, *The National Strategy for the Physical Protection of Critical Infrastructures and Key Assets* (issued in February 2003), articulates a similar focus on physical protection of the U.S. homeland from new-era threats, not deterrence of cyber threats.[2] The same applies to the *National Strategy for Homeland Security*.[3]

Among other U.S. strategy documents, the most important is the *National Security Strategy of the United States of America*, issued by the White House most recently in March 2006.[4] It outlines nine strategic goals ranging from defeating terrorism and preventing proliferation of weapons of mass destruction (WMD) to working with allies and partners while supporting the spread of democracy and a prosperous world economy, but it devotes little discussion to cyber threats. Discussing institutional reforms to the Department of Defense (DOD), it notes that U.S. security faces traditional, irregular, catastrophic, and disruptive challenges; cyber threats are classified as disruptive threats, along with threats from space, biotechnology, and directed energy weapons. The document instructs DOD to build a transformed military force posture that will provide tailored deterrence of a wide spectrum of future threats, including terrorist attacks in the physical and information domains, but it provides no guidance for shaping such deterrence.

The *National Defense Strategy of the United States of America* released in March 2005 identifies four broad goals: assurance, dissuasion, deterrence, and defeat of adversaries for the purpose of protecting the U.S. homeland; securing global freedom of action; strengthening alliances; and fostering favorable security conditions.[5] In order to achieve these goals, it calls for an active, layered defense rather than a passive or reactive strategy against traditional, irregular, catastrophic, and disruptive challenges, including cyber threats. It states that the top U.S. security priority is to dissuade, deter, and defeat those who seek to harm the United States directly, especially extremists who use WMD. It briefly mentions cyber threats but provides no guidance on how to deter them. Neither does *The National Military Strategy of the United States of America* issued by the Chairman of the Joint Chiefs of Staff in 2004.[6] This document is meant to provide strategic principles and operational guidelines for using and building U.S. military capabilities, including ones for homeland defense. While calling for high-technology, networked, and modular forces for full-spectrum dominance, it gives only cursory attention to cyber threats or to strategy for deterring them.

The 2006 Quadrennial Defense Review (QDR) charts future directions for improving U.S. military forces, under the rubric of capability-based planning, for a wide variety of situations.[7] It mandates agility, responsiveness, and battlefield domination. It does provide some useful guidance on dealing with cyber threats. In its section on homeland defense, it notes that the populace, territory, infrastructure, and space assets of the United States are increasingly vulnerable, not only to WMD, but also to electronic or cyber attacks. It declares that DOD "will maintain a deterrent posture to persuade potential aggressors that their objectives in attacking would be denied and that any attack on U.S. territory, people, critical infrastructure or forces could result in an overwhelming response." This statement was intended to underscore deterrence of new-era threats in general; cyber deterrence is explicitly part of the overall strategic calculus. However, the QDR provided no specific guidance on how cyber deterrence could be achieved, or on how requirements for U.S. forces and other instruments of power might be affected.

Current planning for U.S. military operations is greatly influenced by Joint Operating Concepts (JOCs), such as the one on deterrence operations.[8] This 2006 JOC presents a rich conceptual framework for thinking about deterrence in general, and therefore figures prominently in the discussion below of a general model for cyber deterrence. Although it clearly acknowledges cyber threats, however, it says less about deterring them than about deterring use of WMD and similar threats from rogue powers, terrorists, or near-peer competitors.

An official document with specific relevance is the 2007 *National Military Strategy to Secure Cyberspace*.[9] This document is still classified, but official DOD statements have indicated that it calls upon national security planners to:

improve capabilities for attack attribution and response; improve coordination for responding to cyber attacks within the U.S. national security community; and foster the establishment of national and international watch-and-warning networks to detect and prevent cyber attacks as they emerge. Although these statements identify required capabilities for national strategy, they do not amount to a cyber deterrence strategy in themselves.

This brief review of official U.S. documents shows that the dangers posed by potential cyber attacks are officially acknowledged, along with the need for responsive capabilities and the desirability of deterring such attacks. However, a cyber deterrence strategy has not yet been articulated and released, at least publicly. A great deal of effort has been devoted to preparing strategic frameworks for defense and security planning, and therefore many of the basic ingredients for a cyber deterrence strategy already exist. The task is to bring them together to create a cyber deterrence strategy. The next section suggests why.

Growing Vulnerability to Cyber Attacks in a Globalizing World

The cyber attack that was launched on Estonia in spring 2007, which allegedly originated in Russia (which its government denied), helped put the threat of cyber attacks on the front pages of newspapers everywhere. With help from the United States and Europe, Estonia recovered relatively quickly from that attack. But there is no guarantee that future cyber attacks will be confined to small countries such as Estonia or will inflict only transitory damage. Indeed, the United States is vulnerable to such attacks, and they potentially could cause widespread damage.

The damage from cyber attacks could extend far beyond the information systems that they principally affect, because so many spheres of national life depend heavily on modern information systems.[10] The U.S. military, for example, relies upon information networks, including the global information grid, to conduct modern-era combat operations.[11] Many civilian institutions, infrastructures, and essential government services are also highly dependent on the Internet and other information networks. Police, firefighters, and other emergency services providers, public health, education, transportation, banking and finance, water supply, sanitation, and energy systems all depend on computers and information networks, as do the air traffic control system, hydroelectric dams, nuclear power plants, traffic lights, water treatment facilities, and key private sector institutions such as colleges and universities, hospitals, stock markets, business corporations, shopping malls, and credit card companies. An attack on one vulnerable sector could seriously damage other sectors.

Other regions, such as Europe and democratic Asia similarly rely upon information networks and are vulnerable to their disruption. Countries embarked upon economic modernization are also beginning to use cyberspace at growing rates. The entire global economy is becoming increasingly dependent upon modern information systems. Imports, exports, and other international transactions empower growth in many modern national economies, and these rely upon global networks. Modern multinational businesses employ information networks to integrate central headquarters, production lines, and distribution systems that are often scattered across multiple countries and continents. The huge flow of global finance that takes place daily is directly dependent upon the Internet and other systems. Disruption of these activities and their information systems could damage the operations of the world economy, contributing to financial panics, recessions, and even depressions.

Cyber vulnerabilities are thus growing, while cyber attack tools and methodologies are becoming more available, and the technical capacity of malicious actors is improving.

Emerging Cyber Threats

An issue critical to cyber deterrence is understanding what kinds of actors are likely to pose cyber threats, especially threats of major disruptive attacks, to the United States, its military forces, and its allies in coming years. The ability to use cyberspace to create advantages and to influence events in other operational environments and across multiple instruments of power is spreading. Many view cyber attackers today as mainly individual hackers with purely malicious intent, or perhaps criminal groups intending to use information networks for profit-seeking. In addition, however, actors with political or ideological agendas—including terrorist groups, rogue countries, and even big powers such as China and Russia— will also pursue cyberpower and will play roles of growing importance. They may seek to use cyber threats or attacks to pursue strategic and political goals in geopolitical competition with the United States and its allies. Such cyber attacks likely would not be ends in themselves, but rather instruments of persuasion and coercion in pursuit of agendas that extend well beyond cyberspace. These actors and their activities may present bigger cyber threats than we have seen before and thus may require the attention of a U.S. cyber deterrent strategy.

Emerging trends in global security affairs will set the stage on which new and bigger threats may multiply in future years. During the Cold War, the global security structure was static and bipolar, pitting the United States and its democratic allies against the Soviet Union and its communist allies. That period was one of great danger, but bipolarity made the task of designing U.S. national security policy fairly straightforward. Waging the Cold War was difficult and costly, but it was an exercise in clarity and steadfastness rather than uncertainty, adaptability, and endless recalculation about policy basics. America's enemies were militarily powerful, but they were limited in number, their identities were firmly established, and their goals and actions were predictable—all of which facilitated the evolution of U.S. deterrence policies.

Compared to the Cold War, today's world is highly complex. Bipolarity is gone, and no permanent structure has taken its place. Instead, the world is changing rapidly in response to globalization and other information-era dynamics, which bring once-distant parts of the world into close contact with each other and draw the United States into distant regions that once were considered outside its geostrategic perimeter. The changing roles of nation-states and other actors, new political ideologies, shifting security conditions, the hotly competitive world economy, the emergence of new technologies, and transformed military forces all add to the global environment of fast-paced changes and amorphous conditions. Surprises occur frequently, major developments leap suddenly out of a dense fog of uncertainty, and even experts are unable to predict the future.

To the extent that today's international security system has a structure, its most important components have, loosely speaking, three parts. The first part is the wealthy democratic community, composed of the United States, Europe, and democratic parts of Asia, plus much of Latin America, which is mainly democratic albeit not wealthy. For the most part, this democratic community is prosperous, secure, and stable. The second part comprises the "strategic challengers," including big powers such as China, Russia, and India. With nearly one-half of the world's population and a growing share of economic wealth, these three big powers are redefining their identities on the world stage and the imprint that they want to make on global security affairs. India, a democracy with a traditionally independent foreign policy, has recently begun to draw closer to the United States and to play a constructive role in South Asian affairs. Both Russia and China are asserting themselves in global politics, but it is unclear whether they will emerge as partners or rivals of the United States, or something in between. The third part of the global structure is the "southern arc of instability" from the greater Middle East to East Asia. This huge zone is a seething cauldron of chaotic troubles, authoritarian regimes, unstable societies, poverty, turmoil, angry Islamic fundamentalism, and violence. Today's threats of terrorism, WMD proliferation, and rogue countries emerge from this zone, whose future is a big question mark. The difficult wars in Iraq and Afghanistan, the Israeli-Palestinian conflict, and the U.S. search for an effective diplomacy in the region add to the uncertainty.

Given this global structure, the dominant security agenda facing the United States is to preserve the cohesion of the democratic community, to keep relations with the big powers on an even keel, and to muster friends and allies in an effort to quell threats and turbulence along the southern arc, especially in the Middle East. In this endeavor, the United States can hope to influence events but, despite its superpower status, it cannot control the future. Today's world is being heavily shaped by two global dynamics: 10 or 15 years ago, many observers focused on hopeful neo-Kantian trends promising progress in the form of democratization, economic prosperity, and peace. Since then, however, dangerous neo-Hobbesian trends—strife, conflict, turmoil, and stalled progress—have asserted themselves in many places, especially along the southern arc of instability. While neo-Kantian trends are still operating in many ways and places, neo-Hobbesian trends have risen to equal importance. A decade or two from now, the future could witness a world enjoying greater stability if neo-Kantian trends take precedence or one descending into instability and struggle if neo-Hobbesian trends dominate.

Meanwhile, a third trend, empowerment, has gained force in recent years. Economic globalization and the information age give previously weak actors more power to act independently and influentially on the world stage, including by using cyberpower. China, for example, once poverty-stricken and inward-looking, is now on its way to becoming an economic powerhouse, able to build modern military forces and to cultivate ambitious political and strategic appetites in Asia. Some small and mid-sized countries, such as South Korea and Iran, are also deriving greater strategic power from economic growth. Also significant is that nongovernmental actors, including terrorist groups, have been empowered by the Internet and information networks to spread their influence worldwide. Such empowerment trends can help peace-minded countries to become wealthier and more stable and to play increasingly constructive roles on the world scene, but they also enable rogues, aggressors, dictators, and terrorists to pursue troublesome agendas in increasingly potent ways. For example, empowered by access to oil profits, Iran has begun to pursue a more assertive agenda, as has Hugo Chavez's Venezuela. The United States is in no danger of being eclipsed any time soon, but new actors will be able to play more influential roles in global security affairs; geopolitical dramas promise to be correspondingly more complex, and perhaps more dangerous.

Role of Cyberpower

Cyberpower contributes to the growing strength of many actors in global politics; it is a significant reason why a number of previously impoverished countries are becoming wealthier. As many countries acquire greater economic strength, owing partly to cyberpower, they will acquire greater diplomatic and political influence, allowing them to pursue more assertive strategic agendas in their regions and beyond. Mastery of modern networks will also enable some countries to acquire greater military strength by equipping their forces with tools for modern doctrine and operations, even without the expensive ground, air, and naval platforms used by the United States. The enhanced strategic clout of these countries may motivate them to seek greater influence in pursuit of their national interests.

Some countries might also pursue cyberpower as an offensive instrument of intimidation and coercion against neighbors and adversaries. As a strategic tool, cyberpower is attractive and advantageous because it can be acquired inexpensively and can be used in concert with other tools or on its own. It does not require expensive military forces to be influential and effective. Because cyberpower can provide poor countries with potential leverage that far exceeds their strength as traditionally assessed, the future may see a proliferation of cyber predators and of cyber victims too.

Since September 11, 2001, the public literature has commonly viewed major cyber attacks on the United States as most likely to be launched by terrorist groups, perhaps in combination with physical acts of destruction. Al Qaeda, Hamas, and Hizballah are seen as posing cyber threats, as are other terrorist groups that harbor grievances against the United States.[12] Nation-states are not yet widely feared as potential sources for such attacks, even though they are well situated to develop the tools needed to carry out sophisticated cyber attacks. Countries that are adversaries of the United States might decide to pursue this avenue in order to influence American diplomacy and military activity in their regions. Medium-sized powers that might use attacks or threats of attack as instruments of deterrence or compellence include Iran and North Korea; numerous other countries, especially across the greater Middle East, similarly view the United States as an adversary. Among the big powers, China is an obvious potential source of cyber danger. If it begins pursuing an assertive, anti-American agenda in East Asia, it might employ cyber threats or even attacks as strategic instruments. Russia also falls into this category because in recent years its government has become more authoritarian and its foreign policy more assertive and bullying. Its threats in 2007 and earlier to deny natural gas to its neighbors, such as Ukraine, suggests a growing willingness to employ techniques of coercion and intimidation that, as former Russian President Vladimir Putin said, could be expanded to include military power, including nuclear weapons, if Russia perceives a threat to its vital security interests.

A significant issue for deterrence is that because such cyber attacks can be launched largely in secret, the identities of the actors carrying them out often cannot readily be determined. For example, a cyber attack seemingly originating in China might have been launched by the Chinese government, by some unofficial group of hackers in China or elsewhere, or by terrorists in the Middle East who disguise their identities. The alleged but ambiguous Russian cyber attack on Estonia is another obvious example.[13]

Although attribution will remain a serious problem, the fear that the attribution problem wholly cripples any hope of detection and deterrence is misplaced. Many, if not most, big cyber threats or actual attacks on the United States, its military forces, or its allies are not likely to be conducted in a political vacuum. Rather, they will be conducted with an explicit political or strategic goal: as a means to an end rather than an end in themselves. They are most likely to be conducted to exert pressure, intimidation, and coercion on the United States to induce it to acquiesce in the larger agenda being pursued by the attacker. Such an attacker likely would not want to conceal its identity, because that would prevent delivery of the message and thereby dilute prospects for an acquiescent response. How could the United States be expected to buckle to such coercion if it is unable to determine the identity of the attacker and the concessions it is seeking? If the attacker makes its identity known in order to pursue its larger political and strategic agenda, it opens itself to U.S. deterrent mechanisms and retaliatory steps.

Beyond this, a U.S. cyber deterrent strategy would be a construct meant to be applied not only during actual crises, but in peacetime as well. The U.S. preparedness agenda during peacetime merely mandates that it knows the nation-states and other actors that could launch cyber attacks in future crises. Knowledge of potential future adversaries does not require real-time crisis attribution, and it could suffice to help the United States develop many core ingredients of a cyber deterrence strategy aimed at them. During the Cold War, after all, the United States possessed enough evidence of the Soviet Union's potential uses of military forces in a war to justify, in the American government's mind, creation of a deterrent strategy against the Soviet Union even though that country restrained itself from committing actual aggression. The same logic can apply to potential future cyber attackers. Yes, the United States needs concrete attribution to launch retaliatory measures in an actual crisis, but in developing peacetime cyber deterrence mechanisms and plans, its standards of proof of culpability are less demanding. It merely must decide who the potential sources of cyber attacks are, and how to pursue its deterrence agenda accordingly.

Illustrative Crisis Scenarios

Credible prospects for determining attribution of responsibility during many actual cyber attacks can be illuminated by illustrative scenarios. In the first hypothetical scenario, Iran threatens or actually uses cyber attacks to advance its interests in the Middle East, seeking to compel U.S. military withdrawal from the Persian Gulf, to assert control over the Strait of Hormuz, or to intimidate Saudi Arabia and Israel. Such an Iranian effort would not be limited to cyberpower: instead, cyber threats or attacks would probably be part of a larger campaign that would employ other instruments, such as use of declaratory policy, diplomacy, or military forces, or control of access to oil. In this scenario, the Iranian government might try to conceal its identity as a cyber attacker, but equally plausible, it might openly threaten use of cyber tools in order to strengthen its leverage and bargaining power. Even if the attacker tried to conceal its identity in the cyber realm, the source of its cyber attacks probably would not be formidably difficult to determine. Intelligence information about attacker identities can be gathered from sources beyond the cyber activities themselves: the strategic context would reveal a great deal about the attacker, and U.S. officials would be able to use technical data, all-source intelligence, and logical inference.

The second illustrative scenario is that of a North Korean effort to intimidate the Republic of Korea (ROK) into making major concessions, or even to set the stage for a military invasion of the ROK. North Korea might, for example, launch cyber attacks on the United States, Japan, and South Korea in an effort to gain leverage over all three countries. Such cyber attacks would not be conducted in isolation of other events, but would be part of North Korea's overall efforts to use diplomacy, its possession of nuclear weapons and missile delivery systems, its conventional military power, and other instruments at its disposal. If North Korea intended to conduct a military invasion of South Korea, its cyber attacks might try to blind ROK forces, delay the deployment of U.S. reinforcements from the continental United States, and degrade the combat effectiveness of U.S. military forces. Here too, North Korea might not want to conceal its identity as a cyber attacker, but might choose instead to broadcast it clearly in order to strengthen its leverage and bargaining power. Even if it tried to conceal its identity, the source of its activity in the cyber realm most likely could be determined. In such a crisis, it is unlikely that any other potential cyber attacker would choose this particular pattern of activity.

A third scenario is a hypothetical East Asian crisis in which China seeks a showdown over Taiwan in order to intimidate or even to conquer it. In such a crisis, China might resort to major cyber attacks directed against the United States, Taiwan, and Japan. Its cyber attack on the United States might be intended to deter Washington from intervention in the crisis, to prevent it from deploying air and naval reinforcements to the area, and to prevent U.S. military forces from defending Taiwan and from attacking China in event of hostilities. Here again, China's cyber attacks would not be conducted in isolation, but would be a component of its overall strategy and use of its political, diplomatic, and military power. China would have no special incentive to conceal its cyber identity at a time when it is provoking a grand showdown over Taiwan and the future of the entire East Asia security order. Instead, it would be more likely to make its cyber identity known to all of its adversaries in order to enhance its leverage over them. Even if it sought to conceal its cyber identity, it would not have much hope of success under the prying eyes of U.S. all-source intelligence.

As these three scenarios suggest, in the event of major cyber attacks by nation-states on the United States, attribution during crises might be less of a crippling problem than it is commonly presumed to be. Some cyber attacks by terrorists might also fall into this category. To be sure, some terrorist attacks might be conducted purely for vengeance and destruction and therefore might not be directly linked to a specific political-strategic agenda that would motivate the attackers to proclaim responsibility for their actions, or that would make them obvious suspects. Yet even terrorist groups tend to have explicit political agendas such as, for example, driving the United States out of Iraq, Afghanistan, or the entire Middle East. Such an agenda could not be readily pursued by leaving the United States blind to the cyber attacker's strategic intent and demands and thus to its identity. The bottom line is that, while attribution will remain a problem that mandates development of better technical capabilities, many potentially big cyber attacks on the United States are likely to arise out of a specific strategic context, aimed at concrete goals such as altering U.S. foreign policy and defense strategy, and therefore will be possible to attribute to specific attackers. Cyber attacks of this sort fall into the category of events that can be treated by the familiar logic of deterrence.

What the United States must avoid is a crisis situation in which it is confronted by a potential or actual cyber attacker whose identity is known, but for whom the American government does not already possess a well-conceived deterrent strategy showing how it can best respond. In such a situation, the United States could be compelled to resort to improvisation, but without the time to think through the details of response mechanisms or to make the necessary preparations. As a result, it might act incorrectly or weakly in ways that produce serious reversals. By drawing upon deterrence theory, whose components are discussed below, it can reduce the dangers arising from such crisis situations and from cyber threats more generally.

Contributions from Deterrence Theory: Past and Present

What would an effective cyber deterrence theory require? A simple answer would be: strong defenses that can rebuff cyber attacks, and potent cyber offenses that can inflict massive retaliatory damage in return. Such a capability-based approach would presume, however, that cyber wars would occur in isolation from larger surrounding events and could be treated as self-contained, subject to their own logic and requirements. However, the greater likelihood is that many major cyber attacks are likely to appear as one instrument among several aimed at achieving political and strategic goals, not just inflicting damage for its own sake. They would be intended as instruments of bargaining and coercion, to deter the United States from taking actions the attackers do not want, or to compel the United States to acquiesce in the attackers' political-strategic agendas. Dealing with cyber attacks of this sort requires not just offensive and defensive capabilities to deter them in some mechanical sense; it requires, above all, the capacity to influence the motivations and psychology of the attacker, as well as a capacity to integrate U.S. cyber responses—defensive and offensive—with other instruments of national power and crisis response. For these reasons, the issue of cyber deterrence strategy cannot be separated from the rest of U.S. national security policy.

Deterrence during the Cold War

The ingredients for constructing a cyber deterrence strategy can be illustrated by briefly reviewing how deterrence operated during the Cold War and how it operates today. To be sure, the experience of the Cold War cannot be grafted onto the different realities of today, including in the cyber realm. Even so, the process by which Cold War deterrence theory was adopted—for example, awareness of the larger strategic context and adversary motives, the systematic creation of clear strategic concepts, the evolutionary development of new requirements as events changed, and the careful efforts to assemble capabilities that fulfilled these requirements—provides lessons that can be adopted if a credible cyber deterrence strategy is to be built today.

The concept of deterrence first emerged during the 1950s, when the Cold War with the Soviet Union was heating up and rapidly acquiring military components. Some observers, in hindsight, view Cold War deterrence strategy as largely shaped by the U.S. effort to build nuclear offensive forces that could inflict massive retaliation in response to a Soviet nuclear attack on the United States. This is an oversimplification: deterrence was embedded in a more nuanced approach that was entirely focused neither on military nor nuclear calculations. As it evolved during the 1950s and beyond, deterrence became anchored in political calculations aimed at influencing Soviet motivations, underpinning U.S. national defense strategy in Europe, and controlling nuclear escalation. It was isolated from neither larger strategic considerations nor the need to deal with the Soviet adversary in political terms.

Deterrence theory first appeared as part of the West's containment strategy in Europe, which aspired to keep the Soviet Union confined to Eastern Europe and to prevent it from gaining control of Western Europe. When the United States and its European allies created the North Atlantic Treaty Organization (NATO) in 1949 to strengthen their defense capabilities for countering Soviet forces, their new alliance faced a precarious imbalance of military power in Central Europe. The Soviet Union commanded a massive army that was permanently stationed in Eastern Europe, with easy access to exposed West Germany. NATO, by contrast, was able to field only a few combat divisions and air wings. It therefore turned to America's growing fleet of strategic bombers, built to carry nuclear weapons. If the Soviet Army invaded Western Europe with the intent of driving to the English Channel, the United States could launch a devastating nuclear attack not only on Soviet military forces, but also on the

Soviet homeland itself. In the mid-1950s, this strategy was, in fact, based on massive nuclear retaliation, but it was not aimed at responding to a nuclear attack on the United States: although the Soviets possessed nuclear weapons, they had few long-range bombers capable of intercontinental attack. The strategy was aimed at deterring conventional attack on Western Europe by convincing the Soviet government that an invasion would not succeed and that the Soviet Union faced unacceptable risks: if it made such an attack, it would suffer losses that far exceeded any benefits that it might hope to gain.

Even at this early stage, then, deterrence theory did not exist in a political vacuum: it took account of the motives and risk-taking propensities of the adversary. Deterrence theory presumed that the Soviet Union would act rationally in a crisis, that it would be motivated by self-preservation as well as cost-benefit calculations, and that it would not launch a war in which it would inevitably suffer devastating losses. Moreover, deterrence theory, as well as the containment doctrine that was its umbrella political rationale, cautioned the United States to be careful not to threaten an unprovoked western offensive aimed at dislodging the Soviet Union from its stranglehold control over Eastern Europe. As a result, the U.S. deterrence strategy offered the Soviet Union a dual rationale for exercising restraint: whereas military aggression would result in punishing losses, maintaining the peace would allow the Soviets to preserve their principal gain from World War II, their strategic buffer in Eastern Europe. Containment and deterrence thus offered the Soviets a political and strategic bargain. They could retain de facto control of Eastern Europe if they kept their military hands off Western Europe, but if they invaded Western Europe, they would lose both Eastern Europe and their own homeland to nuclear destruction. As events would show, the Soviets were prepared to accept this bargain, and peace was preserved during a period of intense political rivalry and ideological incompatibility that easily could have erupted into full-scale war.

The U.S. deterrence strategy began to change in the 1960s. The Soviet Union started to deploy nuclear-tipped intercontinental ballistic missiles (ICBMs) that could reach U.S. targets within 30 minutes, destroying the U.S.-based bomber force on the ground. This could undermine the precarious logic of deterrence by diminishing the threat that the Soviets would face nuclear punishment if they invaded Western Europe. The United States therefore embarked on an expensive effort to deploy a large force of ICBMs and submarine-launched ballistic missiles (SLBMs) that could survive a surprise Soviet missile attack. The goal was to create a survivable second-strike retaliatory force so as to restore the credibility of retaliatory deterrence.

At the same time, the United States began backing away from its earlier emphasis on massive retaliation in the form of all-out nuclear obliteration of the Soviet Union. A main reason was that, as the Soviets deployed a survivable, second-strike missile force of their own, the United States could not hope to disarm them in a surprise attack. Mutual nuclear vulnerability had arrived. The United States therefore began crafting new nuclear warfighting doctrines that contemplated limited nuclear strikes in the early stages of a war but sought to control subsequent escalation. The threat of nuclear retaliation remained the backbone of deterrence, but ideas for actually waging nuclear war were now developed, along with theories of limiting escalation. The goal would be to halt fighting by political means before the two countries had obliterated each other.

American nuclear theorists therefore outlined a so-called "ladder of escalation" to guide how the United States should prepare to fight at each "rung," so as to offer multiple options and flexibility and avoid domination by the Soviet Union at any step. It postulated that the escalatory process would be characterized on both sides by strategic intentions and political bargaining: each side would employ military strikes to coerce the other into submission to its political objectives. The goal of climbing the ladder gradually and purposefully was to compel the other side to back down, while keeping escalation from spiraling out of control and resulting in massive devastation on both sides. Whether an actual military conflict would have conformed to this hypothetical ladder is uncertain. Many critics doubted that the escalation process, once started, could be controlled at all, let alone in finely tuned ways, but U.S. strategy endeavored to do everything possible to bring escalation under control.

As Cold War deterrence theory matured, it was accompanied by efforts to define its military requirements and to pursue the defense programs mandated by them. In preparing its nuclear offensive forces, the United States created a "triad doctrine" in the 1960s and 1970s. The triad doctrine specified that the U.S. force posture should be composed of three legs—1,000 ICBMs, 656 SLBMs carried by submarines, and about 350 B–52 strategic bombers—each of which could survive a surprise attack and retaliate with sufficient force to devastate Soviet urban areas, so as to deter any Soviet inclination to wage a full-scale nuclear war. Beyond this, the quest for flexibility and options led to decisions to equip all three legs of the triad with accurate warheads that could be used against a range of targets other than cities. As a consequence, the U.S. triad eventually was armed with 12,000 warheads or more, enough to meet almost any need for strike options and target coverage. Meanwhile, the Soviet Union deployed its own version of a triad.[14]

While nuclear forces could deter nuclear attack, they could not reliably deter a conventional attack because the Soviets might judge that if NATO found its conventional defenses buckling, it would not risk nuclear escalation even to save Western Europe.[15] In 1967, therefore, NATO adopted a strategy of forward defense and flexible response that mandated a stronger conventional defense posture. During the 1970s and 1980s, the United States and its European allies invested major sums in conventional defenses. The Cold War ended with Western nuclear and conventional forces stronger than ever, with deterrence solidified, and with the Soviet Union facing bankruptcy partly due to its huge investments in a military buildup that brought fruitless strategic returns.

Cold War Lessons

Deterrence was a risky proposition during the Cold War, but it worked: major war with the Soviet Union was averted, and Western security was safeguarded. It worked for reasons that yield lessons for cyber deterrence. First, it worked because it was credible, and because the United States made efforts to maintain, improve, and adjust it. Second, nuclear war was not viewed in isolation from larger events, but took into account the political and diplomatic motivations of both sides. Third, U.S. deterrence strategy denied the Soviet Union any favorable prospects from aggression, while offering it reasons to conclude that remaining at peace with the West was preferable to war. As deterrence theory matured, it balanced the need of warning the adversary against the imperative of minimizing the risks of unwarranted escalation. Its emphasis on flexibility and options allowed it to respond to a range of situations. Its success was also due to the fact that the United States and its NATO allies took care to meet its military requirements, and because it was crafted to protect not only the United States, but vulnerable allies as well.

All of these lessons provide valuable insights for thinking about deterrence today, including cyber deterrence. The general principles it yields for the contemporary era include the need for focus on the political motivations and risk-taking propensities of potential adversaries, for credible deterrent mechanisms that will work even under great stress, for well-integrated capabilities that are guided by carefully crafted deterrence doctrines and that address the spectrum of challenges likely to be confronted, for flexibility and options, for integration of doctrines of retaliation and compellence with the necessity to control escalation, and for policies that protect allies along with the United States.

Modern-day Problems

What are the implications of contemporary nuclear deterrence theory for deterring cyber attacks? Deterrence theory today continues to focus on influencing the motivations and aspirations of potential adversaries by persuading them that aggression cannot succeed. The principal target of U.S. deterrence strategy has switched, however, from the defunct Soviet Union to rogue countries, terrorists, and other adversaries that menace U.S. and allied interests. While the strategy still is aimed at nuclear attacks and big conventional invasions, such as a North Korean attack on South Korea, it also seeks to deter lesser provocations, including terrorism. This emphasis on multiple adversaries and provocations has given rise to the concept of "tailored deterrence":[16] deterrence must take into account the specific predilections of each individual adversary and its conduct. The U.S. nuclear triad is now composed of offensive forces, defensive forces, and infrastructure. Today, bombers and missiles carrying precision conventional (nonnuclear) warheads figure importantly in the deterrence equation. The entire U.S. conventional military posture is viewed as a major contributor to deterrence, as well as to the other key activities, spelled out in the National Defense Strategy, including assurance of allies, dissuasion of potential rivals from competitive provocative conduct, and defeat of adversaries in wartime.

Since the Cold War ended in 1990, deterrence has continued to work in some places but seems to have failed in others. It failed to prevent Iraq from invading Kuwait in 1990, Serbia from invading Kosovo in 1999, or al Qaeda from using Afghanistan to launch its attack on the United States in 2001. Deterrence has not prevented North Korea and Iran from pursuing nuclear weapons, nor has the presence of large U.S. military forces in Iraq and Afghanistan prevented adversaries from waging guerrilla wars aimed at destabilizing both countries.

Such problems have led many observers to conclude that deterrence theory is inadequate against present-day U.S. adversaries that range from rogue countries to terrorists. Is the problem that the United States does not have a properly conceived deterrence theory, or is it that today's adversaries are more willing to take dangerous risks, and pay heavy prices, than was the Soviet Union during the Cold War? If the success of deterrence could be taken for granted during the Cold War, it cannot be taken for granted today. It has become a variable, not a constant, in the strategic equation. Some threats are harder to deter than others. Recognition of this disturbing reality makes the task of designing an effective cyber deterrence strategy both more necessary and more difficult.

Toward a General Model of Tailored Cyber Deterrence

Given the troubled track record of recent years, can deterrence—including cyber deterrence—be accomplished against multiple potential adversaries with assertive agendas? Some observers argue that modern-era aggressors cannot be deterred, on the grounds that they are not rational: that they are not influenced by the same cautionary mechanisms that motivate normally sensible actors. However, *rationality* is a relative term: while some of today's actors may not be rational by U.S. standards, this does not mean that they are wholly irrational. Although they may perceive high potential payoffs in a confrontation with the United States, and this may lead them to think and act boldly, they are not necessarily oblivious to potential damage and the pain that they may suffer in return. Even today's actors with malevolent agendas tend to be governed by explicit motives, goals, and awareness of costs and risks. This is certainly true of nation-states, and it also applies, to varying degrees, to nonstate actors. Even terrorist groups are motivated not just by ideology and hatred, but also by strategic goals and self-preservation. The decision calculus of such actors may be influenced by U.S. deterrence mechanisms, even cyber deterrence. Cyber attacks are often regarded as not deterrable because they are "free rides"—the attacker has an expectation of impunity—but this calculus could be changed by creating expectations that cyber aggression might be an uncertain or costly act.

No cyber deterrence strategy can hope to be airtight to prevent all minor attacks. However, a strategy can increase the chances that major cyber attacks can be prevented; this could protect the United States and its allies not only from a single major attack but also from serial cyber aggressions and resulting damage. A worthwhile goal of a cyber deterrence strategy would be to transform medium-sized attacks into low-probability events and to provide practically 100 percent deterrence of major attacks.

A cyber deterrence strategy could contribute to other key defense activities and goals, including assurance of allies, dissuasion, and readiness to defeat adversaries in the event of actual combat. The goal of dissuading adversaries is crucially important. Thus far, the United States has not been noticeably forceful in stating its intentions to deter major cyber attacks and, if necessary, to respond to them with decisive force employing multiple instruments of power. Meanwhile, several countries and terrorist groups are reportedly developing cyber attack capabilities. Dissuasion of such activities is not an easy task: it requires investment in technical capabilities as well as building an internal consensus to employ these capabilities. If some of these actors can be dissuaded from entering into cyber competition with the United States and its allies, the dangers of actual cyber aggression will diminish.

How would a cyber deterrence strategy operate, and how can its potential effectiveness be judged? Deterrence depends on the capacity of the United States to project an image of resolve, willpower, and capability in sufficient strength to convince a potential adversary to refrain from activities that threaten U.S. and allied interests. As recent experience shows, deterrence can be especially difficult in the face of adversaries who are inclined to challenge the United States and otherwise take dangerous risks. In cases of failure, deterrence might well have been sound in theory but not carried out effectively enough to work. The aggressions of Saddam Hussein, Slobodan Milosevic, and al Qaeda might not have been carried out had these actors been convinced that the United States would respond with massive military force. These aggressions resulted because of a failure to communicate U.S. willpower and resolve, not because the attackers were wholly oblivious to any sense of restraint or self-preservation, nor because the logic of deterrence had lost its relevance.

A general model of cyber deterrence provides a strategic framework for thinking about tailored deterrence. Such a model is the DOD JOC for deterrence operations, which emphasizes employing instruments of deterrence to affect not only the physical capacities of potential adversaries, but their psychology and motivations as well. The model specifies ends, ways, means, and analytical procedures.

Ends, Ways, and Means

The goal of a cyber deterrence strategy would be to influence an adversary's decisionmaking calculus so decisively that it will not launch cyber attacks against the United States, its military forces, or its allies. Coordinated actions reduce the chances for attacker success, so that the dangers, costs, risks, and uncertainties of a cyber attack are perceived to outweigh any expected success, benefits, or rewards. In the case of an adversary who seeks to use threats of cyber attacks, or actual attacks, to coerce the United States into conduct that would serve its larger interests and goals, a cyber deterrence strategy will work if the adversary judges that this attempted coercion would not succeed and that the attack would provoke U.S. retaliation, resulting in a net strategic setback for the would-be attacker. For example, if Iran were to contemplate cyber attacks to try to coerce the United States into making political concessions in the Persian Gulf and Middle East, it might be deterred from this course if its decisionmakers were to judge that the cyber attack would not physically succeed in inflicting the desired damage; that even if the attack succeeded, the United States would not make the desired concessions; or that the United States would be likely to retaliate in ways that inflict unacceptable damage on Iran in return, in the cyber realm or elsewhere.

The same strategic calculus applies to Chinese use of cyber threats and attacks, as well as actions by other plausible adversaries in the cyber domain. Potential U.S. counteractions in such situations are encapsulated in the three principal ways of pursuing deterrence articulated in the JOC model: deterrence by denying benefits, deterrence by imposing costs, and deterrence by offering incentives for adversary restraint.

Deterrence by denying benefits entails credibly threatening to deprive the attacker of the benefits or gains being sought: convincing it that a cyber attack will not achieve its goals. Deterrence by imposing costs entails credibly threatening to impose costs, losses, and risks that are too painful to accept, thus convincing the adversary that punishment would outweigh any expected successes. Deterrence by encouraging restraint means convincing the adversary that not attacking will result in an acceptable, attractive outcome.

These three deterrence mechanisms can be employed singly, but they are likely to work best when they are combined in mutually reinforcing ways. Potential cyber adversaries may not be unitary actors dominated by a single strategic calculus; decisionmaking may be influenced by multiple actors, such as different parts of a foreign government or terrorist network, that have differing priorities and tolerance for risk. Together, these three mechanisms can influence multiple actors in different ways and to different degrees, enhancing the prospects that the decision will be to reject cyber attacks.

Deterrence by denial or by imposing costs can, in principle, both be carried out purely within cyberspace. For example, the United States could seek to deter cyber attacks both by building strong cyber defenses and by employing cyber offensive capability for retaliatory attack on the information networks of the adversary. This narrow focus may not, however, be appropriate for most strategic confrontations in which cyber attacks are used to pursue larger political and strategic objectives. In such cases, the U.S. strategic calculus of cyber deterrence will need to be broader, too. Efforts to deny benefits will need to focus not only on protecting U.S. cyber networks, but also on ensuring that cyber attacks, even if physically successful, could not compel the United States into making the political concessions being sought. In other words, U.S. cyber defenses must be not only technical but strategic as well.

The same calculation applies to deterrence by imposing costs: the United States might choose to retaliate purely in the cyber realm by taking down enemy information networks, but it can maximize deterrence by applying a full set of other mechanisms—political, diplomatic, economic, and military— to increase the strategic pressures, costs, and risks to adversaries. Indeed, these other instruments may be more potent than cyber retaliation against adversaries that lack sophisticated information networks and thus would not be especially bothered by cyber counterattacks. Retaliatory options must be more than purely cyber; they should be multifaceted and strategic in character.

Encouraging adversary restraint necessitates sophisticated handling of strategic confrontations and crisis management. As a general proposition, cyber deterrence will not work if the adversary is faced with the imminent prospect of total defeat and destruction regardless of whether it launches a cyber attack. For example, a rogue country faced with the imminent prospect of U.S. invasion and conquest has little incentive to refrain from a cyber attack, while it has many incentives to launch one in order to deter, hamper, or exact retaliation for a U.S. invasion. Such an adversary has something to gain and nothing to lose by pursuing offensive cyber warfare. An adversary that may judge itself better off by refraining from cyber warfare, even if it is involved in strategic rivalry, competition, or outright warfare with the United States, can be deterred. Just as deterrence theory during the Cold War required the United States to contemplate how to give the Soviet Union better options than initiating or escalating a nuclear war, cyber deterrence theory requires awareness of adversary interests, and offering adversaries more attractive options than engaging in a mutual effort to destroy each other's information networks and infrastructures. This will be easiest where strategic conflicts are limited and subject to diplomatic resolution. It will be harder to carry out with implacable adversaries that are pursuing duels to the death with the United States.

A cyber deterrence strategy will also need to be aware of thresholds. Cyber attacks can come in many different shapes and sizes, and they will not all merit the same response. Some attacks may be too minor to worry about. Others may merit a retaliatory response, but the degree of that response will depend upon the degree of provocation.

What about the means—the instruments—for pursuing cyber deterrence? A cyber deterrence strategy aimed at handling multiple threats and differing situations cannot rely primarily on any single instrument. It must be able to employ multiple instruments that offer a wide range of response options, that can be packaged and repackaged to serve the specific goals being pursued, and that allow the United States to deal with dynamically evolving situations of complexity. Multiple instruments might be used singly or in combination. Single instruments may be effective against weak adversaries, but multiple instruments are likely to be needed against ambitious, assertive opponents. For each situation, the instruments of retaliation must enable the United States to act credibly and powerfully.

Both cyber defenses and cyber offenses are part of deterrence strategy, but they are not the whole solution or even the most important component of it. In some situations, U.S. cyber defenses may be ineffective, but the United States might choose not to respond with a cyber counterattack. The most effective response to some cyber attacks may be political and economic, perhaps isolating the attacker from the global community, mobilizing nation-states to treat it as a pariah, or imposing economic sanctions. These could inflict more painful penalties than any cyber counterattack. U.S. military strikes might even be carried out, perhaps in retaliation for a truly devastating attack on U.S. information networks, or as part of major combat operations against enemies. Much depends on the identity of the attacker, the nature of the potential attacks, and the nature of a proper response. The United States needs to be able to respond flexibly, to have a portfolio of options that provide adaptability, and to be capable of employing multiple instruments in whatever combination makes best sense for the situation at hand.

Analytical Procedures
The general deterrence model, as derived from the JOC on deterrence operations, offers six analytical steps for pursuing each case of cyber deterrence in peace, crisis, and war:

1. specify the deterrence objectives and the strategic context
2. assess the strategic calculus of adversary decisionmakers
3. identify desired deterrence effects on adversary conduct
4. develop and assess courses of action designed to achieve desired effects
5. develop plans to execute deterrence courses of action and to monitor and assess adversary responses
6. develop capacities to respond flexibly and effectively as the deterrence situation evolves.

These six steps reflect the demands and challenges of achieving tailored deterrence of cyber attacks. Tailored deterrence recognizes that U.S. goals and objectives may vary considerably from one situation to the next, necessitating different types of responses. Thus, step 1 defines U.S. purposes for cyber situations. Step 2 recognizes that, because not all adversaries are the same, the United States must specify the adversary being encountered, the strategic context of the encounter, and the decision calculus being employed by the adversary. Each of the three types of adversaries likely to be faced—near-peer rivals, middle-sized rogue countries, and terrorist groups—would bring different psychologies and motives to confrontations with the United States, as well as different attitudes toward goals, stakes, actions, perceptions of U.S. willpower and resolve, risk-taking propensities, and handling of uncertainties.

Steps 3 and 4 are both critical and challenging. Step 3 entails identifying the desired effects of deterrence on adversary conduct; in step 4, then, courses of action to produce these effects are developed and assessed. Generally, when deterrence has succeeded in the past, the United States was skillful at identifying how its courses of action would produce effects that could influence the motivations and behavior of adversary governments in the desired ways. When deterrence has failed, it was usually because the U.S. Government failed to assemble a portfolio of declaratory policies and actions that strongly influenced the perceptions and motives of the adversaries. In these cases, the problem was not that the United States was blind to the need to send strong deterrence signals, but that it sent the wrong signals, which failed to have the desired effects because they did not credibly signal the will and the capability of the United States.

Because many cyber attack situations will be part of larger geopolitical confrontations, determining how to send credible cyber deterrence signals will entail carrying out multiple actions that, in turn, will need to be embedded in broader U.S. activities aimed at achieving other purposes. When the United States acts weakly in the eyes of adversaries, it may unintentionally signal that cyber attacks can be carried out with impunity or will not be met with a decisive response. However, when the United States acts powerfully in handling a larger crisis that goes beyond the cyber realm, it could risk burying its cyber deterrence signals in a plethora of other activities, thus leading the adversary to overlook or misinterpret them. Beyond this, U.S. actions that powerfully influence one set of adversaries may have little impact on other adversaries, who might be influenced by an entirely different set of measures. For some adversaries, a simple warning might be deterrent enough; for others, a cyber response, or powerful use of other instruments as well as a cyber response, might be appropriate. For some, however, the only effective response might be the use of military power or other non-cyber instruments. For such reasons, cyber deterrence requires that the United States develop its skills in figuring out how to influence each adversary and how to act accordingly.

Step 5, developing plans, and step 6, developing capacities (discussed below), are also important. Plans determine the crucial details of how multiple instruments are to be blended together in a cyber crisis; they also reduce the risks of serious errors in judgment if complex actions had to be cobbled together on the fly. Execution plans are needed for precrisis situations and the initial stages of actual crises, and also for the various stages in which a cyber crisis might unfold, such as a small probing cyber attack, a larger but still limited attack, and so on up the ladder of escalation. This cyber escalation, in turn, might be part of a sequence of political and military steps aimed at bringing pressure on the United States. Thus, a cyber deterrence strategy needs to master the ladder of cyber escalation as well as the other ingredients of cyber crisis management.

Tailored cyber deterrence requires more than realizing that potential adversaries will differ from each other, will harbor different perceptions and motivations, and will employ cyber attacks with differing agendas in mind. It also requires realizing that U.S. goals and objectives will vary from one adversary and situation to the next, that diverse responses may be needed in order to have different types of effects, and that crisis response plans must provide the capacity to act both strongly and effectively. Many cyber attacks will not occur in a vacuum, but instead will arise in a larger context that necessitates multiple U.S. responses in addition to those aimed at ensuring cyber deterrence. Because each cyber situation is likely to be unique, applying tailored deterrence to the cyber domain promises to be complex and challenging.

Strategic Requirements for Cyber Deterrence: Assets and Capabilities

Because a cyber strategy of tailored deterrence must deal with diverse threats, multiple assets and capabilities will be needed. This necessitates a persistent, wide-ranging U.S. Government effort. Key requirements and priorities for achieving an effective capability to carry out a cyber deterrent strategy include:

- a clear and firm declaratory policy spelling out the U.S. intention to deter cyber attacks
- high global situational awareness that is attuned to the full spectrum of potential cyber threats and the circumstances in which they might arise
- good command and control systems that permit coordinated multiregional and homeland responses to cyber threats
- effective cyber defenses that protect both U.S. military forces and the U.S. homeland with a high priority for defending key infrastructure
- a wide spectrum of counter–cyber offensive capabilities, including cyber attack and other instruments for asserting U.S. power in order to enforce deterrence before, during, and after crises
- well-developed U.S. interagency cooperation and collaboration with allies and partners including those in Europe, Asia, and elsewhere
- cyber deterrence methodologies, metrics, and experiments that can help guide the planning process.

Each of these requisites of an effective cyber deterrence policy is examined in this section.

Strong Declaratory Policy

The goal of deterrence of cyber attacks is already stated in some official U.S. documents, but a case can be made for a stronger and clearer U.S. declaratory policy. A good place to present it would be in the next National Security Strategy. The declaratory policy should provide a credible, convincing explanation of why the United States takes cyber threats seriously, why it would regard a major cyber attack as potentially an act of war against it, and the intention of the United States to respond with decisive actions, possibly including force. The declaratory policy should leave no doubt in the minds of potential adversaries that any cyber attacks on the United States would fail to achieve their goals and that the attackers would suffer unacceptable costs, damages, and risks in return.

A U.S. declaratory policy for cyber deterrence needs to be firm, but it also needs to be balanced, sending the right messages regarding possible responses to cyber attack and avoiding inflammatory statements that could contribute to escalation of cyber conflicts. The QDR of 2006 asserts that the deterrent posture should be capable of mounting an "overwhelming response." While this statement clearly is appropriate for major cyber attacks that could cause massive disruption, not all cyber attacks will fall into this category. Some might be smaller, yet still large enough to merit a U.S. response of some magnitude. Above all, the U.S. response should be tailored to the situation. Based on this principle, U.S. declaratory policy could endorse a cyber deterrence strategy of "tailored, decisive, and proportional response."

High Global Situational Awareness

Global situational awareness will be a key requirement for a cyber deterrence strategy. In particular, five types of knowledge are necessary: identification of potential cyber threats around the world, including state and nonstate actors; assessment of the motives, value structures, goals, perceptions, and calculations that different adversaries might bring to the use of cyber attacks, including attacks that are part of broader strategic campaigns aimed at damaging U.S. interests; appraisal of the calculations, judgments, and external pressures that might lead potential adversaries to refrain from launching cyber attacks; awareness of the cyber assets, capabilities, and vulnerabilities that potential adversaries might possess or acquire; and use of all-source intelligence for attributing the source of cyber attacks in crisis situations where attribution is possible.

Especially important for carrying out deterrence is situational awareness of the psychology and motivations that might lead potential adversaries to launch cyber attacks; their attitudes toward benefits, costs, and risk-taking propensities; and the calculations that might lead them to refrain from such attacks. This requires gathering intelligence on the adversaries and developing awareness of how U.S. deterrent actions might affect others' behavior in peace, crisis, or war. The U.S. Intelligence Community must be involved in gathering this information, and it must work closely with U.S. policy agencies in order to evaluate the likely consequences of various courses of action for convincing adversaries to exercise restraint by refraining from committing cyber aggression and from escalating in a crisis. Accurate intelligence on the cyber attack capabilities and activities of potential adversaries is also necessary, to gauge U.S. vulnerabilities, as well as adversary vulnerabilities to U.S. counteraction. Determining the identity of potential attacks requires both technical means and human sources of intelligence.

Effective Command and Control

Preparedness is critical to an effective cyber deterrence strategy and to crisis management. A cyber attack on the United States, especially during an ongoing regional crisis with strategic interests at stake, could impose significant demands on the U.S. command and control system. Simultaneously, the United States would need to orchestrate its cyber defenses at home, to employ counter–cyber actions against the adversary, and to coordinate its cyberspace activities with other instruments of power and actions to manage events that could be taking place anywhere in the world. Beyond this, the United States might have to coordinate its responses to two cyber adversaries at the same time. For example, multiple combatant commands within DOD would need to coordinate their actions, inside as well as outside of the cyber realm, along with homeland defense agencies, the national security interagency community, and U.S. diplomatic activity abroad. Improvements in this arena seem necessary.

Stronger Cyber Defenses

Cyber defenses capable of protecting U.S. information networks are needed both to reduce potential vulnerabilities to cyber attack and to help deter potential attackers. If adversaries conclude that cyber attacks cannot attain their goals of damaging U.S. information networks, they will be less inclined to incur the costs and risks of launching them. Many observers judge that the United States is too vulnerable to cyber attacks. This weakens U.S. hopes for effective deterrence. Improvements in U.S. cyber defenses are thus needed for both defense and deterrence.

The National Strategy to Secure Cyberspace of 2003 sought to foster a partnership between government and the private sector. It outlined five major priorities for strengthening U.S. cyber defenses, along with specific recommendations in each area, many of which remain current. First, it called for a national cyberspace security and response program, establishing the Department of Homeland Security as the main point of contact for cyberspace security efforts with industry. It recommended improvements to cyberspace analysis, warning, information-sharing, major incident management, and national-level recovery efforts.

As a second priority, it called for a program for reducing the national cyberspace security threat and vulnerability. Major recommendations included improved criminal prosecution of cyber attackers, the adoption of improved security protocols and more secure router technology for the Internet, and improved computer software security.

The third priority identified was a national cyberspace security awareness and training program. It recommended improved Federal, state, and local efforts to promote awareness of cyber security, education programs in elementary and secondary schools, and efforts to improve awareness by small businesses and home computer users regarding antivirus software and firewalls.

A fourth priority was to secure government cyberspace with Federal efforts to strengthen the security of computers, software, and information networks, coupled with parallel efforts by state and local governments.

The strategy called, fifth, for national security and international cyberspace security cooperation. Recommendations included improving counter–cyber intelligence and attribution capabilities as well as closer cooperation with foreign governments and multinational organizations in pursuing cyber security.

Preferential defense of the most crucial information networks is a high priority for enhancing cyber deterrence. Safeguarding the information networks of the U.S. military, along with U.S. Government information networks, is clearly critical. Priority efforts to safeguard networks that operate key areas of the domestic infrastructure make sense, too. An example is the electrical power grid, loss of which could have a cascading effect in damaging other key parts of the U.S. economy.[17]

Multifaceted Counter–Cyber Offensive Capabilities

Because America's defenses cannot realistically be made impregnable against major cyber attacks any time soon, creation of offensive retaliatory capabilities is an essential component of a cyber deterrence strategy. Retaliation could be needed to help deter "bolt-out-of-the-blue" attacks confined to cyberspace, or threats of cyber attack during periods of rising political tensions, or major cyber attacks during intense crises or actual shooting wars. Retaliation could take many forms. It could mainly take the form of cyber retaliation against an adversary's networks; this might be launched quickly after an attack began, or later if time is needed to identify the attacker or to create the proper conditions for acting effectively. Retaliation might also include diplomatic, political, or economic responses, or the use of military force. As a general rule, confrontations with adversaries that are strategic in nature, and are focused on regional security affairs elsewhere in the world, are especially likely to require a blend of retaliatory instruments that are embedded in a larger framework of U.S. actions and that extend well beyond the cyber domain.

A major challenge will be to tailor responses to help achieve the specific deterrence goals being sought. A cyber deterrent strategy will require developing a portfolio of capabilities and actions that can be combined to form effective offensive responses tailored to the situations at hand. This requires not only creation of physical capabilities but also development of a wide spectrum of offensive response plans to avoid the risks associated with improvising in a crisis.

Interagency Cooperation and Collaboration with Allies and Partners

A cyber deterrence strategy would be carried out in multiple domains, requiring careful coordination. Strong U.S. interagency cooperation is therefore needed, especially among the intelligence agencies, which are responsible for identifying cyber threats; the homeland security agencies, which handle domestic priorities; and the national security community, which handles external policies. Within the national security community, close cooperation between DOD and the State Department would be needed at home and abroad. The more such agencies collaborate, the stronger the cyber deterrence strategy will be.

Collaboration with allies and partners is also important. Because they are potentially vulnerable to cyber attacks, cooperation in pursuing a cyber deterrence strategy can help reduce their vulnerabilities, as well as the risk that threats of attack against them could be used by adversaries to pressure the United States to make strategic concessions. Multinational cooperation can also increase the pool of assets and capabilities that could be mobilized to deal with cyber attacks. Cooperation with European allies, which already is starting to take place, is especially important.[18] An issue worth examining is whether security collaboration for a cyber deterrence strategy can take place within NATO, which provides the best transatlantic institution for handling threats to its members. It could be argued that a major cyber attack against the United States or its European allies could qualify as an Article 5 contingency that would mandate a strong NATO response in the cyber realm or outside it. If such a judgment is reached, the likelihood of being able to employ NATO increases significantly, but much would depend upon the attitudes of Britain, Germany, France, and other major European allies. Multilateral collaboration with such key Asian allies as Japan, South Korea, and Australia also makes strategic sense. Indeed, collaboration for the purpose of creating a strong cyber deterrence strategy might help set the stage for pursuing broader Asian collective defense and security planning.

Metrics and Experiments

Development of analytical methods and metrics for assessment should be part of any effort to create a cyber deterrence strategy of tailored response. The essence of cyber deterrence—the ability to influence the motives and calculations of potential cyber attackers—requires subjective evaluations and qualitative techniques, but that does not mean that assessment is impossible. Analytical studies might endeavor to calibrate the likely deterrence effects of alternative strategies and capabilities on different types of potential cyber attackers and the situations in which their attacks might occur. Simulation exercises and other experiments could also help build usable knowledge.

Issues for Further Analysis

Efforts to develop an effective cyber deterrence strategy will require further analysis of a number of thorny issues, including developing declaratory policy for multiple audiences; providing better net assessments of adversary cyber capabilities and U.S. vulnerabilities; addressing the attribution problem; learning to deal with nonstate actors; addressing the threshold problem; dealing with intrawar deterrence and control of escalation; and providing extended deterrence coverage and dealing with attacks on third parties. This section briefly outlines each of these issues.

Declaratory Policy for Multiple Audience

During the Cold War, shaping declaratory policy was relatively easy because the United States was dealing mainly with one audience, the Soviet Union, whose motives and aspirations were relatively well known. In the current era, the United States will need to deal with multiple adversaries and wider audiences as it shapes a cyber deterrence strategy. These actors possess differing perceptions, motives, and calculations, and they are likely to be influenced by differing types of U.S. deterrent actions. Thus, the types of U.S. policies to deter one type of adversary may differ from those needed to deter another adversary, with varying degrees of soft and hard rhetoric or of positive incentives and punishing responses. This challenge cannot readily be solved by trying to fine-tune each public declaratory statement so that it somehow addresses all potential adversaries. Instead, the United States will need to use a combination of public and private diplomacy to convey tailored, focused messages to each adversary. Doing so will require Washington to develop a better capacity to communicate with foreign audiences, a challenge that applies to many issues far beyond the cyber realm.

Providing Better Net Assessments of Capabilities and Vulnerabilities

An essential issue is knowing how capable adversaries are of launching major cyber attacks and how vulnerable the United States is to such attacks. Many observers postulate that multiple actors are developing expert attack capabilities in this arena, and that U.S. information networks are highly vulnerable to them. Embracing this assumption is a prudent response to an issue clouded by many technicalities. However, the fact that the United States has not yet been subjected to a major crippling cyber attack may indicate that adversary capabilities and U.S. vulnerabilities are not so great as many fear. Further analysis of this issue is needed because it affects not only future threats, but also how future U.S. cyber deterrence strategy and response options should take shape. During the Cold War, U.S. deterrence strategy did not fully take shape until sophisticated net assessments of the nuclear and conventional military capabilities of both sides had been done. For example, a combination of static techniques and dynamic computer models helped shed analytical light on both nuclear competition and the conventional military balance in Europe. Comparable analyses of capabilities and vulnerabilities in the cyber domain will be needed for a mature and effective U.S. cyber deterrence strategy.

Addressing the Attribution Problem

Earlier, this chapter argued that the perpetrators of many major cyber attacks would likely be identifiable through use of all-source intelligence and strategic reasoning. While this judgment suffices to justify initial efforts to establish a cyber deterrence strategy, it does not mean that we can ignore the critical need to develop better technical attribution capabilities so that the sources of all attacks can be identified. In the cyber realm, attribution is far more difficult than in the realms of nuclear and conventional forces. Perhaps this problem will lessen as better technical means are developed, and as the United States becomes better at employing all-source intelligence to sort out the identity of attackers promptly. Pursuing improved capabilities in this arena is a high-priority goal.

Learning to Deal with Nonstate Actors

Although nation-states seem likely to be the main source of major cyber attacks on the United States, major or minor attacks might also come from nonstate actors, such as al Qaeda, Hamas, Hizballah, and other terrorist groups, or ethnic groups and other political actors whose memberships cut across state boundaries. Their motives and aspirations could be quite different from those of nation-states: they might be more influenced by ideology and anger, and they might be more willing to take risks and to engage in provocations. Whether such groups can be deterred from employing cyber attacks is an open question, but it is not a hopeless proposition: they will typically be pursuing political agendas in order to advance their interests, and they will therefore be vulnerable to counterpressures. In order to carry out a tailored cyber deterrence strategy, the United States will need to learn how to influence such actors. Further research and analysis in this area are an important requirement.

Addressing the Threshold Problem

Cyber attacks can range from small attacks that cause minor damage to very large attacks that can inflict massive damage. It is hard to point to any specific threshold of potential cyber damage below which U.S. strategy should discount an attack, but above which an attack should trigger concern for deterrence, coupled with the possibility of retaliatory response. The ladder of escalation contains many rungs of ascending provocation and damage, each of which could merit a response, of increasing intensity. A U.S. cyber deterrence strategy might be shaped to identify decisive, proportional responses at each rung of the ladder, rather than trying to specify a single threshold that separates nonresponses from strong responses.

Dealing with Intrawar Deterrence and Control of Escalation

While deterring the launching of cyber attacks is a critical imperative, equally important is deterring escalation once a cyber conflict has begun. Some adversaries, for example, might start with a small attack and then gradually scale up to the point at which the United States comes under intense pressure to buckle to the attacker's wishes. Such escalation could happen if U.S. responses at the low rungs of the escalatory ladder are not strong or decisive enough to convince the adversary to desist. If control of cyber escalation is lost, major damage could be inflicted on the United States and its allies. To a degree, this risk can be reduced by preferential defenses aimed at thoroughly safeguarding critical military and governmental networks and by building redundancy into other important networks whose temporary loss could be a calamity. Even so, taking steps such as offensive countermeasures and otherwise holding enemy targets at risk to discourage adversaries from escalating seems likely to be critically important. While no rules exist that guide cyber escalation, a balance will need to be continually struck between responding too lightly, in ways that do not persuade the enemy to desist, and responding too harshly, such as with a massive U.S. retaliation that might provoke a similar counterstrike. U.S. responses, including military responses, might take place in the cyber realm or outside it. The United States will need to learn how to wage cyber conflicts that are strongly affected by escalation dynamics and by the need to preserve deterrence in settings short of all-out war.

Achieving Extended Cyber Deterrence

A final thorny issue is determining how to achieve extended cyber deterrence coverage of allies, and how to deal with other third parties that might be menaced by cyber attacks. Adversaries might choose to attack U.S. allies in Europe and Asia either to coerce them into altering their foreign policies or to exert indirect pressure on the United States to modify its policies. To reduce this risk while preserving alliance cohesion, extended deterrence coverage of these allies, as well as a measure of protection for other friendly countries, may well become an important priority for a U.S. cyber deterrence strategy. Whether this goal can be achieved, and how it can best be pursued, are crucial questions. What types of U.S. commitments might become necessary? Apart from calling for closer multilateral collaboration, answering these questions is not easy, but further research, analysis, and thinking will help produce answers, just as they helped forge extended nuclear deterrence coverage during the Cold War.

Toward a Spectrum of Cyber Deterrence Options

A cyber deterrence strategy is needed because the United States, its military forces, and its allies are vulnerable to major attacks against information networks. Such a strategy should employ a general model or framework from which tailored actions can be created in response to differing threats, situations, and U.S. objectives. As it assesses the need for a cyber deterrence strategy, the United States has a range of options. A limited cyber deterrence strategy would rely mainly on security and defensive measures to achieve its goals, seeking only a gradual, evolutionary improvement in its offensive capabilities. This would be the least demanding and easiest to execute but offers the lowest promise of success. A more ambitious strategy would make robust use of both defenses and offenses and would seek major, rapid improvements in its offensive capabilities. This option is more demanding and harder to execute but could offer better results by combining emphasis on defensive and offensive capabilities. A highly ambitious strategy would not only strengthen U.S. capabilities quickly, but also pursue major improvements in integrated, collaborative planning with allies and partners. This option would be the most demanding and hardest to execute, especially because mobilizing broad international collaboration would be difficult, but it would offer the biggest payoffs because it involves greater U.S. collaboration with allies and partners.

Deciding which of these options to choose requires an appraisal of desirability and feasibility: what the emerging strategic situation mandates, which of the options does the best job of producing an effective strategy, and what the traffic will bear in terms of political consensus and budgetary affordability.

The United States cannot afford to risk drift in this arena. The alternative to a thoughtfully crafted strategy of deterrence is growing vulnerability of America's vital information networks. By contrast, the potential payoff of a well-conceived cyber deterrence strategy is considerably greater security than exists today.

Part IV

Cyberpower: Information

CHAPTER 14

Cyber Influence and International Security

Franklin D. Kramer and Larry K. Wentz

CYBER INFLUENCE is an ongoing source of power in the international security arena. Although the United States has an enormous cyber information capacity, its cyber influence is not proportional to that capacity. Impediments to American cyber influence include the vastness and complexity of the international information environment, multiplicity of cultures and differing audiences to which communications must be addressed, extensiveness and significance of contending or alternative messages, and complexity and importance of using appropriate influential messengers and message mechanisms.

Enhancing the influence of the United States in cyberspace will require a multifaceted strategy that differentiates the circumstances of the messages, key places of delivery, and sophistication with which messages are created and delivered, with particular focus on channels and messengers. To improve in these areas, the United States must concentrate on actions that include discerning the nature of the audiences, societies, and cultures into which messages will be delivered; increasing the number of experts in geographic and cultural arenas, particularly in languages; augmenting resources for overall strategic communications and cyber influence efforts; encouraging long-term communications and cyber influence efforts along with short-term responses; and understanding that successful strategic communications and cyber influence operations cannot be achieved by the United States acting on its own—allies and partners are needed both to shape our messages and to support theirs.

The United States is an information superpower, estimated to produce annually about 40 percent of the world's new, stored information and a similar share of telecommunications.[1] U.S. dominance in information production might be expected to create commensurate influence, yet numerous opinion surveys show that approval of the United States is declining almost everywhere, as is American influence. In 2006, the Pew Global Attitudes Project found that "America's global image has again slipped" and that in only 4 of 14 countries surveyed did the United States have at least a 50 percent favorable rating, as compared to 7 of 10 in 1999–2000.[2] A British Broadcasting Corporation (BBC) poll of some 26,000 people in 24 countries (including the United States) published in 2007 likewise confirmed that the "global perception of the U.S. continues to decline," with the populace of only 3 of the 24 countries surveyed saying the United States had a mainly positive impact on world affairs.[3] The mismatch between U.S. information capabilities and the actuality of U.S. influence is obvious.

This chapter analyzes the factors that affect the generation of influence through cyber capabilities in the international security arena. For the United States to be more effective, a three-part cyber strategy must be developed that combines:

- psychological and marketing expertise in the application of the principles of influence
- domain expertise in the geographic, cultural, linguistic, and other arenas where the principles are to be applied
- technical and management expertise in the use of cyber capabilities and tactics.

Even with such capacities, however, U.S. cyber influence will be affected by numerous factors, including the nature of the information environment, the multiplicity of entities undertaking communications, the actions and policies of the relevant parties (including competing communications strategies of our adversaries), and the impact of culture, belief, and emotion.

Cyberspace Considerations

Cyberspace is "an operational domain characterized by the use of electronics and the electromagnetic spectrum to create, store, modify, and exchange information via networked information systems and associated physical infrastructures."[4] In cyberspace, information communications technologies are used to create and transmit information and thereby generate influence. The capacities of the different technologies overlap, especially as technological convergence continues through ever-greater reliance on digitization, computers, and the

Internet. A look at the technologies reveals both their overlapping natures and their particular virtues.

Classic telecommunications were built on voice-grade, circuit-switched "plain old telephone service," which was oriented to end-to-end connection. Many of these features are now found in or transmitted by wireless platforms and capabilities, such as cell phones, WiFi and WiMax, faxes, smart phones (such as BlackBerry and Treo), text messaging, and voice over Internet protocol. The dominant feature of the phone is speed of communication and, in its newer versions, a close approximation to "anywhere/anytime" contact.

Radio and television are top-down, one-way, broadcast communicators, divided among local, regional, and national systems and increasingly available on a continuous, often global basis through the use of satellite, cable, and streaming audio and video via the Internet. The dominant feature of radio and television is the capability to reach broadly over an area and, accordingly, provide information simultaneously to a very large audience.[5]

The Internet can be a one- or two-way (or more) channel that can have targeted or broad reach. It can create focused groups, establish social networks, engage large populations, and allow for organization across borders. It tends to be a bottom-up, interactive, and instantaneous means of communicating. Its characteristics include "viral distribution" (the quick movement from one or a core to many through the capacity of message recipients to become message distributors), a capacity to search for and provide useful information for action and/or education, and an ability to create influence through the communications empowerment of individuals or groups.

Telecommunications, radio and television, and the Internet have all been enhanced by digitization and the creation of capacities for multiple sources of information—no longer limited to professionals—from cameras, camcorders, iPods, compact discs, digital video discs, and video and audio tapes. User-generated content—and a sort of collective intelligence—has become one of the dynamic and influential aspects of cyberspace via capabilities such as blogs and Wiki sites.[6]

In sum, the ability to use cyber capabilities to communicate in the modern world is substantial and increasing, but communication does not necessarily translate into influence.

From Communication to Influence

Translating communication into influence, particularly in the international arena, requires a full understanding of the factors that bear on the reception and interpretation of the message.

Complex Environment

The international information environment is vast and complex. Multiple messages are being sent and received by multiple entities, simultaneously and generally in an uncoordinated fashion. Even apart from the Internet, in the United States alone, each day there are more than 12 billion display and 184 billion classified advertising messages from newspapers; 6 billion messages from magazines; 2.6 million commercial (radio) messages; 330,000 television commercials; and 40 million direct mail pieces.[7]

Worldwide, in 2002, 18 exabytes (10^{18} bytes) of new information were produced through electronic channels (telephone, radio, television, Internet),[8] and 5 exabytes of new information were produced by print, film, magnetic, and optical storage media.[9] This translates to 800 megabytes of recorded information produced globally per person in 2002.[10] Worldwide, an estimated 25 billion emails per day were sent in 2006—not including spam messages, which account for 60 percent of all email.[11]

Of course, bytes are not the only or the best way to measure the information flow. Video generates more bytes than text; all of Wikipedia will fit on a 100-gigabyte hard drive, which would store less than one day's worth of one channel of broadcast-quality TV programming. Another indicator of information flow is the more than 1.2 billion landline telephones and 2.1 billion cell phones that are in use worldwide.[12] Over 1 billion people (18.9 percent of the world's population) use the Internet.[13] From 2000 to 2007, Internet use jumped 244.7 percent globally, with the greatest percentage increases seen in Africa (874.6 percent) and the Middle East (920.2 percent).[14] More than 50 million blogs are maintained worldwide, a number that has doubled every 6 months for the past 3 years.[15]

As the foregoing suggests, the world is awash in information and means of communication, and the market for attention is highly complicated and competitive. The actors are diverse, ranging from individuals to private entities of all types to governments to supranational entities. The topics include economic, social, governmental, and all forms of human intercourse. Information overload and "noise" are serious problems that contribute to the masking of messages.

Information is continually circulating. Multiple perspectives are regularly presented, and access can be limited in certain areas by, for example, government action. In such an arena, even so substantial an entity as the U.S. Government is only one player. The information environment is not one in which "information dominance" or "information superiority"—in the sense of overwhelming the other players—is likely to be achieved.[16] "Information effectiveness," on the other hand, is achievable.

Target-side Analysis

Communication influence is, of course, intended to affect a target or targets, whether one person or many, similar or divergent. But creating that influence requires much more than aiming communication at targets. Some key factors are considered below.

First, and most importantly, "Communication cannot be conceptualized as *transmission*. . . . The sense people make of . . . messages is never limited to what sources intend and is always enriched by the realities people bring to bear."[17] So instead of a target or an audience, the other party should be considered an active participant. Hence, understanding the target participants is critical to creating the influence the communicator seeks to achieve.

Communicating effectively in the international arena is more difficult than doing so in a familiar culture. Understanding values and belief structures, truly comprehending the language, and being knowledgeable about the information culture are key factors. One has a good feel for one's own culture, but it takes work to achieve a similar feel for another culture. For example, is the culture one where focus on the individual is the best approach, or is the group or the family more of the key influence mechanism? What is the power of the rumor mill and informal networking? What perceptions and biases should be anticipated? All these and many other cultural factors affect the influence of an international message.

Even though culture is a good starting point in thinking about how to create influence, culture is not everything. Interest issues—the political, social, and economic imperatives—also will have huge impact. So, too, will the role of the sources of influence in the society, including key individuals, trusted advisors, and influence networks.[18] The mindset and behavior of such individuals and networks will have significant impact on the interpretation of the message and, hence, on its influence.

In short, the communicator's problem is how to address simultaneously multiple communication partners. This problem is familiar in the context of U.S. political campaigns, where the communicators must reach the political base, the swing vote/neutrals, and the opposition, as well as pundits—all at the same time. This problem is heightened in an international context. In the targeted nation or nations, there will be government officials; other key leaders, both political and private (for example, business and nongovernmental groups); and the population at large, which likely will be divided along racial, cultural, religious, and other lines. In addition, for many international messages, and certainly for the most important, other nations will be interested. That "group," of course, is also likely to be highly divergent, including friends and potential allies, neutrals, and potential or actual enemies. Moreover, the message we deliver to others also will be delivered to ourselves—to the affected portion of the government, the Congress, and the population at large.

Finally, whether the target partners are influenced by the message will be significantly affected by the fact that "research has shown that people inform themselves primarily at moments of need."[19] This has been found to be true in the context of American commercial and domestic political messaging campaigns. The issue of need requires evaluation in the context of an international geopolitical influence effort. Determining the need for information—and therefore the basis for influence—in a different society brings the communicator back to the importance of understanding that society, culture, interests, and entities.

Message Delivery

Understanding the target participants is only part of the communicator's challenge. A second key aspect is the delivery side of messaging: How are the contents of the message chosen? How are the delivery means chosen? How are the messengers chosen?

With respect to content, the most important understanding the communicator must achieve is that what he says is only part of the content. Already noted is the fact that the recipient will participate in shaping the message. Also of crucial importance, however, is what might be called the "message-facts relationship." In speaking of the importance of information as a part of counterinsurgency warfare, David Galula, in his classic book on the subject, points out that "facts speak louder than words"; the counterinsurgent is "judged on what he does, not on what he says"; and "nothing could be worse than promising reforms and being unwilling or unable to implement them."[20]

Counterinsurgency is far from the only circumstance in which international messaging will be undertaken. The point, however, is universal: words can only go so far in the face of real-world evidence that undercuts them or is otherwise more influential.

One important aspect of which the communicator must be aware is the nonverbal message, which often is more influential than the verbal message. As an illustration, Colonel Ralph Hallenback, USA (Ret.), who operated in Iraq as a Coalition Provisional Authority (CPA) civilian, observed, "There has been much subsequent handwringing about CPA's lack of strategic communication with the Iraqi people. [But] a lot of people had no electricity but could look across the river and see the CPA all lit up at night. And that was the way we really communicated."[21] If the nonverbal message is not considered, unintended consequences may overwhelm the intended impact of the message.

Assuming that the message content will not be overwhelmed by the message context, the message must still be chosen to have the desired effect, given the nature of the target audience and the environment. Messages can be delivered directly or indirectly, and sometimes an indirect message may be more effective than a direct one. What might be considered a logical argument may have limited impact because the target participants have strongly held positions for cultural, emotional, or psychological reasons. For example, a campaign for the rule of law may be seen as undercutting the position of elders in a tribal society.

Few new messages have immediate impact, and the role of repetition must be considered—as must the role of timing and whether the message will fill an information need. Direct, hard-hitting confrontational messages also may be appropriate, depending on the results sought. But some messages will not work at all in some environments, although the desired effects may be achievable with a different message.

Different means of delivering messages will achieve different results. Cell phones were the great factor in Ukraine's Orange Revolution. User-generated content such as blogs and digital pictures have had great impact, most notoriously in the Abu Ghraib scandal. Television has had a decided impact on the world's view of the ongoing conflict in Iraq. Such cyber mechanisms, of course, can be complemented or outrun by simple word of mouth—rumor probably is the greatest factor in the views held by many in the Arab world as to who was responsible for the 9/11 attacks. For example, there is continued doubt in the Arab community that Muslims were involved, even after the release of the video in which Osama bin Laden takes credit for the attacks and discusses the hijackers' lack of knowledge of their suicide mission. The effective communicator will analyze the full spectrum of potential message arenas from word-of-mouth discussions, print media, cell and telephone capacities, data networks (including portals and messaging), and radio, television, and movies—all of which are complementary, and many of which are converging because of technological advances.

Different delivery means also may imply different messengers, and the choice of messenger is surely important, as pointed out by Malcolm Gladwell.[22] A messenger may appeal to an audience for many reasons ranging from trust and respect to common interest to celebrity "buzz" to fear. The importance of the culturally attuned messenger is implicit in another point made by Galula, who stresses the importance of finding and organizing the "favorable minority."[23] In his analysis, that minority, working with the outside intervening power, has an important capacity to help resolve the insurgency issue. The reasons, of course, include the minority's understanding of the context for the insurgency and the ability to involve the rest of the country in its resolution. The lesson for the international communicator, more generally, is that communications undertaken with the help of knowledgeable, favorable, local messengers will have a greater chance of success,[24] both because third-party communications are often more effective than those of intervening outsiders, and because the knowledgeable local can help make outsiders more effective.

U.S. Cyber Capacities

The U.S. Government uses a variety of mechanisms to create influence in international cyberspace. For example, public affairs offices at the White House, the Department of State, the U.S. Agency for International Development (USAID), and the Department of Defense (DOD) all use television and radio appearances and maintain Web sites to deliver messages. The information is immediately available worldwide, generally circulated without charge by private media, and increasingly available for review on the Internet. The government's public affairs capacity is enhanced by numerous additional offices and multiple sites. Every Embassy has a public affairs activity, as do numerous DOD commands, and there are many Internet capabilities.

In addition to public affairs, the United States undertakes formal public diplomacy led by the Undersecretary of State for Public Diplomacy. The Public Diplomacy office emails fact sheets, news, event announcements, and electronic journals, and State Department experts are even made available electronically. Embassies also use cyber means, and Embassy Web sites present substantive material.

A third area of U.S. cyber capability is the Broadcasting Board of Governors (BBG).[25] Since October 1, 1999, the BBG has been the "independent federal agency responsible for all U.S. government and government sponsored, non-military, international broadcasting."[26] According to the BBG:

> every week, more than 100 million listeners, viewers, and internet users around the world turn-on, tune-in, and log-on to U.S. international broadcasting programs. . . . Day-to-day broadcasting activities are carried out by individual BBG international broadcasters: the Voice of America (VOA), Alhurra [television], Radio Sawa, Radio Farda, Radio Free Europe/Radio Liberty (RFE/RL), Radio Free Asia (RFA), and Radio and TV Martí, with the assistance of the International Broadcasting Bureau (IBB).[27]

A fourth use of cyber capabilities by the U.S. Government is what DOD calls *information operations*, which include "electronic warfare, computer network operations, psychological operations, military deception, and operations security, in concert with specified supporting and related capabilities."[28] A key function of information operations is "influencing the way people receive, process, interpret, and use data, information, and knowledge."[29]

DOD also makes good use of cyber capabilities to create close partnerships with other countries as part of an overall information campaign. The Partnership for Peace Information Management System was established by DOD in 1996 to support the North Atlantic Treaty Organization's (NATO's) Partnership for Peace members and still seeks to "facilitate collaboration and strengthen relationships in the Euro-Atlantic and Partnership for Peace community."[30]

The Asia-Pacific Area Network was created in 1998. Hosted by U.S. Pacific Command, it is a "World Wide Web portal offering information resources and a collaborative planning environment as a means to greater defense interaction, confidence-building, and enhanced security cooperation in the Asia-Pacific Region."[31] DOD also uses its cyber capacity to plan, support, and conduct exercises on line to work with and influence others.[32]

As the foregoing suggests, the U.S. Government makes extensive use of cyber capacities, particularly the Internet. At the State Department, for example, the USInfo site presents a large amount of information on a daily basis, not only in English, but also in Spanish, French, Russian, Chinese, Arabic, and Persian. State also runs ejournalUSA, which has articles in five thematic areas—Economic Perspectives, Global Issues, Issues of Democracy, Society and Values, and Foreign Policy Agenda—and is available in the same seven languages, plus Portuguese. DOD sponsors a number of information and online news Web sites. Some sites, such as ones maintained by U.S. Central Command, produce information relevant to some of the most difficult issues, particularly the war in Iraq. Others, such as the Southeast European Times (produced in nine languages) and Magharebia (produced in three languages), provide "regional news," and "in-depth analysis" for their respective areas.[33] DOD networks also add to the government cyber use.

Creating a more effective U.S. Government use of cyberspace will involve more than simply getting more information online. To provide the right information at the right time and place to help achieve the desired effect, the government needs a comprehensive strategy and plan to focus on the target audience, including the audience's information culture and needs.

Issues for Cyber Effectiveness

As a general proposition, U.S. Government cyber communications focus on a "mass messaging" approach, seeking to enhance and increase information flow. Mass messages have an important function. It is a very big world, and the government has interests all around it. Simple practicality calls for the use of mass messages.

The downside of mass messages is that they are in transmission mode. As previously discussed, however, virtually no communication is received without the audience "being involved in creating meanings." Moreover, the meanings created will importantly reflect the target's culture. Thus, the issue that arises for the United States is what is often described as *segmentation*, dividing the mass audience to focus on specific receiver needs. Creating segmentation in a real world of multiple, overlapping audiences is a difficult, though not impossible, proposition.

It is not likely that the government will abandon the mass messaging approach. The White House Web site, the daily State Department Washington briefing, and numerous similar activities will continue. Segmentation, and a focus on the culture of less than an "all-world" mass audience, will need to be done by different message channels. One obvious way to segment messages would be through the Embassy posts. There, however, the Government Accountability Office (GAO) has found government performance deficient, stating that posts did a "poor job of answering [the] basic question of whether to direct . . . communications efforts at a mass audience or opinion leaders."[34]

A second problem for creating effective messages arises from what can be called the "problem of multiplicity," almost always an issue for U.S. Government strategic messaging. For any communicator working on behalf of the government, it is important to recognize that the United States has multiple goals and operates in a very complex world. The profusion of messages that the government generates reduces its capacity to have a single, focused message on any particular topic.

A multiplicity of messages follows from a multiplicity of policy, and a multiplicity of policy means that, sometimes, policies must be prioritized, and even apparently inconsistent policies must be followed. Multiple policy objectives can create difficulties for consistent messaging. To take two obvious examples, the United States seeks good relations with both Japan and China. Because these two countries sometimes are at odds, positive messages to one can be seen as negative messages to the other. A similar messaging dilemma has occurred in the context of the Middle East peace process.

It may be possible to help resolve the problem of multiplicity of messages by focusing on a regional or country basis. As a real-world matter, however, the GAO found that U.S. Embassies "did not have a core message or theme to direct their communications efforts." In fact, of the posts reviewed by GAO, none had a detailed communications plan.[35] This absence of thematic messaging is evident in the headline links of Web pages of American Embassies. The entries are perfectly reasonable topics for a Web page, but the pages lack thematic consistency and present very different kinds of messages simultaneously. Part of the reason is that the Embassies are undertaking both long- and short-term messaging. Long-term efforts seek to build credibility and trust sufficient to sustain dialogue even amidst policy disputes. The focus is values-driven, and the expectation is that objective presentation of information will ultimately put the United States in a favorable light. This can be a reasonable function for mass messaging approaches. By contrast, short-term messaging is advocacy- and event-driven and seeks to build support for discrete U.S. policies. It is very unlikely, given the various audiences, values, interests, and actions relevant to a policy, that mass messaging will regularly produce short-term effects. A more tailored approach will be important.

Evaluating U.S. Cyber Influence Effectiveness

U.S. status as an information superpower has not translated to international influence. Both the Pew poll published in mid-2006 and the BBC poll published in January 2007 underscore the declining international perception of the United States. The United States currently has this low standing despite a variety of efforts to improve its image through regular use of the Internet and other communications means to make its points.

The problems associated with mass messaging, multiplicity of messages, and lack of core themes were discussed above. Other impediments to influence were addressed 60 years ago in the seminal research article, "Some Reasons Why Information Campaigns Fail."[36] To understand better how to "promote the free flow of ideas by word and image" on a worldwide basis, the authors focused on the "psychological barriers to the free flow of ideas." Based on the research, they reached some important conclusions.

First, there "exists a hard core of chronic 'know-nothings'"—persons who have little information about events. The study points out that "there is something about the uninformed which makes them harder to reach, no matter the level or nature of information."

Second, "interested people acquire the most information." Noting that "motivation" to acquire information is key, the study also recognizes that large groups in a population will have little or no interest and that "such groups constitute a special problem which cannot be solved simply by 'increasing the flow of information.'"

Third, the study found that "people seek information congenial to prior attitudes."[37] They also "avoid exposure to information which is not congenial."[38] The study's important conclusion is that "merely 'increasing the flow' is not enough, if the information continues to 'flow' in the direction of those already on your side."

The fourth conclusion was that:

> people interpret the same information differently. . . . It is . . . false to assume that exposure, once achieved, results in a uniform interpretation and retention of the material. . . . It has been consistently demonstrated that a person's perception and memory of materials shown to him are often distorted by his wishes, motives, and attitudes. . . . Exposure in itself is not always sufficient. People will interpret the information in different ways, according to their prior attitudes.

Fifth, and perhaps most importantly, "information does not necessarily change attitudes":

The principle behind all information campaigns is that disseminated information will alter attitudes or conduct. There is abundant evidence in all fields, of course, that informed people actually do react differently to a problem than uninformed people do. But it is naïve to suppose that information always affects attitudes, or that it affects all attitudes equally. The general principle needs serious qualification. There is evidence . . . that individuals, once they are exposed to information, change their views differentially, each in the light of his own prior attitude.

Sixth, and in light of the foregoing, the authors concluded that the "above findings indicate clearly that those responsible for information campaigns cannot rely simply on 'increasing the flow' to spread information effectively."

The implications of these conclusions for the effectiveness of U.S. cyber influence are substantial. Information will tend to be accepted and understood in light of prior attitudes; those already supportive of U.S. positions will be most likely to accept information from the United States. Some groups simply will not accept information. If it is important to change their attitudes, more than a direct information approach will be necessary. Determining how to change the positions of those in opposition is more difficult, since these people may interpret the information provided quite differently than intended, according to their prior attitudes. Yet even the best information will not necessarily change attitudes or positions. Information flow is important, but as the authors state, "those responsible for information campaigns cannot rely simply on 'increasing the flow' to spread information effectively."

Enhancing U.S. Cyber Influence

Enhancing the influence of the United States in cyberspace will require a multifaceted strategy that differentiates the circumstances of the message, the key places of delivery, and the sophistication with which the message is created and delivered, with particular focus on channels and messengers.

A useful starting point is to distinguish among three different analytic circumstances. The first might be called the *general condition* under which the United States will have a great many messages on a great many topics that it is regularly delivering. Those messages are normally delivered by the public affairs functions of the government, as exemplified by the State Department spokesperson's briefings. Even though the messages are focused on international topics, quite often the intended first recipient of the message is the American public. For example, at a State Department briefing, numerous U.S. media entities will be present, and they will pass on the message to the American public. Of course, international media are also present, and the messages also will be presented internationally—but the message will always be intended to make sense to the American public.

The key conclusion from this analysis is that public affairs messaging, particularly from the United States, is not a place where tailoring for a non-U.S. audience is easily undertaken. Messages delivered in American English will have a "made in America" tenor. This is not a "bad" result; in fact, it is a "good" result because the American people should have a full understanding of government policy. But it does mean that public affairs undertaken from the United States cannot easily take account of the multiple factors that make international messaging difficult.

Often, in discussions of the effectiveness of U.S. international messaging, there are suggestions that one strategic message should be undertaken top to bottom—so to speak, from the President to the junior foreign service officer and the Army private. But Presidential addresses on international matters are almost always, first and foremost, statements to the American people. Such statements obviously will be the substantive heart of the international message. But they will not be tailored to the international audience. For Presidential addresses and for building on public affairs messages in general, additional international messaging will be necessary for, among other things, reaching the uninformed, those who do not already agree with the substance of the message, and those whose prior attitudes will affect how they understand the message; being part of an influence effort to affect the views of those who will not change their minds simply because of exposure; and generating effective communication with key leaders and organizations.

The second circumstance is what might be called the *focused, non-wartime problem*. Some examples of topics are global warming, responding to radical militant Islam, and promoting free trade in Asia. These problems are focused in that they need to be considered. They are non-wartime in the sense that the violent use of force is not ongoing (or at least not as a major factor). The assumption is that, in a war, the impact of combat generally will overwhelm the use of words.

Effective cyber influence in a focused, non-wartime problem requires taking account of numerous considerations and constraints. The complexity of the environment and the numerous messages can be somewhat simplified because of the focus on particular messages. Consider, for example, an international influence campaign on global warming. A good first step would be for the United States to create an "international map" of individuals and entities important to influence. Not all the world is critical in the same way on every issue. Not only will the "mavens, connectors, and salesmen," to use Gladwell's terminology, be different, but so will the opposition affected by prior attitudes and/or ignorance whose concurrence with U.S. views will be necessary or valuable.

With this map in hand, a cyber influence campaign can be planned. The next step will be to understand the culture in which influence is sought—how will those who get messages view and respond to them? In thinking through message presentation, some questions can be key (and the particular culture may make others important). The following are examples:

- What is the desired effect?
- Should focus be on the individual, or is the group (for example, the family) more the key influence mechanism?
- Will negative messaging work?
- What is the role of religion, and how does that affect messaging?
- What is the meaning of success (for example, is it better for an individual to stand out or to support another)?
- How do you pretest messages and determine what has been successful?
- Who is the correct messenger? Would a third party be more effective?

Likewise, the interests and nature of key entities must be considered. How does the U.S. message, if adopted, affect the political, social, and economic imperatives of the target audience? Who are the important sources of influence in the society, including key individuals and trusted advisors and influence networks? Galula's point about building on the favorable minority surely must be considered, as must Gladwell's point about key influencers.

None of the foregoing can be undertaken effectively unless experts in the geographic and cultural areas where influence is sought (including some experts with a deep understanding of the language) are heavily involved in the development of the message. Those experts can help build the map and describe the culture and relevant interests, as well as the individuals and entities of influence.

Such domain expertise is necessary but not sufficient for effective cyber influence. Understanding the psychological and marketing issues inherent in influence campaigns is also crucial. The insights of "Some Reasons Why Information Campaigns Fail" are good examples of the psychology behind an influence campaign. Marketing expertise likewise should be understood. These matters, however, raise the crucial factor of intercultural expertise. What is true in the United States in terms of psychology and marketing may not be true in another culture. It is the rare person who will combine cultural and geopolitical expertise with psychological and marketing expertise. An interdisciplinary team is needed.

The interdisciplinary team also will need a member with a third expertise, namely, in the use of cyber techniques—how to make effective use of radio and TV, what can be accomplished by cell phone messaging, how to use the Internet.

In the international context, this type of expertise will necessarily have to be combined with cultural, language, and psychological expertise to be effective. As the team generates its approach, it also will need to consider how cyber and noncyber activities interact.

A final point on the focused, non-wartime message is that the concept of focus deserves much more attention. If everything is equally important, it is very hard to give focus. But as the discussion of the Embassy Web sites suggests, the United States has made few attempts to focus its messages in the international arena. In fact, that is the point of the GAO study, which stated that U.S. Embassies "did not have a core message or theme to direct their communications efforts." Of the posts reviewed, none had a detailed communications plan.

The State Department Office of Public Diplomacy has recognized the importance of focus and has identified three key themes: support the President's Freedom Agenda with a positive image of hope, isolate and marginalize extremists, and promote understanding regarding shared values and common interests between Americans and peoples of different countries, cultures, and faiths.[39] If these are to be the key themes, it will be important not only for a Washington office to assert them, but also for posts abroad to do so. It is also important to ask *when and where the themes are relevant.* In some situations, the themes, though most important to Washington and presumably to a number of other countries, may not be the best messages for some target countries. The need to decide the key themes, and when and where to implement them, leads to a requirement for a strategic plan. As the GAO study indicates, such plans are required. For the most part, they are not undertaken. That is a crucial failing—and until it is corrected, it is unlikely that U.S. influence campaigns, including cyber influence campaigns, will become more effective.

The last analytic circumstance to be considered is cyber influence in the *wartime situation,* that is, where the use of violence is a major consideration. The ongoing situations in Iraq and Afghanistan are examples, as is the introduction of the military into so-called stability operations (including counterinsurgency, peace enforcement, and peacekeeping).

Military involvement does not mean that influence is not a critical factor. Clausewitz's observation that war is a continuation of politics by other means emphasized the importance of the intended political outcome over the particular means employed to achieve it. In a wartime situation, a dominant factor in generating influence will be the use or threat of violence. The impact of the normal influence channels, including cyber influence, will be relatively less because the impact of violence will be so great. However, the generation of cyber influence is still applicable, though more complex. A domain expertise in three arenas—geographic and cultural, psychological and marketing, and cyber technical, including planners and implementers—is still needed. But in addition, the interface with the military must be considered. In this regard, several points deserve consideration.

First, the public affairs efforts of the U.S. Government are going to continue in a wartime situation. Those efforts, first and foremost, will be directed toward providing information to the American public. There is no point in asking for such messages to be focused on the theater of operations because, for the most part, that will not happen.[40] What can happen, however, is for the public affairs personnel to be highly aware of the theater requirements and, at a minimum, communicate and, when possible, coordinate messages. As an example, in the Kosovo campaign undertaken under NATO auspices, both interagency and international communications groups undertook such efforts.

Second, the three types of expertise—geographic and cultural, psychological and marketing, and cyber technical—necessary for effective cyber communications need to be organized and coordinated with the military. To accomplish this, two fundamental shortcomings of the current system must be overcome.

The first shortcoming is that the necessary expertise does not exist in sufficient capacity or at high enough levels in either the State Department or DOD. Achieving the necessary level of capacity and expertise can involve a combination of permanent personnel, reserve personnel, and contractors—but the first step is recognizing that we are not even remotely close to the level of expertise we need.

The second shortcoming is that we do not make good use of the capacities we do have. In a wartime situation, the military undertakes to do the best it can in terms of influence operations. A very impressive example is set forth by Colonel Ralph Baker, USA, in his discussion of how he used information operations as one of his "vital tools" to "favorably influence the perceptions of the Iraqi population" in his area of operations.[41] But Baker's story is one of improvisation, not of a strategic campaign effort. As he says, the "traditional tools in my military kit bag were insufficient to successfully compete" in the influence environment.

Unfortunately, it is not only the lone brigade commander who lacks the tools. The State Department generally is not an effective player in influence operations in the theater situation, and DOD does not have adequate theater capacity—or, as Baker makes clear, tactical capability.[42] Contractors have been used, but the results on the whole have not been satisfactory. For example, it is generally agreed that, after the end of major combat operations in Iraq in 2003, it took far too long to generate a U.S.-supported television capability. Achieving better results will require a more coordinated, effective, interagency approach. Up to now, the United States has not been able to accomplish that, even though it is engaged in several wartime situations.

The final point is that even though violence or the threat of violence has a major influence impact, there is also an extremely important role in influencing target populations as to what the impact of violence should mean to them. As an example, in the Israeli-Hizballah conflict in 2006, both sides mounted intensive influence campaigns designed to show they were winning and that they deserved the support of several audiences—their own people, allies, potential intervening states, sympathetic populations and countries, and the world at large. Whenever war will not be fought to a conclusion of unconditional surrender or destruction (and perhaps even then), the method and consequences of conflict termination will be affected by more than one combatant. Hence, influencing the perceptions and consequent actions of relevant target audiences is of greatest importance to the combatants.

Conclusion

Cyber influence is an ongoing source of power in the international security arena. Although the United States has an enormous cyber information capacity, it has less cyber influence than might be desirable. While neither cyber nor any other influence campaign can provide magical results, an effective use of cyber capabilities can do much. A considered approach that recognizes the context in which cyber capabilities will be used; understands the principles of making influence campaigns effective; and provides personnel expertise in the technical management of cyber capabilities, in the domains—particularly cultural and geographic—where they will be applied, and in psychological and marketing expertise relevant to the use of cyber capabilities, should be an important component of international security activities for the United States.

In light of the foregoing, the following actions are offered for consideration as possible ways to help make U.S. cyber influence more effective in the international security arena.

First, and perhaps most important, greater focus must be placed on the nature of audiences and of the societies and cultures into which cyber-transmitted messages will be delivered. In the first instance, the intended recipients of messages need to be clear. For example, in the context of a counterterror effort, there likely will be a difference among messages to populations at large—those who do not support terrorists, those who are terrorist sympathizers, those who are active supporters of terrorists, and those who are terrorists. Moreover, those varying audiences might well be reached by different types of communications—for example, television for broader audiences and Web sites for potential terrorist recruits. In this context of differentiated messaging, a further important consideration needs to be an understanding of the types of persons who have influence with the message recipients and the types of contexts in which that influence will be most effective.

Second, it will be necessary to increase the number of experts in geographic, cultural, and linguistic arenas. Such expertise can help build a societal/cultural map of influencers, key communications nodes, and cultural communications patterns to guide strategic communications and influence operations. Added to these cultural experts should be experts in psychology and marketing who can help generate messages and ensure that communications are effective. Finally, experts are needed in the use of television, radio, the Internet, and cell phones. In short, an interdisciplinary approach is required.

Third, leaders must realize that while there may be a consistent base message, that message will be presented in multiple theaters. These areas will differ significantly, and to be effective, messaging will likewise differ. For example, the society, culture, and influential persons in Indonesia are significantly different from those in Pakistan, and both are significantly different from those in Egypt. It is also worth noting that the Internet has created coherent, nongeographic communities. Numerous studies and reports document the Internet's effectiveness in transmitting messages that sympathize with, give support to, and recruit for terrorist efforts. The Internet must be a focused arena for strategic communications and influence operations.

Fourth, greater resources must be given to overall strategic communications and influence efforts. For example, expanding the capacities of the Broadcasting Board of Governors, Embassies, and other outlets of the State Department would be enormously valuable. As noted, the Internet is a key mechanism. The State Department runs Web sites, but a broader and more multifaceted Internet strategy—both globally and regionally—would be highly desirable. The GAO has found that while Embassy posts are supposed to have a strategic communications plan, they are generally ineffective and lack focus and resources.[43] Enhancing U.S. Government capabilities is a critical requirement.

Fifth, long-term communication efforts must be encouraged along with short-term responses. It is possible to change attitudes over time. As an example, consider the American attitude toward smoking, which has transformed significantly over the last 30 years. In the battle of ideas, the U.S. Government is seeking a long-term change—and so there is a need to adopt long-term policies. Transmitting messages over DOD Web sites and the Web sites Southeast European Times and Magharebia, which provide news, analysis, and information, is a productive, long-term approach that will not affect attitudes immediately but can have significant consequences over time.

Sixth, we must fully appreciate that facts speak louder than words. Some policies generate significant opposition, and strategic communications and influence operations are not panaceas that can overcome all real-world actions.

In the earliest planning stages, the communications consequences of actions must be discussed. In conflicts such as those in Iraq and Afghanistan, the impact of violent activities will significantly change the worldviews of not only those immediately impacted but also those who are indirectly affected and those to whom those impacts are communicated. Every battle commander in these irregular wars soon finds out that the communications battle is critical—because the center of gravity for success is the population. But all too often, our commanders have to learn this on the ground. Especially in this globalized world of instant communications, tactical actions can have strategic consequences. Cyberspace is a creative and cultural commons defined by information, perception, cognition, and belief, and it is becoming the preeminent domain of political victory or defeat. Increased support for training and resources for cyber-enabled communications will be critical elements of effective counterinsurgency and stability operations. As Galula argued, communication—to one's supporters, to the population at large, and to the opposition—is of crucial importance. The government needs resources and training for our people on these issues, and these must be undertaken not only by DOD, but also in a joint DOD-State context.

Seventh, the U.S. Government should not expect to be successful at strategic communications and influence operations acting on its own. Rather, it should use an alliance and partnership approach, both to expand capacities and increase effectiveness. In the business world, it would be the rare American company that would seek to enter another country without the guidance and support of local business, whether as partners, joint ventures, or advisors—and often as all three. In military and diplomatic arenas, our allies and partners are recognized as enormous sources of strength. In the strategic communications and influence operations arena, we need to develop those alliances and partnerships, both to shape our own messages and support theirs.

CHAPTER 15

Tactical Influence Operations

Stuart H. Starr

THIS CHAPTER explores the challenges associated with influence operations at the tactical level. It begins with a framework that identifies five key interrelated areas for the analysis of tactical influence operations options. To illustrate the framework, the creative actions taken by Colonel Ralph Baker, USA, in the early days of Operation *Iraqi Freedom* are examined.[1] The framework then looks forward to identify and explore options for enhancing tactical influence operations by exploiting the opportunities offered by advances in cyberspace.[2] The chapter concludes with a brief summary to guide policymakers and identify residual policy issues that warrant further attention.

Framework: A Mission-oriented Approach to Tactical Influence Operations

A useful framework for assessing influence operations is based on the mission-oriented approach to command and control (C^2) assessment,[3] which addresses five interrelated questions (shown in figure 15–1):

- What is the nature of the problem?
- What are you trying to do operationally?
- How are you trying to do it operationally?
- What gaps in the areas of doctrine, organization, training, materiel, leadership and education, personnel, and facilities (DOTMLPF) impede this operation?[4]
- What steps should we take to ameliorate key DOTMLPF gaps?

The mission-oriented approach has been applied to a variety of C² issues. From 1980 to 2000, these included the development of a North Atlantic Treaty Organization C² plan[5] and the derivation of an advanced battlespace information system to support transformation of the force.[6] The focus of those activities was to formulate and link alternative operational objectives to associated materiel needs and plans, including science and technology initiatives. Here, we extend the mission-oriented approach to address the full spectrum of DOTMLPF factors.

Lessons learned from prior applications of the mission-oriented approach are applied to the analyses of tactical influence operations. First, the nature of the problem demands a mix of skills to implement the approach. Thus, we need to tap the insights of high-level decisionmakers, operational personnel at the tactical level, and experts in DOTMLPF. Second, problems of this nature are generally characterized by the "curse of dimensionality," which requires structured techniques for keeping the problem tractable by deconstructing it, for example, by factors such as geography and range of military operations. Third, it has proven useful to apply the framework iteratively in order to identify and address critical issues systematically. Thus, we employ a broad, shallow cut to analyze tactical influence operations in this chapter. Subsequent iterations would

FIGURE 15-1. Mission-oriented Approach

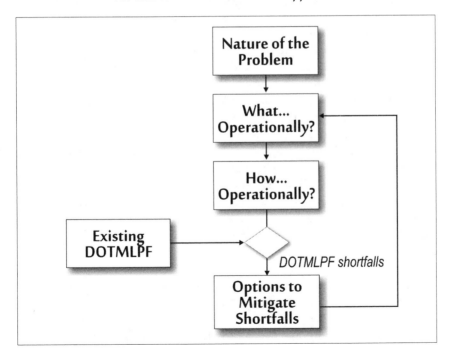

consider narrower, deeper cuts organized around the major policy issues. Fourth, it has proven useful to formulate measures of merit (MOMs) to support analyses of these issues. In this chapter, we identify and discuss key input and output MOMs.

Nature of the Problem

To set the stage for the analysis, we identify and describe the key stakeholders and characterize the environment in which they are interacting. We illustrate the application of the framework with the experiences of Colonel Ralph Baker, USA, in Baghdad.

From 2003 to 2004, COL Baker commanded roughly 5,000 members of the 2^d Brigade Combat Team, part of the 1st Armored Division. The unit was deployed in two of Baghdad's nine major districts, Karkh and Karada, covering an area of 400 square kilometers. This area of responsibility (AOR) is highly varied in sectarian composition, with a mix of Sunni, Shia, and Christian populations, and in the distribution of wealth, with neighborhoods ranging from affluent to poor. Baker found it vital, therefore, to tailor his influence operations to deal with this mix.

Baker divided the indigenous population into three categories. First, he identified those who "would never accept the Coalition's presence," such as insurgents and terrorists. Baker engaged in an "influence operations duel" with that segment of the population. He observed that they were extremely agile at exploiting adverse events for influence purposes. For example, kinetic events such as improvised explosive device (IED) incidents and sniper attacks were deliberately used in order to acquire dramatic video shots for future influence operations activities.[7] Relatively unsophisticated in its employment of influence operations tools in 2003–2004, this segment of the population has since improved its production capabilities considerably to include use of the Internet and mass media. This category has, over the last several years, also become much more complex in its makeup due to a confusing combination of insurgent activity, terrorist actions, civil war, and organized crime.

A second category Baker identified comprised those who "readily accept the Coalition's presence (for example, secular, Western-educated pragmatists)." He viewed them as natural allies who could serve as surrogates to communicate his influence operations message. The deteriorating situation in Iraq, however, subsequently caused many in this category to flee to Jordan, Syria, and other countries.

Baker characterized the third category as undecided: "the vast majority." It is this group that constitutes the "terrain" for tactical influence operations.

Baker identified two major issues with the influence operations campaign that he inherited, from top-down and bottom-up perspectives. First, he noted that higher echelon activities were slow to respond to changes on the ground and were not tailored adequately to selected audiences. This slow, one-size-fits-all approach never fit anyone. From a bottom-up perspective, activities at battalion level and below manifested creativity but were marred by inconsistent and contradictory messages, a problem Baker called "IO [information operations] fratricide."

The nature of the overall problem can also be characterized by employing a simple societal model. In this model, the inputs are the individual levers of national power, including mixes of diplomatic, informational, military, and economic (DIME) actions. The societal outputs can be classified as political, military, economic, social, informational, and infrastructure (PMESII) elements.[8] The following discussion briefly summarizes the PMESII situation that Baker encountered in 2003–2004.

Politically, while COL Baker was in Iraq, the Coalitional Provisional Authority (CPA) was in its early stages, and a national Iraqi government was just emerging. Militarily, security was marginal and on the verge of substantial degradation; at that point, there was a debate as to whether an insurgency was under way. Economically, there was extremely high unemployment; the Iraqi army had been disbanded, and former Ba'athists had been discharged from their jobs. Socially, sectarian schisms were appearing, which subsequently deepened considerably following major acts of violence such as the destruction of the Shi'ite mosque in Samarra. Informationally, a strident tone was emerging from the clergy and segments of the Arab press such as al Jazeera. Perhaps most importantly, the infrastructure was dysfunctional: Coalition commanders had identified the urgent need to improve Iraqi sewage, water, electricity, academic institutions, and trash collection systems.[9] The information communications technology structure was also in disrepair; thus, options to exploit cyberspace to support influence operations were not readily available (an issue further discussed below).

Operational Goals

An operational goal often quoted during the Vietnam War was "to win the hearts and minds" of the population. In Iraq, however, COL Baker concluded that it would not be feasible to realize that ambitious goal, which transcended the tactical, amounting to an operational or strategic goal. More practically, realizing a goal of that magnitude would require developing legitimate friendships, but to do so would take more effort and time than he could afford.

Therefore, Baker adopted an alternative goal: "earn the trust, confidence, and respect of the Iraqis." To achieve that goal, he pursued two themes: "discredit insurgents and terrorists," and "highlight economic, political, social, and security reforms."

For the purposes of this chapter, COL Baker's operational goal is a point of departure for use of the mission-oriented approach to explore the consequences of pursuing each theme. Thus, having answered the first two questions—the nature of the problem, and the operational goals—we seek answers to the third question: how best to pursue this goal?

Accomplishing Operational Goals

This segment considers two answers to the question of how to pursue the chosen operational themes. Looking backward, we examine the choices that COL Baker made to implement an operational plan of attack. Looking forward, we identify how cyberspace might be leveraged for future tactical influence operations.

Looking Backward: Empirical Lessons for Tactical Influence Operations

Baker elected to try to reach the "undecided" population by focusing on five specific audiences: media (the Arab press), clerics (such as imams), sheiks and tribal leaders, local government officials, and university and school leadership. Choice of target audiences is the key to best utilizing limited resources at brigade level for influence operations.

These choices raise several key issues. First, the editorial policies of the Arab press transcend the AOR of a brigade combat team.[10] It might be argued that this is a strategic issue that should be addressed at a higher echelon. A second issue is that there might be other target audiences who could play important roles, such as nongovernmental organizations (NGOs) or the business community. These entities might provide additional avenues for reaching the "undecided" population.

Having chosen his target audiences, Baker employed the following tools: psychological operations; civil affairs; Public Affairs; Combat Camera; Commander's Emergency Response Program; and unit leaders.[11]

COL Baker also relied on many traditional mechanisms of influence operations; for example, he developed leaflets that could be used routinely or modified rapidly to respond to a specific exigency.[12]

Notably, COL Baker elected not to employ military deception, one of the traditional pillars of information operations, as part of his influence operation campaign. In support of this decision, he argued that "being honest in the execution of information operations is highly important. This goes back to developing trust and confidence, especially with target audiences. If you lose your credibility, you cannot conduct effective IO. *Therefore, you should never try to implement any sort of IO 'deception operations'.*"[13]

TABLE 15-1. Output Measures of Merit

CATEGORY	MEASURES
POLITICAL	Political reforms (participation in elections, compromises among sects)
MILITARY	Number and severity of insurgent, terrorist attacks (emphasize Iraqi casualties, damage, impact, in order to discredit)
ECONOMIC	Improvements in economic reforms (reconstruction projects completed)
SOCIAL	Ability of diverse social groups to live in harmony; acceptance of presence of blue forces (measure willingness of Iraqis to work with blue forces; count who is "waving" where)
INFORM-ATIONAL	Increase/decrease of anti-U.S./Coalition graffiti; lack of negative press; number of accurate, positive stories published or aired; clerics' tone in mosque sermons; reaction of undecideds to red force information operations
INFRA-STRUCTURE	Improvements in sewer, water, electricity, academic institutions, trash collection, and information and communications technology

To implement his influence operation campaign, Baker created an IO Working Group (IOWG) that drew on his diverse personnel resources. He adapted individuals to roles for which their prior career training and experience had not specifically prepared them. Thus, for example, he placed the brigade fire support officer in charge of the IOWG, because of his experience in "targeting," although the challenges associated with nonkinetic targeting differ markedly from those of kinetic targeting. He also augmented his team with some indigenous personnel who could support monitoring of the information environment, such as sermons or local news media, and Iraqi "press agents" to assist in working with the Arab press.

To use these personnel and tools, first, he modified his staff processes. He codified almost all influence operations activities in an IO annex, which was developed and issued as a fragmentary order. He mandated weekly or biweekly meetings with the civilian leaders of the targeted audiences, directed the collection of data to support weekly talking points, and required weekly reports and monthly backbriefs from his IOWG.

Second, COL Baker scheduled periodic meetings with others. This included weekly/biweekly meetings with the targeted audiences to listen and communicate. He particularly emphasized eliciting thoughts on what was not going well and sought to respond rapidly. He conducted weekly roundtables with key members of the Arab press, supported by public affairs office activities and his Iraqi press agents.

Baker also implemented a sequence of feedback efforts. Two native Iraqis monitored the Arab satellite news 24 hours a day, and they also monitored the rhetoric of the local imams, graffiti on walls, and the "wave" factor: they noted who among the Iraqi populace was waving to Coalition soldiers on the streets.

To support these operational analyses, Baker kept track of specific metrics including the number of accurate or positive stories published or aired, quantifying a lack of negative press; the number of walk-in or noninformant tips; the "wave" factor; whether there was an increase or decrease of anti-U.S./Coalition graffiti; the tenor of mosque sermons; and the willingness of Iraqis to work with U.S. forces.

Such measures of merit could usefully be augmented and structured into two classes: input measures and output measures. The input measures would be those that characterized influence operations performance, such as the number of meetings held with targeted groups, or the amount of time spent in creating, validating, and disseminating messages to the targeted groups. Such measures would be largely under the control of blue forces.

Even more important would be output measures to characterize the progress toward specific goals such as those that Baker adopted. Such measures could usefully track the dimensions of PMESII, as illustrated in table 15–1.[14]

Looking Forward: Using Cyberspace in Tactical Influence Operations

Cyberspace is likely to play an increasing role in future tactical influence operations. It has the potential to support the rapid dissemination of precision guided messages and to extend the reach of influence operations far beyond the immediate range of the traditional methods of loudspeakers and leaflets.[15]

Examples of the kinds of cyberspace tools that could be used in support of future tactical influence operations campaigns include creative use of the Internet; "E-flets"; the "silent loudspeaker"; inserting messages into existing mass media; social networks; virtual reality; "Megaphone"; ring tones; and video games. Each of these tools is discussed briefly below.

Terrorist groups have exploited the Internet extensively to support a broad variety of functions such as influencing target audiences and facilitating training.[16] General John Abizaid, USA, former Commander, U.S. Central Command, has pointed out that al Qaeda is a master of "recruiting, training, equipping, advertising, manipulating, propagandizing [and] proselytizing" in cyberspace.[17] The United States is currently constrained in its use of the Internet for fear of "blowback" effects on U.S. audiences—that is, U.S. audiences might be influenced by propaganda aimed at our adversaries.[18] Restrictions on U.S. use of the Internet in support of influence operations have meant, however, that we have effectively ceded the use of this mechanism to our adversaries.

"E-flets" are a type of message sent on the Internet, usually through uniform resource locator links to a Web site with a message for the target audience. Attackers can use them anonymously. A "silent loudspeaker" sends text messages tailored to a specific population, generally through their cellular phones or personal digital assistants. The message may contain partially true (or "grey") information or what is called "rumor intelligence."

The United States has developed several mechanisms for inserting messages into existing mass media. For example, it has developed systems to support the broadcast of a live or recorded message on a nation's television or radio airwaves. However, current airborne systems (for example, the EC–130 Commando Solo) are limited in their speed, range, vulnerability to adversary air defense systems, and time on station.[19] In addition, written articles are sometimes generated to be disseminated in the local press or in U.S. media outlets. However, it can prove embarrassing to blue forces when it is revealed that the media have been paid to run those articles.[20] Many of these techniques overlap significantly with operational and strategic influence operations.

Over the last several years, there has been explosive growth in participation in social networks such as MySpace and FaceBook. Information from such sites can provide vital information to support tactical influence operations. Use of social networking techniques could enhance the effectiveness of technical applications of cyberspace.[21] However, there is concern that an adversary could access these social network sites to gain insights that would undermine operations security. Participation in virtual reality sites such as Second Life has surged. Recently, these sites have witnessed increased political agitation as participants have used them to express dissent. It has also been reported that "home-grown jihadis are rehearsing for terror attacks in virtual worlds such as Second Life."[22] Furthermore, in recent clashes, such as the war between Hizballah and Israel, YouTube was employed rapidly by civilians to post still and video imagery to depict alternative perspectives of the conflict.[23]

Israeli sources have developed "Megaphone" software that can send an alert when specified subjects come up in chat rooms or Internet polls. Such a tool could send alerts to an IOWG, which could use the information to help shape discourse and frame key questions.[24] Sometimes, embarrassing pronouncements by important public figures have been surreptitiously recorded and made into cellphone ringtones so that repetition of the message would undermine the reputation of those individuals.[25] New video games glorify jihadi goals and values to indoctrinate young people with the ethos of terrorism. Blue forces need analogous games to counter this trend.

These cyber influence tools raise a set of issues and observations. First, many of these tools are characterized by some level of deception. However, recall that COL Baker instructed his working group that deception should be avoided because it would breed mistrust in the target audience. Second, the use of these techniques requires in-depth understanding of the architecture of cyberspace. For example, the kinetic attack team would have to avoid destroying cellular towers needed to transmit messages to the target audience.

Third, since cyberspace technology features bidirectionality, it offers the opportunity to elicit useful feedback from the target audience. This can be achieved by monitoring key blogs or conducting Internet interviews.[26]

DOTMLPF Gaps

Shortcomings in the areas specified by DOTMLPF factors have been observed and must be addressed. *Doctrinally*, there has been a failure of the organization to be responsive and synchronized for influence operations, top-down and bottom-up. Relationships among strategic, operational, and tactical influence operations must be harmonized to ensure that messages are properly tailored and timely. This is a particular problem with increasing numbers of stakeholders in influence operations (for example, multinational actors, interagency organizations, NGOs). However, this must not constrain our ability to communicate directly and in a timely fashion with the local population.

Organizationally, IOWGs tend to have too few members and an insufficient mix of skills. This suggests that such organizations should be expanded and augmented with well-trained staff members with adequate skills and experience.

Existing IOWGs have very limited *training* in counterinsurgency (COIN) operations and media relations. However, there is a countervailing concern that emphasis in COIN training may lead to the erosion of traditional major combat skills.[27] In addition, there is a serious lack of training in various languages that blue forces are likely to need over the next decades.

From a *materiel* perspective, IOWGs do not have systems to cope with shortfalls. In particular, they lack automated tools to support the timely translation of voluminous written and oral information and decision aids to support formulation and analysis of influence operations courses of action (COAs).

From a *leadership and education* perspective, IOWGs lack adequate education on cultural awareness. Given the diverse areas where these working groups are likely to operate, it is important that reachback capability be established to gain access to experts in cultural subjects. In addition, access should be established to human terrain teams in theater to take full advantage of their social science skills and cultural expertise.[28]

From a *personnel* perspective, the leaders of IOWGs have inadequate capacity to reward individuals with vital skills, such as cultural experts, and thus lack the tools needed to encourage the evolution of needed capabilities.

Finally, IOWGs lack appropriate *facilities* to support information-sharing with the targeted audiences and key stakeholders. Creative use of cyberspace could facilitate this exchange of information without compromising the security of key groups.

Options to Mitigate DOTMLPF Gaps

There are a wide range of options to redress specified DOTMLPF gaps. The following list builds upon and restructures selected recommendations suggested by COL Baker.

Doctrine. First, we should reassess policies and regulations that inhibit tactical units' ability to compete in an influence operations environment. Second, we should explore the potential utility of additional elements of the influence operations toolbox, such as tactical military deception, computer network operations, public affairs, civil affairs, and humanitarian assistance and disaster relief. Third, we should expand and restructure the MOMs to facilitate the formal implementation and analysis of influence operations.

Organization. We should rethink the composition and size of the IOWG to avoid ad hoc assignments. Thus, we should consider expanding the number of people and the seniority of the staff assigned to the IOWG. In addition, we should employ properly educated and trained personnel in the areas of nonkinetic targeting and public affairs, recognizing that the ideal personnel might not always be available.

Training. Two of Baker's recommendations are being partially implemented. First, COIN instruction should be required at all levels in the institutional training base. However, a balance must be struck so that we do not erode the ability to support major combat operations. In addition, we must increase the quality and quantity of media training provided to soldiers.

Materiel. If the United States is to be an effective participant in the "IO duel," constraints on its use of the Internet for influence operations should be reevaluated, particularly for transmissions in languages that have an extremely small linguistic base in the United States (such as Pashtun and Dari). In particular, it would be appropriate to reassess the continued utility of the 60-year-old Smith-Mundt Act.[29]

Second, the need to understand vast amounts of oral information, such as sermons at mosques and radio or television transmissions, and written information, such as newspapers, requires expedited development, transition, and use of automated translation devices (spoken and written). We should also encourage the creation and use of reachback centers of excellence. We should more rapidly develop and field decision aids to support influence operations COA analysis.[30]

Leadership and Education. An urgently needed step is to integrate cultural awareness education as a standard component in our institutional curriculum and to increase the quality and quantity of media training provided to service leaders.

Personnel. We should seek more mature, experienced soldiers to support IOWGs. We should consider vastly increasing the number of authorized culture experts for potential AORs.

Facilities. Currently, there are many facilities to enhance information-sharing in the AOR. We should standardize and populate civil-military operations centers to facilitate information-sharing with nonmilitary participants.[31] These facilities should enable sharing information in cyberspace, to augment the face-to-face physical interactions by which trust can be built most effectively.

Conclusion

This chapter has put forth a number of interlocking frameworks for conceptualizing and analyzing tactical influence operations issues. The proposed mission-oriented approach provides a logical way of organizing and addressing these issues. It incorporates the DIME-PMESII paradigm to provide a systematic means of characterizing the nature of the problem and formulating useful MOMs. The DOTMLPF paradigm provides a systematic means of identifying gaps and formulating integrated packages of actions to redress those gaps. Overall, if the United States is to be effective in future influence operations, "the warfighter must be able to 'pre-empt, react, and be adaptive.'"[32]

Several key policy issues should be addressed as we consider more aggressive use of cyberspace to support tactical influence operations. These include blue force use of the Internet, the value of employing deception operations, and the development of doctrine so that a coalition of multinational and interagency forces can undertake a coherent, effective influence operations campaign.

CHAPTER 16

I-Power: The Information Revolution and Stability Operations

Franklin D. Kramer, Larry K. Wentz, and Stuart H. Starr

INFORMATION and information technology (I/IT) can significantly increase the likelihood of success in stability operations—if they are part of an overall strategy that coordinates the actions of outside intervenors and focuses on generating effective results for the host nation. Properly utilized, I/IT can help create an informed intervention, organize complex activities, and integrate stability operations with the host nation, making those operations more effective.

Key to these results is a strategy that requires that the U.S. Government give high priority to such an approach and ensures that the effort is a joint civilian-military activity; that the military make I/IT part of the planning and execution of the stability operation; that preplanning and the establishment of I/IT partnerships are undertaken with major regular participants in stability operations, such as the United Nations (UN) and the World Bank; that the focus of the intervention, including the use of I/IT, is on the host nation, supporting its governmental, societal, and economic development; and that key information technology capabilities are harnessed to support the strategy. Implementation of the strategy will include development of an information business plan for the host nation so that I/IT is effectively used to support stabilization and reconstruction; agreements among intervenors on data-sharing and collaboration, including data-sharing on a differentiated basis; and use of commercial IT tools and data provided on an unclassified basis.

Over the past 30 years, the information revolution has had an important impact on the conduct of military operations. In the United States, it has produced what is often called *net-centric warfare* or *net-centric operations*[1]—the combination of shared communications, key data, analytic capabilities, and people schooled in using those capacities—that has enabled enhanced joint activities, integrated distributed capabilities, much greater speed, and more effective maneuver. The result has been that the United States and its allies have been able to conduct effective combat operations under a range of conditions, including quick insertion (Panama), maneuver warfare (major combat operations in Iraq), an all-air campaign (Kosovo), and a Special Forces–led effort (Afghanistan).

At the same time that major combat operations have proceeded so successfully, the United States and its allies have undertaken a variety of stability operations in Somalia, Haiti, Bosnia, Kosovo, East Timor, several African countries, Afghanistan, and Iraq.[2] These stability operations generally have included both economic and governance reconstruction and have spanned the full security gamut from nonviolent peacekeeping to full-blown counterinsurgency. Not one of these operations has approached the success achieved in combat operations undertaken in the same period.

This chapter analyzes whether a strategic use of information and information technology (I/IT) in stability operations could lead to more successful outcomes. Certainly, the information revolution has been a dynamic and positive factor in business, government, and social arenas in the Western world. The combination of technology, information content, and people schooled in the use of each has reshaped enterprises and activities of all types. This chapter concludes that utilizing the elements of the information revolution in a strategic approach to stability operations would have positive results and sets forth the strategic and operational parameters of such an effort.

Problems of Stability Operations

Utilizing the fruits of the information revolution for effective stability operations requires a prior understanding of what makes a stability operation effective. As noted above, stability operations have security, economic, and governance reconstruction elements. Yet while it is widely recognized that stability operations go far beyond purely military actions—encompassing security, humanitarian, economic, and governance/rule of law issues—no one has set forth an actual strategic or operational doctrine that promises success in their conduct. As a World Bank staff report put it, "The Bank, like other international partners, is still learning what works in fragile states contexts."[3]

The problems of stability operations are evident. To begin with, no two circumstances are the same. To say that Haiti is different than Somalia is different than Bosnia is different than Afghanistan is only to hint at the depth and breadth of the complexities. These include the causes of the crisis that occasioned the intervention, the host nation culture or cultures, the language or languages, the nature of the economies ante bellum, the influence of neighbors, and a multitude of other factors. By definition, the state structure has collapsed or is severely impaired. Often there has been significant violence. Internal groups have been factionalized and frequently have each other's blood on their hands. Economies are in disarray. Social mechanisms have broken down. Information is lacking, and communications mechanisms are limited.

Prior to almost all interventions, the international community already will have been significantly present in the form of international organizations, nongovernmental organizations, businesses, bilateral governmental activities, and many more venues. Once there is a major international intervention, complexity increases greatly. Regardless of the initial number of international actors, the number and diversity of participants increase. More critical is that their relative importance increases for such functionality as exists or is created in the host country. Additionally, whereas before the intervention, development often had priority, now there are simultaneous challenges in the security, humanitarian, economic, and governance arenas—and, if social needs may be separated from the foregoing, in the social arena as well. Personnel and equipment stream in from civilian and military components of the governments of the United States and other nations, international organizations such as the UN and its many agencies, the North Atlantic Treaty Organization (NATO), the Organisation for Security and Co-operation in Europe, the African Union, the World Bank, and others. Nongovernmental organizations also are involved, many of them in the humanitarian arena, as well as numerous others that participate in myriad aspects of reconstruction and development. Many businesses also get involved, either as contractors to national and international organizations or as participants in private ventures.

A very important aspect of the complexity is that dealing with the host nation has become more difficult. The government, which may have ceased to function, is seen by many as illegitimate and not representative of all the people; its reach is generally limited, and it is ineffective in mobilizing domestic human and other resources.

A further complicating factor is that circumstances on the ground change over time considerably in response to the intervention. (The transformation from liberator to occupier is a well-known problem for intervening forces.) Interventions generally last for years, and a decade is not unusual. Stability operations encompass not only security but also reconstruction, and reconstruction takes time. In addition to actual changes, managing expectations of both the intervenors and the host nation becomes extremely important. For example, there is a so-called golden hour of 6–12 months during which actions must support expectations and the local population must experience improvements in quality of life.

It is in this context that the question arises whether the application of the tools and content of the information revolution can have a positive effect on the outcome of a stability operation.

Opportunities for I/IT Strategy

As difficult as the circumstances of a stability operation are, the very complexity provides significant opportunities for the use of an effective information strategy built around the use of information technology. It is worth underscoring at the outset what may be an obvious proposition: that information and information technology have to be used together to be effective. One will not suffice without the other.

At the most basic level, information technology can be used to distribute information to crucial players in an ongoing stability operation. Making information available can have four important consequences.

First, it can help create an informed intervention. Even before the intervention, and certainly as it progresses, the intervenors will need a range of information about both planned and ongoing respondent activities and about the host nation. For the latter, population characteristics, cultural dynamics, economic structures, and historical governance issues all can be described and analyzed.

The intervenors will first plan and then undertake many activities, with multiple players in each field of endeavor. While it will not be possible for all intervening actors to have the unity of command that is sought by militaries, the use of I/IT may allow for organizing a more common approach—or at least to reduce inconsistent approaches.

An information strategy supported by information technology provides an opportunity to share information among the stability operations respondents themselves. This sharing of information will facilitate the generation of a common approach and can help in the effective use of scarce resources. As an example, the allocation of health care resources might be usefully rationalized once there is at least a working sense of what types of resources are available from the respondents. Also, intervenors working on the rule of law in different sections of the country will be more effective if they adopt closely aligned approaches than if they use significantly different approaches, even if each is valid in and of itself.

A second key element of the strategy will be using I/IT to help organize complex activities. Normally, a stability operation will be undertaken on a countrywide basis. For even the smallest countries, this means a significant geographic area, with all the associated difficulties of maintaining connectivity. The intervention also undoubtedly will be of extended duration, and I/IT will be necessary to maintain an updated approach as conditions on the ground change.

Complexity will be manifested in the requirement to deal simultaneously with security, humanitarian, economic, and governance issues. Many intervenors will be involved in only one or some of these actions, but actions in one field often have consequences for another. Moreover, knowledge of what is happening in each is important for the development of an overall strategy capable of achieving an effective host nation. Even in a single sector, information supported by effective information technology would allow for better in-country coordination; and distributed players would be better able to take focused actions. Furthermore, knowledge is an important element in building trust and commitment among different stability operations players, which can be a vital element in enhancing effectiveness.

The third key use of distributed information will be to integrate the stability operations respondents with the host nation. It bears repeating that the objective of a stability operation is not a "good intervention" but rather an "effective host nation" as a result of the intervention. To accomplish this difficult task, given that the host nation is probably fragmented, disrupted, and not very effective, the intervenors need to stay connected to it so that the results are appropriate for and adoptable by the populace on whose behalf the effort is being undertaken. An I/IT strategy needs to involve the host nation (likely in numerous manifestations) in the ongoing activities of the intervention.

The fourth use of I/IT is to integrate the host nation and make it more effective. Effectiveness can be enhanced by using I/IT to identify key requirements and target scarce resources. Information for a budget process is an important example. I/IT will also be able to facilitate informed senior decisionmaking well beyond budget and budget-type decisions. For example, how best to bring previously warring factions to work together will involve important social and economic issues whose resolution can be enhanced by good information.

Host nation capacity can also be created by the use of I/IT. Government operations can be reestablished with the proper use of information technology. Both the information systems and the training to use them will be required, but information capacity can be generated far more quickly than other infrastructures—and can enable other effective actions.

Key Questions for the I/IT Strategy

An important question in analyzing an I/IT strategy for stability operations is how such a strategy relates to what else is happening in the intervention. As noted by the World Bank staff, no one has developed a truly informed approach to stability operations, which, in World Bank parlance, is one type of activity in fragile states. There are, however, some principles that have been adopted by the international community and the United States that are worth noting here.

First, the international community, through the Organization for Economic Co-operation and Development (OECD) and otherwise, has emphasized the importance of the principles of harmonization and alignment. *Harmonization* refers to having the outside intervenors work in a generally coordinated fashion. As the OECD Development Co-operation Directorate has stated, "Harmonization is taken to refer to common arrangements amongst the donor community, rationalized procedures and information sharing between donors . . . related to the goal of greater coherence between and among donors."[4] *Alignment* refers to having the outside intervenors align their activities with the interests of the host nation. Again, as the OECD Development Co-operation Directorate stated, "Alignment has been defined . . . as a set of practices according to which donor organizations use recipient country strategies, policies, and practices . . . as a guide for their assistance programs."[5] Both these principles are embodied in the so-called Rome Declaration on Harmonization of 2003 and subsequent actions and statements of the major multilateral and bilateral donor entities and countries, including the United States.

I/IT can have an important, positive impact on both harmonization and alignment. Coordination among intervenors is one of the key achievable results of an effective information strategy implemented by information technology. Likewise, an I/IT strategy is a critical element to ensure that the host nation is effectively integrated into the decisionmaking and implementing actions of the outside intervenors.

A second question is the relationship between an I/IT strategy and strategies for security, humanitarian needs, economic development, and governance/rule of law. The U.S. Government, and particularly the Department of Defense (DOD), has often talked about using all elements of national power for success in stability operations, often citing diplomatic, informational, military, and economic (DIME) power as key aspects of the types of power brought to bear by outside intervenors.

This DIME paradigm is a useful model, although it is not meant to be exhaustive. For example, host nation civil society may be affected by outside, nongovernmental, civil organizations that nonetheless are important elements of an intervenor's national power. Social issues also must be considered, and, unless *diplomatic* is read to mean all contacts other than military or economic, there will be important nondiplomatic interactions on matters such as rule of law. What the DIME paradigm shows most importantly, however, is that information needs to be considered in an overall context, just as the principles of harmonization and alignment indicate.

There is a fruitless debate as to whether information only supports other activities or is an activity in and of itself. Certainly, information supports other activities. Military, economic, and governance activities all operate on the basis of information. Conversely, certain aspects of information, such as the establishment of technical structures, can be undertaken apart from other activities. As an example, think of the building of towers to create the infrastructure for a cellular network. Overall, however, information, as every other action in a stability operation, is designed for one purpose: to serve the objective of making the host nation effective. That is the context in which to consider I/IT and to determine whether and how to undertake a particular effort.

The broad challenge for an I/IT strategy for stability operations is to help create effective results from the multitude of players and actions that will be found in a particular situation. No one should think that information is a panacea. If a faction within a country resists working with another faction even after all information is exchanged, then that is a political problem and probably will not be solved by further information. But given that information is not a universal solution to all problems, the question is whether the information revolution can help harmonize, align, and make more effective the outside military and civilian governmental intervenors, international and nongovernmental organizations, businesses, and, especially, the host nation in all its manifestations.

Elements of an I/IT Strategy

Five key elements are required to generate an effective I/IT strategy for the United States to use in stability operations.

Integrate I/IT Strategy Explicitly into Stability Operations

The first requirement is for the U.S. Government to make the fundamental decision that such a strategy is a mandatory element of all stability operations. That is no small statement, because the reality is that the United States has never—in any of its many stability operations—made such a decision. But the rationale for such a conclusion is clear: information and information technology are crucial elements to the success of stability operations, supporting effectiveness, harmonization, and alignment goals.

A coherent U.S. Government I/IT strategy is essential to produce the needed results. This means that the effort has to be truly interagency—and, most importantly, be accepted as a key element by both DOD and the State Department (including the U.S. Agency for International Development [USAID]). While some individuals have acknowledged this point, no such government-wide I/IT strategy exists, although a potential framework for one has been created.

National Security Presidential Directive 44, "Management of Interagency Efforts Concerning Reconstruction and Stabilization," released in December 2005, articulates the basic framework for interagency cooperation. It assigns primary responsibility for stabilization and reconstruction operations to the

Secretary of State (through the Office of the Coordinator for Stabilization and Reconstruction) and mandates close coordination with DOD to integrate stabilization and reconstruction contingency planning with military planning, when relevant and appropriate. The Director of Foreign Assistance, who reports directly to the Secretary of State, also serves as the administrator of USAID, where several offices have been created or restructured to deal with stabilization and reconstruction challenges.

At DOD, the framework was anticipated in November 2005 by the release of Directive 3000.05, "Military Support for Stability, Security, Transition, and Reconstruction Operations," which affirms that such activities represent a core DOD mission and are given a priority comparable to combat operations.

Within this framework, however, the focus on I/IT has been limited. USAID, recognizing the potential of I/IT in stability and reconstruction operations, has taken some steps to include it as a sector and development tool. USAID strategy aims to leverage I/IT in conflict management and mitigation missions and in humanitarian assistance operations. USAID also seeks to promote global access to IT and to assist development through several ongoing projects such as the Leland Initiative for Africa, the Digital Freedom Initiative, and the Administrator's Last Mile Initiative.

Some important Embassies have also taken I/IT steps. The U.S. Embassy in Afghanistan created the position of senior telecom advisor to facilitate coordination among both military and civilian U.S. Government elements in country. In Iraq, DOD established the Iraq Reconstruction Management Office within the Embassy structure, which also has a telecommunications advisor to unify I/IT efforts. These efforts are the beginning of a coherent U.S. Government approach to I/IT. A complete strategy would, however, require the Department of State/USAID to make I/IT a key element of strategy in stability operations. These initiatives are a good start but are not an integrated strategy. They do, however, provide a basis on which to build.

Include I/IT as Part of Military Strategy for Stability Operations

Although the problems of stability operations go far beyond military, the second element of an effective I/IT strategy recognizes that, doctrinally, the military requires an I/IT strategy as part of the planning and execution of any stability operation. Accordingly, in both joint and service documents—plans and the rules and guidance for their development and execution—an I/IT strategy is a required element.

As noted above, this approach is fully consistent with the military analysis of the DIME paradigm. The key point here is that military planners and operators need to include an I/IT strategy in their approaches. A subsidiary—but crucial—

point is that an I/IT strategy is not a traditional function of the J6 (the technical information officer on a military staff, the chief information officer in business terms). Rather, I/IT has to be a function of both the J3 and J5: that is, built into plans and implementation and policy. The J6 will be in a supporting/implementing role to help execute the strategy. There is no reason why the J6 cannot help develop the I/IT strategy, but it cannot be developed apart from the policy, plans, and execution of the larger effort. This is not a technical problem; it is a strategic effectiveness problem to accomplish host nation harmonization, alignment, and effectiveness.

The U.S. military has already taken some important steps in terms of using I/IT as part of a stability operation. Warfighting information technology is available if and when military operations are a required part of the stability operation. This chapter does not deal with those issues and instead focuses on the issue of joint stability operations activity writ large—that is, joint within the U.S. Government and combined with other non–U.S. partners. On the latter, DOD has undertaken some worthwhile efforts under the Combined Enterprise Regional Information Exchange System (CENTRIXS) program.[6]

CENTRIXS is a Web-based network, developed with both commercial-off-the-shelf and government-off-the-shelf tools. It is designed to provide information among coalition partners in activities in which the U.S. military is involved. For example, U.S. Central Command uses CENTRIXS to support coalition military coordination and information-sharing for the Multinational Force in Iraq and the International Security Assistance Force in Afghanistan. CENTRIXS operates on military classified networks, so it is not available to all participants in a stability operation. It is, however, quite useful for information exchange among coalition militaries and is a good step in the direction of using information in stability operations.

Establish I/IT Partnerships with Stability Operations Participants

The third element of an I/IT strategy for the U.S. Government for stability operations is to pre-establish I/IT partnerships with key stability operations participants. It is important to underscore the word *key*. It is not possible, and would not be effective, to try to establish partnerships with all of the many players who will be involved in a stability operation. But there are some critical players from the government perspective.

A few countries can be expected to participate in many and even most operations that the United States does. The United Kingdom is one; Australia is another. Certain key international organizations likewise will be there. The UN would be involved—though dealing with the UN requires dealing with various groups and agencies, since it does not act as a single entity. Thus, planning will be important with the Office for the Coordinator of Humanitarian Affairs, the UN Development Program, the UN Department of Peacekeeping Operations, and perhaps the UN Children's Fund. NATO is often a player, as is the European Union. Major nongovernmental organizations also will be regularly engaged in stability operations. In fact, these organizations will generally be there in advance of the U.S. military. The fact that preplanning includes only some players is meant to allow for creation of a useful framework. An effective I/IT strategy will include many others, and there may be conferences, meetings, and workshops of a broader nature. But real planning will be enhanced by a more limited approach.

Focus on the Host Nation

The fourth element of an effective information strategy is to focus on the host nation. The importance of establishing host nation effectiveness has already been emphasized. Informing host nation decisionmaking, enhancing governmental capacities, and supporting societal and economic development are all crucial elements of an information strategy. Working with I/IT as discussed below can help generate progress in security, humanitarian, economic, and governance/ rule of law arenas. The recognition by the international community of the harmonization and alignment goals is important. However, when information technology is considered, harmonization with respect to the intervenors all too often becomes emphasized as compared to alignment and effectiveness of the host nation. This is backward. An effective I/IT strategy is one that makes the host nation effective. Nothing else will do. Thus, a critical element of the strategy is an I/IT business plan for the host nation and an intervenor support strategy that aims to enable the host nation business plan.

Use Technical Capabilities to Support Mission Goals

The last element of an I/IT strategy will be to work with others to use the key technical capabilities to support the effectiveness, harmonization, and alignment goals. The specifics are discussed below, but a crucial point is that generating the technical part is far less about invention—the information revolution has given us and continues to give us broad capabilities—than it is about developing ways to use those brilliant inventions in an overall effective, collaborative fashion. The planning aspects of the strategy are crucial to effective use of the tools. Common choices can create highly effective capabilities. Divergent choices can undercut well-meaning strategies.

Operationalizing the I/IT Strategy

It is one thing to have a strategy; it is quite another to implement it effectively. The discussion below sets forth how to implement an operational I/IT strategy.

A key point is to remember that both the end goal (creating an effective host nation) and the strategic context (the I/IT strategy itself) must be developed and implemented inside an overall approach of harmonization and alignment that supports enabling the host nation security, humanitarian, economic, and governance activities.

To effectuate those tasks, the U.S. Government needs to adopt an information business model with multiple key elements. Those who have responsibility for the I/IT strategy, which ideally will be a joint effort led by the Department of State (including USAID) and DOD, will need to run the business model in a focused, long-term fashion; otherwise, achievement of the strategic aims will be jeopardized.

The business model breaks down into two broad elements: harmonization among outside intervenors, and effectiveness and alignment for, and with, the host nation.

Harmonization

On the harmonization side, a good place to start oper-ational analysis is to recall the complexity of the problem and the number of intervenors. As discussed earlier, an important element of the strategy is to undertake preplanning with key partners. There are four elements of preplanning to achieve harmonization.

First, joint civil-military information planning will be critical. In the first instance, this needs to be done between the Department of State and DOD, but more important, it needs to be done between the U.S. Government and other major intervenors to harmonize their interventions. It is not an impossible task to keep others informed and aware, but it is a difficult one. Issues arise immediately as to what data can be provided and how information can be exchanged. With respect to the latter, development of agreed management and data standards can fundamentally enhance the provision of information. Pre-event planning and face-to-face meetings can enhance trust and provide important education about others' methods. While the myriad actual stability operations have provided some reasonable knowledge about different actors, on-the-job learning is necessarily more difficult because of the requirement to do one's "day job." Accordingly, some common training, exercising, and/or education away from a stability operation can create potentially significant opportunities to enhance harmonization. None of this will occur unless an element of the government, preferably a joint Department of State–DOD element, focuses on the requirement for preplanning.

Second, improved collaboration depends on both better processes and use of available technical means. The process issue is perhaps the most crucial. As noted above, it is important to decide how, with whom, and how much data are shared. There is a general tendency, particularly at DOD, to come at the problem through a classified lens. That is, since DOD is used to treating data as classified, the question is often framed as how such data can be made available. Often, the answer is given in binary terms: information either can be made available or it cannot. This all too often becomes a least-common-denominator approach because the judgment is made that if the data are not available to some, they cannot be available to any.

A much better approach would be to recognize that, in stability operations, most relevant data are widely available, though often not collected, from other than classified sources. Furthermore, and most important, data can be shared on a differentiated basis. For example, information provided to Japanese civilian officials can be differentiated from information provided to World Bank officials, which can be differentiated from information provided to Red Cross officials. Groups that have engaged in preplanning and have built up trust will find it easier to share information than groups that meet only in the circumstances of the stability operation. Differentiation is one key element to enhancing data-sharing—and working differentiation as an effective operational approach will depend on preplanning.

A second important step to better data-sharing will be better use of technical means. For example, the Internet has become a mechanism for unclassified collaboration and sharing of information among civilian and military elements responding to crisis operations. Furthermore, commercially available collaboration tools and other tools, such as video teleconferencing and Webcams, are being used by them on the Internet. Technologies are improving quickly to enhance data-sharing. In the civilian arena, the growth of Web logs (blogs), file-sharing, Wikipedia, MySpace, and similar sites all attest to the possibilities of sharing, if the desire to use the mechanisms is there. Many organizations already run sites to make information available (for example, the UN-sponsored ReliefWeb). However, the collaborative aspects of these sites are limited.

U.S. Joint Forces Command (USJFCOM) has taken strides to enable the sharing of unclassified information with nontraditional partners. The command has conducted several exercises that explore this challenge, and Multinational Experiment 4 specifically addressed it. The command is also standing up a nonmilitary domain portal outside its firewall that takes an approach more akin to that of a relief organization—many of which are linked to it—than a military one. The portal (<http://harmonieweb.org/>) enables people and organizations who are participating in a relief effort to obtain and post information that may be valuable in providing the needed assistance.[7]

In addition, the United States is encouraging the development of an open-source, collaborative arena, tentatively called "the hub," that would use blogging, file-sharing, and Wikipedia-type approaches to create an open space for collaborative sharing. It is not clear as of this writing what the outcome of that effort will be. However, even assuming its success, it seems probable that a combination of both a fully open site (the hub or some variant) and a more directed approach (for example, NATO–UN–World Bank collaborative sharing) might be useful. Remember the point about differentiation: to try to use only one tool or one kind of approach to allow for all types of collaboration is not necessarily the most successful approach. Transferring the CENTRIXS in some modified form for collaboration among key civil-military players while generating a broader open-source approach is likely to be a useful effort.

The third element required to achieve harmonization is the development of an implementation strategy. Whatever the precise mechanism for improved collaboration, it can be fairly confidently stated that improvements will not occur absent a strategy that designates elements within the government to make them happen. At the moment, there are good but separate efforts. The Office of the Secretary of Defense is working on the hub effort. USJFCOM is seeking to support elements of the Department of State and, through experimentation, is developing new civil-military coalition processes for improved collaboration and information-sharing and assessing commercial information technology tools for enabling the processes. The recent DOD directive on stability operations requires development of a collaborative information-sharing mechanism.[8] But there is no overall directed effort—and this key element is crucial. Otherwise, the efforts will be personality-driven and ad hoc. Such approaches are far better than nothing but are not likely to be sufficiently effective.

An improved approach to collaboration includes broad agreement on the information needed to be collected and exchanged; standards for collection and exchange; technical mechanisms for each that work together; processes; and some education and training together. The final important element of collaboration is the ability to improve data usability. As noted above, it is probably useful to think about data in two broad types of collaborative forums: a more limited network among key partners, and a wider, more open network. In each, capacities for search, aggregation, storage, and retrieval are useful and potentially important. In each, the issues of quality control and information assurance will arise, as will the issue of dissemination.

Technical improvements in recent years have significantly increased the ability to aggregate different types of data, such as the ability to put written information on photographs and to integrate geographic material with other data. That said, there needs to be some data management group that will determine for the collaborating activity just what kind of capacities will be created—or allowed. For example, it is possible to add to a photograph the names of the people in the picture, but in certain circumstances, doing so might be hazardous for the individuals identified. An ongoing data management effort to create rules and manage the activity will be necessary. There is, of course, a technical aspect to this, but some of the key issues will turn out to be policy issues, so the group will need to engage both technicians and policymakers.

Information power derives from a combination of people, content, and technical capabilities. In the technical arena, there is a whirlwind of ongoing activity and innovation. A very useful capability would be to have an "information toolbox" that maintains lists of:

- key information partners, including businesses with technical capabilities
- information and data management tools
- other key tools, such as collaboration and translation.

For the effort that we are focusing on here, commercially developed tools are essential because government-generated tools often will not be available to important partners. There will be debates between proponents of open-source and proprietary tools, and those debates need to be resolved in actual context, based on what the effort is intended to establish. The case will probably be that the broader the activity, the more desirable the use of open-source—but even that statement needs to be evaluated in the particular circumstance.

The Center for Technology and National Security Policy at the National Defense University has generated a first order "tool kits and best practices" analysis in its recently published *ICT Primer.*[9] That discussion includes review of telecommunications capabilities such as satellite communications, creation of a civil-military information environment, data and information management, and best practices. Maintaining and updating such an activity is an important element of an overall strategy.

Effectiveness and Alignment

The fundamental task of an I/IT strategy is to enhance host nation capacity. That is the critical result for which the stability operation is undertaken. To accomplish that result in an effective fashion, the strategy will need to accomplish two tasks, each familiar to the international community: first, assess the host nation, and second, establish a goal toward which to build. To put it more in the vernacular, a cure without a diagnosis will be improbable; directions without destination will be random. In short, an effective approach will require an information business plan for the host nation.

The assessment phase of an information business plan should begin before the intervention. It must include analyses of both information requirements and available information technology. Unlike humanitarian interventions, such as the relief effort for the tsunami of December 26, 2004, stability operations generally have long build-up periods, so there is time to prepare. An assessment would consider the pre-intervention state of information technology and information usage in the host nation. It is important to recognize that baselines will differ in different host nations. What can be accomplished in a country with an austere pre-crisis baseline is likely considerably different from what can be accomplished in a more built-up, moderately established country. As an example, Bosnia would be different from Afghanistan in terms of establishing an information business plan. Different baselines will generate different goals, and there will be no "one-size-fits-all" approach.

Some key elements of an information assessment will include evaluation of the host nation's telecommunications laws and regulations and communication infrastructures—landline telephone system, cell phone capacity, and Internet availability. It should also address usage patterns, language and literacy issues, technical training of locals, and financial resources.

Once an assessment has been undertaken, goals will need to be set for operationalizing the information business plan. Generally, it will be useful to time-phase the goals into an initial deployment phase, a middle (getting-things-going) phase, and a long-term (exit-by-intervenors) phase. A critical point throughout is that the intervenors' information business plan goals need to be in support of the overall goals for the host nation, and the host nation as promptly as possible will need to help generate those goals.

The initial deployment phase will require the intervenors to consider what deployable capabilities will be useful to help establish a host nation element or elements. Both structural information capabilities, such as deployable cell phone capacities and the use of satellites, and functional capabilities, such as "health care in a box," need to be considered.

The virtue of preplanning is that key intervenors can rationalize their capacities in the early, usually chaotic, days of an intervention by considering which capabilities each might focus on. Equally important is to undertake such a discussion remembering that, first, numerous entities will already be in country with some capacities that can be utilized, and that, second, host countries will likely have some, perhaps significant, capacity. Over the entirety of the intervention, the implementation of the information business plan likely will mean that the lead on different aspects of the plan will change. Broadly, one might expect a move from outside military intervenors to outside civilian intervenors to host nation, although the reality is likely to be more coordinated and complex. The transitions will occur over time, so there will be overlaps that need careful management. If it is understood from the beginning that there will be transitions in the way the plan is implemented, it will make for a more realistic and effective approach.

The middle phase of an information business plan for the host country will focus on five elements. First is to align the host country so that it is connected to the collaborative mechanisms used by the intervenors in some fashion. While the key intervenors likely can use high-tech means, it may be that the host country will not be able to do so. An important task of an information business plan will be to allow for low-tech to high-tech connectivity. As an example, in Afghanistan, the literacy rate is so low that Internet use is necessarily limited and cell phone connectivity may be much more important. In fact, in Afghanistan, the cell phone is the lifeline communications capability. These points can be more broadly generalized: if the information business plan is to succeed, it must take account of the host nation's information culture and the related information technology culture.

A second element is to help establish working government agencies. Depending on the overall strategy, these could be central ministries or local/provincial offices. Information technology can be used to improve ministry effectiveness, especially to allow for an analytic approach through budgeting and transparency of expenditures. Those are crucial functions for the establishment of legitimate governance, and information technology can help each.

A third element for many stability operations will be to increase connectivity between the central government and provincial/local governments. Information technology can enhance this connectivity through, for example, the two-way flow of data and finances. Often, the cause of the crisis will have been differences between the central government and a region of the country, and working to bring warring elements together will be important. An information business plan can be an effective part of an overall effort.

A fourth element will often be to provide greater functionalities in certain important government services to the populace. While an information business plan may not be able to improve all functionalities significantly, health and education are two arenas of consequence in which such a plan can make an important difference. In the health arena, information technology can be used to build up local centers of health care, such as hospitals; support training of health care workers; and provide valuable functionalities, such as health surveillance systems. In the education arena, information technology can support curriculum establishment and the provision of instruction, as well as the training of teachers.

The fifth element is to provide for the private sector development of information capabilities. Two of the most important issues are informed regulatory mechanisms and useful seed financing. An overly constrained regulatory environment will make it difficult for private enterprise to operate at a profit. A properly structured set of incentives can help create an environment in which profit-making companies can contribute importantly to economic reconstruction. Seed money may be very important, especially in the early days of a stability operation, particularly to get local involvement in the development of the information business plan.

The middle phase of the plan may be considered the equivalent of the medical "golden hour" for establishing a framework for effective use of I/IT for the host nation. While the information flow may be limited, meeting expectations of the host government and population during this middle phase will be very important to longer term success for the intervention and the host nation.

The middle phase will naturally flow over into the long-term phase for the host nation and the exit strategy for the intervenors. That part of the information business plan strategy should have at least three major elements. First, as noted above, the private sector should become a key element. Creating an environment in which there are commercial opportunities for information technology and information firms will help seed economic revitalization. Second, the host nation will need to consider what role it will play in the development of a national information technology infrastructure. Models range from full privatization to early phase ownership to ongoing involvement. Third, as part of their effort in country, intervenors will have established IT capabilities. Such facilities and datasets should not be automatically dismantled as the intervenors leave. Rather, they should be built as leave-behinds for local partners, both governmental and nongovernmental, whether commercial or nonprofit.

An I/IT strategy includes people, content, and technology. In a stability operation, the information needs—the content of what must be provided in addition to the connectivity—of the host nation require consideration. Broadly speaking, those information content needs will fall into the categories of security, humanitarian, economic, governance/rule of law, and social.

In analyzing how such information needs should be fulfilled, an I/IT strategy will recognize that the information element will support functional strategies for each of these arenas—all of which will have significant subparts. For example, the establishment of prosecutorial, court, and prison functions will have security and rule of law/governance aspects. Significant programs will be under way to help create each of these elements as part of a stability operation. Responding to the information needs of those programs has to be an affiliated strategic effort—or, to use the terms of the international community, needs to be aligned with the overall aims of the functional programs.

The specific needs may be provided with the use of information from one or more of the intervenors. In a variety of ways, information technology can be utilized to provide expert assistance. A simple example is maintaining an online list of experts. More sophisticated efforts can be established, such as a call-in center for the provision of various kinds of information. Research arrangements can be set up online, as can connectivity with key national and international organizations, both governmental and nongovernmental, that are willing and able to provide assistance.

As is true for the technology itself, information needs change over time. In fact, the ability to provide information may become more important as the host nation develops its own capabilities. The capacity to access such information may be developed in two parallel fashions. First, in a traditional approach there could be an office to help facilitate access to expert management. A distributed approach, such as wikis and blogs, may be able to make a great deal of expert information available without a specific data manager, if the right information tools are provided. Issues of trust and reliability will arise, but the community approach to providing information via the Internet has been very powerful in other arenas, and its use in stability operations should be encouraged.

The discussion of the management of information needs raises the important question of how to manage the I/IT strategy in the course of the stability operation. Adoption of a strategic approach and even operational activities will be greatly facilitated by the establishment of a forward field organization. Ideally, this would be a joint Department of State–DOD function with the job of carrying out the information strategy in country. In a stability operation, the organization likely would be collocated with the military command activity.

The role of the organization would include carrying out the U.S. Government aspects of the I/IT strategy. In addition, the organization would collaborate with the organizations with which preplanning took place, including key countries, the UN, and major nongovernmental organizations. As promptly as possible, the organization will want to begin to work with the host nation, though precisely what that means will depend on the circumstances of the operation. As a forward community of interest is being set up, the organization will want to create mechanisms that add to the effort entities that have not been part of the preplanning. As discussed above, a hub-type approach might be very valuable, as might more structured relationships. In addition, the organization will want to work with the public affairs office to facilitate interaction with the media and, most important, provide information for the public at large.

Conclusion

Information and information technology can be important components for success in stability operations. Achieving successful results requires that a purposeful strategy be adopted to use these capabilities to the desired end of building up the host nation and to develop operational activities that effectively implement the strategy. A strategic approach causes coalition participants to undertake five key activities:

- conduct pre-event activities with partners
- implement improved collaboration

- ensure improved data usability
- develop an information toolbox
- create a forward field information office.

Also, creating an overall focus to generate an effective host nation information business plan consists of four actionable items:

- assessing host nation information capacity
- building a host nation information goal
- creating immediate, medium, and long-term information capacities
- analyzing information needs and developing methods to fulfill those needs.

These activities and items can generate an environment in which the information revolution can help create success in stability operations.

CHAPTER 17

Facilitating Stability Operations with Cyberpower

Gerard J. Christman

THE U.S. MILITARY has become involved in a new stability operation every 18 to 24 months since the early 1980s.[1] Each of these operations has consumed Department of Defense (DOD) resources in excess of the original cost of the major combat operation that preceded it. The fact that stability operations have become an increasingly prominent mission for the U.S. military was not acknowledged by the Services, as shown by the lack of doctrine, training, personnel, and equipment to conduct them.

Recent experiences in Iraq and Afghanistan, however, brought recognition of a need for change, as news images of chaos, looting, unrest, and inadequate civil administration in Iraq imparted the painful reality to U.S. policymakers and military leaders: that stability operations were an essential mission that had to be mastered if the United States and the coalition were to be successful. Despite major U.S. military victories, what followed them overshadowed earlier accomplishments. In Afghanistan, after U.S. Special Forces supported the Northern Alliance in deposing the Taliban, there was criticism that the "conflict created conditions that have given warlordism, banditry and opium production a new lease on life."[2] In Iraq, images of Saddam's statue being torn down in Baghdad were followed by images of lawlessness and looting, as relative calm gave way to widespread instability.

Military leaders therefore examined mistakes in actions after the fall of the Taliban and of Saddam Hussein's regime to determine how to correct them in future operations. Stability, security, transition, and reconstruction (SSTR) operations, often referred to more simply as stability operations, became the central theme in the Defense Science Board's Summer Study of 2004.[3] It recommended new policies for stability operations to provide direction to the Services. In the fall of 2005, the Department of Defense issued a new directive that elevated stability operations to the status of "a core U.S. military mission that the Department of Defense shall be prepared to conduct and support" and giving stability operations "priority comparable to combat operations."[4] This was the first time in the history of the U.S. military that a noncombat mission was placed on par with combat. This directive acknowledged that winning the peace was as important as winning the war.

In order to explore how cyberpower could facilitate them, this chapter first reviews the essential functions of stability operations: communication, collaboration, translation, and engagement. It then examines DOD policies pertaining to stability operations to determine if more could be done to fully utilize cyberpower. Next, the chapter describes tools, techniques, and developments of information and communications technology (ICT) that have been adapted to stability operations, reviewing both impediments and methods to engage cyberpower to foster success. Operations at all levels—from the interagency to the tactical—are evaluated to determine how their effectiveness could be improved by better leveraging of cyberpower. The chapter concludes by pointing out that while cyberpower can be a powerful complementary enabler for stability and security operations, the U.S. military must finish developing the necessary underpinnings.

Essential Functions for Stability Operations

Two important works published in 2004 described the application of information and communications technology to enable the kinds of stability operations envisioned in DOD Directive 3000.05, *Military Support to Stability, Security, Transition, and Reconstruction Operations*.[5] I argue that these works should be broadened to make cyberpower itself an enabler of stability operations. Key capacities that support SSTR include communication, collaboration, translation, and engagement: these are cyberpower issues.

Communication
In stability operations, U.S. forces must master communications not only among themselves, but also with civil authorities, the civil populace, nongovernmental organizations (NGOs), international organizations (IOs), and coalition or multinational partners. A number of interoperability issues must be confronted. Purpose-built military communications and information systems will not be adequate for communications with each of these potential partners, nor will commercial-off-the-shelf technology suffice in all cases as the United States

engages with its coalition or multinational partners. Regulations covering information releasability, communications security, and information security prevent unfettered interconnectivity among national military information systems and may block dissemination of information across national network boundaries. Encryption technologies and keying material embedded in U.S communications equipment cannot be released for use by foreign militaries. One approach to this issue is the use of a special force comprising civil affairs personnel who are trained and equipped to bridge the gap between the various military and the civil actors.

By way of illustration, the U.S. Central Command's military information systems—the Maneuver Control System and Global Command and Control System, among others—were initially incapable of interconnecting to all of the nations that entered the coalition against Saddam Hussein in 2002 and 2003. The United States had to pay for and build a new network parallel to its existing infrastructure: the Combined Enterprise Regional Information Exchange System (CENTRIXS), a combination of commercial-off-the-shelf and government-off-the-shelf tools.[6] Although CENTRIXS was successful, once fully implemented across the coalition military, it required the development of information releasability rules and encryption and communications security policy. Moreover, despite its considerable expense, it did not afford the military the vital ability to communicate or collaborate with NGOs, IOs, or civil authorities. The entire cost was borne by the United States, which in the future would like to avoid the cost in time and money of developing parallel networks and systems to achieve interoperability.

Another illustration of communications issues in stability operations pertains to the tactical communications equipment found in most U.S. Army units for command and control (C^2), administration and logistics, and intelligence push-to-talk voice communications (called the single channel ground and airborne radio system). Soldiers and Marines utilized this equipment with great success to communicate among themselves to facilitate military operations. However, these systems have embedded cryptographic technology, so their use must be limited to properly cleared U.S. military personnel. In order to help civil authorities such as police, firefighters, border patrol, and the like, different communications equipment must be procured and delivered along with training and long-term maintenance capability. For the United States to be interoperable with these civil authorities—for example, to plan their transition to authority over a town or region—it would need to possess these others types of systems as well.

When procured and implemented, such alternative systems have performed well and had a major impact on the overall success of stability operations. However, these systems are not part of the organic baseline deployment packages of U.S. forces. Time and treasure are consumed in determining requirements, feeding them to the acquisition community, getting the items into logistics channels, and then installing and implementing them. Introducing this time lag raises the risk of a significant degradation of stability, as seen in Iraq. Thus, the types of communications equipment provided to personnel will have a significant impact on whether or not cyberpower can be applied in a timely and effective manner to enhance the success of stability operations.

Collaboration

Collaboration is defined as people or entities laboring or working together. The demands of communication directly affect the ability to collaborate. The standard issue ICT toolsets provided by the U.S. military are clearly inadequate for fostering collaboration among the variety of potential actors on the civil and military sides of the operation.

Translation

Translation is a third function frequently required in stability operations: U.S. forces must be able to quickly translate written and spoken language in order to communicate intentions, plans, and the need for cooperation with local civil authorities. They must be able to understand and comprehend as well as be understood, in order to avoid conflict, mistrust, and increased risks. The Defense Advanced Research Projects Agency (DARPA) is developing a system called Global Autonomous Language Exploitation; it expects to have a system for Arabic and Chinese by 2010.[7] Another DARPA program, Translingual Information Detection Extraction Summarization, also focuses on Arabic and Chinese. It allows the user to extract critical pieces of information in real time from video, broadcasts, or conversations in order to glean a general understanding of what is being communicated.[8] Numerous commercial translation applications are available; free tools on the Web such as Google Language Tools, for example, allow one to request machine translation of specified text.[9] Many of these tools using machine translation provide only limited results, however; the programs often miss nuance, subtlety, and the true meaning of phrases or idioms in the original text.[10] Errors in translation raise tactical and even strategic risk. High-quality translation products must be used, especially in the absence of or in support of human translation services; users must appreciate the risk and the potential adverse effects of mistranslations.

Engagement

U.S. forces must be able to engage the appropriate local entities in order to effect change on the ground, build trust, and maintain or restore order. Engagement may range from a carefully shaped strategic communication via broadcast radio, to a cell phone call to a local sheik or tribal elder, to face-to-face discussion. At all levels, it can be enhanced by cyberpower. Enhancing engagement was intrinsic to the shift in strategy and the so-called troop surge under General David Petraeus in 2007. "Everywhere, Army and Marine units were focused on securing the Iraqi population, working with Iraqi security units, creating new political and economic arrangements at the local level and providing basic services—electricity, fuel, clean water and sanitation—to the people."[11] Having U.S. forces hold on to neighborhoods after clearing out insurgents and then engaging with locals has become key to instilling trust in local leaders.

Policy Underpinnings for Stability Operations

As Franklin Kramer, Larry Wentz, and Stuart Starr state elsewhere in this volume, "Information and information technology can significantly increase the likelihood of success in stability operations."[12] To do so, they must be part of an overall strategy that coordinates the actions of the community of interest. DOD policies, articulated in National Security Presidential Directives (NSPDs), Homeland Security Presidential Directives, Department of Defense Directives (DODDs), and Department of Defense Instructions, offer some good starting points for the U.S. military to take full advantage of and leverage cyberpower. Overall, however, the results have been mixed. This section reviews the top-level policies, identifies key policy elements, and indicates the foundations on which cyberpower could be applied across all actions required in SSTR operations.

DOD Directive 3000.05
DOD now places stability operations formally on a par with major combat operations.[13] DOD Directive 3000.05, *Military Support to Stability, Security, Transition, and Reconstruction Operations*, gives unprecedented importance to operations other than combat. However, it does not spell out how the Service and combatant commanders should implement the directive. Implementing instructions are needed to ensure that the highest echelons of DOD and the Services are in synch with regard to resourcing and transformational priorities.

DOD Directive 8000.1
DOD Directive 8000.1, *Management of DOD Information Resources and Technology*, establishes the authorities of DOD's chief information officer (CIO) and the need for a strategic vision for the information resources of the enterprise.[14] The CIO is responsible for articulating how the department's infrastructure should be postured, in order to be an effective instrument of cyberpower. However, no DOD directives, instructions, or pamphlets have yet been issued regarding cyberpower.

DOD Directive 8100.1
DOD Directive 8100.1, *Global Information Grid (GIG) Overarching Policy*, assigns

roles and responsibilities for the operation and maintenance of the enterprise information infrastructure so that it can be used and applied to support military operations.[15] One would expect the directive to include DOD's view of how the GIG helps make cyberpower possible as an instrument of power, but it does not treat the GIG as an integral element of cyberpower

DOD Directive 8320.2

DOD Directive 8320.2, *Data Sharing in a Net-Centric Department of Defense*, states that users of DOD's information infrastructure must begin to think of data as a commodity that must be accessible, visible, understandable, and trusted by all who have a need to know.[16] The intention is that data can be entered just once and then be available to the enterprise, so that others may take full advantage of it. This requires data consumers to agree on common definitions, especially for data that apply across the range of mission areas.[17] Each of the communities of interest (COIs) must agree on the meaning of each term in the metadata registry so as to ensure interoperability. This will be a challenge; the cost and difficulty of dedicating resources and fencing them off to get data-sharing aspects right may be a hard sell.

One problem with this policy is that it does not limit the number of COIs; it presumes that such communities will somehow self-organize and that some will eventually consolidate. "DOD's data-sharing strategy has led to a proliferation of COIs and competition among them—a situation that could require DOD to map dozens of data models to one another."[18] The DOD Director of Information Management, who is responsible for this data strategy, stated that "we haven't decided what the appropriate number of COIs is. We are letting the market do its work."[19]

DOD Directive 2205.02

DOD Directive 2205.2, *Humanitarian and Civic Assistance Provided in Conjunction with Military Operations*, specifies DOD activities associated with humanitarian operations or training missions.[20] The list of activities does not specifically mention cyberpower or ICT. Clarifying language in the 109th Congress conference report on the defense authorization bill, however, permits the directive to be interpreted to mean that a basic information and communications technology capacity can be developed as part of the military efforts and that such a capacity can be left behind.[21] This is a significant development; its ramifications are beginning to be felt within the combatant commands as they execute humanitarian and civic assistance missions. U.S. forces can now incorporate ICT as they construct schools and clinics abroad, which will vastly improve the effectiveness of such facilities and thus the success of the U.S. forces.

National Security Presidential Directive 44

NSPD 44, *Management of Interagency Efforts Concerning Reconstruction and Stabilization*, provides for the establishment of a Coordinator for Stability and Reconstruction within the State Department for the purposes of having a single U.S. government perspective.[22] It was hoped that the directive would result in a strong coordination role for the State Department in Iraq and Afghanistan. In reality, as of this writing, working groups were just forming to determine how this organization will function, how it will be staffed, and what sorts of logistics and communications support it will require to sustain operations. Moreover, it was unclear what budgetary support this office would receive from the Office of Management and Budget.

DOD Information Sharing Strategy

The *Department of Defense Information Sharing Strategy* established four goals for DOD: promote, encourage, and incentivize sharing; achieve an extended enterprise; strengthen agility in order to accommodate unanticipated partners and events; and ensure trust across organizations.[23] Its focus is on information-sharing across the Federal enterprise as well as with IOs and NGOs that offer valuable capacity or functionality. The strategy document sheds light on the goals and the vision of the CIO established by DOD Directive 8000.1. An Information Sharing Executive position was established to develop these instructions, in conjunction with the Joint Staff and the Services. However, no implementation had been issued as of the summer of 2008.

Summary of Policy Initiatives

The results of the various policy tools, which can either assist or impede cyberpower in the stability operations domain, are mixed. Overall, a fairly good start has been made with regard to policy, and positive steps have been taken to address some of the shortfalls. Unlocking the full potential of cyberpower in support of stability operations can be further enabled through various policy improvements—for example, focusing on the development of implementing instructions for stability operations; improving the implementation of the data-sharing directive; making explicit provisions for ICT in conjunction with humanitarian civic assistance activities (not leaving it as a matter of interpretation); making the State Department Coordinator for Reconstruction and Stabilization into a stronger interagency intermediary; and developing implementation instructions for the visionary information-sharing strategy. The roles of the CIO and the GIG should also be reexamined in the context of cyberpower as an instrument of power and as an enabler of stability operations.

Cyberpower can be applied to all phases of a campaign, not just in a post-conflict context. Every consideration must be given to these tools and issues across all five phases of current campaign planning. If these tools could be applied in phase zero and deter instability and avoid combat, this would clearly be a preferable outcome.

Policy Obstacles to Cyberpower

The Services and DOD have vastly improved communications capabilities due to advances in technology, changes in acquisition rules, and improvements in policy. However, there are areas that could be improved in order to improve the likelihood of success in stability operations. In particular, inflexible rules and regulations will hinder the application of cyberpower.

DOD, the Services, the combatant commands, and various Defense agencies have a range of enterprise-wide approaches for knowledge management, Web services, email, access control, collaboration, and other aspects of utilizing the DOD Intranet to support operations. In general, the Services have gotten much better at communicating with and among each other since the Goldwater-Nichols Department of Defense Reorganization Act of 1986. However, much remains to be done to harmonize approaches even to such simple tools as email. For example, some servers limit the size of messages to roughly 1 megabyte and prevent a user from sending any more email without deleting mail from the server. Some offices require secure access card–enabled sign-on, others do not. Some offices will not permit the use of convenient, cheap "thumb drives" for portable data storage. Commands in Afghanistan and elsewhere have had to mandate that they not be used, because they were too easily stolen; they were being offered for sale in local markets in Kabul, and many held sensitive and operationally relevant files.[24] Some firewalls and antivirus software will not allow .ZIP, .EXE, or other fairly common file extensions to pass through, leaving some email undeliverable. Some Services allow the use of certain types or makes of software, such as "Groove" collaboration software, while others do not. These differences in implementation of regulations and directives can become a significant hindrance to leveraging cyberpower. This is especially true in stability operations, which are often conducted in an austere environment with limited ICT options. The more flexibility that can be afforded to the operator, the more likely success will be achieved. Imposing rules and restrictions, however well meant, may impede success.

Security restrictions and classification of information can similarly prevent the full use and potential of cyberpower. DOD operates on a "need to know" basis and not a "need to share" basis. Often, however, unclassified information is fed into a classified system for transmission and sharing, which inadvertently renders it virtually classified and thus unusable. The security classification process is cumbersome and often abused. The penalties in the system cause many people to err on the side of caution, overclassifying information in order to avoid being dubbed a security violator. There is no penalty for overclassification of information that should have remained more usable in an unclassified and sharable manner. Security is a risk-management process. It should not be so prohibitive to block appropriate people from having access to critical, time-sensitive information so they can save lives or mitigate the effects of a disaster. Adding coalition partners only further complicates releasability criteria. The Defense Department CIO must grapple with these issues and recognize their adverse impact on operations, and then enact changes for the department as an enterprise. This uniform approach will result in a common set of tactics, techniques, and procedures across the department.

NGOs, IOs, and intergovernmental organizations (IGOs) are critical actors; they must be engaged, enabled, and leveraged in order to maximize the probability of success of stability operations. If information is going to be shared with these entities, and these entities are going to be afforded access to portals outside the DOD Intranet, there is the risk that a rogue element will be among them and seek to do harm. Procedures will have to be developed to vet organizations as well as individuals. Individuals might, for example, be granted access only on an invitational and sponsored basis. Once the entity or individual is granted access (for example, to a portal or a Web-based database), network security procedures should be in place and monitoring should be performed to safeguard the data. When any sort of malevolent behavior is detected, access should be immediately blocked and an investigation begun. An advisory should be posted to ensure that there is an awareness of a potential threat to data and to the operation. DOD must develop a vetting process for organizations that join an operation, and organizations must be accountable for their personnel. If someone in an organization is suspected of malicious activity on a network, the organization must know that it will be held responsible for those actions and that it risks being removed from the operation, with potential loss of involvement in future operations and damage to its reputation.

In the interagency arena, there have been efforts to improve communications, especially with regard to the employment of tools such as Information Work Space at the State Department and DOD. However, former Chairman of the Joint Chiefs of Staff General Peter Pace stated that improvements must be made in interagency cooperation; he indicated that legislation analogous to the Goldwater-Nichols Act, which reformed joint warfighting, is needed in this arena.[25]

U.S. Joint Forces Command (USJFCOM) has spent considerable time and effort in developing information technology–based tools to enhance interagency planning and collaboration. These tools were developed to support a new USJFCOM civil-military coordination group called the Joint Interagency Coordination Group. Its proposed functions include:

- participating in combatant command staff crisis planning and assessment
- advising the combatant command staff on civilian agency campaign planning
- working on civilian-military campaign planning issues
- providing civilian agency perspectives during military operational planning activities and exercises
- presenting unique civilian agency approaches, capabilities, and limitations to military campaign planners
- providing vital links to civilian agency campaign planners
- arranging interfaces for useful agency crisis planning activities
- conducting outreach to key civilian international and regional contacts.[26]

These initial efforts are leading to promising results, but a great deal more needs to be done to integrate other departments and agencies to improve communications, collaboration, and information-sharing.

Structured data exchange is possible to a degree among Federal agencies and departments, but unstructured data is becoming increasingly important as an information source. More and more unstructured data is created through blogs, wikis, chat sessions, email, video teleconferences, Web-based video, and other sources. Homeland Security Presidential Directive 11, *Comprehensive Terrorist-related Screening Procedures*, issued August 27, 2004 provides for implementation of plans to share information pertinent to terrorism among Federal agencies.[27] However, no similar directive gives the government, as an enterprise, impetus to improve information-sharing as a means to increase productivity and efficiency in general. Coordination and collaboration issues have plagued the interagency process in Iraq and Afghanistan. In response, the Bush administration created and filled the position of Assistant to the President and Deputy National Security Advisor for Iraq and Afghanistan, as well as creating the post of Department of State Coordinator for Reconstruction and Stabilization. Thus, significant coordination and collaboration issues remain despite implementation of some of the best technologies and improvements in policy, suggesting that these issues are based not in technology but in culture, policy, and politics.

The new U.S. Africa Command (USAFRICOM) is meant to be a combatant command with a strong interagency emphasis and focus. The Principal Deputy Under Secretary of Defense for Policy has stated that USAFRICOM will be different from other U.S. military commands in that it is not meant to fight wars.[28] Its unprecedented organization structure may aid in the integration and sharing of information across the U.S. Government over the long term as new procedures, systems, and policies are put in place to facilitate operations. This will be extremely important from a stability operations perspective. The objective is to construct a well-coordinated and synergized program of humanitarian and civic assistance activities, security cooperation programs, foreign military sales, international training, and other measures in order to facilitate stability, increase security, and avoid conflict. It will only work well if the U.S. Agency for International Development (USAID), the Department of State, DOD, and other pertinent agencies are involved.

Tools and Approaches

This section reviews some of the cyberpower tools and approaches that could enhance stability operations.

Web 2.0

The term *Web 2.0*, when used in the DOD context, generally refers to social networking sites and online collaboration tools.[29] The term encompasses online collaboration tools such as wikis, blogs, video hosting, Real Simple Syndication (RSS), file sharing, and chat. The Defense Intelligence Agency's (DIA's) rollout of Intellipedia was widely reported as a success.[30] It is a tool to "provide information that our analysts and warfighters need in a timelier and more usable fashion."[31] It uses wikis and other networking tools to create a dynamic interactive and collaborative intelligence capability. The State Department also developed a wiki, known as Diplopedia, for use by its employees.[32]

These tools can be combined in *mashups*, a term referring to an application or Web site that combines data from multiple sources into a single integrated tool. For example, DIA can combine cartographic information from Google Earth (which now provides fixed and live street views of some locations using Web cams) with tools provided by geospatial information programs such as the Environmental Systems Research Institute's ArcGIS Explorer to provide geospatially referenced views of structures, streets, and other items represented on maps.[33] Many vendors now supply high-resolution imagery, whereas, for example, "ten years ago, if you wanted a high-resolution picture of Moscow, you would need to work for the CIA [Central Intelligence Agency]. Now you can buy it from 20 different sources, including the Russians, France, India, or China."[34] As these tools develop, they offer considerable potential for stability operations.

Objections have been raised to the release of high-resolution geospatial data by the National Geospatial-Intelligence Agency. However, a big incentive for non-DOD actors to share information with DOD is precisely that DOD can provide such high-resolution data in exchange. In this context, cyberpower could be applied to providing highly precise, geospatially related information on any waypoint of interest to all who need it. There is a risk that such data could be exploited and used against the United States and its allies. However, there are ways to mitigate risk.

There are clear advantages to leveraging the capabilities of Web 2.0 with regard to stability operations. A recent study by the Center for Strategic and International Studies (CSIS) explores the use of tools and capabilities associated with Web 2.0 for "conflict-prone settings, such as wikis, blogs, tagging, and online social-networking web sites.[35] It emphasizes the importance of creating "communities of practice" in which NGOs and other relevant organizations can develop techniques and procedures to solve problems. Larry Wentz emphasizes the use of open-source, open-standard products wherever possible in order to promote interoperability.[36] Both point out that industry is the driver of the technology: actors in the stability operations domain must take what industry is offering to the public—cell phone, personal digital assistant, and WiFi technologies—and adapt them for use in the stability operations environment.

There are disadvantages associated with Web 2.0. For example, the Defense Information Systems Agency (DISA) had to block access by DOD employees and Servicemembers to 13 social networking Web sites, on the basis that these Web sites were consuming too much bandwidth and, more seriously, that they posed a security risk by allowing Servicemembers to post anything they wanted, even information from hostile areas.[37]

Joint C3 Information Exchange Data Model

As noted above, CENTRIXS focused on a C^2 system meant to provide a common platform to support coalition operations on a secure network separate from the U.S. Secure Internet Protocol Router Network. This was acquired, designed, built, deployed, and maintained by the United States at great cost. An alternative approach would be to build to an interface standard: what takes place before the interface is immaterial, as long as what crosses the interface is compatible with the agreed standards. This is the approach taken by the Joint Consultation Command and Control Information Exchange Data Model (JC3IEDM), adopted as the data model for both U.S. Army and Marine Corps C^2 systems of the future; a similar model supports the Army's current C^2 system, the Maneuver Control System. The model is developed by working groups in the Multilateral Interoperability Program (MIP), a multilateral body with 26 member nations. All have agreed to the requirements established by the operations and data working groups and published as standards for systems operations.

The Office of the Assistant Secretary of Defense for Networks and Information Integration (OASD–NII) partially sponsored the development of a prototype system based on this model for interoperable online communications in support of operational level deployment in the North Atlantic Treaty

Organization.[38] That system was on track for deployment to Afghanistan in 2006, but a resurgence of the Taliban caused a postponement of the demonstration. Developers for these JC3IEDM systems continued testing and expected to deploy systems to Afghanistan in the fall of 2008.

This "data model provides an evolved, shared, common set of semantics and concepts that reduces complexity."[39] It can be viewed as a "mechanism to tear down the 'tower of Babel'" resulting from the variety of data types and formats from the various battle command systems acquired over the years.[40] Twenty-six nations are now developing systems based upon this standard, and other nations are being encouraged to join the standards body.

Shared Operational Picture Exchange Services

Although industry was part of the MIP, it did not specify a model that the software industry could readily use. To encourage the development of commercial standards, therefore, the OASD–NII, among others, has sponsored development of Shared Operational Picture Exchange Services (SOPES), an effort that takes standards derived in the MIP community and expresses them in a manner compatible with the best practices of the commercial software industry. This is intended to allow the private sector to develop commercial products for other entities with which the United States and coalition partners must exchange data to support future operations. The SOPES effort seeks to bridge MIP standards to industry practices, "to enhance the ability of first responders, government, military and civilian organizations to develop and sustain a complete, timely and accurate awareness of the operational situation (Common Operational Picture)."[41]

SOPES will "enable users to selectively share information across and between participating organizations" so as to improve the "visibility of the operational environment affecting decisions and resource commitments." It is also intended to "protect sensitive, private, confidential or legally significant information from general dissemination." The goal of the system is to "enable all participants within a coalition to have the same understanding of the operational scenario and environment within their area of interest."

Agent-based Technologies

Potential real-time data sources within various agencies of the Federal Government could help support stability operations. Treasury, State, Defense, Justice, Homeland Security, and other departments are each involved in stability operations in Iraq and Afghanistan, which confront them with the challenges of a rapid growth of information volume and complexity. As these organizations attempt to become more productive through the application of information systems, growth in productivity can be inhibited by the type of available data:

enormous quantities of semistructured and unstructured data are now generated by email, file attachments, wikis, blogs, and files in heterogeneous formats that are stored on shared organizational drives or data warehouses.

The potential value of the knowledge and information contained in this semistructured and unstructured data might be harnessed through the implementation of a "metadata" layer where "tagging" allows the extraction and translation of this data into a useful form. Quality metadata can play a significant role in benefiting decision processes.[42] The metadata are discoverable by automated "intelligent agents" and thus made available to decision support systems, easing the cognitive load on the policymaker or decisionmaker. As computing power continues to grow, software agents with greater sophistication will make decision support system components more effective.

The methodology of metadata and intelligent agents is being applied across a range of domains of the U.S. Government, from hydrology to military intelligence and law enforcement. For example, the Consortium of Universities for the Advancement of Hydrologic Science has developed the Hydrologic Data Access Center, which draws data from six different departments or agencies of the Federal Government for hydrologic analyses on behalf of the National Science Foundation.[43] The intelligence and law enforcement communities use XML metadata tagging to process data from 20 different sources. These represent up to 300 data feeds that generate more than half of the Intelligence Community's data. This enables them to draw on previously untapped semistructured and unstructured data buried in vast repositories and data warehouses.[44] A law enforcement program known as OneDOJ is a vendor-neutral approach that uses a standard XML data model that will be built into the joint Department of Justice—Department of Homeland Security National Information Exchange Model. This effort involves the 93 U.S. Attorneys, the Federal Bureau of Investigation, the Drug Enforcement Administration, the U.S. Marshals Service, the Federal Bureau of Prisons, and the Bureau of Alcohol, Tobacco, Firearms, and Explosives.[45] Agent-based technologies are also being applied to crisis management and disaster response.[46]

Geostrategic Considerations and Market Forces to Create Stability

Use of the military is not the only way to leverage cyberpower to conduct stability operations; market forces can also bring cyberpower to help enable a stable and prosperous civil populace. The International Telecommunication Union (ITU), for example, is seeking to extend cyberpower connectivity to the disconnected and underserved countries of the world (as discussed in chapter 21, "Internet Governance," and elsewhere in this volume). The ITU-sponsored World Summit for an Information Society (WSIS) developed a series of actions and programs to improve the degree of connectedness around the world from 2005 onward. A program introduced at the WSIS Convention in Tunis in 2005 was the "$100 Laptop," a creation of Nicholas Negroponte and a team of Massachusetts Institute of Technology researchers and engineers along with the One Laptop Per Child (OLPC) Foundation.[47] The computers are LINUX-based (free and open source) and are meant to serve as a conventional laptop, e-book reader, or game system. The computer, dubbed the "XO," hosts a variety of software applications for education plus an Internet browser. The display is capable of being read in daylight or darkness, and the computer has built-in recharging and WiFi capability. The WiFi capability will permit peer-to-peer "mesh" networks to be formed. It will take an additional step to connect to the Internet; in remote villages, the only alternative is the Very Small Aperture Terminal, a two-way satellite ground station with a dish antenna, but there are more options where some telecommunications infrastructure exists. A growing number of countries have signed up to purchase these computers for school-age children.[48] Intel developed a low-cost computing solution called Classmate, which it sought to market where OLPC had not.[49] Intel's position was that reaching the next billion computer users would require a range of hardware vendors; however, press coverage suggested that Intel was encroaching for profit on charitable work done by a nonprofit organization. Intel backed off and agreed to join the board of the charitable organization in order to complement rather than compete with the OLPC vision established by Negroponte and his team.[50] The company's membership on the board has since ended with Intel seeking a place in the market for their product. Market forces prevailed in 2007 as price points for the OLPC decreased from $150 for initial units to a projected $50 per unit in 2009. The first units were shipping to Libya for every school-age child in the country. In 2007, there were orders for 3 million XO computers for use in Argentina, Brazil, Libya, Nigeria, and Thailand.[51]

A framework for postconflict reconstruction tasks developed by CSIS included the task of "development of Social and Economic Well-Being."[52] Part of this task was "Employment Generation through Microenterprise," that is, "creating microenterprise mechanisms with appropriate credit mechanisms; soliciting proposals at local level; and identifying funding sources and implementing priority projects."[53] This general framework can be applied in India and Latin America in environments that are not "postconflict" but where additional stability and security are sought. C.K. Prahalad discusses the notion of applying elements of cyberpower to assist those he calls the bottom of the pyramid (BOP)—the 4 billion poorest people at the lowest rungs of society, those who live on $2 per day.[54] Prahalad argues that low-cost, readily available cyberpower-based technologies can allow the BOP along with banks and businesses to rethink commerce and arrive at a solution where everyone wins through a fair profit. Microcredit and microfinance in conjunction with applied technology and connectivity open doors to the poor and provide them access to the global marketplace. Although as individuals the BOP are poor, this stratum of society as a whole does have money. They are eager to use video teleconferencing, chat, email, personal computers, and cell phones to compare and analyze loan rates and commodity prices and to negotiate transactions.[55] It is of note that Prahalad's illustrations show companies, not government, leveraging cyberpower. He predicts that "poverty alleviation will become a business development task shared among the large private sector firms and local BOP entrepreneurs."[56] This approach suggests that the combination of market forces and cyberpower can be an important aid to stability.

Operations Centers and Provincial Reconstruction Teams

Typically, military operations are characterized by positive control: all characteristics of operations are monitored and influenced through command and control. Order and discipline are maintained as much as possible through coordination and unity of command. Military organizations participating in stability operations are hierarchical and are led top-down. However, this is not necessarily the case with NGOs, IGOs, and IOs that play roles in stability operations. Such entities rely on their own experience and decisionmaking to deliver their goods and services. In order to work together, both sides must understand the differences in their cultures and how each functions and disseminates information. Military officials will seek to "control" entities in their respective areas of operations, while entities such as NGOs or IOs may resist the efforts of the military to control them. Civil-military operations centers have been one successful approach to coordinating activities of military and civilian organizations. Much has been developed in terms of doctrine in the U.S. Army Civil Affairs branch and, perhaps surprisingly, from the UN Office of the Coordinator for Humanitarian Affairs with regard to instructional civil-military coordination courses. The portals discussed earlier are a natural extension in cyberspace of these types of operations centers. Some have used the term *collaborative information environment* to characterize the intent of these portals.[57] ReliefWeb, sponsored by the United Nations, is an example of this type of collaborative environment: it is intended to be "the global hub for time-critical humanitarian information on Complex Emergencies and Natural Disasters."[58] To coordinate operations, the UN has created the Virtual On-Site Operations Coordination Centre, a Web portal whose purpose is to "facilitate decision-making for international response to major disasters though real-time information exchange by all actors of the international disaster response community."[59] The Department of State has created the Global Disaster

Information Network, intended to complement the work achieved elsewhere by adding information available only to the United States through national means of reconnaissance. The State Department indicates that its primary functions would be:

> First, to enable disaster managers, relief workers and others to systematically and rapidly access existing information, to include in situ and remote sensing data, maps, situation reports, etc., that is pertinent to their specific needs; Second, to serve as a mechanism whereby, in the absence of sufficient relevant existing information, disaster managers and relief workers can promptly communicate with reliable sources (e.g. governments, international organizations) to request the needed information in a usable form.[60]

The World Food Programme's Humanitarian Early Warning Service is intended to be a "global multi-hazard watch service to support humanitarian preparedness."[61] It tracks drought, floods, storms, locusts, volcanoes, severe weather, tsunamis, and the like.[62] All of these portals seek to coordinate, collaborate, and share information to facilitate the mission of providing relief and saving lives. The World Food Programme also uses online games to generate donations of rice and other food for the needy of the world.[63]

Provincial reconstruction teams (PRTs) are a newer type of organization for civil-military engagement. First used in Afghanistan with much success, PRTs were introduced into Iraq after Zalmay Khalilzad, who had been U.S. Ambassador to Afghanistan, was appointed Ambassador to Iraq in 2005. PRTs in recent operations have been led by personnel from the State Department, DOD, and the International Security Assistance Force in Afghanistan. They have differed in terms of the mission, their composition, how well they have been equipped, and how well they have been integrated into the military mission.[64] CSIS analyses indicate a need to give these teams better information and communications technology capacity so they can communicate, collaborate, translate, and engage with the host nation and local leaders, and so they can communicate the needs of the local leaders and host nation to the strategic programmers in Kabul, Baghdad, Washington, and elsewhere.[65]

Sending out PRTs without needed information and communications technologies and equipment is a recipe for failure, and there have been shortfalls in practice. A PRT leader indicated after her return from Iraq that she had not been given any sort of ICT support as she departed Baghdad for her post in Diyala Province. Eventually, her team members pooled resources and assembled computers, organized Internet service from a local provider, and procured cellular phones from another local provider. No set, kit, or outfit had been provided to the PRT members or leaders as they departed for their posts.

USAID, the State Department, and DOD have purchased a variety of commercial-off-the-shelf satellite-based communications equipment for operations centers and PRTs in austere environments. Leaders must do better to ensure that this type of kit is issued to the teams before they are assigned to a emote posting.[66] Advances in bandwidth availability continue to make these technologies attractive when less expensive alternatives, such as local cellular phones or Internet providers, are unavailable.[67] The ability to bridge the gap between the military and civilian authorities to enable stability operations is a critical task.

PRTs and civil-military operations centers are both important to strategic communications and information campaigns.[68] While each has different compositions and methodologies, each can send the message that the military operation is here to help create an environment to foster stability and reconstruction. Strategic communications are a requirement of DOD Directive 3000.05. Success in stability operations requires the support of the local populace. Garnering that support is the task of strategic communications, but it has to be accomplished at the tactical level, as part of a tactical information campaign communicating to people that it is in their interest to cooperate with the United States and its coalition partners, rather than resist or engage in combat.

The United States has had the ability for years to broadcast AM, FM, and television programming to pass on information as an indigenous capability in the military's inventory. In the past, the U.S. military distributed AM radios to inform, educate, and advise the populace in advance of an operation in order to avoid confrontation and to solicit support. The World Wide Web and Internet can now accomplish this via email and instant messaging on personal computers and cell phones. This activity is in the realm of information operations and influence operations. Political blogs, wikis, and other social networking tools are also useful for advocating and promoting reconstruction, stability, and security. Streaming video, images, text, and music can be employed to share U.S. ideals and goals. The U.S. message has competition: Islamic jihadists use YouTube as a recruiting tool to show that the U.S. military is vulnerable to sniper fire and improvised explosive device attacks. The United States, too, must leverage this medium as part of its cyberpower toolkit to advance stability around the world.

Conclusion and Recommendations

A good start has been made to harmonizing policy to coincide with the reality that stability operations are indeed a core mission for DOD. However, precise instructions to the Services about how to implement Directive 3000.05 are wanting.[69] A redoubling of efforts and scrutiny should be applied to developing the implementation instruction. Instructions will affect the resources and the way in which we organize, train, and equip our forces as well as how we develop doctrine, tactics, techniques, and procedures.

Stability operations require engagement of coalition partners as well as NGOs, IOs, and IGOs. The U.S. Government in general, and DOD in particular, needs to guard against inflexible and restrictive procedures that will preclude these valuable partners from exchanging information with the United States. The sooner participants other than DOD entities can perform their functions to improve water and food distribution, medical support, security, and the like, the sooner the U.S. military can disengage and refit for the next contingency. Lessons of other operations can identify best practices to mitigate the risks of information-sharing, such as sponsored membership to secure Web sites, digital invitations for shared workstations, agreed ICT architectures, vetting of organizations and holding organizations responsible for their personnel, trust with verification through monitoring, and restrictive write permissions. Declassification procedures can be reassessed to ensure information is not overly classified to the detriment of operations. What is being recommended is a move to a "need to share" culture rather than restrictions based on "need to know."

Design of organizations for stability operations is an important consideration. A civil-military operations center or a provincial reconstruction team must have the correct mix of civilian and military members, along with access to information and communications technology to leverage cyberpower. The crucial functions of stability operations—communications, collaboration, translation, and engagement with the local populace—require a proper mix of satellite communications, cellular communications, and information systems tools.

Teamwork is also critical. It cannot be left to just one department in the Federal Government to be successful in the next stability operation: the strengths of all necessary Federal departments must be brought to the operation.

DOD is improving its ability to share information and leverage new technologies to enhance situational awareness and improve decisionmaking. However, only recently has operating with NGOs, IGOs, and IOs been examined in such detail, and much more could be done to foster trust and collaboration with these entities. Education, joint training and exercises, and social networking with these organizations could be an immense help in identifying policy flaws and necessary procedural improvements and cultural changes. Involvement by these nongovernmental, intergovernmental, and international organizations with the U.S. military in stability exercises could lead to more effectiveness in real operations. Improving the familiarity of these organizations with U.S.-sponsored Web portals and their capabilities will also serve to improve interoperability and efficiency.

New coursework and educational materials have already been developed to train and educate future U.S. military leaders on the nature of stability operations.

The Naval Postgraduate School has the Center for Reconstruction and Stabilization Studies and has developed a distance learning module on Hastily Formed Networks. Stability operations are integrated into the coursework at the School of National Security Executive Education at the National Defense University. The Peacekeeping and Stability Operations Institute at the U.S. Army War College focuses on stability operations training and education for all government personnel who are a part of the community of interest. In addition to formal classroom instruction, tools emerging on the Internet—such as "Peacemaker," "Darfur Is Dying," and "Third World Farmer"—stimulate thought as gamers work through some of the issues that befall stability operations.[70] Training and education must continue to include nonmilitary aspects of stability operations.

Leveraging the power of the semistructured and unstructured data generated by collaborative efforts will be the next area of development, offering new tools for stability operations as they have for the intelligence and law enforcement communities. This will be the next great addition to the cyberpower toolkit.

Since the 2004 Defense Science Board Summer Study recommended an examination of the notion of stability operations, there have been many new developments. With regard to cyberpower, the conclusions, issues, and recommendations discussed in this chapter represent a step in the right direction. Much remains to be accomplished with regard to policy, doctrine, programs, cultural changes, tactics, techniques, and procedures. Cyberpower can be a powerful complementary enabler for stability and security, but the U.S. military must finish developing the necessary underpinnings. An understanding of the challenges of efficient stability operations is just emerging. Changing cultures and organizations and resolving policy and legal impediments will take much more work within the community of interest.

Part V
Cyberpower: Strategic Problems

CHAPTER 18

Cyber Crime

Clay Wilson

CYBER CRIME is becoming a highly organized underground business on the Internet, where criminals advertise a variety of disruptive software products and malicious technical services for sale or rent. High-end cyber crime groups use modern business practices to keep their software products updated with the latest antisecurity features while seeking to recruit new software engineering talent into their organizations. Cyber criminals use the Internet to direct large networks of remotely controlled "zombie" computers to attack in swarms, attempting to infect additional computers, distribute unwanted spam, or deny Internet access and services to legitimate users. Attribution of cyber crime to perpetrators is problematic, and new technologies outpace law enforcement capabilities. As malicious code grows in sophistication and the consequences of cyber crime expand, this emerging threat to national security may also alter discussions about cyber terrorism.[1]

This chapter begins by describing the characteristics of cyber crime and offering examples of how it has evolved over the past few years. Next is a discussion of the tools of cyber crime, such as botnets, malicious code on Web sites, and identity theft, which has also been linked to terrorist activity. An examination of cyber espionage shows how Internet technology has caused a dilemma: this form of "cyber crime" may also be viewed as a necessity in business competition or maintenance of national security. Discussion includes insider threats, piracy of intellectual property, and money laundering (especially associated with drug traffickers).

The next section describes law enforcement issues, including problems in measuring the scope and economic effects of cyber crime and in tracing evidence associated with a cyber crime. The problem is addressed but not solved by the Convention on Cybercrime, the first international agreement to coordinate the work of cyber crime law enforcement agencies in different countries.

The chapter then examines organized crime, which is increasing its operations in cyberspace, and the future of organized cyber crime, including potential attacks on infrastructure control systems and links with terrorism.

The chapter ends by encouraging decisionmakers to pay more attention to the urgent need for improvements to cyber security. The conclusion presents crucial policy questions and warnings (in particular, the possibility that extremists can now employ sophisticated cyber crime tools for cyber terrorism without the need to develop their own hard-to-obtain technical skills).

Characteristics of Cyber Crime

Cyber crime is usually enabled and conducted through a connection to the Internet but can also involve unauthorized removal of data on small, portable storage devices (known as flash drives or thumb drives). Crime in cyberspace can be committed anonymously with relative ease and sometimes even can occur without detection by the victim. Cyberspace allows criminals to extend their reach across national borders, putting at risk a wider population of potential victims. Consumers who use new "Web 2.0" tools for sharing data on social networking Web sites such as MySpace and YouTube, and on business networking Web sites such as LinkedIn, are increasingly at risk as criminals capture personal information and corporate data for purposes of fraud and extortion.[2] Problems of coordination among law enforcement agencies of different countries, and sometimes conflicting national policies about crime in cyberspace, combine to aid cyber criminals who may choose to operate from geographic locations where penalties for some forms of cyber crime may not yet exist.

The possibility of illicit profits, together with a low probability of detection or identification, can make cyber crime attractive. Criminal groups that lack the technical skills needed to manipulate computer code may hire the services of individual (or groups of) hackers. Profitable alliances of hackers and criminals can be rapidly created as needed and then just as quickly dissolved. Where illicit profits are potentially large, some criminal groups have adopted standard information technology (IT) business practices to systematically develop more efficient and effective computer code for cyber crime. Cyber criminals reportedly now sell or rent software products in online markets for customers to use to support their own cyber crimes. For example, some security experts suspect that such services may have been used in the April 2007 attack in Estonia (discussed below). When illicit profits become the only concern, it is possible that future customers of cyber criminals may comprise anyone who can pay for services, possibly including terrorist groups.

Some argue there is no agreed definition for *cyber crime* and that *cyberspace* is just a new instrument used to commit crimes that are not new at all. For example, cyber crime may involve theft of intellectual property in violation of existing patent, trade secret, or copyright laws. Press releases on the U.S. Department of Justice's Web site indicate the variety of activities that fit into the category of cyber crime:[3]

- "'Phisher' Sentenced to Nearly Six Years in Prison after Nation's First Can-Spam Act Jury Trial Conviction" (June 14, 2007)
- "Man Indicted for Illegally Transmitting Electronic Funds from Various Banks to Ameritrade and E*Trade, Totaling Approximately $3,348,000.00" (May 9, 2007)
- "Digital Currency Business E-Gold Indicted for Money Laundering and Illegal Money Transmitting" (April 27, 2007)
- "Man Charged with Computer Fraud and Aggravated Identity Theft: Internet 'Phishing' Scheme Used to Steal Thousands of Credit and Debit Card Numbers, Social Security Numbers" (April 26, 2007)
- "Couple Charged with Criminal Copyright and Trademark Violations for Distributing Counterfeited Microsoft Software" (June 12, 2007)
- "Man Sentenced to Five Years in Prison for Conducting a Multi-Million Dollar International Cable Piracy Business" (June 8, 2007)
- "Former Computer Contractor Pleads Guilty to Hacking Daimler Chrysler Parts Distribution Wireless Network" (June 1, 2007)
- "Man Charged with Leaking Season Premier of Popular Television Show by Uploading to the Internet" (June 1, 2007)
- "Ex-Employee of the Coca Cola Company and Co-Defendant Sentenced for Stealing Trade Secrets" (May 23, 2007)
- "Software Piracy Crackdown 'Operation Fastlink' Yields 50th Guilty Plea" (May 14, 2007)
- "Man Receives Federal Sentence for Copying Copyrighted Movies" (May 11, 2007).

Evolution of Cyber Crime

Most cyber crime has taken the form of massive, widespread attacks intended to affect all users of the Internet. Increasingly, however, cyber crime involves the use of remotely controlled software that can focus the power of many hacked zombie computers to attack a specific target. Thousands of individual computers infected with malicious code are remotely directed via the Internet to attack in swarms, called *botnets*. Two examples illustrate how cyber crime has evolved from randomly targeted attacks to sophisticated, controlled attacks focused on specific targets. The first example describes a single Internet worm that, in 2005, spread randomly to infect thousands of computers worldwide.

An 18-year-old Moroccan national and a 21-year-old resident of Turkey were arrested in 2005, and sentenced in 2006, for creating and spreading computer worms that disrupted services on computer networks of major U.S. news organizations and other institutions during August 2005. The Zotob worm and its variants were designed to remotely instruct computers to send email spam, steal personal data, or attack other computers without the user's knowledge. According to Federal Bureau of Investigation (FBI) Assistant Director Louis Reigel, who at the time headed the cyber division, investigators believe the malicious code was created by one hacker and sold to the other hacker for financial gain. The Zotob worm was an example of a widespread cyber attack that did not show evidence of specific targets for identity theft, bank fraud, or forgery. It is estimated to have cost $500 million in lost productivity and other nuisance damage to many corporate and individual users.[4]

The Zotob incident was an example of the type of widespread and random cyber attack in which hackers seemed to be looking less for monetary gain than for notoriety. Subsequently, however, Department of Justice officials indicated they were observing a change in the apparent motives of people who attack computer networks away from bragging rights and toward monetary motives.[5] Now, cyber crime is apparently becoming a fee-for-service business operation, where criminals offer technical skills and malicious code products for sale or rent. Such an arrangement may be behind a recent cyber attack that involved thousands of computers worldwide simultaneously attacking government computer systems in Estonia.

On April 27, 2007, officials in Estonia relocated a Soviet-era war memorial commemorating an unknown Russian who died fighting the Nazis, and the move stirred emotions. Ethnic Russians in Estonia rioted, and the Estonian embassy in Moscow was blockaded. Several large and sustained distributed denial-of-service (DDOS) attacks were launched against many Estonian national Web sites, including those of government ministries and the prime minister's Reform Party.[6] The attacks, which flooded computers and servers and blocked legitimate users, were described as crippling to Estonia's limited resources for support of its communications infrastructure.

As in any cyber attack, accurate identification of the attacker was difficult. This uncertainty means that it is difficult to name a target for retaliation (which in turn affects deterrence, as discussed in chapter 13 in this volume, "Deterrence of Cyber Attacks"), and creates uncertainty over whether a retaliatory or other response should come from law enforcement or the military. In the Estonia case, the North Atlantic Treaty Organization and the United

States sent computer security experts to Estonia to help recover from the attacks, analyze the methods used, and attempt to determine their source.

Initially, some Estonian officials blamed the Russian government for the cyber attacks and even made charges of cyberwarfare. Other observers linked the cyber attacks to transnational cyber criminals who had made large botnets available for short-term rent. It was noted that as the rented time expired, the intensity of the persistent cyber attacks against Estonia also began to fall off.[7] However, not all security experts agree, and it remains unclear whether the cyber attacks were sanctioned or initiated by the Russian government or a criminal botnet was involved.

Some network analysts later concluded that the cyber attacks targeting Estonia were not a concerted attack but instead were the product of spontaneous anger from a loose federation of separate attackers. Technical data showed that sources of the attack were worldwide rather than concentrated in a few locations. The computer code that caused the DDOS attack was posted and shared in many Russian-language chat rooms, where the moving of the war memorial was an emotional topic. These analysts stated that although access to various Estonian government agencies was blocked by the malicious code, there was no apparent attempt to target national critical infrastructure other than Internet resources, and no extortion demands were made. Their analysis led them to believe that there was no Russian government connection to the attacks against Estonia.[8] However, investigation into the incident continues, and U.S. officials view some aspects of the event as a possible model for future cyber attacks against other nation-states. In February 2008, an Estonian court convicted a 20-year-old ethnic Russian living in Estonia of participating in the cyber attack and ordered him to pay a fine of €1,120. To date, this is the only conviction associated with the cyber attack.[9]

Cyber crime, and the accompanying publicity, has given some practitioners a celebrity status within the hacking community. Authors of malicious code now collaborate to produce annual conferences and seminars where hacking methods are showcased and potential security vulnerabilities are publicly exposed.[10] Organized crime groups are also actively recruiting skilled IT students into cyber crime. These recruits include college graduates and technical expert members of computer societies, who might be sponsored to attend IT courses to further their technical expertise. However, in some cases, the targeted student may not realize that a criminal organization is behind the recruitment offer or the support for their education.[11]

Anonymity is part of another recent trend, as cyber attacks are increasingly designed to silently steal information without leaving behind any damage that a user would notice. These types of attacks are designed to escape detection in order to remain on host systems for longer periods of time. Cyber criminals can also work out in the open, rather than in their basements, because the pervasiveness of the Internet helps maintain anonymity. For example, Internet cafes often clean their computers by automatically rebooting and wiping all nonstandard files between each customer.

Cyber criminals post update information about their computer exploits as a type of advertising, so their business customers can be sure they purchase the latest malicious code with new features to elude newer commercial antivirus tools. Criminals put legitimate Web sites where Web crawlers will inspect them, but innocent users who later visit the site are routed to infected sites.[12] Another trick is to customize the malicious code so that each visitor to an infected Web site is infected by a differently encrypted version of the code; this helps defeat newer antivirus tools. Thus, criminals can evade detection while continuing to spread malicious code.

Counterfeit software is sold to U.S. and foreign consumers with features that facilitate later infections by computer viruses. Sale of counterfeit goods is on the increase as eBay and similar Web sites gain prominence outside the United States in countries where laws are unsettled or are unfavorable to U.S. crime victims.

Criminals use "phishing" techniques, masquerading as a trustworthy entity in an attempt to acquire sensitive information for fraudulent purposes. Phishing is typically carried out by an email or instant message requesting that recipients respond with user names, computer passwords, and credit card or banking details, or that they expose sensitive information by visiting a Web site. Users of eBay, online banks, and investment services are common targets. Criminals also use the services of popular payment networks such as PayPal and E-Gold for money laundering and masking illegal activities. Some cyber criminals may engage in cyber crime to finance terrorist schemes (discussed further below; also see chapter 19 in this volume, "Cyber Terrorism: Menace or Myth?").[13]

Tools of Cyber Crime

Increasing in use are botnets, malicious code on Web sites, identity theft, cyber espionage, theft or abuse of insider information, piracy and trade in counterfeit goods, and money laundering.

Botnets

Bot (from *robot*) *networks* or *botnets* are made up of vast numbers of computers that are infected and remotely controlled to operate, in concert, through commands sent via the Internet. They are used to block or disrupt the computers of targeted organizations or to distribute spam, viruses, or other malicious code. Botnets have been described as the "Swiss Army knives of the underground economy" because they are so versatile.

Jeanson Ancheta, a young hacker and member of a group called the "Botmaster Underground," reportedly made more than $100,000 from Internet advertising companies who paid him to download their malicious "adware" code onto more than 400,000 vulnerable personal computers (PCs) he had secretly taken over.[14] He also made tens of thousands of dollars renting his 400,000-unit "botnet herd" to companies that used it to send out spam, viruses, and other malicious code on the Internet. In 2006, Ancheta was sentenced in U.S. District Court in California to nearly 5 years in prison after pleading guilty under an indictment for conspiring to violate the Computer Fraud Abuse Act; conspiring to violate the Controlling the Assault of Non-Solicited Pornography and Marketing Act; causing damage to computers used by the Federal Government in national defense; and accessing protected computers without authorization to commit fraud, in the first U.S. case to target profits derived from use of botnets.[15]

Botnet code was originally distributed as infected email attachments. When users click to view a spam message, botnet code can be secretly installed on their PC. As users have grown more cautious, cyber criminals have turned to other methods. A Web site may spread infection by means of an ordinary-looking advertisement banner or a link to an infected Web site. Clicking on any of these may install botnet code. Botnet code can be silently uploaded, even if the user takes no action while viewing the Web site, if the browser has certain unpatched vulnerabilities. Firewalls and antivirus software do not necessarily inspect all data that is downloaded through browsers, and some bot software can disable antivirus security.

Once a PC has been infected, the malicious software (or *malware*) establishes a secret communications link to a remote botmaster or bot-herder by which it receives commands to attack a specific target. The malicious code may also automatically probe the infected PC for personal data or may log keystrokes and transmit the information to the botmaster.

The Shadowserver Foundation monitors the number of bot networks being controlled online at any given time by monitoring command-and-control servers. From November 2006 through May 2007, it found approximately 1,400 active command-and-control servers. The number of individual infected drones or zombies controlled by such servers reportedly grew from half a million in March 2007 to more than 3 million in May 2007. Symantec, another security organization, reported that it detected 6 million bot-infected computers in the second half of 2006.[16] Some botnet owners reportedly rent out huge networks for $200 to $300 an hour. Botnets are increasingly used for fraud and extortion.[17]

Newer methods for distributing bot software may complicate law enforcement efforts to identify and locate the originating botmaster. Authors of software for Botnets are increasingly using modern open-source techniques for software development, including use of multiple contributors to the design, new releases that fix bugs in the malicious code, and modules that make portions of the code reusable for newer malicious software. This behavior mirrors the code development techniques used to create commercial software products and is expected to make future botnets more robust and reliable, making malware more attractive to criminals.[18]

Malicious Code Hosted on Web Sites

Users who lacked important software security patches and who visited the popular MySpace and YouTube Web sites in 2005 may have had their PCs infected. If they clicked on a particular banner advertisement, it silently installed malicious code on their computers to log keystrokes or capture sensitive data. During the first half of 2006, the Microsoft Security Team reported that it removed 10 million pieces of malicious software from nearly 4 million computers and Web servers.[19] When analysts at Google examined several million Web pages for the presence of malicious software, they determined that 4.5 million of the Web pages examined were suspicious in nature. After further testing of those pages, over 1 million were found to launch downloads of malicious software, and more than two-thirds of those programs were bot software that, among other things, collected data on banking transactions, which it emailed to a temporary (and thus hard to trace) email account.[20]

Researchers at Finjan, Inc., a California security firm, reviewed security data from the first quarter of 2007. Based on an analysis of more than 10 million unique Web sites from Internet traffic, they found that attacks are increasingly using code obfuscation through diverse randomization techniques, making them almost invisible to pattern-matching or signature-based methods in use by traditional antivirus products; and that more and more, malicious code is embedded within legitimate content, with less dependence on outlaw servers in unregulated countries. Finjan found that 90 percent of the Web sites it examined that contained malware resided on servers located in the United States or the United Kingdom.[21] This finding contradicts the common perception that malicious code is primarily hosted in countries where e-crime laws are less developed.

Identity Theft

Individual users may become victims of cyber crime if they are lured into clicking on tempting links in email or on Web sites, such as offers to "buy Rolex watches cheap" or "check out my new photos." These links might be configured to place malicious software onto a user's system by exploiting Web browser vulnerabilities.

Malicious code placed in this way can scan a victim's computer for sensitive information, such as name, address, telephone number, place and date of birth,

Social Security number, and answers to commonly used security questions such as mother's maiden name. Identity information obtained this way is then sold in online markets. Purchasers might use it to create false identity documents: readily available equipment such as a digital camera, color printer, and laminating device might be used to make official-looking driver's licenses, birth certificates, reference letters, or bank statements.[22]

Inadequate computer security practices within organizations sometimes facilitate identity theft involving thousands of victims. Over 218 million records containing sensitive personal information were involved in U.S. security breaches between January 2005 and March 3, 2008. For example, on February 27, 2008, 103,000 individual records were compromised when personal information, including Social Security numbers, for thousands of doctors in 11 states was openly posted on a company Web site.[23] In June 2006, officials from the U.S. Department of Energy acknowledged that personal information belonging to more than 1,500 employees of the National Nuclear Security Administration had been stolen in a network intrusion that apparently took place starting in 2004 and was not discovered until a year later.[24]

Stolen credit card numbers and bank account information are now traded online in a highly structured arrangement involving buyers, sellers, intermediaries, and service industries. Services offered include changing the address of a stolen identity through manipulation of stolen personal identification numbers or passwords. Some observers estimated that in 2005, such services for each stolen MasterCard number cost between $42 and $72.[25] The cost has apparently gone down: other studies show that in 2007, a stolen credit card number would sell online for $1, while an identity complete with U.S. bank account number, credit card number, date of birth, and government-issued ID number sold for $14 to $18.[26]

Cyber Espionage

Cyber espionage involves the unauthorized probing of a target computer's configuration to evaluate its system defenses or the unauthorized viewing and copying of data files. If a terrorist group, nation, or another organization uses computer hacking techniques for political or economic motives, such intrusions could be criminal. If there is disagreement about this, however, it is because technology has outpaced policy in cyberspace. In some views, industrial cyber espionage is considered a necessary part of global economic competition, and secret monitoring of the computerized functions and capabilities of potential adversary countries may be considered essential for national defense.

In 2001, a special committee of inquiry established by the European Parliament accused the United States of using a Cold War–era electronic spy network to engage in industrial espionage against European businesses.[27] The United

States set up the Echelon network in 1971; Britain helps operate the system, and there are listening posts in Canada, Australia, and New Zealand. Echelon is described as a global spy system capable of intercepting phone calls, electronic mail, and fax messages made from almost any location around the world. The European Parliament charged that information gathered on Echelon helped the United States beat the European Airbus Consortium in selling aircraft to Saudi Arabia in 1994. The State Department denied that the U.S. Government was engaged in industrial espionage. However, the former director of the Central Intelligence Agency, James Woolsey, reportedly justified the possibility of doing so on the basis that European companies use bribery. This prompted an outraged response from officials of the European Parliament, but no denial that companies sometimes used bribery to secure a deal.[28]

Reliance on technology has changed the nature of both military and industrial espionage, and the Internet offers new low-cost and low-risk opportunities for espionage. Some government officials warn of an increased risk to U.S. national security due to cyber espionage by other countries since criminals now sell or rent malicious code tools to conduct it. One industry official, arguing for stronger government agency computer security practices, stated, "If gangs of foreigners broke into the State or Commerce Departments and carried off dozens of file cabinets, there would be a crisis. When the same thing happens in cyberspace, we shrug it off as another of those annoying computer glitches we must live with."[29]

In 2003, a series of computer attacks designed to copy sensitive data files was launched against Department of Defense (DOD) systems and computers belonging to DOD contractors. The cyber espionage attack apparently went undetected for many months. DOD suspected that this series of cyber attacks, later labeled Titan Rain, originated in China. The attacks were directed against the Defense Information Systems Agency, the Redstone Arsenal, the Army Space and Strategic Defense Installation, and several computer systems critical to military logistics. Although no classified systems were breached, many files were copied containing sensitive information that is subject to U.S. export-control laws.

In 2006, an extended computer attack against the U.S. Naval War College in Newport, Rhode Island, prompted officials to disconnect the entire campus from the Internet.[30] A similar attack against the Pentagon in 2007 led officials to temporarily disconnect part of the unclassified network from the Internet.[31]

Accurate attribution is important when considering whether to retaliate using military force or police action. DOD officials suspect that the majority of cyber attacks against DOD and U.S. civilian agency systems originated in China, and these attacks are consistently more numerous and sophisticated than cyber attacks from other malicious actors.[32] The motives appear to be primarily cyber espionage against civilian agencies, DOD contractors, and DOD systems. The espionage involves unauthorized access to files containing sensitive industrial technology and unauthorized research into DOD operations. Some attacks included attempts to implant malicious code into computer systems for future use by intruders.[33]

Security experts warn that all U.S. Federal agencies should now be aware that some malicious actors in cyberspace make no distinction between military and civilian targets. According to an August 2005 computer security report by IBM, more than 237 million overall security attacks were reported globally during the first half of that year.[34] Government agencies were targeted the most, reporting more than 54 million attacks, while manufacturing ranked second (36 million), financial services ranked third (around 34 million), and then health care (over 17 million). The United States was the most frequent target, with 12 million attacks in the first half of 2005 on U.S. Government agencies and industries, followed by New Zealand (1.2 million) and China (1 million). Moreover, the number of incidents reported is only a small fraction of the total number of attacks that actually occur.

The Insider Threat

A major threat for organizations is the ease with which data can be copied and carried away using small storage devices such as thumb drives. Future advances in technology that allow installed computer applications to be run entirely from the thumb drive mean that the entire contents of a PC might be copied to a small, portable, easily concealed device.[35]

A 2003 study of security incidents conducted by the U.S. Secret Service and the Carnegie Mellon Software Engineering Institute found that attacks on computer systems committed by insiders with authorized access have cost industry millions of dollars in fraud and lost data.[36] Insider employees with access to sensitive information systems can initiate threats by inserting malicious code into software as it is being developed, either locally or under offshore contracting arrangements. The risk is suggested by the January 2003 arrest and eventual conviction of 20 employees of subcontractors working in the United States at the Sikorsky Aircraft Corporation; they were charged with possession of false identification, which they had used to obtain security access to facilities containing restricted and sensitive military technology.[37]

Piracy and Counterfeit Goods

Anything that can be digitized can be transmitted rapidly through the Internet from one computer to another, with no reduction of quality for second-generation or subsequent copies. *Piracy* is the term used to describe theft of intellectual property, or the illegal copying of software, music, movies, and other digital items protected by copyright, trade secret, or patent laws.

The U.S. State Department cites data that show global losses from piracy of creative works and software at $30 billion–$35 billion per year.[38] Some estimate that up to 92 percent of all computer software currently used in mainland China is counterfeit.[39] Theft of intellectual property affects the entire U.S. economy, through lost employment and taxes, as well as the economies of all countries that protect digital products. Sources in Europe estimate that economic losses related to counterfeiting are around €500 billion per year. Additionally, some counterfeit food or medical products present a serious health threat.[40] Concerns over digital piracy are rising as terrorist groups collaborate with cyber criminals trafficking in counterfeit goods, products, and intellectual property, activities potentially even more lucrative than drug trafficking. Former Attorney General Alberto Gonzales noted that this is "more than just a question of protecting IP [intellectual property], it's a question of [national] security."[41]

Pirated digital copies of copyrighted work transmitted over the Internet are sometimes known as *warez*, and *warez groups* illegally copy and distribute hundreds of millions of dollars' worth of copyrighted material each year. Pirated trade secrets are sold to other companies or to criminal groups who use the information to extort money from legitimate companies. Pirated software is sold at prices that undercut legitimate digital products. It is especially vulnerable to attack from malicious code because important security patches and updates distributed by the legitimate software company are never installed.

Money Laundering
In April 2007, the E-Gold company was indicted by the U.S. Government for money laundering.[42] E-Gold is one of a number of Internet services that allow users to deal in shares of precious metal and avoid government tracking of currency. E-Gold was started in 1996 as one of several pioneer Internet Web payment systems that converted different forms of conventional money into a form of digital Web currency. E-Gold was intended to become an easily accepted, independent currency that would enable persons from countries all over the world to exchange products at stable prices and without the negative effects of inflation usually associated with government paper money. Customers of E-Gold were not required to prove their identities, so they were able to use false names when opening an account. By using a wire transfer, a credit card, or a digital cash card, a customer would buy units of E-Gold and could transfer them to anyone else with an E-Gold account, exchange E-Gold units for regular money, or transfer E-Gold value onto a portable digital cash card. Banks are legally required to monitor customers and report suspicious transactions to the U.S. Government, but E-Gold is not bound by these regulations, and therefore it attracted online criminals who wanted to move money quickly without detection. Reportedly, the cyber crime group known as ShadowCrew was one of several

suspicious groups that used E-Gold to launder money in 2004.[43] Many Web sites that sell stolen bank account and credit card information or that deal in child pornography requested payment via E-Gold. However, E-Gold reportedly cooperated with watchdog organizations, such as the National Center for Missing and Exploited Children, in attempts to crack down on payment schemes used by child pornography Web sites.[44]

Other electronic payment services also let users operate accounts anonymously, sometimes using only phone cards for identification. These Internet payment services closely resemble the money-changing system known as *hawala* that has been used by Middle Eastern terrorists. A customer gives money to a hawala service located in one area; that service telephones a similar service located in another city or country, which gives out money to a designated recipient. Some terrorism experts believe that terrorist groups increasingly will use Internet payment services to move funds without government detection.[45]

Virtual casinos, Internet auctions, online banking, and the sale of shares, bonds, and futures online also offer ample opportunities for money laundering.[46] Internet gambling is reportedly a $12-billion-a-year industry that relies heavily on international online payment services. Many U.S. credit card companies started refusing to process gambling transactions in 2001, and U.S. law now bars financial institutions from processing illegal gambling transactions. However, it would be difficult for the United States, or any other country, to prohibit the processing of financial transactions that are legal in the nation from which a business operates. It is also problematic for U.S. law enforcement to stop Internet payment services from processing illegal gambling transactions made from U.S. computers. Cyber criminals continue to exploit numerous advantages arising from such differences in jurisdictions.[47]

Other methods for money laundering include the use of "e-purses" such as smart cards that store and transport funds in memory chips. Internet payment services, such as PayPal and Neteller, operate outside traditional banks or credit card companies. Neteller was said to process over $5 billion in transactions in 6 months in 2006.[48] In May 2007, 143 million consumers reportedly had PayPal accounts, and PayPal "handled more than $11 billion in payments through all its services in the first quarter of 2007, up 30% from a year ago."[49]

Another method uses "money mules," individuals who are hired to assist international wire fraud and other illicit operations by helping to move money around. Some are naive teenagers who work from home for part-time pay and may not know that they are part of an international fraud ring. Criminals who have stolen sensitive financial account information from a victim's PC using a trojan horse, spyware, or adware direct the mule to make a cash withdrawal from the financial account and then wire the stolen money to a bank account overseas.[50]

Insiders, such as in-house financial specialists, accountants, or bank employees in offshore zones or major financial centers, may also help cyber criminals evade the scrutiny of bank regulators and international investigators, deliberately or sometimes unwittingly.[51]

Law Enforcement Issues

According to Secret Service Director Ralph Basham, "With just a few keystrokes, cyber criminals around the world can disrupt our economy."[52] However, according to some experts, statistics describing the extent of cyber crime are not reliable, partly because cyber crime is a vast area with innumerable crimes where no common statistics system exists. The Government Accountability Office (GAO) estimates that losses associated with cyber crimes include \$49.3 billion in 2006 for identity theft and \$1 billion annually due to phishing. These projected losses are based on direct and indirect costs that may include actual money stolen, estimated cost of intellectual property stolen, and recovery cost of repairing or replacing damaged networks and equipment.[53]

In one example of costs associated with a computer security breach, TJX, the parent company of retailer TJ Maxx, took a \$12 million charge in its fiscal first quarter of 2008 due to the theft, starting in 2006, of more than 45 million credit and debit card numbers. The costs were for investigating and containing the intrusion, improving computer security, communicating with customers, and other fees. TJX estimates that, adding damages from future lawsuits, the breach may eventually cost \$100 per lost record, or a total of \$4.5 billion.[54]

It is estimated that only 5 percent of cyber criminals are ever arrested or convicted, because the anonymity associated with Web activity makes them hard to catch and the trail of evidence needed to link them to a cyber crime is hard to follow. In response to numerous security breaches that can lead to credit card or checking account fraud, a number of states have enacted various identity theft laws to protect consumers. Many states now require notification by a business when there is evidence that consumer information may have been stolen by cyber criminals.[55] Fighting cyber crime requires cooperation between law enforcement and private industry, according to FBI Director Robert Mueller, who told a conference of computer security professionals in 2006 that "maintaining a code of silence" does not benefit a company in the long run. Steven Martinez, Deputy Assistant Director of the FBI's cyber division, pointed out that partnerships between law enforcement, the academic community, and the private sector are the key to reducing cyber crime.[56]

Each year, a survey of thousands of security practitioners from U.S. corporations, government agencies, financial institutions, and universities is conducted by the Computer Security Institute (CSI) with help from the computer intrusion team of the FBI's San Francisco office.[57] The CSI Computer Crime and Security Survey, published annually, is a widely used source of information about how often computer crime occurs and how expensive these crimes can be. Preliminary key findings from the 2007 CSI survey were that "the average annual loss reported more than doubled, from $168,000 in last year's report to $350,424 in this year's survey. Reported losses have not been this high in the last five years. Financial fraud overtook virus attacks as the source of the greatest financial loss."[58] However, some observers question the statistical validity of the CSI survey methodology.[59]

The Computer Emergency Response Team Coordination Center (CERT–CC) at Carnegie Mellon University has for years collected information about computer security incidents occurring nationwide, and until 2004 also published summary information about the number and types of computer security incidents reported. However, as Internet cyber attacks rapidly became more sophisticated, the methodology used by CERT–CC for capturing and reporting intrusions could not keep up. In 2004, the CERT–CC Web site stated, "Given the widespread use of automated attack tools, attacks against Internet-connected systems have become so commonplace that counts of the number of incidents reported provide little information with regard to assessing the scope and impact of attacks. Therefore, beginning in 2004, we stopped publishing the number of incidents reported."[60]

With the uncertainties of survey results concerning the financial costs of computer crime and of reports about the number and types of computer security incidents, there may yet be no statistically valid way to understand the real scope and intensity of cyber crime. The growing evidence of botnets and of other automated attacks suggests that the percentage of undetected and unreported cyber crime may be going up.

Problems Tracing Cyber Crime

Law enforcement officials concede that they face major obstacles in tracing the profits and finances of cyber criminals. Online payment services, such as PayPal and E-Gold, enable criminals to launder profits. Although some companies have been convicted and fined for distribution of spyware (which silently captures personal information from users' PCs), other adware and spyware purveyors can still make millions of dollars per year. Law enforcement officials argue that even legitimate technology companies are lax in enforcing standards to determine the veracity of online advertisers who may be distributing spyware. Many spyware companies are hard to subject to legal action because they typically also offer some legitimate services. The finances that back cyber crimes are so distributed that they are difficult for law enforcement to figure out.[61]

International Convention on Cyber Crime

The ability of cyber criminals to ignore borders allows them to exploit obstacles to international law enforcement. Cyber crime is a major international challenge, and attitudes and laws about what amounts to a criminal act of computer wrongdoing vary from country to country. However, the Council of Europe, a consultative assembly of 43 countries based in Strasbourg, France, adopted the Convention on Cybercrime in 2001. Effective July 2004, it was the first international treaty to deal with breaches of law "over the Internet or other information networks." The convention requires participating countries to update and harmonize their criminal laws against hacking, infringements on copyrights, computer facilitated fraud, child pornography, and other illicit cyber activities.[62] (The convention is discussed further in chapter 21 in this volume, "Internet Governance.")

The Electronic Privacy Information Center, in a June 2004 letter to the U.S. Senate Foreign Relations Committee, objected on privacy grounds to U.S. ratification of the convention, arguing that it would "create invasive investigative techniques while failing to provide meaningful privacy and civil liberties safeguards."[63] However, a coalition of U.S. industry associations, including the Business Software Alliance, the Cyber Security Industry Alliance, the American Bankers Association, the Information Technology Association of America, InfraGard, Verisign, and several others, urged the Foreign Relations Committee to recommend ratification of the convention,[64] which the Senate did on August 3, 2006. The United States will comply with the convention based on existing U.S. Federal law; no new implementing legislation was expected to be required. Legal analysts say that U.S. negotiators succeeded in scrapping most objectionable provisions, thereby ensuring that the convention tracks closely with existing U.S. laws.

The United States did not sign a complementary protocol that contained provisions to criminalize racist language on the Internet.[65] The Department of Justice has said that the protocol would be contrary to the guarantee of freedom of expression contained in the first amendment to the U.S. Constitution.

Organized Cyber Crime

Some large cyber criminal groups are transnational networks; members reportedly operate from locations all over the world to hack into systems, steal credit card information, and sell identities.[66] Organized crime is also recruiting teenagers who apparently feel safer doing illegal activity online than in the streets. A useful source of information is the "Virtual Criminology Report" from McAfee, which draws on input from European high-technology crime units and the FBI.[67] It suggests that criminal outfits are targeting top students from leading academic institutions and helping them acquire more of the skills needed to commit high-tech crime on a massive scale. It also finds that cyber criminals are being drawn to social networking and community sites where they load fake profiles and pages with adware, spyware, and trojan horses. Some cyber criminals collate personal information found online to formulate virtual twin identities for fraudulent purposes; innocent users of these sites often expose such data, obviating the need for sophisticated attacks. Password proliferation for consumer and work devices means that simple guesswork often unlocks the door. Removable media devices like flash drives make it easier to steal inside information. At least 12 million computers around the world are now compromised for use in botnets and are used for phishing schemes, illegal spamming, the spread of pornography, and the theft of passwords and identities. Smartphones and multifunctional mobile devices are making portable computers ubiquitous; cyber criminals will increasingly mine them for valuable information. The increasing use of Bluetooth and voice over Internet protocol will also lead to a new generation of phone hacking.[68]

In the future, we may see new and different modes of criminal organizations evolve in cyberspace. Cyberspace frees individuals from many of the constraints that apply to activities in the physical world. Cyber crime requires less personal contact, less need for formal organization, and no need for control over a geographical territory. Therefore, some researchers predict, the hierarchical structures of organized crime groups may adapt, and online criminal activity may instead emphasize lateral relationships and networks.[69] Instead of assuming stable personnel configurations that can persist for years, online criminal organization may reflect a "swarming" model: individuals coalesce for a limited period of time in order to conduct a specific task, or set of tasks, and afterward go their separate ways. This can make the task of law enforcement much more difficult. If cyber criminals evolve into the "Mafia of the moment" or the "cartel of the day," police will lose the advantage of identifying a permanent group of participants who engage in a set of repeated activities.[70]

Terrorism and Cyber Crime

The proportion of cyber crime that can be directly or indirectly attributed to terrorists is difficult to determine. Linkages between criminal and terror groups may allow terror networks to expand internationally by leveraging the computer resources, money laundering activities, and transit routes of criminals. The 2005 subway and bus bombings and the 2007 attempted car bombings in the United Kingdom also indicate that groups of terrorists are active within countries that have large communications networks and computerized infrastructures, along with a large, highly skilled information technology workforce. London police officials reportedly believe that terrorists obtained the high-quality explosives used for the 2005 bombings through criminals based in Eastern Europe.[71]

A recent British trial revealed a significant link between Islamic terrorist groups and cyber crime. In June 2007, three British residents, Tariq al-Daour, Waseem Mughal, and Younes Tsouli, pled guilty and were sentenced for using the Internet to incite murder. The men had used 110 different stolen credit cards at online Web stores to purchase items such as night vision goggles, tents, global positioning satellite devices, hundreds of prepaid cell phones, and more than 250 airline tickets to be used by terrorists. Another 72 stolen credit cards were used to register over 180 Internet domains at 95 different Web hosting companies. The group laundered money charged to more than 130 stolen credit cards through online gambling Web sites. Their fraudulent charges totaled more than $3.5 million from a database containing 37,000 stolen credit card numbers along with account holders' names and addresses, dates of birth, credit balances, and credit limits.[72]

Regions with major narcotics markets, such as Western Europe and North America, have optimal technology infrastructure and open commercial nodes that are increasingly used for transnational trafficking by both criminal and terrorist groups.[73] Officials of the U.S. Drug Enforcement Administration (DEA) reported in 2003 that 14 of the 36 groups found on the U.S. State Department's list of foreign terrorist organizations were also involved in drug trafficking. A 2002 report by the Library of Congress Federal Research Division described a "growing involvement of Islamic terrorist and extremist groups in drug trafficking," along with some evidence of cooperation between terrorist groups involving both drug trafficking and trafficking in arms.[74] Consequently, DEA officials argued, the war on drugs and the war on terrorism are and should be linked.[75]

State Department officials stated at a Senate hearing in March 2002 that terrorist groups may be using drug trafficking as a way to both gain financing and to weaken their enemies in the West by spreading addictive drugs.[76] The poppy crop in Afghanistan reportedly supplies resin to produce over 90 percent of the world's heroin, supporting a drug trade estimated at $3.1 billion, some of which goes to fund terrorist and insurgent groups in Afghanistan. Intelligence reports in 2007 stated that al Qaeda in Afghanistan had been restored to its pre–September 11, 2001, operation levels, and may be in a better position now to strike Western countries.[77]

Drug traffickers are reportedly among the heaviest users of encryption for Internet computer messaging and have the wherewithal to hire high-level computer specialists to help evade law enforcement, coordinate drug shipments, and launder money. Such technologies also enable terrorist organizations to transcend borders and operate internationally with less chance of detection. Many highly trained technical specialists are located in the countries of the former

Soviet Union and the Indian subcontinent. Some technical specialists would not willingly work for criminal or terrorist organizations, but many may be misled or unaware of their employers' terrorist objectives, while some agree to provide assistance because well-paid legitimate employment is scarce in their region.[78]

Future Targets: Infrastructure Control Systems

Evidence has not yet been published showing a widespread focus by cyber criminals on attacking the control systems that operate the U.S. civilian critical infrastructure. Disabling infrastructure controls for communications, electrical distribution, or other infrastructure systems is often described as a way terrorists might seek to amplify the effects of a simultaneous conventional terrorist attack involving explosives. (See the discussion of critical infrastructure protection in chapter 23 in this volume, "Cyberpower and Critical Information Protection: A Critical Assessment of Federal Efforts.")

Criminal extortion schemes in which attackers have exploited control system vulnerabilities for economic gain have already occurred. In January 2008, officials from the Central Intelligence Agency stated:

> We have information, from multiple regions outside the United States, of cyber intrusions into utilities, followed by extortion demands. . . . We have information that cyber attacks have been used to disrupt power equipment in several regions outside the United States. . . . We do not know who executed these attacks or why, but all involved intrusions through the Internet.[79]

In December 2006, malicious software for an automated control system vulnerability scanner reportedly was made available on the Internet; this software would enable individuals with relatively little experience in control systems to scan a critical system and identify its vulnerabilities quickly.

Many, if not most, automated control systems are connected to the Internet or to corporate administrative systems and are vulnerable to a cyber attack. Because many of these systems were not originally designed with security as a priority, it is often difficult to implement new security controls to reduce known security vulnerabilities.[80] On the basis that hackers and cyber criminals will always seek to take advantage of easy vulnerabilities, some analysts now predict that cyber criminals will exploit vulnerabilities in critical infrastructure control systems.[81] The Idaho National Laboratory, one of 10 multiprogram National Laboratories operated by the Department of Energy, has been tasked to study and report on technology risks associated with infrastructure control systems.[82]

Some experts argue that cyber terrorism does not suit the objectives of terrorists because it does not cause the horrific visible effects of blood, smoke, and fire that cause terror. However, botnets might be used strategically to amplify the effects of a conventional terrorist attack, such as one using bombs, or perhaps by delaying or diverting first responders from such an attack.

The Urgency of Improving Cyber Security

In recent years, many software vendors have taken major steps to improve the security of their commercial products and to distribute software patches rapidly to fix newly discovered problems. However, much is still needed to help improve the computer security policy and practices of businesses and home users of these products. Cyber criminals continue to search for new vulnerabilities, and there is still far too much opportunity for them to take advantage of weaknesses in networks and systems that persist, despite publicity warning about the increasing threat of cyber crime.

As early as 1991, the National Research Council published a report titled "Computers at Risk" and another in 1993, titled "Trust in Cyberspace." Both warned that computer networking would allow cyber attacks to affect more users and would increase the number of potential attackers. The National Infrastructure Advisory Council, now a part of the Department of Homeland Security (DHS), was created in 2001 to improve cooperation for cyber security between banking, manufacturing, and other businesses and local and state governments and law enforcement. In 2002, Congress passed the Federal Information Security Management Act (FISMA), which was intended to improve computer and network security for Federal Government agencies. FISMA required yearly audits in which agencies must report on their compliance with specified standards and rules to strengthen cyber security, set by Congress, the executive branch, and the National Institute for Standards and Technology (NIST). The Cybersecurity Research and Development Act of 2002 authorized appropriations for the National Science Foundation and NIST to improve information-sharing between the private sector and government, and to increase the number of information security professionals. The 2003 White House statement, "The National Strategy to Secure Cyberspace," warned that cyber attack tools are becoming more sophisticated and widely available and that future organized cyber attacks could severely disrupt the Nation's civilian critical infrastructure, cripple the economy, and adversely affect national security.

Other reports specifically describe security vulnerabilities of computers that operate the civilian critical infrastructure. Water supply, electrical distribution, communications, and other industry sectors are operated by computerized control systems that are vulnerable to cyber attack. Such an incident could be used as a threat to extort money, could be damaged by an attack like the 2007

DDOS cyber attack in Estonia, or could be used to amplify the effects of a simultaneous physical terrorist attack.

Most infrastructure control systems are privately owned, but because of the risk to national security, Homeland Security Presidential Directive 7 directed DHS to coordinate efforts to protect the cyber security for the Nation's critical infrastructure. In 2005, DHS issued the "Interim National Infrastructure Protection Plan" and the "National Plan for Research and Development in Support of Critical Infrastructure Protection," providing a framework for identifying, prioritizing, and protecting each infrastructure sector.

However, many observers point out that there is still no apparent sense of national urgency to close the gap between cyber security and the threat of cyber attack. For example, despite FISMA, security remains a low priority or is treated almost as an afterthought at some domestic Federal agencies.[83] In 2004, a GAO report stated that cyber security risks had actually increased for attacks against infrastructure control systems for water, electricity, communications, and other sectors.[84] However, a more recent GAO report stated that the private sector had made progress for improving computer security, although that progress varied by industry sector.[85] Even as corporations and individual users gradually become more cautious in their policies and actions, critical infrastructure control systems may become more attractive as targets for cyber crime.

Cyber crime is one of the risks of doing business, but many decisionmakers currently seem to view it as a low-probability threat. Perhaps the information dangers have not been presented compellingly enough, or perhaps future possibilities are discounted, partly because the future costs of current inaction will not be borne by current decisionmakers.

Nevertheless, IT vendors must somehow be persuaded to regard security as a product attribute that is coequal with performance and cost; to value cyber security research as much as they value research into high performance or cost-effective computing; and to incur present-day costs in order to obtain future protection.[86]

The low risk of detection and identification will continue to embolden cyber criminals and will encourage them to further expand the scope of cyber crime, along with its consequences. Cyber criminals will continue to use new technologies and select new priorities and objectives to guide their cyber attacks. Cyber crime may give even more support to extremist groups in the future. Vulnerabilities in critical infrastructure control systems could attract new criminal activity to extort money or meet terrorist demands.

Cyber criminals are likely to make profitable alliances involving trade in lucrative items such as counterfeit goods or pirated intellectual property. Future cyber criminal organizations may have no central geographic base and may function effectively solely through network technology, taking on new forms that may be more difficult for law enforcement organizations to counter.

Policy issues for reduction of cyber crime include seeking new ways for private industry and government to cooperate for reporting cyber crime and increasing cyber security; encouraging more international cooperation among law enforcement agencies to improve attribution of cyber crimes and for pursuing malicious actors across national borders; and developing more accurate methods for measuring the effects of cyber crime.

As cyber crime is recognized by government and industry officials as a growing threat to national security, each business and government agency must be held more accountable for protecting against cyber crime by following best practices to improve computer security in their organizations. This may be problematic as long as the reporting of computer security vulnerabilities is viewed as a threat to customers' or users' confidence. Thus, businesses and government may need to create new ways to anonymously report cyber intrusions, while still holding management accountable for cyber security. Education programs to change public attitudes about reporting cyber intrusions may also help. Ultimately, reducing the threat to national security from cyber crime depends on a strong commitment by government and the private sector to follow best management practices that help improve computer security.

Security experts generally believe that terrorist groups collectively will not, at least in the near future, have the technical skills required to launch an effective, widespread cyber attack. However, the events in Estonia in 2007 and the growing threat from cyber crime may soon alter that sense of safety. Extremists may take advantage of criminal botnets and begin to employ cyber attack as a weapon, perhaps against critical civilian infrastructure of Western nations.

Cyber crime is likely to increase in variety, scope, and consequences until both government and industry decisionmakers make cyber security research and measurement a high priority, increase international coordination between governments and with business for reporting and investigating cyber attacks, and devote more resources to best practices to reduce computer security vulnerabilities.

CHAPTER 19

Cyber Terrorism: Menace or Myth?

Irving Lachow

CYBER TERRORISM is often portrayed as a major threat to the United States. Articles, books, and reports discussing the subject conjure images of infrastructure failures, massive economic losses, and even large-scale loss of life.[1] Fortunately, the hype surrounding this issue outpaces the magnitude of the risk. Terrorists use the Internet extensively, but not to launch massive cyber attacks. In fact, while there is clear evidence that terrorists have used the Internet to gather intelligence and coordinate efforts to launch physical attacks against various infrastructure targets, there has not been a single documented incidence of cyber terrorism against the U.S. Government.[2] Why is that? Is it just a matter of time until terrorists launch a massive cyber attack against the United States, or are current trends likely to continue? If terrorists are not using the Internet to attack us, what are they using it for? This chapter addresses these questions.

The chapter begins by providing a framework for assessing the risks of cyber terrorism. It uses this framework to develop a good understanding of the factors that terrorists must consider when deciding whether to pursue cyber-based attacks. It also facilitates a general assessment of the overall risks posed by cyber terrorists, today and in the next few years.

Terrorist use of the Internet is common, even though cyber terrorism is rare. The Internet provides an almost perfect tool for enabling the goals of many terrorist organizations. The second part of this chapter examines how terrorists are using the Internet to thrive in the modern world. The chapter closes with a series of recommendations for responding to these two aspects of the threat.[3]

What Is Cyber Terrorism?

The Department of Defense (DOD) defines *terrorism* as "the calculated use of unlawful violence or threat of unlawful violence to inculcate fear, intended to coerce or to intimidate governments or societies in the pursuit of goals that are generally political, religious, or ideological."[4] Definitions from the Federal Bureau of Investigation (FBI) and State Department are similarly worded. Thus, there is general agreement within the U.S. Government that terrorism is focused on obtaining desired political or social outcomes through the use of tactics that instill fear and horror in target populations. By extension, *cyber terrorism* can be defined as:

> a computer based attack or threat of attack intended to intimidate or coerce governments or societies in pursuit of goals that are political, religious, or ideological. The attack should be sufficiently destructive or disruptive to generate fear comparable to that from physical acts of terrorism. Attacks that lead to death or bodily injury, extended power outages, plane crashes, water contamination, or major economic losses would be examples. . . . *Attacks that disrupt nonessential services or that are mainly a costly nuisance would not [be cyber terrorism]*.[5]

Some experts have extended the definition of cyber terrorism to include physical attacks on information technology (IT) systems.[6] This author does not consider such attacks to be cyber terrorism. Cyber terrorism refers to the *means* used to carry out the attacks, not to the nature of the *targets* of a "classical" terrorist attack. Otherwise, the term *cyber terrorism* loses all value, and analyses of cyber terror threats become diffuse and lacking in rigor. This leads to a larger point: one of the reasons that cyber terrorism is often perceived to be such a threat is that the term is frequently applied (or rather misapplied) to a wide range of activities. A typical example is in a *USA Today* article, "Cyberterror Impact, Defense Under Scrutiny," which begins: "A terrorist threat is out there—and not just against physical infrastructure."[7] However, a few paragraphs later, the article acknowledges that "Al-Qaeda doesn't see cyber terrorism as achieving significant military goals." Declaring that other groups and nations are looking at using cyber terrorism to damage the United States, it quotes a senior government official: "There are a large number of threats: hackers, cyber criminals, other countries." Reading this article, it is not clear exactly what the term *cyber terrorism* refers to. It seems to say that hackers, criminals, and nation-states are engaging in cyber terrorism, while terrorist groups are not.

There are many other examples of this confusion in terminology. To cite just one more: an article on the Council on Foreign Relations Web site describes the cyber attacks conducted against Estonia in 2007 as a case of "cyber espionage;" however, the attacks were clearly focused on shutting down systems rather than stealing information (more on this later).[8]

In order to clarify terminology for this chapter, table 19–1 illustrates the similarities and differences between six types of cyber threats: cyber terrorism, hacktivism, hacking, cyber crime, cyber espionage, and state-level information warfare.

Hacktivism is usually understood as the manipulation of digital information to promote a political ideology. In general, acts of hacktivism are aimed at leveraging use of code to have "effects similar to regular activism or civil disobedience."[9] Unlike cyber terrorism, hacktivism is not focused on creating a sense of fear or horror. Hacktivists often target decisionmakers directly to express their dissatisfaction with various policies, whereas terrorists usually target innocent victims or third parties. For example, it is commonplace for "patriotic hackers" of one country to express their anger at foreign governments by launching cyber protests (which usually involve Web defacements and denial-of-service attacks). In several cases, national governments have specifically asked such hackers to cease their activities for fear of escalating tensions with other countries.[10]

TABLE 19-1. Cyber Threats: Defining Terms

	MOTIVATION	TARGET	METHOD
CYBER TERROR	Political or social change	Innocent victims	Computer-based violence or destruction
HACKTIVISM	Political or social change	Decisionmakers or innocent victims	Protest via Web page defacements or distributed denial of service (DDOS)
BLACK HAT HACKING	Ego, personal enmity	Individuals, companies, governments	Malware, viruses, worms, and hacking scripts
CYBER CRIME	Economic gain	Individuals, companies	Malware for fraud, identity theft; DDOS for blackmail
CYBER ESPIONAGE	Economic and political gain	Individuals, companies, governments	Range of techniques to obtain information
INFORMATION WAR	Political or military gain	Infrastructures, information technology systems and data (private or public)	Range of techniques for attack or influence operations

The term *hacking* generally refers to the activity of illegal computer tres-passing.[11] Hacking is sometimes done to uncover weaknesses in computer systems or networks in order to improve them (often with permission from the owners of these targets). Such hacking is called "white hat" hacking and is not usually malicious. In contrast, "black hat" hacking refers to malicious exploitation of a target system. Although hacking techniques can be used for a variety of purposes (including hacktivism, cyber terror, or cyber crime), black hat hackers can defined as those who exploit weaknesses in computer systems for personal gain. In some cases, that gain may be financial, in which case the activity would be classified as cyber crime; however, many hackers are motivated by the prospect of aggrandizement, by the challenge of breaking into high-value systems, or by personal vendettas against a specific target. According to one computer security expert: "The most common motivation [for hacking] is ego-gratification and it drives all the script-kiddots to deface Web sites—digitally spray-painting their name on the Internet and brag to their friends. Usually, the sites they hit are pretty easy targets and the defacement is a yawn to the rest of us. A more compelling motivation is retaliation."[12]

There is no single, widely accepted definition of cyber crime. However, the majority of definitions focus on the use of computers or networks to facilitate criminal acts such as spamming, fraud, child pornography, and data theft. The methods used for cyber crime can sometimes be the same as those used for hacktivism or hacking; what distinguishes these from each other is the motivation of the perpetrator. In the case of cyber crime, the goal is economic gain, not political change, ego gratification, or civil disobedience.

Cyber espionage can be defined as the use of information technology systems and networks to gather information about an organization or a society that is considered secret or confidential without the permission of the holder of the information.[13] Cyber espionage is conducted by a wide range of actors, including individuals, groups, companies, and nation-states. Although cyber espionage is often cloaked in secrecy, the world was given a glimpse at the magnitude of the problem when it was revealed in late 2007 that the British intelligence agency MI5 had sent a letter to over 300 senior executives in industry warning them about Chinese cyber espionage activities. In the letter, the British government "openly accused China of carrying out state-sponsored espionage against vital parts of the Britain's economy, including computer systems of major banks and financial services firms."[14] The FBI has also identified Chinese espionage activities as being a major threat to U.S. national security.[15]

In this chapter, the term *information war* encompasses two concepts that were defined by John Arquilla and David Ronfeldt in 1997: netwar and cyberwar.

Netwar refers to the information-related conflict at a grand level between nations or societies. It means trying to disrupt, damage, or modify what a target population "knows" or thinks it knows about itself and the world around it. . . . In other words, netwar represents a new entry on the spectrum of conflict that spans economic, political, and social as well as military forms of "war."[16]

The term *cyberwar* is more focused on the military aspects of competition:

> *Cyberwar* refers to conducting, and preparing to conduct, military operations according to information-related principles. It means disrupting if not destroying the information and communication systems, broadly defined to include even military culture, on which an adversary relies in order to "know" itself.[17]

Thus, the term *information war* can be understood to refer to cyber conflict at the nation-state level involving either direct military confrontation or indirect competition via disruption and deception. Many nations across the globe are developing doctrine for information warfare, and there are indications that activities of this kind are already occurring. For example, a recent report notes that sophisticated attacks against several Western nations have originated in China.[18] While this does not prove that the Chinese government is conducting information warfare, the circumstantial evidence is fairly strong.

The distinctions among these six threats are somewhat artificial. The boundaries between cyber terrorism and hacktivsim, or between cyber crime and cyber espionage, may be blurry. Similarly, single actors can engage in multiple activities: terrorist groups can also commit cyber crime or hacktivism, criminal groups can conduct cyber terror or cyber espionage, and nation-states can undertake cyber espionage or information warfare. However, the distinctions are still useful for analytic purposes. For example, the recent cyber attack against Estonia has been called everything from a "cyberwar" to a "cyber terror attack." Using our framework to examine a series of after-action reports about the incident, we see that the attacks against Estonia were clearly an instance of hacktivism. Hacktivism directed at a nation-state is not new; Chinese hacktivists have launched attacks against both the United States and Taiwan several times over the last 20 years in response to a number of incidents, such as the accidental U.S. bombing of the Chinese embassy in Yugoslavia in 1999. Palestinian and Israeli hackers have engaged in a mutual battle of nationalistic hacktivism for years. What makes the Estonian case interesting is that the consequences of the attack were more serious than in previous instances, that botnets were used for the attack (thus tying hacktivism to cyber crime), and that servers from the Russian government were implicated in the attack (although they were likely just unwitting nodes in the botnets).[19] To paint the Estonian cyber attacks as the first instance of either state-sponsored information war or cyber terror is misleading and unhelpful.

By placing a cyber attack in the proper context, it becomes easier to assess the risks it poses and to select appropriate policies for responding. This is especially important for cyber terrorism, which is usually mischaracterized. Cyber terrorism is quite distinct from hacking, cyber crime, hacktivism, or cyber espionage, all of which are exceedingly common and some of which pose serious threats to U.S. national security.

Assessing the Risks of Cyber Terrorism

Many assessments of cyber terrorism focus strictly on the threat that such attacks pose to the United States. However, to truly understand the seriousness of the issue, one needs to examine the vulnerabilities that such threats can exploit and the consequences that such attacks would have if they were successful. To perform this comprehensive assessment, we utilize a risk management framework developed by the RAND Corporation.[20] The RAND framework defines the risk of terrorism in terms of three variables: threat, vulnerability, and consequence.

Threat (T) is the probability that a specific target is attacked in a specific way during a specified time period. In other words, Threat = P (attack occurs).

Vulnerability (V) is the probability that damage (which may involve fatalities, injuries, property damage, or other consequences) occurs given a specific attack type, at a specific time, on a given target. Thus, Vulnerability = P (attack results in damage/attack occurs).

Consequence (C) is the expected magnitude of damage given that a specific attack type, at a specific time, on a given target, results in damage. In mathematical terms, Consequence = E (damage/attack occurs and results in damage).

The overall risk is a product of the three terms defined above. In other words:

$$Risk (R) = T*V*C.$$

Or, to put things in terms of probabilities:

Risk (R) = P (attack occurs)
   *P (attack results in damage/attack occurs)
   *E (damage/attack occurs and results in damage).

Threat
To determine the level of threat posed by cyber terrorism, one has to examine the resources, capabilities, structure, and motivations of a given terrorist group in terms of a specific type of attack. To that end, it useful to group cyber terrorism

threats in three broad categories: simple unstructured (simple), advanced structured (advanced), and complex coordinated (complex).[21] Each of these threat levels is associated with a given set of capabilities, resources, structures, and motivations. Table 19–2 summarizes the characteristics of these levels.

The following discussion explores what it takes for terrorists to operate at each of the three levels described in table 19–2. We then assess where terror groups are operating today and where they may be headed in the future.

Simple threats. Carrying out cyber attacks of any kind requires two kinds of capabilities: analytical and technical.[22] Analytical capability refers to the ability to analyze a potential target in order to identify its critical nodes and vulnerabilities (and potentially its connections to other targets). Technical capability refers to knowledge of computer software and hardware, networks, and other relevant technologies.

Simple cyber attacks can be carried out by anyone who has basic computer skills and rudimentary analytical capabilities. No special resources or organizational structures are needed; a single individual could download hacker tools from a Web site, pick a target, and launch an attack. Such attacks are generally focused on a specific target. Web defacements are a good example of this type of attack. Simple attacks are extremely common on the Internet today; anyone willing to devote a few hours of time researching hacker tools can perform such attacks.

Advanced threats. Advanced cyber attacks differ from simple ones in their sophistication. At this threat level, the attacker has the ability to write programs or to modify those of others, and also has a working knowledge of networks, operating systems, and possibly even defensive techniques. For example, such an attacker often understands the functioning of common firewalls and intrusion detection systems. This allows the attacker to develop more sophisticated attacks than those found in the previous category. According to a Naval Postgraduate School study, people at this level must have technical capabilities equivalent to a Microsoft Certified Systems Engineer.[23] To reach this threat level, a terrorist group would need to recruit or hire at least one person with a solid education in computer science or a great deal of experience working with computer systems.

In addition to stronger technical skills, advanced threats require more sophisticated analysis and planning than simple attacks. Terrorists at this level would need to analyze target networks and systems to find vulnerabilities or circumvent defenses. They might also want to model the possible effect of a successful cyber attack to determine what would happen in different scenarios. For both of these reasons, groups wishing to operate at this level would likely need to create a simple testbed to allow the attackers to rehearse their attack plans or to experiment with different scripts.

While advanced threats are clearly more sophisticated than simple ones and can cause a great deal of economic damage, they still fall short of the kind of massive cyber attacks often portrayed in the press. Frequently developed and launched by an individual or perhaps a small team, they generally target known vulnerabilities and are aimed at a single type of system or network. Thus, advanced attacks would likely be used against a single organization or against a number of organizations that use similar technologies. Multiple attacks, if they occur, would likely occur in sequence rather than simultaneously. An example of an advanced cyber attack was the Nimda computer virus, which caused billions of dollars of damage worldwide.[24]

Complex threats. Complex attacks are significantly more difficult to accomplish than the previous two attack types, but they pose by far the biggest threat to U.S. assets. In contrast to the previous two threat levels, complex attacks cannot be carried out by a single hacker or even a small team of computer experts. These attacks require a team of individuals (or perhaps multiple teams) with expertise in a number of technical areas, including but not limited to: networks, operating systems, programming languages, infrastructure topologies and control systems (for example, supervisory control and data acquisition systems), intelligence-gathering and analysis, and planning. Obtaining the depth and variety of technical expertise alone would pose a daunting challenge for most terrorist groups.

Because attacks of this nature require the coordination of multiple attack vectors, a sophisticated testbed would be needed to test attack methods and rehearse the attack itself.[25] The testbed alone would be expensive and would

TABLE 19-2. Cyber Threat Levels

	SIMPLE	ADVANCED	COMPLEX
TARGET SCOPE	Single system or net	Multiple systems or nets	Multiple networks
TARGET ANALYSIS	None	Elementary	Detailed
EFFECTS CONTROL	Unfocused	Focused	Scalable
RESOURCES REQUIRED	One or more computer-literate people	One or more sophisticated programmers; simple testbed	Several expert programmers, analysts, and planners; sophisticated testbed
STRUCTURES REQUIRED	None	None	Synchronized teams
POTENTIAL USE	Harassment	Tactical attacks	Strategic attacks

Source: This table is based on material found in Bill Nelson et al., *Cyberterror: Prospects and Implications* (Monterey, CA: Center for the Study of Terrorism and Irregular Warfare, 1999). A similar table can be found in Joseph F. Gustin, *Cyber Terrorism: A Guide for Managers* (Lilburn, GA: Fairmont Press, 2004).

require dedicated manpower for upkeep and maintenance. In addition, the planning and coordination skills required to pull off a complex attack are not trivial. A terrorist group would need an estimated 6 to 10 years to develop such a capability internally.[26]

Vulnerability

We have examined the ability of terrorist groups to launch attacks against different types of targets. To assess the risks facing the United States from such attacks, we must determine the likelihood that a given attack would actually cause damage. This depends on two key variables: the characteristics of a specific system or network, and the range of countermeasures employed to protect that system or network. Because most organizations use a variety of computer systems and networks, a large number of characteristics must be examined to assess the vulnerability of an organization's cyber assets. A partial list of key technical factors includes the operating systems, all user applications, and network architectures and configurations.

Every computer technology has inherent vulnerabilities that could be exploited. For this reason, all security-conscious enterprises employ a range of countermeasures that seek to mitigate these vulnerabilities. Countermeasures can be technical, process-oriented, or people-oriented. Typical technical countermeasures include firewalls, intrusion detection systems, encryption, hardware tokens, and biometrics. Process-oriented countermeasures focus on policies and procedures, such as access control policies, authentication procedures, and configuration management practices. People-oriented countermeasures focus on minimizing vulnerabilities associated with human behavior, the single biggest risk in any organization. Countermeasures of this type might include background checks on employees, training requirements, physical barriers, and the use of monitoring software.

It is evident that one cannot assess the vulnerability of a given target to a specific attack without delving into the details of both the attack and the target. However, we can make some general statements about the ability of different types of attackers to exploit the vulnerabilities inherent in different types of targets. Simple threats could take advantage of well-publicized vulnerabilities found in standard operating systems (for example, Windows Vista), applications (such as Internet Explorer), and networks (for example, wireless standards such as 802.11g). Many enterprises do not spend the time and money needed to block all such vulnerabilities, so it is possible that a simple attack could succeed against some organizations. However, organizations that are strongly focused on security will be much less vulnerable to these simple types of attacks.

While advanced threats can take advantage of well-publicized vulnerabilities, they might also use their more extensive knowledge to find less well known vulnerabilities in a given system. In fact, the real danger with these threats is that they might find and exploit a weakness quietly, without fanfare or bragging on hacker Web sites. Advanced attackers might be able to find vulnerabilities in applications and networks that affect multiple organizations, but they are limited in their ability to exploit those vulnerabilities in a coordinated and systematic manner. They usually target one organization or system at a time. An example of this type of attack is the Nimda virus, a worm designed to exploit vulnerabilities found in Windows IIS Web servers. If a given Web server was not properly patched, then the worm infected the local files of that server as well as network drives connected to it, created copies of itself, and emailed those copies to other servers and clients. While the Nimda virus spread extremely quickly throughout the world and caused a fair amount of financial damage, it was designed to exploit a single vulnerability, and it spread sequentially from machine to machine.

Complex threats can identify and exploit vulnerabilities in multiple organizations simultaneously. Like advanced threats, these experts can find vulnerabilities that are not well known and exploit them to gain entry into networks and computer systems. By coordinating their efforts across multiple networks or systems, they could leverage vulnerabilities found in the connections and dependencies between organizations. This could cause more damage, as ripple effects spread the attack throughout the network of targeted organizations, such as those comprising the electric power grid.

The challenge of actually exploiting different vulnerabilities across multiple organizations is tremendous. In order to launch a well-coordinated complex attack, an attacker would need a team of experts to analyze the network and system vulnerabilities of each potential target and then model how those targets are related in order to develop a good idea of what would happen when the attacks were launched. Of course, attackers could choose simply to launch a series of different scripts against different vulnerabilities and hope that the results would be to their liking. However, such attacks would fall under the advanced category and are more characteristic of individual hackers than well-organized terrorist groups, which would generally prefer to plan a major attack meticulously to maximize the chances of success.

The discussion so far has focused on vulnerabilities inherent in the system being attacked, but one must also consider the range of countermeasures that have been or could be implemented in response to an attack. For example, if an organization that is a target of a distributed denial-of-service (DDOS) attack can rapidly ramp up its bandwidth dramatically, the attack could fail. A whole range of technologies and processes in use today could, if implemented in a timely and proper manner, prevent many of the most common network attacks. That being said, there is no question that the attacker has the advantage against the defender when it comes to information security. Attackers (as a whole) outnumber defenders by a large margin, they do a better job of sharing information on successful attack strategies than defenders do with defense strategies, and they only need to succeed a small fraction of the time to achieve their goals. This is one reason why having a defense-in-depth strategy and a good recovery capability is so important for targeted organizations—topics that we will address again later in this chapter.

In summary, simple attacks exploit known vulnerabilities. Examples include DDOS attacks and downloadable scripts that can be launched by anyone. Advanced attacks can identify new vulnerabilities but are limited in how they can exploit them due to constraints in knowledge and resources. Examples include new viruses and zero-day attacks (exploits of vulnerabilities that take place the same day as knowledge of the vulnerability becomes available) of applications and operating systems. Complex attacks can identify and exploit vulnerabilities across multiple networks, systems, and organizations. A hypothetical example would be an attack against multiple infrastructure targets (logistics, communications, transportation) in the United States to hinder military deployments.

The likelihood of a given attack being successful depends on the nature of attack, the nature of the system being attacked, and the countermeasures (if any) that have been put in place to prevent such attacks from succeeding. This game of cat-and-mouse is highly dynamic because attackers and defenders are constantly developing new techniques and technologies to defeat each other.

Consequences

To assess the consequences of a specific attack against a given target, one must analyze how the system fails (does it degrade gradually or dramatically?), the response processes and procedures that are in place (how quickly can system administrators patch the exploited vulnerability and get the system working normally?), the continuity of operations measures or backup alternatives that may exist (if a secondary site backs up the targeted system continuously, the impact of the attack might be minimal even though it was completely successful in bringing down the targeted application or network), and the resilience of the affected population.

If an attack is successful and damage occurs, one needs to examine two issues: the magnitude of damage and the type of damage. It is fairly obvious why the scale of damage resulting from an attack must be determined, but why is the type of damage important? The answer to this question goes to the heart of the debate about why cyber terrorism has not occurred. Terrorists seek to achieve political, social, or religious goals through the use of violence that instills a sense of fear and horror. To that end, terrorist attacks tend to be extremely violent, bloody, and photogenic. They want to hurt or kill their victims in a way that disturbs as many people as possible and is seen by as many people as possible. It is obvious that explosives can achieve these goals. The question is: Can cyber attacks do so as well? In the case of both simple and advanced attacks, the answer is probably no.

History shows that the majority of cyber attacks, even viruses that cause billions of dollars of damage to an economy, are not going to cause the levels of fear and/or horror desired by most terrorists. Even the temporary disablement of a component of a critical infrastructure may not cause the desired emotions— such disruptions occur rather frequently due to human error and natural disasters, and people generally do not panic. On the other hand, the U.S. populace appears to have an irrational fear of terrorism (based on actual versus perceived risks), and thus it is possible that a cyber terror attack, if sufficiently newsworthy, could create a sense of fear.[27] In addition, a complex attack causing serious damage to the U.S. economy would likely engender a genuine feeling of fear and panic in the population.[28]

Overall Assessment of Current Cyber Terror Risks

It is difficult to assess with certainty the risks posed by cyber terrorism. However, there is strong circumstantial evidence pointing to the conclusion that terrorist groups are limited to launching simple cyber attacks and exploiting existing vulnerabilities. For example, a recent assessment of terrorist capabilities to launch cyber attacks found the following:

> Any cyber attacks originating with terrorists or cyber jihadists in the near future are likely to be conducted either to raise money (e.g., via credit card theft) or to cause damage comparable to that which takes place daily from Web defacements, viruses and worms, and denial-of-service attacks. While the impact of these attacks can be serious, they are generally not regarded as acts of terrorism. Terrorists have not yet demonstrated that they have the knowledge and skills to conduct highly damaging attacks against critical infrastructures. . . . their capability is at the lowest level, namely that required to carry out simple-unstructured attacks.[29]

Another key indicator of the limited cyber knowledge and skills found in jihadist terrorist groups was their heavy reliance on a single individual who had a moderate level of ability in this area: Irhabi 007 (real name: Younis Tsouli). This 22-year-old living in London became "the top jihadi expert on all things Internet-related" after 9/11.[30] Despite this ominous sounding label, Irhabi's skills were quite mundane by hacker standards: he was able to hack Web sites and servers using standard toolkits found on the Internet. More importantly, Irhabi spent much of his time showing fellow jihadists how to perform such simple tasks as posting videos to Web sites and joining anonymous chat rooms. He also provided tutorials on the fundamentals of hacking Web sites to launch basic denial-of-service attacks.[31] The fact that he was functioning as *the* Internet expert for a number of major terrorist and insurgent groups until his arrest in 2005 implies that these groups had limited education and expertise in computer attack methods and practices. While Irhabi's tutorials have almost certainly raised the overall cyber capabilities of terrorists, which is worrisome, there is little evidence that these groups have progressed beyond the simple attack category.

This tentative conclusion is further bolstered by an analysis of terrorist activities and cyber attacks from 1996 to 2003.[32] The data in table 19–3 show three things. First, cyber attacks were extremely common.[33] Second, terrorists were quite active; they conducted an average of over 200 attacks per year. And third, the fact that there were no known cases of cyber terrorism during a period in which terrorists were quite active and hundreds of thousands of cyber attacks were occurring suggests that terrorists either are not trying to conduct cyber attacks or are trying and failing.

While it is possible that a small number of cyber terror attacks did happen and were simply not reported, the overall trend is clear: terrorists were not focused on conducting cyber attacks. Similar patterns hold true for 2003 through 2007. For example, it was reported early in 2008 that "every day, the Defense Department detects three million unauthorized probes of its computer networks; the State Department fends off two million."[34] In 2006, the State Department cataloged 14,352 terrorist incidents around the world, none of which were classified as cyber terrorism.[35] Both hackers and terrorists are keeping quite busy, but their activities are not intersecting in any meaningful way. Why?

It is not possible to provide a definitive answer to this question, but a reasonable explanation can be pieced together. First, it appears that terrorist groups in general do not have the expertise to conduct advanced or complex cyber attacks. This means that terrorists are currently limited to exploiting the same basic vulnerabilities that are constantly being targeted by thousands of hackers around the world. While such attacks can work—they succeed all the time against poorly defended systems—it does mean that cyber attacks conducted by terrorists would have roughly the same impact as techniques used by ordinary hackers, hacktivists, and cyber criminals. To put things in context, DOD alone faced 80,000 intrusion attempts in fiscal year 2007. The presence of a few simple cyber attacks from terrorist groups would be lost in the sea of cyber attacks, some of them quite serious, already faced by DOD.

A similar story holds true for the private sector. For example, in 2006, the Department of Homeland Security warned U.S. financial services companies about "an al Qaeda call for a cyber attack against online stock trading and banking Web sites."[36] Did the financial community respond with alarm and fear? Hardly. The financial sector's reaction was "muted, with markets showing little or no reaction."[37] The threat was simply not viewed as being worthy of panic. In the words of one executive, "I'm not saying that there aren't precautions to be taken, but I just can't fathom how there would be serious havoc."[38] Given the constant stream of cyber attacks that the financial sector faces on a daily basis, and the lack of sophistication found in terrorist hacking circles, this executive's assessment should not be surprising. It also turned out to be accurate: either no attacks occurred or they occurred but failed to work, because the financial companies operated as usual during the period in question.

In comparison to cyber terrorism, using physical means to create terror is fairly easy to do and is quite effective.[39] Put in these terms, it is not surprising that terrorists prefer to inflict damage with physical means and then use the Internet to magnify the results of their handiwork.[40] In fact, al Qaeda's own training manual makes the point that explosives are the preferred weapons of terrorists because "explosives strike the enemy with sheer terror and fright."[41] They also create carnage that is highly photogenic and inspires strong emotions, horrifying victims and inspiring allies and supporters. Indeed, despite its sophisticated planning and analytic capabilities, all of al Qaeda's operations to date have focused on high explosives; what have changed are the delivery mechanisms and the targets.

From a terrorist perspective, cyber attacks appear much less useful than physical attacks: they do not fill potential victims with terror, they are not photogenic, and they are not perceived by most people as highly emotional events. While it is possible that a complex attack on a critical infrastructure would create some of these desired effects, including a sense of panic or a loss of public confidence, terrorists appear to be incapable of launching such attacks in the near future. Faced with a choice between conducting cyber attacks that would be viewed mostly as a nuisance or using physical violence to create dramatic and traumatic events, terrorists have been choosing the latter. This choice is not surprising given our assessment earlier in this chapter. Other security experts have reached similar conclusions:

> Cyber terrorism has grabbed the headlines recently, but most of that is overblown. . . . We know what terrorism is. It's someone blowing himself up in a crowded restaurant or flying an airplane into a skyscraper. It's not infecting computers with viruses, disabling the Internet so people can't get their e-mail for a few hours, or shutting down a pager network for a day. That causes annoyance and irritation, not terror. . . . Stories of terrorists controlling the power grid, or opening dams, or taking over the air traffic control network and colliding airplanes, are unrealistic scare stories. This kind of thing is surprisingly hard to do remotely. Insiders might have an easier time of it, but even then they can do more damage in person than over a computer network.[42]

Assessment of Future Cyber Terror Risks

Is the risk of cyber terrorism likely to change in the future? In the spirit of policy analysts everywhere, this author must answer: "It depends." There are several factors at play—some of which favor the prospects for cyber terrorism and some of which oppose them.

Threat. One of the key considerations that might push terrorists toward a greater use of cyber attacks is having the ability to launch either a complex cyber attack or a series of sustained and well-targeted advanced attacks. In order to achieve such capabilities, terrorist groups would have to obtain the services of several highly educated or experienced computer scientists, engineers, or self-taught hackers. There are two options for getting there: insourcing or outsourcing. The former option would require terrorist groups either to recruit experts or to grow them internally through education and training. Historically, terrorist groups have had trouble doing either. One trend that works in their favor is the growth of computer literacy across the world. As computer know-how spreads, the chances that terrorist groups will be able to recruit people with strong computer skills (or induce potential recruits to obtain such skills) will likely increase over time. The fact that the jihadist movements are attracting to their cause well-educated young men in Europe further increases these odds.[43]

Terrorists have a second option: they could choose to obtain computer expertise through outsourcing. The main benefit of this approach is that it would allow the groups to access needed knowledge quickly and relatively cheaply. On the other hand, there are numerous risks associated with outsourcing cyber attacks to experts outside of a terrorist group. For example, one avenue to pursue would be to hire people from the hacking community. Some hackers are quite skilled and could help terrorist groups launch an advanced attack. However, hackers and terrorists often have different personalities, skill sets, and group cultures.[44] By going outside of their group, terrorists increase the risk of being caught because many hackers like to brag about their exploits.

TABLE 19-3. Number of Cyber and Terrorist Attacks, 1996–2003

TYPE OF INCIDENT	NUMBER OF OCCURRENCES
Computer security attack	217,394
Conventional terrorist attack	1,813
Cyber terrorist attack	0

Source: James Lewis, "Cyber Terror: Missing in Action," *Knowledge, Technology, and Policy* 16, no. 2 (Summer 2003).

Another approach for terrorist groups looking for computer skills would be to hire criminal organizations for assistance with cyber attacks. This strategy is probably less risky than working with hackers, and it has the added benefit of the apparent willingness of some cyber criminals to work with any paying customer. Criminal groups might also be willing to launch attacks for terrorist organizations in order to bolster their reputations. Cyber criminals could provide terrorists with fairly sophisticated capabilities for delivering cyber attacks. For example, many criminal organizations have created large botnets in order to perform (or threaten to launch) DDOS attacks. In addition, cyber criminals are constantly developing malicious code attacks that can take over a target system in order to steal valuable information that the criminals can use or sell. For example, according to one IT research company, "Phishing attacks are becoming more surreptitious and are often designed to drop malware that steals user credentials and sensitive information from consumer desktops."[45]

The downside of this strategy is that cyber criminals are in the business of making money, not taking down national infrastructures. In fact, these groups rely heavily on several U.S. infrastructures, such as telecommunications and financial services, to conduct their operations. While some of their capabilities, such as botnets and malicious code, could be used by terrorists to attack critical systems, these capabilities alone are unlikely to cause large-scale damage of any lasting impact. Launching a complex attack requires detailed analysis, planning, and rehearsal and, as several studies have indicated, it would take a dedicated and well-financed team several years of effort to prepare a truly serious strategic attack on U.S. infrastructures. Criminal groups are simply not in that business. Their capabilities might allow terrorists to launch advanced attacks against companies or countries—and such attacks are certainly worrisome—but companies and countries already face such threats on a daily basis. It is not clear how much benefit terrorists would gain by using such attacks against their desired targets.

A final avenue for terrorist groups to bolster their attack capabilities is to obtain state sponsorship. There is little question that nation-states have the potential to pose the most serious threat to U.S. national security. Many nations have the resources, personnel, and motives to develop the ability to launch complex cyber attacks against other countries. The key question is: Would such nations choose to aid and abet terrorist groups, either directly or indirectly, in obtaining the capacity to launch cyber attacks that could truly cripple another nation? There are numerous factors (some leading to benefits and others to risks) that nations must weigh when deciding what relationship to have with terrorist groups. At present, it appears that the nations with the most advanced cyber capabilities are unlikely to support terrorist groups directly, while nations that have a history of supporting terrorist groups are more limited in their cyber capabilities. However, a deeper analysis is required to assess the possible future risks of state-sponsored cyber terrorism.

Vulnerabilities and consequences. One trend that increases the likeli-hood of cyber terrorism is growing reliance of critical infrastructures on com-mercial-off-the-shelf software and the Internet—both of which increase the number of vulnerabilities that can be exploited. A related trend is the growing interconnectedness of organizations (both private and public) via the Internet. This connectivity, while beneficial for economic efficiency and productivity, can create points of vulnerability that, if properly targeted and attacked, could cause real economic, physical, or psychological harm to U.S. citizens.[46] In addition, the tight coupling between different infrastructures and organizations might lead to a "ripple effect" that magnifies the consequences of a particular attack. This ripple effect was evident in both Hurricane Katrina and the cyber attacks against Estonia in 2007.

On the other hand, the growing complexity and connectedness of in-frastructure targets make them harder to target and take down. The kinds of networks that terrorists would need to attack (usually referred to as scale-free networks) are robust against random failures but vulnerable to failures in key nodes.[47] The trick is to know which nodes to attack. In some networks, this is an extremely difficult thing to figure out due to the sheer complexity of the system. In other kinds of networks, identifying such nodes can be straightforward, but as society moves toward greater complexity and connectedness, identifying these nodes may also become difficult. This, in turn, would make the system as a whole more robust against random (or badly aimed) attacks. Then again, the growing availability of Internet-based information and of sophisticated software tools that can be used for network analysis may counteract the growing complexity of infrastructure networks. It is hard to predict which trend will come out on top.

Summary. There are strong reasons why cyber attacks have not been the weapons of choice for terrorists. Many of those reasons will hold in the future, but there are some trends that may make cyber terrorism both more attractive and feasible in the future. Dorothy Denning has identified five key indicators of cyber terror activity: computer network attack incidents; cyber weapons acquisition, development, and training; official statements; formal education in IT; and general experience in cyberspace.[48] Her analysis of these indicators found little evidence that terrorists have developed comprehensive and significant capabilities for cyber attacks against the United States. What is more surprising is that her analysis showed that terrorists made little progress in this area in the 5 years after 9/11. This is a critical finding because if terrorists were serious about exploiting the Internet for attacks (rather than for operational effectiveness or influence operations), one would have expected to see signs of that during a period that has seen an explosion in the number of terrorist groups, a rise in anti-American sentiment internationally, and a tremendous increase in Internet connectivity across the globe. One could legitimately ask of cyber terrorism: If not now, when?

Of course, one must be careful in extrapolating too much from an analysis of a 5-year window. Denning's analysis *has* shown the terrorists are growing more interested in cyber attacks, if only for fund-raising and low-level attacks. Cyber terrorism could become a more serious risk at some point in the future.

Terrorist Use of the Internet

Terrorists are using the Internet to harm U.S. national security, but not by attacking infrastructure or military assets directly. Instead, terrorists are using the Internet to improve their operational effectiveness while simultaneously undermining U.S. military and diplomatic efforts to win the war of ideas. There is little doubt that they are doing both things well. The Internet enables terrorist groups to operate either as highly decentralized franchises or as freelancers. Much like information-age businesses, these groups use the Internet to create a brand image, to market themselves, to recruit followers, to raise capital, to identify partners and suppliers, to provide training materials, and even to manage operations. As a result, these groups have become more numerous, agile, and well coordinated, which makes them harder to stop.[49] Further, these groups have become experts at using the Internet to manipulate both public opinion and media coverage in ways that undermine U.S. interests. In short, rather than attacking the Internet, terrorists are using it to survive and thrive.

Why the Internet?
The Internet has five characteristics that make it an ideal tool for terrorist organizations. First, it enables rapid communications. People can hold conversations in real time using instant messaging or Web forums. Instructions, intelligence information, and funds can be sent and received in a manner of seconds via email. Second, using the Internet is a low-cost proposition. Terrorist organizations can now affordably duplicate many of the capabilities needed by modern militaries, government organizations, and businesses: a communications infrastructure, an intelligence-gathering operation, a training system, and a media-savvy public affairs presence. Third, the ubiquity of the Internet means that small terrorist groups can have a global cyber presence that rivals that of much larger organizations. Terrorist members can communicate with each other from almost anywhere in the world. A small terrorist cell may create a Web site that is viewed by millions of people and even examined daily by media outlets for news stories.[50] Fourth, the growth in bandwidth combined with development of new software has enabled unsophisticated users to develop and disseminate complex information via the Internet. For example, "In December 2004, a militant Islamic chat room posted a twenty-six-minute video clip with instructions on how to assemble a suicide bomb vest, along with a taped de-

monstration of its use on a model of a bus filled with passengers."[51] Finally, modern encryption technologies allow Internet users to surf the Web, transfer funds, and communicate anonymously—a serious (though not insurmountable) impediment to intelligence and law enforcement organizations trying to find, track, and catch terrorists. To do this, terrorists can download various types of easy-to-use computer security software (some of which is commercial and some of which is freely available) or register for anonymous email accounts from providers like Yahoo! or Hotmail.[52]

The combination of characteristics described above makes the Internet a valued strategic asset for terrorists. In fact, one could argue that the Internet, in conjunction with other modern communications technologies, is a sine qua non of the modern global extremist movement.[53] What follows is an examination of how terrorists are using the Internet to influence target audiences and to improve their operational effectiveness.

Influence Operations

The Internet allows terrorist groups to control their image with target audiences and the media. Usually this is accomplished via Web sites: "A typical terrorist Web site usually includes information about the history of the group or organization; biographies of its leaders, founders, heroes, and commanders; information on the political, religious, or ideological aims of the organization; and news bulletins and updates."[54] This information is presented in the best possible light. For example, most terrorist Web sites avoid mentioning the violent means used by that group to achieve its aims and instead focus on their justifications and valor in resisting whatever political, religious, or social repressions are driving their actions. Some Web sites are quite sophisticated; they feature high-quality graphics and up-to-date information and can be read in multiple languages. In addition to Web sites, terrorist groups use a variety of collaboration tools, such as chat rooms, to help foster a spirit of unity and collectivism among their followers similar to that found in many political campaigns.[55]

One goal of terrorist influence campaigns is to build a sustaining level of support and tolerance among their constituents. The Internet allows extremists to deliver well-coordinated propaganda campaigns that increase the levels of support among the general public; this in turn allows the terrorists to operate freely in these societies. For example, one of al Qaeda's goals is to use the Internet to create "resistance blockades" in order to prevent Western ideas from "further corrupting Islamic institutions, organizations, and ideas."[56] One technique is to distribute Internet browsers that have been designed to filter out content from undesirable sources (for example, Western media) without the users' knowledge.[57]

In addition to influencing the general public and media, terrorist groups need to recruit active members who will work in direct support of the cause.

In other words, successful terrorism requires the transformation of interested outsiders into dedicated insiders.[58] Once someone has become an insider, less intense but still continuous interactions are required to maintain the needed level of commitment to the cause. Before the advent of advanced communications technologies, this process was entirely based on face-to-face interactions, which limited the scope of a given group. However, the Internet allows groups to create and identify dedicated insiders, and to maintain fervor in those already dedicated to the cause, on a global scale.[59]

Operational Effectiveness

There is no doubt that the Internet has revolutionized how businesses, governments, and nonprofit institutions conduct their affairs. The same is true with terrorist organizations. By using the Internet, terrorist groups that used to operate as small localized cells with limited capabilities can now operate on a global scale. We have seen how cyberspace abets terrorist recruiting. The same medium can be used to train those recruits and turn them into effective fighters for the cause:

> Using the Internet, jihadists have created a virtual classroom that teaches the online jihadist community how to produce and construct weapons ranging from simple IEDs [improvised explosive devices] to nuclear, biological, and chemical weapons. Not only are jihadists taught military tactics; they also learn how to mine the Internet for information, protect their anonymity online, encrypt the contents of their computers, and use the Internet to benefit the global jihadist movement.[60]

This points to several other benefits terrorists gain from the Internet. For example, they can use it as an effective intelligence-gathering tool: "Terrorists have access not only to maps and diagrams of potential targets but also to imaging data on those same facilities and networks that may reveal counterterrorist activities at a target site."[61] They can use anonymous communications mechanisms to conduct planning and operational command and control. Al Qaeda did just that for the 9/11 attacks. Terrorists can use the Internet to raise funds, without which they cannot operate effectively. The Internet allows terrorist groups to obtain money through a variety of means, including targeted donations (funds given directly to organizations such as al Qaeda, Hamas, or Hizballah), indirect donations (funds given to religious groups or other ideological/political organizations that can pass along the money to terrorists), and even through cyber criminal activities (such as identity theft or fraudulent scams).

Last but not least, the Internet enables terrorists to alter their organizational structures. In the words of one team of terrorism experts:

Terrorists will continue moving from hierarchical toward information-age network designs. Within groups, 'great man' leaderships will give way to flatter decentralized designs. More effort will go into building arrays of transnationally internetted groups than into building stand-alone groups.[62]

This move from "hierarchical" to "horizontal" greatly complicates the counterterrorism problem facing the United States.[63] The United States knows how to take down traditional hierarchical organizations: it targets the center of gravity, removes it, and watches the group (military, criminal, or terrorist) descend into chaos. Unfortunately, this approach is not optimal against a highly networked, horizontal organizational structure that has no center of gravity. In fact, attempting to take out the leader of a leaderless organization may actually make things worse because decisionmaking authority may devolve to the next layer, or more accurately, the next circle, of the organization.[64]

Recommendations

This section begins with prescriptions addressing the issue of cyber terrorism. It then offers recommendations for dealing with terrorist use of the Internet.

While cyber terrorism does not pose a serious risk to U.S. national security at this time, the other cyber threats described in table 19–1—especially crime, espionage, and state-sponsored information warfare—are more worrisome. The U.S. Government is taking these threats seriously and is acting to minimize the risks they pose.[65] Of course, many if not most of these attacks are aimed at organizations in the private sector where the Federal Government has little day-to-day involvement in cyber security. The response of the private sector to these cyber threats has been mixed: some organizations have developed outstanding cyber defenses, while others have fallen woefully short. Overall, though, there is a clear understanding across all parts of the Nation that cyber threats are a real problem that will only get worse over time. As a result, most public and private sector organizations are taking steps to improve their cyber defenses. Although these efforts are primarily aimed at countering cyber crime and espionage, they work equally well against hacktivism and cyber terrorism. While the offense generally has the advantage over the defense in such a cyber arms race, the fact that organizations are running to stay ahead of motivated and well-funded cyber criminals and thousands of hackers means that these organizations are probably moving fast enough to stay ahead of cyber terrorists.

Thus, it is imperative for organizations across the U.S. economy to continue bolstering their defenses against cyber attacks, and they should do so using a defense-in-depth strategy that focuses on protection, detection, and response. The latter in particular often receives insufficient attention. Security professionals tend to focus on preventing cyber attacks from succeeding, so most of their time, energy, and resources is spent on perimeter defenses such as firewalls and intrusion detection systems. The problem with this approach is that, sooner or later, an attack will succeed and the targeted system will go down or its integrity will be called into question. Another problem is that perimeter defenses do not help against malicious insiders, human errors, natural disasters, or systemic failures.[66] At that point, the key issue is availability: How can people get access to the information they need? Perimeter defenses and intrusion detection systems cannot help with that problem. That is why focusing on response is so critical.

Systems that are resilient can respond quickly after facing cyber attacks, human errors, and even natural disasters. Building in such resilience is expensive, inefficient (unless something bad happens), and time consuming. Organizations will need to conduct their own risk assessments to determine if such expenditures are worthwhile. However, the benefits of resilience are often underestimated by many organizations until it is too late. This is especially true for critical infrastructures that are possible targets of cyber terrorists or nation-states.[67] Because most of these infrastructures are owned and operated by the private sector, the issue of infrastructure resilience is a complex public policy problem that requires tradeoffs among options that all carry serious risks or costs. The risks of not acting are growing with each passing day.

On another front, the United States must make every effort to prevent terrorist groups from recruiting or hiring people with strong technical and analytical skills. If terrorists wish to develop the ability to perform complex and coordinated attacks, they will need to obtain the expertise somewhere. This is a vulnerability that the United States can exploit. Groups trying to grow their own experts may send members to universities in the United States or Europe. It may be possible for the United States and its allies to identify and track students who are affiliated with these groups. If terrorists attempt to hire outside experts, they could become vulnerable to infiltration by Western agents (professional or amateur) posing as IT experts with sympathetic beliefs. There is a window of opportunity right now. The Irhabi 007 incident shows that terrorist groups are currently lacking in deep IT expertise, but that situation is likely to change in the future. Once such expertise is resident within terrorist groups, it will be easier for them to develop internal training programs, and they will be less likely to seek outside training and education.

Finally, the United States needs to explore the potential utility of preemption and deterrence (cyber or kinetic) for preventing cyber terror attacks from occurring in the first place.[68] These options offer a number of benefits but they also pose a number of technical, operational, and legal challenges. Further study is needed to determine if, how, and when such options can be pursued.

Terrorist Use of the Internet

The Internet enables terrorist organizations to operate as transnational, virtual organizations. They can use it to do fundraising, recruiting, training, executing command and control, intelligence-gathering, and information-sharing. Clearly, it is in the interest of the United States to disrupt or undermine these activities. The good news is that relying on the Internet is a two-edged sword for terrorist organizations: despite the many benefits associated with using this technology, it also carries liabilities. For example, terrorist reliance on Web sites and discussion forums allows outsiders to monitor their methods and track trends. It creates the opportunity for outsiders to pose as insiders in order to provide misinformation or simply to create doubt among the terrorists about whom to trust. The bad news is that terrorists are doing their best to minimize the liabilities associated with heavy reliance on the Internet. They are quick to learn from mistakes and to disseminate best practices on how to defeat the tactics used by intelligence and law enforcement agencies.[69]

The remainder of this chapter explores different strategies that the United States can pursue to counter terrorist use of the Internet. It does so by examining the strengths and weaknesses of targeting the three components of the "information environment" as defined by DOD: physical (infrastructure), information (content), and cognition (perceiving and deciding).[70]

Physical Infrastructure

One approach to counter extremists' use of the Internet is to target their communications infrastructure to deny or disrupt their ability to communicate or to maintain an Internet presence. The benefit of this strategy is that it would seriously harm their ability to operate effectively precisely because of their heavy reliance on this medium. It might also force the extremists to use other means of communication that are potentially more cumbersome for them and easier for the United States to monitor.

While attacking the Internet infrastructure of terrorist groups carries clear benefits, it also brings significant challenges. The majority of extremist organizations depend on commercially owned infrastructure for their communications needs. Most of that infrastructure, especially the elements that provide Web-based services, is hosted in the United States or Europe. As a result, a strategy of countering extremist activities by attacking their infrastructures would require the United States to target itself or its allies. There may be cases where the infrastructure in question is owned or operated by a company that resides in a country that is not allied with the United States. In such cases, a direct attack (either via physical or cyber means) on the targeted information infrastructure might prove to be useful in certain circumstances. The United States would have to weigh the perceived benefits of such an attack against the political and military risks associated with a potential act of war against another sovereign nation.

Another option would be for the U.S. Government to ask infrastructure providers to identify extremist clients and selectively terminate or disrupt their activities. Unfortunately, this is harder than it sounds. Extremists often pose as legitimate companies or use false information to register for accounts. They also tend to move between providers frequently. To complicate matters further, the issue of monitoring terrorist activities inside the United States requires both government and industry to weigh the rights of free speech against the needs for national security. There is no clear consensus on where to draw the line between these competing demands.

Finally, in the cases where infrastructure providers can identify extremists that are using their services, it might make more operational sense for the United States to monitor or eavesdrop on the extremists rather than just shut them down (in which case they would simply move to another provider). This approach— which could be called "tolerate, monitor, and exploit"—could provide the United States with valuable intelligence. It could also open the door to the planting of disinformation.

Content

A second approach to countering extremists' use of the Internet is to target their content. The goal here is to affect one or more of the three components of information assurance: confidentiality, integrity, and availability. By attacking the *confidentiality* of information, the United States would deny the terrorists the ability to communicate secretly and securely. This could be accomplished by using wiretaps, breaking encryption algorithms, or using undercover agents to gain access to secure chat rooms and Web sites (these sites are usually password protected and their locations are revealed only to trusted members via secure email or other covert means). While government agencies will clearly play a key role in such activities, nonprofit organizations such as the SITE Institute are also contributing to the cause by monitoring terrorist Web sites and providing information to a range of interested parties, including elements within the U.S. Government.[71]

By attacking the *integrity* of information, the United States would be able to do two things: secretly plant misleading information in order to get the extremists to take desired actions or to begin mistrusting each other; and openly reveal that they had compromised critical information (for example, by hacking into databases or Web sites) in order to raise doubts in the minds of the terrorists about the validity of all of their content. Surprisingly, nongovernmental organizations appear to be conducting these types of activities as well. For example, there are cases of individual citizens who have infiltrated terrorist networks via chat rooms and then worked with government agencies to bring about several arrests.[72]

Finally, by attacking the *availability* of their content, the United States would deny the extremists effective and timely access to their information. This could be accomplished in numerous ways, including both physical and cyber means such as denial-of-service attacks.[73] Given their heavy reliance on the Internet, limiting terrorist access to the content available via that medium alone would limit the effectiveness of these groups.

While attacking extremist content is generally easier than taking out the physical infrastructure upon which it depends, this strategy still requires the United States to overcome several challenges. One problem is that terrorist groups are adept at quickly moving their Web sites from host to host, which makes them difficult to track and shut down (trusted members of these groups use chat rooms, email, and other forums to share information about the new location of a moved Web site). Some of their activities masquerade as legitimate business operations. A related challenge is that the number of relevant Web sites is growing extremely quickly. Thus, significant resources would be required to keep track of the tremendous amount of extremist content appearing online. This also means that compromising some data, or denying access to a few Web sites or databases, might have a small impact on the overall extremist movement. In the words of cyber terrorism expert Gabriel Weimann: "Those who think that we can stop terrorism by removal of Web sites are either naive or ignorant about cyberspace and its limitations for interference."[74]

A final problem is that terrorists tend to use secure chat rooms and encrypted emails to transmit critical pieces of information. Many use free anonymous email accounts provided by companies like Yahoo! and Microsoft. This allows them to use public computers at any location, such as a cyber café, to communicate. It is much harder to find and disrupt, alter, or deny these messages than it is to track Web sites, which is itself a challenge.

Cognition

A third approach to countering terrorist use of the Internet is to focus on the cognitive domain rather than on either the infrastructure or the content per se. The goal is to influence how people perceive information and how they make decisions. In order for this approach, sometimes referred to as perception management, to be successful, it must be tied closely to the broader war of ideas against the extremist Islamic movement. For example, attempts to alter the perceptions of target audiences must consider factors such as language, culture, values, and context.

There are a number of advantages associated with perception management. First, it can be used to reduce the perceived legitimacy and attractiveness of terrorist movements. This, in turn, could have a cascading effect on the ability of terrorist groups to recruit, raise funds, maintain operational security, influence the media, and operate training bases. Perception management can also be used to influence allies and nonaligned parties in order to build support for U.S. policies and actions targeted against these groups. Another benefit of using perception management, especially the public diplomacy component, is that it can help spread U.S. values around the world. This reduces the likelihood of military conflict and improves the chances for beneficial economic relations, both of which reduce factors that can contribute to the success of terrorist groups.

The United States faces two significant challenges in the area of perception management. The first is that its current ability to operate a well-coordinated, government-wide strategic perception management campaign is limited. Short-comings in the area of public diplomacy have been well documented, but many efforts on the military side have also come up short.[75] Developing a robust strategic perception management capability will require time and resources at the agency level (specifically at the State Department and DOD), and an effective interagency process for the development and coordination of coherent themes and messages—a significant challenge given the government's current structure. Former Secretary of Defense Donald Rumsfeld admitted as much when he said, "If I were rating, I would say we probably deserve a D or D+ as a country as to how well we're doing in the battle of ideas that's taking place. . . . So we're going to have to find better ways to do it and thus far we haven't as a government. The government's not well organized to do it."[76]

Finally, perception management campaigns, even ones that are well funded and organized, take many years to reach fruition. Changing how people think is not easy; it may take a generation or more. The United States needs to take a long-term view of the problem, much as it did during the Cold War. Unfortunately, such long-term thinking is rare in the current political climate because incentives work against spending money now to achieve benefits that will not accrue for years or even decades.

Despite the challenges associated with perception management, the "war of ideas" cannot be ignored; it is a critical component of U.S. efforts to counter terrorist movements. The following suggestions should be helpful no matter what specific strategy the United States decides to follow in this area.

First, U.S. efforts to influence must be tied to real-world actions. While it is easy to focus purely on the principles of effective communications strategies, our words will ring hollow if they are not related to the realities experienced by the target audience. Thus, it should go without saying that what the United States does is as (if not more) important as what it says. To that end, diplomatic and military influence operations must ensure that target audiences are aware of the positive actions undertaken by the United States in the Muslim world, while simultaneously highlighting the negative actions being taken by our enemies. The corollary to this point is that the United States must effectively get its story out before the terrorists or insurgents can use the Internet to spin events in their favor. It is much harder to respond to or discredit initial stories, even ones that are untrue, than to establish the baseline facts or perceptions in the first place. Elements of the U.S. Government are making efforts in this area. For example, the State Department maintains a Web site in a number of languages (including Arabic, Farsi, and French) that is devoted to countering false stories that appear in extremist sources. It also focuses on countering disinformation likely to end up in the mainstream media. U.S. Embassies have used the Web site's resources to counter disinformation in extremist print publications in Pakistan and elsewhere. There are also military units deployed overseas that are exhibiting "best practices" in operational level influence operations.[77] Unfortunately, much work remains to be done for such examples to become the rule rather than the exception.

A related point is that the United States must view the war of ideas as being equally important as the military and law enforcement aspects of the war on terror. The "war of ideas" aspects of any decision involving the global war on terrorism must be considered at the highest levels of U.S. policymaking. That emphasis must then be communicated down the chain so that all players understand the importance of "message" in this war. Strategic communications cannot be seen as an afterthought of a military operation or as the sole responsibility of an office buried within the State Department. Similarly, information operations cannot be viewed simply as a set of activities done by a local commander in support of tactical objectives. Countering terrorist use of the Internet will require a government-wide approach to designing and implementing perception management strategies.

Third, the United States must reframe the terms of the war of ideas. Words like *jihad* and *mujahideen* are part of the popular lexicon describing antiterrorist operations in Iraq, Afghanistan, and elsewhere. However, such terms disempower the United States while legitimizing the terrorists' story line. *Jihad* literally means *striving* and is frequently used to describe every Muslim's responsibility to strive in the path of God. *Mujahideen* is closely translated to mean *holy warriors*. These terms may have worked to the U.S. advantage when Osama bin Laden was fighting against the Soviet Union in Afghanistan; however, use of those same words now paints the United States as a legitimate enemy of holy warriors who are engaged in a just war. The United States needs to adopt a formal lexicon of Arabic terms for referring to various players and concepts in the global war on terror.[78] For example, we should use terms such as *hirabah*, meaning *unholy war*, and *irhabists*, meaning *terrorists*, when talking about extremist groups.[79] Such words reframe the conflict between groups such as al Qaeda and the United States in ways that will resonate with Muslim audiences. Similarly, the United States can leverage values that are grounded in Islamic theory and traditions, such as honor, to emphasize peaceful ways to achieve political ends.[80]

As important as it is for the United States to improve its own communications efforts, a key part of countering extremist misinformation and propaganda is to have messages come from a variety of sources, some of them preferably local. For example, it is critical for the United States to promote the views of well-respected Muslim clerics to counter the claims made by Islamic terrorists and extremists. There are examples of this type of activity taking place, including some efforts by the government of Saudi Arabia, but more needs to be done.[81] The United States should do everything possible to enable moderate Muslims to develop a strong, healthy, and responsive Internet and media presence of their own.

Last but not least, resources must be made available to support all of these efforts, plus others that are not mentioned here but are equally important, such as training and education to improve understanding of Muslim cultures and languages. Current U.S. resources dedicated to strategic communications, public diplomacy, and information operations are woefully inadequate.[82] On the military side, the lack of training and education in information operations at all levels—strategic, operational, and tactical—often requires commanders to both learn on the job and to build information operations teams "out of hide."[83] While some leaders will certainly rise to the occasion, this approach is not a recipe for success in a complex, media-heavy war effort against adversaries who are highly adept at conducting their own influence operations.

Conclusion

Terrorists are using the Internet to harm U.S. national security interests, but not by conducting large-scale cyber attacks. Instead, they are using it to plan and conduct physical attacks, spread their ideology, manipulate the general public and the media, recruit and train new terrorists, raise funds, gather information on potential targets, and control operations. As a result, terrorist groups can easily operate on a global front and use the networked nature of cyberspace to become both more effective and robust. Thus, it is critical for the United States to combine its cyber defense efforts with a well-developed strategy for countering terrorist use of the Internet. Such a strategy must be well resourced, developed, and executed in an interagency context, and flow coherently up and down the chain of command. It must address the war of ideas occurring between extremist groups and the West, and it must attempt to counteract the operational effectiveness that these groups gain by using the Internet. This task will not be easy, but it must be done. Technological and demographic developments portend a future in which the power of individuals and groups continues to grow relative to that of the nation-state. The United States will need to confront this reality if it wishes to thrive in the coming century.

CHAPTER 20

Nation-state Cyber Strategies: Examples from China and Russia

Timothy L. Thomas

AN EARLY adopter of cyberspace concepts in the United States was the Air Force, which established a cyberspace command in November 2006. That same year, U.S. policymakers developed the *National Military Strategy for Cyberspace Operations*, which lays out national strategy in the form of ends, ways, and means with the goal of ensuring U.S. military strategic superiority in cyberspace. However, not all nation-states approach the new capabilities of cyberpower in the same way. This chapter describes how China and Russia are implementing cyber doctrine and practice; the challenges each country's cyber strategy presents to current U.S. practices; and what weaknesses those strategies reveal in the U.S. approach.

The cyber strategy of China is focused as much on the use of information warfare (IW) stratagems and reconnaissance of foreign sites as on attacking others' Web sites. Nationalists do most of the hacking that causes disruptions, often during crises in China; whether they are state-directed is not clear.

The cyber strategy of Russia focuses on ensuring information security by managing the flow of information to its citizens, as well as on securing its physical information infrastructure.

This chapter first discusses how China uses what it terms *informationization* (the word *cyber* is not widely used in China but has been noted as a cognate of *informationization*), and the role of informationization in the strategic thought of the People's Liberation Army (PLA). Then, Russia's potential cyber strategy is illuminated through an examination of its cyber terminology and its understanding of the term *strategy*. The chapter concludes with a brief statement of lessons for U.S. cyber strategy.

China

In recent years, Chinese cyber capabilities have become more visible and troubling. China has launched an unknown number of cyber reconnaissance and offensive events with unknown intent against a variety of countries. Episodes reported publicly include espionage conducted in 2005 against U.S. Department of Defense (DOD) computers in operations that Federal investigators code-named Titan Rain.[1] China also reportedly attempted to blind a U.S. satellite using high-powered laser attacks in 2006.[2] Attacks on the U.S. Naval War College's net capability, reportedly originating from China, shut down email and computer systems for several weeks in 2006.[3] When an old Chinese weather satellite was destroyed with an antisatellite missile, a Beijing People's University commentator related this capability both to "the development of missiles" and to "an IW capability."[4] China has also been accused of backing hacker attacks against Japan and Taiwan.[5] These attacks were perceived as retaliation: in the case of Japan, for its anti-Chinese interpretations of history, and in Taiwan, for its claims of independence.

The growing intensity of these cyber attacks demands a closer look at China's cyber philosophy and how it has evolved. Of particular interest is how cyber issues have been embedded into the peacetime strategic activities of the PLA and China's potential use of cyberpower as a preemptive strategy.

Development of Cyber Philosophy

The word *cyber* does not enjoy widespread use in China, which instead generally employs the word *informationization*. However, the latter term may be a cognate for *cyber*. In 2005, the Chinese military translated its own publication, *The Science of Military Strategy*, into English.[6] Chinese translators added a few pages at the back of the book titled "Selected Chinese-English Terms," in which the Chinese word for *information attack* had the alternate translation *cyber attack*. The Chinese word for *informationization* had next to it the alternate translation *cyberization*. Two other related Chinese words were expressed in English as *age of cyber information* and *cyber war*. The main text also dedicated one sentence to the concept of *comprehensive cyberized war*. The editors state that "information production modes keep developing and global integration moves on. Political elements, modes of violence, and even the intension [sic] of war will all be updated. A new pattern of comprehensive cyberized war is going to appear."

In February 2007, *China National Defense News* defined *cyber warfare* broadly as a "struggle between opposing sides making use of network technology and methods to struggle for an information advantage in the fields of politics, economics, military affairs, and technology."[7] Cyber warfare would be "a series of actions like network surveillance, network attack, network defense, and network support by opposing sides using network technology in the area of combat command, weapons control, combat support, logistical support, intelligence reconnaissance, and combat management." Cyber warfare was identified as an important action toward achieving "network control." Control is a vital aspect of China's information operations theory: whoever controls the network can take preemptive actions, either in a propaganda war or in real confrontations such as computer network attacks. Both the cases of Titan Rain and the attacks on the Naval War College are potential examples of confrontational Chinese activities on the Internet, although no U.S. official has confirmed Chinese involvement at a government level.

Cyber technology potentially has advanced Chinese thinking with regard to preemption. Chinese military academics state that those who do not preempt lose the initiative in what may be a very short-lived war; combatants in present-day conflicts, they argue, will find it easier to obtain the objective of war through a single campaign or battle than at any other time in history.[8] The idea of sudden attack has changed. It no longer simply means surprise in the old sense; rather, it means that one side cannot react even if the situation is known, because the other side possesses more advanced technology.

As a result, Chinese analysts argue, preparation and mobilization are more important than ever before.[9] War preparations, to include the recruitment of information talent, must be made in advance, so that a cyber operation, if needed, can be conducted suddenly with the use of all civil-military links.[10] Launching preemptive attacks to gain the initiative includes "striking the enemy's information center of gravity and weakening the combat efficiency of his information systems and cyberized weapons."[11] This allows one to weaken the enemy's information superiority and reduce its holistic combat efficiency.[12]

It appears that the PLA does not expect to go along this path alone. In March 2007, PLA National Party Congress deputy Chen Zuoning declared that the army and civilians together must strengthen state information security cooperation. He suggested they join hands and share resources in the creation of a national cyber information security coordinating institution.[13]

In May 2006, China published its *2006–2020 State Informationization Development Strategy*. Although it is not specifically military, it is in many ways a counterpart to the *National Military Strategy for Cyberspace Operations*. It called for China to:

- provide a nationwide cyber infrastructure[14]
- strengthen capacities for the independent innovation of cyber technologies
- optimize the cyber industry structure
- improve cyber security
- make effective progress in building a cyber-oriented national economy and society

- establish new industrialization models
- build and perfect national policies and systems for the cyberization process
- enhance capabilities to apply cyber technologies among the public
- promote the cyberization of the national economy
- popularize e-government
- establish an advanced Internet culture
- accelerate social cyberization.[15]

To understand China's cyber strategy, it is necessary first to understand how the Chinese definition of *strategy* differs from that of the United States, which defines *strategy* as "a prudent idea or set of ideas for employing the instruments of national power in a synchronized and integrated fashion to achieve theater, national, and/or multinational objectives."[16] The *Chinese Military Encyclopedia* defines *strategy* as "the analytical judgment of such factors as international conditions, hostilities in bilateral politics, military economics, science and technology, and geography as they apply to the preparation and direction of the overall military/war plan." The definition notes that it is "advantageous to study the occurrences and developments in war forecasting/predictions; to formulate strategic policy, strategic principles, and strategic plans; to make warfare preparations; and to put into place directives on the actual principles and methods of warfare."[17] Thus, the major difference is the U.S. concept of a set of ideas for employing the instruments of military power to achieve military objectives versus China's perception of an analytical judgment of factors applicable to a war plan.

One of China's most prominent military strategists, Li Bingyan, discussed strategy in terms of the use of information, a crucial component of cyber processes, to influence or control the direction of an opponent's decisionmaking activities.[18] It involves the wisdom, intelligence, and intellect of decisionmakers and how they gain the upper hand in a competitive environment by calculating the future, grasping the situation, making comprehensive plans, and seeking gains while avoiding harm.[19] Li wrote that military strategy should absorb new methodologies, including cybernetics and information theory.[20] If absorbed and understood properly, strategy will be able to take advantage of new conditions. Li thus emphasized the innovative use of information strategies in war.

The best strategy, according to Li, tries to entice the opponent to adopt a strategy that will lead China to the greatest gains. In this sense, risk and opportunity coexist.[21] The fog of war is used to execute, conceal, and develop strategy; strategists hope to know the situation on the other side, while using strategy and concealment to increase the fog affecting the opponent. Planning and designing strategy calls for knowing the enemy, while implementing strategy requires use of information channels to send the information, or misinformation, that one wants the opponent to know or perceive.[22]

To thwart the enemy's plans, friendly forces must analyze the size of the interests and contradictions of the two sides. One should arrange factors and see if one's own interests and objectives can be realized by influencing or destroying the opponent's cognition systems or by changing the opponent's decision-making.[23]

Li described the development of information warfare as a process of escalation. The way that the United States uses battlefield IW, he argued, still relies mainly on data and understanding, seeking to cut off an opponent's flow of information and to assure information flows for its side.

For China, in contrast, Li argued that high-technology warfare requires that Eastern military strategy must shed some old thinking and take into account new features: methods are new; information is abundant; content is vast; summaries are strong; preplanning is detailed; and resolution is quick. This implies that the revolution in military affairs (RMA) is changing the commander's concept of time, space, and strategy. Military theory can now emerge from laboratories, and military strategy can be previewed there.[24]

Li explained how a weak country could fight a technologically superior opponent by using superior knowledge of the other side. Metaphorically, he asked, "How could a mouse hang a bell around a cat's neck?" His answer is that the mouse could "entice the cat to put on the bell himself." In another metaphor, he posed, "How do you make a cat eat a hot pepper?" He suggested three possible ways: "You can stuff it down his throat (the most difficult). You can put the pepper in cheese and make him swallow it. Or you can grind the pepper up and spread it on his back, which makes the cat lick himself and receive the satisfaction of cleaning up the hot pepper."[25] In the last method, the cat is oblivious to the end goal and, said Li, this makes it a useful strategy. One must understand how an opposing side reacts to certain criteria.

Integrating High-tech Cyber Weaponry with Traditional Military Stratagems

One of China's foremost experts on IW is Dai Qingmin, who was director of the PLA Communication Department of the General Staff with responsibility for IW and information operations (IO). Discussing the importance of using RMA-generated information in shaping strategies, he said, "Today we should grasp the historical opportunity afforded by making these transformations in this information age . . . and formulate an effective threat and IW combat capability as soon as possible, thereby gaining the strategic initiative in the military struggles of this new century and even in international struggles."[26]

The topic of developing information warfare or cyber warfare strategies and tactics has taken center stage in China's discussions over the past few years. Dai wrote that "new technologies are likely to find material expression in informationized arms and equipment which will, together with information systems, sound, light, electronics, magnetism, heat, and so on, turn into a carrier of strategies."[27]

Dai's comments imply that China may intend to use packets of electrons as it once used forces. Stratagems such as "kill with a borrowed sword" and "exhaust the enemy at the gate and attack him at your ease" suggest how information operations might, for example, use packets of electrons to help country A destroy country C's information infrastructure after passing the packets through country B, the borrowed sword. Packets of electrons thus serve as the implementers of stratagems.

Dai defined an *information operation* as "a series of operations with an information environment as the basic battlefield condition, with military information and an information system as the direct operational target, and with electronic warfare and a computer network war as the principal form."[28] Since these operations are a confrontation of forces and arms as well as a trial of strength focusing on knowledge and strategies, Dai recommended a "focus on strategies."

Dai noted that scientific and technological developments have given strategies a new playing field. A strategy may carry different contents under different technological conditions. Thus, there is room for both traditional strategies and for mapping out new strategies using new technological means. Options include new information confrontation strategies.[29] Overall, said Dai:

> [A good strategy may] serve as a type of invisible fighting capacity; may make up inadequate material conditions to a certain extent; may narrow a technological or equipment gap between an army and its enemy; and may make up a shortage of information fighting forces or poor information operational means.[30]

Some specific strategies that Dai suggested include:

- jamming or sabotaging an enemy's information or information system
- sabotaging an enemy's overall information operational structure
- weakening an enemy's information fighting capacity
- dispersing enemy forces, arms, and fire while concentrating one's own
- confusing or diverting an enemy and creating an excellent combat opportunity for oneself
- diverting an enemy's reconnaissance attempt and making sufficient preparations for oneself
- giving an enemy a false impression while simultaneously launching a surprise information attack
- blinding or deafening an enemy with all sorts of false impressions

- confusing an enemy's mind or disrupting an enemy's thinking
- making an enemy believe that what is true is false and what is false is true
- making an enemy come up with a wrong judgment or take a wrong action.[31]

Dai emphasized that future operations must integrate the use of both military and civilian information forces. Information systems are offering more modes for people to take part in IO as well as giving people a chance to serve as a major auxiliary information fighting force.[32]

Dai pointed out that traditional tactics can help shape a strategy before a war so they can sabotage and weaken a superior enemy while protecting or enhancing China's own fighting capacity, serving as a type of invisible fighting capacity, and even helping China to evade combat with a stronger enemy.[33] Dai stated that new developments had created challenges to some traditional strategies while improving conditions for others. He did not specify which strategies he had in mind. However, if defeating strong forces with weak forces in future IW is a goal, then stratagems may suggest useful asymmetric means for China to combat U.S. high technology.[34] In this sense, stratagems would be one of the "magic weapons" that the Chinese stress.

Dai broke with Chinese tradition when he advocated gaining the initiative and seizing information superiority by attacking first. This active offensive strategic emphasis contradicts China's traditional strategy of active defense and indicates new missions for IW/cyber forces. Dai noted that integrated and joint IO, two subjects rarely discussed by other Chinese military specialists until recently, gives more scope and purpose to a people's war. His support of stratagem-based activities and the writings of other Chinese analysts on the subject should be closely followed by Western analysts.

Information Warfare Stratagems

Another important article offered several ways to apply IO stratagems in the information/cyber age.[35] Authors Niu Li, Li Jiangzhou, and Xu Dehui defined *information warfare stratagems* as "schemes and methods devised and used by commanders and commanding bodies to seize and maintain information supremacy on the basis of using clever methods to prevail at a relatively small cost in information warfare."[36] Niu, Li, and Xu compare how East and West view the combination of stratagems and technology in different ways based on their different military and social cultures, not to mention their economic prosperity, and evaluate how this has resulted in different thought processes:

> Traditionally, Oriental people emphasize stratagems, and Occidental people emphasize technology. . . . Occidental soldiers would seek technological

means when encountering a difficulty, while Oriental soldiers would seek to use stratagems to make up for technological deficiencies without changing the technological conditions. An Oriental soldier's traditional way of thinking is not conducive to technological development, but can still serve as an effective way of seeking survival in a situation of danger.[37]

A Western proclivity to look for technological fixes has been recognized and critiqued by both Chinese and U.S. analysts. Little has been written or published in the West, however, on IW stratagems. Western audiences have underappreciated the Eastern focus on strategic sophistication and perhaps their importance in general. A proper mix of the two may be required to ensure that all sides of a situation are properly assessed.

Niu, Li, and Xu argue that clever stratagems can help China make up for its deficiencies in high-technology–based weaponry. Stratagems may combine human qualitative thinking with computer-assisted quantitative calculations. One goal, for example, may be to cause enemy commanders to make mistakes by influencing their cognitive elements and system of beliefs. The idea is to force enemy commanders to develop decisions in the direction desired by the Chinese side, as suggested earlier by the scenario of the cat and the bell.[38]

Stratagems must be devised to be compatible with the characteristics of different networks, and they must be used by a system capable of ensuring information acquisition, transmission, and processing. They must control the entire process in a targeted manner, which requires an understanding of how an information contest develops over different stages and times. Chinese authors place emphasis on attacking first; this indicates that, in the information age, an active offense may be more important than an active defense.[39]

In the acquisition or preparation phase, stratagems might be devised to interfere with, damage, or destroy listening and antilistening, camouflage and anticamouflage, reconnaissance and antireconnaissance, or stealth and antistealth devices, among other items. Perhaps this is the current stage of development of China's cyber philosophy. Stratagems may be included in information flows to block channels of communication while keeping friendly flows of information secure. Some of the methods of influencing information flows are to carry out interference and anti-interference, deciphering and antideciphering, and destruction and antidestruction efforts. The processing phase requires stratagems that, in addition to the transmission task, include misleading and antimisleading efforts targeting the enemy's information processing system, to cause the enemy to make decisionmaking errors.[40]

Stratagems can be used to intimidate, employ perception management, and create fictitious objects (such as fake networks and equipment in an information system) as part of a deception plan whose intent is to hide true reality. The intellectual battle is now more important than contests in bravery, the authors note, and wide-ranging knowledge and superior wisdom, boldness, and scheming ability are required.[41]

A stratagem can be as simple as misleading the enemy by pretending to follow his wishes. If one knows the enemy's intentions, the enemy can be led into a trap:

> A contest in information warfare stratagem is usually conducted in a non-contact manner, and contains efforts to create cognitive errors on the part of the enemy and to influence the contents, process, and direction of thinking on the part of the enemy's commanders and relevant personnel for information warfare; the purpose is to make enemy commanders make wrong decisions or even stop fighting, so as to achieve the objectives of information warfare without fighting.[42]

The effectiveness of this strategy would need to be evaluated based on the enemy's perceived awareness of the strategy's intent and subsequent response. Niu, Li, and Xu noted that "there are many ways of seizing information supremacy and the initiative in IW, and the use of stratagems is one of the most efficient ways." They suggest 10 specific stratagems that can be applied to IW.[43]

Thought-directing. Direct others' thinking toward the wrong decision by attacking cognitive and belief systems and force commanders to make errors. Use schemes with regard to enemy doubts and exploit information relays between enemy units and departments.

Intimidation through momentum-building. Generate psychological pressure via intimidation by signaling inevitable victory, concentrating forces, and coordinating information networks. This is achieved by creating a situation favorable to China and unfavorable to the enemy. Intimidation is to be achieved via momentum-building: enhancing one's own position, situation, and posture while blocking the flow of information to the enemy.

Information-based capability demonstrations. Intimidate by demonstrating capabilities in actions that should not appear to be intentional. The right time, occasion, and modality must be chosen to make information believable to the enemy. One's own true strength should not be revealed, and one should be unpredictable, using both true and false information.

Prevailing over the enemy with extraordinary means. Adopt active and effective measures to generate surprise, and use decisive technical equipment and means of information warfare. Develop and hide information warfare "killer weapons."

Using fictitious objects to hide the true picture. Hide true reality by creating a fictitious reality. Simulate combat forces using high-tech means, to include the creation of nonexistent objects, such as fictitious networks or information systems, as well as fictitious strategic and operational objectives.

All-encompassing deception. Apply deceptive schemes simultaneously or consecutively according to strategic or operational intentions. Actions taken should be coordinated to ensure the enemy will have no suspicion.

Prevailing over the enemy with all-around strength. Use all means of information warfare to maintain supremacy, including electronic soft attacks by use of reconnaissance satellite systems and the like, hard attacks such as informationized precision guidance weapons or strategic bombings, and command, control, communications, and information battlefield control and management.

Going with the flow. Mislead the enemy by pretending to follow his wishes. Pretend to "go with the flow" by exploiting one's knowledge of an enemy's intentions and the detection of enemy moves in order to lead the enemy into a trap.

Releasing viruses to muddy the flows. Release viruses to contaminate information flows. Using viruses, the authors note, is an important combat operation. A virus attack is "a technical act, which will have to be based on the use of stratagems in order to play an important role in IW." Stratagems should be used to create a favorable time for releasing viruses. It is important not only to seize opportunities but also to create opportunities and to "attack first."

Controlling the time element. Control of the time element is crucial. Information inducement, deception, concealment, and containment operations will help achieve the desired amount of control.[44]

The goal of the use of stratagems, write Niu, Li, and Xu, is to force an opponent to refrain from deciding to launch information attacks in order to achieve objectives without direct fighting; to create cognitive errors in the enemy; to influence the content, process, and direction of thinking on the part of enemy commanders; and to create a multidimensional threat with which the enemy must contend.[45]

China is already a cyber competitor of the United States. Hopefully, it will not become a cyber enemy. However, China is making significant strides in tying its cyber capabilities to its strategic concepts and is taking a more active (some would say threatening) posture. The Chinese use a different cyber vocabulary and different definitions, analyses, and institutions for the study of cyber-related strategic issues than the United States. China's definition of strategy encompasses basic and applied theory as well as the objective and subjective aspects of strategy and discusses ways to apply stratagems familiar from traditional Chinese military thought in new ways to shape information warfare. China's Academy of Military Science (a comparable institution does not exist in the United States) studies the science of information operations (an academic discipline that does not exist in the United States); and the University of Information Security proposed by Shen Weiguang (China's father of information warfare) will study cyber issues and strategy. An updated version of Mao Tse Tung's people's war strategy includes cyber techniques and procedures. China seeks to develop cyber countermeasures, both technical and cognitive, to Western cyber strengths. China frequently practices information-related mobilization exercises.

It is important for the United States to continue to examine how China is developing and applying its cyber-related strategic concepts and to prepare to adapt to them or develop countermeasures to them. Of particular concern is the Chinese movement in the direction of a preemptive strategy. Discussing strategic guidance, the editors of *The Science of Military Strategy* stated that information operations are directly linked to the gain or loss of the initiative in war and thus "priority should be given to the attack and combining the attack with the defense."[46]

China's extensive computer reconnaissance in the United States and other countries should cause other nation-states to take note. Cyber issues such as these should be seen in light of the ancient dictum that "a victorious army first wins and then seeks battle." It is possible that China's cyber strategy is already preparing to preempt U.S. systems if Beijing perceives a need to do so. More importantly, China's ability to hide the form of its attack will make it difficult to recognize a preemptive action as it unfolds.

Russia

Russia, like China, has been accused of conducting cyber activities against foreign states. The main U.S. accusation was a series of incidents between 1998 and 2000 that came to be known as Moonlight Maze. These intrusions were reportedly traced to a mainframe in Russia. Moscow denied any involvement, and the actual state sponsor (if any) or origin of the attack apparently remains unknown.[47]

More recently, a 3-week wave of cyber attacks against Estonia reportedly originated primarily from Russia. This attack came at a time when Estonia and Russia were in dispute over the planned Estonian removal of a Soviet war memorial from Tallinn. The main targets of the attacks were the Estonian presidency and parliament, government ministries, political parties, three of the country's six news organizations, two of the biggest banks, and firms specializing in communications.[48] European Union and North Atlantic Treaty Organization (NATO) officials did not accuse Russia formally. Estonian officials, however, identified specific Russian Internet addresses, including some from Russian state institutions.

Russia denied any involvement. Kremlin spokesman Dmitry Peskov stated that in "no way could the state be involved in terrorism."[49] Direct Russian responsibility for the attack became even more questionable when Estonia arrested one of its own citizens (an ethnic Russian) and charged him with complicity in the attack. It was reported that he was simply angry over the war memorial issue.[50]

In response to the attack on Estonia, NATO stated its intention to establish a Cyber-Security Center in Estonia.[51] The agreement for such a center was signed on May 14, 2008. The center will develop standards and key directions for NATO's cyber protection system and carry out expert analyses of suspected cyber attacks.[52]

In light of these episodes and in the absence of any formal charges, Russia's complicity remains uncertain. But that is not to say that Russia does not have a national cyber-related strategy. On February 7, 2008, President Vladimir Putin signed a document titled, "The Strategy of Information Society Development in Russia." When briefing the strategy in early April 2008, Vladimir M. Vasilyev, deputy director of the Department of Information Society Strategy of the Ministry for Information Technologies and Communications, used the term *cyber* several times in his charts that explained the strategy.[53] Developments such as these indicate that Russia's cyber and information strategy deserve examination for the direction they are headed and for basic content. Perhaps more than any other country, Russia is alarmed over the cognitive aspects of cyber issues as much as their technical aspects, which make its strategy of further interest.

In Russia, *military strategy* has been defined as a system of scientific knowledge about the objective laws of war as armed combat to achieve certain class interests.[54] Military strategy prepares for and wages war and conducts various forms of strategic operations.[55] Strategy organizes, directs, and guides the deployment of forces during war, proceeding from and serving the needs of policy.[56]

Officially, Russia does not use the word *cyber*. In unclassified publications on information warfare and information operations, the term seldom appears, and then only when referring to other countries. Instead, like the Chinese, Russian military and civilian communities prefer the term *informationization*.[57]

A related term is *electronification*. In a plan called "Electronic Russia," the Ministry of Information and Communications is studying the formation of an information society and its electronification to address the Moscow region's information security plan and other issues.[58] The purpose is to thwart aggression against Russian systems by criminals, terrorists, or nation-states.

Concerns regarding criminal use of cyber actions are illustrated by comments of the First Deputy Head of the Russian Interior Ministry, Konstantin Machabeli, who stated in October 2006 that Russia had the ability to combat high-tech crime but that there was no law that would regulate it. He described cyber terrorism as "the use of the Internet aimed at recruiting new members of terrorist organizations and spreading information that calls for interethnic strife and racial intolerance."[59]

However, use of the term *cyber*, while not widespread, is growing in colloquial speech and even in some military journals. A November 2006 journal article noted that:

> In recent years certain socio-economic, scientific-technical, and cultural prerequisites have formed in our country for the development of an information society and its essential attribute—cyberspace. The latter has today essentially become a new front for global confrontation and all of humanity has become a target for a possible cyber attack.[60]

Russia recognizes that informationization topics greatly influence the modes and methods of the conduct of war. For example, virtual simulations influence what strategy a Russian commander might take. In 1995, General Vladimir Slipchenko stated that the Russian General Staff Academy was no longer doing force-on-force simulations but rather system-on-system simulations, to include cyber and other information-related systems.[61] This suggests that cyber issues influence strategic planning from its earliest stages in Russia.

Reflexive Control, Stratagems, and Perception Management

Russia views the cognitive aspect of cyber issues as more important than do most other nations. Some Russian policymakers feel that the disintegration of the Soviet Union was due to a cognitive attack or deliberate information operation. Many Russian books discuss the "Third World War" as a war of information in which the West conquered the Soviet Union.

While the Chinese use stratagems to alter the reasoning of decisionmakers, the Russian preference is for a concept known as *reflexive control*, a process in which the controlling actor conveys to the target various motives and reasons that cause the latter to reach the decision sought by the controlling actor.[62] The decision itself must be made independently. In this sense, reflexive control is very much like the stratagem concept employed by the Chinese. A *reflex* involves the specific process of imitating the enemy's reasoning or possible behavior and causing it to make a decision unfavorable to itself:

> In fact, the enemy comes up with a decision based on the idea of the situation which he has formed, to include the disposition of our troops and installations and the command element's intentions known to him. Such an idea is shaped above all by intelligence and other factors, which rest on a stable set of concepts, knowledge, ideas and, finally, experience. This set usually is called the "filter," which helps a commander separate necessary from useless information, true data from false, and so on.[63]

The chief task of reflexive control is to locate the weak link of the opponent's filter and to exploit it. Accordingly, during a serious conflict, the two opposing actors (countries) analyze their own ideas and those of the perceived enemy and then attempt to influence one another. A reflex refers to the creation of certain model behavior in the system it seeks to control (the objective system). It takes into account the fact that the objective system has a model of the situation and assumes that it will also attempt to influence the controlling organ or system. Reflexive control exploits moral, psychological, and other factors, as well as the personal characteristics of commanders. (Thus, biographical data, habits, and psychological deficiencies could be used in deception operations.[64]) In a war in which reflexive control is being employed, the side with the highest degree of reflex (the side best able to imitate the other side's thoughts or predict its behavior) will have the best chances of winning. The degree of reflex depends on many factors, the most important of which are analytical capability, general erudition and experience, and the scope of knowledge about the enemy. Military author Sergei Leonenko added that, in the past, stratagems were the principal tool of reflexive control, but today camouflage and deception (*maskirovka*) have replaced stratagems; however, this conclusion is not universally accepted.

In his writings, Leonenko integrated information technologies and reflexive control theory. He noted that the use of computers could hinder the use of reflexive control by making it easier to process data and calculate options, allowing an opponent to see through a reflexive control measure by an opposing force because the computer's speed and accuracy in processing information could detect it. On the other hand, in some cases, this may actually improve the chances for successful reflexive control, since a computer lacks the intuitive reasoning of a human being.[65]

Computer technology could increase the effectiveness of reflexive control by offering new methods. Writing in 1995 from a military perspective, Leonenko defined reflexive control as:

> consist[ing] of transmitting motives and grounds from the controlling entity to the controlled system that stimulate the desired decision. The goal of RC [reflexive control] is to prompt the enemy to make a decision unfavorable to him. Naturally, one must have an idea about how he thinks.[66]

Leonenko assessed the new opportunities afforded by the use of computer (cyber) technology:

> In present conditions, there is a need to act not only against people but also against technical reconnaissance assets and especially weapons guidance systems, which are impassive in assessing what is occurring and do not perceive to what a person reacts.[67]

If an IW or IO operation system cannot perceive what a person reacts to and is unable to assess what is occurring, does this mean that it provides only insignificant data? Or does it mean that there are two layers of data to reflexively control? The first layer consists of the "eyes, nose, and ears" of sensors, satellites, and radars. The second layer is the "brain software" of humans, which gathers, processes, and produces knowledge from the information or makes decisions based on it. But what happens if the "eyes, ears, and nose" are manipulated? How does that affect the input into decisions and knowledge? Using such principles (perhaps from studying Russian actions), Yugoslav forces in the Balkans fooled NATO sensors over Kosovo into shooting at fake targets.

In the end, some decisions are left to computers and are made automatically without human intervention. To Leonenko, this indicates that we live in a much more frightening environment than we may have thought: decisions may be made by machines that are "incapable of assessing what is occurring and do not perceive what a person reacts to." Leonenko noted that "how the enemy thinks" is shaped by combat intelligence and a collective image set made up of concepts, knowledge, ideas, and experience.

Leonenko's definition of reflexive control contains many of the elements of another term, the *information weapon*, defined by Sergei Markov as a "specially selected piece of information capable of causing changes in the information processes of information systems (physical, biological, social, etc., in this case, decision-making information) in accordance with the intent of the entity using the weapon."[68] Accordingly, it causes change in the information processes of an opponent by persuading it to make decisions according to the design of the controller, and it affords the information weapon a methodology for controlling an opponent. So defined, the information weapon, like reflexive control, can be applied in the modeling and decisionmaking contexts of various types of conflicts. It can also be used in social processes and systems.

The concept of reflexive control is influencing approaches to various branches of knowledge in Russia, including philosophy, sociology, psychology, pedagogy, and problems of artificial intelligence and computer science in general, as well as military affairs, intelligence, counterintelligence, and a number of other areas.[69]

Definitions of Information Warfare and Information Operations

No Russian definitions of IW and IO utilize the term *cyber*, although several discuss informationization. In general, Russian military theorists view information-related topics in two categories: information-technical and information-psychological. Russia does not separate information-related topics into the same kinds of categories that the United States and China do, such as psychological operations, computer network operations, operational security, deception, and the like.

The technical aspect is of greatest interest in most countries, but the psychological aspect is the area of most attention in Russia. A Russian book titled *Secret Weapons of Information War* stated that the primary threat to a nation's security in the 21ˢᵗ century is to its psychophysical security. Threats may take the form of psychological, suggestive, or "technotronic" effects (such as computer games, virtual reality, acoustical and video equipment, computer technology, and lasers and other effects).[70]

In 2002, Russian information warfare expert S.P. Rastorguyev defined *IW* as "a battle between states involving the use of exclusively information weapons in the sphere of information models." An *information operation* was defined as a "sequence of actions to use an information weapon to achieve an assigned task."[71]

An article in the Russian navy publication *Morskoy Sbornik* in October 2003 defined the two parts of IW further. The "information-psychological" part consisted of the mass media, the Internet, computer network attacks, leaflets, and religious propaganda. The "information-technical" part consisted of deception; misinformation; radio-electronic intelligence, attack, deception, and defense; counterintelligence; cryptology; and steganography.[72]

In October 2005, Konstantin Nikolskiy defined the principal object and meaning of IW to consist of "a disorganization of the structure of society and distortion of public consciousness, as a result of which society loses moral-psychological and scientific-technological potential and thereby is deprived of the capability to wage armed warfare." He defined information threats as "ideological-religious, scientific-technological, and emotional-psychological." He argued for viewing the world as an aggregate of specific properties of systems.[73]

The Initial Russian Policy on Information Security

In contrast to the Chinese approach, the Russian focus has been on the development of a state information security doctrine, international information security laws, and the "Electronic Russia" program, and on the study of U.S. cyber programs. The Russian strategic concept appears to focus on protecting the state from "harmful" information and from the effects of informationization while simultaneously focusing on international laws limiting the use and development of "information weapons," a term often used in Russia.

Russian authorities closely follow cyber developments in the United States. Pavel Shumilo described the U.S. cyberspace concept as the establishment of a national system to counter cybernetic security threats, and noted that other U.S. priorities were:

- a national program to prevent threats and decrease vulnerability in cyber-space

- the development of a conscious awareness among the population of cyber threats
- ensuring the security of the government's infrastructure in cyberspace
- cooperation in the sphere of international cybernetic security.[74]

Shumilo declared the U.S. approach, as he described it, to be similar to that of the Russian Federation's Information Security Doctrine.

Russia's Information Security Doctrine in 2000

The Information Security Doctrine was first developed in 2000, years before publication of the first official U.S. cyberspace document. It presented the purposes, objectives, principles, and basic directions of Russia's information security policy. Its 11 sections cover, first, the national interests of the Russian Federation in the information sphere, including observance of constitutional liberties of man and citizen, information backing for Russian Federation policy, development of information technology and industry, and protection of information resources from unsanctioned access.

The second section examines types of threats to Russia's information security. These include constitutional rights in spiritual life, information support for state policy, the development of the information industry, and the security of information. Third, it identifies external and internal sources of threats to Russia's information security. Fourth, it outlines the state of information security in the Russian Federation and objectives supporting it, discussing tension between the need for the free exchange of information and the need for restrictions on dissemination of some information.

General methods of information security of the Russian Federation—legal, organizational-technical, and economic—are outlined in the information security doctrine. The document next discusses features of information security: economics, domestic policy, foreign policy, science and technology, spiritual life, information and telecommunications systems, defense, law enforcement, and emergency situations. Goals of international cooperation in the field of information security include such issues as a ban on information weapons, support for information exchanges, coordination of law enforcement activities, and prevention of unsanctioned access to confidential information.

Another topic of Russia's information security doctrine is a description of two provisions of state policy on information security: guidelines for federal institutions of state power and for balancing the interests of the individual, society, and the state in the information sphere. Priority measures in implementing information security are identified, including mechanisms to implement the rule of law and increase the efficiency of state leadership, and programs to provide access to archives of information resources, training, and harmonizing standards in the field of computerization and information security. The functions of the system of information security are discussed. Finally, organizational elements of Russia's information security system are described; these include the president, Federation Council of the Federal Assembly, the State Duma of the Federal Assembly, the government of the Russian Federation, the Security Council, and other federal executive authorities, presidential commissions, judiciary institutions, public associations, and citizens.[75]

Russia's Information Security Doctrine defines *information security* as "the state of protection of its national interests in the information sphere defined by the totality of balanced interests of the individual, society, and the state." Just a few months earlier, in a resolution to the United Nations, Russia had defined information security somewhat differently as the "protection of the basic interests of the individual, society, and the State in the information sphere, including the information and telecommunications infrastructure and information per se with respect to its characteristics, such as integrity, objectivity, availability, and confidentiality."

Information security in the defense sphere was highlighted in the doctrine. The sphere involves:

- the information infrastructure of the central elements of military command and control, and the elements of military command and control of the branches of the armed forces and the scientific research institutions of the Ministry of Defense
- the information resources of enterprises of the defense complex and re-search institutions
- the software and hardware of automatic systems of command and control of the forces and weapons, arms, and military equipment furnished with computerization facilities
- information resources, communications systems, and the information infra-structure of other forces and military components and elements.[76]

External threats to the Ministry of Defense (MOD) are spelled out in the next part of the section. They include the intelligence activities of foreign states; information and technical pressure (electronic warfare, computer network penetration, and so forth) by probable enemies; sabotage and subversive activities of the security services of foreign states, including information and psychological pressure; and activities of foreign political, economic, or military entities directed against the interests of the Russian Federation in the defense sphere. Internal threats included the violation of established procedure for collecting, processing, storing, and transmitting information within the MOD; premeditated actions and individual mistakes with special information and telecommunications systems, or unreliability in their operation; information and propaganda activities that undermine the prestige of the armed forces; unresolved questions of protecting intellectual property of enterprises; and unresolved questions regarding social protection of servicemen and their families.[77]

Ways to improve the system of information security for the armed forces included the systematic detection of threats and their sources, and structuring the goals and objectives of information security; certification of general and special software and information protection facilities in automated military control and communications systems; improvement of facilities and software designed to protect information; improvement in the structure of functional arms in the system of information security; training of specialists in the field of information security; and—most important, it seems, in light of the Russian military doctrine's views on information security—refinement of the modes and methods of strategic and operational concealment, reconnaissance, and electronic warfare, and the methods and means of active countermeasures against the information and propaganda and psychological operations of a probable enemy.[78]

The discussion of the defense sphere in the information security document varies in many ways from the general military doctrine of the Russian Federation. The latter is quite specific that information-psychological and information-technical matters are the two greatest informationization (cyber-related) external threats to Russia, and that disruptive plans or technologies are the greatest internal threats. The terms *information-technical* and *information-psychological* are not used in the information security doctrine, perhaps because military people did not write it. However, its sections on the spiritual and cultural sphere and the scientific research sphere do cover the gist of the military's concerns in information-psychological and information-technical realms. While not citing information-psychological issues explicitly, several sections implied that they were a concern. For example, under constitutional rights, it was noted that one threat was the unlawful use of special techniques of influencing individual, group, or social consciousness, and the disruption of cultural values. Under foreign policy concerns, one internal threat was identified as propaganda activities of political forces, public associations, the news media, or individuals who would distort or disrupt the strategy and tactics of the foreign policy activity of the Russian Federation. An important spiritual sphere of concern in the information security doctrine was the prevention of unlawful information or psychological influences on the mass consciousness of society, and another was the uncontrolled commercialization of culture and sciences.

The doctrine declared that the "implementation of the guarantees of the constitutional rights and liberties of man and citizen concerning activity in the information sphere is the most important objective of the state in the field of information security."[79] While this sounds reassuring enough, Russian citizens are concerned over the interpretation of this notion. Some citizens fear the government's ability to convey reliable information to the Russian and international community, since they fear that what is "reliable" information would be determined by the state. The record of the government's handling of information on the *Kursk* incident and the war in Chechnya causes some to question the idea of reliable government information. The government considers the "information war," conducted by the press for public opinion, to be a very important aspect of keeping the emotions and loyalties of its people in check during crises. All governments do this to a certain degree, but the Russian government appears to have gone quite far, especially in these two cases.

The doctrine stated near its conclusion that a basic function of the system of information security of the Russian Federation is "the determination and maintenance of a balance between the need of the citizens, society, and the state for the free exchange of information, and the necessary restrictions on the dissemination of information."[80] The last paragraph of the document stated:

> The implementation of the priority measures in support of the inform-
> ation security of the Russian Federation enumerated in this doctrine
> presupposes the drafting of the corresponding federal program. Certain
> provisions of this doctrine may be made more specific with reference to
> particular spheres of the activity of society and the state in the appropriate
> documents approved by the President of the Russian Federation.[81]

Little was written about the Information Security Doctrine after 2000. One of the first doctrine-related articles to appear was generated by an October 23, 2000, conference on information security. Anatoliy Streltsov, deputy head of the six-member Information Security Department of the staff of the Russian Security Council, said that the doctrine might promote a dialogue between the authorities and the press. The conference wanted to create a data bank for shaping state policy in the sphere of the mass media and the formation of an effective basis for cooperation between the press services of ministries and agencies, on the one hand, and the mass media on the other.[82]

In another report, First Deputy of the Security Council Vladislav Sherstyuk, who helped draft the doctrine, claimed that it would not be used to restrict independent media or control television channels, but asserted that the state must supervise all media, state or private.[83] The Speaker of the Upper House of the Federation Council, Yegor Stroyev, stated that the doctrine did not contradict freedom of speech but was aimed at "consolidating the Russian state as a whole."[84] Anatoly Streltsov noted that the components of the doctrine provide for the constitutional rights and freedoms of citizens to obtain and use information, while providing for Russia's spiritual renewal, the development of moral values, patriotic and humanistic traditions, and cultural and scientific potential. The doctrine's components also provide information support to Russia's state policy, notifying the Russian and international public about state policy and offering citizens access to open state information. Most important, according to Streltsov, is that the doctrine would improve an individual's information security, since in 2000:

> [t]he doctrine drafters believe that the level of Russia's information security does not fully comply with the needs of society and the state. The constitutional rights of citizens to the inviolability of private life, personal and family secrecy, and secrecy of correspondence do not have sufficient legal, organizational and technical backing. The protection of information about individuals, which is collected by federal and municipal institutions, is inferior.[85]

Thus, the doctrine was presented as having the best of intentions, according to the official spokesmen.

Other Views
On October 5, 2000, Sherstyuk took part in an Internet chat with citizens from all over the country. He defined information security as the state of protection of national interests in the information sphere, dictated by the aggregated balance of interests of the individual, society, and the state. Asked if the doctrine threatens freedom of the press, he replied:

> The state doesn't plan to control the independent mass media, let alone, as some journalists say, establish complete and comprehensive control over the television airwaves and infringe on freedom of mass information. You won't find such provisions in the Doctrine; they simply aren't there. You will agree that controlling the mass media and strengthening the state mass media is not one and the same thing.[86]

A participant in the Internet discussion asked if the balance between the individual, society, and the state was upset by this emphasis on the state, and also whether the doctrine signaled Russia's admission that it had lost the "information war" in Chechnya and the Balkans.[87]

Sherstyuk's reply to these questions was abrupt and unconvincing. He said it would be improper to talk about Russian defeat in "information wars" since there are no precise criteria for such defeats and victories. (Actually, the perceived requirement to publish an information security doctrine is arguably an indication of Russian defeat in this sphere.) Sherstyuk's denials notwithstanding, many Russian leaders and analysts have openly referred to the "information defeat" at the hands of the Chechens. Sherstyuk's answer was that fears about a disturbance of the balance of interests among the individual, society, and the state are simply groundless; however, many Russians were raising concerns about this very idea.[88]

June 2006 Military Policy Proposal

By 2006, Russian analysts were stating that the military policy of the Russian Federation needed to be updated, due to concern over the development, manufacture, introduction, preparation, and deployment of information weapons and the resulting endangerment of military security. Issues included restraining foreign states from deploying the means and methods of IW against Russia, promoting and developing international information security concepts with friendly states (including within the United Nations and other regional organizations, such as in Geneva or in accord with the Okinawa or Tunisia accords on the development of an information society), and arranging for equitable and reliable information exchanges based on the norms and principles of international law.[89] Another concern was that because "hundreds of millions of people have never been harnessed by the uniform world-wide electronic information space," they were "unprotected against the 'mass effect weapon' attack." Concern about critically important infrastructure systems was also mentioned, as "the triggering of production-induced, energy-oriented, financial catastrophes [would] creat[e] chaos and panic aimed at bringing the indomitable enemy [meaning Russia], after all, to its knees."[90]

Russian cyber strategy has accepted that the task of preserving internal stability in Russia is a priority. Books and articles claim that the death blow to the Soviet Union came, not from NATO conventional forces, but from an imperialist "information war" that Russia lost. By 2000, therefore, Russian state specialists had written the country's first information security doctrine (perhaps the first of any nation in the world), focused on laws and regulations and the information security of individuals as much as on the information security of industry.

This does not mean that Russia avoids attacking or conducting reconnaissance of foreign sites. Russia's fingerprints seemed to be all over both the Moonlight Maze incident and the cyber attacks on Estonia, even if conclusive proof of Russian involvement was not found. Russian nationalist hackers, as in China, may be behind many of the reconnaissance or offensive attacks on foreign sites.

For Russian information warfare specialists, the use of information weapons is a key component of success. This effort is aimed as much at disrupting an adversary's information as it is at obtaining information supremacy. Targets of disorganization are not only weapons and decisionmakers on the field of battle but also the minds of average citizens. An article in *Morskoy Sbornik* listed, as aspects of the information-psychological aspect of information warfare, theories of the mass media, the Internet, computer network attacks, leaflets, and religious propaganda.[91] It is rare indeed to find computer network attacks listed more for their psychological than their technical impact, but this is the case in Russia.

With its talented corps of mathematicians, Russia is expected to remain a strong cyber power for the coming years. Of interest will be to see whether Russia's cyber plans are oriented more toward the information-psychological or the information-technical direction as it conducts future missions. Nation-states should expect to encounter Russia's electronic presence on the virtual battlefield, in plain sight or disguised by reflexive control principles.

Russia has also been aggressive in pushing an international understanding of informationization/cyber issues. They are active participants in discussions to define cyber-related (information/cyber aggression, information/cyber territory, cyber strategy, and so on) issues in the United Nations and among other international organizations such as the Shanghai Cooperation Organization. In this manner, Russia is leading the drive to shape the world's opinions regarding information-technology issues.

Lessons for U.S. Cyber Strategy

If U.S. cyber strategists expect to continue to lead the way in the cyber age, then they cannot afford to ignore the methods that other nation-states are using to advance their agendas or to implement cyber-age concepts. They must learn from these methods as well, both their offensive and defensive techniques. These methods reflect characteristics and approaches that differ, sometimes dramatically, from U.S. approaches. Chinese efforts to move packets of electrons through wires in accordance with 5,000-year-old stratagems come immediately to mind, as do Russian attempts to use international organizations to shape the world's understanding of cyber technology. Without close study of these and the approaches of other nation-states to cyber issues, it would be akin to playing a game of basketball in which your focus was solely on your team's offensive and defensive philosophy while disregarding your opponent's skill set and strategy. This can only result in defeat. Sun Tzu recognized this important aspect of potential conflict years ago, noting, "Know the enemy and know yourself and you will never fail in battle." Of particular importance in both the Chinese and Russian cases is their emphasis on cognitive aspects of cyber issues, an aspect to which the United States pays less attention than these nations.

A lack of agreement on international cyber terminology could also result in misunderstanding. One nation's understanding of cyber warfare could differ greatly from another's due to cultural or organizational differences. U.S. cyber strategists must continue to attempt to overcome this potential weakness in their assessment of the international environment, its actors, and the interpretations of events by these actors. The coming years could be ones of understanding or of tension and unanticipated circumstances. Hopefully, nation-states will work for the former and not leave our world to chance and at the mercy of the latter.

Part VI
Institutional Factors

CHAPTER 21

Internet Governance

Harold Kwalwasser

INTERNET GOVERNANCE: the concept is a challenge to understand. No single body dominates collective decisionmaking about the Internet. No one type of decision process repeats itself in different venues. As a result, cyberpower—in the sense of having the power to influence collective decisionmaking about the Internet—is easy neither to exercise nor to describe.

Two predominant and related facts define this subject. First, governments exercise relatively little control over the Internet, even though it has a tremendous impact on society. Second, the key forums for Internet governance are evolving, not fixed. One of the impulses driving the forums' evolution is the tension between their legitimacy and the pressure by some governments to increase their roles; the pressure—and the likelihood that it will yield some success—will become greater if the current structures' legitimacy ever declines or disappears. Conversely, the pressure will diminish only if and when the structures' legitimacy becomes firmly and permanently established.

Internet governance is complex, with collective decisionmaking distributed among various organizations that have different structures. Few aspects of the Internet's operations are subject to typical government or even intergovernmental decisionmaking. Instead, in many of the key forums, particularly those related to the standards process that is fundamental to the Internet, private parties dominate and governments play only a subordinate role.

The structure of each of these organizations and the scope of its jurisdiction generally came about by a combination of short-term decisions and historical accident. Power, or the ability to influence particular policies, arises not from the sovereign might of states, but rather from the persistence of participants—entities and individuals—and their technical expertise, alliance-building among operators and users, and sheer financial capability to participate in multiple forums around the world.

Further complicating this picture is the fact that some of the most important organizations are new and their rules and working procedures are still evolving. The Internet Corporation for Assigned Names and Numbers (ICANN), which oversees the Domain Name System (DNS), was organized as a nonprofit corporation in 1998.[1] The original predecessor to the organization now known as the Internet Engineering Task Force (IETF), which resolves key standards for the operation of the core of the Internet, dates only from 1979.

Governments other than that of the United States have realized how little they can control what happens in and around the Internet. As it has grown into a powerful engine of economic growth and political speech, Internet issues have taken on a significance they did not have just a few years ago. What were once considered technical questions to be left to scientists and engineers have become matters of public policy that greatly interest large numbers of people who claim a stake in the decisions. It has been said that "'technical issues' become 'public policy' whenever voters think they should."[2] The Internet's great ability to foster globalized free market competition and free speech cuts across traditional geographic boundaries and challenges historic notions of national sovereignty. This transnational effect diminishes governments' control over the activities of their own people and their own economies, and some governments see this change as a challenge to their national sovereignty and domestic power.

Governmental control of the Internet is impeded, however, by the existing governance structure, and therefore some governments have called for changes in that structure. Others, notably the United States, want the current system to remain largely in place, provided that they can deal with a limited number of pressing problems such as child pornography and cyber crime.

The main part of this chapter describes the components of Internet governance, what each governs, and how each is organized and governed internally. The first three sections describe the most prominent organizations involved in Internet governance. These organizations' agendas are significantly or exclusively focused on Internet-related questions. The first section describes ICANN and the management of the DNS. The second section addresses the IETF, the Internet Society, and the other bodies that it supports, and offers a brief review of the independent World Wide Web Consortium that oversees the Web. The third section examines the International Telecommunication Union (ITU), a specialized agency of the United Nations (UN) that predates the Internet but whose decisions particularly affect the telecommunications companies that carry Internet traffic.

The next three sections describe institutions whose focus is broader than the Internet but that nonetheless play significant roles in Internet-related decisionmaking. Because they have generally been established longer, they are less subject to issues of legitimacy and the kind of evolutionary pressure described above. The fourth section describes the role of international entities such as the Organization for Economic Co-operation and Development (OECD), the UN (other than the ITU), and the Council of Europe. The fifth section looks at the role of national governments, particularly the U.S. Government. The sixth section briefly describes other international standards-setting bodies whose decisions may affect the Internet, including the Institute of Electrical and Electronics Engineers, the International Electrotechnical Commission, and the International Organization for Standardization.

Table 21–1 summarizes the organizations and their subject matter concerns.

The Internet Corporation for Assigned Names and Numbers

For a variety of reasons, many people see ICANN as the governance body for the Internet, but this view is a misperception. ICANN oversees the DNS and operates the Internet Assigned Numbers Authority (IANA). These are important Internet-related functions, but other institutions are just as vital to other equally significant decisionmaking. Nonetheless, ICANN has been the center of the international political debate about Internet governance, most likely because of the existence of three agreements with the U.S. Government that affect its operations. ICANN is, therefore, an appropriate place to begin.

ICANN coordinates the allocation and assignment of three sets of unique identifiers for the Internet: domain names, Internet Protocol (IP) addresses, and protocol port and parameter numbers.[3] ICANN also "coordinates the operation and evolution of the DNS root name server system; [and] coordinates policy development . . . related to these technical functions."[4]

The DNS is the addressing function of the Internet, translating a typical uniform resource locator, such as <www.aol.com> or <www.ndu.edu>, into the unique numeric IP address that is actually used to route messages. "Each domain name is made up of a series of character strings (called 'labels') separated by dots. The right-most label in a domain name is referred to as its 'top-level domain' (TLD),"[5] such as *.org* or *.com*. "Most TLDs with three or more characters are referred to as 'generic' TLDs, or 'gTLDs,'"; these also include *.edu*, *.int*, *.mil*, *.net*, and *.org*.[6] TLDs also include country-code TLDs (ccTLDs); these generally have two letters, such as *.uk* for the United Kingdom or *.cn* for China.[7] ICANN has the right to authorize new gTLDs and ccTLDs and to review changes to the domains' registries, which operate them.

The Internet Assigned Numbers Authority was originally created by the Defense Information Systems Agency (DISA) in the early days of the Internet to

TABLE 21-1. Internet Governance Organizations

Organization	Subject Matter Jurisdiction
Internet Corporation for Assigned Names and Numbers, which includes functions referred to as the Internet Assigned Numbers Authority	Supervises the Domain Name System, allocates Internet protocol address space, and oversees the root zone servers that provide basic finding information for Internet traffic
Internet Society and related organizations: Internet Engineering Task Force, Internet Engineering Steering Group, and Internet Architecture Board	Develops standards for operation of Internet and its overall architecture
World Wide Web Consortium	Develops standards for the World Wide Web
International Telecommunication Union	Develops standards for telecommunications, including interface of Internet and telecommunications systems
Organization for Economic Co-operation and Development, European Union, Council of Europe, United Nations agencies	Ad hoc policy development on issues of critical interest to members
National governments acting individually or through joint agreements	Ad hoc policy development chiefly related to cyber crime, use, and commercial regulatory issues
Institute of Electrical and Electronics Engineers, International Electrotechnical Commission, International Organization for Standardization	Standards for products and for manufacturing and testing processes (operations of these entities relate only peripherally to the operation of the Internet itself)

assign addresses to Internet users, meaning that it significantly predates ICANN. Much of that work has now devolved elsewhere, but IANA still deals with the policy-related functions of TLD and address block management. Its most prominent function—and its most politically charged one—is to make changes to the master root zone file.[8] The Internet Architecture Board also designated IANA to carry out the technical registration functions associated with IETF protocol parameters and other technical assignments. Currently, "the IANA function," which ICANN performs under a no-cost contract with the U.S. Department of Commerce (DOC), represents primarily administrative or book-keeping functions. The three most important of these are coordination of the assignment of technical protocol parameters; administrative functions associated with root management; and allocation of IP address blocks.[9]

ICANN and IANA issues

The kinds of questions ICANN addresses provide a sense of what is at stake, particularly the implications for the security and stability of the Internet itself.

One current issue is that of Domain Name System Security Extensions (DNSSec), a suite of IETF specifications for securing certain kinds of DNS information on IP networks. DNSSec is a set of extensions to DNS that provide for origin authentication and data integrity. When one types in an Internet address, one has to have faith that the message is going to the intended recipient or Web site and that the message received is actually from the person or organization identified as the sender. False addresses, improper routing instructions, or other disruption of Internet addressing and routing would undermine the faith of users in the accuracy of the system. The system faces significant threats from people with the capability to disrupt this process. Individual operators can apply DNSSec tools within their own systems, but promoting and coordinating the process of adoption of DNSSec over the entire system needs a central focus.

Another prominent ICANN issue is internationalized domain names. The DNS utilizes American Standard Code for Information Exchange, which relies on the Latin alphabet. If one reads only Chinese or Hindi or Arabic, using the Internet can be a challenge. If the Internet and the DNS are to be truly universal, other scripts must be incorporated into the DNS. Research and development is not complete, and the policy issues are nettlesome; for example, which of India's multiple scripts should the Internet use? If internationalized domain names are not successfully implemented, it could lead to the balkanization of the Internet and limit its universality.

A third issue involves information about IP address holders. The so-called WHOIS database is a publicly available source about those who hold IP addresses, designed to offer a means to find out who is accountable for each one. However, the WHOIS database has been challenged by privacy advocates. The resolution of these two goals must balance the interests of law enforcement and others who want the identifying information to be available against assertions of privacy rights in the information.

The list of issues is much longer, including the adoption of a new addressing scheme, Internet Protocol version 6 (IPv6), and the creation of new gTLDs. Even without further elaboration, the point is clear: numerous significant issues are decided at ICANN.

ICANN Governance Structure

Prior to the formation of ICANN, the Defense Advanced Research Projects Agency (DARPA) and the National Science Foundation were responsible for managing critical parts of the Internet. By the mid 1990s, much of the operational responsibility had been contracted out to the University of Southern California's Information Sciences Institute. However, the U.S. Government wished to stop overseeing the growing commercialization of the Internet DNS, especially the burden of deciding when to authorize new TLDs during the "dot-com" boom or resolving disputes around "cyber-squatting" and other trade name and copyright problems. In a 1997 document called "Framework for Global Electronic Commerce," President Bill Clinton directed the DOC to privatize the DNS in a manner that would increase competition and facilitate international participation in its management.

The resulting Internet community discussions of management of the DNS considered both a private sector–lead model and an international treaty–based organization. The DOC proposed a transition to private sector management and sought public comment. However, the private sector model provoked considerable concern among foreign governments and others who were uncomfortable with the idea of an oversight function that was not controlled by a governmental or intergovernmental entity. Nevertheless, in 1998, DOC called for transition to independent, private sector management, based on a new private sector entity, ICANN.[10] The Department of Commerce Memorandum of Understanding (MOU) with ICANN called for ICANN to develop a management scheme that reflected the principles of "stability," "competition," "private control," "bottom-up coordination," and "representation." The transition process would be overseen by the Department of Commerce.[11] The original 1998 agreement ran until 2000 but has been repeatedly extended; it is now called the Joint Project Agreement (JPA).

The issues related to trade name and copyright infringement, such as cyber-squatting, became a joint project of ICANN and the World Intellectual Property Organization. The latter organization eventually developed the Uniform Dispute Resolution Procedure, an alternative to traditional litigation that has been generally successful in handling these problems.

U.S. Government Contracts for DNS

There are now three major U.S. Government agreements with regard to Internet DNS: the DOC agreement with ICANN (the MOU/JPA), a procurement contract for IANA functions between DOC and ICANN, and a cooperative agreement with VeriSign, a publicly held corporation, which provides for maintaining and administering the root zone file, among other things.

The MOU/JPA with ICANN provides the framework of the transition to private sector management of the DNS.[12] It does not, however, give DOC any authority over ICANN's policymaking process.[13] Commerce's role is limited to oversight of development of the management and policy process.[14] The MOU/ JPA contemplates that DOC will cease to have an oversight role once there is a stable governance arrangement that meets the goals stated in the MOU/JPA. As of 2007, DOC oversight of ICANN continued; even though the agreement has been extended and modified several times, the DOC role has not yet changed. At the time of the most recent extension in 2006, the administrator of DOC's National Telecommunication and Information Administration (NTIA), which administers the agreement, stated that the U.S. Government remained committed to an "independent" ICANN and suggested that it might allow the MOU/JPA to expire at the end of the current contract period in 2009.[15]

Another way in which the U.S. Government is involved with ICANN is through a procurement contract between DOC and ICANN for management of the IANA functions, such as assigning IP address space and processing requests for delegation and redelegation of management of TLDs.[16] After ICANN processes any proposed change to the root zone file, DOC must approve it before it is entered. A private company, VeriSign, then enters the change in the authoritative root zone file, which it maintains on a master root zone server, pursuant to a third U.S. Government agreement described below.

DOC reportedly intends to continue to contract for IANA services into the future (although leaving open the question of who might be its contracting partner), thereby maintaining U.S. Government oversight of changes to the master root zone file.[17]

Although DOC has generally not interfered with root zone changes, in 2005 the U.S. Government had to decide whether to concur in ICANN's tentative approval of a change in the root zone in order to create a new gTLD, *.xxx*, which would have hosted adult sites.[18] Rather than veto the proposed change itself, however, the Government and conservative interest groups worked successfully to have ICANN reverse its decision. The ICANN Board rejected *.xxx* in May 2006[19] and again in March 2007.[20] The episode was proof to critics that the United States had excessive leverage over the ICANN process. However, there are no reported cases of actual DOC rejection of proposed changes, and critics generally complain about potential rather than actual abuse of power.

Under a cooperative agreement with Commerce, VeriSign (formerly Network Solutions, Inc. [NSI]) maintains and updates the authoritative root zone file.[21] When this cooperative agreement was initially executed in 1992, it included management of the *.com*, *.net*, *.org*, *.edu*, *.gov*, and *.us* domain names, giving the company a virtual monopoly in registry services. Upon the creation of ICANN, the cooperative agreement was revised.[22] VeriSign was required to separate its registry and registrar businesses, give up several of its registries, and enter into agreements with ICANN for management of its remaining registries.[23] DOC retained the right to review and approve any *.com* registry agreement between ICANN and VeriSign because of concerns over the importance of *.com* to the Internet and monopoly pricing due to *.com*'s extraordinary size and impact.[24] DOC also continues its oversight regarding any changes in the authoritative root zone file: "While NSI [now VeriSign] continues to operate the root zone server, it shall request written direction from an authorized U.S. government official before making or rejecting any modifications, additions or deletions to the root zone file."[25] The U.S. Government's agreement with VeriSign is expressly acknowledged in the provisions of the ICANN MOU/JPA and its amendments, which affords the Government a role in overseeing this particular TLD, *.com*, that it does not have with regard to any other private registry.[26] The agreement with VeriSign runs through 2012 and may be further renewed.

ICANN Internal Governance

The ICANN Board of Directors, with 15 voting members, is at the pinnacle of the organization's structure, which has now grown large and complex. ICANN has incorporated the Regional Internet Registries (RIRs), some of which existed prior to ICANN. The RIRs are essentially regional groupings of IP users, as well as others, that administer much of the system, particularly allocations of blocks of IP addresses. In many respects, they function independently of ICANN, as they did before ICANN's creation, but they have agreements with ICANN and must seek the board's approval for common policies. The RIRs, ccTLDs, and gTLDs have been organized into supporting organizations. Each of these three organizations selects two members of the Board. ICANN has also sought to provide a forum for a broader group of those involved with the Internet, such as Internet service providers, commercial and noncommercial users, and intellectual property interests. All participate with the gTLDs' registrars and registries in the Generic Number Support Organization (GNSO). An at-large advisory committee, which meets monthly, provides a way for individual users to participate. As of the fall of 2007, three board members were American.[27]

Governments have no direct voting role in ICANN. A governmental advisory committee (GAC), which advises the board, is open to any national government. The GAC has the right to advise the board on the public policy aspects of any decisions it considers. ICANN's bylaws require the board to explain any decision it takes contrary to the GAC's advice. Until recently, participation in the GAC was sparse and its influence weak. However, after calls for a new ICANN governance structure were turned aside at the meeting of the World Summit on the Information Society in 2005, both ICANN and many of the world's leading governments promised to reinvigorate the GAC process.[28] The GAC nominates a nonvoting member of the board nominating committee, and there is a nonvoting GAC liaison on the board itself.

ICANN has become a robust political forum. Three 4-day board meetings are held every year around the world. Board committees and supporting and advisory organizations meet and also conduct work by email.

The ICANN structure represents an audacious attempt to incorporate the views of thousands of interested parties from around the world. The presumption underlying the MOU/JPA is that it can be done, but the evidence is thus far mixed. During the public comment period prior to the completion of the 2006 MOU/JPA between ICANN and the U.S. Department of Commerce, there was considerable criticism of ICANN for lack of transparency and accountability and other governance deficiencies (discussed further below).[29] As a result, the MOU/JPA pushed ICANN to do better on both fronts.

Who Has Power within ICANN?

Given this context, *power*—defined as the capacity to influence a particular decision or result—is difficult to quantify. For nations other than the United States, governments' power is constrained. Governments have no vote on ICANN's decisions. Their influence through the GAC has been weak. They may try to invigorate it, but that possibility remains an open question. Alternatively, they may be able to increase their influence by spending more time and effort participating in board committees or supporting organizations, although they would have no greater status than nongovernmental members. Whichever route they choose, their influence will have to come from the level of expertise and effort they put forward.

Governments can also attempt to exercise power or influence in two other ways. One is through the use of surrogates: the corporations, Internet providers, and registries that are active in ICANN affairs can, if they choose, carry the banner for governments' preferred policies. The practice has likely benefited the United States more than anyone else.

Local Internet societies[30] and ccTLD[31] registries may be more under the control of their respective national governments, and they may have less incentive than companies to act independently of their governments' interests in ICANN or other Internet governance forums. The United States has recognized the right of national governments to manage their own ccTLDs.[32] Over time, ccTLDs under control of their national governments may become, in essence, government representatives at ICANN.

A wedge between governments and their potential proxies or representatives is the effect of globalization. As companies become more citizens of the world than citizens of one country, it is more likely that narrow nationalist policies will be decreasingly consistent with companies' own goals. Governments may be less able to influence firms to support positions contrary to those goals.

Another way governments can exercise power is by threatening to create a separate DNS, essentially ignoring the ICANN regime. China has already exercised this option to some extent. By separating itself technically from the global Internet, it has achieved significant internal control over Internet access and content.

During the WSIS in 2005, Brazil, China, India, Iran, Russia, South Africa, and others denounced ICANN and IANA principally because of the contracts with the U.S. Government. Brazil, for example, complained that "on Internet governance, three words tend to come to mind: lack of legitimacy. In our digital world, only one nation decides for all of us."[33] They demanded that the Internet be truly internationalized, at least by ending the U.S. Government agreements, and preferably by coming up with an entirely new governance structure in which governments would have a greater role. They played on anti-American feeling, elevated due to the Iraq War. Some threatened to go their own way, like China, creating their own separate Internets using their own rules.

While no government (other than China to some extent) carried through on the threat, and the proposals were defeated, the overall issue has not gone away. As part of the final compromise at the WSIS, there was an agreement to create an Internet Governance Forum, a multi-stakeholder body for discussion, not decisionmaking. At the first forum, in the fall of 2006 in Athens, there was some discussion about changing ICANN's structure, but it was not a major issue. At the second forum in Rio de Janiero in 2007, the issue was more prominent, but there was no consensus among the multi-stakeholder participants on a way forward. A Russian proposal made at the end of the conference to consider placing the Internet under some form of international structure did not draw significant attention.

Because the United States created ICANN, as well as the Internet, it has a distinct position among government actors. First, it holds the three contracts described above: the MOU/JPA with ICANN, the contract with ICANN for management of IANA functions, and the agreement with VeriSign regarding the root zone file. Through those contracts, the U.S. Government can influence ICANN's process. During the 2006 MOU/JPA renewal negotiations, the Government asked for comments about ICANN's performance. There were complaints about transparency and participation. ICANN's promises to improve were incorporated into the MOU/JPA.

The more fundamental question is whether or not the three contracts give the U.S. Government excessive leverage over policy decisions. Those who want to reshape ICANN's structure play upon such concerns. Whether evidence of such influence is genuinely important to the political debate, however, is open to question. The fierceness of the attack by governments (such as those of Russia and Brazil) and some academics seems to have less to do with actual malevolent use of influence than with the possibility of such influence.[34] The evidence of actual influence is meager: the *.xxx* episode, but little else.[35] The practical reality is that whatever influence the contracts give the U.S. Government is limited.

If it overreaches, there would be considerable damage to ICANN's legitimacy, making the cost likely greater than any benefit.

The U.S. Government's use of surrogates and its direct participation through individuals present a more complicated story. Its view is that the extensive deployment of a stable and secure Internet best advances its larger political and economic interests. Its philosophy, reflected in policies of the Clinton and George W. Bush administrations, is that a relatively unregulated atmosphere that relies on competition, open markets, and corporate self-interest best achieves that end. The corporate world can easily work under those assumptions. Nonetheless, there are potential differences. For example, in the discussion over the WHOIS database, a corporation's interest in assuring its customers of their privacy may be inconsistent with the desire of law enforcement to be able to identify IP address holders who hack or commit cyber crime.

U.S. Government employees from the National Institute of Standards and Technology, DOC, Department of Homeland Security, and DOD, among others, are involved in ICANN's committees and, to some degree, in the North American Regional Internet Registry (ARIN). Although identified as government employees, they have no particular status as such and participate generally as individuals. It is their expertise, which is often extensive, and their long involvement in the process that affords them influence. However, it is somewhat difficult to evaluate the power associated with their participation. Is it the ongoing DOC–ICANN connection, the individuals' influence, or the significant continuing U.S. presence on the board—or some combination of those—that has helped resolve many recent issues in U.S. favor?

One question is whether the U.S. Government's influence can continue. Undoubtedly, its reluctance to terminate the MOU/JPA reflects the view that the contractual arrangement provides for U.S. guidance that might be lost or become subject to other influences if the agreement were to be terminated. However, there is considerable pressure, even from some European allies, to do so. It is also inevitable that with the retirement of U.S. individuals—the founders of the Internet and of ICANN—people from other countries will eventually have as much history and expertise as Americans. When that happens, the principal source of continuing U.S. influence may be through the Government's individual representatives and the U.S. companies who can act as Government surrogates. Unless they are extraordinarily vigorous, it would seem unlikely that the Government's distinct ability to influence outcomes can remain the same as it has been.

The power of nongovernmental participants in ICANN is also difficult to gauge. The 15 voting members of the board currently include 8 incumbents who are associated with businesses involved with the Internet. A former Australian government official and businessman sits on the board as the President of

ICANN; the other board members are academics, researchers, lawyers, and a representative of a standards body. Only three of the members in the fall of 2007 were American; no other country had more than two.

The public comments prior to the 2006 MOU/JPA renegotiation suggest a measure of how well ICANN is meeting its goals. The board is generally seen as fair, or at least not dominated by one faction or another. ICANN's mechanisms to legitimize board selection seem to be successful. ICANN has published extensive ethics rules and has taken steps at the board level to manage conflicts of interest.[36] While concerns have been expressed that there may be undisclosed conflicts or that the nominating committee might fail to assure that all candidates have been thoroughly vetted, there is little evidence of any actual problem or of public concern.

The board itself sits atop a structure that has been frequently attacked. There have been complaints about financial reporting and the budget, about appeals from board decisions, and about the openness of the board's own meetings. Other challenges about issues such as transparency, accountability, and participatory decisionmaking figured prominently in comments directed to DOC during the MOU/JPA renewal discussions.

ICANN has not satisfied those who criticize its lack of transparency. In 2003, for example, VeriSign and ICANN became embroiled in an extended dispute about what services VeriSign, as the *.com* registry, could offer. The parties could not resolve the disagreement, and the case wound up in court. The settlement agreement was not popular with many groups active in ICANN.[37] Two lawsuits sought to stop the settlement, and a number of Internet registrars who rely upon the VeriSign registry actively criticized the board.[38] By approving the deal, albeit with some additional safeguards incorporated into the cooperative agreement, the U.S. Government became a target of the settlement's opponents, who attacked it for endorsing "monopoly pricing."[39]

In response to criticism during the renewal discussions, the board commissioned a nongovernmental organization (NGO) based in the United Kingdom, the One World Trust, to prepare a report on its efforts at transparency, accountability, and participation.[40] That report, delivered in March 2007, suggested several improvements to ICANN's process, but gave ICANN relatively high marks for transparency.[41]

However, the unhappiness with ICANN over transparency continues. A posting on June 20, 2007, of responses to ICANN's request for public comments and dialogue on its performance reflected 14 comments. Even though the number was small, some responses were from significant ICANN participants, including GoDaddy (a registrar), the Internet Commerce Association, and the Canadian Internet Registration Authority, which "raised concerns over the transparency and accountability of governance at ICANN including how it conducts its public consultations."[42]

The key method of board consultation for a large number of issues is an online forum combined with formal and informal discussions. The electronic consultation process is open to all those who wish to submit views, and many people take a considerable amount of time to set out positions. As with all online forums, discussion can proceed through exchanges, but the structure is not optimal for getting consensus from initially disparate reviews. Nonetheless, ICANN's online forum on transparency and accountability operating principles had (as of July 2007) reflected no major complaints with the process for registering comments.[43]

ICANN created a policy development process (PDP) several years ago to investigate and articulate positions for consideration by the board affecting the interests of the gTLDs, ccTLDs, or regional registries.[44]

The PDP starts by request of the board, the Supporting Organization (SO) Council, or one of the SO's advisory groups. If either the GNSO (for gTLD registries and others) or the ccNSO (for ccTLD registries) initiates a PDP, an elaborate effort is made to solicit the views of SO constituent groups and the public, with a specific requirement for votes by the constituent groups on the recommendations. If the SOs propose a policy (by supermajority for the GNSO, by consensus or supermajority for the ccNSO), the board essentially is required to adopt it unless two-thirds oppose it.

In September 2006, the London School of Economics Public Policy Group published a study at the request of ICANN that reviewed the GNSO's representativeness, transparency, effectiveness, and compliance with ICANN's bylaws.[45] The report was mixed. Among several substantive negatives were that the "external visibility of the GNSO Council is poor" and that the "information costs [are high] for anyone who is not already a deep insider in ICANN." However, it concluded, "The processes and policy development exchanges of the GNSO Council are highly transparent, more so than most similar organizations," despite "some signs that Constituencies are hard to penetrate for newcomers and that baseline standards such as disclosure of interests are not adequately enforced." In addition, said the study, "Many PDPs take quite a long time to complete," and thus the "process of reaching 'consensus' on major policy issues is often arduous," while "current arrangements for voting introduce further complexities by assigning double-weight votes to two Constituencies (Registries and Registrars)."[46] The report prompted discussion of changes to the GNSO, but these remained inconclusive as of the fall of 2007.

Evaluating the PDP as it currently stands yields a complicated picture. The PDP is an attempt to balance pure participatory democracy against organizational coherence and efficiency. The procedure heightens the value of coalition-building and inclusive outreach; there has to be extensive vetting of ideas before each of the constituent elements of the SO; a public comment period provides an opportunity for individuals who are not involved in the SOs to speak; and deliberations by the constituent elements, seeking consensus or supermajority on the recommendations, are followed by consideration by the SO councils.

The process inhibits any one entity's ability to push a proposal forward unilaterally. In its attempt to reach out to any interested party, anywhere in the world, the PDP creates a lengthy, difficult process that is likely to founder in the face of any significant dissent. As a result, the system will work only if it can avoid problems that require immediate attention where no consensus is in place. However, business and Internet users share an overriding interest in pragmatic solutions that keep the system running. Any other interests they may have in the DNS are probably secondary to their fundamental commitment to a functional and constantly improving system. If, however, other players, such as governments, were introduced into the decisionmaking, their interests might not so consistently favor pragmatic technical solutions, and the PDP or some equivalent would be more prone to fail.

The One World Trust Report issued in March 2007 similarly called upon ICANN to make changes to increase its effectiveness and legitimacy, such as improving ways to publicize how the board makes its decisions, particularly its use of public and advisory input; improving availability of meeting agendas; and more consistent handling of public outreach during the PDP. ICANN has promised to implement some of the changes and to consider others.[47]

Any participant must have specific attributes if it intends to promote a particular policy or point of view within ICANN. An extraordinary commitment of time and effort is required to participate not just at the board level, but also at the board committee, supporting organization, and constituency levels. There has to be a willingness and an ability to go to meetings all over the world, draft papers, and otherwise take time to share ideas with the many participants whose consent is needed to move an issue forward. Corporations have understood the value of such expenditures, but few governments, apart from those of the United States, Australia, and New Zealand, have done so. Individual members of the European Union (EU), and the EU itself, have become more active, and other governments will almost inevitably reevaluate their level of activity as the Internet grows in importance in their home markets.

Effective participation also requires one to be an "insider." The process is so diffuse that those who have not built relationships and credibility are unlikely to have much influence in the decisionmaking. The organization may have aspirations of incorporating global views, but that it functions reasonably well is probably only because the same 200 to 250 people keep coming to the meetings and emailing each other.

Nontechnical issues pose a different challenge in decisionmaking, because they have no technical focus that could create convergence around a single answer. The security and stability of the DNS do not, for example, depend on whether a new gTLD is created (although the creation of a vast number might have an effect). Consensus is more difficult to achieve where there is no one technically best solution or even a technical framework on which to make such a judgment. In the absence of objective data, longstanding representatives who have built up relationships over time have an advantage in navigating the policy process. Even so, they have had to expend large sums over a long period, going to meetings and otherwise participating constantly, regardless of whether their employer or institution has a direct interest in a particular issue under consideration. Few companies or other institutions can support that level of activity, which winnows down the number of players.

The Value Structure Underlying ICANN Governance

A number of social forces and values influenced how ICANN took shape. Deregulation had a real impact on the current structure of ICANN, which also reflects the broadening acceptance worldwide of participatory democracy. The 1990s were a time of spreading democracy and growing political commitment to direct public participation. The ICANN structure might not have been accepted if the significance of the Internet had been better understood. ICANN may also have benefited from timing. Had the Clinton or Bush administrations proposed ICANN just a few years later, when the power of the Internet had become clearer, other governments might have objected. Another influence on ICANN's structure was the U.S. Government's distinctive laissez-faire attitude toward the Internet. Although the Government, chiefly DARPA and the National Science Foundation, had paid for the initial research, development, and operation of the Internet, the Government refrained from seeking to control its evolution.

Another distinct influence is the power of academia. The Internet reflects the emergence of academics and researchers into an influential role in the "knowledge economy." In fact, the distinction between academia and corporate activity has been virtually erased. For example, whenever the history of Google is recited, it inevitably includes the comment that it was conceived by two graduate students at Stanford University.

A final distinction is the continuing influence of the U.S. Government—which, even if not exercised, may have forestalled the exercise of less benign control by others. During WSIS in 2005, the Government argued that ending its contracts and allowing other governments greater participation could be destabilizing. For a variety of countries—such as Africans nations who wanted to end the digital divide far more than they wanted to humble the United States—the point was persuasive.

The Internet Society and the World Wide Web Consortium

Most of the key organizations for collective decisionmaking about core technical standards and issues of the Internet are now grouped under the umbrella of the private, nonprofit Internet Society. They include the Internet Engineering Task Force (IETF), the Internet Engineering Steering Group (IESG), and the Internet Architecture Board (IAB).[48] Although it is a separate private, nonprofit organization, the World Wide Web Consortium (W3C), which sets standards for the Web (such as Hyper Text Markup Language [HTML], File Transfer Protocol [FTP], and Extensible Markup Language [XML]), is also discussed in this section, because of the Web's distinct and significant function as a principal Internet service.[49]

There are three main working elements of the Internet Society: the IETF, the IESG, and the IAB.

The IETF is an organization of designers, operators, vendors, researchers, and users that anyone may join; it has no formal membership and no membership requirements. All participants and leaders are volunteers, though their work is usually funded by their employers or sponsors. Its mission is to produce technical and engineering documents to help make the elements of the Internet work together better (in other words, to assure interoperability), including protocols, standards, and statements of best current practices. In particular, it develops the standards for the transmission control protocol and IP suite.

An area director oversees each subject area; the directors, together with the IETF chair, make up the IESG, which handles technical management of IETF activities and the Internet standards process. The IAB is responsible for defining the overall architecture of the Internet; it is both a committee of the IETF, providing it with guidance, and an advisory body to the Internet Society. The Internet Society was formed in 1992 to support these Internet standards activities.

These organizations grew out of the Internet Configuration Control Board (ICCB), formed in 1979 by DARPA's Internet project manager.[50] The ICCB was filled with U.S. Government employees and their contractors. Over a quarter-century later, it has evolved into multiple related organizations that create the protocols and other standards and identify best practices in the Internet's operations.[51] There is close cooperation between these organizations and ICANN, ITU, and the other Internet governance organizations.

The Internet Engineering Task Force

The IETF is "a large open international community of network designers, operators, vendors, and researchers concerned with the evolution of the Internet architecture and the smooth operation of the Internet." Its mission is "to produce high quality, relevant technical and engineering documents that influence the way people design, use, and manage the Internet in such a way as to make the Internet work better. These documents include protocol standards, best current practices, and informational documents of various kinds."[52]

The IETF has over 100 working groups in 8 broad subject areas.[53] Working groups address specific issues, mostly by telecommunicating. The IETF as a whole meets three times a year. The areas are overseen by the area directors, who are themselves volunteers, and a small secretariat.

The working groups of the IETF and its standards development process have been central to the evolution of the Internet's core functions. The documents produced by the IETF (known as requests for comment [RFCs]) cover practically every technical specification relevant to the operation of the Internet itself. Any change in the basic Internet protocols, whether relevant to security, capacity, or robustness, must come though the working groups.

The Internet Engineering Steering Group

The area directors of the IETF, together with its chair, form the IESG, which handles "technical management of IETF activities and the Internet standards process. . . . The IESG is directly responsible for the actions associated with entry into and movement along the Internet 'standards track,' including final approval of specifications as Internet Standards."[54] As of the summer of 2007, only one area director was a U.S. Government employee, but many of them were drawn from U.S. corporations.[55]

The Internet Architecture Board

The IAB, a committee of the IETF, is responsible for "defining the overall architecture of the Internet, providing guidance and broad direction to the IETF."[56] It does not focus on specific technical topics but develops documents on general technical principles to support the proper functioning of the Internet and its protocols or creates ad hoc panels to develop ideas in a particular area. The IAB can also convene a workshop or ad hoc panel outside the IETF's standards process.[57] The IAB handles editorial management and publication of the RFC series of publications; confirms the IETF chair and area directors from nominations provided by the IETF nominating committee; serves as the appeal board if there are complaints about improper execution of the standards process in a decision by the IESG; and selects the chair of the Internet Research Task Force, which addresses long-term Internet-related research projects.[58]

The IAB has 13 members. Six are elected each year for 2-year terms based on nominations from the IETF nominating committee that have been approved by the Internet Society's Board of Trustees. The 13th member is the IETF chair. The board has had only two non-U.S. chairs since 1981; the most recent U.S. chair took office in March 2007. Eight of the IAB members as of mid-2007 were U.S. residents.

The Internet Society

When the IETF grew concerned about continuation of its U.S. Government funding, it created the Internet Society in 1992 to raise money to help support its operations and to handle administrative functions that the engineers viewed as a distraction from their primary focus on technical standards development.[59] As of 2007, the organization had an annual budget of approximately $9 million. In addition to supporting IETF, IESG, and IAB, it sustains a range of policy and education projects, focusing on national Internet organizations and operators. Most of its budget comes from the private sector, but DISA is a major contributor.[60]

Governance of the IETF and Related Bodies

The IETF's governance process is a mixture of straightforward direct participation and complicated policy development. On the one hand, it is broadly participatory: the IETF is open to anyone. As befits that open spirit, the introductory manual for new members is entitled "The Tao of the IETF."[61] However, influence requires continuous, high-quality, technically competent participation. Most of the area directors are senior officials with major corporations or senior researchers at government or academic institutions. The process of creating a new Internet standard has been characterized as arduous; it often takes years to go from IAB approval of a new working group charter to a final RFC that has been approved by the IESG.

The significant U.S. presence in the leadership of the IETF and the IAB provides some protection of U.S. interests. When working groups are so open and diffuse, the area directors and working group chairs derive influence from being able to direct the work and to shape, to some extent, the draft documents. They are probably most influential in determining which new questions will be studied and how the issues are framed. They also have some ability to resolve final outcomes. The adoption process requires only "rough consensus,"[62] which has been defined in many ways; "a simple version is that it means that strongly held objections must be debated until most people are satisfied that these objections are wrong."[63]

To the extent there is government participation, it is as technically oriented as other participation. The fact that any government proponent must present a case that will persuade technical experts who could deny a "rough consensus" makes political appeals not just useless, but counterproductive. As a consequence, when there were attacks on ICANN at WSIS, there was no similar pressure to change the working methods of the IETF. On the contrary, to the extent IETF was a subject of discussion, governments generally applauded its work.

Process at the IETF or other standards bodies is not pristine. It can matter a great deal to companies' competitive positions which standards are selected; that has led at times to accusations of unethical conduct. For example, Microsoft was accused in September 2007 of vote-buying in connection with a decision by the Swedish Standards Institute regarding a document format known as Open Office XML.[64]

The World Wide Web Consortium

The Web is just one element of the Internet and it has its own standards structure, which is under the control of a much smaller number of participants than is the IETF. The W3C, not the IETF, sets standards for the World Wide Web, and W3C is not part of the Internet Society. However, the W3C involves some of the same people and corporate organizations as the IETF. They coordinate, but rarely need to collaborate, given their separate technological spheres. Governments are not particularly active in the W3C's deliberations, although DOC's National Institute for Standards and Technology and some government agencies from other countries are members of the W3C.

The Consortium was created in 1994 by Tim Berners-Lee (who developed original World Wide Web standards such as HTML, HTTP, and FTP) to promote the Web by creating guidelines and standards to facilitate its use.[65] Today, the consortium is jointly sponsored by the Massachusetts Institute of Technology, the European Research Consortium in Informatics and Mathematics, and Keio University in Japan. Membership is limited to organizations, many of which are academic institutions, consultants, and software companies. Over one-third of the members are from the United States.[66]

The W3C's working methods resemble those of the IETF, but there is more staff involvement and direction. A broad-based approval process relies on literal consensus. Working groups set up to address specific issues include consortium members, staff, and invited experts. The W3C uses member-donated funds to pay for a share of the research and development itself, while participating parties pay the rest. The groups work on a proposed recommendation until there is a consensus. The final version is put before the advisory committee, which has a representative from each member. If there is a consensus, the proposal is adopted as a new guideline.[67]

The International Telecommunication Union

The ITU was founded in 1865 and is now a UN agency.[68] Although the ITU allows private sector companies to participate in deliberations, it is unlike ICANN and the IETF in that only governments vote on final decisions. The distinction is one source of tension in the evolution of Internet governance.

The ITU's Telecommunication Standardization Sector (ITU–T) issues technical and operating standards for telecommunications networks and addresses tariff questions that can affect the Internet.[69] It does not address the technical issues integral to the internal operation of the Internet itself. Its

Secretary-General and senior staff have speculated that the ITU could assume a larger role in Internet governance, perhaps taking over some of ICANN's functions.[70] Hence, both for what it does and what it might do, the ITU has a major role in Internet decisionmaking.

The worldwide telecommunications system depends upon the standards and tariff work in the ITU–T. The Internet has always been dependent on telecommunications networks for delivery, and the relationship between the two grows closer with the convergence of technologies, especially increasing use of voice over IP (VoIP) communications.

The range of questions under consideration in the ITU–T in mid-2007 demonstrated the scope of its influence over the Internet. At least 20 questions before the ITU–T's 13 study groups directly would affect some aspect of Internet policy. Many more would have some collateral effect on the delivery or quality of Internet service.

ITU Collective Decisionmaking

The ITU operates differently from ICANN and the IETF, both because it is part of the UN and because it developed when telephone service was, in most of the world, a government-run function. Only governments vote in the ITU, making it a true intergovernmental organization.

That voting power creates a complicated process for the adoption of new standards. The practical reality is that private companies have the lead role in ITU deliberations, particularly in the ITU–T. The union has created "sector members," a membership category for nongovernmental entities that have an interest in the ITU's deliberations. These may be "recognized operating agencies" that operate a public correspondence or broadcasting service; scientific or industrial organizations that study telecommunications problems or that design or manufacture telecommunications equipment; other entities dealing with telecommunications matters; and regional and other international telecommunication, standardization, financial, or development organizations.[71] There are 191 national government administrations that are full members of the ITU and over 700 "sector members," including practically every major corporation with an interest in the telecommunication industry.

The ITU–T's method of doing business is worthy of close examination in this era of privatization and globalization. With the end of state-run telephone companies in most of the developed world, governments no longer have the expertise to provide much of the technical work that is the basis for the ITU's standards and other recommendations. They also have little direct incentive to participate, except insofar as the stability and security of their own national or intragovernmental networks are at issue.[72] The result is a need for close cooperation between the sector members, who do the actual investigation and drafting of the recommendations—and who have the economic interest in their passage—and the governments that vote on their adoption.[73]

Every 4 years, at the World Telecommunication Standardization Assembly (WTSA), all national administrations and the nonvoting sector members meet to define general policy and adopt working methods and procedures for the telecommunications sector. The WTSA determines many of the topics to be addressed by each study group; the study groups can identify additional matters. The study group chairs then develop work plans to address the questions posed under each topic. They take into account the directions of the WTSA and the recommendations of the Telecommunication Standardization Advisory Committee, which holds regular meetings of all government and sector members to advise the sector's bureau director.[74]

The chairs of the ITU study groups select the leaders of working parties, may appoint rapporteurs to investigate a particular issue, and may provide a report or draft text for a new recommendation. The study groups or the director of the Telecommunication Standardization Bureau may also create focus groups for the quick development of standards on specific subjects. According to the ITU–T, "the key difference between Study Groups and Focus Groups is the freedom that they have to organize and finance themselves."[75] The study group chairs have the power to appoint leaders of the subgroups and to determine the number and timing of meetings for each subject; this gives them considerable power to control the groups' work.

A sector member may submit contributions directly to a working party or propose instead that the submission be made in the name of its government. A government may submit a paper itself, or it may seek the endorsement of one of five regional groupings, such as the Inter-American Telecommunication Commission of the Organization of American States (*Comisión Interamericana de Telecomunicaciones,* or CITEL).

For example, in the United States, the formal interaction between sector members and the Department of State (which represents the United States at the ITU) occurs in the International Telecommunication Advisory Committee (ITAC), which is composed of interested private sector companies. However, because of the nature of the ITU–T's work, much of the public-private collaboration actually occurs at the Federal Communications Commission (FCC), whose International Bureau works closely with the State Department and private companies.[76] Following ITAC deliberations on a proposal, the U.S. Government reviews it in an all-government "national committee" that includes State, the NTIA, the FCC, and at times other agencies. If the proposal raises security and stability concerns that conflict with some other interest, the ITAC recommendation may go nowhere or be sent back for further negotiation. Although there is considerable one-to-one contact between company and government representatives during this process, rules of procedure under the Federal Advisory Committee Act slow down the ability to resolve issues.

The United States usually submits proposals to the ITU in its own name, but it has sometimes looked to CITEL for support. CITEL and the other four regional groupings have grown more active in recent years. They represent large blocs of votes, and thus a CITEL endorsement indicates wide support. However, the time and effort needed to win national and regional approval for a proposal may sometimes be impractical.

Whether a proposal comes from a private sector member or a government, after it has been considered in an ITU study group, a unanimous vote of the study group is required before final drafts of recommendations are adopted. The unanimous consent requirement gives nations leverage to negotiate even if, like the United States, they are not closely allied with a regional grouping. Unilateral vetoes have been rare.

In 2000, however, the WTSA adopted a rule for a fast-track alternative, called the Alternative Approval Process (AAP), for recommendations that were deemed not to have a regulatory or policy implication. A majority of Study Group activities appear to be on the AAP fast-track list.[77] WTSA later revised AAP to provide that proposals under fast-track consideration could be adopted despite the objection of a single national administration, but the United States strongly objected. The fast-track proposal was then further revised to allay concerns about loss of national sovereignty, effectively returning to the requirement of unanimity.[78]

The ITU–Radiocommunication Bureau (ITU–R), which deals with radio spectrum management, is not as central to issues related to Internet governance. However, broadband wireless communication is within its jurisdiction and is an important means of expanding the Internet's reach. The working methods of the ITU–R generally are similar to those of the ITU–T, but the relative power of the actors is somewhat different. Because national governments have significant interests in the radio spectrum, both for military and public safety uses, and they retain control over civilian spectrum allocation, they take a more active role in ITU–R deliberations. Their interests are more often at odds with the private sector, and ITU–R decisions reflect national security concerns more than in the ITU–T.

Although ICANN, IETF, and the ITU recognize each other and try to cooperate and coordinate standards activity, there is inevitable overlap in some areas, particularly on hot-button issues such as stability, security, and internationalized domain names. That can lead to forum-shopping.[79]

Exercise of Power at the ITU

In the ITU–T, private sector companies, which draft and advocate most of the recommendations developed by the study groups, have the most influence. Power in the ITU is more of a mix of technical expertise, commercial pressures, and national political interests than in the IETF or ICANN. Political issues do not necessarily have primacy: governments with privatized phone service or a desire for a better system or wider Internet service will often do what is technically logical, although they may try to provide their corporate "national champions" with opportunities to capitalize on the standards.

The United States has done well over the years at the ITU. Both its national security interests and its commercial goals have been advanced. Success is generally attributed to the State Department's leadership of U.S. delegations and the active involvement of U.S. corporations in study group meetings. Here, as with the IETF, U.S. influence comes from its considerable presence among study group chairs.[80] Also as with the IETF, these bodies are dispersed globally, and thus those who control the work flow and the appointment of subordinate leadership have considerable power. Many of the U.S. chairs and cochairs will be stepping down in the near future; unless new U.S. leaders replace them, the U.S. ability to shape events will decline.

More significantly, there are considerable pressures to diminish U.S. influence by increasing the ITU's role in Internet governance. In early 2007, the new ITU secretary-general invited comment on Plenipotentiary Resolution 102, which instructed the secretary-general to "continue to take a significant role in international discussions and initiatives on the management of Internet domain names and addresses and other Internet resources within the mandate of the ITU."[81] Many responses came from countries that were also active at WSIS in calling for an overhaul of Internet governance.[82] For example, Brazil's response pressed for the ITU to assure that governments play a role "on equal footing" in Internet public policy issues. Iran drew attention to the fact that only the United States has more than an advisory role in Internet governance mechanisms. Saudi Arabia, too, argued for a greater ITU role in "worldwide coordination of technical and policy issues related to the management of Internet domain names and addresses."

A second force for change within the ITU was reflected in the WSIS Tunis Agenda for the Information Society (the Tunis Final Acts). It identifies various UN agencies to take the lead in coordinating specified Internet-related subject matters (called *action lines*), as originally described in the 2003 WSIS Action Plan.[83] Two action lines were assigned to the ITU: information and communication infrastructure, and building confidence and security in the use of Information and Communication Technologies.

In early 2007, the newly elected secretary-general announced initiatives for each of the WSIS Action Lines. The ITU, along with the World Bank and others, planned a "Connect Africa" conference in Rwanda for that year. The secretary-general also published the ITU Global Cyber-security Agenda to implement the cyber security action line.[84]

The question is whether these activities will eventually involve the ITU in decisionmaking now done elsewhere. At present, the ITU has a formal agreement with the IETF intended to foster collaboration and prevent duplication of effort.[85] There are regular meetings between IETF and ITU–T leadership, and there have been joint workshops. The ITU is also active at ICANN but, except as noted, has not attempted to take over any of its functions.[86] Numerous ITU study group questions acknowledge work done at ICANN or IETF and promise not to duplicate their efforts. The secretary-general has repeatedly disclaimed any interest in changing the balance among the organizations.[87] However, projects such as the ITU's Global Cyber-security Agenda may eventually alter the division of labor.

A third force for change is the ITU's own staff. The former secretary-general and the director of the TSB have suggested that the ITU should take on additional Internet functions, such as running the IP addressing function.[88]

The U.S. Government, many other governments, and the overwhelming majority of ITU private sector members strongly opposed such ideas, and those proposals did not move forward. The secretary-general recognized that it was such a major issue for the United States that he had to address it directly during his campaign for office, but it remains to be seen whether he can honor that promise against pressure from some governments and ITU staff.

Other International Organizations

Discussion to this point has focused on agencies that set the Internet's common operating standards. However, the Internet has also created some issues and problems that have prompted action by governmental or international bodies. This section highlights what may be the most influential of these actions: the antispam toolkit developed by the Organization for Economic Co-operation and Development (OECD); the Council of Europe's Cybercrime Convention; and UN development activities.

OECD Spam Toolkit

The OECD is a 30-nation organization devoted to promoting sustainable economic growth and employment, economic expansion, and world trade. Information and communication technologies, electronic commerce, and the wider economic implications of the Internet have for many years been regular elements of the OECD work program. The organization regularly issues reports and other information about the Internet to support economic development. Because of the extraordinary burden on electronic commerce and communications created by unwanted Internet solicitations known as *spam*, OECD members decided to go further and to create a series of recommendations to governments about how to combat the problem, which they called the "Spam Toolkit."[89]

The toolkit reflects the fact that the Internet does not recognize national boundaries.[90] However, while it encourages international cooperation, it does not suggest any kind of international treaty or binding commitment by governments.[91] Instead, it focuses on suggestions for national legislation, regulations, and private sector initiatives. This reflects the limits of common action when, due to variations in views on commercial and political free speech, privacy, and consumer protection, governments are unable to arrive at a common definition of the actions they want to curb.

There has, however, been some progress toward shared goals in combating spam. For example, over two dozen antispam agencies and more industrial partners developed the London Action Plan, an initiative to promote international enforcement cooperation.[92] There is a similar agreement among several European antispam enforcement agencies. Where adequate agreement to create a treaty is lacking, however, the OECD's toolkit encourages governments and industry to create more cross-border programs.

The Council of Europe Convention on Cybercrime

The Council of Europe is an organization of 47 European states that was created to promote democracy, human rights, and the rule of law in Europe. Although its focus is not the Internet, its antiterrorism, anticrime, and human rights efforts have led it to make proposals that affect Internet use and abuse. In particular is its Convention on Cybercrime, opened for signature in 2001.[93] As of December 2007, the convention had been signed by 43 countries and ratified by 21, including the United States. Its goal is to improve governments' ability to deal with cyber crime by harmonizing national laws and facilitating international cooperation against cross-border criminal acts. Parties to the convention agree to pass national legislation to outlaw specified cyber crimes, to take responsibility for crimes within their jurisdictions, and to authorize necessary investigative techniques. The convention also provides for assisting other nations' criminal investigations and the extradition of cyber criminals.

An example of the difficulty of drafting international legal rules for the Internet was a proposed provision to the convention, sought by many European nations, that would ban racist language. It was removed at the insistence of the United States, which saw it as an infringement on free speech guaranteed by the U.S. Constitution. There is now a separate protocol on racist language, which the United States has refused to sign.[94]

The convention has facilitated tracking down cyber criminals among signatories. However, cyber criminals will still have safe havens in countries such as North Korea or Yemen that do not sign the agreement.[95] Hence, while something like the convention is necessary to control international cyber crime activities against victims in the United States, it will never be totally effective because adversaries can evade it.

One recent high-profile example of the problem occurred in May 2007, when numerous denial-of-service attacks threatened to paralyze Estonia's economy. Estonia was able to identify several Russian IP addresses as the likely sources of the attacks, but the Russian government was unwilling to help track down the responsible individuals.[96] The Estonians had no choice but to shut down large parts of their networks temporarily in order to defend against the intruders.

The Council of Europe has several joint projects with the European Commission; some of these, such as privacy protection, affect the Internet.[97] The European Union's involvement in the Internet is considered below, but it should be noted here that the EU now participates in ICANN, and it has had a particular impact on the Internet through the enforcement of its privacy guidelines.[98]

UN Development Activities

The WSIS and the UN's Millennium Development Goals committed the organization to promoting the expansion of the Internet in the developing world.[99] In April 2007, the UN secretary-general reported on activities designed to follow up on the organization's WSIS commitments, which reflected the Millennium Development Goals for economic growth in the developing world.[100]

The report is a snapshot of a great many activities, but they have had far less effect than market forces on Internet expansion. The WSIS had identified various action lines for the expansion of different aspects of the Internet in the developing world, specifying UN agencies for lead roles. As of the fall of 2007, however, the UN Department of Economic and Social Affairs had not gotten much beyond the consultation stage in its work on action lines. The one organization that had made real progress was the ITU.

Although the UN has laudably embraced an information technology development agenda, it is not likely to play a pivotal role in the actual expansion of the Internet. The UN's work may ultimately yield real benefits, especially in capacity-building and information-sharing, but those efforts will be dwarfed by competitive market forces

The UN's Internet activities are not exclusively focused on development. The UN Commission on International Trade Law has devoted extensive efforts to electronic commerce and has in particular spent several years working on a draft convention.[101] The challenge to the successful completion of the document is finding common ground among different legal systems for activities that may have a pervasive effect in local economies.

There is one other UN-related organization whose activities are worth noting: the World Intellectual Property Organization (WIPO). While its attempts to resolve intellectual property protections for material on the Internet are not fundamental enough to the functioning of the Internet to justify extensive discussion in this chapter, WIPO's deliberations have a vast impact on content providers who place materials on the Internet for use or sale. For any entity interested in influencing the economic results of using the Internet, the ability to achieve results at WIPO is extraordinarily important.

This discussion of intergovernmental organizations' activities is illustrative rather than exhaustive. It does suggest three significant points.

First, there may be political pressure to take action, even where no consensus exists. Intergovernmental agencies have adapted by finding ways to move forward without calling for mandatory regulation. Second, governments still have considerable power based on their national sovereignty, and they can exercise it to frustrate the ability of others to control aspects of the Internet within their own territory. Third, the private sector and users are quickly deploying the Internet, for which they need an "enabling environment" from government. That is, they need to be able to operate without undue regulation in a free market and be supported by adequate infrastructure such as the power grid. Although governments seek to support deployment of the Internet, their more significant role in Internet governance may be in constraining some aspects of its use rather than in promoting it.

National Governments

Where can national governments have impact on the Internet? How, and how much, can they influence the exercise of cyberpower by others? Governments have not always acknowledged the logic of the globalized nature of the Internet. They have acted based on their longstanding notions of national sovereignty, with varying degrees of success.

For example, the NTIA has pushed U.S. registrars to limit the practice of "tasting," which allows someone to use a domain name for a brief period at no cost. Although the practice is sanctioned by ICANN, it has become an attractive device to cyber criminals as a way to avoid being identified.

The suppression of free speech is another contentious issue. The U.S. Government's position on free speech led it to oppose the ban on racist language proposed in the Convention on Cybercrime. At the same time, it has adopted antipornography laws to shield children from adult content. While Americans can reconcile those positions, others see contradictions.

The U.S. Government, the press, civil rights advocates, and other free-speech proponents have attacked the Chinese government for attempting to filter out words such as *democracy* from Web sites.[102] Chinese authorities have defended the practice, claiming the need to protect civil order, and have cracked down on Web sites containing what they consider politically troublesome content. Some U.S. companies have acceded to Chinese requests to eliminate the troublesome words and to reveal the identities of the Web site operators. Recently, Burma used an even heavier hand, shutting down its international Internet connections entirely during civil unrest in the fall of 2007.[103]

In other areas, governmental capability to control the Internet remains unclear. For example, debate in Congress on the issue of "net neutrality" leaves open the question of whether national legislation will work on a problem that is really Internet-wide. Some Internet service providers have raised the possibility of creating tiers of service, prioritizing some packets over others. Opponents call for net neutrality. So-called net-neutrality legislation has been proposed that would ban or limit tiered service. However, any prioritization program would only work if adopted worldwide, or at least broadly enough to allow faster delivery of priority traffic.[104] Eventually, U.S. activity around this issue may be a test of how far a nation can push its own policies without degrading the worldwide standards necessary for the system to function.

Other Standards Organizations

The Institute of Electrical and Electronics Engineers (IEEE), the International Organization for Standardization (ISO), and the International Electrotechnical Commission (IEC) are involved in standards work on a broad range of issues, not just the Internet.[105] Each of these organizations encompasses specific concentrations on standards for devices, hardware, and software related to the Internet. The IEEE, for example, developed the 802 standard for wireless device connections to the Internet and has a focus on Internet best practices. The three organizations work closely with each other. A Joint Technical Committee on Information Technology combines the IEC's work on hardware with ISO's work on software. Each has a memorandum of understanding with the ITU. The ISO and IEC have agreed upon a common patent policy with the ITU to address how to deal with patented technology in standards.[106] While the three organizations have somewhat different processes for standards development, influence in each requires technical competence, as well as continuous and long-term participation.

The IEEE is a professional organization that develops industrial standards in a broad range of disciplines, including electric power and energy, biomedical technology and health care, information technology, information assurance, telecommunications, consumer electronics, transportation, aero-space, and nanotechnology. Open to anyone (although full membership requires attainment of specified educational standards), it has over 300,000 members and 10 technical divisions. The IEEE's Standards Association has 20,000 members who can join the standards process and participate in the standards coordinating committees. Their consensus recommendations are reviewed by a review committee and then by the association's standards board.

The ISO is an international standards-setting body that acts as a consortium of various national standards associations. Countries are represented by national committees; the American National Standards Institute (ANSI) is the U.S. member.[107] Within ISO, national committees propose standards that are negotiated and then voted upon. Two-thirds of the ISO members that have participated actively in the standards development process must approve the standard; if so, and if 75 percent of all members that vote approve it, the standard becomes an ISO standard.

The IEC is a not-for-profit, nongovernmental international standards organization that sets standards for electrical, electronic, and related technologies, such as power generation, home appliances, semiconductors, batteries, and marine energy. Its members are called national committees, and each represents its nation's interests in the IEC. The U.S. committee operates through ANSI. Approximately 10,000 people working through 179 technical committees and 700 project teams develop standards that are then voted upon by the national committees. The IEC publishes standards with the IEEE and develops standards jointly with the ISO as well as the ITU.

These three organizations coordinate their activities to reduce subject matter overlap. ISO is less specialized than IEEE or IEC, but because of the closeness of their subject matters, ISO and IEC set up a Joint Technical Committee on Information Technology a quarter-century ago.

The significance of these standards is commercial; they have much less impact on national cyberpower than do the decisions of ICANN or IETF. The similarities in their processes underscore the difficulty and expense of participation in standards-making decisions, which may limit a participant's ability to manipulate the process to particular advantage.

Conclusion

All of the collective international decisionmaking processes that affect the Internet share some traits:

- they are not speedy, and swift decisionmaking is unlikely
- they stress technical competence and a long-term commitment to the process, and while political considerations are not unknown, outside the ITU, they are not generally influential
- they are worldwide processes, designed to incorporate a range of views
- all the standards bodies except ISO and the ICANN Board require unanimity, or close to it, for adoption of policies
- private, chiefly commercial, interests dominate the processes, even the ITU's standards process

- governments participate on equal footing with others, except within the ITU where governments formally dominate
- decisionmaking processes are fairly transparent, but leaders have considerable discretionary power, and it is not always apparent how that power has been exercised
- overlap of subject matters creates some incentive to forum-shop.

The process of Internet governance has worked reasonably well. The Internet has rapidly expanded around the world and, at least at the technical level, there is good reason to believe that the current collective decisionmaking processes can accommodate additional incremental changes. Internet governance should receive good marks on several measures: openness, democracy, transparency, dynamism, adaptability, accountability, efficiency, and effectiveness. However, a fair assessment would also identify some problems that could eventually erode its overall legitimacy. Both positives and negatives are reviewed in this concluding section.

What Internet Governance Is

Open. Overall, the Internet governance process is remarkably open. IETF and ICANN both have formal outreach mechanisms to encourage individuals and entities to join and participate in the decisionmaking process. The ITU and the other organizations are not as open, but any motivated business, organizational, or academic interest can participate in ITU, IEEE, ISO, or IEC deliberations.

Generally democratic in spirit, if somewhat less so in practice. Two particular issues arise with regard to democracy: the role of the United States, especially at ICANN, and the relatively small number of people and institutions that are consistently at the center of all the collective decisionmaking.

The role of the United States at ICANN has prompted complaints that it may compel particular decisions against others' views. While there is no doubt that contractual mechanisms give the United States extra influence, recent cases have demonstrated that U.S. exercise of its power can also have negative consequences and is subject to limits.

Most of the positive results in the development of the DNS would have happened even if the U.S. Government had not exercised a supervisory role. The goals of the business interests that would, in any event, have dominated the process are generally aimed at the expansion and development of an open, stable, and secure Internet, all consistent with the goals of the U.S. Government.

The more important value of the U.S. contracts may be in preventing others from asserting some alternative form of control. At WSIS, the demands for changes in the governance of the DNS were not based on complaints about the quality of ICANN's technological decisions. These complaints could fairly be summarized as political: nations either called for removal of the U.S.

Government from ICANN management as an expression of anti-American sentiment, or they wanted their political rather than their technical views more effectively included. That would be a problem. It is difficult enough to achieve consensus under the current structure, but affording governments—with their broad range of political interests—greater influence in the mix would undercut the openness, transparency, efficiency, and effectiveness of the current structure, without any compensating benefit to the operation of the DNS.

The second democracy issue is that of the small number of players. Notwithstanding the dispersed and diffuse nature of Internet governance, the system has worked. A fundamental reason is that a relatively small number of people, representing a relatively small number of governments, international organizations, and corporations, participate in all of the work. The process depends not upon strangers from around the world getting together, but on a core group whose members know each other well, doing business together on a regular basis.

The question is whether this small group of active participants in Internet governance could somehow use its influence adversely against the rest of the world. Thus far, that does not seem to have been a significant complaint. Part of the reason is that all participants, particularly businesses, are aware of the constraints imposed by competition policies in the United States, EU, and Japan. So long as there is vigilance about price-fixing and patent abuse, Internet decisions are unlikely to have anticompetitive aspects that would pit users against providers or operators against manufacturers. The key is the continued enforcement of a vigorous set of competition policies.

Reasonably transparent. The decisionmaking processes at ICANN, IETF, the ITU study groups, IEEE, IEC, and ISO have reasonable transparency. Part of that transparency is organizational commitment; part of it is due to the power of the Internet itself, which allows virtual worldwide conversations in real time. There are shortcomings, and some processes are under review. Administrative and management decisions by study group chairs or their equivalents are not as well documented as other parts of the process.

One problem is lack of trust in decisions of the ICANN board, partially because of suspicions about U.S. Government involvement. It is an ongoing challenge for a small group of ICANN participants to convince a worldwide audience that it has taken their views into account to come to a reasonable decision.

Another problem with transparency is the lack of coverage of many issues by the mainstream media. Much of the news about the Internet winds up on specialized Web sites or on the business or technology pages of the newspaper. For issues that have the potential to be highly visible to the general public, that may be the equivalent of little coverage at all.

Generally dynamic, but with some challenges. The Internet has grown rapidly and has scaled remarkably well. However, it has some potential weaknesses. First, the structure does not generally rely on laws or regulations to which states can compel compliance but rather rests largely on agreed standards. Their force comes in the logic of the system: participants must either follow them or lose the Internet's interoperability. The system has worked well, but it depends on the primacy of interoperability and related values. As an alternative, a nation might, for its own political reasons, create its own alternative Internet in order to better filter traffic from the rest of the world. One other potential source of weakness is that many of ICANN's goals are not even subject to contract: implementation of DNSSec and IPv6, for example, depend on the enlightened self-interest and economic judgment of the parties. The system has worked thus far, but there is no guarantee it will do so in the future.

Second, dynamism is also about coping with the negative consequences of growth. Here, Internet governance is somewhat deficient. The lack of a truly worldwide agreement on how to deal with spam or cyber crime is a major problem. The deficiency is not just a process problem; the Internet has brought various cultures and political systems closer together technologically than they are socially.

Third, other issues may soon demand more dynamism. Net neutrality, for example, calls for a decision on whether to institute a worldwide standard for tiered or neutral provision of service. The issue is ripe for decision in the United States and in Europe (even if the decision is to do nothing). Similarly, there is concern about the need for extensive changes to the core Internet structure to accommodate major increases in traffic, such as implementing higher capacity algorithms and more capable routers and other hardware. The problems are apparent, but the responses may not be in place when needed.

Adequately adaptable so far. The greatest current challenges to adapt-ability of the Internet governance system have to do with Internet security, such as increases in spam and more technologically sophisticated denial-of-service and other attacks. The problem centers upon coordination of the law enforcement and regulatory activity that could curtail security problems. Only a minority of nations have ratified the Cybercrime Convention. Antispam legislation is more effective in some places than in others, but in many countries there is no effective control. Until there is greater consensus on these issues, the response to spam and cyber crime will have to focus on technological fixes.

Accountable, somewhat. All of the Internet governance standards organizations described in this chapter operate on a consensus or strong super-majority basis, except for the ICANN board and ISO. In the IETF, it is easier to stop a proposal than to try to hold others accountable for its adoption, but that structure is sufficient to satisfy questions of legitimacy. ICANN's policy development process makes it easy to stymie a contentious policy; however, someone who is unhappy with a decision and is unable to get satisfaction from any of ICANN's internal accountability mechanisms cannot do much to turn out those who voted for it. At the ITU, there is no way to remove a government from participation in the process, but one could simply wait for a change of study group chairs, which takes place every 4 years. The greatest lack of accountability overall may be with regard to spam and cyber crime. There is no way to force governments to work together to reduce threats to Internet security and stability. The system is not presently prepared to cut any of them off, and as a result, they can benefit from the system even as they, or some of their citizens, may pose threats to its smooth and reliable functioning.

Efficient enough—for now. The Internet governance process can seem slow. Decisions can take years to work their way through the various study groups and other decision processes. Judgment about whether the process is efficient in that sense may need to be tempered by the recognition that the decisionmakers are attempting to achieve worldwide consensus.

Efficiency is more of an issue at the level of national governments. First, resolution of security issues has not kept pace with the growth of the problems. Second, with regard to the developing world, the private sector has long complained that many governments have failed to foster "enabling environments" for the Internet—that is, regulatory structures that foster market solutions and competition. Moreover, such environments require education and capacity-building, both of which can take time.

Overall, effective. In sum, Internet governance should be given high marks. Whether one looks at it by scrutinizing each decisionmaking process or by looking at the overall results, the conclusion is positive. Some issues could, nonetheless, raise problems.

First, ICANN must solve its remaining transparency problems, and it must also continue to perform well.

Second, the U.S. Government must work to reduce the international tension surrounding its ICANN contracts, either by convincing the world that the current arrangement, whatever its deficiencies, is better than any alternative, or by terminating its agreements, if it can continue to protect ICANN from less benign influence.

Third, all of the collective decisionmaking bodies must continue to cooperate and collaborate. Attempts by the ITU to take over subject areas now dealt with by ICANN or IETF could be disruptive.

Fourth, national governments and the EU must continue to scrutinize all collective decisionmaking closely to ensure that competition policies are enforced and that Internet governance decisions promote fair competition and a level playing field. There will inevitably be more Internet-related enterprises as growth continues in Asia, Latin America, and Africa. Those governments must be encouraged to give priority to competition over protection.

Fifth, the key players, who are few in number, must continue to focus on the overall good of the Internet. Any attempts to gain undue advantage for a few would risk destroying support for systems that are now private sector–dominated.

Sixth, there must be much more international dialogue on spam and cyber crime. In particular, civil society and the private sector must take more of a lead in developing a consensus on what needs to be controlled and how to control it.

Finally, governments, business, and civil society should be encouraged to recognize that the Internet and its governance rely on widespread acceptance of the values of deregulation, private enterprise, free markets, free speech, and participatory democracy. Participatory democracy must constantly be reconciled with more vertical structures: the pledge of broad participation at ICANN, for example, cannot be allowed to destroy the representative structure that makes decisions possible. If the U.S. Government determines that it is time to terminate the ICANN contracts, it is going to have to rely on these values to create whatever environment will make it feel comfortable that ICANN can continue to function in the way it intended when ICANN was first created.

The dominance of the United States, and the U.S. Government in particular, is likely to decline, whether or not the Government gives up its ICANN contracts. It should worry about that decline only if it believes that without its current influence, the Internet's decisionmaking would no longer support the fundamental U.S. goals of a secure, stable, and competitive system. In the short term, that question is likely to lead to a discussion of the ICANN contracts; eventually, it leads to longer term questions about the configuration of a mature Internet governance structure. The best way for the U.S. Government to promote one that serves its interests is to assure that none of the problems enumerated above come about.

The challenge to those who do not like the status quo is to convince people there is a better alternative. At present, those who want change can make no persuasive case that they could do better. As awkward as aspects of the current system are, it has embraced the powerful values of democracy, the free market, free speech, and private enterprise, and it has delivered a powerful, inexpensive tool for economic, social, and political life.

CHAPTER 22

International Law and Information Operations

Thomas C. Wingfield

FUTURE WARS will feature information operations with novel weapons, techniques, and targets. Such information operations and cyber attacks will raise unprecedented legal questions to discriminate the lawfully compliant from the negligent, reckless, or intentionally maleficent.

The multiple denial-of-service attacks carried out against Estonia in April and May 2007 provide a rich fact pattern to test the emerging law of information conflict. Three legal issues proved particularly problematic. First, it may be very difficult to determine what person, organization, or country is ultimately responsible for any given cyber intrusion. Computer forensics may quickly and reliably identify the last server used in a multiserver attack, but the first server, its operator, and owner may never be known. Second, it is difficult to measure, or even properly characterize, the damage done in a cyber attack. In Estonia, the immediate damage to specific systems was fairly limited and rarely rose above the level of inconvenience. The second-order effects, however—fear, loss of confidence in banking and communications systems, and a national awareness of vulnerability—could lead to even more enduring negative consequences than a limited military incursion. Third, Estonian, Russian, and American authorities demonstrated, by their comments, an uncertain grasp of the applicable rules of law, variously describing the Estonian attacks as criminal activity, covert operations, or military actions. Each of these would implicate different legal regimes and would demand widely divergent responses. Thus, there is a need for greater clarity and certainty with respect to the principles of law that apply in cyber conflict. That is the subject of this chapter.

A first distinction is between peacetime (*jus ad bellum*) standards regulating the resort to force and wartime (*jus in bello*) principles governing conduct in war. These two rule sets are quite different, and specific terms have different definitions under the peacetime and wartime regimes; deciding which of the two rule sets to apply is the first task of attorneys advising decisionmakers in nations under attack.

Jus ad Bellum: Standards Governing the Resort to Force

The first question in applying peacetime standards is to determine whether an information operation or cyber attack rises to the level of a "use of force" prohibited under international law. Ample precedent exists for answers where attacks involve kinetic means such as bombs and bullets, but the novelty of information operations, with its innovative digital weapons, modes of attack, and target lists, is more problematic.

Until recently, there were two broad schools of thought. The common sense approach postulated, quite reasonably, that the international legal regime was in place to keep operations short of war from escalating into full-blown wars, and to identify war-level activities as soon as possible so as to attach the appropriate legal protections to the participants. Under this premise, the simplest and most sensible approach to applying the kinetic legal regime to the digital battlefield was to disregard the means of attack and concentrate solely on the quantum of damage done. It should be immaterial whether a refinery was destroyed by a 2,000-pound bomb or by a line of malicious code in its pressure regulation subroutine; what did matter was the size of the hole left in the ground after the attack.

This quantitative approach had the benefit of simplicity, clarity, and logic, but it is inconsistent with the prevailing structure of international law, the United Nations (UN) Charter paradigm. Article 2, paragraph 4 of the UN Charter states, "All Members shall refrain in their international relations *from the threat or use of force* against the territorial integrity or political independence of any state, or in any other manner inconsistent with the Purposes of the United Nations."[1]

Thus, a second approach followed the logic of the charter's framers to its literal conclusion: that anything other than an armed attack—something like the tanks-across-the-border threat the charter was written to address—was not prohibited by international law.[2] The quantity of force was less important than the quality of force: military coercion was discouraged, with a very low threshold for prohibited activity, while diplomatic, economic, or political coercion would not be discouraged by the UN Charter, because they amount to a peaceful alternative to war. This approach had the advantage of academic consistency and consonance with mainstream international legal thinking. Unfortunately, as a half-century-old legal theory, it failed to take into account the newly destructive capacities of what had once been mere messages and signals.

Michael Schmitt noted that "as the nature of a hostile act becomes less determinative of its consequences, current notions of 'lawful' coercive behavior by states, and the appropriate responses thereto, are likely to evolve accordingly."[3] Schmitt examined why the framers of the UN Charter chose to characterize each type of coercion as they did:

> In the current normative scheme the consequences of an act are often less important than its nature. For instance, a devastating economic embargo is not a "use of force" or an "armed attack" justifying forcible self-defense, even though the embargo may result in enormous suffering. On the other hand, a relatively minor, armed incursion across a border is both a use of force and an armed attack. This contrary result derives from the law's use of "acts" as cognitive shorthand for what really matters—consequences. Acts are more easily expressed (to "use force" versus to cause a certain quantum and quality of harm) and more easily discerned than an effects-based standard, based on the harm suffered. This cognitive shorthand does not work well in the age of information operations because information attacks, albeit potentially disastrous, may be physically imperceptible.[4]

Schmitt suggested, instead, applying a quantitative scale to seven factors that he specified in order to locate any given operation along a spectrum between prohibited and permitted. Schmitt thus translated the qualitative charter paradigm into its quantitative components, providing a useful framework for scholars and practitioners to organize analysis.

Schmitt's brief description of the importance or distinctiveness of each of the seven factors is fleshed out below with some additional questions that would satisfy the requirements of the factor. Three qualitative answers to each question range between relatively clear cases at each qualitative extreme, with a central area of uncertainty. Results for these seven factors are then averaged for an overall score to give an indication of an operation's qualitative status as a use of force under international law. Schmitt's work thus offers a structure for discussion of the Estonia case.

Severity

According to Schmitt, "Armed attacks threaten physical injury or destruction of property to a much greater extent than other forms of coercion. Physical well-being usually occupies the most basic level of the human hierarchy of need."[5] Results of attacks might be categorized by:

- people killed; severe property damage
- people injured; moderate property damage
- people unaffected; no discernible property damage.

In other words, one must ask: How many people were killed? How large an area was attacked (scope)? How much damage was done within this area (intensity)?

Immediacy

Schmitt writes, "The negative consequences of armed coercion, or threat there-of, usually occur with great immediacy, while those of other forms of coercion develop more slowly. Thus, the opportunity for the target state or the international community to seek peaceful accommodation is hampered in the former case."[6] One might assess immediacy as:

- seconds to minutes
- hours to days
- weeks to months.

In other words, what was the duration of the action? How soon were its effects felt? How long until its effects abate?

Directness

Schmitt's third criterion is directness: "The consequences of armed coercion are more directly tied to the *actus reus* [culpable act] than in other forms of coercion, which often depend on numerous contributory factors to operate. Thus, the prohibition on force precludes negative consequences with greater certainty."[7] Results could range as follows:

- action sole cause of result
- action identifiable as one cause of result, and to an indefinite degree
- action played no identifiable role in result.

Another way to ask the question is: Was the action distinguishable from parallel or competing actions? Was the action the proximate cause of the effects?

Invasiveness

Schmitt next assesses the invasiveness of an attack:

> In armed coercion, the act causing the harm usually crosses into the target state, whereas in economic warfare the acts generally occur beyond

the target's borders. As a result, even though armed and economic acts may have roughly similar consequences, the former represents a greater intrusion on the rights of the target state and, therefore, is more likely to disrupt international stability.[8]

Thus, one could categorize operations as:

- border physically crossed; action has point locus
- border electronically crossed; action occurs over diffuse area
- border not crossed; action has no identifiable locus in target country.

Did the action involve physically crossing the target country's borders? Was the locus of the action within the target country?

Measurability

A fifth standard is measurability:

> While the consequences of armed coercion are usually easy to ascertain (e.g., a certain level of destruction), the actual negative consequences of other forms of coercion are harder to measure. This fact renders the appropriateness of community condemnation, and the degree of vehemence contained therein, less suspect in the case of armed force.[9]

Assessing measurability means putting operations into one of these categories:

- effects can be quantified immediately by traditional means (such as bomb damage assessment) with high degree of certainty
- effects can be estimated by rough order of magnitude with moderate certainty
- effects cannot be separated from those of other actions; overall certainty is low.

One might, therefore, ask how the effects of the action could be quantified, whether the effects of the action are distinct from the results of parallel or competing actions, and what the level of certainty was.

Presumptive Legitimacy

Next is the question of presumptive legitimacy:

> In most cases, whether under domestic or international law, the application of violence is deemed illegitimate absent some specific exception such as

self-defense. The cognitive approach is prohibitory. By contrast, most other forms of coercion—again in the domestic and international sphere—are presumptively lawful, absent a prohibition to the contrary. The cognitive approach is permissive. Thus, the consequences of armed coercion are presumptively impermissible, whereas those of other coercive acts are not (as a very generalized rule).[10]

Presumptive legitimacy might be assessed as follows:

- action accomplished by means of kinetic attack
- action accomplished in cyberspace but manifested by a "smoking hole" in physical space
- action accomplished in cyberspace and effects not apparent in physical world.

Presumptive legitimacy thus depends on whether this type of action has achieved customary acceptance within the international community and whether the means are qualitatively similar to others presumed legitimate under international law.

Responsibility

Finally, Schmitt would examine the factor of responsibility:

> Armed coercion is the exclusive province of states; only they may generally engage in uses of force across borders, and in most cases only they have the ability to do so with any meaningful impact. By contrast, non-governmental entities are often capable of engaging in other forms of coercion (propaganda, boycotts, etc.). Therefore with armed coercion the likelihood of blurring the relative responsibility of the State, a traditional object of international prescription, and private entities, usually only the object of international administration, narrows. In sum, the consequences of armed coercion are more susceptible to being charged to the State actor than in the case of other forms of coercion.[11]

One may ask whether:

- responsibility for action is acknowledged by acting state; degree of involvement large
- target state government is aware of acting state's responsibility; public role unacknowledged; degree of involvement low
- action unattributable to acting state; degree of involvement low.

Is the action directly or indirectly attributable to the acting state? But for the acting state's sake, would the action have occurred?

Overall Analysis

Have enough of the qualities of a use of force been identified to characterize the information operation as a use of force that is prohibited under Article 2(4) of the UN Charter; as arguably a use of force or not; or as certainly not a use of force under Article 2(4)? These issues are illustrated by a recent case.

The Estonia Cyber Attack: A Prohibited "Use of Force" under International Law?

Under these criteria, did the cyber intrusions of April–May 2007 rise to the level of a use of force? Despite the widespread and continuing nature of the cyber attacks in Estonia, it appears that no one was killed or even wounded, nor was any tangible property destroyed, although a great deal of intangible property was lost. Assuming that economic value in euros or dollars is a suitable means of comparing intangible and tangible property losses, the severity of the attack appears to be in the moderate range of Schmitt's severity scale.

The speed with which the attack developed, beginning precisely at the midnight separating May 8 (the date on which Western Europe and the United States celebrate the end of World War II in Europe) from May 9 (the date celebrated by Russia), shows high levels of immediacy for the onset of the attacks. It appears that only minutes, perhaps just seconds, passed between the initiation of the cyber attacks and their culmination against their targets. Furthermore, the attacks were intensified and moderated at least three times in response to Estonian reactions, demonstrating a very brief time lag between offensive tactical decisionmaking and the resulting effect on the targets. Immediacy, then, appears to be in the high range.

The directness of the attacks is difficult to characterize. In such denial-of-service attacks, anywhere from several hundred thousand to several million individually harmless requests for access combine to overwhelm a system. If the widely distributed botnets that enable such attacks are themselves controlled by a single actor, then it is appropriate to characterize that actor's initiation of the attack as the single cause.[12] The damage done to the targeted banks, newspapers, government offices, or public utilities is the direct effect of this cause. Since a relatively small number of actors affected a relatively small number of large, institutional systems, the directness of the attack would be considered moderate.

Invasiveness may be characterized as the physical crossing of a border, which in this case was low, or as the focusing of attacks inside the territory of a particular nation, which in this case was high. Although no identifiable forces violated Estonia's border, the exclusive locus of the attacks was in Estonia: its newspaper Web sites were defaced, its large banks were shut down, and its national emergency telephone system was interfered with for several hours. On balance, the invasiveness of the attack was moderate.

The measurability of the attacks was likewise difficult to evaluate. Although there were several large, clearly identifiable targets, and although many of these targets suffered quantifiable damage in revenue lost, there is a great uncertainty in quantifying the resulting loss of confidence in the integrity of commercial systems and the reliability of public infrastructures. As in terror attacks, the immediate target is of less value to the aggressor than the fear instilled in the wider population. Paradoxically, the confident, even defiant, response by the Estonian government, and the prompt support lent by the North Atlantic Treaty Organization and the European Union, may have left Estonia in a stronger technical, political, and moral position after the attacks than before. The challenge of measuring the damage done by cyber attacks is less a matter of determining the degree of damage than of deciding what to measure. Overall, then, the measurability of theses attacks was low.

The presumptive legitimacy of the Estonian attacks was low. While targets may have been selected with an eye toward reminding Estonia of Russia's vastly greater power, the attacks themselves were not of such size or complexity that they could only have been mounted by a nation-state. Investigators identified several botnets used in the attacks, and these were available for hire by any government, corporation, organized crime ring, political group, or even individual with adequate means to employ them. The wide availability of this means of attack, and the common nature of these means, results in a low presumptive legitimacy rating.

Finally, the element of responsibility is low. It may be that the Russian government participated in, or even directed, the attacks, but it did not claim responsibility for them. Such a claim is a prime discriminator between military and nonmilitary actions. The Russian government was either uninvolved or chose to hide its role in the attacks. In either case, an immediate or emphatic claim of national responsibility was absent.

The overall picture, then, is one factor in the high range (immediacy), three factors in the moderate range (severity, directness, and invasiveness), and three factors in the low range (measurability, presumptive legitimacy, and responsibility). This suggests that the attacks were quantitatively damaging enough, or qualitatively "military" enough, to be properly characterized under international law as uses of force.

There are two caveats to this conclusion. First, this analysis was performed on the attacks of April–May 2007 and not on any larger campaign by Russia against Estonia. Enlarging the scope of the analysis could identify a strategic use of force that comprised multiple elements that were, individually, below that threshold. Second, such actions in cyberspace, regardless of their initiator, are clearly unlawful because of their end result—destruction of property (whether tangible or intangible) or blocking access to emergency services, to give only two examples, would be illegal based on Estonian, U.S., or Russian law, regardless of the instrumentality employed. They also are potentially threatening to international peace and security, and, to the extent committed or permitted by a state, they are a violation of the UN Charter. Although they do not rise to the level of a use of force, this does not render them permissible; it merely requires that the initial response be other than military. Whether that response takes the form of a lawsuit, an arrest, a diplomatic offensive, or a covert operation is the choice of the victim state.

Jus in Bello: International Law on the Conduct of War

The novelty of many information operations—their targets, means, even "shooters"—has led to a great deal of confusion about what kind of conduct is lawful under the rules of war. It took many centuries to develop the certainty applicable to kinetic operations; as weapons evolved, their effects became different in degree but not kind. Certain information operations still fit this paradigm: the kinetic "kill" of a radio transmitter or the destruction by a special operations team of a computer complex would involve no new intellectual challenges. However, civilian contractors emplacing and then triggering a trojan horse in another country's governmental mainframe computer would raise a host of new issues: the action's character as mere espionage or the first stage of a full-blown military action, the contractors' status as combatants or civilians accompanying the military or purely private actors, and the degree of attributability of the contractors' actions to the contracting government, to name just a few.

To the extent these actions are properly characterized as military operations, traditional principles of the law of armed conflict apply: belligerents must distinguish between combatants and noncombatants, must avoid targeting civilians and civilian property, and must take all reasonable precautions against injuring civilians or damaging their property in the course of striking military targets. The *Commander's Handbook on the Law of Naval Operations* captures this rule as three interrelated proscriptions: "1. The right of belligerents to adopt means of injuring the enemy is not unlimited. 2. It is prohibited to launch attacks against the civilian population as such. 3. Distinctions must be made between combatants and noncombatants, to the effect that noncombatants be spared as much as possible."[13] The authoritative articulation of this principle under international law is found in the Geneva Conventions: "In order to ensure respect for and protection of the civilian population and between civilian objects, the

Parties to the conflict shall at all times distinguish between the civilian population and combatants and civilian objects and military objectives and accordingly shall direct their operations only against military objectives."[14]

In war, combatants and other military objectives are, under these rules, lawful targets. Combatants are defined as:

> those persons who have the right under international law to participate directly in armed conflict during hostilities . . . includ[ing] all members of the regularly organized armed forces of a party to a conflict . . . [as well as] irregular forces who are under responsible command and subject to military discipline, carry their arms openly, and otherwise distinguish themselves clearly from the civilian population.[15]

However, "medical personnel, chaplains, civil defense personnel, and members of the armed forces who have acquired civil defense status" are not counted as combatants.[16]

Military objectives that may lawfully be attacked include:

> Combatants and those objects which, by their nature, location, purpose, or use, effectively contribute to the enemy's warfighting or war sustaining capability and whose total or partial destruction, capture, or neutralization would constitute a definite military advantage to the attacker under the circumstances.[17]

Noncombatants and civilian objects are unlawful targets:

> The term noncombatants may, however, also embrace certain categories of persons who, although members of or accompanying the armed forces, enjoy special protected status, such as medical officers, corpsmen, chaplains, technical (i.e., contractor) representatives, and civilian war correspondents. . . . The term is also applied to armed forces personnel who are unable to engage in combat because of wounds, sickness, shipwreck, or capture.[18]

Civilian objects that are not lawful targets include "all civilian property and activities other than those used to support or sustain the enemy's warfighting capability." Specifically, for example, it is unlawful to destroy "food, crops, livestock, drinking water, and *other objects indispensable to the survival of the civilian population*, for the specific purpose of denying the civilian population of their use."[19]

Weapons that cannot be used in such a way as to discriminate between lawful and unlawful targets are themselves unlawful, under the doctrine of indiscriminate effect.[20] As this prohibition is explained by the *Commander's Handbook on the Law of Naval Operations*, "any weapon may be set to an unlawful purpose when it is directed against noncombatants and other protected persons and property."[21]

Although the concept of indiscriminate effect and the distinction between the armed forces and the civilian populace are clear in theory, their application to real-world targeting issues can become hazy and complex. This is clearly true in the world of information operations, where "shooters" rarely "see" their targets, where interconnected, dual-use infrastructures support civilian customers and military users, and where unintentional secondary and tertiary effects can cause results unforeseeable, or at least unforeseen, by the attacker. Separating military targets from civilian sites presents a special problem in intelligence collection, legal analysis, and operational execution.

The increasing interconnectedness of information systems vital to a nation's critical infrastructure, and the special reliance placed by developing countries on the dual use of such systems, renders discrimination far more complex in cyberspace than in physical space. There are two keys to following the prescriptions of international law. First, an attacker must gather finely sifted intelligence so that competent decisions can be made regarding which computers or, indeed, which programs within computers, are lawful targets.

Second, information weapons sufficiently precise to attack specifically selected cybernetic targets must be developed. While a nondiscriminating approach would remain perfectly lawful for an attack against a standalone system, a more discriminating attack would have to be mounted against a system of systems, if the attacker wishes to comply with international law and prevent unanticipated secondary and tertiary consequences far more destructive than the primary attack.

The concept of military necessity, more quantitative than qualitative, limits the force that may lawfully be used: "Only that degree and kind of force, not otherwise prohibited by the law of armed conflict, required for the partial or complete submission of the enemy with a minimum expenditure of time, life, and physical resources may be applied."[22]

Excessive force beyond that required to accomplish a lawful mission is unlawful. In addition, infliction of unnecessary suffering is prohibited; this proscription was "first applied very narrowly, to poisons, burning agents, or bullets of a certain size, shape, or composition."[23] However, approaches to limiting unnecessary suffering have become more broadly categorical.[24]

Just as the principle of necessity prohibits the use of excess force against combatants, the complementary principal of proportionality limits the effects of an attack against noncombatants.[25] While the principle of discrimination prohibits attacks against civilians per se, "it is not unlawful to cause incidental injury to civilians, or collateral damage to civilian objects, during an attack upon a legitimate military target."[26] The principle of proportionality, however, prohibits those attacks that "may be expected to cause incidental loss of civilian life, injury to civilians, damage to civilian objects, or a combination thereof, which would be excessive in relation to the concrete and direct military advantage anticipated."[27]

This prohibition is expressed as a balancing test between the anticipated "concrete and direct" military advantage on one hand, and the expected civilian losses on the other.[28] As the value of a potential target increases, so does the level of permissible collateral damage. A corollary of this principle, stated in article 57 of protocol I of the Geneva Protocols, is that "commanders must take all reasonable precautions, taking into account military and humanitarian considerations, to keep civilian casualties and damage to the minimum consistent with mission accomplishment and the security of the force."[29]

These decisions must be based on an "honest and reasonable estimate of the facts,"[30] available at the time the decision is made. The International Committee of the Red Cross (ICRC) explicates the standard as:

[T]he identification of the objective, particularly when it is located at a great distance, should be carried out with great care. Admittedly, those who plan or decide upon such an attack will base their decision on information given them, and they cannot be expected to have personal knowledge of the objective to be attacked and of its exact nature. However, this does not detract from their responsibility, and in case of doubt, even if there is only a slight doubt, they must call for additional information and if need be give orders for further reconnaissance. . . . The evaluation of the information obtained must include a serious check of its accuracy.[31]

A commander must consider whether to adopt an alternative method of attack, if reasonably available, to reduce civilian casualties and damage.[32]

Schmitt cites the three ways in which proportionality is frequently violated: a lack of full knowledge as to what is being hit; the inability to surgically craft the amount of force being applied to the target; and the inability to ensure the weapon strikes precisely the right point.[33] The calibration of force has been almost completely refined with modern technology, and the ability to steer toward a selected target is scarcely less advanced. The lack of complete intelligence, however, has been and will remain a problem. From the al Amariyah bunker in Baghdad to the Chinese embassy in Belgrade, examples abound of high-technology weapons being guided with flawless precision to an inappropriate target.

These issues have even greater application in cyberspace, where it may be extremely difficult to distinguish the code in a computer that governs delivery of electrical power to an early warning radar (which may be a lawful target of a cyber attack) from the code that controls power to a hospital intensive care unit. The risk of unintended consequences complicates the targeting picture. In cyberspace, the principle of proportionality may call for a fidelity and granularity of intelligence collection and analysis beyond current demonstrated capabilities, and may also call for modeling and simulation of attacks to give the commander at least minimal assurances that the attack will hit the intended target and not produce unlawful collateral damage.

Ruses and Treachery

The traditions of chivalry have informed the development of the principles of discrimination, necessity, and proportionality, applying to such issues as the protections accorded noncombatants and the amount of damage that may be done in "just" pursuit of a military objective. The chivalric code remains most unchanged in the distinction between lawful ruses and unlawful or "treacherous" perfidy, and these distinctions are particularly applicable to understanding what information operations are lawful in war.

Schmitt describes the standard: treachery is "a breach of confidence by an assailant." However, he points out:

> [O]ne must be careful not to define treachery too broadly. Use of stealth or trickery, for instance, is not precluded, and will not render an otherwise lawful killing [unlawful]. . . . Treachery exists only when the victim possessed an affirmative reason to trust the assailant. . . . [Lawful] ruses are planned to mislead the enemy, for example, by causing him to become reckless or choose a particular course of action. By contrast, [unlawful] perfidy involves an act designed to convince the enemy that the actor is entitled to protected status under the law of war, with the intent of betraying that confidence. Treachery, as construed by early scholars, is thus broader than the concept of perfidy; nevertheless, the same basic criteria that are used to distinguish lawful ruses from unlawful ruses can be applied to determinations of treachery.[34]

The criteria for discriminating lawful ruses from unlawful perfidy are essential to understanding what types of information operations are lawful or unlawful. The modern military effort involves attempts to limit the physical violence of war by affecting the analysis and options of the opposing commander, for example, by persuading an opponent that it is surrounded, or that the arrival of a superior force is imminent when it is not. These are practically a synonym for "ruses of war." Precisely what in the realm of information operations is permissible and what is not, given the almost unlimited technical capabilities on the horizon, may be the principal legal question of operational military lawyers in the next century.

These criteria arise out of the European chivalric system, which was based on a complex network of personal obligations, especially the trustworthiness of knights, but it was loyalty of a precisely defined form. "Where no prior agreement was involved . . . surprise and guile might be considered perfectly legitimate. Low cunning was not itself dishonorable; what brought shame was perjury of an oath promising to abstain from certain acts."[35] For example, when "a party of armed knights gained entrance to a walled town by declaring themselves allies and then proceeded to slaughter the defenders, chivalry evidently was not violated, no oath having been made to the burghers."[36]

This doctrine slowly evolved from the end of the Middle Ages to the beginning of the modern era. Balthazar Ayala, a 16th-century commentator, proposed that a general duty to avoid treachery existed, whether or not a specific understanding existed between aggressor and defender. The key for Ayala was a distinction between permissible "trickery," similar to our understanding ruses of war, and impermissible "frauds and snares."[37]

Alberico Gentili, in the early 17th century, extended the concept of treachery to include not just those who took advantage of a reasonably placed trust in safety, but also those who encouraged or commissioned violations of that trust.[38] His contemporary, Hugo Grotius, removed the presumption of legality for acts perpetrated by the "just" party in a conflict, eliminating an excuse for atrocious behavior by those claiming their cause of war was just.[39] Later commentators, such as Vattel and Lieber, would sharpen and refine this doctrine, but Grotius' analysis of the distinction between ruses of war and perfidy is virtually indistinguishable from the modern standard. That standard is codified in article 37 of protocol I of the Geneva Conventions:

> It is prohibited to kill, injure or capture an adversary by resort to perfidy. Acts inviting the confidence of an adversary to lead him to believe he is entitled to, or is obligated to accord, protection under the rules of international law applicable in armed conflict, with intent to betray that confidence, shall constitute perfidy.[40]

Stratagem is a term encompassing both ruses of war and perfidy; it is addressed by the three principal U.S. reference manuals on the operational aspects of the law of war.[41] The U.S. Army manual states that among permitted stratagems are "ruses of war and the employment of measures necessary for obtaining information about the enemy and the country are considered permissible."[42] Good faith is required in all dealings with the enemy, except those that the enemy can reasonably foresee and against which it can reasonably defend.[43]

This suggests that a key question for information operations is the breadth of the measures against which the enemy is expected to protect himself. If the area is broadly drawn, defining one such area as to "protect all computer systems from all intrusion," then the enemy is on constructive notice against almost any conceivable computer network attack. If, however, one defines the duty to protect as applying to more narrowly defined systems or against more narrowly defined techniques, then this aspiration toward good faith may be violated.

For example, suppose a nation sought to conduct psychological operations, perhaps including false statements alleging an enemy dictator's scandalous personal conduct, and, using a new technology, inserted this information into the Cable Network News data stream reaching every TV set in the enemy country.[44] If a broad definition of *psychological operations* is accepted, then any psychological operation would be one against which the enemy could be expected to defend itself. If a narrow definition is chosen, perhaps limited to known technologies, then the duty of good faith would be violated because the enemy would not be protecting his civilian television system from "attack." On the other hand, where such targets and techniques were widely discussed in the open press, one could argue that the enemy was on constructive notice to protect any system now susceptible to attack. This type of notice would satisfy the rule's requirement for good faith in these operations.

U.S. Army Field Manual 27–10, *The Law of Land Warfare*, addresses treachery and perfidy: "Ruses of war are legitimate so long as they do not involve treachery or perfidy on the part of the belligerent resorting to them. They are, however, forbidden if they contravene any generally accepted rule."[45] The paragraph closes with the reason behind the rule: "Treacherous or perfidious conduct in war is forbidden because it destroys the basis for a restoration of peace short of the complete annihilation of one belligerent by the other."[46] This explanation is consistent with the article 37 definition from protocol I of the Geneva Conventions, prohibiting killing, injuring, or capturing an adversary "by resort to perfidy."

The U.S. Army manual provides a long list of permissible ruses, including: "surprises, ambushes, feigning attacks, retreats, or flights, simulating quiet and inactivity, use of small forces to simulate large units, transmitting false or misleading radio or telephone messages, [and] deception of the enemy by bogus orders purporting to have been issued by the enemy commander."[47] The Navy and Air Force manuals have similar lists.[48] On the Air Force list, the most important for the law of information conflict is the "imitation of enemy signals," a category under which many information operations could be accurately placed. The Air Force manual explains that:

> no objection can be made to the use by friendly forces of the signals or codes of the adversary. The signals or codes used by enemy aircraft or by enemy ground installations in contact with their aircraft may properly be

employed by friendly forces to deceive or mislead an adversary. However, misuse of distress signals or distinctive signals internationally recognized as reserved for the exclusive use of medical aircraft would be perfidious.[49]

Camouflage is sometimes lawful, including disguising a military objective as a civilian object. The important distinction, for the purposes of likenesses that may be appropriated for ruses of war, is between protected symbols, discussed below, and ordinary civilian objects. It can be unlawful to use identifying devices improperly.[50] The Army manual says that: "[I]t is especially forbidden to make improper use of a flag of truce, of the national flag, or of the military insignia and uniform of the enemy, as well as the distinctive badges of the Geneva Convention."[51] These insignia are protected because they directly induce the reliance of the enemy, and endanger those who legitimately rely on such symbols for protection.[52] The Army manual prohibits misuse of flags of truce,[53] of Geneva Convention symbols, such as the emblem of the Red Cross,[54] and of national flags, insignia, and uniforms.[55] The rationale is to avoid dilution of the absolute nature of these symbols, reinforcing the legal protections they bestow and the legal obligations they exact. The use of these protected symbols in information operations would be included in the general prohibition.

It has been argued that "analogy strongly weighs against sending a logic bomb disguised as e-mail from the International Committee of the Red Cross (ICRC) or even from Microsoft Software Support—where such a message might be permissible without perfidious labels."[56] However, this statement incorrectly equates two kinds of information attacks. Such a message purporting to be the ICRC is clearly perfidious, in that it delivers a weapon under the protection of the Red Cross symbol—an action analogous to delivering a car bomb in an ambulance. The second, however, is clearly lawful, in that Microsoft Corporation enjoys no protected status under international law: a message from Microsoft would be no different from a message from any other firm with which a belligerent is doing business, although it might violate national laws or treaties intended to limit spam, viruses, and the like. The analogy here would be a commando team emplacing a bomb in enemy headquarters while disguised in the coveralls of a local plumbing company.

Intelligence operations in wartime—whether information-gathering (espionage) or destruction of property (sabotage)—are governed by two legal principles. One defines who, under international law, is a spy:

A spy is someone who, while in territory under enemy control or the zone of operations of a belligerent force, seeks to obtain information while operating under a false claim of noncombatant or friendly forces status with the intention of passing that information to an opposing belligerent.

The definition applies to "members of the armed forces who penetrate enemy-held territory in civilian attire or enemy uniform to collect intelligence," but "personnel conducting reconnaissance missions behind enemy lines while properly uniformed are not spies;" nor are "crewmembers of warships and military aircraft engaged in intelligence collection missions in enemy waters or airspace. . . . unless the ship or aircraft displays false civilian, neutral, or enemy markings."[57]

There is no clear consensus on the application of the term "zone of operations of a belligerent force" to cyberspace. Until clearly distinguishable norms arise, it is probably best to apply, as closely as possible, the standards of the physical world by analogy.

The second legal principle regulates treatment of a captured spy. Cyber "entries" into and "exits" from the enemy country were not contemplated in the formulation of this rule of law and do not appear to provide the basis for liability. However, not all information operations are mounted from outside enemy borders, and those that require physical entry to enemy territory, and that could be characterized as intelligence operations, will expose the operator to traditional liability.

In summary, whatever use is made of the enemy commander's information environment, the techniques employed must resemble or be analogous to the Army list of permissible ruses, or the Navy or Air Force equivalents. Although there are exceptions due to specific circumstances, the general rule is that military forces may masquerade as civilians or civilian objects until engaging in hostilities, but they may not use protected symbols (such as the Red Cross or the UN flag) in any way that would induce the enemy's detrimental reliance or dilute the effect of those symbols and the safety of those depending on their protection.

Conclusion

A review of the international law governing information operations leads to several provisional conclusions. First, it is imperative to actually identify the governing body of law. There are three overlapping legal regimes—law enforcement, intelligence collection, and military operations—that may apply to any given activity in cyberspace. Each of these legal regimes operates at multiple levels: in addition to international law (treaty and customary), there is the domestic law of the United States (Federal and state), that of the target nation, and that of any intermediate nation through which an operation is routed. This creates a Rubik's Cube of potential liability that must be solved at the threshold of any information operation.

Second, determining the military nature of an information operation is crucial to fashioning an appropriate response. Here, the seven factors of the Schmitt analysis (severity, immediacy, directness, invasiveness, measurability, presumptive legitimacy, and responsibility) offer a principled means of determining if an intrusion rises to the level of a "use of force" or an "armed attack" under international law, or if it is merely a criminal act.

Third, if an information operation is sufficiently destructive to be considered an armed attack, then the response must be guided by the four customary principles of the law of armed conflict: discrimination, necessity, proportionality, and chivalry. These principles, while formulated for application in the kinetic world, apply equally well to the results of information operations. They provide clarity for combatants wishing to mount a robust defense without themselves becoming war criminals.

These conclusions are, in reality, merely points of departure for even more thorough analyses in the years ahead. As new weapons and tactics are developed, as new organizations are designed and created, and as an increasingly professional corps of information operators are recruited and trained, clarity on these legal issues will provide the greatest operating space and the largest number of options for military commanders and political decisionmakers in the future.

CHAPTER 23

Cyberpower and Critical Infrastructure Protection: A Critical Assessment of Federal Efforts

*John A. McCarthy with Chris Burrow,
Maeve Dion, and Olivia Pacheco*

IN THIS CHAPTER, we examine the cyber infrastructure of the United States, which has become vital to national defense infrastructures, the U.S. Government, and the global economy. Due to the increased speed and efficiency of cyber systems and networks, military supply and logistics chains have been automated; government emergency services rely increasingly on electronic processes; and critical business services have migrated to technology that depends on Internet protocol.

These developments have created the potential for a catastrophic cyber incident on a scale comparable to Hurricane Katrina in 2005. As a result of the increasing pervasiveness of cyber and communications technology, many critical pieces of national infrastructure now rely on complex, interconnected cyber systems. An accident, attack, or natural disaster could impact infrastructure that is critical to public safety, national security, or economic security. Such an incident could be devastating to the lives of Americans or to the security of the Nation itself. Although the exact type or likelihood of catastrophic cyber incidents is unknown, the consensus is that the potential results of such incidents could be dire. Thus, prevention and preparedness efforts, response procedures, and recovery plans are required.

Unfortunately, the Federal Government has displayed irresolute and inconsistent leadership regarding cyber critical infrastructure protection. Much of its effort has been directed at general outreach and awareness activities, rather than at developing robust and comprehensive prevention, response, and reconstitution programs for attacks against critical cyber systems. Federal policy has neither clearly defined factors that would comprise a cyber incident of national significance nor specified triggers and thresholds for action during an emergency. Vague policies have resulted in little operational guidance for Federal response entities if such an event were to occur. The existing guidance does not clearly delineate roles and responsibilities for stakeholders in the Federal Government or provide expectations for private sector entities. In addition, the Government has shifted its focus and resources away from issues critical to national security, such as a cyber attack with catastrophic consequences, and toward criminal and consumer protection issues, such as identity theft and data breaches. In this chapter, we give some historical background, detail the reasons for our conclusions, and provide some recommendations.

Background of Critical Infrastructure Protection

During the two World Wars, the United States instituted civil defense programs that related directly to the fear of domestic invasion by the nation-state enemy being fought abroad. The focus was primarily on preventing a physical attack by conventional means. Today's concept of critical infrastructure protection (CIP) similarly reflects the fear of attacks by foreign enemies against domestic assets, but it incorporates threats from native saboteurs and from nature. CIP also integrates a new threat spectrum, which includes attacking through complex cyber systems.

The first major policy document on CIP was the 1997 report of the President's Commission on Critical Infrastructure Protection (PCCIP).[1] Since then, numerous CIP offices have been established within Federal, state, and local governments, as well as within research institutions.

There have also been various laws and regulations relating to CIP. In 1998, Presidential Decision Directive 63 (PDD 63) identified principles for protecting the United States from cascading disruptions that could result from the interdependence of critical infrastructures, and for guarding against attacks on our information technology.[2] In addition, PDD 63 called for a National Infrastructure Assurance Plan, but such a plan was not created until 8 years later, in 2006.[3]

After the terrorist attacks of September 11, 2001, Congress passed the USA PATRIOT Act. In this legislation, Congress defined *critical infrastructure* as "systems and assets, whether physical or virtual, so vital to the United States that the incapacity or destruction of such systems and assets would have a debilitating impact on security, national economic security, national public health or safety, or any combination of those matters."[4]

It could be said that the 1997 report of the PCCIP conceptualized infrastructure protection; PDD 63 in 1998 attempted to implement those concepts;

and in 2001, the USA PATRIOT Act codified them. Then, in 2003, President George W. Bush released the *National Strategy to Secure Cyberspace* and in the same year issued Homeland Security Presidential Directive 7 (HSPD 7), which mandated the development of a national CIP plan as PDD 63 had requested 5 years earlier.[5]

In the meantime, cyber issues were again rising to the forefront among policymakers. In 2005, the leadership of the Department of Homeland Security (DHS) cyber office, formerly a position at the division director level, was elevated to Assistant Secretary for Cyber and Telecommunications Security. This position was filled late in 2006.

Responding to the HSPD 7 mandate, the Department of Homeland Security finalized its National Infrastructure Protection Plan (NIPP) in 2006.[6] The NIPP is meant to be a comprehensive risk management framework for the protection of U.S. infrastructure. However, the early drafts of the plan did not do much to address cyber issues. While cyber concerns were incorporated in the final NIPP, the document lacks specific guidance as to how to integrate physical and cyber protection plans.

The U.S. Government's critical infrastructure efforts span many different aspects of the threats and vulnerabilities facing the Nation. The question of what specific assets and processes comprise critical infrastructure is itself the subject of intense debate; a thorough examination of all aspects of critical infrastructure is not attempted here. Rather, this chapter reviews stakeholder efforts to protect cyber and communications infrastructure, pressing cyber CIP concerns, and shortfalls in adequately addressing those concerns.

Importance of Cyber CIP

Paraphrasing the 2003 *National Strategy to Secure Cyberspace*, DHS has described cyberspace as "the nervous system of the Nation's critical infrastructures, the control system of our country and the global economy."[7] Congress has explicitly recognized the role of information technologies (IT), noting that "[p]rivate business, government, and the national security apparatus increasingly *depend on an interdependent network of* critical physical and *information infrastructures*, including telecommunications, energy, financial services, water, and transportation sectors."[8]

Cyber CIP and Government Emergency Response
The cyber infrastructure plays a large role in the government's emergency response capabilities, serving as an enabler in critical processes and procedures. Organizations and personnel responsible for the health and safety of citizens rely on cyber technology at almost every turn. As the Business Roundtable emphasized in a report on cyber preparedness, first responders use the IT infrastructure to

coordinate and manage responses to catastrophic events, including dispatching emergency personnel, communicating with law enforcement, health, and fire professionals, and tracking essential supplies via the global positioning system.[9] Thus, protection of the cyber infrastructure is essential to emergency response capabilities.

The role of cyber infrastructure in emergency response is also critical to areas such as transportation of supplies and personnel, government communication with the populace, and the restoration of public confidence during an emergency. The cyber infrastructure is an integral part of the Nation's communications infrastructure, due in part to the convergence of communications and cyber capabilities and infrastructure. If the cyber infrastructure that supports communications capabilities were to fail, there would be a large impact on the government's ability to warn and inform citizens during an emergency. The government's ability to coordinate messages and information among multiple emergency response entities would also be affected. The lack of coordinated information and guidance from the government harms public confidence and could possibly cause physical danger to citizens, as illustrated by the problematic evacuation processes during Hurricane Katrina in 2005.

Another vital part of the government's emergency response structure is its ability to move supplies and personnel through areas quickly and efficiently. Areas in crisis need everything from medical supplies and food, to engineers and computer experts. The Federal Government's report on lessons learned after Hurricane Katrina highlighted the fact that resource managers did not have a clear idea of what was needed and what was available, due to poor management of assets and logistics. The government's supply chain was highly bureaucratic and outdated.[10] Cyber CIP has a major role in the systems and networks used to update and modernize the government's supply chain capabilities. If advanced cyber security solutions are not integrated as core processes within these updated and modernized supply networks, we will simply be increasing the quantity and dependency of such vital systems, and thus enhancing their vulnerability.

Cyber CIP and the Military

The U.S. military is one part of the Federal Government that does possess a well-developed and modernized supply chain and logistics system. In order to be able to carry out its mission of protecting the United States, the Department of Defense (DOD) needs to be able to transport large amounts of materiel and personnel quickly, safely, and efficiently. It operates a massive supply chain system that stretches around the world. Cyber capabilities play a large role in operating and maintaining this structure, making cyber CIP a critical component of DOD's warfighting capability.

Technology also supports other important DOD functions in addition to supply and logistics. It is a vital part of many of the military's weapons systems, directly supporting warfighting capability. Everything from tanks and missiles to fighter planes and ships relies on cyber technology. Accordingly, the military has recognized the importance of this aspect of its fighting capability and has taken some steps to protect vulnerable systems and assets.

In regard to the protection and defense of cyber systems and data, DOD has formulated clear policy, constructed operational structures, and acquired the technological capabilities to protect its systems. DOD policy requires strict oversight of cyber security, including asset identification and management. Formal procedures delineate roles and responsibilities and provide guidance on how to implement policy. The military not only purchases significant amounts of information security technology, it also integrates information security into the entire asset life cycle process for all purchases.[11] The DOD model could be leveraged by other governmental entities seeking to improve security for cyber assets.

Recognizing that both the threats against its systems and information and their vulnerabilities are growing daily, the military is conducting research and development, operations, and exercises to test its weaknesses and enhance its capabilities. DOD has taken a proactive approach to addressing cyber issues that should be adopted by other organizations, both public and private, that have significant responsibilities for protecting critical cyber systems. Given the role that technology plays in DOD's mission to defend the security of the Nation, the military is attempting to address the risks associated with its cyber reliance. However, there are other major aspects of national security that the military does not control.

Cyber CIP in the National and Global Economy
The danger from threats to cyber and communications infrastructure is not limited to lives and physical assets. The Nation's economy is a crucial piece of the national security landscape. Financial markets are very dependent upon cyber technology, and this reliance can cause cascading problems.

For example, a massive selloff of stocks occurred on one day in February 2007. The extraordinary trading volume carried its own inherent problems, but several cyber incidents exacerbated these problems. A computer glitch caused a time lag of more than an hour in calculating the value of the Dow Jones Industrial Average. When calculating operations were shifted to a backup computer, prices suddenly caught up and were processed all at once, and as a result there appeared to be an immediate 200-point drop in the Dow Jones average. With all this confusion, the Dow suffered its biggest drop since the first trading day after the terrorist attacks of September 11, 2001.[12]

In addition to the Dow Jones computer problems, intermittent systems problems and communications delays occurred at the NASDAQ, American

Stock Exchange, and New York Stock Exchange, and numerous online brokerage companies suffered slowdowns in their networks. For a time that day, it was estimated that one out of four online stock transactions could not be completed.[13]

There are technological and human safeguards in place to prevent such glitches from becoming uncontrolled and wreaking havoc on the markets, but these measures are not infallible. Plans should be in place not only for protection, but also for response and reconstitution, of all assets—including public trust.

Some experts question whether the U.S. National Response Plan (NRP), to be utilized after natural disasters and terrorist attacks, is relevant to cyber incidents that cause market harm. Public trust is a huge factor in any response to a damaged financial system. Any cyber incident that results in Internet disruptions could also have a major impact on financial markets. Thus, for cyber incidents, some experts have called for a national response mechanism that balances traditional first-responder priorities of the NRP with market and public trust priorities.[14]

In addition to its role in the U.S. economy, cyber infrastructure plays a major role in trade and financial services in markets and economies around the world. A major cyber incident could have impacts similar to or worse than the Dow Jones glitch of February 2007. The global system of finance is now so interconnected that actions and events in one market or location often result in widespread ripple effects.

As new connections are established and new stakeholders join daily, the global system becomes more and more complex, thereby increasing the chances that the impact of an incident could ripple into the U.S. economy from an unexpected source. The critical cyber infrastructure that helps operate the financial networks and systems in countries outside of the United States can still have impacts on U.S. economic security. These effects, and the behavior of the whole global economic system, are not receiving adequate attention from the policymakers dealing with cyber CIP. The United States and its financial partners should intensify efforts to understand the interconnections and the cyber vulnerabilities of the global economy and should include both market effects and public trust impacts in future response plans and guidance.

Potential for Catastrophic Cyber Incidents

An accident, a natural disaster, or an attack on elements of critical infrastructure that depend on cyber technologies could have Hurricane Katrina–level results. Damage could be caused by disruption of cyber systems or by weaponization of the cyber infrastructure. Disruption could result from either a natural disaster or a manmade situation. There is no agreement on the probability of, or timeframe for, such an incident, or on what a cyber catastrophe would look like.[15] There is no doubt, however, that such an incident is possible due to the vulnerabilities inherent in the hardware and software critical to the Internet and the threats facing the Nation's cyber infrastructure.

Despite its resiliency, significant vulnerabilities exist in the infrastructure of the Internet. Attacks on the 13 root servers, submarine cables, or telecommunications hotels could affect significant portions of the Internet. There are also vulnerabilities in the software supporting Domain Name System servers that permit Internet traffic to flow. These vulnerabilities present many different opportunities to those looking to damage the United States. The range of threats confronting the safety and security of America includes threats from organized nation-states as well as various terrorist groups. Security experts are aware that the plans of attack of particular nation-states include strikes on cyber infrastructure.[16] There are also indications that terrorist groups such as al Qaeda are considering cyber-based attacks on electrical grids and financial institutions.[17]

An attack on cyber infrastructure that has consequences at the national level moved beyond abstract possibility in the spring of 2007. The small Baltic country of Estonia experienced "massive and coordinated cyber attacks on Web sites of the government, banks, telecommunications companies, Internet service providers and news organizations."[18] Like most countries, Estonia relies heavily on its cyber infrastructure, and the attacks did serious damage—from the crashing of government computers that had to be taken offline to the disabling of payment systems, which prevented citizens from making non-cash purchases.[19]

If similar attacks were to take place in the United States, damage could be extensive. Attacks or incidents could impact public safety (for example, an attack on the control systems of a dam to facilitate the sudden and unexpected flooding of a downstream city); national security (such as an attack that gained access to U.S. intelligence or military information); or economic security (such as a misinformation and systems attack that undermined confidence in the integrity of U.S. financial networks). Each type of attack is addressed in turn here.

Public Safety

More than ever, the public's health and welfare are dependent on cyber infrastructure. In addition to the major role cyber technology plays in the missions of first responders, it is also vital to operating and maintaining critical infrastructure on which the physical safety of thousands of people may depend. For example, a cyber incident or attack affecting the systems that control nuclear facilities or dams could be devastating if it resulted in the flooding of a city downstream from a dam, or an explosion that spread radiation over a wide radius.

Supervisory control and data acquisition (SCADA) systems, or process control systems, control the operations of many different critical infrastructures, such as powerplants, chemical and nuclear facilities, oil and gas pipelines, and water treatment plants. In the past, several SCADA attacks have posed direct threats to health and safety, including a 1997 attack in Worcester, Massachusetts, that disabled a telephone network that served fire departments, an airport, and local residents.[20] The "Slammer" worm of 2003 disabled a safety monitoring system at a nuclear power plant and blocked control system traffic at five other utilities.[21] Although the attacks on SCADA systems so far have not caused catastrophic damage, they demonstrate the vulnerability of systems that affect the safety and health of thousands of people. Larger and more determined attacks, such as those inflicted upon Estonia, could do far more damage.

National Security

Also included in the realm of cyber CIP are Federal systems that contain sensitive information. These systems may contain data critical to national security, such as military capabilities and foreign intelligence. If such information were compromised, the effects might damage the military's ability to protect the Nation or the government's ability to detect threats.

There have been many attempts to probe the cyber defenses of the government; for example, a series of attacks have targeted Federal agencies ranging from DOD to the National Aeronautics and Space Administration.[22] Departments possessing highly sensitive information have experienced data breaches and hacks. State Department networks were breached in June 2006, resulting in a potential loss of information, as well as a chance that the perpetrators had opened hidden, backdoor paths of attack into the system.[23]

These attacks have been significant, but they are largely discrete and separate attacks. No massive, coordinated effort to take down military, intelligence, and diplomatic systems has yet been identified. However, judging by the damage caused by the individual attacks that have occurred to date, an attack on the scale of the Estonia campaign could have serious ramifications for national security. An attack of this nature could reveal the potentially large gaps in U.S. policy and doctrine about how the Nation would respond to cyber attacks.

Economic Security

In the event of an attack, public confidence in U.S. financial and monetary stability could be harmed in the absence of adequate guidance and reassurance from the government. If citizens are not assured that their money is safe and available, the economic effects could be severe. The financial and economic system relies on the trust of its citizens as well as international stakeholders. The government has a responsibility to communicate situational and other information in such a way that incidents will not needlessly damage national or global financial institutions.

Given the vital role that cyber technology plays in national and international economic systems, an attack on Internet hardware or software could also have a major impact on the global economy. The ripple effects of the Dow Jones computer glitch described above affected other exchanges at the national level, and subsequent drops in value affected stock exchanges abroad. Although this glitch was not an intentional attack, it had global consequences. An intentional and targeted attack, building on the lessons learned from the Dow Jones incident, could be far more detrimental to the international system of trade and finance.

The danger from cyber attacks or accidents comes not just from incidents originating in financial systems abroad or within domestic stock exchanges. Due to the convergence of cyber technology, many of the businesses that comprise the U.S. economy utilize the same cyber and communications infrastructure. The interconnection of systems brings many benefits, including improved efficiency, speed, and capability. However, the technology that underpins these capabilities may contain vulnerabilities that can be exploited.

Not only do businesses rely on the same technology for critical business functions, they also rely on *other* businesses and sectors. Any attack or incident that caused a major failure in a critical infrastructure, such as the power or telecommunications sectors, could affect other businesses and sectors nationwide. Thus, a single business can have multiple key dependencies and interdependencies, and it might not even be aware of all of them. Understandably, then, the extent of cyber and communications dependencies across one sector of the economy, much less those dependencies across the Nation, can be difficult to comprehend. A disruption within any cyber or communications technology that supports businesses could ripple up from the individual business and sector level to affect the national economy.

Federal Leadership

Although the private sector will lead the effort to develop solutions to cyber and communications infrastructure vulnerabilities, it is the government that must lead efforts in the preparedness for, response to, and recovery from catastrophic incidents. This is the first time that the private sector has had such a large role in protecting national security and the first time that it has been asked to shoulder such a large burden. In the case of cyber and communications CIP, the Federal Government must rely extensively on the private sector. However, it cannot delegate its inherently governmental responsibility for the protection of life and property.

The best way forward is for the government to serve as an organizational model, develop and test emergency practices, and subsequently bring its expertise to the private sector to be leveraged as best practices. For the Federal Government to guide the private sector, however, it will need to provide clear policy direction, develop operational guidance that specifies roles and responsibilities, and shift its research and development priorities and its distribution of resources to the task of preventing and managing catastrophes. The Federal Government must lead by example, by offering an effective model for preparedness, response, and recovery. However, its efforts to date have fallen short.

Misdirected and Ambiguous Federal Policy

Federal leadership is crucial to cyber-related CIP issues because cyber threats and incidents will rarely be limited to local or state effects. The 2003 *National Strategy to Secure Cyberspace* specifies that the Federal Government is responsible for such cyber issues as "forensics and attack attribution, protection of networks and systems critical to national security, indications and warnings, and protection against organized attacks capable of inflicting debilitating damage to the economy."[24]

However, cyber issues have suffered from a lack of consistent leadership from the Federal Government. Despite language in the USA PATRIOT Act that emphasizes virtual as well as physical systems and assets, the Federal spotlight has been on the protection of the latter. Cyber-related CIP issues have not received focused or consistent attention. In its first major policy document, DHS took steps toward developing a national plan for CIP: it issued the *National Strategy for the Physical Protection of Critical Infrastructures and Key Assets* but, as its title indicated, this document focused on physical assets, not cyber assets or protection against cyber threats.

The strategic objectives of the 2003 *National Strategy to Secure Cyberspace* are to prevent cyber attacks against critical infrastructures, reduce national vulnerability to cyber attacks, and mitigate against damage and improve recovery time from cyber attacks.[25] However, the primary focus of DHS is still on awareness—spreading the word that cyber security is an important concern. In a speech in early 2007, the new DHS Assistant Secretary for Cyber and Telecommunications Security encouraged the private sector to perform vulnerability assessments and implement security policies.[26] Such advice and awareness are inarguably important but fail to differentiate between the majority of everyday security issues, which are not critical, and the security of those systems and assets that, in the words of the USA PATRIOT Act, are "so vital to the United States that [their] incapacity or destruction . . . would have a debilitating impact on security, national economic security, national public health or safety." The policy and operational issues regarding the security of such vital systems or assets must be examined.

One example is the Federal authority to declare an incident of national significance. The NRP Cyber Annex states that "[c]yberspace is largely owned and operated by the private sector; therefore, the authority of the federal Government to exert control over activities in cyberspace is limited."[27] Since no new laws have been passed regarding authorities during a cyber incident, the extent of Federal power during such an incident has not been openly delineated. An analysis of the extent of Federal authority in such circumstances would encompass not only disaster response authorities but also Federal powers under the Defense Production Act, such as setting priorities for access to cyber assets and for reconstitution.[28] There is no clear sign that the Federal Government has yet undertaken such an analysis.

Moreover, the phrase *cyber incident of national significance* may be anomalous because, although an incident may have a national effect, a catastrophic cyber incident would likely be global in nature. Here, too, the Federal Government has not yet provided leadership on international cyber response and recovery issues.

The government must provide a clear definition of the factors that determine a cyber incident of national significance, including specific triggers and protocols for response escalation. This policy should clarify the legal authorities of the Federal Government during a cyber incident and set goals for expected Federal interactions with the private sector and with government entities at the state and local level. It should strengthen international understanding of and cooperation on cyber issues and establish initiatives to engage the international community in discussion of appropriate actions during cyber crises.

The Federal Government should also set expectations for the private sector. The business community plays a major role in critical infrastructure protection, but there is widespread confusion as to how it should prepare for, respond to, or recover from catastrophic cyber incidents. The private sector owns and operates a large share of the critical infrastructure in the United States, but the Federal Government, too, owns and operates much of it. As part of its traditional role of managing catastrophic incidents, the government has a responsibility to protect this infrastructure. The U.S. Government should leverage its extensive global networks to establish early warning and information-sharing protocols that could be used by both the government and private sector in the event of emergency.

In serving as a leader to the private sector, the Federal Government should inform the private sector of what it can expect from government departments and agencies; establish minimum expectations for actions from the private sector; and mandate liabilities for failure to perform in a satisfactory manner. It should also establish central points of contact that are easily accessible to private sector stakeholders. These government actions to manage catastrophic incidents should be clearly defined, so as to provide clear guidelines to the private sector.

The private sector also has a responsibility to protect its infrastructure. The business community must take the initiative and not simply wait for guidance from the Federal Government. Private sector stakeholders must join to form their own points of contact. The Information Sharing and Analysis Centers (ISACs) now established in several critical industry sectors are a start, but more is needed.

The private sector should communicate with the government and establish joint expectations that are acceptable to both the public and private sectors. Business leaders should focus efforts on learning how to manage important economic issues that may be affected by a cyber disruption, such as public trust and confidence in the markets.[29] CEOs and other senior business officials must plan within their own companies and industries in order to maintain business functionality during catastrophic incidents.

Lack of Federal Operational Guidance

While some Federal policy documents have recognized the importance of cyber CIP issues, there has been little government follow-through or implementation. High-level policy discussion has been lacking within DHS to formulate specific plans and guidance for dealing with cyber catastrophes. The National Infrastructure Protection Plan contains cyber language at the strategic level but does not address the operational level. Similarly, the Cyber Annex to the National Response Plan contains little specific guidance. As of early 2007, DHS was still working "to refine written documentation establishing a concept of operations" for how Federal departments and organizations and the private sector would work together during a cyber incident.[30] Further, although the NRP states that the administration has the authority to declare a cyber incident of national significance, it does not specify the factors that indicate what would constitute such an incident, nor has the DHS spelled these out. The departments and agencies of the Federal Government do not currently have plans for how to respond if such an incident were declared, nor do they have a unified plan for how to coordinate their response with other agencies, state and local level government, the private sector, or international organizations.

The Federal Government must move forward to generate operational guidance. In particular, it must delineate the roles and responsibilities of DOD and other Federal entities for emergency response to a cyber incident. These roles and responsibilities should be based on an escalating scale of triggers and thresholds that are clearly set forth in policy that includes definitions of emergencies and missions and identification of essential personnel. Across two administrations, Presidents have signed national strategies mandating results in this area, but cyber remains one of the least developed areas of homeland security policy. This must change.

Allocation of Resources

As the Cold War ended, a new and complex set of challenges arose, and U.S. leaders realized that priorities and assets at the national level would have to be reoriented. However, in the cyber realm, the government has shifted its priorities and resources away from national security issues such as preparing for a catastrophic cyber incident, instead focusing funding on cyber crime, identity theft, and consumer protection issues.

DHS seems to spend more time on outreach and awareness activities than on identification of critical assets and critical infrastructure protection issues. This imbalance reflects congressional appropriations. For fiscal year 2007, Congress appropriated as much for "Critical Infrastructure Outreach and Partnership" within DHS ($101.1 million) as it did for both critical infrastructure "Identification and Evaluation" and "Protective Actions" combined.[31] By these numbers, Congress gave outreach the same funding priority as actual protection.

While recognizing these external mandates, DHS's internal allocation of its cyber security budget could still improve to address what is truly critical in a meaningful and efficient manner. For example, in 2005, the National Cyber Security Division (NCSD) at DHS spent $15 million on a SCADA security program.[32] But NCSD also spent $3 million, or one-fifth as much, on a single 4-day tabletop exercise called Cyber Storm.[33] It may be questioned whether one 4-day exercise was worth one-fifth of a year's expense for a program to improve control system security. The value of Cyber Storm may be further cast into doubt when one considers its purpose and major findings. One main goal was to exercise the established response policies, procedures, and communication mechanisms during a cyber crisis. However, as already discussed, there are no clear, formal operating procedures for Federal cyber incident response. Thus, it should not be surprising that one conclusion from Cyber Storm was that we need clearly defined, well-thought-out, formalized response plans for such contingencies.[34] It is unclear, however, why DHS apparently needed to spend $3 million to reach that conclusion.

Positive Steps

While the Federal Government has not provided consistent leadership in cyber issues in the past, there is still hope that we may be moving onto the right path. In February 2007, nearly a decade after the President's Commission on Critical Infrastructure Protection, DHS announced that it would be collocating its watch and warning personnel at the U.S. Computer Emergency Readiness Team with private sector warning teams from the Communications ISAC. DHS also expects to collocate government staff with private sector staff from the Information Technology ISAC warning teams, with the goal of establishing a "collaborative, real time and trusted information sharing environment that enables us to see what's happening on our networks and take immediate steps to fend off attacks."[35] DHS eventually expects to strengthen this capability with other sectoral ISACs, to give a "synthesized, cross-sectoral view and incident response capability."[36] Although there have been delays in arriving at these steps, such programs are encouraging.

Conclusion and Recommendations

The Federal Government must now move beyond a focus on awareness to identify what is truly critical in cyber CIP: an incident that could create a catastrophic result in terms of physical or economic harm. That which is critical to a state or locality needs only a commensurate level of preparedness and response. That which is critical to the Nation, or to the global economy and communications systems, needs a much greater level of preparedness and response.

The Federal Government must, therefore, overhaul its current position and do better at preparing for cyber incidents, update its approach to partnering with the private sector, and shift resources toward emergencies at the national and global levels. It must embrace its role and responsibility to lead preparedness and response efforts for catastrophic cyber and communications incidents. It should start by establishing policy that clearly defines what constitutes a cyber incident of national significance and follow it with operational guidance that outlines Federal roles and responsibilities during such an incident. Guidance should also include a set of expectations for the private sector and international stakeholders. The Federal Government should establish a system for response to economic and market disruption resulting from a cyber incident.[37] And it would also be helpful to develop Federal operational guidance to implement existing strategic policy and engage global stakeholders.

Cyber and communications critical infrastructure protection plays a crucial role in the Nation's economic and national security, as well as the critical functions that the government provides. These technologies are embedded in processes that are vital to the Nation and its citizens—from the processes that operate the financial markets, to the systems that run tanks and planes, to the devices used by first responders. The new and ever-expanding role of such cyber systems, combined with their inherent vulnerabilities, has resulted in the potential for a catastrophic cyber incident. Interdependencies and the pervasive nature of cyber infrastructure mean that unexpected cascading effects can undermine these vital processes. The possibility of such an incident grows greater as cyber and communications technologies are increasingly interwoven into national and economic security, as well as core emergency response functions. The Federal Government can, and must, do better at protecting the critical cyber infrastructure of the United States.

CHAPTER 24

Cyberpower from the Presidential Perspective

Leon Fuerth

THIS CHAPTER makes two fundamental points. First, cyberpower is an attribute not just of military strength, but of the strength and vitality of our society as a whole. An approach to national policy that dealt with cyberpower mainly as an element in the struggle for physical safety and survival would completely miss the point that the dynamism of our economy is also a manifestation of cyberpower. It would also neglect the extent to which the cyber age is influencing how we live, how we view the world, and what kind of people we are. The White House—and ultimately the mind and the office of the President—are where that kind of panoramic view must exist.

The second point is that cyberpower is an example of a new order of "wicked" public issues that reflect the axioms and postulates of complexity theory.[1] Such issues involve ceaseless interaction of systems within systems, the constant possibility of surprise, and the primacy of the law of unintended consequences. The design and management of policy for this class of issues is a new type of challenge for American governance and in particular for the President.

The experts who wrote this book have aimed to present cyberpower from the many perspectives offered by their specializations. My knowledge of this subject is general and derivative, but my experience as national security advisor to Vice President Al Gore allows me to speak with some authority about how cyberpower presents itself to national leaders. And since the ultimate objective of all those who have contributed to this book is sound national policy, that gives me an opportunity to add value to the discussion.

Cyber Society and Cyberpower

Cybernetics is the study and creation of machines that regulate themselves. Initially, this was accomplished by means of feedback through internal mechanical linkages, but now it is done by means of computer-mediated data that is sometimes generated by on-board systems but increasingly by globally networked systems. Cybernetic control makes possible electronic and mechanical devices that operate at speeds exceeding human capacity by orders of magnitude, rapidly narrowing the gap between machine and human intelligence. Cybernetics is the means by which every layer of our civilization is able to regulate itself and synchronize its relations with all other layers. States that make the most intense use of cybernetics for military or civilian applications have important competitive advantages over their peers, but they are also profoundly vulnerable to failures of these systems, whether caused by flaws of design or by malice.

Classical economics identified three basic sources of national power: land, labor, and capital. In our time, the list has been expanded to include information, which in many ways trumps the other categories. We have already become a cyber society, wherein cybernetic technology is the key driver of progress, expanding collective and individual wealth, but may also be its Achilles' heel. In the final years of the 20th century, the Y2K scare alerted us to the extent of our dependence on the performance of networked cybernetic systems. That dependency continues to grow as cyber systems become ubiquitous and indispensable in every aspect of our daily lives as individuals and as a society.

People are increasingly living within the cyber world and developing a cyber culture. Our civilization's vital processes would be unstable and inoperable without the intervention of cybernetic systems. At the leading edge of this process in our social lives, systems for human socialization that are exclusively based in cyberspace are being developed. Virtual reality begins to compete with reality as we have known it, evident in the burgeoning growth of phenomena ranging from e-commerce to social networking sites. To remain at the forefront of the cyber age requires an unprecedented readiness not just to embrace but to promote deep, societal change.

Cyberpower arises from the ability of individual nations to develop, apply, and benefit from cybernetics, in the form of increasingly sophisticated economic, social, political, and military behavior. Any nation that fell behind in the capacity to develop cyberpower would cede enormous competitive advantage to its rivals, and any nation or entity that could deny the use of cyberpower to others, or to force others to pay monopoly rates for its use, could occupy a position of dominance.

Policymaking for Complex Priorities

Cyberpower thus reflects the sum of our ability to make use of information of all kinds. It cannot be understood as a fixed condition but rather as the ongoing consequence of an interplay of forces at the scientific, economic, and cultural levels of society. Thus, any governmental organization that aims to create and manage policy for complex priorities of this type must be able to deal with the whole of the system, not just its parts. This supposition points straight to the need for a national policy orchestrated from the White House—which, in turn, points to the need for innovations in the policy process itself. The creation and management of national policy require investments of scarce intellectual, political, and, ultimately, material resources. From the White House perspective, there are many claimants for this kind of investment, and they are often in competition with each other. The odds of survival are steep in part because of the structure and mindset of the White House itself: in an age of specialists, the White House is a redoubt of generalists. In a policy field such as cyberpower, there will a short supply of policymakers who have the requisite blend of technical and political acuity.

Although specialized scientific and technical knowledge is on call within the White House, it generally is not part of the personal background of the highest tier of officials. There is, to be sure, the Office of the Science Advisor to the President, but it has only nominal equivalence to other senior positions, and its domain is normally restricted, with the management of the societal consequences of science and technology left to others. They, however, are already struggling to keep pace with identified priorities relating to problems of every imaginable kind, and often enough with challenges that were unimaginable before they thrust themselves forward in the form of a crisis.

The White House Principals' and Deputies' Committees are critical for the integration of issues and policies at the national level. However, these bodies are struggling to deal with multiple, concurrent, and interacting issues of major consequence. Each of these bodies comprises only as many people as can be seated comfortably around a conference table of modest size, and all of these individuals carry an extraordinary burden of executive responsibility in their respective agencies. Out of necessity, this system will give priority to what is important and imminent at the expense of what is important but long-range. There is a partial exception to this rule in the first year of most administrations, when it is customary to do a kind of "open-season" review of existing policy. Even during that short period, however, priority will usually be assigned to situations that are imminent, if not already ongoing. There is also a bias in favor of attending to situations involving the threat of conspicuous loss, rather than to situations involving the prospect of longer term gain.

National policymaking tends to suffer from not only myopia but also tunnel vision.[2] It is unable to recognize interactions among subjects, especially once these have been assigned to or claimed by specific constituencies in the bureaucracy. In theory, the interagency system is an answer to this problem, but too often, it functions as a kind of appellate process within which executive agencies litigate their interests at successively higher levels, using tactics that are collectively zero-sum rather than win-win. This tendency works against comprehensive vision in the formation and execution of policy. It is reinforced by the symbiosis between executive branch agencies and the Congress, with its own multiple, overlapping committee jurisdictions.

In the White House, like the general bureaucracy, organizational firewalls separate what are thought to be substantively distinct domains of policy: economics from defense, for example, or domestic policy from international. There are both formal and informal systems designed to alleviate the resulting shortcomings, but they are relatively ineffective because they are ad hoc rather than systemic.

In particular, the White House has not yet recognized, and therefore has not responded to, a fundamental change that is occurring in the very nature of the challenges it faces. The issues that the White House handles are no longer merely complicated; it must now deal with issues and priorities that are complex. Merely complicated problems may be disentangled and successfully resolved by linear processes; models of these problems can be formed and used with some degree of confidence. In these models, changes of input produce proportionate changes of output; operations may be executed sequentially according to a program; issues, properly handled, will tend toward equilibrium solutions.

Complex problems, on the other hand, are not linear. Minor changes of input can produce drastic levels of surprise. Solutions generate new problems. Policies interact with each other across conventionally accepted firebreaks. Events occur spontaneously and can overwhelm sequential operations.

These are the problems we call *wicked*, meaning that they have "incomplete, contradictory, and changing requirements." Moreover, their "solutions are often difficult to recognize as such because of complex inter-dependencies."[3]

Wickedness in the White House

The White House is where wicked issues come to roost, but it is no better organized than the rest of the executive branch for dealing with wicked problems. It lacks systems for long-range assessment of issues at the stage of early visibility. It does not have mechanisms to grapple with issues that involve dissimilar yet interactive components, especially where these cut across customary organizational boundaries. It lacks systems to identify and track interactions. It is, therefore, at a disadvantage when trying to establish a sense of the shape and momentum of complex issues. Neither does the White House have the means to track the consequences of policy decisions as these are interpreted and set into motion by the bureaucracy. It is particularly ill suited for problems that lack definitive solutions but are instead both permanent and always changing.

The first impulse may be to focus responsibility for such issues in yet another "czar" at the White House level. Paradoxically, however, wicked issues will require White House arrangements that disperse authority rather than concentrating it. Wicked issues do not lend themselves to centralized management. What they require, rather, is broad strategic guidance—what the military calls "commanders' intent"—applied to a flattened network of stakeholding organizations designed to permit rapid adaptation to circumstances, with the capacity to learn from error before it becomes calamity and to exploit opportunity while it is there for the taking. Upgrading the capability of government to handle wickedness depends on innovative use of principles of networked organization, which we have already seen applied in the private sector and in the uniformed military. It is the civilian sector of government that lags behind in recognizing the need for deep change.

In the first chapter of this book, Franklin Kramer called for the establishment of a "Cyber Policy Council along the lines of the Council of Economic Advisors," to "integrate or at least coordinate and review key issues."[4] This would be a very important institutional means by which a President—and the government as a whole—could attain full situational awareness concerning the scope and importance of cyberpower as a factor in the continued growth and security of the United States.

As Kramer points out, however, this proposal represents only a tentative first step toward a form of organization within the White House that could do justice to the subject. Cyberpower, as a wicked issue, has complex causes and effects that will exceed the capacity of a single advisory body. The management of this class of challenge requires a fully networked framework for the development and execution of many policies, which would be dealt with as systems operating within larger systems; the most extensive system involves the economic well-being and the physical security of the United States.

To meet this kind of challenge, there are calls for a broad reorganization of the national security function in government, picking up where the Goldwater-Nichols Department of Defense Reorganization Act of 1986 left off and extending well beyond the concept of security as synonym for defense. It is a daunting proposition that could take years to bring to fruition. Meanwhile, the speed and force of wicked problems represent a growing threat to the capacity of governance to respond with the requisite agility and effectiveness. Here again, therefore, the focus shifts to the President, who can jump-start this process at the top by instituting networked processes within the White House itself.

I have addressed this question by suggesting that a President can establish in the White House "a networked, small, flexible, task-oriented managerial 'supra-structure' designed to be retrofitted to the existing system."[5] I recommended that a President could use the existing advisory and management system of the White House for this purpose and could employ the Cabinet itself in different configurations to provide overall executive management of complex policy from the top.

Addressing this question in detail, my students coined the very useful term "complex priorities" to suggest the possibility of organizing to encircle and embrace wicked issues.[6] They proposed the establishment of specific White House machinery for this purpose, to operate at the principals' and deputies' levels as complements to the existing system. They point out that:

> [d]ue to the increasing pace and impact of technological change, we have entered a time of unprecedented uncertainty and possibility. These changes have significantly expanded the range of issues and trends with the potential to impact the very core of our nation, and have necessitated that we move beyond the traditional understanding of national security as a function of national defense. To serve and protect U.S. interests going forward the federal government must become more adaptive and flexible, and better capable of anticipating and responding to complex and inter-related realities. The Executive Branch must take the lead in transforming the U.S. government to meet the challenges—and exploit the opportunities—of the 21st century.

It is to that end that I have offered the recommendations of this chapter.

Conclusion

Cyberpower cannot be appreciated as an aggregate of its properties. It transcends its components to become a thing in itself, demanding conceptualization as a whole. Such a conceptualization must be captured in the form of a broad, formal statement of national policy. That national policy should be centered on the promotion and rapid incorporation of cyber culture, defined as the total capacity of the United States to develop and exploit cyber technology. National defense is a component of this challenge, but so too are the economic and societal dimensions. It will be necessary to have a policy and management system dedicated to cyberpower, but it must also be fully integrated into all other systems that exist for the purpose of sustaining the power of the United States and the well being of its citizens. The management system needed for cyberpower must demonstrate what is called *requisite complexity*, or it will fail. In short, cyberpower is a wicked problem and should be handled as a complex priority.

Notes

Introduction
1. Department of Defense, *2006 Quadrennial Defense Review Report* (Washington, DC: Department of Defense, February 6, 2006).
2. Recently, the Chairman of the Joint Chiefs of Staff has recommended that the term *cyberspace* be defined as a "global domain within the information environment consisting of the interdependent network of information infrastructures, including the Internet, telecommunications networks, computer systems, and embedded processors and controllers."
3. As noted above, emphasis was placed on the military and informational levers.
4. Daniel Gonzales et al., "Network-centric Operations Case Study: Air-to-Air Combat with and without Link 16" (Santa Monica, CA: RAND/National Defense Research Institute, 2005).
5. Daniel Gonzales et al., "Network-centric Operations Case Study: The Stryker Brigade Combat Team" (Santa Monica, CA: RAND/National Defense Research Institute, 2005).
6. Ralph Baker, "The Decisive Weapon: A Brigade Combat Team Commander's Perspective on Information Operations," *Military Review* (May-June 2006).

Chapter 1
1. For example, see chapter 2 in this volume, "From Cyberspace to Cyberpower: Defining the Problem."
2. The White House, *The National Strategy to Secure Cyberspace* (Washington, DC: The White House, February 2003), xi.
3. Gregory C. Wilshusen, director, Government Accountability Office, "Information Security: Persistent Weaknesses Highlight Need for Further Improvement," testimony before the Subcommittee on Emerging Threats, Cybersecurity, and Science and Technology, Committee on Homeland Security, House of Representatives (April 19, 2007), GAO–07–75IT, 2.
4. Committee on Prospering in the Global Economy in the 21st Century, *Rising Above the Gathering Storm: Energizing and Employing America for a Brighter Future* (Washington, DC: The National Academies Press, 2007), 16. There are disputes over the numbers, though China, India, and other countries are certainly graduating increasing numbers of science and engineering students. See Gary Gereffi et al., "Getting the Numbers Right: International Engineering Education in the United States, China, and India," *Journal of Engineering Education* 97, no. 1 (January 2008), 13.
5. General James E. Cartwright, USMC, comments at Air Force Association Air Warfare Symposium, February 8, 2007, accessed at <www.afa.org/events/aws/post_orlando/scripts/Cartwright_Printer.asp>.

6. See chapter 21 in this volume, "Internet Governance."
7. Department of Defense, *The National Defense Strategy of the United States of America* (Washington, DC: The Pentagon, March 2005), available at <www.au.af.mil/au/awc/awcgate/nds/nds2005.pdf>, 15.
8. See chapter 10 in this volume, "An Environmental Approach to Understanding Cyberpower."
9. Keith B. Alexander, "Warfighting in Cyberspace," *Joint Force Quarterly* (Issue 46, 3ᵈ Quarter 2007), 60.
10. Ronald Keys, quoted in *Defense News*, February 26, 2007, 8.
11. Cartwright.
12. Ibid.
13. This section was derived from chapter 14 in this volume, "Cyber Influence and International Security."
14. British Broadcasting Company, "'Listen More' is World's Message to U.S.," World Service Poll, January 23, 2007, available at <http://news.bbc.co.uk/2/hi/americas/6288933.stm>.
15. Jesse T. Ford, director, International Affairs and Trade, "U.S. Public Diplomacy, State Department Efforts to Engage Muslim Audiences Lack Certain Communication Elements and Face Significant Challenges," testimony before the Subcommittee on Science, the Departments of State, Justice, and Commerce, and Related Agencies, House Committee on Appropriations, GAO–06–707T (Washington, DC: U.S. Government Accountability Office, May 2006), 21, available at <www.gao.gov/new.items/d06535.pdf>.
16. This section was derived from chapter 16 in this volume, "I-Power: The Information Revolution and Stability Operations."

Chapter 2

1. The research for this effort provided a wide range of approaches to this definition, some of which are summarized in table 2–1.
2. While some in the U.S. Air Force have argued that the aerospace is a seamless environment that extends from the Earth's surface to infinity, the fact is that the air and outer space are subject to not only differing legal regimes—overflying a nation's sovereign airspace could be a violation of international law, while orbiting the Earth in space is not—but physical ones as well. Movement in the air is governed by lift, while in space, the laws of orbital mechanics rule. Thus, air and space are two very different domains.
3. Joint Publication 1–02, *DOD Dictionary of Military and Related Terms* (Washington, DC: The Joint Staff, dated April 12, 2001, and amended through November 9, 2006), available at <www.dtic.mil/doctrine/jel/new_pubs/jp1_02.pdf>.
4. See, in roughly chronological order: Winn Schwartau, *Information Warfare: Chaos on the Electronic Superhighway*, 2ᵈ ed. (New York: Thunder's Mouth Press 1996); Ed Waltz, *Information Warfare: Principles and Operations* (Boston: Artech House, 1998); Walter Gary Sharp, *Cyberspace and the Use of Force* (Falls Church, VA: Aegis Research, 1999); Dorothy Denning, *Information Warfare and Security* (Reading, MA: Addison-Wesley, 1998); and Gregory Rattray, *Strategic Warfare in Cyberspace* (Cambridge: MIT Press, 2001).
5. The White House, *The National Strategy to Secure Cyberspace* (Washington, DC: The White House, 2003).
6. During the initial meeting of the task force that wrote this book, a representative of the Joint Staff (J6X) effort to develop the *National Military Strategy for Cyberspace Operations* presented a concept for cyberspace that was unacceptable to almost everyone in attendance. To their credit, the J6X team—of which the author of this chapter was a member—reworked its approach, perhaps influenced by concepts presented by this author at that initial meeting, to the point where the final J6X effort was very similar to that presented during the meeting and to that suggested in this chapter. While this author

had some minor quibbles with the definition that was used in the final product, it comes so close to many of the key points he offered during the drafting process that we were clearly on the same sheet of music. The same is essentially true of the 2008 definition of cyberspace signed by Deputy Secretary of Defense Gordon England and Chairman of the Joint Chiefs of Staff Admiral Mike Mullen.

7. Both definitions are contained in the Deputy Secretary of Defense Memorandum to the Military Departments et al., "The Definition of Cyberspace," May 12, 2008, and its accompanying staff papers.

8. The term *domain* has taken on a near-theological significance in the Department of Defense, with intelligent and well-intended people trying to parse differences between words such as *domain, realm,* and *environment.* This can be seen in the Deputy Secretary of Defense definition, which characterizes cyberspace as a domain within an environment.

9. The role of the human element in cyberspace is the subject of an ongoing debate as to whether humans are an integral part of cyberspace, or whether we are merely the users—some would add creators—of cyberspace. While this author feels that the importance of the human element can hardly be overemphasized, we are no more "part" of cyberspace than we are of the aerospace or outer space, since the essence of the definition of these different environments flows from their unique physical characteristics.

10. The current (February 2006) Joint Publication 3–13, *Information Operations,* available at <www.dtic.mil/doctrine/jel/new_pubs/jp3_13.pdf>, defines this environment as "the aggregate of individuals, organizations, and systems that collect, process, or act on information," then further refines this definition with the observation that this environment functions via the interrelated effects of three dimensions: the physical (which is described in this chapter as connectivity), the informational (content), and the cognitive. This author finds the approach toward the three dimensions the most instructive and thus has concentrated on them.

11. The debate about whether cyberspace is a "place we go" stems from the need to use manmade technologies to operate in cyberspace. But this is no different than most of our other physical environments in that we require technologies such as motors to use those environments. Submarines, airliners, and spacecraft—and computers—operate in different physical environments, yet all use motors in the process of "entering" and operating in those environments.

12. The author is indebted to Dave Clark for suggesting this perspective on cyberspace. His point about interconnectivity cannot be stressed too strongly.

13. *Operational* is being used in the sense of it being practical and useful, a place where things actually happen, and not as one of the levels of war such as *tactical* or *strategic.*

14. The observation was made during the 2008 Democratic Presidential primary, that while Senator Hillary Clinton told supporters to visit her Web page, Senator Barack Obama told supporters to text-message their five closest friends and thus gained advantages through his exploitation of "viral networking."

15. We are seeing an enormously increased use of cyberspace and the Internet by the terrorists and radical Islamist organizations. See, for example, Gabriel Weimann, "Hezbollah Dot Com: Hezbollah's Use of the Internet During the 2006 War," presented at the International Institute for Counterterrorism's "International Conference on Terrorism's Global Impact," Herzliya, Israel, September 2006, or Weimann's book *Terror on the Internet: The New Arena, the New Challenges* (Washington, DC: U.S. Institute of Peace Press, 2006). Even terminology has come into play, with some specialists suggesting that we use the wrong terms to describe the enemy and that calling terrorists "jihadists" legitimizes them, while words such as "irhabists" speak to Islamic audiences in different ways. See the work of Jim Guirard and the "Truespeak Institute," available at <www.truespeak.org/> or Douglas E. Streusand at Marine Corps Command and Staff College for more. Also

see Irving Lachow and Courtney Richardson, "Terrorist Use of the Internet: The Real Story," *Joint Force Quarterly* 45 (2^d Quarter 2007), available at <www.ndu.edu/inss/Press/jfq_pages/editions/i45/24.pdf>.

16. The U.S. concept of network-centric warfare dates to 1998 and the pathbreaking article by Arthur K. Cebrowski and John J. Garstka, "Network-Centric Warfare: Its Origin and Future," United States Naval Institute *Proceedings* (January 1998), available at <www.usni.org/Proceedings/Articles98/PROcebrowski.htm>. The Chinese have been prolific writers about "informationized" warfare for at least a decade; see Michael Pillsbury, *Chinese Views of Future Warfare* (Washington, DC: National Defense University Press, 1998), available at <www.ndu.edu/inss/Press/NDUPress_Books_Titles.htm>.

17. See, for example, David C. Gompert, Irving Lachow, and Justin Perkins, *Battle-Wise: Seeking Time-Information Superiority in Networked Warfare* (Washington, DC: National Defense University Press, 2006); also Myriam A. Dunn, "The Cyberspace Dimension in Armed Conflict," *Information and Security* 7 (2001), 145–158, available at <www.isn.ethz.ch/crn/_docs/ACF18D.pdf>.

18. Some radio waves are blocked by dense material such as water or earth, while other waves are best transmitted via those dense materials. It depends on the type of radio waves and their frequency ranges.

19. In 2007, a team sponsored by Carnegie Mellon University's Software Engineering Institute published a compendium of papers titled *Preparing to Fight in Cyberspace*. The first paper, "On the Security of the Cyber Battlefield," by William L. Fithian, suggested that "cyberspace is just as much a physical space as air, sea, land, or outer space." That is precisely the same argument made in this chapter.

20. There are obvious limits to this: we have not yet learned how to express the emotion of the human heart or the intellect of the human mind as a string of ones and zeroes, until they are turned into observable phenomena in the physical world—at which point we can capture those phenomena in multiple ways. Another question that arose during the writing of this definition concerned the words *exchange* and *transmit*. *Exchange* was chosen as being more inclusive: you cannot have an exchange of information without its transmission, and transmission without reception is meaningless.

21. The term *information-communication technology* (ICT) has been in use worldwide for more than a decade, and our failure to use it is a strange omission. ICT neatly blends two critical dimensions of cyberspace—the information itself and its exchange.

22. See Tom Standage, *The Victorian Internet* (New York: Walker, 1998), and Daniel R. Headrick, *The Invisible Weapon* (New York: Oxford, 1991). While it is true that we had earlier ways of transmitting information—balloons, signal fires, flags—the origins of modern information technology began with the telegraph little more than a century and half ago. The same holds true for the use of the subsurface of the sea: while the *Turtle* dates to the Revolutionary War, and the CSS *Hunley* to the Civil War, they were powered by hand cranks and hardly permitted useful employment of the subsurface.

23. Dave Clark has observed that in India, WiFi base stations have been mounted in vehicles that are then driven from village to village, to enable local cyber cafes to make temporary connection to the Internet. What is interesting is not the form of physical transport—the WiFi station could even have been elephant-mounted, perhaps—but the astronomical expansion of connectivity that results in each separate location when that WiFi base arrives.

24. This definition of information operations was first published in the *Information Operations Roadmap* approved by the Secretary of Defense in October 2003 and became part of the formal joint doctrinal lexicon with the issuance of Joint Publication 3–13, *Information Operations*, in February 2006; available at <www.dtic.mil/doctrine/jel/new_pubs/jp3_13.pdf>.

25. If one tried to capture this visually as a Venn diagram, the connectivity dimension would include three related and touching yet separate elements, reflecting technologies dependent on cyberspace (the Internet or television), technologies not dependent on cyberspace (the office "snail mail" distribution system), and human interaction. The content dimension would also include three distinct yet related and touching elements, again reflecting technologies dependent on cyberspace (a Web page), technologies not dependent on cyberspace (the content of an office memo tacked to the bulletin board), and human interaction.

26. See David T. Fahrenkrug, "Cyberspace Defined," in *The Wright Stuff* (Maxwell Air Force Base, AL: Air University Press, May 17, 2007), available at <www.au.af.mil/au/aunews/archive/0209/Articles/CyberspaceDefined.html>. The Air University portal has a number of viewpoints on cyberspace; see <www.au.af.mil/info-ops/cyberspace.htm> for a list.

27. The author is indebted to Dave Clark, who suggested this "layered" approach to cyberspace.

28. See Rati Bishnoi, "Navy Eyes Fighting in Cyberspace," *InsideDefense.com*, November 29, 2006.

29. Naval War College Strategic Studies Group XXVI briefing, "Convergence of Sea Power and Cyber Power," July 13, 2007.

30. See Sebastian M. Convertino II, Lou Anne DeMattei, and Tammy M. Knierim, *Flying and Fighting in Cyberspace*, Maxwell Paper 40 (Maxwell Air Force Base, AL: Air University Press, July 2007); and "Cyber-Commander: Preparing Combat Forces for the Electromagnetic Spectrum," *Military Information Technology* 12, no. 3 (April 2008), 25–27.

31. Michael Wynne and General T. Michael Moseley, "Establishment of an Operational Command for Cyberspace," memorandum, September 6, 2006; General Moseley, "Operational Cyberspace Command 'Go Do' Letter," memo to 8th Air Force Commander, November 1, 2006; John T. Bennett and Carlo Munoz, "Wynne, Moseley Tap 8th Air Force as First-Ever 'Cyberspace Command," *Inside the Air Force*, November 3, 2006; Marcus Weisgerber, "Cybercommand Expected to Reach IOC in May," *Inside the Air Force*, January 26, 2007.

32. Bob Brewin, "Air Force Suspends Cyber Command Program," *Nextgov.com*, August 12, 2008, available at <www.nextgov.com/nextgov/ng_20080812_7995.php>.

33. Until early 2008, in fact, the Army's institutional position was that cyberspace was NOT a distinct warfighting domain.

34. The U.S. Strategic Command Web page at <www.stratcom.mil/organization-fnc_comp.html> has a thumbnail sketch of each of these organizations and others, including the Joint Information Operations Warfare Command.

35. Executive Working Group, "NATO Policy on Cyber Defence," C–M (2007) 0120, December 20, 2007.

36. NATO press release, "NATO opens new centre of excellence on cyber defence," May 14, 2008, available at <www.nato.int/docu/update/2008/05-may/e0514a.html>. As an indicator of the level of interest in the topic, a quick Google search on the combined terms *NATO* and *cyber* yielded over a million hits.

37. Dancho Danchev, "Coordinated Russia vs. Georgia cyber attack in progress," *ZDNet.com*, August 11, 2008, available at <http://blogs.zdnet.com/security/?p=1670>. Also see John Markoff, "Before the Gunfire, Cyberattacks," *The New York Times*, August 13, 2008, and David Ho, "Web Sites Hit as War Uses Bytes and Bullets," *Atlanta Journal-Constitution*, August 15, 2008.

38. Air Force Doctrine Document (AFDD) 2–5, *Information Operations*, January 11, 2005, 7. A planned revision to this doctrine was shelved until the entire issue of cyberspace and the Air Force is clearer. AFDD 2–11, *Cyberspace Operations*, is in development, although it may not be completed until 2009.

39. Alfred Thayer Mahan, *The Influence of Sea Power upon History, 1660–1783* (Boston: Little, Brown and Company, 1890).

40. William Oliver Stephens and Allan Westcott, *A History of Sea Power* (New York: Doubleday, 1920), 443.

41. Although Douhet used the terms *aerial power* and *air power* within the first few pages of *The Command of the Air* (originally published in 1921, reprinted by the Office of Air Force History in 1983), he never clearly defined the term. In his editor's introduction to the 1983 reprint, Air Force historian Richard Kohn described airpower as "the use of space off the surface of the earth to decide war on the surface." The very first use of the term actually came with the onset of powered flight, in H.G. Wells' futuristic novel *The War in the Air*, published in 1908, which predicted some of the massed aerial attacks on cities and civilians seen later in the 20th century.

42. While the concept of cyber superiority offered here is clearly a comparison between competitors, the concept of cyberpower offered here is by no means a comparison and is not intended to be seen in a zero-sum context. Indeed, one of the oft-cited attributes of cyberspace is its ability to augment and empower many users simultaneously.

43. See Thomas L. Friedman, *The World is Flat: A Brief History of the Twenty-first Century* (New York: Farrar, Straus and Giroux, 2005); it is curious that the term *cyberspace* is not listed in the index, because cyberspace's impact on the 21st century drips from every page of this marvelous analysis of the future.

44. One of the assignments the author gives students at the National Defense University is to watch international and non-U.S. television to gain a perspective on how information is being used by others in the global battle for ideas. How do they access television from dozens of countries all over the globe? Via the Internet, of course, and by going to Web sites such as <www.yourglobaltv.com/portal.htm>, they can access television programming from all over the Earth.

45. Indeed, one of the criticisms that can be made of the National Security Presidential Directive 54–type approach is that it focuses too narrowly on military and governmental information networks without sufficient appreciation of their growing reliance on civilian networks and infrastructures.

46. Mahan, 25; for Possony's list, see Charles M. Westenhoff, *Military Air Power* (Maxwell Air Force Base, AL: Air University Press, 1990), 24.

47. For a cogent analysis of the cyber event in Estonia in May 2007, see Joshua Davis, "Hackers Take Down the Most Wired Country in Europe," *Wired* 15, no. 9 (August 22, 2007), available at <www.wired.com/print/politics/security/magazine/15-09/ff_estonia>.

Chapter 3

1. Department of Defense, *2006 Quadrennial Defense Review Report* (Washington, DC: Department of Defense, February 6, 2006).

2. Charles D. Lutes, "INSS Project Summary: Towards a Theory of Spacepower," August 28, 2007.

3. Terms of Reference for study of "A Theory of Cyberpower," March 2006.

4. Harold R. Winton, "An Imperfect Jewel," presentation to Institute for National Strategic Studies workshop on theory of warfare, National Defense University, Washington, DC, September 2006.

5. Jim Holt, "Unstrung," *The New Yorker*, October 2, 2006.

6. An enumeration of key cyber events is provided in the appendix to this chapter.

7. Strategic Studies Group XXVI, "Convergence of SeaPower and CyberPower," July 24, 2007.

8. William Gibson, *Neuromancer* (New York: Ace Science Fiction, 1984).

9. *National Military Strategy for Cyberspace Operations* (Washington, DC: The Joint Staff, December 2006). More recently, Chairman of the Joint Chiefs of Staff Admiral Michael G. Mullen has proposed an alternative definition of *cyberspace*: "A global domain within the information environment consisting of the interdependent network of information technology infrastructures, including the Internet, telecommunications networks, computer systems, and embedded processors and controllers" (Joint Staff Action Processing Form, Action Number J–7A 00067–08, May 30, 2008).

10. Chairman of the Joint Chiefs of Staff, *The National Military Strategy of the United States of America—A Strategy for Today, A Vision for Tomorrow* (Washington, DC: The Joint Staff, 2004).

11. Joint Publication 3–0, *Joint Operations* (Washington, DC: The Joint Staff, September 17, 2006, incorporating change 1, February 13, 2008).

12. George E.P. Box, "Robustness in the Strategy of Scientific Model Building," in *Robustness in Statistics*, ed. R.L. Launer and G.N. Wilkinson (New York: Academic Press, 1979).

13. For each category, we briefly cite the chapters of the book that are relevant. Furthermore, in the appendix to this chapter, we introduce a brief timeline of major events that characterize each category.

14. In-depth theoretical discussions of cyberspace are provided in the following chapters of this book: chapter 4, "A Graphical Introduction to the Structural Elements of Cyberspace"; chapter 5, "Cyberspace and Infrastructure"; chapter 6, "Evolutionary Trends in Cyberspace"; chapter 7, "Information Security Issues in Cyberspace"; and chapter 8, "The Future of the Internet and Cyberpower."

15. As a bounding case, note that the fastest U.S. computer, Roadrunner (built by IBM and Los Alamos National Laboratory), is capable of more than 1 petaflop (1 quadrillion floating point calculations per second). John Markoff, "Military Supercomputer Sets Record," *The New York Times*, June 9, 2008.

16. The Nobel Prize in Physics for 2007 was awarded to Albert Fert of France and Peter Grunberg of Germany, who independently discovered this phenomenon.

17. IPv6 will provide 2^{128} addresses. This would provide 5×10^{28} addresses for each of the 6.5 billion people alive today.

18. See Jeremy M. Kaplan, *A New Conceptual Framework for Net-centric, Enterprise-wide, System-of-systems Engineering*, Defense and Technology Paper 29 (Washington, DC: Center for Technology and National Security Policy, National Defense University, July 2006).

19. To put this change in context, note that in 1971, processor speeds were on the order of 4×10^5 hertz (or 400 kilohertz) and the cost of 1 megabyte of dynamic random access memory (DRAM) was approximately $400 (in 2006 dollars). By 2006, commercial processor speeds were on the order of 4×10^9 hertz (or 4 gigahertz) and the cost of 1 megabyte of DRAM was $0.0009. Sally Adee, "37 Years of Moore's Law," *IEEE Spectrum* (May 2008).

20. In-depth theoretical discussions of the military and informational dimensions of cyberpower are provided in the following chapters of this book: chapter 10, "An Environmental Approach to Understanding Cyberpower"; chapter 11, "Military Cyberpower"; chapter 14, "Cyber Influence and International Security"; chapter 15, "Tactical Influence Operations"; and chapter 17, "Facilitating Stability Operations with Cyberpower."

21. Carl von Clausewitz, *On War*, ed. and trans. Michael Howard and Peter Paret (Princeton: Princeton University Press, 1975).

22. Charles J. Dunlap, "Neo-Strategicon: Modernized Principles of War for the 21st Century," *Military Review* (March-April 2006).

23. Halford J. Mackinder, "The Geographical Pivot of History," *The Geographical Journal* (1904).

24. Alfred Thayer Mahan, *The Influence of Sea Power upon History, 1660–1783* (Boston: Little, Brown and Company, 1890).

25. Giulio Douhet, *The Command of the Air*, trans. Dino Ferrari (New York: Coward-McCann, 1942).
26. Colin S. Gray and Geoffrey Sloan, eds., *Geopolitics, Geography, and Strategy* (London: Routledge, 1999).
27. David S. Alberts and Richard E. Hayes, "Power to the Edge," Command and Control Research Program, June 2003. Note that the figure does not explicitly depict the social domain.
28. David T. Signori and Stuart H. Starr, "The Mission Oriented Approach to NATO C² Planning," *Signal* (September 1987), 119–127.
29. George Gilder, "Metcalfe's Law and Legacy," *Forbes ASAP*, September 13, 1993.
30. Bob Briscoe, Andrew Odlyzko, and Benjamin Tilly, "Metcalfe's Law is Wrong," *IEEE Spectrum* (July 2006). To illustrate the differences in these results, assume that one has a network of 100 users. According to "Metcalfe's Law," the "value" of the network is on the order of 10,000. However, the revised "law" suggests that the value is on the order of 100 x 2 = 200.
31. Daniel Gonzales et al., "Network-centric Operations Case Study: Air-to-Air Combat with and without Link 16" (Santa Monica, CA: RAND/National Defense Research Institute, 2005).
32. In-depth theoretical discussions of cyberspace are provided in the following chapters of this book: chapter 13, "Deterrence of Cyber Attacks"; chapter 18, "Cyber Crime"; chapter 19, "Cyber Terrorism: Menace or Myth?"; and chapter 20, "Nation-state Cyber Strategies: Examples from China and Russia."
33. *Hacktivism* (a portmanteau of *hack* and *activism*) is often understood as the writing of code, or otherwise manipulating bits, to promote political ideology. "Hacktivism," *Wikipedia*, available at <http://en.wikipedia.org/wiki/Hacktivism>.
34. Marc Sageman, "The Homegrown Young Radicals of Next-Gen Jihad," *The Washington Post*, June 8, 2008, B1.
35. Frank Cilluffo et al., "NETworked Radicalization: A Counter-Strategy," Homeland Security Policy Institute and Critical Incident Analysis Group Task Force on Internet-facilitated Radicalization, Washington, DC, May 2007, available at <www.gwumc.edu/hspi/reports/NETworked%20Radicalization_A%20Counter%20Strategy.pdf>.
36. Joseph S. Nye, Jr., *Understanding International Conflicts: An Introduction to Theory and History* (New York: Pearson-Longman, 2005).
37. M. Elaine Bunn, *Can Deterrence Be Tailored?* Strategic Forum No. 225 (Washington, DC: National Defense University Press, January 2007).
38. AFEI Conference on Cyber Deterrence, Tysons Corner, VA, November 1–2, 2007.
39. For example, the United States might respond to a cyber attack through a variety of levers of power including diplomacy (for example, a demarche) or economic actions (restricting the flow of technology).
40. In-depth theoretical discussions of institutional factors are provided in the following chapters of this book: chapter 21, "Internet Governance"; chapter 22, "International Law and Information Operations"; chapter 23, "Cyberpower and Critical Infrastructure Protection: A Critical Assessment of Federal Efforts"; and chapter 24, "Cyberpower from the Presidential Perspective."
41. OASD (NII)/DOD CIO Globalization Task Force, "Development of an Internet Influence/Evolution Strategy for the Department of Defense," October 19, 2007.
42. John Soat, "IT Confidential: Is There Anything That Can Be Done About E-mail?" *Information Week*, February 17, 2007.
43. Audi Lagorce, "Clearwire, Sprint Nextel Scrap WiMax Network Agreement," *Market Watch*, November 9, 2007.
44. Michael J. Riezenman, "Melding Mind and Machine," *The Institute*, June 2008, available

at <www.ieee.org/portal/site/tionline/menuitem.130a3558587d56e8fb2275875bac26c 8/index.jsp?&pName=institute_level1_article&TheCat=2201&article=tionline/legacy/ inst2008/jun08/featuretechnology.xml&>.

45. Council of Europe, Convention on Cybercrime, November 23, 2001, available at <http://conventions.coe.int/Treaty/en/Treaties/Word/185.doc>.

46. Emad Aboelela, *Network Simulation Experiments Manual*, 3ᵈ ed. (San Francisco: Morgan Kaufmann, June 2003).

47. Ira Kohlberg, "Percolation Theory of Coupled Infrastructures," presentation at 2007 Homeland Security Symposium, "Cascading Infrastructure Failures: Avoidance and Response," National Academy of Sciences, Washington, DC, May 2007.

48. Strategic Multi-Layer Analysis Team, "Deterrence in the 21ˢᵗ Century: An Effects-Based Approach in an Interconnected World, Volume I," sponsored by USSTRATCOM Global Innovation and Strategy Center, October 1, 2007.

49. William Wimbish and Jeffrey Sterling, "A National Infrastructure Simulation and Analysis Center (NISAC): Strategic Leader Education and Formulation of Critical Infrastructure Policies," Center for Strategic Leadership, U.S. Army War College, August 2003.

50. Chairman of the Joint Chiefs of Staff, *Joint Vision 2010* (Washington, DC: The Joint Staff, July 1996).

51. Arthur Cebrowski and Anita Jones, "Advanced Battlespace Information System: Volume I," 1996.

52. Arthur Cebrowski and John Garstka, "Network Centric Warfare: Its Origin and Future," U.S. Naval Institute *Proceedings* (January 1998).

53. Josh Rogin, "Air Force to Create Cyber Command," *FCW.COM*, November 13, 2006.

54. Thomas L. Friedman, *The World Is Flat: A Brief History of the Twenty-first Century* (New York: Farrar, Straus and Giroux, 2005).

55. Walter Pincus, "State Department Tries Blog Diplomacy," *The Washington Post*, November 19, 2007, A15.

56. ICANN Factsheet, "Root Server Attack on 6 February, 2007," March 1, 2007.

57. Joshua Davis, "Hackers Take Down the Most Wired Country in Europe," *Wired* 15, no. 9 (August 22, 2007).

Chapter 4

1. While IP-based networks are packet-switched technologies, individual links, especially stable point-to-point links with constant connectivity, are usually carried over circuit-switched technology provided by legacy telecommunications, cable, or cellular networks.

2. IPv6 uses 128-bit addresses.

3. The hierarchical file system may or may not be visible to the user. Some operating systems and applications hide this organizational structure from users, trying to simplify human interactions with the machine.

4. Queries for relational databases are usually formatted in the Structured Query Language (SQL), a standardized language for interacting with databases. Relational database software is available from a large number of commercial software companies, such as Oracle and Microsoft. An open-source relational database called MySQL is also popular.

5. The Slashdot Web site is <http://slashdot.org>; Ars Technica is available at <www. arstechnica.com>; and the Gizmodo Web site is <http://gizmodo.com>.

Chapter 5

1. Stuart Chase, *Men and Machines* (New York: Macmillan, 1929), 288–289, 297.

2. Mark Clodfelter, "Pinpointing Devastation: American Air Campaign Planning before Pearl Harbor," *The Journal of Military History* 58 (January 1994), 75–101; United States

Strategic Bombing Survey (hereafter USSBS), *Over-All Report (European War)* (Washington, DC: U.S. Government Printing Office, 1945); USSBS, *The Effects of Strategic Bombing on the German War Economy* (Washington, DC: U.S. Government Printing Office, October 31, 1945); USSBS, *The Effects of Strategic Bombing on Japan's War Economy* (Washington, DC: U.S. Government Printing Office, December 1946).

3. USSBS, *Statistical Appendix to Over-All Report (European War)* (Washington, DC: U.S. Government Printing Office, February 1947).

4. USSBS, *The War against Japanese Transportation, 1941–1945* (Washington, DC: U.S. Government Printing Office, May 1947).

5. Attacks against Japan's oil infrastructure were judged, by contrast, to have been "almost superfluous" because the war on transportation had already largely idled the refineries for want of feedstocks. USSBS, *The Effects of Strategic Bombing on Japan's War Economy*, 46–47.

6. Thomas A. Keaney and Eliot A. Cohen, *Gulf War Air Power Survey: Summary Report* (Washington, DC: Air Force Historical Studies Office, U.S. Government Printing Office, 1993).

7. James Glanz, "Iraq Insurgents Starve Capital of Electricity," *The New York Times*, December 19, 2006.

8. Network theory is an active research field, and a number of important discoveries have been made in recent years. See Albert-László Barabási, *Linked: How Everything Is Connected to Everything Else and What It Means for Business, Science, and Everyday Life* (New York: Plume Books, 2003), for an excellent nontechnical overview by a leader in modern network theory. For a more technical summary, see Réka Albert and Albert-László Barabási, "Statistical Mechanics of Complex Networks," *Reviews of Modern Physics* 74 (January 2002), 47–97. Duncan J. Watts, *Six Degrees: The Science of a Connected Age* (New York: Norton, 2003) is another sound nontechnical overview by a prominent scientist, oriented more toward social networks than infrastructures.

9. The terms *link*, *edge*, and *line* are used interchangeably in discussing networks. Similarly, *node*, *vertex*, and *point* all refer to the same thing. Networks are also referred to as *graphs*.

10. The most fundamental statistic describing a complex network is p_k, the proportion of the network's nodes having exactly k links connecting to other nodes. Naturally, k has to be a whole number; a node cannot have $2\frac{1}{2}$ or 4.38 links. A node having k links is said to have *degree k*, and the table or set of values of p_k for all values of k is called the degree distribution of the network.

11. It seems odd to speak of "random" networks in connection with infrastructures, where the design choices are not made by rolling dice or drawing from a hat. But infrastructures do tend to develop through a sequence of choices reflecting a variety of changing considerations, and this gives them a certain statistical or random-like character.

12. Dmitri Krioukov et al., "The Workshop on Internet Topology (WIT) Report," *Computer Communication Review* 37, no. 1 (2007), 69–73.

13. Computer Science and Telecommunications Board, *The Internet Under Crisis Conditions: Learning from September 11* (Washington, DC: National Academies Press, 2003).

14. For an overview of the electricity grid, see Jack Casazza and Frank Delea, *Understanding Electric Power Systems: An Overview of the Technology and the Marketplace* (Hoboken, NJ: IEEE Press and Wiley-Interscience, 2003).

15. In electrical terminology, any equipment or system that draws electric power is a *load*.

16. The advent of new transmission technology such as high-temperature superconductors may reduce but not eliminate the advantage of high-capacity transmission.

17. Transformers do not work for direct current (DC), and there is no simple DC equivalent.

18. To distribute current from high-voltage direct current lines, it is necessary first to convert it to alternating current.

19. There is a partial exception to this, in that one of the synchronous regions, that in

northeastern Canada operated by Hydro-Québec, is a major power exporter from its large hydroelectric generating facilities. The power is almost all exported via a high-voltage direct current line that prevents frequency disturbances from spreading, but a sudden major voltage disturbance, either in this region or in the northeastern U.S. region to which it sells power, would put the other region under stress.

20. Richard F. Hirsh, *Power Loss: The Origins of Deregulation and Restructuring in the American Electric Utility System* (Cambridge: MIT Press, 1999).

21. Frank A. Wolak, "Diagnosing the California Electricity Crisis," *The Electricity Journal* 16, no. 7 (August 2003), 11–37.

22. Secretary of Energy Advisory Board, *Maintaining Reliability in a Competitive U.S. Electricity Industry: Final Report of the Task Force on Electric System Reliability* (Washington, DC: Department of Energy, September 29, 1998).

23. The comprehensive official report is illuminating about the mechanisms of failure. U.S.-Canada Power System Outage Task Force, *Final Report on the August 14, 2003, Blackout in the United States and Canada: Causes and Recommendations* (Washington, DC, and Ottawa: U.S. Department of Energy and Natural Resources Canada, April 2004). Also useful is North American Electric Reliability Council (NERC), *Technical Analysis of the August 14, 2003, Blackout: What Happened, Why, and What Did We Learn?* (Princeton: NERC, July 2004). Also see Richard Pérez-Peña, "Utility Could Have Halted '03 Blackout, Panel Says," *The New York Times*, April 6, 2004, A16. "Blackout 101," a series of tutorial presentations developed by experts to inform Congress, is available at <www.ieee.org/portal/site/pes/menuite m.2b4756efb9a16c58fb2275875bac26c8/index.jsp?&pName=pes_level1&path=pes/ subpages/meetings-folder/other_meetings&file=Blackout_101.xml&xsl=generic.xsl> or <http://tinyurl.com/yur6o4>.

24. In many cases, the lines and generators were not actually immediately threatened but only appeared to be due to the large power surges triggered by the cascade. If the safety relays had been better able to discriminate between real and apparent threats, the outage could have been much less widespread.

25. U.S.-Canada Power System Outage Task Force, 131–137.

26. S. Massoud Amin and Philip Schewe, "Preventing Blackouts," *Scientific American* 296, no. 5 (May 2007), 60–67; S. Massoud Amin and Bruce F. Wollenberg, "Toward a Smart Grid," *IEEE Power and Energy Magazine* 3, no. 5 (September-October 2005), 34–38; and Clark W. Gellings and Kurt E. Yeager, "Transforming the Electric Infrastructure," *Physics Today* 57, no. 12 (December 2004), 45–51. See also "Ideas Generated for Transforming the Electric Infrastructure," *Physics Today* 58, no. 5 (May 2005), 13–15.

27. Supramaniam Srinivasan et al., "Fuel Cells: Reaching the Era of Clean and Efficient Power Generation in the Twenty-first Century," *Annual Reviews of Energy and the Environment* 24 (1999), 281–328.

28. John M. Deutch and Ernest J. Moniz, "The Nuclear Option," *Scientific American* 295, no. 3 (September 2006), 76–83; James A. Lake, Ralph G. Bennett, and John F. Kotek, "Next-generation Nuclear Power," *Scientific American* 286, no. 1 (January 2002), 72–81.

29. George W. Crabtree and Nathan S. Lewis, "Solar Energy Conversion," *Physics Today* 60, no. 3 (March 2007), 37–42; Ken Zweibel, James Mason, and Vasilis Fthenakis, "A Solar Grand Plan," *Scientific American* 298, no. 1 (January 2008), 64–73; Daniel M. Kammen, "The Rise of Renewable Energy," *Scientific American* 295, no. 3 (September 2006), 84–93.

30. Kammen; Karl Stahlkopf, "Taking Wind Mainstream," *IEEE Spectrum* (June 2006).

31. W. Wyatt Gibbs, "Plan B for Energy," *Scientific American* 295, no. 3 (September 2006), 102–114.

32. The United States has 4 million miles of public roads, 100,000 miles of Class I rail lines, and 26,000 miles of waterways that also represent networked infrastructures, but they are not discussed here because they are less vulnerable to cyber attack.

33. Department of Transportation, "National Transportation Statistics, 2007," table 1–10, available at <www.bts.gov/publications/national_transportation_statistics/>.
34. Paul W. Parfomak, "Pipeline Safety and Security: Federal Programs," CRS Report RL33347 (Washington, DC: Congressional Research Service, July 11, 2007), 1–2.
35. Ellen Nakashima and Steven Mufson, "Hackers Have Attacked Foreign Utilities, CIA Analyst Says," *The Washington Post*, January 19, 2008, A4.
36. Andy Greenberg, "America's Hackable Backbone," August 22, 2007, available at <www.forbes.com/2007/08/22/scada-hackers-infrastructure-tech-security-cx_ag_0822hack.html>.
37. John Rollins and Clay Wilson, "Terrorist Capabilities for Cyberattack: Overview and Policy Issues," CRS Report RL33123 (Washington, DC: Congressional Research Service, January 22, 2007).
38. Howard F. Lipson, Nancy R. Mead, and Andrew P. Moore, "Can We Ever Build Survivable Systems from COTS Components?" CMU/SEI–2001–TN–030 (Pittsburgh: Carnegie Mellon University, Software Engineering Institute, December 2001).
39. It may be objected that attackers do routinely find and exploit important design flaws in the software on Internet-connected computers. However, EMS and SCADA systems are much less available for examination and probing. Moreover, the relative simplicity of SCADA systems, in particular, allows less opportunity for serious hidden flaws. Thus, devastating attacks on these systems are far less likely. This is borne out by experience, as attacks on EMS and SCADA systems by hackers have thus far been much less common and generally less serious than those directed at Internet computers and servers.
40. Control Systems Security and Test Center, "A Comparison of Electrical Sector Cyber Security Standards and Guidelines," INEEL/EXT–04–02428, Revision 0, Idaho National Engineering and Environmental Laboratory, October 28, 2004.
41. See, for example, Richard A. Clarke, *Breakpoint* (New York: Putnam, 2007); Will O'Neil, *The Libyan Kill* (New York: W.W. Norton, 1980).
42. Since the March 2003 American invasion, insurgents have targeted Iraq's infrastructure, especially its oil and electricity infrastructure. There have been repeated physical attacks on oil production facilities and especially pipelines. See Iraq Pipeline Watch, available at <www.iags.org/iraqpipelinewatch.htm>. Electric grid attacks have been aimed at high-voltage transmission lines. Many people have been killed. There are no reports of cyber attacks, but neither the oil nor electrical system has much in the way of SCADA or operational management systems as potential cyber targets. The identities of the attackers and their strategies, goals, and incentives are unclear; their motives may be profit as much as politics. They have not destroyed the oil or electrical systems, but it is not clear whether that is their intention; they certainly have imposed major problems and costs. The lack of adequate and reliable electrical power has been a factor in demoralizing and angering the population and undercutting support for U.S. objectives. Loss of oil revenues has significantly weakened the Iraqi government and forced the United States to subsidize it. Substantial U.S. forces have had to be devoted to protection of infrastructure. The limitations of domestic production of petroleum products and electricity have forced large-scale trucking of fuels from Iran, Kuwait, and Turkey, and substantial effort is required to protect the fuel convoys. The problems of fuels logistics have been greatly exacerbated by an ill-considered American decision at an early stage to boost Iraqi electrical generating capacity with combustion turbines (turbogenerators driven by the exhaust from aircraft-type jet engines), which were ill suited to Iraqi needs and conditions and which required fuel that must be trucked in because it is not available in Iraq. Glenn Zorpette, "Re-engineering Iraq," *IEEE Spectrum* 43, no. 2 (February 2006), 22–35. Advance examination of Iraq's real needs on a total-system basis would have paid significant dividends.

43. Daniel Jackson, Martyn Thomas, and Lynette I. Millett, eds., *Software for Dependable Systems: Sufficient Evidence?* (Washington, DC: National Academies Press, 2007).

44. President's Commission on Critical Infrastructure Protection, *Critical Foundations: Protecting America's Infrastructures: The Report of the President's Commission on Critical Infrastructure Protection*, October 1997, available at <www.fas.org/sgp/library/pccip.pdf>.

45. Parfomak.

46. The latest Network Reliability and Interoperability Council concluded its work in 2005. See <www.nric.org/>.

47. U.S. Department of Energy, Secretary of Energy Advisory Board, *Maintaining Reliability in a Competitive U.S. Electricity Industry*, available at <www.seab.energy.gov/publications/esrfinal.pdf>.

48. *Mandatory Reliability Standards for Critical Infrastructure Protection*, FERC Docket No. RM06–22–000, Order No. 706, issued January 18, 2008.

49. See <www.dhs.gov/xprevprot/committees/>.

50. The Tennessee Valley Authority is the most prominent exception.

51. Steven L. Schwarcz, "Private Ordering," *Northwestern University Law Review* 97, no. 1 (January 2002), 319–349.

52. It is in some way similar to the problem of regulating hedge funds and like entities, which can have very infrequent but extremely costly failures. See Dean P. Foster and H. Peyton Young, "The Hedge Fund Game," Brookings Institution Center on Social and Economic Dynamics Working Paper No. 53, November 14, 2007.

53. Based on data in "National Transportation Statistics," available at <www.bts.gov/publications/national_transportation_statistics/>.

54. Centers for Disease Control and Prevention, "Web-based Injury Statistics Query and Reporting System (WISQARS)," available at <www.cdc.gov/ncipc/wisqars/>.

55. Clark R. Chapman, "The Hazard of Near-Earth Asteroid Impacts on Earth," *Earth and Planetary Science Letters* 222, no. 1 (May 2004), 1–15.

56. M. Granger Morgan, "Risk Analysis and Management," *Scientific American* 269, no. 1 (July 1993), 32–41; Paul Slovic et al., "Risk as Analysis and Risk as Feelings," *Risk Analysis* 24, no. 2 (April 2004), 311–322.

57. "What would we do if the United States were attacked and New York menaced? . . . A deafening roar—another and another. . . . There is another blast—and the rush to the streets begins. . . . The streets are tightly filled before a third of the office workers have poured out. Tardy ones claw and clutch and scramble, clambering on top of those who have fallen. Before long there is a yelling, bloody, fighting mass of humanity." William Mitchell, "When the Air Raiders come," *Collier's*, May 1, 1926.

58. Christopher Gelpi, Peter D. Feaver, and Jason Reifler, "Success Matters: Casualty Sensitivity and the War in Iraq," *International Security* 30, no. 3 (Winter 2005/2006), 47–86, provides a guide to earlier literature. See also Louis J. Klarevas, Christopher Gelpi, and Jason Reifler, "Casualties, Polls, and the Iraq War," *International Security* 31, no. 2 (Fall 2006), 186–198, for a critique and response. For a survey of data on support for wars between 1942 and 1993, see Eric V. Larson, *Casualties and Consensus: The Historical Role of Casualties in Domestic Support for U.S. Military Operations*, MR–726–RC (Santa Monica, CA: RAND, 1996), 105–120.

59. Lee Clarke, "Panic: Myth or Reality?" *Contexts* 1, no. 3 (Fall 2002), 21–26.

60. "Risk as Analysis and Risk as Feelings: Some Thoughts about Affect, Reason, Risk, and Rationality," *Risk Analysis* 24, no. 2 (April 2004), 311–322.

61. Antonio R. Damasio, *The Feeling of What Happens: Body and Emotion in the Making of Consciousness* (New York: Harcourt Brace, 1999).

Chapter 6

1. Two examples come to mind: the Pointcast fad of 1996 and the rise and fall of Napster in 2001. Pointcast was a much-hyped screen saver that delivered news updates across the World Wide Web. The Pointcast company eventually collapsed and delivery of news via screen savers never caught on, but the underlying trend of gathering, researching, and disseminating news via the Internet itself has grown rapidly. Similarly, Napster and free file sharing were much ballyhooed concepts in 2000, but the original Napster disappeared in a flurry of lawsuits over music copyright issues. However, both file sharing and online music sales have flourished since.

2. Intel Corporation, "Moore's Law," available at <www.intel.com/technology/mooreslaw/index.htm.>

3. This practice of naming certain technological industry observations or principles as "laws" is common in the information technology industry, probably modeled on Moore's law.

4. Bob Briscoe, Andrew Odlyzko, and Benjamin Tilly, "Metcalfe's Law Is Wrong," *IEEE Spectrum* (July 2006).

5. International Telecommunication Union, "Broadband Penetration by Technology, Top 20 Countries Worldwide, 2004," available at <www.itu.int/ITU-D/ict/statistics/at_glance/top20_broad_2004.html>.

6. "What Is the Speed of Standard Data Rates?" Whatis.com, available at <http://whatis.techtarget.com/definition/0,,sid9_gci214198,00.html>.

7. The role of the Internet Engineering Task Force in the development of Internet technology is explained in chapter 21 in this volume, "Internet Governance."

8. Bugs in IPv4 stacks, which allowed an attacker to crash a target system by sending a large ping packet, lead to the Ping of Death attack in 1996. Similarly, the Land attack of 1997 let an attacker drive a target system's central processing unit to 100 percent across the network by sending a spoofed packet with unusual settings to the target system. This vulnerability was originally discovered in most major operating systems in 1997 and was quickly patched. Yet in 2005, the vulnerability reappeared in a patch update to Microsoft Windows, forcing Microsoft to issue yet another patch to fix this recurrent flaw.

9. In an example of search directives, Google's "filetype:" allows a search for specific types of files: Microsoft Excel spreadsheets, where "filetype:xls" is a search term, or MS Word documents, if a search includes filetype:doc, while "site:" limits search results to a given Web site. An operator such as "-" (NOT) filters out all Web pages with a given term; using the operator "AND" allows a search limited to results containing both of the terms on either side of the operator.

10. Rich Gordon, "Convergence Defined," *USC Annenberg Online Journalism Review*, available at <www.ojr.org/ojr/business/1068686368.php>.

11. John Borland, "iTunes Outsells Traditional Music Stores," CNET News, November 2005, available at <http://news.com.com/iTunes+outsells+traditional+music+stores/2100-1027_3-5965314.html>.

12. Marshall Kirkpatrick, "YouTube Serves 100m Videos Each Day," TechCrunch, July 2006, available at <www.techcrunch.com/2006/07/17/youtube-serves-100m-videos-each-day/>.

13. See chapter 18, "Cyber Crime," in this volume.

14. Bots and their associated botnets are described in detail at <http://en.wikipedia.org/wiki/Botnet>.

15. Miniwatts Marketing Group, "World Internet Usage and Population Stats," available at <www.internetworldstats.com/stats.htm>.

16. Robert Lemos, "Zotob Suspects Arrested in Turkey and Morocco," *Security Focus*, August 2005, available at <www.securityfocus.com/news/11297>.

17. Nathan Thornburgh, "Inside the Chinese Hack Attack," *Time*, August 2005, available at <www.time.com/time/nation/article/0,8599,1098371,00.html>.

18. Brian McWilliams, "North Korea's School for Hackers," *Wired*, June 2003, available at <www.wired.com/news/politics/0,59043-0.html>.

19. "MySpace," Wikipedia, available at <http://en.wikipedia.org/wiki/Myspace>.

20. "Weblogs Cumulative," *Technorati*, January 2006, available at <www.sifry.com/alerts/archives/000419.html>.

21. United States Institute of Peace, "www.terror.net: How Modern Terrorists Use the Internet," March 2004, available at <www.usip.org/pubs/specialreports/sr116.html>. Also see chapter 19 in this volume, "Cyber Terrorism: Menace or Myth?"

22. Thomas L. Friedman, *The World is Flat: A Brief History of the 21ˢᵗ Century* (New York: Farrar, Straus and Giroux, 2005).

23. "Linden Dollars" can be bought and sold in the online community using U.S. dollars.

Chapter 7

1. The transmission control protocol and Internet protocol are standards that make the Internet possible.

2. For the purposes of this chapter, differentiating a medium scale is not necessary. Intermediate-sized attacks can be considered either smallish large-scale attacks or big small-scale attacks.

3. Data from the Anti-Phishing Working Group, a nonprofit organization created to track phishing attacks and educate users in methods for avoiding such scams. See <www.antiphishing.org>.

4. A nontechnical discussion of the Estonian attack is Mark Landler and John Markoff, "Digital Fears Emerge After Data Siege in Estonia," *The New York Times*, May 24, 2007. For technical details of the attack, see Beatrix Toth, "Estonia Under Cyber Attack," at <www.cert.hu/dmdocuments/Estonia_attack2.pdf>.

5. The 13 root servers are housed in multiple sites worldwide; some are single-site installations with a single machine constituting the DNS server, while others use a technology called *anycast* to have multiple distributed machines function as a single root DNS server. The root servers that rely on anycast are less prone to outages from packet floods because they distribute the load across multiple separate machines. See <http://root-servers.org/>.

6. ICANN Fact Sheet, "Root Server Attack on 6 February 2007," March 2007, available at <www.icann.org/announcements/factsheet-dns-attack-08mar07.pdf>.

7. Legitimate TCP traffic follows the pattern SYN, SYN–ACK, ACK, followed by a connection. SYN floods have a SYN and a SYN–ACK, but no completion of the three-way handshake or the follow-on connection.

8. Examples of some significant router vulnerabilities include: May 2001, vulnerability in routing protocol update (using the Border Gateway Protocol) could have been used to crash router (see <www.kb.cert.org/vuls/id/106392>); August 2003, four specially crafted packets could have stopped routers from routing (see <http://nvd.nist.gov/nvd.cfm?cvename=CVE-2003-0567>); April 2004, method for resetting routing updates could have made communications gradually decay as routers could not receive network topology updates (see <www.us-cert.gov/cas/techalerts/TA04-111A.html>); July 2005, method found for exploiting router coding flaws that lets an attacker control router (see <http://nvd.nist.gov/nvd.cfm?cvename=CVE-2005-3481>); May 2007, error in crypto library in major routers could have been used to take over routers (see <http://nvd.nist.gov/nvd.cfm?cvename=CVE-2006-3894>).

9. For technical details of this attack, see <http://kerneltrap.org/node/3072>.

10. See <www.wired.com/politics/security/news/2005/08/68365>.

11. Examples of significant domain name system (DNS) server vulnerabilities include: November 2002, DNS vulnerability could have let attacker take over DNS server (see <http://nvd.nist.gov/nvd.cfm?cvename=CVE-2002-0029>); April 2005, DNS cache poisoning attacks could have let attackers redirect traffic by tricking servers into loading bogus DNS records (see <www.ncs.gov/library/tech_bulletins/2005/tib_05-4.pdf>); April 2007, protocol used for management of Windows DNS servers was vulnerable, allowing for takeover of DNS server (see <www.us-cert.gov/cas/techalerts/TA07-103A.html>); July 2007, flaw in DNS server allowed attackers to load bogus record and redirect traffic (see <www.isc.org/index.pl?/sw/bind/bind-security.php>).

12. Examples of such protocol-converting gateways include IP-to-IPX converters, as well as IP to Signaling System 7 gateways that convert IPv4 to the protocol used to control public telephone network switches.

13. See, for example, Seth Mydans, "Monks are Silenced, and for Now, Internet is Too," *The New York Times*, October 4, 2007.

14. The Internet Engineering Task Force calls itself "a large open international community of network designers, operators, vendors, and researchers concerned with the evolution of the Internet architecture and the smooth operation of the Internet." See <www.ietf.org/overview.html>.

15. The security of a certificate authority (CA) depends on how carefully the CA checks a given user's or enterprise's identity before issuing a certificate and how the CA protects the encryption keys used to sign the certificates. If a CA were to issue a certificate to an imposter that claimed, for example, to be a government agency, all users who relied on that CA's certificate would be exposed to the imposter.

16. Similarly, Microsoft built rudimentary file encryption technologies into Windows 2000 and later with a feature called the Encrypting File System (EFS). Other companies offer far superior encryption functions, but because a baseline capability is available for most Windows users, consumers can choose to use these security tools. While the Windows personal firewall is in widespread use because it is activated by default, EFS is seldom used, likely because it is off by default.

17. Microsoft's decisions about which security features to bundle into Windows and which to leave to third-party vendors require careful balancing of the interests of the company and its competitors, regulators, enterprises, and consumers.

Chapter 8

1. See Steven Cherry, "Winner: Nothing but Net," *IEEE Spectrum* (January 2007), available at <www.spectrum.ieee.org/jan07/4831>; and Paul V. Mockapetris, "Telephony's Next Act," *IEEE Spectrum* (April 2006), available at <www.spectrum.ieee.org/apr06/3204>.

2. See the discussion in chapter 6, "Evolutionary Trends in Cyberspace."

3. Two proposals currently funded by the National Science Foundation that explore this concept are Jon Turner et al., "An Architecture for a Diversified Internet," National Science Foundation grant CNS-0626661, accessed at <www.nets-find.net/DiversifiedInternet.php>; and Nick Feamster, Jennifer Rexford, and Lixin Gao, "CABO, Concurrent Architectures are Better than One," National Science Foundation Networking Technology and System grant CNS-0626771, accessed at <www.nets-find.net/Cabo.php>.

4. See, for example, the Defense Advanced Research Projects Agency (DARPA) Networking in Extreme Environments Program, available at <www.darpa.mil/sto/strategic/netex.html>; and the DARPA Next Generation Program, available at <www.darpa.mil/sto/smallunitops/xg.html>.

5. See, for example, the Gumstix computers at <http://gumstix.com/platforms.html> or the iButton computer at <www.maxim-ic.com/auto_info.cfm>.

6. Classical supercomputing combines specialized and typically custom-built hardware and software, including algorithms that may be associated with complex models of the physical world. See Computer Science and Telecommunications Board, *Getting Up to Speed: The Future of Supercomputing* (Washington, DC: National Academies Press, 2005).

7. Examples of volunteer activities include SETI@home (searching for extraterrestrial radio signals), available at <http://setiathome.berkeley.edu/>, and Folding@home (research into protein folding), available at <http://folding.stanford.edu/>.

8. Botnets involve the surreptitious placement of malicious software into personal computers (PCs), which are then mobilized into "nets" to perform attacks. The "@home" research projects suggest the potential for legitimate commercial botnets. This also raises questions about what might happen if PC owners willingly rent out their excess computational capacity. Such a practice might have implications for network capacity planning as well as liability and other practical issues.

9. A commodity server in this context refers to a mass-produced commercial computer, in contrast to a special-purpose machine.

10. Google is rumored to have almost a half-million commodity servers in operation. Rick Rashid of Microsoft has suggested that 75 percent of all servers in the United States are operated by just three companies: Google, Yahoo!, and Microsoft. Rick Rashid, remarks at 20th Anniversary Symposium of the Computer Science and Telecommunications Board, October 17, 2006.

11. There are also longer term trends, such as quantum computing, but we believe these will not be relevant to a discussion in the next decade.

12. Google has multiple server sites, but any one query is processed at one physical location. In that respect, the processing is centralized.

13. See <http://robotics.eecs.berkeley.edu/~pister/SmartDust/>.

14. See, for example, UCLA's Center for Embedded Networked Sensing, a National Science Foundation Science and Technology Center, at <http://research.cens.ucla.edu/>.

15. See, for example, U.S. Department of Transportation Intelligent Transport Systems Joint Project, available at <www.its.dot.gov/index.htm>. An overview can be found in Jonathan Fahey, "Car Talk," *Forbes,* January 29, 2007, 52–54.

16. The Center for Embedded Network Sensing at UCLA has a new program on "participatory sensing" as part of its efforts in urban sensing. See <http://research.cens.ucla.edu/projects/2007/Urban_Sensing/Applications/>.

17. Today, except for a few consumer items such as motion-sensing lights, sensors are in the hobbyist category.

18. For example, cell phone encryption is known to have limitations; WiFi deployments often lack any encryption, leaving them open to "wardriving" as people in cars search out networks to exploit (see <http://www.wardriving.com/>); and Bluetooth interception has also become recreation for the mischievous; see <http://seclists.org/lists/isn/2005/Feb/0085.html>.

19. See Weather Underground at <www.wunderground.com/>.

20. See, for example, the National Ecological Observatory Network at <www.neoninc.org/> and Earthscope at <www.earthscope.org/> in the United States.

21. A mashup combines data or functions from multiple sources into a single integrated tool; a mashup might add location information from Google Maps (<http://maps.google.com/maps?hl=en&tab=wl>) to real estate data from Craigslist (<www.craigslist.org/about/sites.html>) to create a service not available from either by itself.

22. This issue has been discussed and debated by observers of the social context of information. See Computer Science and Telecommunications Board, *Global Networks and Local Values* (Washington, DC: National Academies Press, 2001).

23. Today's proliferation of blogs and communal sites for sharing video clips, photos, and so on points to a seeming flowering of creative output led by individuals; this activity, in turn, has generated additional growth in associated business data.
24. See Wikipedia at <http://wikipedia.org/>.
25. See, for example, Jaron Lanier, "Digital Maoism: The Hazards of the New Online Collectivism," and the responses the article generated, available at <www.edge.org/3rd_culture/lanier06/lanier06_index.html>.
26. For example, the OptIPuter project, "named for its use of optical networking, computer storage, processing and visualization technologies," is meant "to enable collaborating scientists to interactively explore massive amounts of previously uncorrelated data." The hope is that:

    > the OptIPuter, when linked with remote "data generators," whether the TeraGrid, instrumentation, or data storage devices, will prove to be an enabling technology for large-scale networked science facilities, as well as for broader societal needs, including emergency response, homeland security, health services and science education.
    >
    > The TeraGrid comprises "resources at eleven partner sites to create an integrated, persistent computational resource. . . . Using high-performance network connections, the TeraGrid integrates high-performance computers, data resources and tools, and high-end experimental facilities around the country."

    See Faith Singer-Villalobos, "The OptIPuter: 21st-century E-science," available at <www.teragrid.org/news/news06/tg06_opti.html>.
27. See, for example, Department of State press release, "Secretary of State Establishes New Global Internet Freedom Task Force," available at <www.state.gov/r/pa/prs/ps/2006/61156.htm>.
28. See, for example, W3C Semantic Web site, available at <www.w3.org/2001/sw/>.
29. It is possible to tag a site in a way that diverts the crawlers used by search systems, and it is possible for crawlers to be programmed to ignore those tags. These possibilities create a space of contention for control surrounding search.
30. See "EU: Quaero—a European multimedia search engine project to rival world leaders in Internet search," accessed at <http://ec.europa.eu/idabc/en/document/5554/194>. For a skeptical assessment of its prospects, see Philip E. Ross, "Loser: What's the Latin for 'Delusional'?" *IEEE Spectrum* (January 2007), available at <www.spectrum.ieee.org/jan07/4842>.
31. A prominent example is Baidu, which in early 2008 expanded its operations to Japan, signaling international ambitions. See <http://ir.baidu.com/phoenix.zhtml?c=188488&p=irol-homeprofile>.
32. See K. Sollins, ed., "Architectural Principles of Uniform Resource Name Resolution," RFC 2276, Internet Engineering Task Force, 1998. For a discussion of confusion over terms, see "URIs, URLs, and URNs: Clarifications and Recommendations 1.0," available at <www.w3.org/TR/uri-clarification/>.
33. See Corporation for National Research Initiatives, "Handle System: Unique Persistent Identifiers for Internet Resources," available at <www.handle.net/>.
34. See, for example, Bryan Ford et al., "User-relative Names for Globally Connected Personal Devices," available at <http://publications.csail.mit.edu/abstracts/abstracts06/baford/baford.html>.
35. The TIA program (Total [or Terrorism] Information Awareness) begun at the Defense Advanced Research Projects Agency in 2002 explored ways to draw from multiple information stores on an ad hoc basis; some of that work continues under various auspices.
36. This function is often provided by third-party providers such as Akamai, discussed below.

37. The term *cloud computing* is being used to describe the idea of commodity computing service available within the Internet.
38. The Open Net Initiative at <www.opennetinitiative.org/> is one of several organizations tracking current content controls on the Internet.
39. See examples noted in Reporters without Borders, *Handbook for Bloggers and Cyber-Dissidents*, September 14, 2005, available at <www.rsf.org/rubrique.php3?id_rubrique=542>.
40. Applications being explored range from outer space to the battlefield. For pointers to current research, see <www.dtnrg.org/wiki> and <www.darpa.mil/sto/solicitations/DTN/>.
41. One illustration is "a camera phone visual tag reader" that acts as "the glue that connects the two halves of your application, the physical world deployment and the virtual world application software." See <http://semacode.com>.
42. See, for example, Second Life at <http://secondlife.com/>; Edward Castronova, *Synthetic Worlds: The Business and Culture of Online Games* (Chicago: The University of Chicago Press, 2006). For commentary and critique, see Jim Giles, "Life's a Game," *Nature,* 445 (January 4, 2007), 18–20.
43. These issues were discussed by Jon Kleinberg and, to some extent, Richard Karp at the 20th Anniversary Symposium of the Computer Science and Telecommunications Board, October 17, 2006.
44. Much attention has been given to the $100 laptop "one laptop per child" project (see <www.laptop.org/>) and, recently, Intel's similar effort, although some argue that for the foreseeable future, approaches that capitalize on the fact that in some cultures there is a greater level of comfort with shared technology, such as cell phones, may be more realistic.
45. Of course, it can be argued that not becoming overly dependent on cyberspace might convey a different kind of resourcefulness, one that may be important in the event of disruption of access.
46. Recent research programs have focused on making information technology more resilient: assuming failure of prevention (itself also a research focus), improved technology would better detect security problems, resist damage from them, continue to operate at some level despite damage, and even recover from them or regenerate damaged components.
47. See the final report of the Future-Generation Internet Architecture Project (NewArch) at <www.isi.edu/newarch/>.
48. This mechanism, once designed and deployed, might be usable by many actors for many purposes.
49. See, for example, P. Gutmann, "Simplifying public key management," *IEEE Computer* 37, no. 2 (February 2004).
50. U.S. Department of Defense, *5200.28-STD Trusted Computer System Evaluation Criteria* (December 1985), also known as the Orange Book.
51. For one speculation on this approach, see Butler Lampson, "Accountability and Freedom," available at <http://research.microsoft.com/~risaacs/blampson.ppt>.
52. See the discussion of pressures toward such outcomes in chapter 21 of this volume, "Internet Governance."
53. The standards-development process displays such rivalry regularly. Disputes over the open systems interconnection versus the transmission control protocol/Internet protocol suites and over standards for wireless communication, such as China's recent attempt to promote indigenous technology, have had international dimensions reflecting concerns ranging from classical competitiveness to cyberpower.
54. Korea has already experienced the challenge of slowing revenue flow due to market saturation, leading providers to consider usage-based pricing or other steps to preserve revenue flow. See Broadband Working Group, MIT Communications Futures Program,

"The Broadband Incentive Problem," September 2005, available at <http://cfb.mit.edu/groups/broadband/docs/2005/Incentive_Whitepaper_09-28-05.pdf>.

55. There are different degrees of openness in cell phone systems and conflicting trends. Different countries have more differences in cell phone service than in Internet service.

56. Constraints on innovation may promote monocultures, themselves a source of vulnerability.

57. The apparent failure of the much-heralded AOL–Time Warner merger provides but one cautionary tale about the uncertainties of predicting industry trends, which reflect, among other things, technology change, consequent shifts in buyer behavior and the costs of doing business, and what the government does and does not do.

58. See <www.akamai.com/>.

59. An example of such a site is <http://mycoke.com>.

60. See <www.tivo.com>.

61. The DVR situation is an instance of a larger battle associated with digital rights management: content generators have used the threat of withholding contracts and other legal maneuvers to induce consumer electronics manufacturers to produce devices that assist in the protection of content, although such devices also limit access and use of content that has fewer or no protections. See Julie E. Cohen, "Normal Discipline in the Age of Crisis," Georgetown University Law Center, Public Law and Legal Theory Research Paper No. 572486, August 4, 2004.

62. Growth in the Internet marketplace has attracted government attention to competitive conduct there, as evidenced by attention to antitrust issues on the occasion of certain mergers or acquisitions.

63. The International Telecommunication Union's promotion of "Next Generation Network" standards suggests an effort that combines traditional players and governments in promoting seemingly benign customary features such as priority access in emergencies, as well as law enforcement access (wiretapping) that may have broader implications. See <www.itu.int/ITU-T/ngn/index.phtml>.

64. See Federal Communications Commission, The Telecommunications Act of 1996, available at <www.fcc.gov/telecom.html>.

65. See <www.fcc.gov/calea/> and <www.cdt.org/digi_tele/>.

66. Similar kinds of concerns have been raised even for seemingly benign applications: the development of the Platform for Internet Content Selection (PICS) Web standard was more or less derailed when critics expressed concern that PICS could be used by governments to achieve censorship.

67. See, in this volume, chapter 5, "Cyberspace and Infrastructure," and chapter 23, "Cyberpower and Critical Information Protection: A Critical Assessment of Federal Efforts."

68. The effects of the 9/11 attacks on conventional telecommunications and the Internet reinforced the value of diversity, among other things, and should have boosted Internet service provider interest in this subject. See Computer Science and Telecommunications Board, *The Internet Under Crisis Conditions: Learning from September 11* (Washington, DC: National Academies Press, 2002).

69. Such decisions as have been made are limited to subjects such as articulation of principles and definitions (for example, of Internet governance).

70. See Computer Science and Telecommunications Board, *Broadband: Bringing Home the Bits* (Washington, DC: National Academies Press, 2002).

71. See Computer Science and Telecommunications Board, *Renewing U.S. Telecommunications Research* (Washington, DC: National Academies Press, 2006).

72. See, for example, <http://europa.eu.int/information_society/research/index_en.htm>.

73. See <www.nets-find.net/>.

74. See Global Environment for Network Initiatives Web site at <www.geni.net/>.

Chapter 9

1. Fred Cohen, "Experiments with Computer Viruses," 1984, available at <http://all. net/books/virus/part5.html>; Judith Klein-Seetharaman, "The Use of Analogies for Interdisciplinary Research in the Convergence of Nano-, Bio-, and Information Technology," National Science Foundation Report on Societal Implications of Nanoscience and Nanotechnology, 2004, available at <www.cs.cmu.edu/~judithks/ Klein-Seetharaman.2005.pdf>.
2. Daniel Geer et al., "CyberInsecurity: The Cost of Monopoly," September 2003, available at <http://cryptome.org/cyberinsecurity.htm>.
3. "Phylogenetic tree," *Wikipedia*, available at <http://en.wikipedia.org/wiki/Phylogenetic_ tree>.
4. Argentina, Brazil, Canada, China, South Africa, and the United States accounted for 99 percent of genetically manipulated crops in 2003; Pew Initiative on Food and Biotechnology fact sheet, "Genetically Modified Crops in the United States," August 2004, available at <www.pewtrusts.org/news_room_detail.aspx?id=17950>.
5. U.S. Department of Agriculture Economic Research Service Data Sets, "Adoption of Genetically Engineered Crops in the U.S.," July 2007, available at <www.ers.usda.gov/ Data/BiotechCrops>.
6. Judy Siegel-Itzkovich, "Scientists Use Gene Therapy to Cure Immune Deficient Child," *British Medical Journal* 325, no. 7354 (July 6, 2002), available at <www.pubmedcentral.nih. gov/articlerender.fcgi?artid=1123542>.
7. See Basic Local Assignment Search Tool at <www.ncbi.nlm.nih.gov/BLAST>. Harvard University provides a similar tool called QueryGene, available at <http://llama.med. harvard.edu/~jklekota/QueryGene.html>.
8. David A. Vise and Mark Malseed, *The Google Story* (New York: Bantam Dell, 2005), chapter 26, "Googling Your Genes."
9. 23andMe Web site, available at <www.23andme.com>.
10. University of Michigan news release, "New Cochlear Implant Could Improve Hearing," February 6, 2006, available at <www.umich.edu/news/index.html?Releases/2006/ Feb06/r020606a>.
11. Ray Kurzweil, *The Age of Spiritual Machines* (New York: Penguin Books, 1999).
12. Kristin Weidenbach, "Pacemaker for the Brain May Offer Control for Severe Depression," *Stanford Report*, October 11, 2000, available at <http://news-service.stanford.edu/ news/2000/october11/brain_pace-1011.html>; BBC Report, "Health: Latest News 'Pacemaker' for Parkinson's Disease," May 20, 1998, available at <http://news.bbc. co.uk/2/hi/health/97057.stm>.
13. Elizabeth A. Thomson, "Monkey Controls Robotic Arm Using Brain Signals Sent over the Internet," MIT News Office, December 6, 2000, available at <http://web. mit.edu/newsoffice/2000/monkeys-1206.html>; Duncan Graham-Rowe, "Monkey's Brain Signals Control 'Third Arm'," *New Scientist*, October 2003, available at <www. newscientist.com/article/dn4262-monkeys-brain-signals-control-third-arm.html>.
14. Tony Fitzpatrick, "Teenager Moves Video Icons Just by Imagination," Washington University in St. Louis News and Information, October 9, 2006, available at <http:// news-info.wustl.edu/news/page/normal/7800.html>.
15. Neural Signals Web site, available at <www.neuralsignals.com>.
16. Freeman Dyson, "Our Biotech Future," *The New York Review of Books*, July 19, 2007.

Chapter 10

1. Also see Gregory J. Rattray, *Strategic Warfare in Cyberspace* (Cambridge: MIT Press, 2001), 11–12.
2. Key early works addressing information warfare and the possibilities of conflicts based

on network attacks include Alvin and Heidi Toffler, *War and Anti-War: Survival at the Dawn of the 21ˢᵗ Century* (Boston: Little, Brown, 1993); John Arquilla and David Ronfeldt, "Cyberwar Is Coming!" *Comparative Strategy* 12, no. 2 (Spring 1993), 141–165; and Winn Schwartau, *Information Warfare: Chaos on the Electronic Superhighway* (New York: Thunder's Mouth Press, 1994).

3. *The National Security Strategy of the United States of America* (Washington, DC: The White House, September 2002), 1.
4. *The National Defense Strategy of the United States of America* (Washington, DC: Department of Defense, March 2005), 3.
5. *The National Strategy to Secure Cyberspace* (Washington, DC: The White House, February 2002).
6. See chapter 2 in this volume, "From Cyberspace to Cyberpower: Defining the Problem."
7. National Defense Strategy, 13.
8. See discussion of the International Telecommunication Union in chapter 21 of this volume, "Internet Governance."
9. See, for example, Seth Mydans, "Monks are Silenced, and for Now, Internet Is Too," *The New York Times*, October 4, 2007, available at <www.nytimes.com/2007/10/04/world/asia/04info.html?emc=etal>.
10. Rattray, 43–44.
11. For discussion of government control of the Internet and its limits, see chapter 21 in this volume, "Internet Governance."
12. Halford John Mackinder, "The Geographical Pivot of History," *The Geographical Journal* 23, no. 4 (1904), 421–437.
13. Nicholas Spykman, *Geography of the Peace* (New York: Harcourt and Brace, 1944).
14. Ibid., 43.
15. Alfred Thayer Mahan, *The Influence of Sea Power upon History, 1660–1783* (Boston: Little Brown, 1890), reprinted in David Jablonsky, ed., *Roots of Strategy*, vol. 4 (Mechanicsburg, PA: Stackpole Books, 1999).
16. Ibid., 28.
17. Ibid., 85.
18. Julian S. Corbett, *Some Principles of Maritime Strategy* (London: Longmans, Green, 1911).
19. Ibid., 55.
20. Heather Timmons, "Two Communication Cables in the Mediterranean Are Cut," *The New York Times*, January 31, 2008, available at <www.nytimes.com/2008/01/31/business/worldbusiness/31cable.html>.
21. Giulio Douhet, *Command of the Air*, trans. Dino Ferrari (New York: Coward-McCann, 1942), 61.
22. Hugh M. Trenchard, "Report on the Independent Air Force," January 1, 1919, 1334–1335.
23. William Mitchell, *Skyways: A Book on Modern Aeronautics* (Philadelphia: J.B. Lippincott, 1930), 255–256.
24. The need for a national effort is the primary focus of William Mitchell, *Winged Defense: The Development and Possibilities of Modern Airpower—Economic and Military* (New York: G.P. Putnam's Sons, 1925).
25. Douhet, 181.
26. Ronald Reagan, "Address to the Nation on National Security by President Ronald Reagan," March 23, 1983, available at <www.fas.org/spp/starwars/offdocs/rrspch.htm>.
27. "Report of the Commission to Assess United States National Security Space Management and Organization," January 11, 2001, available at <www.fas.org/spp/military/commission/report.htm>.
28. National Defense Strategy, 3.

29. William J. Broad and David A. Sanger, "China Tests Anti-Satellite Weapon, Unnerving U.S.," *The New York Times*, January 18, 2007, available at <www.nytimes.com/2007/01/18/world/asia/18cnd-china.html>.

30. Colin S. Gray and Geoffrey Sloan, *Geopolitics, Geography, and Strategy* (London: Frank Cass, 1999).

31. Mark E. Harter, "Ten Propositions Regarding Space Power: The Dawn of a Space Force," *Air and Space Power Journal* 20, no. 2 (Summer 2006), 68.

32. Ibid., 67.

33. Ibid.

34. Marshall McLuhan and Quentin Fiore, *War and Peace in the Global Village* (New York: Bantam Books, 1968).

35. Larry Greenemeier, "Estonian Attacks Raise Concern Over Cyber 'Nuclear Winter'," *Informationweek.com*, May 24, 2007, available at <www.informationweek.com/news/showArticle.jhtml?articleID=199701774>.

36. David Eshel, "Hezbollah's Intelligence War: Assessment of the Second Lebanon War," *Defenseupdate.com*, available at <www.defense-update.com/analysis>.

37. "Falun Gong Hijacks Chinese TV," *Wired*, September 24, 2002, available at <www.wired.com/politics/law/news/2002/09/55350>.

38. Gabriel Weimann, "www.terror.net: How Modern Terrorism Uses the Internet," U.S. Institute of Peace Special Report No. 116, March 2004, available at <www.usip.org/pubs/specialreports/sr116.html>.

39. Kathryn Westcott, "Transport Systems as Terror Targets," *BBC News*, July 7, 2005, available at <http://news.bbc.co.uk/1/hi/world/europe/4659547.stm>.

40. Tim Wilson, "Experts: U.S. Not Prepared for Cyber Attack," *DarkReading.com*, April 26, 2007, available at <www.darkreading.com/document.asp?doc_id=122732>.

41. Japanese Ministry of Information, "Basic Guidelines on the Promotion of an Advanced Information and Telecommunications Society," November 9, 1998, available at <www.kantei.go.jp/foreign/990209guideline-aits.html>.

42. Steve Coll and Susan B. Glasser, "Terrorists Turn to the Web as Base of Operations," *The Washington Post*, August 7, 2005, A1.

43. National Defense Strategy, 5.

44. Douhet, 196–197.

45. Ellen Knickmeyer and Jonathan Finer, "Insurgent Leader Al-Zarqawi Killed in Iraq," *The Washington Post*, June 8, 2006, available at <www.washingtonpost.com/wp-dyn/content/article/2006/06/08/AR2006060800114.html>.

46. The Slammer worm in 2003 caused major disruption across the Internet in less than 15 minutes. Paul Boutin, "Slammed! An Inside View of the Worm that Crashed the Internet," *Wired*, July 2003, available at <www.wired.com/wired/archive/11.07/slammer.html>.

47. "U.S. Passes Up Chance to Strike Taliban: Predator had Suspected Fighters in its Sights, but Military Passed on Shot," *MSNBC.com*, September 13, 2006, available at <www.msnbc.msn.com/id/14823099>.

48. Harter, 72.

49. David Leppard, "Al-Qaeda Plot to Bring Down UK Internet," *The Sunday Times*, March 11, 2007, available at <www.timesonline.co.uk/tol/news/uk/crime/article1496831.ece>.

50. Kenneth Neil Cukier, "Who Will Control the Internet?" *Foreign Affairs* 84, no. 6 (November-December 2005).

51. See, for example, Wayne Rash, "Cyber-Security Office Calls for More Clout," *Eweek.com*, December 10, 2004, available at <www.eweek.com/article2/0,1895,1739061,00.asp>; and Scot Petersen, "Wanted: Cyber-Security," *Eweek.com*, October 18, 2004, available at <www.eweek.com/article2/0,1895,1675483,00.asp>.

Chapter 11

1. The use of cyberspace to influence perceptions by carrying messages does not depend on other military media for its effect, but this is a different dimension of power and is not the subject of this chapter. For discussion of that dimension, see chapter 14 in this volume, "Cyber Influence and International Security."

2. The observe-orient-decide-act loop is also known as the Boyd cycle, after Air Force Colonel John Boyd who first articulated it. See John Coram, *Boyd: The Fighter Pilot Who Changed the Art of War* (Boston: Back Bay Books, 2004). On swarming, see Sean Edwards, *Swarming on the Battlefield: Past, Present, and Future* (Santa Monica, CA: RAND, 2000).

3. Martin van Creveld, *Command in War* (Cambridge: Harvard University Press, 1985), dwells on the difficulty that commanders have had in simply knowing where their forces were.

4. It might help indirectly, insofar as units that knew precisely where their cohorts were could coordinate actions better on a peer-to-peer basis, even if their means of communications were no more advanced than those available to U.S. soldiers in World War II.

5. See David Talbot, "How Technology Failed in Iraq," *Technology Review*, November 2004.

6. John J. Garstka presented a list of experiments in "Network Centric Operations: An Overview of Tenets and Key Concepts," presentation to the NCO Short Course at the National Defense University, May 18, 2005.

7. David Gonzales et al., "Network-Centric Operations Case Study: The Stryker Brigade Combat Team," MG 267–1–OSD (Santa Monica, CA: RAND, 2005).

8. Results drawn from briefing slides presented by Jack Forsyth, "Network-Centric Operations: Air-Air and Air-Ground Case Studies," delivered to NCO Short Course at the National Defense University, May 18, 2005.

9. The report suggests that the Stryker Brigade Combat Team was able to deceive and thus surprise the town's defenders as well, but it did not explain whether their communications capabilities played a role in their being able to do so when the Light Infantry Brigade could not.

10. To achieve statistical significance, one would have to run the experiment repeatedly with similar outcomes, as well as eliminating the Hawthorne effect (the tendency for people to perform better when they are subjects of an experiment).

11. Richard Overy, *Why the Allies Won* (New York: Norton, 1996), makes the case that it was worthwhile because it forced Germany to waste resources on air defense that it could ill afford.

Chapter 12

1. Defining the Internet broadly, this includes email and the World Wide Web as well as military and government Internet protocol–based networks. These include networks that have access to the Internet architecture—for example, the Nonsecure Internet Protocol Router Network—and those that do not—such as the Secret Internet Protocol Router Network and Joint Worldwide Intelligence Communications System, which are secure networks.

2. Department of Military Strategy, Planning, and Operations, "Campaign Planning Primer AY 07," U.S. Army War College, 2006, available at <www.carlisle.army.mil/usawc/dmspo/Publications/Campaign%20Planning%20Primer%20AY07.pdf>.

3. The "three-block war" concept is credited to General Charles Krulak, former Commandant of the Marine Corps.

4. Department of Defense, "Capstone Concept for Joint Operations," Version 2.0, August 2005, available at <www.dtic.mil/futurejointwarfare/concepts/approved_ccjov2.pdf>.

5. Joint Publication 3–13, *Information Operations* (Washington, DC: The Joint Staff, February 13, 2006), available at <www.dtic.mil/doctrine/jel/new_pubs/jp3_13.pdf>.

6. M.P. Fewell and Mark G. Hazen, "Network-Centric Warfare—Its Nature and Modeling," Australian Defence Science and Technology Organisation, September 2003, available at <www.dsto.defence.gov.au/publications/scientific_record.php?record=3310>.

7. David S. Alberts and John J. Garstka, "Network-centric Warfare: Department of Defense Report to Congress," July 2001, available at <www.dodccrp.org/files/ncw_report/report/ncw_cover.html>.

8. Josh Rogin, "Cartwright: Cyber Warfare Strategy 'Dysfunctional'," U.S. Air Force Aim Points, February 12, 2007, available at <http://aimpoints.hq.af.mil/display.cfm?id=16609>.

9. Lieutenant General Robert J. Elder, Jr., "The Fifth Dimension: Cyberspace," briefing, Headquarters, U.S. Air Force.

10. *The Air Force Transformation Flight Plan* (Washington, DC: Headquarters, U.S. Air Force, November 2003), B–6, available at <www.af.mil/library/posture/AF_TRANS_FLIGHT_PLAN-2003.pdf>.

11. *United States Army 2003 Transformation Roadmap* (Washington, DC: Department of the Army, November 2003), B–3, available at <www.army.mil/2003transformationroadmap/>.

12. Warfighter Information Network–Tactical Operational Requirements Document, November 1999, available at <www.fas.org/man/dod-101/sys/land/docs/WIN-T5NOV.htm>.

13. Government Accountability Office, "Defense Acquisitions: Key Decisions to Be Made on Future Combat System," Report to Congressional Committees 07–376, March 16, 2007, available at <www.gao.gov/new.items/d07376.pdf>.

14. Kenneth Jordan, "The NMCI Experience and Lessons Learned: The Consolidation of Networks by Outsourcing," Case Studies in National Security Transformation No. 12 (Washington, DC: Center for Technology and National Security Policy, September 2007), available at <www.ndu.edu/ctnsp/Case%20Studies/Case%2012%20%20The%20NMCI%20Experience%20and%20Lessons%20Learned.pdf>.

15. Richard W. Mayo and John Nathman, "Sea Power 21 Series, Part V: Turning Information into Power," U.S. Naval Institute *Proceedings* (February 2003), 42.

16. Naval Research Advisory Committee, "Naval S&T in FORCEnet Assessment," Report 04–2, July 2004, 15, available at <www.onr.navy.mil/nrac/docs/2004_rpt_navy_st_forcenet.pdf>.

17. Office of Force Transformation, *The Implementation of Network-Centric Warfare* (Washington, DC: U.S. Government Printing Office, January 2005), available at <www.maxwell.af.mil/au/awc/awcgate/transformation/oft_implementation_ncw.pdf>.

18. The *global information grid* is defined in DOD Directive 8100.1, "Global Information Grid Overarching Policy," September 19, 2002, available at <www.dtic.mil/whs/directives/corres/pdf/810001p.pdf>. See also David S. Alberts and Richard E. Hayes, *Power to the Edge: Command and Control in the Information Age* (Washington, DC: Department of Defense Command and Control Research Program, June 2003), 187.

19. Alberts and Hayes, 196.

20. "Global Information Grid," National Security Agency Web site, available at <www.nsa.gov/ia/industry/gig.cfm?MenuID=10.3.2.2>.

21. National Research Council, *FORCEnet Implementation Strategy* (Washington, DC: National Academies Press, 2005).

22. Frank Tiboni, "Army Stuck in a WIN–T Quandary," *FCW.com*, February 2006, available at <www.fcw.com/article92437-02-27-06-Print>.

23. Center for Technology and National Security Policy, *Report to the Congress: Information Technology Program* (Washington, DC: Center for Technology and National Security Policy, January 2006).

Chapter 13

1. The White House, *The National Strategy to Secure Cyberspace* (Washington, DC: The White House, February 2003).
2. The White House, *The National Strategy for the Physical Protection of Critical Infrastructures and Key Assets* (Washington, DC: The White House, February 2003).
3. The White House, *The National Strategy for Homeland Security* (Washington, DC: The White House, February 2003).
4. The White House, *The National Security Strategy of the United States of America* (Washington, DC: The White House, March 2006).
5. Department of Defense, *The National Defense Strategy of the United States of America* (Washington, DC: The Pentagon, March 2005).
6. Chairman of the Joint Chiefs of Staff, *The National Military Strategy of the United States of America: A Strategy for Today; A Vision for Tomorrow* (Washington, DC: The Joint Chiefs of Staff, 2004).
7. Department of Defense, *2006 Quadrennial Defense Review Report* (Washington, DC: Department of Defense, February 2006).
8. Department of Defense, *Deterrence Operations, Joint Operating Concept* (Washington, DC: Department of Defense, December 2006).
9. *The National Military Strategy to Secure Cyberspace* (classified), issued by Department of Defense in early 2007.
10. See, in this volume, chapter 7, "Information Security Issues in Cyberspace," and chapter 23, "Cyberspace and Critical Information Protection: A Critical Assessment of Federal Efforts."
11. See, in this volume, chapters 10–13 on military uses of cyberpower.
12. For analysis of the motivations and actions of terrorist groups, see Jessica Stern, *Terror in the Name of God: Why Religious Militants Kill* (New York: Ecco, 2003).
13. The cyber attack on Estonia in May 2007 was attributed, but not with certainty, to hackers within Russia:

    > The Russian government has denied any involvement in the attacks, which came close to shutting down the country's digital infrastructure, clogging the Web sites of the president, the prime minister, Parliament and other government agencies, staggering Estonia's biggest bank and overwhelming the sites of several daily newspapers.

    Mark Landler and John Markoff, "Digital Fears Emerge After Data Siege in Estonia," *The New York Times*, May 29, 2007, available at <www.nytimes.com/2007/05/29/technology/29estonia.html>.
14. The Soviet Union had more ICBMs and SLBMs than the U.S. force posture, but fewer strategic bombers; ultimately it deployed about 2,400 launchers and 10,000–12,000 warheads.
15. For details, see Richard L. Kugler, *Commitment to Purpose: How Alliance Partnership Won the Cold War* (Santa Monica, CA: RAND, 1993).
16. Tailored deterrence is a central concept of current U.S. deterrent strategy, and is discussed in detail in the *Deterrence Operations, Joint Operating Concept*.
17. See chapter 23 in this volume, "Cyberspace and Critical Infrastructure Protection: A Critical Assessment of Federal Efforts."
18. The official NATO Web site provides a valuable source for tracking NATO activities across the full spectrum of preparedness measures.

Chapter 14

1. University of California Berkeley, *How Much Information? 2003*, Executive Summary, available at <www2.sims.berkeley.edu/research/projects/how-much-info-2003/execsum.htm>.

2. Pew Global Attitudes Project, "America's Image Slips, But Allies Share U.S. Concerns over Iran, Hamas," June 13, 2006, available at <http://pewglobal.org/reports/display. php?ReportID=252>.

3. British Broadcasting Company, "'Listen More' is World's Message to U.S.," January 23, 2007, available at <http://news.bbc.co.uk/2/hi/americas/6288933.stm>.

4. See chapter 2 in this volume, "From Cyberspace to Cyberpower: Defining the Problem."

5. The proliferation of channels in some areas has allowed for greater market segmentation and somewhat less "mass" mass marketing.

6. Wiki is server software that allows users to freely create and edit Web page content using any Web browser. Wiki supports hyperlinks and has simple text syntax for creating new pages and crosslinks between internal pages on the fly.

7. Michael Pfau and Roxanne Parrott, *Persuasive Communication Campaigns* (Boston: Allyn and Bacon, 1993).

8. Two exabytes equals the total volume of information generated in 1999; five exabytes equals all words ever spoken by human beings. *How Much Information? 2003*, table 1.1.

9. Ibid., Summary of Findings I.1.

10. Ibid. "It would take about 30 feet of books to store the equivalent of 800 MB of information on paper."

11. "Industry Statistics," Ferris Research, available at <www.ferris.com/research-library/ industry-statistics>.

12. *The 2007 World Fact Book* (Washington, DC: Central Intelligence Agency, 2007), available at <www.cia.gov/cia/publications/factbook/geos/xx.html>.

13. "Internet Usage Statistics," Internet World Stats, available at <www.internetworldstats. com/stats.htm>.

14. Ibid.

15. "State of the Blogosphere, August 2006," *Sifry.com*, available at <www.sifry.com/alerts/ archives/000436.html>.

16. *Information superiority* is "the operational advantage derived from the ability to collect, process, and disseminate an uninterrupted flow of information while exploiting or denying an adversary's ability to do the same." *DOD Dictionary of Military and Associated Terms,* April 12, 2001, as amended through April 14, 2006, available at <www.dtic.mil/ doctrine/jel/doddict/data/i/02656.html>. See, generally, Martin Libicki, *Information Dominance*, Strategic Forum No. 132 (Washington, DC: National Defense University Press, November 1997), available at <www.ndu.edu/inss/strforum/SF132/forum132. html>.

17. Pfau and Parrott, 53.

18. See, generally, Malcolm Gladwell, *The Tipping Point: How Little Things Can Make a Big Difference* (Boston: Back Bay Books, 2002).

19. Pfau and Parrott, 54.

20. David Galula, *Counterinsurgency Warfare: Theory and Practice* (London: Praeger, 1964), 14, 104.

21. Quoted in Thomas Ricks, *Fiasco: The American Military Adventure in Iraq* (New York: Penguin Press, 2006), 326.

22. Malcolm Gladwell describes different types of influential messengers based on the category of what they are doing: *mavens*, who validate the message; *connectors*, who link different parties and groups; and *salesmen*, who are effective at marketing. All of these may play roles in the international influence arena.

23. Galula, 75–77.

24. Gladwell, 219: "Simply by finding and reaching those few special people who hold so much social power, we can shape the course of social epidemics." Local assistance can help in both pretesting messages and assessing their impact.

25. The Broadcasting Board of Governors was created by the 1998 Foreign Affairs Reform and Restructuring Act (Public Law 105–277).

26. "About the Broadcasting Board of Governors," *BBG Online*, available at <www.bbg.gov/bbg_aboutus.cfm>.

27. Ibid.

28. Joint Publication 3–13, *Information Operations* (Washington, DC: Office of the Joint Chiefs of Staff, February 13, 2006), GL–9.

29. Ibid., I–9.

30. Partnership for Peace Information Management System, available at <http://www.pims.org>.

31. Asia-Pacific Area Network, available at <http://www1.apan-info.net/About/tabid/54/Default.aspx>.

32. Ibid. The home page lists several exercises supported by the Asia-Pacific Area network.

33. The Southeast European Times Web site averages 5 million hits a month, with average visits exceeding 20 minutes. Charles F. Wald, "The Phase Zero Campaign," *Joint Force Quarterly* 43 (4th Quarter 2006), 72.

34. Jesse T. Ford, director, International Affairs and Trade, "U.S. Public Diplomacy, State Department Efforts to Engage Muslim Audiences Lack Certain Communication Elements and Face Significant Challenges," testimony before the Subcommittee on Science, the Departments of State, Justice, and Commerce, and Related Agencies, House Committee on Appropriations, GAO–06–707T (Washington, DC: U.S. Government Accountability Office, May 2006), 21, available at <www.gao.gov/new.items/d06535.pdf>.

35. Ibid., 20, 21, 24, 26.

36. Herbert H. Hyman and Paul B. Sheatsley, "Some Reasons Why Information Campaigns Fail," *The Public Opinion Quarterly* 11, no. 3 (Autumn 1947), 412–423.

37. Ibid., 417.

38. Ibid.

39. Ford, 27.

40. Public affairs activities at the local and regional level, for example, at Embassies, that can be focused on the theater of operations.

41. Ralph O. Baker, "The Decisive Weapon: A Brigade Combat Team Commander's Perspective on Information Operations," *Military Review* (May-June 2006), 13. See also chapter 15 in this volume, "Tactical Influence Operations."

42. Chapter 15 in this volume, "Tactical Influence Operations," discusses how such operations might be improved.

43. Ford, 20.

Chapter 15

1. Ralph O. Baker, "The Decisive Weapon: A Brigade Combat Team Commander's Perspective on Information Operations," *Military Review* (May-June 2006), 13–32.

2. The discussion of cyberspace opportunities for enhancing tactical influence operations draws extensively on the ideas advanced by Timothy L. Thomas, "Hezballah, Israel, and Cyber PSYOP," *IOsphere* (Winter 2007), 36–44.

3. David T. Signori and Stuart H. Starr, "The Mission-oriented Approach to NATO C² Planning," *SIGNAL* (September 1987), 119–127. This article discusses the development of the approach and applies it to NATO command and control planning.

4. The acronym *DOTMLPF* was introduced in *Joint Vision 2020*, which was issued by the Chairman of the Joint Chiefs of Staff on May 30, 2000. The framework is used extensively by the Services and the joint community as a problem-solving construct for assessing current capabilities and managing change.

5. See Brigadier K.T. Hoegberg, "Toward a NATO C³ Master Plan," *SIGNAL* (October 1985).

6. Joint Staff, Director of Command, Control, Communications, and Computers, and Director, Defense Research and Engineering, *Advanced Battlespace Information System (ABIS) Task Force Report*, vol. 2, *Major Results*, report no. A859313, May 1996, available at <http://stinet.dtic.mil/cgi-bin/GetTRDoc?AD=ADA313958&Location=U2&doc=G etTRDoc.pdf>.

7. Chuck de Caro, "Killing Al Qaeda: The Destruction of Radical Islam Using SOFTWAR and AMOEBA," paper no. 031, 12th International Command and Control Research and Technology Symposium, Newport, RI, June 19–21, 2007.

8. Societal models of this type are discussed and analyzed in Greg L. Zacharias et al., *Behavioral Modeling and Simulation: From Individuals to Societies* (Washington, DC: National Academies Press, 2008), issued by the Board on Behavior, Cognitive, and Sensory Sciences and Education.

9. Thom Shanker, "Success in Iraq Depends on Services and Jobs, General Says," *The New York Times*, August 22, 2005.

10. Steven P. Carney, "This is Al Jazeera," *IOsphere* (Winter 2007), 22–29.

11. It is notable that only one of these tools, psychological operations, is considered a "pillar" of information operations. The other four "pillars" of information operations include computer network operations, electronic warfare, military deception, and operations security. The remaining tools (civil affairs, public affairs, Combat Camera, and the Commander's Emergency Response Program) are generally regarded as supporting or related capabilities (see DOD Directive 3600.1, "Information Operations," August 14, 2006).

12. For example, standard leaflets were used to disseminate information about repetitive events such as improvised explosive device incidents or house raids. Conversely, tailored leaflets were used to respond to specific incidents (for example, a specific insurgent incident that killed or wounded Iraqi citizens in a selected neighborhood).

13. Baker, emphasis added.

14. From a visualization perspective, it might be useful to senior leadership if these measures are depicted in "stoplight charts" (red, amber, green). In addition, it would be useful to depict aggregate values and trends.

15. Thomas.

16. See chapter 19 in this volume, "Cyber Terrorism: Menace or Myth?"

17. Fawzia Sheikh, "Abizaid: U.S. Military Has Failed to Embrace Cyberspace in Terror War," *Inside the Army*, July 2, 2007.

18. Note that the Smith-Mundt Act of 1948 has been invoked to limit U.S. use of the Internet. However, that law was focused on the Department of State. Policies in the Department of Defense (DOD) have been ambiguous about the use of the Internet. For example, "Policy for DOD Interactive Internet Activities" (June 8, 2007) enables use of a system accessible via the Internet that allows two-way communications. However, the Joint Task Force–Global Network Operations announced on May 14, 2007, that DOD access will be blocked to 13 "entertainment sites" on the Internet (for example, YouTube, MySpace). Consequently, workarounds are needed to implement waivers and independent arrangements to access the Internet.

19. For example, slow-moving EC–130 aircraft broadcast for up to 10 hours a day in Afghanistan. Douglas Waller, "Using PsyWar against the Taliban," *Time*, December 10, 2001.

20. Lynne Duke, "The Word at War," *The Washington Post*, March 26, 2006, D1.

21. M. Craig Geron, "Editorial: IO in an Unpredictable World," *IOsphere* (Winter 2007), 3–4.

22. Natalie O'Brien, "Terrorists Practice on Cyber Game," *The Australian*, July 31, 2007.

23. Dennis M. Murphy, "New Media and the Warfighter," Center for Strategic Leadership Issue Paper, Volume 3–08, March 2008, available at <www.carlisle.army.mil/usacsl/publications/IP3-08NewMediaandtheWarfighter.pdf>.

24. "[Israel's] Foreign Ministry has ordered trainee diplomats to track websites and chatrooms so that networks of U.S. and European groups with hundreds of thousands of Jewish activists can place supportive messages. . . . [S]pecial 'megaphone' software . . . alerts [subscribers] to anti-Israeli chatrooms or internet polls to enable them to post contrary viewpoints . . . [and] influence an opinion survey or the course of a debate." Jonit Farago, "Israel backed by army of cyber-soldiers," *Times* (London), July 28, 2006, available at <www.timesonline.co.uk/tol/news/world/middle_east/article693911.ece>.

25. At a November 2007 summit in Chile, King Juan Carlos of Spain asked Venezuelan president Hugo Chavez to "shut up" after Chavez said Spain's ex-Prime Minister Jose Maria Aznar was a "fascist." An estimated 500,000 people have downloaded the insult for their ringtones. As a 21-year-old student in Caracas told the *Miami Herald*, "It's a form of protest. It's something that a lot of people would like to tell the president." BBC News, accessed at <http://news.bbc.co.uk/go/pr/fr/-/2/hi/Europe/7101.386.stm>, November 19, 2007.

26. Thomas.

27. Marina Malenic, "Army Concerned that COIN is Displacing Conventional Training," *Inside the Army*, July 2, 2007.

28. Monte Morin, "Cultural Advisers Give U.S. Teams an Edge," *Stars and Stripes, Mideast Edition*, June 28, 2007.

29. The Smith-Mundt Act of 1948, amended in 1972 and 1998, prohibits the U.S. Government from propagandizing the American public with information and psychological operations directed at foreign audiences.

30. A new generation of useful tools to support course of action analysis is emerging. For example, the Defense Advanced Research Projects Agency has been developing a family of "plug and play" models that can be assembled to model a society through the Conflict Modeling, Planning and Outcomes Experimentation program (Alexander Kott and Peter Corpac, "Technology to Assist Leaders in Planning and Executing Campaigns in Complex Operational Environments," paper no. 232, 12th International Command and Control Research and Technology Symposium, Newport, RI, June 19–21, 2007). However, additional work is required to verify, validate, and accredit these models for their intended use (Robert Clemence et al., "Verification, Validation, and Accreditation of Complex Societal Models," paper no. 165, 13th International Command and Control Research and Technology Symposium, Bellevue, WA, June 17–19, 2008).

31. See also chapter 17 in this volume, "Facilitating Stability Operations with Cyberpower."

32. Murphy.

Chapter 16

1. *Net-centric warfare*, as defined by the Department of Defense Functional Capabilities Board, refers to warfighting that networks all elements of an appropriately trained joint force, and integrates their collective awareness, knowledge, and experience in order to rapidly create new capabilities, make superior decisions, and achieve a high level of agility and effectiveness in dynamic and uncertain operational environments.

2. Department of Defense (DOD) Directive 3000.05, *Military Support for Stability, Security, Transition, and Reconstruction (SSTR) Operations*, Section 4.2, says:

> Stability operations['] . . . immediate goal . . . is to provide the local populace with security, restore essential services, and meet humanitarian needs. The long-term goal is to help develop indigenous capacity for securing essential services, a viable market economy, rule of law, democratic institutions, and a robust civil society.

In this chapter, the term *stability operations* is used per the DOD directive to mean the full spectrum of stabilization and reconstruction activities.

3. World Bank, *Operations Policy and Country Services, Fragile States—Good Practices in Country Assistance Strategies,* December 19, 2005, vii, available at <www-wds. worldbank. org/external/default/WDSContentServer/IW3P/IB/2005/12/22/000090341_ 20051222094709/Rendered/PDF/34790.pdf>.

4. Organisation for Economic Co-operation and Development, Development Cooperation Directorate, "Senior Level Forum on Development Effectiveness in Fragile States, Harmonisation and Alignment in Fragile States," December 17, 2004, 14, available at <www.oecd.org/dataoecd/20/56/34084353.pdf>.

5. Ibid.

6. Jill L. Boardman and Donald W. Shuey, "Combined Enterprise Regional Information Exchange System (CENTRIXS): Supporting Coalition Warfare World-Wide," available at <www.au.af.mil/au/awc/awcgate/ccrp/centrixs.pdf>.

7. Robert K. Ackerman, "Unclassified Information New Key to Network Centricity," *SIGNAL* (September 2006), available at <www.afcea.org/signal/articles/templates/ SIGNAL_Article_Template.asp?articleid=1185&zoneid=52>.

8. DOD 3000.05, Sections 5.1.9, 5.7.1.

9. Larry Wentz, *An ICT Primer: Information and Communication Technologies for Civil-Military Coordination in Disaster Relief and Stabilization and Reconstruction,* Defense and Technology Paper 31 (Washington, DC: Center for Technology and National Security Policy, July 2006), available at <www.ndu.edu/ctnsp/Def_Tech/DTP31%20ICT%20Primer.pdf>.

Chapter 17

1. Department of Defense, *Report to Congress on the Implementation of DOD Directive 3000.05* (Washington, DC: U.S. Department of Defense, April 2007).

2. Seymour M. Hersh, "The Other War: Why Bush's Afghanistan Problem Won't Go Away," *The New Yorker,* April 12, 2004.

3. Defense Science Board 2004 Summer Study, *Transition to and from Hostilities* (Washington, DC: Department of Defense, December 2004), available at <www.acq.osd.mil/dsb/ reports/2004-12-DSB_SS_Report_Final.pdf>.

4. Department of Defense (DOD) Directive 3000.05, *Military Support to Stability, Security, Transition, and Reconstruction Operations,* November 28, 2005, available at <www.dtic.mil/ whs/directives/corres/pdf/300005p.pdf>.

5. Hans Binnendijk and Stuart E. Johnson, eds., *Transforming for Stabilization and Reconstruction Operations* (Washington, DC: National Defense University Press, 2004); Robert C. Orr, ed., *Winning the Peace: An American Strategy for Post-Conflict Reconstruction,* Significant Issues Series (Washington, DC: Center for Strategic and International Studies, 2004).

6. See chapter 16 in this volume, "I-Power: The Information Revolution and Stability Operations."

7. Richard Chait, Albert Sciarretta, and Dennis Shorts, *Army Science and Technology Analysis for Stabilization and Reconstruction Operations,* Defense and Technology Paper No. 37 (Washington, DC: Center for Technology and National Security Policy, October 2006), 11.

8. Charles L. Wayne, *Human Language Technology TIDES, EARS, Babylon* (Defense Advanced Research Projects Agency, 2002), available at <www.darpa.mil/darpatech2002/ presentations/iao_pdf/slides/WayneIAO.pdf>.

9. "How to Use Google's Language Tools as a Proxy Server," available at <www. downloadsquad.com/2005/12/20/how-to-use-googles-language-tools-as-a-proxy-server/>.

10. Chait, Sciarretta, and Shorts.

11. Michael E. O'Hanlon and Kenneth M. Pollack, "A War We Just Might Win," *The New York Times*, July 30, 2007, available at <www.nytimes.com/2007/07/30/opinion/30pollack. html>.
12. Kramer, Wentz, and Starr.
13. DOD Directive 3000.05.
14. DOD Directive 8000.1, *Management of DOD Information Resources and Information Technology*, February 27, 2002, available at <www.dtic.mil/whs/directives/corres/pdf/800001p. pdf>.
15. DOD Directive 8100.1, *Global Information Grid (GIG) Overarching Policy*, September 19, 2002, available at <www.dtic.mil/whs/directives/corres/pdf/810001p.pdf>.
16. DOD Directive 8320.2, *Data Sharing in a Net-Centric Department of Defense*, December 2, 2004, available at <www.defenselink.mil/cio-nii/coi/docs/832002p.pdf>.
17. For example, the word *bark* may be something a dog does, a covering on a tree, or a class of British sailing vessel. Explicit agreement must be reached on how such a term should be used, so as to avoid ambiguity and confusion. This example comes from community of interest training conducted by the Directorate of Information Policy of the Office of the Assistant Secretary of Defense for Networks and Information Integration.
18. Peter Buxbaum, "COIs: Too Much of a Good Thing?" *Federal Computer Week*, July 16, 2007, available at <www.fcw.com/print/13_24/news/103210-1.html>.
19. Ibid.
20. DOD Directive 2205.02, *Humanitarian and Civic Assistance Provided in Conjunction with Military Operations*, October 6, 1994, available at <www.dtic.mil/whs/directives/corres/ pdf/220502p.pdf>.
21. Joint explanatory statement, 109th Congress, Defense Authorization Bill:
    The conferees acknowledge that restoring basic information and communications capacity is a fundamental element of humanitarian and civic assistance, and that a functioning information and communications infrastructure is vital to the successful conduct of humanitarian missions. Accordingly, the conferees note that rudimentary construction and repair of public facilities, under section 401(e)(4) of title 10, United States Code, includes information and communications technology as necessary to provide basic information and communications services.
22. National Security Presidential Directive 44, *Management of Interagency Efforts Concerning Reconstruction and Stabilization*, December 7, 2005, available at <www.fas.org/irp/offdocs/ nspd/nspd-44.html>.
23. Department of Defense, *DOD Information Sharing Strategy*, May 4, 2007, available at <www.defenselink.mil/cio-nii/docs/InfoSharingStrategy.pdf>.
24. John E. Dunn, "U.S. Military Struggles with Data Loss," *Techworld*, April 17, 2006, available at <www.techworld.com/security/features/index.cfm?featureid=2436>.
25. Jim Garamone, "Pace Urges Interagency Cooperation in Government," American Forces Press Service, August 8, 2007, available at <www.defenselink.mil/news/newsarticle. aspx?id=46991>.
26. U.S. Joint Forces Command fact sheet, "Joint Interagency Coordination Group: A Prototyping Effort," January 2005, available at <www.ndu.edu/itea/storage/683/ Fact%20Sheet%20JIACG%20-%20Jan%2005.pdf>.
27. Homeland Security Presidential Directive 11, *Comprehensive Terrorist-related Screening Procedures*, August 27, 2004, available at <www.whitehouse.gov/news/releases/2004/ 08/20040827-7.html>.
28. Tony Perry and Edmund Saunders, "Security Brings Technology to Africa," *Los Angeles Times*, August 6, 2007.
29. Jason Miller, "DoD Is Caught in the Web 2.0," *Federal Computer Week*, May 21, 2007, available at <www.fcw.com/print/13_16/news/102757-1.html>.

30. Peter Buxbaum, "DIA Embraces Web 2.0: Wikis, RSS Feeds and Mashups are Among the Favored Tools of Information Sharing," *Federal Computer Week*, July 30, 2007, available at <www.fcw.com/print/13_26/news/103324-1.html>.
31. Ibid.
32. Ben Bain, "Diplopedia 'One-Stop Shop' for Foreign Affairs Data," *Government Computer News*, July 26, 2007, available at <www.gcn.com/online/vol1_no1/44734-1.html?topic= workflow#>.
33. Buxbaum, "DIA Embraces Web 2.0."
34. Wyatt Kash and Joab Jackson, "Michael Jones: Geospatial Democracy," *Government Computer News*, July 30, 2007, available at <www.gcn.com/print/26_19/44745-1.html>.
35. Frederick Barton, Karin von Hippel, and Rebecca Linder, *Wikis, Webs, and Networks: Creating Connections for Conflict-prone Settings* (Washington, DC: Center for Strategic and International Studies, October 2006).
36. Larry Wentz, *Information and Communication Technologies for Civil-Military Coordination in Disaster Relief and Stabilization and Reconstruction*, Defense and Technology Paper No. 31 (Washington, DC: Center for Technology and National Security Policy, July 2006).
37. Miller. The vice director of the Defense Information Systems Agency announced that with DOD having 5 million computers worldwide, there was no way to support the bandwidth requirements scaled across the enterprise with regard to these social networking sites. Former director Lieutenant General Harry D. Raduege, Jr., USAF (ret.), stated the blockage was meant to forestall "inadvertent activity that the enemy can pick up on."
38. Gerard J. Christman and Mark Postal, "Coalition Interoperability: A Modeled Approach," *Proceedings of the 11th Command and Control Research and Technology Symposium,* Cambridge, United Kingdom, September 2006.
39. Ibid.
40. Ibid.
41. Shared Operational Picture Exchange Services (SOPES) Information Exchange Mechanism (IEM) RFP, *Industry Links,* available <http://c4i.omg.org/C4I_RFPs&RFIs. htm#SOPES_IEDM>.
42. Ganesan Shankaranarayanan and Adir Even, "The Metadata Enigma," *Communications of the ACM* 49, no. 2 (February 2006), 88–94.
43. Robert P. Hooper, "Hydrologic Information System," Consortium of Universities for the Advancement of Hydrologic Science, May 22, 2007.
44. Larry Greenemeier, "Defense Intelligence Agency Boosts Search Firepower," *Information Week*, March 22, 2007, available at <www.informationweek.com//.jhtml?articleID=198 500124>.
45. Dave Gradijan, "Justice Department Pushes FBI to Hasten Data Sharing," *Computerworld*, January 9, 2007, available at <www2.csoonline.com/blog_view.html?CID=28055>.
46. *Proceedings of the 4th International Conference on Information Systems for Crisis Response and Management* (Delft, The Netherlands: ISCRAM, May 2007).
47. One Laptop Per Child Web site, available at <http://laptop.org/>.
48. One Laptop Per Child world map, "Those countries we plan to pilot: Argentina, Brazil, Ethiopia, India, Libya, Nepal, Nigeria, Pakistan, Peru, Romania, Russia, Rwanda, Thailand, Uruguay, USA," available at <http://wiki.laptop.org/go/OLPC_world_map>.
49. Bobbie Johnson, "Which Laptop Per Child?" *The Guardian,* May 31, 2007, available at <www.guardian.co.uk/technology/2007/may/31/guardianweeklytechnologysection. olpc>.
50. On January 3, 2008, Intel "quit the One Laptop Per Child project, which provides low-cost laptops to the world's poorest children. The chip giant said it couldn't abide by OLPC founder Nicholas Negroponte's demand that it discontinue making a similar

laptop and argues that there's plenty of room in the marketplace for different brands." Wendy Tanaka, "Intel's Laptop Flap," *Forbes*, January 5, 2008, available at <www.forbes. com/technology/2008/01/05/olpc-laptop-intel-tech-ebiz-cx_wt_1205intel.html>.

51. Tom Espiner, "$100 Laptop Goes into Mass Production," *Business Week*, July 24, 2007, available at <www.businessweek.com/globalbiz/content/jul2007/gb20070724_323018. htm?chan=globalbiz_europe+index+page_top+stories>.

52. Orr, 316.

53. Ibid., 320.

54. C.K. Prahalad, *The Fortune at the Bottom of the Pyramid* (Upper Saddle River, NJ: Wharton School Publishing, 2005).

55. Ibid., 14–16.

56. Ibid., 5.

57. Wentz.

58. UN Office for the Coordination of Humanitarian Affairs, *ReliefWeb*, accessed at <www. reliefweb.int/rw/dbc.nsf/doc100?OpenForm>.

59. UN Office for the Coordination of Humanitarian Affairs, *Virtual OSOCC*, available at <ocha.unog.ch/virtualosocc/(zabvxeehxq3mig45s0scdhjb)/VOLogin.aspx>.

60. U.S. Department of State Web site, *Global Disaster Information Network*, available at <www. state.gov/www/issues/relief/gdin.html>. The State Department says the network could also:

> foster increased sharing of disaster information among governments, international organizations, NGOs and other entities; to promote standardization and integration of disaster information; to provide an incentive for disaster prone countries and regions that have poor communications facilities to upgrade them so as to be in a position to receive alerts or request information in a timely manner; to encourage greater interaction and collaboration among providers, disseminators, and users of disaster information through electronic and other means.

61. United Nations World Food Programme Web site, available at <www.wfp.org/english/>.

62. Humanitarian Early Warning Service Web site, available at <www.hewsweb.org/home_page/default.asp>.

63. "FreeRice is a creative web-based vocabulary game that ties every correct answer to the donation of rice to WFP." See <www.wfp.org/how_to_help/ways_to_donate/freerice. asp?section=4&sub_section=5>; <http://www.freerice.com/>

64. Anthony Cordesman, *Reconstruction in Iraq: The Uncertain Way Ahead*, Center for Strategic and International Studies, January 19, 2007, working draft available at <www.csis.org/media/csis/pubs/070119_iraq_reconstruction.pdf>.

65. Frederick D. Barton, statement before House Committee on Armed Services, hearing on Provincial Reconstruction Teams, Washington, DC, September 5, 2007, available at <http://armedservices.house.gov/pdfs/OI090507/Barton_Testimony090507.pdf>.

66. International Maritime Satellite, Very Small Aperture Terminal, GlobalStar, and Iridium are examples of systems used in recent operations and in the U.S. inventory.

67. For an excellent discussion of considerations and best practices with regard to satellite-based communications, see Wentz, 75–92.

68. For more on these issues, see in this volume chapter 15, "Tactical Influence Operations," and chapter 16, "I-Power: The Information Revolution and Stability Operations."

69. The directive was published and no implementing instructions have been produced as is usually the case. The Services and combatant commanders are left to discern how to implement the directive on their own.

70. *PeaceMaker*, <www.peacemakergame.com>; *Darfur Is Dying*, <www.darfurisdying.com>; *Third World Farmer*, <www.arcadetown.com/3rdworldfarmer/game.asp>.

Chapter 18

1. See also chapter 19 in this volume, "Cyber Terrorism: Menace or Myth?"
2. Bruce Schneier, "Attack Trends: 2004 and 2005," *Schneier on Security* blog, June 6, 2005, available at <www.schneier.com/blog/archives/2005/06/attack_trends_2.html>.
3. The Computer Crime and Intellectual Property Section of the U.S. Department of Justice is responsible for implementing national strategies in combating computer and intellectual property crimes worldwide. U.S. Department of Justice Cybercrime Web site, available at <www.cybercrime.gov/>.
4. "Turk, Moroccan nabbed in huge worm case," *CNNMoney.com*, August 26, 2005, available at <http://money.cnn.com/2005/08/26/technology/worm_arrest/index.htm>; Allen Wastler, "Virus angst, thy name is us," *CNNMoney.com*, August 25, 2005, available at <http://money.cnn.com/2005/08/17/commentary/wastler/wastler/index.htm>.
5. Reuters, "Cybercrime is Getting Organized," *Wired*, September 15, 2006, available at <www.wired.com/techbiz/media/news/2006/09/71793>.
6. Robert Vamosi, "Cyberattack in Estonia—What It Really Means," *CnetNews.com*, May 29, 2007, available at <http://news.com.com/Cyberattack+in+Estonia-what+it+really+me ans/2008-7349_3-6186751.html>.
7. Iain Thomson, "Russia 'Hired Botnets' for Estonia cyber-war," *VnuNet.com*, May 31, 2007, available at <www.vnunet.com/vnunet/news/2191082/claims-russia-hired-botnets>.
8. Heise Security, "Estonian DDoS—A Final Analysis," May 31, 2007, available at <www.heise-security.co.uk/news/print/90461>.
9. "Cyber attack Fallout in Estonia," February 4, 2008, *The Budapest Times*, February 4, 2008, available at <www.budapesttimes.hu/index.php?option=com_content&task=view&id= 5081&Itemid=26>.
10. Examples are Defcon (<www.defcon.org/>) and the Blackhat Security Conference (<www.blackhat.com/>), both held annually.
11. "McAfee Virtual Criminology Report: Organized Crime and the Internet," December 2006, available at <www.sigma.com.pl/pliki/albums/userpics/10007/Virtual_Criminology_Report_2006.pdf>.
12. A Web crawler (also known as a Web spider or Web robot) is a program or automated script that browses the World Wide Web systematically. Web crawlers are mainly used to create a copy of all the visited pages for later processing by a search engine that will index the downloaded pages to provide fast searches. "Web Crawler," *Wikipedia*, available at <http://en.wikipedia.org/wiki/Web_crawler>.
13. Gregory Crabb, U.S. Postal Service Global Investigations, and Yuval Ben-Itzhak, CTO Finjan, presentation at the Gartner IT Security Summit 2007, Washington, DC, June 4, 2007.
14. Trojan horses, spyware, and adware are forms of malicious software that can secretly infect a computer, record sensitive information residing on that computer, or log keystrokes (including passwords), and then transmit that information through the Internet to a temporary location where it is collected for fraudulent use by a third party.
15. Bob Keefe, "PC Security Still More of a Wish than a Promise," *Atlanta Journal*, February 3, 2007, 1A; U.S. Department of Justice for the Central District of California, "'Botherder' Dealt Record Prison Sentence for Selling and Spreading Malicious Computer Code," Release 06–051, May 8, 2006, available at <www.usdoj.gov/criminal/cybercrime/anchetaSent.htm>.
16. Julie Bort, "Attack of the Killer Bots," *Network World*, July 2/9, 2007, 29.
17. Susan MacLean, "Report Warns of Organized Cyber Crime," *ItWorldCanada*, August 26, 2005, available at <www.itworldcanada.com/a/IT-Focus/39c78aa4-df47-4231-a083-ddd1ab8985fb.html>.
18. "McAfee Virtual Criminology Report: Organized Crime and the Internet."

19. Elise Ackerman, "Hackers' Infections Slither Onto Web Sites," *Mercury News*, January 3, 2007, 1.

20. Jeff Hecht, "Web Browsers Are New Frontline in Internet War," *NewScientistTech*, May 5, 2007, available at <www.newscientisttech.com/article.ns?id=mg19426026.000&print=true>; Niels Provos et al., "The Ghost in the Browser: Analysis of Web-based Malware," available at <www.usenix.org/events/hotbots07/tech/full_papers/provos/provos.pdf>.

21. Finjan, Inc., "Web Security Trends Report, Q2 2007," June 2007, available at <www.finjan.com/Content.aspx?id=827>.

22. Lou Bobson, "Identity Theft Ruining Lives," *The Sunday Mail*, May 20, 2007, 62.

23. "A Chronology of Data Breaches," Privacy Rights Clearinghouse, available at <www.privacyrights.org/ar/ChronDataBreaches.htm#CP>. See also David Bank and Christopher Conkey, "New Safeguards for Your Privacy: Bank Regulators are Latest to Push for Alerts to Consumers When Personal Data Get Breached," *The Wall Street Journal*, March 24, 2005, D1, available at <http://online.wsj.com/article/SB111162452521088223.html>.

24. Dawn Onley and Patience Wait, "DOD's Efforts to Stave Off Nation-state Cyberattacks Begin with China," *Government Computer News*, August 21, 2006.

25. Computer Crime Research Center, "Russia, Biggest Ever Credit Card Scam," July 8, 2005, available at <www.crime-research.org/news/08.07.2005/1349/>.

26. David Hayes, "A Dollar Goes a Long Way in Swiping Private Data," *Kansas City Star*, March 20, 2007, 1.

27. "European Parliament resolution on the existence of a global system for the interception of private and commercial communications (ECHELON interception system) 2001/2098(INI)," approved on September 5, 2001, available at <www.cyber-rights.org/interception/echelon/European_parliament_resolution.htm>; Ron Pemstein, "Europe Spy System," GlobalSecurity.org, March 30, 2000, available at <www.globalsecurity.org/intell/library/news/2000/03/000330-echelon1.htm>; Gerhard Schmid, "Report on the existence of a global system for the interception of private and commercial communications (ECHELON interception system)," Document A5-0264/2001, May 9, 2001, available at <www.statewatch.org/news/2001/sep/02echelon.htm>.

28. James Woolsey, "Intelligence Gathering and Democracies: The Issue of Economic and Industrial Espionage," Federation of American Scientists, March 7, 2000, available at <http://ftp.fas.org/irp/news/2000/03/wool0300.htm>.

29. James Lewis, testimony before the House Committee on Homeland Security, Subcommittee on Emerging Threats, Cybersecurity, and Science and Technology, April 15, 2007.

30. Chris Johnson, "Naval War College Network, Web Site Back Up Following Intrusion," *Inside the Navy*, December 18, 2006.

31. Robert McMillan, "Pentagon Shuts Down Systems After Cyber-Attack," *PC World*, June 21, 2007, available at <www.pcworld.com/article/id,133301-pg,1/article.html>.

32. In addition, some estimates say that up to 90 percent of computer software used in China is pirated and thus open to hijack through computer viruses. James Lewis, "Computer Espionage, Titan Rain and China," Center for Strategic and International Studies, December 14, 2005.

33. Josh Rogin, "Cyber Officials: Chinese Hackers Attack 'Anything and Everything'," *FCW.com*, February 13, 2007, available at <www.fcw.com/article97658-02-13-07-Web&printLayout>.

34. The Global Business Security Index reports worldwide trends in computer security from incidents that are collected and analyzed by IBM and other security organizations. IBM press release, "IBM Report: Government, Financial Services and Manufacturing Sectors Top Targets of Security Attacks in First Half of 2005," August 2, 2005.

35. "McAfee Virtual Criminology Report: Organized Crime and the Internet."

36. Marisa Randazzo et al., "Insider Threat Study: Illicit Cyber Activity in the Banking and Finance Sector," Carnegie Mellon Software Engineering Institute, August 2004, available at <www.sei.cmu.edu/pub/documents/04.reports/pdf/04tr021.pdf>.

37. U.S. Attorney's Office, District of Connecticut, Antiterrorism Advisory Council, available at <www.usdoj.gov/usao/ct/attf.html>.

38. Jaroslaw Anders, "Copyright Violations Threaten Cultural Diversity," U.S. Department of State, April 26, 2007, available at <http://usinfo.state.gov/xarchives/display.html?p=washfile-english&y=2007&m=April&x=20070426164247zjsredna0.739773>.

39. Frederick Balfour et al., "Fakes!" *Business Week*, February 7, 2005, 54–64.

40. "MEPs back criminal sanctions for counterfeiters," *EurActiv.com*, April 25, 2007, available at <www.euractiv.com/en/innovation/meps-back-criminal-sanctions-counterfeiters/article-163380>.

41. Nancy Gohring, "Feds Renew Cybercrime Fight," *PC World*, June 28, 2007, available at <www.pcworld.com/article/id,133523-c,cybercrime/article.html>.

42. U.S. Department of Justice Press Release, "Digital Currency Business E-Gold Indicted for Money Laundering and Illegal Money Transmitting," April 27, 2007, available at <www.usdoj.gov/opa/pr/2007/April/07_crm_301.html>.

43. "ShadowCrew was an international crime message board that offered a haven for carders or 'hackers' to trade, buy, and sell anything from stolen personal information, to hacked credit card numbers and false identification. ShadowCrew emerged from another underground site, counterfeitlibrary.com in early 2002 and would be followed up by carderplanet.com, a primarily Russian site. . . . The site flourished from the time it opened in 2002 until its demise in late October 2004." "ShadowCrew," *Wikipedia*, available at <http://en.wikipedia.org/wiki/ShadowCrew>.

44. Brian Grow et al., "Gold Rush," *Business Week*, January 9, 2006, 68–76.

45. Ibid.

46. Council of Europe Octopus Programme, *Summary of the Organised Crime Situation Report 2004: Focus on the Threat of Cybercrime* (Strasbourg: Council of Europe, September 6, 2004), 47.

47. Catherine Holahan, "Policing Online Money Laundering," *Business Week Online*, November 6, 2006, 4, available at <www.businessweek.com/technology/content/nov2006/tc20061106_986949.htm?campaign_id=bier_tcv.g3a.rssf1106u>.

48. "Neteller, the market-leading 'virtual wallet' payment processor, closed down its American operations after the arrest this week of its two Canadian founders. . . . Over six months last year, Neteller processed transactions worth \$5.1bn (£2.6bn), with about 85% involving American customers." "Arrests prompt Neteller to quit U.S. gaming," *Guardian Unlimited*, January 19, 2007, available at <www.guardian.co.uk/technology/2007/jan/19/news.newmedia>; Reuters, "Company Reaches Deal with U.S. in Internet in Internet Gambling Case," *The New York Times*, July 19, 2007, available at <www.nytimes.com/2007/07/19/business/worldbusiness/19neteller.html>.

49. "PayPal Express Looks for More Pals as it Battles Google Checkout," *Internet Retailer*, May 18, 2007, available at <www.internetretailer.com/dailyNews.asp?id=22446>. It was reported that "61% of [PayPal's] payment volume came from eBay.com, the auction site that owns PayPal." See also Holahan, 4.

50. Ken Dunham, "Money Mules: An Investigative View," *Information Systems Security* (March-April 2006), 6.

51. Louise I. Shelley and John T. Picarelli, "Methods Not Motives: Implications of the Convergence of International Organized Crime and Terrorism," *Police Practice and Research* 3, no. 4 (2002), 311, available at <www.american.edu/traccc/Publications/Shelley%20Pubs/To%20Add/MethodsnotMotives.pdf>.

52 Marcia Savage, "Private-public Sector Rallies Against Organized Cybercrime," *SCMagazine.com*, February 17, 2005, available at <www.scmagazineus.com/Private-public-sector-rallies-against-organized-cybercrime/article/31800/>.

53. U.S. Government Accountability Office, "Cybercrime: Public and Private Entities Face Challenges in Addressing Cyber Threats," Report GAO–07–705, June 2007, available at <www.gao.gov/new.items/d07705.pdf>.

54. Sharon Gaudin, "Breach Costs Soar at TJX," *Information Week*, May 21, 2007, 19.

55. "State PIRG Summary of State Security Freeze and Security Breach Notification Laws," available at <www.pirg.org/consumer/credit/statelaws.htm>.

56. Marcia Savage, "Companies Still Not Reporting Attacks, FBI Director Says," *SearchSecurity.com*, February 15, 2006, available at <http://searchsecurity.techtarget.com/originalContent/0,289142,sid14_gci1166845,00.html>.

57. "Virus Attacks Named Leading Culprit of Financial Loss by U.S. Companies in 2006 CSI/FBI Computer Crime and Security Survey," Computer Security Institute, July 13, 2006, available at <www.gocsi.com/press/20060712.jhtml>.

58. Robert Richardson, "CSI Computer Crime and Security Survey 2007," available at <http://i.cmpnet.com/v2.gocsi.com/pdf/CSISurvey2007.pdf>.

59. The survey is limited to CSI members, and thus respondents may not be representative of all security practitioners, and their employers may not be representative of employers in general. In addition, as the 2006 CSI/FBI survey itself points out, most companies are continuing to sweep security incidents under the rug. Bill Brenner, "Security Blog Log: Has CSI/FBI Survey Jumped the Shark?" *SearchSecurity.com*, July 21, 2006, available at <http://searchsecurity.techtarget.com/columnItem/0,294698,sid14_gci1202328,00.html>.

60. CERT Coordination Center, Carnegie Mellon University, 2004, accessed at <www.cert.org/stats/>.

61. Matt Hines, "Malware Money Tough to Trace," *Eweek*, September 18, 2006, 14.

62. Full text of the Convention on Cybercrime is available at <http://conventions.coe.int/Treaty/en/Treaties/Html/185.htm>.

63. Marc Rotenberg, Cedric Laurant, and Tara Wheatland, letter to Richard G. Lugar and Joseph R. Biden, Jr., June 17, 2004, available at <www.epic.org/privacy/intl/senateletter-061704.pdf>.

64. Patience Wait, "Industry Groups Urge Senate Ratification of Cybercrime Treaty," *Government Computer News*, June 6, 2005, available at <http://appserv.gcn.com/vol1_no1/web/36257-1.html>; Declan McCullagh, "Tech Firms Call for Approval of Cybercrime Treaty," *CNet News.com*, June 29, 2005, available at <http://news.com.com/2102-7348_3-5768462.html?tag=st.util.print>.

65. The U.S. Senate Committee on Foreign Relations held a hearing on the convention on June 17, 2004. Kristin Archick, "Cybercrime: The Council of Europe Convention," Congressional Research Service Report RS21208, April 26, 2002, available at <http://digital.library.unt.edu/govdocs/crs/permalink/meta-crs-2394:1>; Estelle Durnout, "Council of Europe Ratifies Cybercrime Treaty," *ZDNet*, March 22, 2004, available at <http://news.zdnet.co.uk/business/legal/0,39020651,39149470,00.htm>.

66. Kevin Poulsen, "Feds Square Off with Organized Cyber Crime," *SecurityFocus*, February 17, 2005, available at <www.securityfocus.com/news/10525>.

67. McAfee Virtual Criminology Report, "Cybercrime: The Next Wave," 2007, available at <www.mcafee.com/us/local_content/reports/mcafee_criminology_report2007_en.pdf>.

68. Bill Brenner, "Criminals Find Safety in Cyberspace," *SearchSecurity.com*, December 18, 2006, available at <http://searchsecurity.techtarget.com/originalContent/0,289142,sid14_gci1235455,00.html?bucket=NEWS&topic=299990>.

69. "Summary of the Organised Crime Situation Report 2004: Focus on the Threat of Cybercrime," 48.

70. Susan Brenner, "Organized Cybercrime? How Cyberspace May Affect the Structure of Criminal Relationships," *North Carolina Journal of Law and Technology* 4, no. 1 (Fall 2002), available at <www.jolt.unc.edu/Vol4_I1/Web/Brenner-V4I1.htm>.

71. Conal Walsh, "Terrorism on the Cheap—and with No Paper Trail," *The Guardian*, July 17, 2005, available at <www.guardian.co.uk/business/2005/jul/17/alqaida.money>; Rollie Lal, "Terrorists and Organized Crime Join Forces," *International Herald Tribune*, May 25, 2005, available at <www.iht.com/articles/2005/05/23/opinion/edlal.php>; Barbara Porter, "Forum Links Organized Crime and Terrorism," *By George!*, Summer 2004, available at <www2.gwu.edu/~bygeorge/060804/crimeterrorism.html>.

72. Brian Krebs, "Three Worked the Web to Help Terrorists," *The Washington Post*, July 6, 2007, D1.

73. Glenn Curtis and Tara Karacan, "The Nexus Among Terrorists, Narcotics Traffickers, Weapons Proliferators, and Organized Crime Networks in Western Europe," Federal Research Division, Library of Congress, December 2002, 22, available at <www.loc.gov/rr/frd/pdf-files/WestEurope_NEXUS.pdf>.

74. LaVerle Berry, Glenn E. Curtis, Rex A. Hudson, and Nina A. Kollars, "A Global Overview of Narcotics-Funded Terrorist and Other Extremist Groups," Federal Research Division, Library of Congress, May 2002, available at <www.loc.gov/rr/frd/pdf-files/NarcsFundedTerrs_Extrems.pdf>.

75. Authorization for coordinating the Federal war on drugs expired on September 30, 2003. For more information, see Mark Eddy, "War on Drugs: Reauthorization of the Office of National Drug Control Policy," CRS Report RL32352 (Washington, DC: Congressional Research Service, June 1, 2005), available at <www.fas.org/sgp/crs/misc/RL32352.pdf>. Also see D.C. Préfontaine and Yvon Durand, "Terrorism and Organized Crime: Reflections on an Illusive Link and its Implication for Criminal Law Reform," International Society for Criminal Law Reform Annual Meeting, Montreal, August 8–12, 2004, available at <www.icclr.law.ubc.ca/Publications/Reports/International%20Society%20Paper%20of%20Terrorism.pdf>.

76. Rand Beers and Francis X. Taylor, U.S. State Department, "Narco-Terror: The Worldwide Connection Between Drugs and Terror," testimony before the U.S. Senate Judiciary Committee, Subcommittee on Technology, Terrorism, and Government Information, March 13, 2002, available at <www.state.gov/p/inl/rls/rm/8743.htm>.

77. Matthew Lee and Katherine Shrader, "Al-Qaeda Has Rebuilt, U.S. Intel Warns," *Associated Press*, July 12, 2007, available at <http://news.yahoo.com/s/ap/20070712/ap_on_go_pr_wh/us_terror_threat_32;_ylt=AuURr2eP8AhBrfHyTOdw714Gw_IE>; Associated Press, "Afghanistan's poppy crop could yield more than 2006's record haul, UN says," *International Herald Tribune*, June 25, 2007, available at <www.iht.com/articles/ap/2007/06/25/asia/AS-GEN-Afghan-Drugs.php>.

78. Louise Shelly, "Organized Crime, Cybercrime, and Terrorism," Computer Crime Research Center, September 27, 2004, available at <www.crime-research.org/articles/Terrorism_Cybercrime/>.

79. "CIA Confirms Cyber Attack Caused Multi-City Power Outage," *SANS NewsBites* X, no. 5, January 18, 2008, available at <www.sans.org/newsletters/newsbites/newsbites.php?vol=10&issue=5>.

80. Aaron Turner, testimony to House Committee on Homeland Security, Subcommittee on Emerging Threats, Cybersecurity, and Science and Technology, hearing on "Cyber Insecurity: Hackers are Penetrating Federal Systems and Critical Infrastructure," April 19, 2007, available at <http://homeland.house.gov/SiteDocuments/20070419153130-95132.pdf>.

81. Ibid.
82. Idaho National Laboratory, "National Security: Energy Security," available at <www.inl. gov/nationalsecurity/energysecurity/>.
83. James A. Lewis, statement to Committee on House Oversight and Government Reform Subcommittee on Government Management, Organization, and Procurement, Subcommittee on Information Policy, Census, and National Archives, June 7, 2007.
84. U.S. General Accounting Office, "Critical Infrastructure Protection: Challenges and Efforts to Secure Control Systems," GAO–04–354, March 2004, available at <www.gao. gov/new.items/d04354.pdf>.
85. U.S. Government Accountability Office, "Critical Infrastructure Protection: Progress Coordinating Government and Private Sector Efforts Varies by Sectors' Characteristics," GAO–07–39, October 16, 2006, available at <www.gao.gov/new.items/d0739.pdf>.
86. Seymour Goodman and Herbert Lin, eds., *Toward a Safer and More Secure Cyberspace* (Washington, DC: Committee on Improving Cybersecurity Research in the United States, National Research Council, 2007), 261–267, available at <http://books.nap.edu/ openbook.php?isbn=0309103959>.

Chapter 19

1. For example, "Our water and sewer systems, electricity grids, financial markets, payroll systems, air and ground traffic control systems . . . are all electronically controlled, electronically dependent, and subject to sophisticated attacks by both state-sponsored and freelance terrorists." Joel Brenner, U.S. National Counterintelligence Executive, quoted in Jeanne Meserve, "Official: International Hackers Going after U.S.," *CNN.com*, October 19, 2007, available at <www.cnn.com/2007/US/10/19/cyber.threats/>.
2. Evidence of terrorist use of the Internet is described in Stephen Ulph, "Internet Mujahideen Intensify Research on U.S. Economic Targets," *Terrorism Focus* 3, no. 2 (January 18, 2006). The observation about the absence of cyber attacks comes from several sources, including Gabriel Weimann, *Terror on the Internet: The New Arena, the New Challenges* (Washington, DC: U.S. Institute of Peace, 2006); Dorothy E. Denning, "A View of Cyberterrorism Five Years Later," in Kenneth Himma, ed., *Internet Security: Hacking, Counterhacking, and Society* (Sudbury, MA: Jones and Bartlett, 2006), 123–139; James Lewis, "Cyber Terror: Missing in Action," *Knowledge, Technology, & Policy* 16, no. 2 (Summer 2003), 34–41; and Joshua Green, "The Myth of Cyber-Terrorism," *Washington Monthly*, November 2002, available at <www.washingtonmonthly.com/features/2001/0211. green.html>.
3. This chapter focuses on terrorism associated with various fundamentalist Islamic movements.
4. Department of Defense, Joint Publication 1–02, *Department of Defense Dictionary of Military and Associated Terms* (Washington, DC: The Joint Staff, April 12, 2001, as amended through October 17, 2007), 544.
5. Dorothy E. Denning, "Is Cyber Terror Next?" in *Understanding September 11*, ed. Craig Calhoun, Paul Price, and Ashley Timmer (New York: The New Press, 2002), 193. Emphasis added.
6. For example, see Dan Verton, *Black Ice: The Invisible Threat of Cyber-Terrorism* (Emeryville, CA: McGraw-Hill/Osborne), 2003, xx.
7. Jon Swartz, "Cyberterror Impact, Defense under Scrutiny," *USA Today*, August 3, 2004, available at <www.usatoday.com/tech/news/2004-08-02-cyber-terror_x.htm>.
8. Greg Bruno, "The Evolution of Cyber Warfare," Council on Foreign Relations Backgrounder, February 27, 2008, available at <www.cfr.org/publication/15577/>.
9. "Hacktivism," *Wikipedia*, available at <http://en.wikipedia.org/wiki/Hacktivism>.

10. For example, see BBC News, "U.S. Hackers Told to Leave Iraq Alone," February 14, 2003, available at <http://news.bbc.co.uk/2/hi/technology/2760899.stm>.

11. "Hacker," *Wikipedia*, available at <http://en.wikipedia.org/wiki/Hacker>.

12. Carole Fennely, "Motivation to Hack," *Internet Security News*, available at <http://seclists.org/isn/2000/Nov/0039.html>.

13. "Espionage," *Wikipedia*, available at <http://en.wikipedia.org/wiki/Espionage>.

14. Rhys Blakely et al., "MI5 Alert on China's Cyberspace Spy Threat," *Times Online*, December 1, 2007, available at <http://business.timesonline.co.uk/tol/business/industry_sectors/technology/article2980250.ece>.

15. "FBI Thinks China is Greatest Threat," *Newsmax.com*, November 4, 2007, available at <http://www.newsmax.com/insider_report/China_Is_Greatest_Threat/2007/11/04/46612.html>.

16. John Arquilla and David Ronfeldt, *In Athena's Camp: Preparing for Conflict in the Information Age* (Santa Monica, CA: RAND, 1997), 28.

17. Ibid., 30.

18. McAfee Virtual Criminology Report, "Cybercrime: The Next Wave," 2007, available at <www.mcafee.com/us/local_content/reports/mcafee_criminology_report2007_en.pdf>.

19. A *botnet* is a network of *bots*. A *bot* (short for *robot*) is a computer that has been compromised by a hacker with software that allows the hacker to control it remotely. Botnets can be quite large; some include more than a million machines.

20. Henry H. Willis, *Guiding Resource Allocations Based on Terrorism Risk*, WR–371–CTRMP (Santa Monica, CA: RAND, 2006). This framework is quite similar to the one currently in use by the Department of Homeland Security. For a detailed analysis of the DHS approach, see Todd Masse, Siobhan O'Neil, and John Rollins, "The Department of Homeland Security's Risk Assessment Methodology: Evolution, Issues, and Options for Congress," CRS Report RL33858 (Washington, DC: Congressional Research Service, 2007), available at <http://fpc.state.gov/documents/organization/80208.pdf>.

21. Bill Nelson et al., *Cyberterror: Prospects and Implications* (Monterey, CA: Center for the Study of Terrorism and Irregular Warfare, 1999), 15.

22. Ibid., 77.

23. Ibid., 86.

24. For a good description of the Nimda virus, see <www.symantec.com/security_response/writeup.jsp?docid=2001-091816-3508-99&tabid=2>.

25. The United States is still developing its own testbeds. In 2007, U.S. Joint Forces Command began working on an Information Operations Range, and the Defense Advanced Research Projects Agency solicited proposals for a computer attack "firing range."

26. Nelson, xi. Another study conducted by Gartner and the Naval War College reached similar conclusions. Richard Hunter, "Digital Pearl Harbor: Getting Real with Cyber-War," presentation at National Defense University, Washington, DC, April 2005.

27. For a discussion of the huge gap between actual risks and perceived risks of terrorism in the United States, see John Mueller, *Overblown: How Politicians and the Terrorism Industry Inflate National Security Threats, and Why We Believe Them* (New York: Free Press, 2006).

28. For a discussion of this topic, see Robert A. Miller and Irving Lachow, *Strategic Fragility: Infrastructure Protection and National Security in the Information Age*, Defense Horizons No. 59 (Washington, DC: Center for Technology and National Security Policy, 2007).

29. Denning, "A View of Cyberterrorism Five Years Later," 135–136.

30. Rita Katz and Michael Kern, "Terrorist 007, Exposed," *The Washington Post*, March 26, 2006, B1.

31. Evan F. Kohlman, "The Real Online Terrorist Threat," *Foreign Affairs* 85, no. 5 (September-October 2006), 121.

32. Lewis, 36.
33. In fact, there were probably more actual cyber attacks during this period than indicated here; data on cyber incidents almost always underrepresents the actual problem because organizations are often reluctant to admit that they have been attacked.
34. Lawrence Wright, "The Spymaster: Can Mike McConnell Fix America's Intelligence Community?" *The New Yorker*, January 21, 2008, 51.
35. Office of the Coordinator for Counterterrorism, "A Strategic Assessment of Progress against the Terrorist Threat," *Foreign Policy Agenda* 12, no. 5 (May 2007), 46–50. See also U.S. Department of State, *Country Reports on Terrorism 2006*, available at <www.state.gov/s/ct/rls/crt/2006/>.
36. Kristin Roberts, "U.S. Warns of Possible Qaeda Financial Cyberattack," *Reuters*, December 1, 2006, available at <www.alertnet.org/thenews/newsdesk/N30222160.htm>.
37. Ibid.
38. Ibid.
39. This conclusion has been reached by a number of renowned security experts, including James Lewis, Bruce Schneier, and Ira Winkler. For example, see Ira Winkler, *Zen and the Art of Information Security* (Rockland, MA: Syngress, 2007), 76–79.
40. An excellent example of the effectiveness of this approach is the fact that al Zarqawi was able to accelerate the withdrawal from Iraq of about 50 Philippine soldiers by kidnapping a Philippine citizen and threatening to behead him. Clearly, the posting of previous beheadings on the Internet had its intended effect in this case. See Evan Osnos, "Philippines Begins Withdrawal," *The Chicago Tribune*, July 15, 2004, available at <www.globalsecurity.org/org/news/2004/040715-philippines-withdrawal.htm>.
41. Quoted in Lewis, 36.
42. Bruce Schneier, *Beyond Fear: Thinking Sensibly About Security in an Uncertain World* (New York: Copernicus, 2006), 237.
43. See Marc Sageman, *Understanding Terror Networks* (Philadelphia: University of Pennsylvania Press, 2004).
44. Nelson, 76.
45. Gartner, "Gartner Survey Shows Phishing Attacks Escalated in 2007; More than $3 Billion Lost to These Attacks," press release, December 17, 2007, available at <www.gartner.com/it/page.jsp?id=565125>.
46. See Miller and Lachow.
47. For an excellent discussion of scale-free networks, see Albert-Laszlo Barabasi, *Linked* (New York: Plume, 2003), or chapter 5 in this volume, "Cyberspace and Infrastructure."
48. Denning, "A View of Cyberterrorism Five Years Later," 127.
49. Henry A. Crumpton, Coordinator for Counterterrorism, Department of State, "The Changing Face of Terror: A Post-9/11 Assessment," statement before Committee on Senate Foreign Relations, June 13, 2006.
50. Weimann, 110. For example, many news services reported the 2004 beheading video of Nick Berg, which was originally uploaded on the Web site of the militant Islamist group Muntada al-Ansar (a group associated with al Qaeda). The popularity of the video can be inferred from the fact that "Nick Berg" was the second most frequent search term in Google in May 2004.
51. Ibid., 126–127, citing Lisa Myers, "Web Video Teaches Terrorists to Make Bomb Vest," *MSNBC News*, December 22, 2004, available at <www.msnbc.msn.com/id/6746756>.
52. Some terrorist Web sites provide guides on how to use the Internet "safely and anonymously." See Jarret M. Brachman, "High-Tech Terror: Al-Qaeda's Use of New Technology," *The Fletcher Forum of World Affairs* 30, no. 2 (Summer 2006), 156.
53. For an excellent discussion of the impact of the Internet on terrorist recruitment, see Frank Cillufo et al., "NETworked Radicalization: A Counter-Strategy," report of the

George Washington University's Homeland Security Policy Institute and the University of Virginia's Critical Incident Analysis Group, 2007.

54. Weimann, 52.

55. For a discussion of the similarities between political activism and terrorism, see Weimann, 23–31.

56. Brachman, 160.

57. Ibid., 152.

58. This process, and the impact of the Internet upon it, is described in Sageman, 158–161.

59. The recruiting process is usually not entirely done in cyberspace. At some point, face-to-face interactions are used to assess the level of commitment of potential members. See Sageman, 163.

60. Rita Katz, Director, SITE Institute, "The Online Jihadist Threat," testimony before the Homeland Security Committee, Subcommittee on Intelligence, Information Sharing and Terrorism Risk Assessment, U.S. House of Representatives, November 6, 2007.

61. Weimann, 113.

62. John Arquilla, David Ronfeldt, and Michele Zanini, "Networks, Netwar, and Information-Age Terrorism," in *Countering the New Terrorism*, ed. Ian O. Lesser et al. (Santa Monica, CA: RAND, 2001), 41.

63. See Ori Brafman and Rod A. Beckstrom, *The Starfish and the Spider* (New York: Penguin Group, 2006).

64. Ibid., 143.

65. For example, there was a series of closed congressional hearings in early 2008 on a new classified Presidential Directive designed to improve the cyber security of all Federal Government networks.

66. Some high-risk systems are almost guaranteed to fail at some point. See Charles Perrow, *Normal Accidents: Living with High-Risk Technologies* (Princeton: Princeton University Press, 1999).

67. For a good discussion of this issue, see Stephen Flynn, *The Edge of Disaster* (New York: Random House, 2007).

68. See chapter 13 in this volume, "Deterrence of Cyber Attacks."

69. For example, see Abdul Hameed Bakier, "The Evolution of Jihadi Electronic Counter-Measures," *Terrorism Monitor* 4, no. 17 (September 8, 2006).

70. Department of Defense, Joint Publication 3–13, *Information Operations* (Washington, DC: Department of Defense, 2006).

71. See Benjamin Wallace-Wells, "Private Jihad," *The New Yorker*, May 29, 2006, available at <www.newyorker.com/archive/2006/05/29/060529fa_fact>.

72. For example, see Blaine Harden, "In Montana, Casting a Web for Terrorists," *The Washington Post*, June 4, 2006, A3.

73. The goal here is to deny access to information without going after infrastructure. Clearly, destroying or disrupting the Internet infrastructure of terrorist groups would also affect the availability of their content. However, because targeting infrastructures is not easy, going after data directly may often be easier technically, legally, and politically.

74. Greg Goth, "Terror on the Internet: A Complex Issue, and Getting Harder," No. 0803-03003, *IEEE Distributed Systems Online* 9, no. 3 (2008).

75. See, for example, U.S. Government Accountability Office, "U.S. Public Diplomacy: Interagency Coordination Efforts Hampered by the Lack of a National Communication Strategy," GAO–05–323, 2005, available at <www.gao.gov/new.items/d05323.pdf>.

76. CBS News, "Rumsfeld: U.S. Losing War of Ideas," March 27, 2006, available at <http://www.cbsnews.com/stories/2006/03/27/terror/main1442811.shtml>.

77. An excellent example is found in Ralph O. Baker, "The Decisive Weapon: A Brigade Combat Team Commander's Perspective on Information Operations," *Military Review*

(May-June 2006), 13–32. This article should be required reading for everyone in the U.S. Government remotely involved in the Long War, and especially for Active-duty forces heading to Iraq and Afghanistan. Chapter 14 in this volume, "Cyber Influence and International Security," also has a nice discussion of tactical influence operations.

78. Jim Guirard, "Petraeus Aide's Call for a 'New Lexicon'," *TrueSpeak.org*, available at <www.truespeak.org/print.php?id=petraeusaidescallforanewlexicon>.

79. For more detail, see Douglas E. Streusand and Harry D. Tunnell IV, "Choosing Words Carefully: Language to Help Fight Islamic Terrorism," Center for Strategic Communications, National Defense University, May 23, 2006, available at <www.ndu. edu/csc/docs/Choosing%20Words%20Carefully--Language%20to%20Help%20Fig ht%20Islamic%20Terrorism%2024%20May%2006.do >; and Jim Guirard, "Hirabah versus Jihad: Rescuing Jihad from the al Qaeda Blasphemy," *The American Muslim*, July 6, 2003, available at <http://theamericanmuslim.org/tam.php/features/articles/ terrorism_hirabah_versus_jihad_rescuing_jihad_from_the_al_qaeda_blasphemy/>.

80. On the role of honor in Islam, see Akbar S. Ahmed, *Islam under Siege* (Cambridge, UK: Policy Press, 2003).

81. For more details, see Robert Spencer, "Losing the War of Ideas," *FrontPageMagazine. com*, February 5, 2004, available at <www.frontpagemag.com/Articles/Read. aspx?GUID=3D75E317-8475-4677-97C8-4A5136A4C72>.

82. See, for example, Office of the Under Secretary of Defense for Acquisition, Technology, and Logistics, *Report of the Defense Science Board Task Force on Strategic Communication* (Washington, DC: Department of Defense, September, 2004).

83. Baker, 20.

Chapter 20

1. Nathan Thornburgh, "The Invasion of the Chinese Cyberspies," *Time*, August 29, 2005, available at <www.time.com/time/magazine/article/0,9171,1098961,00.html>.

2. Vago Muradian, "China Tried to Blind U.S. Sats with Laser," *Defense News*, September 25, 2006, 1.

3. Josh Rogin, "Network Attack Disables Naval War College," *Federal Computer Week*, November 30, 2006, available at <www.fcw.com/online/news/96957-1.html>.

4. Anthony Kuhn, National Public Radio, January 19, 2007, interview with Beijing People's University commentator.

5. "Chinese Hackers Attack Taiwan Military Computers," *Taipei P'ing-kuo Jih-pao* (Internet version), May 15, 2006, Open Source Center Report no. CPP20060516310002.

6. Peng Guangqian and Yao Youzhi, eds., *The Science of Military Strategy* (Beijing: Military Science Publishing House, Academy of Military Science of the Chinese People's Liberation Army), 2005.

7. Pu Duanhua, "Network Control: New Access Control Concerning Outcome of Future War," *China National Defense News*, February 8, 2007.

8. Peng and Yao.

9. Ibid., 418–419.

10. Ibid., 345.

11. Ibid.

12. Ibid.

13. Yang Zurong, "Military Deputy Appeals to Army-Civilian Joint Efforts to Guard 'Information Border'," *Jiefangjun Bao*, March 7, 2007, 4, Open Source Center Report no. CPP20070307710014.

14. The word *cyber* was used in place of the term *informationization* here based on a glossary in *The Science of Military Strategy* where it was noted that the two words are cognates.

15. Report on Chinese Military, Science and Technology Developments, May 1–15, 2006,

Open Source Center Report No. CPP20060612478001, Department of Defense, in English, June 7, 2006.

16. Joint Publication 1–02, *Department of Defense Dictionary of Military Terms* (Washington, DC: The Joint Staff, April 12, 2001, as amended through March 4, 2008).

17. *Chinese Military Encyclopedia*, vol. 3 (Beijing: Military Science Publishing House, July 1997), 699.

18. Li Bingyan, "Applying Military Strategy in the Age of the New Revolution in Military Affairs," in *The Chinese Revolution in Military Affairs*, ed. Shen Weiguang (Beijing: New China Press, 2004), 2–31.

19. Ibid.

20. Ibid. He also listed dispersion theory, function theory, intelligence theory, optimality theory, homology theory, and fuzzy theory.

21. Ibid.

22. Ibid.

23. Ibid.

24. Ibid.

25. Ibid.

26. Dai Qingmin, "Discourse on Armed Forces Informationization Building and Information Warfare Building," in Shen, 39–47. The chapter also appeared as an article in *China Military Science*, 2002.

27. Dai Qingmin, "Innovating and Developing Views on Information Operations," *Zhongguo Junshi Kexue* (China Military Science), no. 4, August 2000, 72–77, Foreign Broadcast Information Service, document no. CPP2000911000150.

28. Ibid.

29. Ibid.

30. Ibid.

31. Ibid.

32. Ibid.

33. Ibid.

34. Ibid.

35. Niu Li, Li Jiangzhou, and Xu Dehui, "Planning and Application of Strategies of Information Operations in High-Tech Local War," *Zhongguo Junshi Kexue* (China Military Science), no. 4 (2000), 115–122, Foreign Broadcast Information Service document no. CPP 20010112000141. The authors of this article teach at an unidentified communications and command institute in China.

36. Ibid.

37. Ibid.

38. Ibid.

39. Ibid.

40. Ibid.

41. Ibid.

42. Ibid.

43. Ibid. The Chinese use the phrase *thought directing* in this article in the way a U.S. analyst might use *perception management*.

44. Ibid.

45. Ibid.

46. Peng and Yao.

47. See, for example, "Moonlight Maze," *Wikipedia*, available at <http://en.wikipedia.org/wiki/Moonlight-Maze>.

48. Ian Traynor, "Russia Accused of Unleashing Cyberwar to Disable Estonia," *The Guardian*, May 17, 2007, available at <www.guardian.co.uk/russia/article/0,,2081438,00.html>.

49. Patrick Jackson, "The Cyber Pirates Hitting Estonia," *BBC News*, May 17, 2007, available at <http://news.bbc.co.uk/2/hi/europe/6665195.stm>.
50. Kevin Poulsen, "We Traced the Cyberwar—It's Coming from Inside the Country!" *Wired*, available at <http://blog.wired.com/27bstroke6/2008/01/we-traced-the-c.html>.
51. *Moscow Interfax*, May 17, 2007, Open Source Center document no. CEP 20070517950094.
52. *Moscow Interfax*, May 14, 2008, Open Source Center document no. CEP 20080514950059.
53. The author of this chapter was present for Mr. Vasilyev's briefing.
54. V.D. Sokolovskiy, *Soviet Military Strategy* (New York: Crane, Russak, and Company, Inc.), 1963.
55. S.N. Mikhalev, *Military Strategy: Preparation and Conduct of New and Latter-Day Wars* (Moscow: Kuchkovo Polye, 2003), 22, 23, quoting A.A. Danilevich's 1992 definition of strategy.
56. S.F. Akhromeev, *Military Encyclopedic Dictionary* (Moscow: Military Publishing House, 1986), 711, 712.
57. A Russian information operations specialist confirmed this use of *informationization* in place of *cyber* to this author in an October 2006 interview in Moscow.
58. S.V. Belking and S.N. Navolokin, "Conceptual Foundations of the Moscow Oblast's Information Security," *Nauchno-Tekhnicheskaya Informatsiya. Seriya 1. Organizatsiya I Metodika Informatsionnoy Raboty*, no. 3, 2005, Open Source Center translation.
59. *ITAR-TASS*, "Russian Interior Ministry Calls for Legislation to Combat Cyber Terrorism," October 19, 2006, Open Source Center document no. CEP 20061019950025.
60. Pavel Shumilo, "A Cyber Attack on Humanity Is in Progress," *Armeyskiy Sbornik*, November 30, 2006, Open Source Center translation no. CEP 20070502322005.
61. Author's discussion with Major General (retired) Vladimir Slipchenko in Moscow.
62. S. Leonenko, "*Refleksivnoe upravlenie protivnikom* (Reflexive control of the enemy)," *Armeyskiy Sbornik*, no. 8 (1995), 28.
63. Ibid.
64. Ibid., 29–30.
65. Ibid., 29.
66. Ibid., 28. This is akin to how British and American perception management theorists view the purpose of deception.
67. Ibid.
68. S.V. Markov, "*O nekotoryk podkhodakh k opredeleniyu sushchnosti informatsionnogo oruzhiya* (Several approaches to the determination of the essence of the information weapon)," *Bezopasnost* no. 1–2, (1996), 53.
69. Vladimir E. Lepsky, *Refleksivnoe upravlenie v polisubektnikh i mnogoagentnikh sistemakh* (Reflexive control in multi-object and multi-agent systems)," copy of an unpublished manuscript provided by Lepsky to this author, 2.
70. V.F. Prokof'ev, *Secret Weapons of Information War* (Moscow: Sinteg), 2003.
71. S.P. Rastorguyev, *An Introduction to the Formal Theory of Information War* (Moscow: Vuzovskaya Kniga, 2002). In an earlier book (*Information War* [Moscow: Radio and Communication, 1998]), Rastorguyev discussed the use of algorithms to put "psycho viruses" into people's heads. His focus over the years has been on computer methods to accomplish both information-technical and information-psychological goals.
72. R. Bikkenin, "Information Conflict in the Military Sphere: Basic Elements and Concepts," *Morskoy Sbornik*, no. 10 (October 2003), 38–40.
73. Konstantin Nikolsky, "When They Shoot with Words," *Krasnaya Zvezda*, October 19, 2005, 2.
74. Pavel Shumilo, "A Cyber Attack on Humanity Is in Progress," *Armeyskiy Sbornik*, November 2006, Open Source Center document no. CEP 20070502322005.
75. *Information Security Doctrine*, Russian Federation Security Council (Internet version), September 13, 2000, Open Source Center translation.

76. Ibid.
77. Ibid.
78. Ibid.
79. Ibid.
80. Ibid.
81. Ibid.
82. ITAR-TASS, "Conference on Information Security, Mass Media Held in Russia," October 23, 2000.
83. "Russia Calls for International Information Security System," *Interfax*, October 12, 2000.
84. Lyudmila Yermakova, ITAR-TASS, September 12, 2000, Foreign Broadcast Information Service.
85. Mikhail Shevtsov, ITAR-TASS, September 12, 2000, Foreign Broadcast Information Service.
86. V.P. Sherstyuk's responses to questions from Internet users, October 5, 2000, Foreign Broadcast Information Service.
87. Ibid.
88. Ibid.
89. I.N. Dylevskii, S.A. Komov, S.V. Korotkov, S.N. Rodionov, and A.V. Fyodorov, "Russian Federation Military Policy for the Provision of International Information Security," *Military Thought*, June 30, 2006.
90. Ibid.
91. Bikkenin.

Chapter 21

1. "The Internet's domain-name system (DNS) allows users to refer to web sites and other resources using easier-to-remember domain names (such as 'www.icann.org') rather than the all-numeric IP [Internet Protocol] addresses (such as '192.0.34.65') assigned to each computer on the Internet." "Top Level Domains," Internet Corporation for Assigned Names and Numbers Web site, available at <www.icann.org/tlds/>.
2. Comments by David Hendon, European Union chief negotiator at the World Summit on the Information Society (WSIS), before a meeting of the Information Technology Association of America's Government Affairs Committee, April 25, 2007, at which the author was present. The two WSIS conferences were convened by the United Nations in 2003 in Geneva and in 2005 in Tunis to address the "digital divide" between the developed and developing worlds.
3. See Joyce K. Reynolds and Jon Postel, "Assigned Numbers," October 1994, available at <www.ietf.org/rfc/rfc1700.txt>.
4. "Bylaws for Internet Corporation for Assigned Names and Numbers," available at <www.icann.org/general/bylaws.htm#I>.
5. "Top Level Domains," available at <www.icann.org/tlds/>. "Each TLD includes many second-level domains (such as 'icann' in 'www.icann.org')."
6. Ibid. "Domain names may be registered in three of these (.com, .net, and .org) without restriction; the other four have limited purposes."
7. Ibid. "The responsibility for operating each TLD (including maintaining a registry of the second-level domains within the TLD) is delegated to a particular organization . . . referred to as 'registry operators,' 'sponsors,' or simply 'delegees'.' . . . [These] designated managers . . . operate the ccTLDs according to local policies that are adapted to best meet the economic, cultural, linguistic, and legal circumstances of the country or territory involved."

8. Root zone servers are directories that can be queried for the location of Internet protocol addresses for top level domains (they do not route the traffic themselves). There are 13 root zone servers, of which the "A" server is the master; 10 are in the United States. Because of concerns about robustness and reliability, most of the root zone servers now make use of multiple "anycast" servers distributed around the world, which hold duplicate files. See <www.root-servers.org/>.

9. The Internet Architecture Board has tried to remind ICANN that the technical registration functions for IETF protocol parameters and other technical assignments are separate from IANA's other functions, but the distinctions have long been blurred. The significance of this caution is that in performing what are generally referred to as the "IANA functions," ICANN is not solely responsible to the U.S. Government. It may complicate how to resolve disputes between the United States and various foreign governments about the ICANN–U.S. Government IANA contract, a significant issue in Internet governance that is discussed below.

10. When ICANN was formed in 1998, the intent was that it would initially be under the direction of Jon Postel, a member of the University of Southern California's Information Sciences Institute, which had previously performed much the same work under contract to the U.S. Government. Although Postel died shortly after, ICANN came into existence as a continuation of his previous work.

11. See "Memorandum of Understanding between the U.S. Department of Commerce and Internet Corporation for Assigned Names and Numbers," available at <www.icann. org/general/icann-mou-25nov98.htm>. The memorandum has been amended several times.

12. "Domain Names," National Telecommunications and Information Administration Web site, available at <www.ntia.doc.gov/ntiahome/domainname/icann.htm>.

13. See below. Critics dispute that characterization.

14. The memorandum of understanding/joint project agreement does require ICANN to seek governmental advice, which it does through its Governmental Advisory Committee, discussed below. The U.S. Government is a member of the committee.

15. See "ICANN to Cut U.S. Apron Strings?" *Business Week,* July 28, 2006, available at <www. businessweek.com/technology/content/jul2006/tc20060728_701788.htm>; Associated Press, "US Extends ICANN Agreement Three Years," October 2, 2006, available at <http://entmag.com/news/article.asp?EditorialsID=7846>.

16. NTIA, "Domain Names: Management of Internet Names and Addresses," available at <www.ntia.doc.gov/ntiahome/domainname/iana.htm>. "The responsibility for operating each TLD (including maintaining a registry of the second-level domains within the TLD) is delegated to a particular organization. . . . [These organizations are] referred to as 'registry operators,' 'sponsors,' or simply 'delegees.'. . . [D]esignated managers . . . operate the [country-code] ccTLDs according to local policies that are adapted to best meet the economic, cultural, linguistic, and legal circumstances of the country or territory involved."

17. "United States Announces Intention to Maintain Control Over Internet," *Globalization101.org,* August 9, 2005, available at <www.globalization101.org/index. php?file=news1&id=14>.

18. Declan McCullagh, "Porn-friendly '.xxx' domains approved," C/netNews.com, June 1, 2005, available at <http://news.com.com/Porn-friendly+.xxx+domains+approved/210 0-1030_3-5728713.html>.

19. ICANN Press Release, "ICANN's Board of Directors has voted against a proposed agreement for creating a new Top Level Domain, Dot xxx," May 11, 2006; "ICANN meeting passes on .com, .xxx decisions," *CBROnline,* December 5, 2005, available at <www.cbronline.com/news/icann_meeting_passes_on_com_xxx_decisions>.

20. Eric Bangeman, "ICANN shoots down .xxx yet again," March 30, 2007, available at <http://arstechnica.com/news.ars/post/20070330-icann-shoots-down-xxx-yet-again.html>.

21. "Cooperative Agreement Between the Department of Commerce and VeriSign (Network Solutions)," NTIA Web site, available at <www.ntia.doc.gov/ntiahome/domainname/nsi.htm>.

22. Ibid. See particularly Amendments 11 (October 6, 1998) and 19 (September 28, 1999). The amendments required NSI (later VeriSign) to enter into the agreements with ICANN.

23. VeriSign is still a registry for other TLDs. It won the right to continue with *.net* following an open competition in 2005. Kieren McCarthy, "VeriSign wins back .net registry," *The Register*, March 29, 2005, available at <www.theregister.co.uk/2005/03/29/verisign_keeps_net/>; ICANN, "ICANN Publishes Telecordia Report on their Findings and Rankings for .NET," March 28, 2005, accessed at <www.icann.org/announcements/announcement-28mar05.htm>.

24. According to recent figures, *.com* now has 112 million registrations. Andrew Allemann, "Domain Registrations Hit 112 Million," *CircleID*, November 30, 2006, available at <www.circleid.com/posts/domain_registrations_hit_112_million/>. Also see remarks by Secretary of Commerce William M. Daley, September 28, 1999, available at <www.ntia.doc.gov/ntiahome.domainname/agreements/92899spicann.htm>.

25. Amendment 11, October 6, 1998.

26. In 2006, the Deparment of Commerce approved a new agreement between ICANN and VeriSign. However, the approval process drew it into a dispute over the agreement, which had been the subject of considerable dissatisfaction in the Internet community. NTIA eventually forced VeriSign to agree to certain changes, reflected in amendments to the Cooperative Agreement. NTIA, "NTIA Approves New .Com Domain Name Registry Agreement," November 30, 2006, available at <www.ntia.doc.gov/ntiahome/press/2006/icanncom_113006.htm>. Issues included "competition and Internet security and stability issues" and "proposed increase in prices for .com registrants."

27. ICANN Web site. The non-U.S. voting members come from Canada, Australia (two, including the president of ICANN), France, Kenya, New Zealand (chair), Italy (vice-chair), Norway, Chile, Brazil, Ireland, and India. Of six non-voting liaison members, three are American.

28. See, for example, Governmental Advisory Committee Secretariat, "The Internet Domain Name System and the Governmental Advisory Committee (GAC) of the Internet Corporation for Assigned Names and Numbers (ICANN)," available at <http://gac.icann.org/web/about/gac-outreach_English.htm>.

29. See <www.hrea.org/lists/huridocs-list/markup/msg01354.html>.

30. The Internet Society has local chapters, often referred to as Internet societies. The term may also loosely refer to groups composed of Internet users, some of which may be recognized participants in the ICANN At Large Advisory Committee.

31. A range of institutions operate country code top level domain (ccTLD) registries. Initially, few, if any, had government ties; most were technical specialists or academics who had the requisite skills. There has been a trend toward more government control in recent years, although it is not clear how many ccTLD registries are now effectively under such influence.

32. One of the four principles the NTIA announced in 2005 regarding the DNS was, "Governments have a legitimate interest in the management of their ccTLDs. The United States recognizes that governments have legitimate public policy and sovereignty concerns with respect to the management of their ccTLD." NTIA, "U.S. Principles on the Internet's Domain Name and Addressing System," June 30, 2005, available at <www.ntia.doc.gov/ntiahome/domainname/USDNSprincipleso6302005.htm>.

33. T. Wright, "EU and U.S. clash over control of Net," *International Herald Tribune*, September 30, 2005, 1. The story points out that the European Union briefly also pushed for a replacement to ICANN that would have given governments more control. See Kenneth Neil Cukier, "Who Will Control the Internet?" *Foreign Affairs* 84, no. 6 (November-December 2005), 7.

34. For example, the Internet Governance Project (IGP) published an extended critique of U.S. Government influence shortly before the 2005 WSIS. IGP, "Political Oversight of ICANN: A Briefing for the WSIS Summit" (November 1, 2005), 3. IGP later criticized the 2006 JPA on the grounds that: "ICANN still gets general policy guidance from the DoC." IGP, "ICANN's New MoU: Old Wine in New Bottle," September 30, 2006, accessed at <www.internetgovernance.org/news.html>. As evidence to support its complaint, IGP pointed to a provision in the 2006 JPA that required ICANN to continue its current practice regarding disclosure of information about IP address holders reflected in its WHOIS database. IGP saw this as dictating substantive decisionmaking. However, ICANN Board member Susan Crawford, defending her vote in favor of the JPA, wrote that she had considered the provision a potential departure from longstanding policy and practice but was specifically assured that the provision would not be enforced if the ICANN Board decided to change WHOIS policy. Susan Crawford, "ICANN and the DOC," *CircleID*, September 29, 2006, available at <www.circleid.com/posts/icann_and_the_doc/>. The WHOIS database has since become the subject of significant internal debate, suggesting that the JPA did not foreclose consideration of major changes.

35. The author was present at a working group at the Rio de Janeiro Internet Governance Forum in 2007 where ICANN was strenuously attacked. Various conspiracy theories involving the U.S. Government were advanced to explain other decisions, such as the failure to deploy IPv6, but little proof was offered.

36. ICANN Bylaws, Article VI, Section 6, available at <www.icann.org/en/general/bylaws.htm#VI>.

37. Wired, "ICANN, VeriSign Reach Accord," *Wired*, October 25, 2005, available at <www.wired.com/science/discoveries/news/2005/10/69346>.

38. "Lawsuits Filed Against ICANN-VeriSign Settlement," *CircleID*, November 29, 2005, available at <www.circleid.composts/lawsuits_filed_against_icann_verisign-settlement/>; Justin Lee, "ICANN Closes Deal, Upsets Registrars," *WHIRnews*, March 3, 2006, available at <www.thewhir.com/features/030306_ICANN_Closes_Deal_Upsets_Registrars.cfm>. See also Non-Commercial Users Constituency, "NCUC response to the ICANN-VeriSign settlement," available at <www.ncdnhc.org/policydocuments/ncuc-icann-verisignsettlement.pdf>.

39. VeriSign has subsequently received NTIA approval for renewal of its *.com* registry agreement through 2012, with a presumption that it will continue thereafter. Amendment 30 to NCR 92–18742, <www.ntia.doc.gov/ntiahome/domainname/agreements/amend30_11292006.pdf>.

40. One World Trust, "Independent Review of ICANN's Accountability and Transparency—Structures and Procedures," London, March 2007, available at <www.icann.org/announcements/announcement-4-29mar07.htm>.

41. Ibid., 5.

42. "Independent Review of ICANN's Accountability and Transparency."

43. See <www.icann.org/lists/principles-comments>.

44. There are two policy development processes; the Generic Names Supporting Organization considers more requests for PDPs because of its broader constituency base, while the ccNSO, PDPs focus on issues related to global ccTLD issues. The Address Supporting Organization, composed of the regional registries, also provides advice on IP address

allocations, but has no equivalent process in its bylaws, although they outline opportunity for public comment. See Address Supporting Organization Web site at <www.iso.icann. org>.

45. London School of Economics Public Policy Group and Enterprise LSE, *A Review of the Generic Names Supporting Organization (GNSO)*, London, September 2006.

46. Ibid., 9–10.

47. ICANN, "ICANN Response to One World Trust Review of ICANN's Accountability and Transparency—Structures and Practices," June 7, 2007, available at <www.icann. org/transparency/mop-update-07jun07.htm>.

48. See "Internet Architecture Board," *Wikipedia*, available at <http://en.wikipedia.org/ wiki/Internet_Architecture_Board>. The IAB grew out of the Internet Configuration Control Board formed by the Defense Advanced Research Projects Agency in 1979; it became the Internet Advisory Board in 1984, the Internet Activities Board in 1986, and the Internet Architecture Board in January 1992. The Internet Engineering Task Force began in 1986 as a meeting of 21 U.S. Government–funded researchers. See <www.isoc. org/internet/history/brief.shtml>.

49. "The Internet and the World Wide Web are not synonymous. The Internet is a collection of interconnected computer networks, linked by copper wires, fiber-optic cables, wireless connections, and so forth. In contrast, the Web is a collection of interconnected documents and other resources, linked by hyperlinks and URLs. The World Wide Web is one of the services accessible via the Internet, along with many others, including email [and] file sharing." "Internet," *Wikipedia*, available at <http://en.wikipedia.org/wiki/ Internet>.

50. Anick Jesdanun, "Internet Board Picks New Zealander Chair," Associated Press, November 2, 2007, available at <www.newsvine.com/_news/2007/11/02/1069437- internet-board-picks-new-zealander-chair>.

51. See <www.isoc.org/internet/history/brief.shtml>.

52. Request for Comment 3935.

53. These are Applications; General; Internet; Operations and Management; Real-time Applications and Infrastructure; Routing; Security; and Transport. "Active IETF Working Groups," available at <www.ietf.org/html.charters/wg-dir.html>.

54. "Glossary," available at <www.ietf.org/glossary.html>.

55. As of summer 2007, 11 of the 16 area directors were American or employed by American- based organizations.

56. Ibid. See also <http://222.iab.org/index.html>.

57. See <www.iab.org/about/overview.html>; Request for Comment 4677, Part 3.2.4.

58. The Internet Research Task Force mission is "to promote research of importance to the evolution of the future Internet by creating focused, long-term and small Research Groups working on topics related to Internet protocols, applications, architecture and technology." There is a steering group whose members are chosen by the chair "in consultation with the rest of Steering Group on approval of the IAB." See <www.irtf. org>; Request for Comment 2014.

59. See <www.isoc.org/isoc/related/ietf>.

60. See <www/isoc/org/members-php>.

61. Request for Comment 4677, Part 4.

62. Ibid. "The exact method of determining rough consensus varies from Working Group to Working Group. Sometimes consensus is determined by 'humming'—if you agree with a proposal, you hum when prompted by the chair; if you disagree, you keep your silence. Newcomers find it quite peculiar, but it works. It is up to the chair to decide when the Working Group has reached rough consensus."

63. Request for Comment 4677, Part 5.2.

64. John Markoff, "Software via the Internet: Microsoft in 'Cloud' Computing," *The New York Times*, September 3, 2007, available at <www.nytimes.com/2007/09/03/technology/03cloud.html>.

65. See <www.w3c.org/Consortium>.

66. See <www.w3c.org/AboutW3C.mht>.

67. See the World Wide Web Consortium's Web site, <www.w3c.org>, for a more extended discussion of the process.

68. A formal treaty, the International Telecommunication Regulations, governs some aspects of international telephone service. It has not been open for revision or amendment for almost 20 years, so it does not directly address the Internet, although its language has been adapted for IP communication. At the ITU's Plenipotentiary Conference in 2006, there were several proposals to reopen the treaty. There may well be a treaty conference on the document in 2012, depending on future ITU decisions.

69. The bulk of the ITU's Internet-related work is in the ITU–T. The ITU has two other bureaus, Radiocommunication, which deals with some Internet issues related to wireless communication, and Telecommunication Development, which is involved in promoting expansion of the Internet in the less developed world.

70. See, for example, letter, Houlin-Zhou, Director of the Telecommunication Standardization Bureau, to NTIA, March 3, 2006 (suggesting ITU could operate the IANA function); Circular Letter, Houlin-Zhou, Document CO6/4, March 2006 (suggesting to ITU members that the ITU could operate a dual parallel system of address allocations).

71. See <www.itu.int/ITU-T/membership/join-itut.html>.

72. Governments take an active role in the management of the ITU, even if not in the development of individual recommendations. The ITU Council, made up of 46 member-nations elected at the Plenipotentiary every 4 years, oversees the union. Sector members do not participate in the council meetings and only recently have been allowed to have a limited number of "observers."

73. See Telecommunication Standardization Bureau, "ITU–T Guide for Newcomers," available at <www.itu.int/ITU-T>.

74. The ITU–T and ITU–R also participate in the Global Standards Collaboration (GSC), an annual meeting of the major national and regional telecom standards bodies that discuss issues where there are both national and international interest, such as next generation networks (which focus on converged IP-based services), broadband rural access, and networked radio frequency identification. An ad hoc group in Intellectual Property Rights advises the TSB director on issues such as the Common Patent Policy adopted by the ITU along with the International Organization on Standardization and the International Electrotechnical Commission. See <www.itu.int/ITU-T/othergroups/ipr-adhoc/index.html>.

75. See <www.itu.int/ITU-T/focU.S.governmentgroups/index.html>.

76. Sector members often disagree with each other, offer competitive positions for consideration, and lobby their fellow private sector members and government officials outside the ITAC process. When negotiations lead to no conclusion, the individual private sector member must fend for itself or find an international partner to bring forward the same proposal through some other government.

77. See <www.itu.int/ITU-T/app>.

78. The main approval process is set forth in WTSA–04 Resolution 1, Section 9. The Alternative Approval Process is contained in ITU–T Rec. A.8, and its revision is in TSB Circular Letter 110 (August 18, 2006). See <www.itu.int/ITU-T/tap> or <www.itu.int/ITU-T/app>.

79. A recent example of the overlap creating a problem involved multiprotocol label switching (MPLS), which is designed to provide a unified data-carrying service for both circuit-

based clients and packet-switching clients. See <www.wikipedia.org/wiki/MPLS>. The IETF had been working on MPLS for 8 years, the ITU–T for 3. The resolution of the overlap reflects how complex the conflicts can be; the proposal states, "Future work will be progressed by first analyzing the requirements and desired functionality." Since T [Sector]-MPLS utilizes MPLS functionality extensively, the experts recommend that "the IETF Standards Process will be used for extensions or modifications of IETF MPLS Technology." It was clearly noted that there are aspects of the problem space that lie outside the domain of expertise in the IETF or straddle both organizations— for example, management of transport equipment, and some aspects of OAM and survivability. The working team will be tasked to help identify which of these aspects are best standardized in IETF RFCs and which in ITU–T Recommendations." See <www. itu.int/ITU-T/newslog/TMPLS+Agreement+ITUT+And+IETF.aspx>.

80. As of mid-2007, there were three U.S. ITU–T study group chairs and seven U.S. vice chairs. See <www.itu.int/ITU-T/study groups>.

81. Resolution 102, Final Acts, ITU Plenipotentiary Conference, Antalya, Turkey, November 2006, available at <www.itu.int/osg/spu/wtpf/wtpf2009/documents/ ITUresolution102_publicpolicy_IPB>.

82. See <www.itu.int/osg/spu/mina/consultations/contributions_memberstates.html>.

83. WSIS Plan of Action, available at <www.itu.int/wsis/docts/geneva/official/poa.html>; Article 102, WSIS Tunis Agenda for the Information Society and Annex A, available at <www.itu.int/wsis/documents>.

84. ITU, "Connect Africa Summit to be held in Kigali, Rwanda, 29–30 October 2007, Marshall Plan for ICT to meet 2015 development goals," July 11, 2007, available at <www.itu.int/ newsroom/press_releases/2007/18/html>;TMCnet, "International Telecommunication Union (ITU); Connect Africa Summit to be held in Kigali, Rwanda, 29–30 October 2007," July 11, 2007, available at <www.tmcnet.com./usubmit/2007/07/11/2775508. htm>; ITU Global Cyber-security Agenda, available at <http://222.itu.int/osg/csd/ cybersecurity/gca/background.html>.

85. Request for Comment 3356; Supplement to ITU–T A-series Recommendations, available at <www.itu.int/ITU-T/recommendations>.

86. The ITU also has formal agreements setting up collaboration with the International Organization for Standardization and the International Electrotechnical Commission; these are discussed below. ITU–T Resolution 7, "Collaboration with ISO and IEC;" ITU–T Recommendation A.23, "Collaboration with ISO and IEC on Information Technology."

87. For example, the secretary-general made such comments before the U.S. International Telecommunication Union Association meeting held in Washington, DC, March 5, 2007, at which the author was present.

88. See, for example, Circular Letter C06/4 from Houlin Zhao, "ITU Activities related to the Internet Protocol (IP) based networks and management of internet domain names and addresses; including activities related to internet governance," March 2006.

89. See <www.oecd-toolkit.org>.

90. Ibid., 6.

91. Ibid., 15.

92. See <http://londonactionplan.org>.

93. See also chapter 22 in this volume, "International Law and Information Operations."

94. Kristin Archick, *Cybercrime: The Council of Europe Convention,* Congressional Research Service Report RS21208 (Washington, DC: Congressional Research Service, July 22, 2004), 3. Also see the 2001 Council of Europe report on the protocol, available at <http://assembly.coe.int/Documents/WorkingDocs/doc01/EDOC9263.htm>. Some European nations and Canada have now signed the protocol. "Canada signs protocol to

fight online hate," *OUT-LAW News*, December 7, 2005, available at <www.out-law.com/ page-5901>. For U.S. concerns, see, for example, "Protocol to Cybercrime Convention," *American Journal of International Law* 96 (October 2002), 973–975; Michelle Madigan, "Internet Hate-Speech Ban Called 'Chilling'," *PC World*, December 2, 2002, available at <www.pcworld.com/article/id,107499-page,1/article.html>.

95. Archick, 3.

96. Mark Landler and John Markoff, "Digital Fears Emerge After Data Siege in Estonia," *The New York Times*, May 24, 2007.

97. "Joint Programmes between the Council of Europe and the European Commission," available at <www.jp.coe.int>.

98. EU privacy guidelines have, among other things, significantly complicated the debate over the WHOIS database. The European Commission's position is set forth in "Opinion 2/2003 on the application of the data protection principles to the Whois directories," 10972/03/EN final WP 76 (June 13, 2003). See also Declan McCullagh, "Is it time to get rid of the WHOIS directory," *C/NET News*, October 30, 2007, available at <www.news. com/8301-13578_3-9807356-38.html>.

99. The Millennium Development Goals were adopted in 2000. Goal 8 called for a partnership for global development, "in cooperation with the private sector, [to] make available the benefits of new technologies—especially information and communications technologies." See <www.un.org/millenniumgoals/>.

100. Report of the Secretary-General to the Economic and Social Council, "Promoting the building of a people-centred, development-oriented and inclusive information society: Progress made in the implementation of and follow up to the World Summit on the Information Society outcomes," E/CN 16/2007/2, April 3, 2007.

101. See, for example, "Summary of Activities, Working Group IV, 1997 to present: Electronic Commerce," <www.uncitral.org.uncitral.en.commission.working_groups/4Electronic_ Commerce>.

102. Jonathan Zittrain and Benjamin Edelman, "Internet Filtering in China," *IEEE Internet Computing* (March-April 2002); Open Net Initiative, "Internet Filtering in China in 2004– 2005: A Country Study," available at <www.opennetinitiative.net/studies/china/>; Rebecca McKinnon, "China's Internet: Let a Thousand Filters Bloom," *Yale Global Online*, June 28, 2005, available at <http://yaleglobal.yale.edu/display.article?id=5928>; Amnesty International, "Censorship in China," <www.amnestyusa.org/Internet_Censorship/ Implicated_companies/page.do?id=11015>; Rita Desai, "China Filters the Internet," *The Bivings Report*, October 10, 2006, available at <www.bivingsreport.com/2006/china- filters-the-internet>.

103. Steve Gibbard, "Myanmar Internet Shutdown," CircleID, October 4, 2007, available at <www.circleid.com/posts/710413_myanmar_internet_shutdown/>.

104. Both the ITU and the OECD have cautioned that the problem is complex. See ITU Study Group 13, discussion of quality of service for Next Generation Networks, available at <www.itu.int/ITU-T/studygroups/com13/sg13-q4.html>; OECD Working Party on Telecommunication and Information Services Policies, "Internet Traffic Prioritisation: An Overview," DSTA/ICCP/TISP(2006)4/Final (6 April 2007), 5, available at <www. oecd.org/dataoecd/43/63/38405781.pdf>.

105. See <www.iso.org>; <www.iee.org>; <www.iec.ch>.

106. "IEC, ISO and ITU, the world's leading developers of international standards, agree upon common patent policy," March 19, 2007, available at <www.itu.int/newsroom/ press_releases/2007/05.html>.

107. Although ANSI is private nonprofit organization, its membership comprises both government and nongovernment organizations, as well as corporations, academic and international bodies, and individuals.

Chapter 22

1. "Charter of the United Nations," United Nations Web site, available at <www.un.org/aboutun/charter/>; emphasis added.

2. Ibid., article 51. "Nothing in the present Charter shall impair the inherent right of individual or collective self-defence if an armed attack occurs against a Member of the United Nations."

3. Michael N. Schmitt, "Bellum Americanum: The U.S. View of Twenty-first Century War and Its Possible Implications for the Law of Armed Conflict," *Michigan Journal of International Law* 19 (1998), 1051.

4. Ibid.

5. Michael N. Schmitt, "Computer Network Attack and the Use of Force in International Law: Thoughts on a Normative Framework," *Columbia Journal of Transnational Law* 37 (1999), 887, at 914–915.

6. Ibid.

7. Ibid.

8. Ibid.

9. Ibid.

10. Ibid.

11. Ibid.

12. See the discussion of botnets in chapter 7 of this volume, "Information Security Issues in Cyberspace," and chapter 18, "Cyber Crime."

13. Department of the Navy, NWP 1–14M, *The Commander's Handbook on the Law of Naval Operations* (Newport, RI: Naval War College, 1995), sec. 8.1 (hereafter *Commander's Handbook*). See also Department of the Army, Field Manual 27–10, *The Law of Land Warfare* (Washington, DC: Department of the Army, 1956); and Department of the Air Force, AFP 110–31, *International Law—The Conduct of Armed Conflict and Air Operations* (Washington, DC: Department of the Air Force, 1993), secs. 5–3, 11–2.

14. "Protocol Additional to the Geneva Conventions of 12 August 1949, and Relating to the Protection of Victims of International Armed Conflicts," art. 48, December 12, 1977, 1125, in *Documents on the Laws of War*, ed. Adam Roberts and Richard Guelff (London: Oxford University Press, 1989); hereafter Geneva Protocol.

15. *Commander's Handbook*, 109, at sec. 5.3

16. Ibid. This distinction is critical to the laws distinguishing permissible "ruses" from impermissible treachery, discussed below.

17. *Commander's Handbook*, sec. 8.1.1. It goes on to list lawful targets:

    > Proper targets for naval attack include such military objectives as enemy warships and military aircraft, naval and military auxiliaries, naval and military bases ashore, warship construction and repair facilities, military depots and warehouses . . . lines of communication and other objects used to conduct or support military operations. . . . Proper naval targets also include geographic targets, such as a mountain pass, and buildings and facilities that provide administrative and personnel support for military and naval operations such as barracks, communications and command and control facilities, headquarters buildings, mess halls, and training areas.
    >
    > Also lawful as "economic targets" would be "enemy lines of communication . . . industrial installations producing war-fighting products, and power generation plants. Economic targets of the enemy that indirectly but effectively support and sustain the enemy's war-fighting capability may also be attacked."

18. Ibid., sec. 5.3.

19. Ibid., sec. 8.1.2.

20. Geneva Protocol I, arts. 51, para. 4(b), and 51, para. 5.

21. *Commander's Handbook*, secs. 9.1–9.1.2. However, a "weapon is not indiscriminate simply

because it may cause incidental or collateral civilian casualties, provided such casualties are not foreseeably excessive in light of the expected military advantage to be gained."

22. Ibid., sec. 5.2. It quotes a seminal elaboration on this definition from *The Hostages Case (United States v. List et al.)*, 11 TWC 759, 1253–54 (1950):

> The destruction of property to be lawful must be imperatively demanded by the necessities of war. Destruction as an end in itself is a violation of international law. There must be some reasonable connection between the destruction of property and the overcoming of the enemy forces. It is lawful to destroy railways, lines of communication, or any other property that might be utilized by the enemy . . . [even] [p]rivate homes and churches . . . if necessary for military operations. It does not admit the wanton devastation of a district or the willful infliction of suffering upon its inhabitants for the sake of suffering alone.

23. Schmitt, "Bellum Americanum," 1084.
24. *Commander's Handbook,* sec. 9.1.2 (emphasis added): "Antipersonnel weapons are designed to kill or disable enemy combatants and are lawful notwithstanding the death, pain, and suffering they inflict. *Weapons that are designed to cause unnecessary suffering or superfluous injury are, however, prohibited* because the degree of pain or injury, or the certainty of death they produce is needlessly or clearly disproportionate to the military advantage to be gained by their use."
25. See generally William J. Fenrick, "The Rule of Proportionality and Protocol I in Conventional Warfare," *Military Law Review* 98 (1982), 91; and Judith G. Gardam, "Proportionality and Force in International Law," *American Journal of International Law* 87 (1993), 391.
26. *Commander's Handbook,* sec. 8.1.2.1.
27. Geneva Protocol I, arts. 51, para. 5(b,) and 57, para. 2(a)(iii).
28. Robert G. Hanseman, "The Realities and Legalities of Information Warfare," *Air Force Law Review* 42 (1997), 173, at 182: "The military advantage gained by attacking military structures is generally minuscule compared to the resulting loss of human life and culture, and thus runs afoul of proportionality. This is why attacking hospitals, schools, religious structures and other cultural institutions is banned [under the doctrine of discrimination], unless the enemy is taking advantage of the situation by hiding military assets there."
29. Geneva Protocol I, arts. 51, para. 5(b), and 57, para. 2(a)(iii); quotation from *Commander's Handbook,* sec. 8.1.2.1.
30. *Commander's Handbook,* sec. 8.1.2.1.
31. The International Committee of the Red Cross (ICRC), Commentary on Protocol I, at 680–681.
32. *Commander's Handbook,* sec. 8.1.2.1.
33. Schmitt, "Bellum Americanum," 1080.
34. Michael N. Schmitt, "State-Sponsored Assassination in International and Domestic Law," *Yale Journal of International Law* 17 (1992), 609, 617.
35. Michael Prestwich, *Armies and Warfare in the Middle Ages: The English Experience* (New Haven, CT: Yale University Press, 1996), 128.
36. Barbara Tuchman, *A Distant Mirror: The Calamitous 14th Century* (New York: Knopf, 1978), 64.
37. Balthazar Ayala, *Three Books on the Law of War and the Duties Connected with War and on the Military Discipline,* in *The Classics of International Law,* trans. J. Bate (Washington, DC: Carnegie 1933; reprint Buffalo, NY: Hein, 1995), 84–85. See also Schmitt, "State-Sponsored Assassination," 614.
38. Alberico Gentili, "De Iure Belli Libre Tres," in *The Classics of International Law,* vol. 16, trans. John Rolfe (Washington, DC: Carnegie 1933), 168. See also Schmitt, "State-Sponsored Assassination," 615.

39. Hugo Grotius, *The Law of War and Peace*, in *The Law of War: A Documentary History*, ed. Leon Friedman (New York: Random House, 1972), 39.

40. Geneva Protocol I, arts. 51, para. 5(b), and 57, para. 2(a)(iii). Protocol I offers four examples of perfidious behavior: "1. feigning a desire to negotiate under a truce or surrender flag; 2. feigning incapacitation by wounds or sickness; 3. feigning civilian, noncombatant status; 4. feigning protected status by the use of signs, emblems or other uniforms of the United Nations, neutral states, or other states not party to the conflict."

    Schmitt expands as follows: "Offering a bounty, equivalent to a ransom, is treacherous. So, too, is launching an attack in civilian clothes, unless the enemy is not deceived by or does not rely upon the civilian clothing worn by the attacker." Schmitt, "State-Sponsored Assassination," 635–639. See also 1907 Hague Convention IV, Customs of War on Land, art. 23, para F.

41. *The Law of Land Warfare*, 22–23; *Commander's Handbook*, secs. 12.1–12.10; *International Law—The Conduct of Armed Conflict and Air Operations*, 8–1 to 8–5. An excellent distillation of the rules is Ashley J. Roach, "Ruses and Perfidy: Deception during Armed Conflict," *University of Toledo Law Review* 23 (1992), 395. See also Mary T. Hall, "False Colors and Dummy Ships: The Use of Ruse in Naval Warfare," *Naval War College Review* 42, no. 3 (Summer 1989), 52–62.

42. *The Law of Land Warfare*, 22.

43. Ibid., 22:

    > Absolute good faith with the enemy must be observed as a rule of conduct; but this does not prevent measures such as using spies and secret agents, encouraging defection or insurrection among the enemy civilian population, corrupting enemy civilians and soldiers by bribes, or inducing the enemy's soldiers to desert, surrender, or rebel. In general, a belligerent may resort to those measures for mystifying or misleading the enemy against which the enemy ought to take measures to protect himself.

44. Such an operation would not be mounted by the United States, which scrupulously adheres to a policy of disseminating selected facets of the truth in its psychological operations. The United States would mount such an operation only if the allegations were grounded in fact.

45. *The Law of Land Warfare*, 22:

    > The line of demarcation between legitimate ruses and forbidden acts or perfidy is sometimes indistinct, but the following examples indicate the correct principles. It would be an improper practice to secure an advantage of the enemy by deliberate lying or misleading conduct which involves a breach of faith, or when there is a moral duty to speak the truth. For example, it is improper to feign surrender so as to secure an advantage over the opposing belligerent thereby. So similarly, to broadcast to the enemy that an armistice has been agreed upon when such is not the case would be treacherous. On the other hand, it is a perfectly proper ruse to summon a force to surrender on the ground that it is surrounded and thereby induce such surrender with a small force.

46. Ibid.

47. Ibid., 22–23. Also permitted are "use of the enemy's signals and passwords, pretending to communicate with troops or reinforcements which have no existence, deceptive supply movements, deliberate planting of false information . . . removing unit identifications from uniforms, use of signal deceptive measures, and psychological warfare activities."

48. *Commander's Handbook*, arts. 51, para. 5(b), and 57, para. 2(a)(iii), similarly lists, as permitted, "camouflage, deceptive lighting . . . false intelligence information, electronic deceptions, and utilization of enemy codes, passwords, and countersigns" and "allowing false messages to fall into enemy hands."

49. *International Law—The Conduct of Armed Conflict and Air Operations*, 8–2.

50. *The Law of Land Warfare*, 23. See also *Commander's Handbook*, secs. 12.2–12.5. Although

land and ground forces are prohibited from using neutral flags, insignia, or uniforms, naval forces are permitted more latitude before hostilities commence; they may "fly false colors and disguise its outward appearance in other ways. . . . However, it is unlawful for a warship to go into action without first showing her true colors. Use of neutral flags, insignia, or uniforms during an actual armed engagement at sea is, therefore, forbidden."

51. *The Law of Land Warfare,* 23.
52. *See Commander's Handbook,* secs. 12.6, 12.7. For the same reason, feigning distress in order to attack a rescuing enemy, and falsely claiming noncombatant status, are perfidious and punishable as war crimes. See also Michael Bothe, Karl Josef Partsch, and Waldemar A. Solf, *New Rules for Victims of Armed Conflicts* (The Hague, Boston, London: Martinus Nijhoff Publishers, 1982), 207: "It would be a legitimate ruse to use the electronic transponder aboard a combatant aircraft to respond with the code used for identifying friendly aircraft (IFF), but it would be perfidious to use for this purpose the electronic signal . . . for the exclusive use of medical aircraft . . . [or] distress signals established under the Radio Regulations of the International Telecommunication Union."
53. *The Law of Land Warfare,* 23.
54. Ibid. Paragraph 55 prohibits using personnel, vehicles, and facilities displaying these symbols "for cloaking acts of hostility."
55. Ibid. Paragraph 54 states: "It is certainly forbidden to employ [another's flag, insignia, or uniform] during combat, but their use at other times is not forbidden."
56. Mark R. Schulman, "Discrimination in the Laws of Information Warfare," *Columbia Journal of Transnational Law* 37 (1999), 939, 959.
57. *Commander's Handbook,* sec.12.8.

Chapter 23

1. President's Commission on Critical Infrastructure Protection, *Critical Foundations: Protecting America's Infrastructures* (Washington, DC: U.S. Government Printing Office, 1997), available at <http://permanent.access.gpo.gov/lps15260/PCCIP_Report.pdf>.
2. Presidential Decision Directive/NSC 63, "Critical Infrastructure Protection," May 22, 1998, available at <www.fas.org/irp/offdocs/pdd/pdd-63.htm>.
3. Department of Homeland Security, *National Infrastructure Protection Plan* (2006), available at <www.dhs.gov/xprevprot/programs/editorial_0827.shtm>.
4. USA PATRIOT Act, Public Law No. 107–56, sec. 1016(e), October 26, 2001 (prior to 2006 reauthorization), available at <http://frwebgate.access.gpo.gov/cgi-bin/getdoc.cgi?dbname=107_cong_public_laws&docid=f:publ056.107.pdf>.
5. The White House, *The National Strategy to Secure Cyberspace* (Washington, DC: The White House, February 2003), available at <www.whitehouse.gov/pcipb/>; Homeland Security Presidential Directive 7 (HSPD 7), December 17, 2003, available at <www.fas.org/irp/offdocs/nspd/hspd-7.html>.
6. The National Infrastructure Protection Plan is available at <www.dhs.gov/xlibrary/assets/NIPP_Plan.pdf>.
7. Department of Homeland Security, "National Infrastructure Protection Plan, Information Technology Sector," available at <www.dhs.gov/xlibrary/assets/nipp_it.pdf>.
8. USA PATRIOT Act, sec. 1016(b)(2). Emphasis added.
9. Business Roundtable, *Essential Steps to Strengthen America's Cyber Terrorism Preparedness: New Priorities and Commitments from Business Roundtable's Security Task Force* (2006), available at <www.businessroundtable.org/pdf/20060622002CyberReconFinal6106.pdf>.
10. The White House, *The Federal Government's Response to Hurricane Katrina: Lessons Learned* (Washington, DC: The White House, February 2006), 56.
11. See Department of Defense Directive 8500.01E, "Information Assurance" (October 24,

2002); Department of Defense Instruction No. 8500.2, "Information Assurance (IA) Implementation" (February 6, 2003).

12. Keith Regan, "Computer Glitches Heaped Fuel on Stock Sell-Off," *E-Commerce Times*, March 1, 2007, available at <www.ecommercetimes.com/story/56032.html>; Jessica Dickler, "Technical Glitches Plague Wall Street," *CNNMoney.com*, February 27, 2007, available at <http://money.cnn.com/2007/02/27/markets/dow_drop/index.htm>; Thomas S. Mulligan, "A Computer Glitch Distorts Dow's Drop, Then Exacerbates It," *Global Technology Forum*, February 28, 2007, available at <http://ebusinessforum.com/index.asp?layout=rich_story&doc_id=10212>; Associated Press, "Computer Glitch Triggered Dow Jones Plunge," February 27, 2007, available at <www.kstp.com/article/stories/S33513.shtml?cat=1>.

13. Mulligan.

14. Business Roundtable, 14.

15. See chapter 7 in this volume, "Information Security Issues in Cyberspace."

16. See, for example, Century Foundation Task Force, *The Forgotten Homeland* (New York: Century Foundation Press, 2006), 112–113.

17. Justin Blum, "Hackers Target U.S. Power Grid," *The Washington Post*, March 11, 2005, E1; Agence France-Presse, "Police Foil al-Qaida Net Attack," March 12, 2007, available at <http://australianit.news.com.au/story/0,24897,21365277-26199,00.html>; David Leppard, "Al-Qaeda Plot to Bring Down UK Internet," *Times Online*, March 11, 2007, available at <www.timesonline.co.uk/tol/news/uk/crime/article1496831.ece>.

18. Peter Finn, "Cyber Assaults on Estonia Typify a New Battle Tactic," *The Washington Post*, May 19, 2007, A1.

19. Larry Greenemeier, "Estonian Attacks Raise Concern Over Cyber 'Nuclear Winter,'" *InformationWeek*, May 24, 2007, available at <www.informationweek.com/news/showArticle.jhtml?articleID=199701774>; Jaikumar Vijayan, "Hackers Evaluate Estonia Attacks," Computerworld, August 4, 2007, available at <www.pcworld.com/article/id,135503-page,1/article.html>.

20. Cyber Security Industry Alliance, "SCADA: Get the Facts," April 2007, 3–4, available at <www.csialliance.org/publications/csia_whitepapers/CSIA_SCADA_Get_Facts_April_2007.pdf>.

21. Ibid.

22. James A. Lewis, Director and Senior Fellow, Technology and Public Policy Program, Center for Strategic and International Studies, statement, "Addressing the Nation's Cybersecurity Challenges: Reducing Vulnerabilities Requires Strategic Investment and Immediate Action," hearing before the Subcommittee on Emerging Threats, Cybersecurity and Science and Technology of the House Committee on Homeland Security, 110th Congress, 2007, 1–2.

23. Sean McCormack, Spokesman, U.S. Department of State, daily press briefing, July 12, 2006, available at <www.state.gov/r/pa/prs/dpb/2006/68924.htm>.

24. *The National Strategy to Secure Cyberspace*, ix.

25. Ibid., viii.

26. Gregory Garcia, Assistant Secretary for Cyber Security and Communications, U.S. Department of Homeland Security, remarks at the RSA Conference on IT and Communications Security, San Francisco, CA, February 8, 2007, available at <www.dhs.gov/xnews/speeches/sp_1171386545551.shtm>.

27. Department of Homeland Security, "National Response Plan, Cyber Incident Annex CYB–5" (2006), available at <www.dhs.gov/xpreparedp/committees/editorial_0566.shtm>.

28. 50 U.S. Code App. Sec. 2061 et seq.; see also Lee M. Zeichner, "Use of the Defense Production Act of 1950 for Critical Infrastructure Protection," *Security in the Information*

Age: New Challenges, New Strategies, Joint Economic Committee, U.S. Congress (May 2002), 74–88, available at <www.house.gov/jec/security.pdf>.

29. Business Roundtable, 2.
30. Garcia.
31. House of Representatives Report No. 109–699, "Making Appropriations for the Department of Homeland Security for the Fiscal Year Ending September 30, 2007, and for Other Purposes" (2006), 158. The amounts are $69,000,000 and $32,043,000, respectively.
32. Caron Carlson and Paul F. Roberts, "DHS Progress Proves Elusive," *eWeek*, September 12, 2005, available at <www.eweek.com/article2/0,1895,1858740,00.asp>.
33. Wade-Hahn Chan, "Cyber Storm Finds Weaknesses," *FCW.com*, October 2, 2006, available at <www.fcw.com/article96277-10-02-06-Print>.
34. See, generally, Department of Homeland Security, National Cyber Security Division, "Cyber Storm Exercise Report," September 12, 2006, available at <www.dhs.gov/xlibrary/assets/prep_cyberstormreport_sep06.pdf>.
35. Garcia.
36. Ibid.
37. "[T]he public and private sectors must have a single plan for shoring up the financial markets and public trust and confidence following an event." Business Roundtable, 16.

Chapter 24
1. "Wicked problem," *Wikipedia*, available at <http://en.wikipedia.org/wiki/Wicked_problem>.
2. See Leon Fuerth, "Strategic Myopia: The Case for Forward Engagement," *The National Interest*, no. 83 (Spring 2006), 58–63.
3. "Wicked problem."
4. See chapter 1 in this volume, "Cyberpower and National Security: Policy Recommendations for a Strategic Framework."
5. Fuerth, 58–63.
6. "Management and Decision-Making in an Age of Complexity," accessed at <www.forwardengagement.org>.

About the Contributors

EDITORS

Franklin D. Kramer is an independent consultant and a former Distinguished Research Fellow in the Center for Technology and National Security Policy, National Defense University. Mr. Kramer has been a senior political appointee in two administrations, most recently as Assistant Secretary of Defense for International Security Affairs for President William Clinton, Secretary of Defense William Perry, and Secretary of Defense William Cohen, and previously as Principal Deputy Assistant Secretary of Defense for President Jimmy Carter and Secretary of Defense Harold Brown.

Stuart H. Starr is a Distinguished Research Fellow in the Center for Technology and National Security Policy, National Defense University. Concurrently, he serves as President of Barcroft Research Institute, where he consults on command and control (C^2) issues, serves on senior advisory boards to defense industry, lectures to audiences worldwide on C^2 issues, and participates on blue ribbon panels. Previously, Dr. Starr has worked with the MITRE Corporation, the Institute for Defense Analyses, and the Office of the Secretary of Defense.

Larry K. Wentz is a Senior Research Fellow in the Center for Technology and National Security Policy at the National Defense University and consults on command and control (C^2) issues. He previously served as Technical Director for Joint and Defense-Wide Command, Control, and Communications at the MITRE Corporation. He is an experienced manager, strategic planner, and command, control, communications, computers, intelligence, surveillance, and reconnaissance (C^4ISR) systems engineer with extensive experience in nuclear C^2, continuity of government C^2, multinational military C^2 and command, control, communications, and intelligence systems interoperability, civil-military operations and information operations support to peace operations, and numerous other military C^4ISR activities.

CONTRIBUTING AUTHORS

Charles L. Barry is a Senior Research Fellow in the Center for Technology and National Security Policy at the National Defense University. He is also the principal of Barry Consulting, a strategic planning, national security, and information management firm. Dr. Barry's career in the U.S. Army included operational leadership positions and 9 years as a high-level strategic planner in Europe and Washington. His research covers command and control networks, multinational forces, and civil-military organizational design.

Marjory S. Blumenthal has been Associate Provost, Academic, at Georgetown University since August 2003. Between July 1987 and August 2003, she was the Executive Director of the National Academy of Sciences' Computer Science and Telecommunications Board, where she designed, directed, and oversaw collaborative study projects, workshops, and symposia on technical and policy issues in computing and telecommunications. Ms. Blumenthal has taught and advised students on Internet policy, an area where she continues to pursue personal research.

Chris Burrow was a Research Associate with Zeichner Risk Analytics when this book was written.

Gerard J. Christman is a Program Manager with Femme Comp Incorporated (FCI) supporting the Assistant Secretary of Defense for Networks and Information Integration. He served 23 years as an officer in the U.S. Army Signal Corps before joining FCI in 2003.

David D. Clark has been leading the development of the Internet since the 1970s. From 1981 to 1989, he was Chief Protocol Architect in this development and chaired the Internet Activities Board. He is a former chairman of the Computer Science and Telecommunications Board of the National Research Council and is a Senior Research Scientist at the Massachusetts Institute of Technology.

Maeve Dion is a Program Manager at the Critical Infrastructure Protection Program at George Mason University School of Law.

Leon Fuerth is Research Professor of International Affairs at The George Washington University's Elliot School of International Affairs. He was the national security advisor to Vice President Al Gore and served on the Principals' Committee of the National Security Council.

Daniel T. Kuehl teaches military strategy and national security policy at the Information Resources Management College at the National Defense University. He is the Director of the Information Strategies Concentration Program, a specialized curriculum on the information component of national power, offered to select students at the National War College and the Industrial College of the Armed Forces.

Richard L. Kugler is a former Distinguished Research Professor in the Center for Technology and National Security Policy at the National Defense University. His specialty is U.S. defense strategy, global security affairs, and the North Atlantic Treaty Organization (NATO). Dr. Kugler advises senior echelons of the Office of the Secretary of Defense, the Joint Staff, and the interagency community. He is the author of multiple books, articles, and official studies on U.S. defense strategy and programs as well as NATO and global security affairs.

Harold Kwalwasser is an independent telecommunications consultant based in Washington, DC. He is Chair of the U.S. International Telecommunication Union Association, an organization of telecommunications-related companies and consultancies that have an interest in the operation of the International Telecommunication Union. Previously, Mr. Kwalwasser practiced law for 16 years.

Irving Lachow is a Senior Research Professor at the Information Resources Management College at the National Defense University, where he teaches courses on information assurance and critical infrastructure protection, international perspectives in information operations, global enterprise networking, and telecommunications. Dr. Lachow has also worked for Booz Allen Hamilton, the RAND Corporation, and the Office of Deputy Under Secretary of Defense (Advanced Systems and Concepts).

Martin C. Libicki has been a Senior Policy Analyst at RAND since 1998, where he works on the relationship between information technology and national security. Previously, he was a senior fellow in the Institute for National Strategic Studies at the National Defense University for 12 years. Dr. Libicki has written on information technology standards, the revolution in military affairs, and information warfare.

John A. McCarthy was Director of the Critical Infrastructure Protection Program (now the Center for Infrastructure Protection) at George Mason University School of Law when this book was written. The center integrates law, policy, and technology to conduct comprehensive infrastructure protection research relevant to domestic and international security, providing critical infrastructure stakeholders with valuable analysis of the cyber, physical, human, and economic frameworks of U.S. critical infrastructures.

William D. O'Neil is a private consultant and author. He has served as a naval officer and civilian official in the Department of Defense as well as an engineer and executive in private industry.

Olivia Pacheco is Editor of *The CIP Report* at the Center for Infrastructure Protection at George Mason University School of Law.

Gregory J. Rattray is a Partner at Delta Risk Consulting, where he establishes risk management strategies and cyber security capacity-building approaches for government and private sector clients. During 23 years as a U.S. Air Force officer, he served on the White House National Security Council Staff as Director for Cyber Security, leading national policy development and National Security Council oversight for cyber security, and he directed oversight of Iraqi telecommunications reconstruction. He is a full member of the Council on Foreign Relations.

Edward Skoudis is a founder of and Senior Security Consultant for Intelguardians Network Intelligence, LLC, a Washington, DC–based network security consulting firm. He is also a handler at the SANS Internet Storm Center. His expertise includes hacker attacks and defenses, the information security industry, and computer privacy issues. He has performed numerous security assessments, designed information security governance and operations teams for Fortune 500 companies, and responded to computer attacks for clients in financial, high technology, health care, and other industries.

Timothy L. Thomas is a senior analyst at the Foreign Military Studies Office at Fort Leavenworth, Kansas. Before retiring from the U.S. Army as a lieutenant colonel in 1993, he was a Foreign Area Officer who specialized in Soviet/Russian studies. Mr. Thomas has done extensive research and publishing in the areas of peacekeeping, information war, psychological operations, low-intensity conflict, and political military affairs.

Clay Wilson retired as a Research Specialist in Technology and National Security in the Foreign Affairs, Defense, and Trade Division of the Congressional Research Service (CRS). Previously, he taught computer security and risk analysis at the University of Maryland University College and at National-Louis University. Dr. Wilson served as a government representative to the Critical Infrastructure Coordination Group to improve industry and government cooperation under U.S. Presidential Decision Directive 63.

Thomas C. Wingfield is an Associate Professor at the Fort Belvoir, Virginia, campus of the U.S. Army Command and General Staff College. He is also a Lecturer in Law at the Catholic University of America's Columbus School of Law, an Adjunct Research Fellow at the Potomac Institute of Policy Studies, and an Adjunct Professor at the Georgetown Public Policy Institute. A national security attorney, Mr. Wingfield specializes in use-of-force issues, specifically the application of the law of armed conflict to information operations.

Elihu Zimet is a former Distinguished Research Fellow in the Center for Technology and National Security Policy at the National Defense University. Previously, Dr. Zimet headed the Expeditionary Warfare Science and Technology Department at the Office of Naval Research, where he directed science and technology programs in missiles, directed energy, aircraft, and stealth as well as science and technology support to the Marine Corps.

Index